ALEXANDER

A History of the Origin and
Growth of the Art of War
from the Earliest Times
to the Battle of Ipsus,
301 BC, with a Detailed
Account of the Campaigns
of the Great Macedonian

Theodore Ayrault Dodge

DA CAPO PRESS
A Member of the Perseus Books Group

To
THE AMERICAN SOLDIER

Who, not bred to arms, but nurtured by independence,
has achieved the proudest rank among the veterans of history.

THIS VOLUME IS DEDICATED

Cataloging-in-Publication data for this book is available from the Library of Congress.

ISBN 0-306-81361-0

This Da Capo Press paperback edition of *Alexander* is an unabridged republication of the edition first published in 1890.

Published by Da Capo Press
A Member of the Perseus Books Group
http://www.dacapopress.com

Da Capo Press books are available at special discounts for bulk purchases in the U.S. by corporations, institutions, and other organizations. For more information, please contact the Special Markets Department at the Perseus Books Group, 11 Cambridge Center, Cambridge, MA 02142, or call (800) 255–1514 or (617) 252–5298, or e-mail special.markets@perseusbooks.com.

2 3 4 5 6—08 07 06 05

PREFACE.

THE basis of this history is the Anabasis of Alexander by Arrian of Nicomedia, who lived in the second century of our era. Arrian was surnamed in Athens the Younger Xenophon, because he occupied the same relation to Epictetus which Xenophon did to Socrates. This historian is by far the most reliable, plain and exact of all those who have told us of the great Macedonian. Arrian, though a Greek, was long in the service of the Roman state, having fallen into the good graces of the Emperor Hadrian, whom he accompanied to Rome, and who later appointed him prefect of Cappadocia. Under Antoninus Pius, Arrian rose to the supreme dignity of consul. He wrote several philosophical and historical treatises, among them an account of his own campaign against the Alani. Arrian was himself a distinguished soldier, and it is this which enables him to make all military situations so clear to us. Of the fifteen works which we know he wrote, the Anabasis is the most valuable.

Arrian had in his hands the histories of Ptolemy, son of Lagus, one of Alexander's most distinguished officers, later king of Egypt, and of Aristobulus, a minor officer of Alexander's. He also used the works of Eratosthenes, Megasthenes, Nearchus, Alexander's famous admiral, Aristus, and Asclepiades, as well as had access to all which had been written before him, a large part of which he rejected in favor of the testimony of those who served under Alexander in person. He quotes from the king's own letters, and from the diary of Eumenes, his secretary, which he appears to have had at hand.

Next to Arrian's history comes that of Quintus Curtius, who wrote in the first century. Of ten books, the eight last are extant. This work is far behind Arrian's in credibility. Curtius is somewhat of a romancer, though he gives local color, and occasionally supplies a fact missing in Arrian. But he is neither clear nor consistent. He draws his facts largely from Clitarchus, a contemporary of Alexander.

Plutarch (50 to 130 A. D.) is always interesting, and his short life of Alexander is just and helpful. Many stray facts can be gleaned in the other Lives.

Diodorus Siculus, a contemporary of Cæsar and Augustus, in his Historical Library, gives us many items of worth. Out of his forty books, only fifteen have survived. Diodorus is suggestive, but must be construed in the light of other works.

Justinus, a Roman historian who lived in the second or third century A. D., wrote a History of Macedonia. This ranks with Diodorus in usefulness. The chapters relating to Philip and Alexander supply some gaps, and give an occasional glimpse into the character of these monarchs, lacking elsewhere. But one cannot rely on Justin unsupported.

Strabo's Geography (first century) contains material which ekes out what we glean elsewhere, and there are in many of the old authors — Dionysius, Livy, Josephus, Frontinus, Ammian, and others — frequent references to Alexander which can be drawn from. Vegetius' *De re militari* is somewhat mixed, but very valuable. Onosander's *Strategos* can be put to use in explaining tactical manœuvres.

Polybius, one of the most valuable of all our ancient sources of information, military and political, in his Universal History, strays off to Greece, Asia Minor, and Egypt, and we find some material in his pages. He lived in the third century.

There were numberless historians of Alexander. Very few have survived. Rafael Volteran quotes Clitarchus, Polycrates, Onesicritus, Antigenes Istrus, Aristobulus, Chares, Hecatæus Eritreus, Philip the Chalcidian, Duris the Samian, Ptolemy, Anticlides, Philo the Theban, Philip, Hisangelus, Antisthenes, Menechmus the Sicyonian, Nymphis of Heraclea, Potamon the Mitylenæan, Sotericus Arsites, Arrian, Plutarch, Quintus Curtius. Plutarch quotes most of the above, and Callisthenes, Eratosthenes, Polyclitus, Hermippus, and Sotion, beside. Most of these authors did not long survive their own era; but they were known to those whose works have remained to us, and were by them accepted or rejected, according to the credibility of each. It may be claimed that Arrian furnishes us the main body of all histories of Alexander. Other sources are, as it were, appendices. And this, because the trained military mind of Arrian enabled him to distinguish clearly between what was valuable and consistent, and what was manifestly incredible or unimportant.

The early chapters, about the military art preceding Philip, come mainly from Herodotus, Thucydides and Xenophon. Cornelius Nepos draws a clever character, and we all know what a fund of riches Plutarch lays before us, available for all purposes, if not always exact.

So much for the facts. But the ancient authors rarely give more than just the bald facts in dealing with military matters. They tell us where Alexander went and what he did, with sketches of character and interesting incidents ; but they furnish no clue to the special why and wherefore which the soldier likes to know; or if a clue, quite frequently a wrong one. What to us is clear, because the art which Alexander created has since been expanded by the deeds of the other great captains and elucidated by their commentators, was, even to Arrian, a sealed book. Arrian did not understand what Alexander did as Jomini would have understood it; for it needed the remarkable campaigns of a Frederick and a Napoleon to enable Jomini to compass the inner meaning of the art of war. This meaning we must seek in modern military criticism.

There is by no means a perfect sequence to the origin and growth of the art of war. Its continuity has been interrupted by periods of many centuries. But as all great soldiers have acknowledged their indebtedness to their predecessors, though they themselves have been able to improve upon the art, so it is interesting and instructive to study what these predecessors did, and see from what small beginnings and through how many fluctuations the art has grown to its present perfect state.

There have been many lives of Alexander written in modern times, some within this generation. Much of the best of military criticism has been devoted to this subject. It is hard to say anything about Alexander that some one may not already have said. But a good deal contained in this volume in the way of comment is new, and the author does not know of a life of Alexander, which, by the use of such charts and maps as abound in the histories of our own Civil War, makes the perusal of his great conquests an easy task. The military student is willing to devote his days to research; he should not rely on others; the general reader has no leisure for such work. He has a right to demand that his way should be made plain. The author has tried to do just this, while not neglecting the requirements of those who wish to dwell upon the military aspect of Alexander's campaigns.

There is no mystery about the methods of great captains. A hundred years ago there was; but Jomini and his followers have brushed away the cobwebs from the secret and laid it bare. The technical details relating to war are intricate and difficult, nor are they of interest to the general reader. They take many years to learn. No officer, who drops for an instant his studies, can save himself from falling behind his fellows. Especially is this true to-day. This, however, relates chiefly to the minutiæ of the profession. The higher the art of the soldier goes, the simpler it is, because it becomes part of his own individuality; but the captain must first have mastered every detail of the profession by the hardest of work. He must be familiar with the capacities and limitations of every arm of the service, and be able to judge accurately what ground each needs for its march, its manœuvres, and its fire. He must be so apt a business man as never to fail in providing for his troops, however fast he moves or however far from his base. He must be an engineer of the first class. Almost all great generals have been able to drill a company, or serve a gun, or throw up a breastwork, or conduct a reconnoissance better than most of their subordinates. Intimate knowledge of detail is of the essence. *Ad astra per aspera.*

Having reached the top, the captain's work is less intricate in one sense. Nothing is more beautifully simple than the leading features of the best campaign of Napoleon. We may all understand them. But to few, indeed, has the power ever been given to conceive and execute such a masterpiece. A bare half-dozen men in the world's history stand in the highest group of captains. The larger operations of war are in themselves plain, but they are founded on complicated detail. War on the map, or strategy, appears to us, in the event, easy enough; but to conceive and develop, and then move an army in pursuance of, a strategic plan requires the deepest knowledge of all arts and sciences applicable to war, and such exertion, mental, moral and physical, as is known to no one but the commander of a great army in time of war. The simple rests upon the difficult. What is treated of in this book is not, as a rule, the minutiæ, but the larger operations, though details have sometimes to be dwelt on for their historical value. What is difficult to do may be easy to narrate.

There is no pretense to make this a military text-book. It contains nothing but what the professional soldier already knows. A military text-book is practically useless to the general reader. Even Jomini acknowledged that he could not make his books interesting except to professionals; and there are now enough good text-books accessible to those who wish to study the technical side of war. But it is hoped that the presentation may commend itself to those military men whose studies in their peculiar branch of the profession have led them in other directions, and who may wish to refresh their knowledge of Alexander's campaigns, even if they do not agree with all the conclusions reached.

It is assumed by some excellent military critics that there are no lessons to be learned from antiquity. This was not what Frederick and Napoleon thought or said. It is certainly difficult to develop a text book of the modern science from ancient campaigns alone; illustrations and parallelisms must for the most part be sought in the campaigns of the last three centuries. But it will not do to forget that Frederick's victory at Leuthen was directly due to his knowledge of Epaminondas' manœuvre at Leuctra, or that the passage of the Hydaspes has been the model for the crossing of rivers in the face of the enemy ever since. All gain is bred of the successes and failures of our predecessors in the art; it is well to know what these were. While all the principles of the modern science of war are not shown in the old campaigns, because the different conditions did not call for their development, as well as because history is full of gaps, the underlying ones certainly are ; and these can be best understood by tracing them from their origin. It is believed that when the series of volumes, of which this is the first, shall have reached our own times, the entire body of the art of war will have been well covered. This volume can include but a small part of it.

This is not a political history. If any errors in the description of the intricate political conditions of Alexander's age have crept in, the author begs that they may be pardoned as not properly within the scope of the work. Time has been devoted to manœuvres and battles ; politics has been treated as a side issue.

Individual prowess was a large part of ancient war. In Homeric times it was especially prominent. A narrative of Alexander is apt to abound in instances of his personal courage rather than of his moral or intellectual force. The former seemed to appeal more strongly to the ancients. The old historians deal almost exclusively in details of this kind, and in following them, one is instinctively led into giving much prominence to acts of individual gallantry. In olden days troops had to be led, and the commander-in-chief was called on to give a daily example of his bravery. Troops are now moved. Brigades are mere blocks. While he needs courage as much as ever, the commander should avoid exposure to unnecessary risk. His moral and intellectual forces are more in demand than the merely physical.

There are singular discrepancies between all atlases, ancient and modern. The best of maps vary in their details to an annoying extent. The maps in this volume do not aim at infallibility. They are accurate enough not to mislead. The charts are original. In many cases topography has been

created to conform to the relations of the authorities. Such
is the chart of Aornus. The larger part of the Eastern conquests of Alexander are practically inaccessible to the modern
traveler, and no geographer has been able to secure more
than general accuracy. The local topography is quite unknown. In such cases the chart is merely suggestive, and is
inserted as it were as a part of the text. Helpfulness to the
reader has been sought rather than artistic excellence. There
are some slight variations between charts and maps, but none
of moment. The scales of miles may not in all cases be
quite exact. There is an occasional variation between chart
and text. In such cases the text is to be followed. The
maps and charts are usually north and south. The relative
sizes of the blocks of troops are not meant to be accurate.
Sometimes exaggeration is resorted to to make the meaning
of a manœuvre more plain. Accuracy is not always possible.
The peculiar use of the charts is to elucidate the text. Between charts and text it is hoped that the book will be easy
to read, and the author believes that a single perusal of the
battle of Arbela will make its general features as plain as
those of the battle of Gettysburg. Lest any part of the
book should prove dull, so that the reader may desire to exert
his right to skip, short arguments at the heads of the chapters have been provided, specific enough to preserve the continuity of the narrative.

The cuts of uniforms, arms and siege-devices will be found
interesting. Most of them have their origin in old architec-
tural or ceramic decoration. The dress and arms of the soldiers are largely taken from Kretchmar-Rohrbach's Trachten
der Völker, whose materials are copied from the ruins and the
relics of the ancient world.

Among very recent writers, the author desires to acknowledge his indebtedness to Prince Galitzin, whose just com-

pleted History of War is a well-digested and admirably
classified work, drawn from all sources, ancient and modern.
It has been laid under free contribution. Droysen's History
of Alexander is accurate, full and complete, but lacks the
advantage of charts and maps. It has been equally utilized.
From the middle of the last century, when Folard and Guish-
ard began their commentaries and discussions on the ancient
historians, up till now, there has been such a mass of matter
published, often of highest value and often trivial, that its
mere bibliography is tiresome. But there is no existing com-
mentary on the great Macedonian, known to the author to be
of acknowledged value, which has not been consulted. The
facts, however, have been uniformly taken from or compared
with the old authorities themselves. The labors and commentaries of many philologists, geographers and soldiers have
now moulded the ancient histories into a form easily accessible to him who possesses but a tithe of the knowledge and
patience they have so freely placed at the service of their
fellow-man.

TABLE OF CONTENTS.

LIST OF ILLUSTRATIONS.

———◆———

" *Faites la guerre offensive comme Alexandre, Annibal, César,* *Gustave Adolphe, Turenne, le prince Eugène et Frédéric ; lisez, reli-* *lisez l'histoire de leur quatre-vingt-huit campagnes ; modélez-vous sur* *eux,* — *c'est le seul moyen de devenir grand capitaine et de surprendre* *le sécret de l'art ; votre génie, ainsi éclairé, vous fera rejeter des max-* *imes opposées à celles de ces grands hommes.*" — NAPOLEON.

" *La tactique, les évolutions, la science des l' officier de génie, de* *l'officier d'artillerie peuvent s'apprendre dans les traités ;* — *mais la* *connaissance de la grande tactique ne s'acquiert que par l'expérience* *et par l'étude de l'histoire des campagnes de tous les grands capitaines.*" — NAPOLEON.

ALEXANDER.

I.

IN GENERAL.

ALL early history is a record of wars. Peace was too uneventful to call for record. But mere record cannot fashion a science. The art of war has been created by the intellectual conceptions of a few great captains; it has been reduced to a science by the analysis of their recorded deeds. Strategy is war on the map; tactics is battlefield manœuvring. Both depend less on rules than on the brain, courage, and activity of the captain. Strategy has been of slow growth, and was, as a science, unknown to the ancients; tactics was highly developed, as were, within given limits, logistics and engineering. No study is so fruitful to the soldier as that of the history of great captains. From their deeds alone can the true instinct of war be gleaned. These pages propose to sketch briefly the typical events and the status of armies antedating Alexander, to show what then was already known of war; and, by a relation of Alexander's campaigns, to illustrate his influence upon the art.

THE earliest histories are but a record of wars. The seasons of peace were too uneventful to call for historians. The sharply defined events which arrest attention, because followed by political or territorial changes, have always been wars, and these have been the subject-matter of nearly all early writings. The greatest of poems would never have seen the light had not Homer been inspired by the warlike deeds of heroes; nor would Herodotus and Thucydides have penned their invaluable pages had not the stirring events of the Persian and Peloponnesian wars impelled them to the task. Xenophon, Arrian, Cæsar, are strictly military historians; and the works of the other great writers of ancient history contain only the rehearsal of wars held together by a network of political conditions influencing these struggles. It is indeed peculiarly in the fact that war is now subordinated to peace that our modern civilization differs from that of the ancients; and but within a couple of generations can it be truly claimed that the arts of peace have assumed more prominence than the arts of war. So long as war remains the eventual arbitrament of all national disputes, so long must the arts of peace contribute to the art of war, and so long must this be studied, and an active interest in the deeds of the great captains be maintained.

The art of war has been created by the intellectual conceptions of a few great captains. It is best studied in the story of their triumphs. The memorizing of technical rules can teach but the detail of the art. The lessons contained in what the masters did can be learned only by an intelligent analysis of the events themselves; the inspiration essential to success can be caught only by assimilation of their methods. Nothing is so fruitful to the soldier as to study closely the character and intellect of these great men, and to make himself familiar with the events which they have illustrated. Few topics have greater interest for the layman. Less than a generation since, we Americans were a nation of soldiers. In four years something like four millions of men had worn the blue or gray. In the autumn of their life many of these veterans may enjoy the comparison of their own campaigns with those of the men whom all unite in calling the masters of the art. To such my work is principally addressed.

Strategy has been aptly described as the art of making war upon the map. Nor is this a mere figure of speech. Napoleon always planned and conducted his campaigns on maps of the country spread out for him by his staff, and into these maps he stuck colored pins to indicate where his divisions were to move. Having thus wrought out his plan, he issued orders accordingly. To the general the map is a chessboard, and upon this he moves his troops as players move queen and knight. Strategy is, in other words, the art by which a general so moves his army about the country in relation to but beyond the proximity of the enemy, that when he finally reaches him, the enemy shall be placed in a disadvantageous position for battle or other manœuvre. The movements of an army in the immediate presence of the enemy, or on the field of battle, belong to the domain of grand tactics. Strategy is the common law or common sense of war. As the common law has arisen from the decisions of great judges relating to the common affairs of life, so strategy has arisen from the action of the great masters of war in the events they were called on to control. The word is very properly derived from *strategos*, the name given by the Greeks to the leader of a certain unit of service — to a general. It is not the army, nor the people, nor the territory, nor the cause which are the origin of strategic movements, though, indeed, all these bear their due part in the calculation. It is the head and heart of the leader which always have furnished and always must furnish the strategic values of every campaign. From his intellectual and moral vigor — in other words, his personal equipment — must ever come the motive power and direction.

Strategy has its rules, like every science. Until within a little over a century these have been unwritten. They are in principle inflexible, in practice elastic. They are but the tools of the trade, the nomenclature of the science ; the " Barbara Celarent " of logic. The strictness or laxity of the maxims of strategy is measured by the ability of the general. The second-rate commander transcends them at his

peril. For the great captain they vary as the conditions
vary, The man who can rise superior to mere rules, and
succeed, has always a spark of genius. But as these maxims
are, like those of the common law, nothing but a statement
of what is the highest common sense, the genius who makes
exceptions to them does so because the circumstances warrant
the exception, or because he feels that he can control circumstances. The great captain will never permit mere rules to
tie his hands; but his action will always be in general, if not
specific, accordance with them. The one thing which distin-
guishes the great captains of history from the rank and file
of commanders is that they have known when to disregard
maxims, and that they have succeeded while disregarding
them, and because of their disregard of them. But in all
cases their successes have proved the rule.

The first requisite of oratory, said Demosthenes, is action;
the second, action; the third, action. In this generation of
conversational speeches the saying is less applicable to oratory than to strategy and tactics. It is the general who can
think rapidly and move rapidly; who can originate correct
lines of manœuvre, and unceasingly and skillfully follow
them, who becomes great. The few instances of Fabian tactics are but the complement to this rule. They prove its
truth. Fabius Maximus was in one sense as active as Hannibal. It was mainly in the avoidance of armed conflict that
he differed from the great Carthaginian. How, indeed, could
he follow each movement of his wonderful antagonist, — as
he did, — unless his every faculty was in constant action?
Incessant action is not of necessity unceasing motion; it is
motion in the right direction at the right moment; though,
indeed, it is the legs of an army, as much as its stomach, which
enable the brain tissue and throbbing blood of the captain
to conduct a successful campaign or win a pitched battle.

Strategy has been a growth, like other sciences. Its earliest manifestation was in the ruthless invasion by one barbarian tribe of the territory of another, in search of bread, metals, wives, or plunder of any kind. The greater or less skill or rapidity of such an invasion, by which the population attacked was taken unawares or at a disadvantage, meant success or failure. Thus grew offensive strategy. The invaded people cut the roads, blocked the defiles, defended the fords of the rivers, lay in ambush in the forests. The ability shown in these simple operations originated the strategy of defense. Often the strong, relying on their strength, showed the least ability ; the weak, conscious of their weakness, the most. From such simple beginnings has grown up the science and art of war, which to-day, among the greatest nations, — saving always our own happily exempt America, — embraces all arts and sciences, and makes them each and all primarily subservient to its demands.

As with strategy, so tactics, logistics and engineering came to perfection by a slow growth in ancient and modern times. The tactics of organization and drill rose to a high degree among the ancients ; the tactics of the battlefield were sometimes superb. Logistics were simpler, for armies were neither large, nor carried such enormous supplies of material. Engineering, as exemplified at the sieges of Tyre, Rhodes, and Alesia, has rarely been equaled in the adaptation of the means at hand to the end to be accomplished. War is scarcely more perfect to-day, according to our resources in arts and mechanics, than it was twenty odd centuries ago among the Greeks, according to theirs.

It is not, however, the purpose of these pages to discourse upon the art of war. It will be a far more pleasant task to tell the story of the great captains whose deeds have created this art, and through them, by unvarnished comment, to lay open to the friendly reader the rules and maxims which govern or limit strategy and tactics. And before coming to the first, — and perhaps the greatest of all, — Alexander of Macedon, it is proposed to describe briefly the armies antedating his, to say something about his predecessors in the art, and to give a short account of a very few of their campaigns or battles, in order to show what equipment this wonderful soldier possessed when, a mere lad, he undertook, as captain-general of the smallest and yet greatest nation on earth, Greece, the expedition against the stupendous power of the Persian empire, and thus placed the weight of the world upon his youthful shoulders. This cannot readily be done in a well connected historical narrative. Many noted wars and brilliant generals must be omitted. The instances and commanders to be quoted will be but typical of the rest, and will illustrate the gradual advance from unintelligent to intellectual warfare. A history of war must embrace all wars and battles, small and great. A history of the art of war may confine itself to narrating such typical wars and battles as best illustrate its growth.

Persian Noble.

II.

EARLY HISTORY OF WAR.

THE first reliable history of war is found in the Bible ; the next comes from Homer, Herodotus, Thucydides, and Xenophon. All ancient historians are properly military historians. During the Middle Ages chronicles were kept, but no history was written, and war as an art was at a low ebb. It was the French Revolution which first developed the national sentiment and the study of war as a science. The world's wars may for our uses be conveniently divided into Ancient Wars, Middle Age Wars, Modern Wars, Recent Wars. The eras of Alexander, Hannibal, Cæsar, Gustavus, Frederick and Napoleon contain the names of nearly all the great captains. — Man is a fighting animal. His club was the first hand-to-hand weapon ; his slung-stone the early long-range arm. The organization of armies came about in a perfectly simple manner, just as the first stockade around a barbarian village was the origin of the stupendous walls of Babylon. The beginning of all military devices was in the East ; they have been perfected in the West. The character of all Oriental wars was that of huge raids, accompanied by extravagant cruelties and devastation. Entirely unmethodical, they contain no lessons for us to-day.

THE first reliable history of war may be said to have come to us from the Jews. The historical books of the Bible give us the earliest written glimpse into very ancient methods of warfare, as the Egyptian monuments give us the pictorial. This narrative was followed by the Iliad, which portrays the condition of war twelve hundred years before Christ. Herodotus († 418 B. C.) next appeared, and by his faithful description of the Persian wars justly earned the title of Father of History ; and following him closely came Thucydides († 384 B. C.), who narrated the great political and interesting, though in instruction meagre, military events of the Peloponnesian War. Xenophon († 360 B. C.) graphically, if sometimes imaginatively, described the deeds of the elder

Cyrus, and capped all military-historical works in his wonderful Anabasis. The same character was kept up by Polybius, Diodorus, Dionysius, Arrian, Plutarch, among the Greeks, and by Cæsar, Sallust, Livy, Tacitus, Nepos, among the Romans. That the works of all these and many other authors should deal mostly with war was a necessity. It was war which was, as a rule, the precursor of advancing civilization.

From the decline of Rome throughout the Middle Ages there was no history, properly speaking. Only chronicles and partial notes were kept; nor did history emerge from its hiding until the revival of learning and the arts in the fifteenth and sixteenth centuries. It was then patterned, as was everything else, on ancient models. The invention of gunpowder gave a new direction to war and its records, though the classical influence and a certain pedantry in historical work remained until the eighteenth century. The systems of war partook of this same pedantry, with the exception of what was done by a few great masters, and it was not until the French Revolution overturned all preconceived notions on every subject that the art of war, as we understand it, arose and throve. The worship of the ancient models gave way to a national sentiment, and the growth of scientific war became assured and permanent, as well as the fruitful study of what the great captains had really done. Military history had been but a record. It became an inquiry into the principles governing the acts recorded.

Prince Galitzin's splendid work divides the history of war into four sections : —

A. *Ancient War.*

1°. Down to 500 B. C.

2°. From the beginning of the Persian wars, 500 B. C., down to the death of Alexander, 323 B. C.

3°. From the death of Alexander, 323 B. C., to the death of Cæsar, 44 B. C.

4°. From the death of Cæsar, 44 B. C., to the fall of the West Roman Empire, A. D. 476.

B. *Wars of the Middle Ages.*

1°. From A. D. 476 to the death of Charles the Great, A. D. 814.

2°. From A. D. 814 to the introduction of firearms, A. D. 1350.

3°. From A. D. 1350 to the Thirty Years' War, A. D. 1618.

C. *Modern Wars.*

1°. The Thirty Years' War, A. D. 1618 to 1648.

2°. Wars from A. D. 1648 to Frederick the Great.

3°. Frederick's era to the beginning of the French Revolution, A. D. 1740 to 1792.

D. *Recent Wars.*

1°. From the French Revolution to 1805.

2°. Napoleon's wars, A. D. 1805 to 1815.

3°. Wars since 1815.

Of these several periods the most important by far to the military student are those which contain the deeds of Alexander, Hannibal, Cæsar, in ancient days, and those of Gustavus, Frederick and Napoleon in modern times. Few of the other great generals fall without these periods. To narrate the military achievements of these great masters, and incidentally a few others, and to connect them by a mere thread of the intervening events, will suffice to give all which is best in the rise and progress of the science of war. " Read," says Napoleon, " re-read the history of their campaigns, make them your model ; this is the sole means of becoming a great captain and of guessing the secret of the art."

So long as man has existed on the earth he has been a fighting animal. After settling his quarrels with the weapons of nature, he resorted to clubs and stones, that is, weapons

for use hand to hand and at a distance; and no doubt at
an early day built himself huts and surrounded them with
stakes, stones and earth, so as to keep away aggressive neighbors. Herein we have the origin of weapons and of fortification. As men joined themselves into communities, the arts
of attack and defense, and their uses as applied to numbers,
grew. The citizen was always a soldier. But often only a
portion of the citizens required to be sent away from home
to fight, and this originated standing armies, which became
a well-settled institution when conquerors made themselves
kings. As man invented useful arts, these were first applied
to the demands of war. Bows and arrows, lances, slings,
swords, breastplates and shields came into use, and horses
were tamed and employed for war, first as beasts of burden,
and then in chariots and for cavalry. Chariots and horses for
cavalry were first adopted because they afforded the fighters
a higher position from which to cast their weapons, as well
as rendered their aspect more dreadful. Elephants and camels came into warfare for a similar reason. No doubt chariots antedated cavalry. Troops began by fighting in masses,
without settled order, and the victory was won by those who
had the bravest, strongest, or most numerous array. With
better weapons came greater order. The best-armed warriors were placed together. The slingers could not do good
work side by side with the pikemen, nor the charioteer or
mounted man with the foot-soldier. Thus certain tactical
formations arose, and as the more intelligent soldiers were
put in charge of the less so, rank and command appeared.
It was soon found that the light-armed, bowmen and slingers, could best use their weapons and most rapidly move in
open, skirmishing order; that the heavy-armed, pikemen and
swordsmen, could best give decisive blows when ployed into
masses. The growth of army organization came about in a

perfectly natural sequence, and grew side by side with all other pursuits.

Fortification originated in a similar manner. Tribes built their villages in inaccessible places, — on rocks or hills, — and surrounded them with ditches, stockades or loosely-piled walls. Such simple habitations gradually grew into fortified cities, and the walls and ditches increased in size and difficulty of approach. Inner citadels were built; and towers crowned the walls, to enable these to be swept by missiles if reached by the besiegers. The art of sieges was of much later and more formal growth. For many generations fortified cities were deemed inexpugnable, and artifice or hunger were resorted to for their capture. But gradually it was found that walls could be undermined or weakened or breached, or that they could be mounted by various means, and the art of besieging cities began to take on form.

As tribes grew into nations war assumed larger dimensions. As a rule, it was brute weight alone which accomplished results, but sometimes the weaker party would resort to stratagems to defend itself, — such as declining battle, and making instead thereof night or partial attacks, defending river fords or mountain passes, and falling on the enemy from ambush or from cities. Out of such small beginnings of moral opposition to physical preponderance has come into existence, by slow degrees and through many centuries, what we now know as the science of war.

Except the Phœnicians and Jews, the Oriental nations of remote antiquity were divided into castes, of which the most noble or elevated were alone entitled to bear arms, and to this profession they were trained with scrupulous care. The military caste in some nations was wont to monopolize all offices and political control; in others it wielded a lesser sway.

The existence of such castes gave rise to what eventually became standing armies, and from the ranks of these were chosen the king's body-guard, always an important factor in Oriental government.

The Phœnicians first employed mercenary troops. A paid force enabled the citizens to continue without interruption the commercial life on which their power rested. But such troops were of necessity unreliable. Egypt and Persia in later times employed mercenaries in large numbers.

In addition to these methods of recruitment, drafts of entire districts, or partial drafts of the country, were usual. These swelled the standing armies, caste or mercenary, to a huge size, but furnished an unreliable material, which, against good troops, was in itself a source of weakness, but which often won against similarly constituted bodies.

The methods of conducting war, in organization and tactics, were always on a low scale in the Orient. The origin of every military device is in the East; successive steps towards improvement were made in Europe by the Greeks and Romans. Despite that a certain luxurious civilization rose to a higher grade among the Orientals, the military instinct of these down-trodden races was less marked than among the freemen of the West. In one respect alone — cavalry — were the Oriental nations superior. This superiority was owing to the excellence of their horses and to the prevalence of horsemanship among them. In all other branches they fell distinctly below the Europeans.

The chief characteristic of the operations of the ancient Orientals was that of huge raids or wars of conquest, which overran vast territories, and often led to the conflict of enormous armies, to the extinguishment or enslaving of nations, or to long drawn-out sieges of capitals or commercial cities. In battles, it was sought by stratagem to fall on, and, by preponderance of force, to surround and annihilate the enemy. All such operations were accompanied by dire inhumanity to individuals and to peoples, by the shedding of blood and destruction of property beyond compute. But they have furnished no contribution to the art of war.

Assyrian Mounted Archer.

III.

EARLY ORIENTAL ARMIES.

AMONG the ancient Oriental nations, military service was generally confined to a caste. Infantry was the bulk, cavalry the flower, of the Oriental armies. Light troops came from the poorer classes and were miserably clad, and armed with bows and slings. The heavy foot, drawn from the richer classes, was, as a rule, splendidly armed and equipped. There was plenty of courage in the Eastern armies, but small discipline and *ensemble*. There was no strategic manœuvring; armies simply met and fought. Battle was opened by the light troops; the chariots then charged, and were followed up by an advance of the heavy foot, while the cavalry sought to surround the flanks of the enemy. The parallel order was universal, and open plains were chosen as battlefields. The Jews had, even under Moses, a fine organization. There was a sort of landwehr of two hundred and eighty-eight thousand men, of which a twelfth was always on duty. While using other arms, the sling remained a favorite weapon. The Jews learned much of war from the Philistines. The Egyptians were excellent soldiers in early times; but their chariots and cavalry were gradually driven out by the extension of the canal system, which prevented their manœuvring; and mercenaries crept into use to the detriment of the service. The Egyptian formation was generally in huge squares of one hundred files one hundred deep. The Persians had a hereditary warrior caste, and were in early history very warlike. Cyrus began his wonderful career of conquest with but thirty thousand infantry. Cavalry he accumulated afterwards. The Persians learned much from the conquered Medes in the way of technical skill. Their army contained many fine bodies of troops.

Assyrians, Babylonians and Medes. — The army organization of the Assyrians, Babylonians and Medes had a similar origin and much common likeness in form. Military service was the sole right of a certain caste, and among the Medes was looked on as the highest of pursuits. The standing armies consisted of the king's body-guard, often very large; particular corps under command of nobles of high degree, which helped to sustain the centralized government; and provincial troops. The population was divided into bodies of ten, one hundred, one thousand, ten thousand, each of which furnished its quota of men; and the army was itself organized on a decimal basis. A vast horde of nomads, mostly horse, and excellent of its kind, was wont to accompany the regular army, either for pay or in hope of plunder.

Infantry constituted the bulk, cavalry the flower, of the

Assyrian Warriors.

Oriental armies. For many generations after the Greek infantry had shown to the world its superiority over any other, the Oriental cavalry was still far ahead of that of Greece. The Greeks were not horsemen, nor their hilly country as well suited for horse-breeding as the level plains of Asia. It is a truism, however, that a nation of horsemen overrun, a nation of footmen conquer a country. The Greeks and Romans were examples of this.

The armament of the light troops consisted of bows and

slings ; they wore no defensive armor. The nobles and well-
to-do, who served as heavy troops, were superbly armed and

Babylonian Heavy Foot.   Babylonian Slinger.

equipped. They bore a sword, battle-axe, javelins, pike and
dagger, or some of these. Though few in number, the heavy-

Babylonian Chariot.

armed were the one nucleus of value. There was no idea of
strategic manœuvring ; armies marched out to seek each
other and fought when they met. The troops were ranked
for battle by order of nationalities, generally in a long and

often more or less concave order, so as, if possible, to surround the enemy. The foot stood in the centre, the cavalry on the wings; the front was covered by chariots. The formation was in massed squares, often one hundred or more deep. The archers and slingers swarmed in the front of all, and opened the battle with a shower of light missiles. They then retired through the intervals between the squares of the advancing main line, or around its flanks, and continued their fire from its rear. The chariots then rushed in at a gallop and sought to break the enemy's line, generally by massing a charge on some one point. These were followed by the heavy footmen, who, covered with their shields and

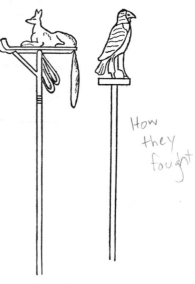

Military Insignia.

pike in hand, under the inspiration of the trumpet, and led by bearers of insignia, such as birds and beasts of prey or sacred emblems, mounted on long lances like our battle-flags, sought to force their way, by weight of mass, into the breaches made by the chariots; while the cavalry swept round the flanks and charged in on the rear of the enemy. Fierce hand-to-hand fighting then ensued. The Orientals were far from lacking courage. It was mobility and discipline they wanted. That army which could overlap the enemy or had the stronger line — unless the enemy protected its front and flanks with chariots or chosen troops — was apt to win; and the beaten army was annihilated. Battles were generally fought on open plains. It never seemed to occur to these peoples to lean a flank on a natural obstacle, such as a wood or river.   An unfortunate turn in a battle could not be retrieved.

The capital cities were splendidly fortified.   Nineveh, Bab-

Median Scythed Chariot.

ylon, Ecbatana, had stone walls of extraordinary thickness and height.   Those of Nineveh were still one hundred and fifty feet high in Xenophon's time.   Babylon had two walls, an outer one stated by Herodotus as three hundred and thir-

Assyrian Archer.

ty-five feet high and eighty-five feet thick, and by Ctesias at almost these dimensions, and with a correspondingly wide ditch.   The citadel was a marvel of strength, so far as massiveness was concerned.   The art of engineering, as applied to sieges, was not highly developed.   The mechanical means of the day were not as well adapted for besieging as for fortification, and the defense of a city was rendered desperate by the uniform penalty of its surrender or capture, which was death or slavery.   The Assyrians are said to have fortified their temporary camps, generally in circular form.

Jews. — Among the Jews, every man over twenty years of age, with certain stated exceptions, was a warrior.   The twelve tribes each furnished a corps, which, at the time of the flight from Egypt, was, on the average, fifty thousand strong. From this corps, in times of war, the needed number

of recruits was selected by lot or rote. It was a draft pure and simple. Saul first established a body-guard. In David's time (1025 ? B. C.) the number of Jews fit for war was one million three hundred thousand, and each tribe furnished twenty-four thousand men for active duty. One of these bodies

Hebrew Pikeman.

Hebrew Pikeman.

served each month, under a captain who reviewed it, and was held responsible for its effectiveness. The whole body of two hundred and eighty-eight thousand men was a sort of landwehr, of which one twelfth was constantly under arms. The organization was on a decimal basis of tens, hundreds and thousands. Solomon largely increased the number of cavalry and chariots, and perfected their organization and discipline.

Hebrew Heavy Footman.

On the flight from Egypt the Israelites were in possession of no weapons. They partially armed themselves from those cast up by the sea after the destruction of the Egyptians. Their arms, during the later part of their wanderings, were bows, slings and darts. Until they reached the promised land, they had no forged weapons. The Philistines, or dwellers in Palestine, were better provided, and were familiar with both cavalry and chariots. At a

later day the Jews acquired and
used short, wide, curved swords and
lances.   But the sling always remained a favorite weapon, and in
its use they were curiously expert.
In the *corps d'élite* of the time of
the Judges, which consisted of twenty-six thousand men who drew the
sword, was a body of seven hundred
left-handed slingers, who could cut a
hair hung up as a target.   So early
as the time of Moses, even, the drill

Hebrew Archer.

and discipline of the Jewish army was considerable.   The
method of battle was similar to that of other nations.   The
light troops in the van opened the battle in loose order ; the
heavy infantry in deep masses followed after.   They fought
under the inspiration of horns and battle-cries.   They sometimes stood in three lines, light troops, main body ten to thirty
men deep, and a reserve of
picked troops.   Martial insignia representing animals
were usually carried in the
ranks.

Slinger.

The Jews had great num-
bers to encounter. The Philistines came against Saul
with six thousand cavalry,
thirty thousand chariots, and
foot like to the sands of the
seashore in number.   In the
war against Hadadeser, son

of Rehob, King of Zobah, David captured one thousand chariots, seven hundred horsemen, and twenty thousand infantry.

Solomon kept on foot fourteen hundred chariots and twelve thousand cavalry. He had stalls for forty thousand chariot-horses, which probably included the equipages for the royal household and the army trains. These figures, compared with the numbers of chariots at Thymbra and Arbela, seem exaggerated; but they serve to show that the main reliance for the day was on chariots rather than on cavalry.

A careful military organization no doubt existed. We read in Holy Writ that David appointed Joab captain-general over his army, with twenty-seven lieutenants under him, and that his army was divided into three corps. There was clearly an established rank and command.

Hebrew Irregular.

Under Moses, the Jews fortified their daily

camp in form of a square. But permanent fortification of cities they only learned after conquering Palestine. Jerusalem was strongly fortified by David, on the method then usual among the Orientals.

Egyptians. — Thebes and Memphis appear to have had the earliest Egyptian military organization, but shortly after 1500 B. C. the first Pharaoh welded Egypt into one body. The warrior caste was at the head of society, second only to the priestly caste. Under the Sesostridæ (1500–1200 B. C.) the army organization grew in effectiveness. The father of

Egyptian King in War-Dress.

Sesostris, at the time of this great king's birth, selected all the boys in Egypt born on the same day, and made of them a military school, out of which later grew Sesostris' confidential body-guard. Among the number were many of his generals. Sesostris first gave rewards in land to his soldiers, as feudal kings did in later centuries, and obliged these dependents, as a consideration for their tenure, to go to war with

Egyptian Soldier, in Scale Armor.   Egyptian Soldier, in Linen Breastplate.

him at their own cost, and always to be prepared to perform this duty. The Egyptian army was over four hundred thousand strong. The youths of the warrior caste were carefully trained. All records and traditions agree that the Egyptians were excellent soldiers. The chief punishment for breach of discipline was loss of honor, which, however, the warrior could, by signal acts of bravery, regain. By 1200 B. C. came the decline of the Egyptian power, and, under Psammeticus, mercenary troops from Asia Minor and Greece gradually supplanted the warrior caste.

Infantry constituted the bulk of the forces. Chariots were

common, even in remote antiquity, as well as cavalry. These decreased in usefulness, however, as the canal-system of Egypt grew and left small room for manœuvring. The weapons were the usual arms, — bows, lances, slings, axes, darts and swords. The Egyptian soldiers were light and heavy, irregular and regular. Some carried shields covering the entire body, and wore helmets and mail. The army had martial music, and the emblem of the sacred bull or crocodile was carried on a lance as a standard. Xenophon, in the Cyropædia, describes their tactics at the battle of Thymbra. They stood in large, dense masses, very deep, often in squares of one hundred files of one hundred men, and, covered by linked shields and protruded lances, were dangerous to attack. The Egyptians fortified their camps in rectangular form, and built extensive walls to protect their borders. Sesostris erected one extending from Pelusium to Heliopolis. Their cities were fortified with walls of several stories. But, as with other nations at this period, the art of sieges was little advanced. Ashdod, though not strongly fortified, resisted Psammeticus twenty-nine years.

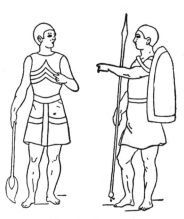

Egyptian Soldiers.

Sesostris is supposed to have had six hundred thousand infantry, twenty-seven thousand chariots and twenty-four thousand horse. He is said to have conquered Ethiopia, then crossed from Meroë to Arabia Petrea, and thence made excursions as far as India. He later sailed to Phœnicia, and overran a large part of Asia Minor. Sesostris is alleged to have conquered territory as far east as the Oxus and Indus,

and to have levied contributions on the populations of these countries. But his conquests had no duration, even if what is related of him by tradition has a more than problematical basis of truth.

Persians. — Under Cyrus the warrior caste was not only the uppermost, but was hereditary, and at all times thoroughly prepared for war. Assuming the Cyropædia to be exact, Cyrus undertook his great conquests with but thirty thousand men, which later increased to seventy thousand, and still more by accessions from the conquered provinces. In all these provinces a kernel of

Persian Soldier.

Persian troops was stationed, but the local government was uniformly preserved. This proceeding testifies to the keen good sense of Cyrus, who left behind him contented peoples, under satraps closely watched by his own Persian officers. His course was later imitated by Alexander the Great, with equally satisfactory results. Cyrus subdued as large a part of Asia as Alexander did after him, holding the cities as *points d'appui* as he went along. During his lifetime, Persian discipline was excellent. After his death, contact with the luxury of the Medes destroyed much of his structure.

Persian Irregular.

The Cyropædia is, however, a sort of military romance, into which Xenophon has woven his own military experience and astuteness. It is full of exaggerated hero-worship. While its main features are correct, its details are unquestionably dressed up. But it has none the less as great value as it has charm.

The Persians fought mainly on foot. There were few horses in Persia proper. But Cyrus found cavalry necessary against the Asiatics, who had much which was excellent. He collected ten thousand horsemen from various sources, and at Thymbra used the body to good advantage. This was the origin of the superb Persian cavalry of later days. The foot had bows, slings, darts and small shields, to begin with, but gradually bettered these weapons as they hewed their way into Asia, and thereafter used battle-axes and swords, and wore helmet and mail. Thus, from what was at first but a species of light infantry grew up a later body of heavy foot, in addition to much that remained light. The Persian foot had been marshaled thirty deep ; Cyrus reduced it to twelve ranks. The cavalry was divided in a similar manner, — the bulk was light horse, coming mainly from the nomad allies ; a lesser part was heavy-armed. Cyrus also

Persian Warrior.

had scythed-chariots, and Xenophon describes at the battle of Thymbra the use of towers on wheels, filled with armed men, together with other curious devices, and camels carrying archers and catapults, — questionable but interesting assertions.

In the art of fortification and sieges the Persians had made little or no advance, but they learned something from the Medes and other Asiatics, and gradually acquired the use of catapults and rams. But stratagem, as at Sardis after the battle of Thymbra, had generally to be put into practice to capture towns, unless hunger speedily reduced them. Nebuchadnezzar besieged old Tyre thirteen years and failed to take it.

Cambyses, son of Cyrus, divided the male population of his kingdom into children, youths, men, old men. Each class had twelve chiefs, chosen from among the last two classes. Every lad of ten began his career by entering the first. Here he stayed till twenty; among the youths till thirty; among the men till forty; and until fifty-five he was in the last class. After this he was free from military duty. Each class had its special occupations and discipline. This distribution is rather curious than valuable.

Assyrian Armsbearer.

IV.

EARLY GREEK ARMIES AND WARS.

EVERY Greek citizen was a soldier and trained as such. In Homeric times the great warriors fought in chariots, the lesser ones on foot. There was no cavalry. Distinct organization is traceable as far back as the times of the Seven against Thebes; tactics is observable in the Trojan war. The siege of Troy was a mere blockade, though its walls were very poor, for there was small knowledge of the means of siege. Religion, education, and public games combined to maintain the honor of the warrior's life. He was on duty from eighteen to sixty years of age, and only through arms could political preferment be reached. The phalanx was the main reliance of the Greeks; light troops were insignificant, cavalry poor. Chariots disappeared after the Trojan war. Battles were uniformly in parallel order, and decided as a rule by one shock. The Greek armies were very nimble; but sieges were long drawn out. Command was divided, much to the loss of directness. The men were not paid. Booty replaced emoluments. Rewards were mere marks of honor, punishments outward marks of disgrace. Sparta was noted for the severity of its discipline and the simplicity of its habits, but lacked the broad intelligence requisite to continued success in war. The infantry was perfect; the cavalry worthless. The kings, though in command, were subject to the whims of civil officials, known as ephors. The Spartans had no idea of strategy, though they practiced ruse. Peace to the soldier was incessant labor and deprivation to prepare his body for war; he went to war as to a feast, decked with flowers and singing hymns of joy. The Athenian citizen was equally bound and bred to arms. From eighteen to forty he must serve anywhere, from forty to sixty be prepared to fall in to resist invasion. The phalanx was the chief reliance, as in Sparta. The Athenian soldier was more fiery, less constant, than the Spartan. Few early wars call for any notice. The Messenian wars were noteworthy on account of the able defense made against the Spartans, and the marked skill of Euphaës and Aristomenes. Not Sparta's skill or courage, but her excess of strength, subdued the Messenians.

THE ancient Greeks borrowed the germs of all they knew of the art of war from the East, but with true national intelligence they rejected the useless and improved the valuable up to its highest utility for the conditions of their age.

The early kings of Greece held both the civil and military power. Every freeman was a soldier, and was trained as such from his youth up. Bronze weapons were already familiar to the Greeks at the time of the Trojan war. The nobles

and chiefs used thrusting pike, casting lance and sword, and left missile-weapons — bows and slings — to the less brave or expert. The Trojan chiefs did not disdain bows. Helmets, breastplates and large shields were likewise made of bronze. Fighting on foot and in chariots — the latter was the prerogative of the great — were the

Paris, from Ægina Marbles.

usual methods. There was no cavalry, for the hilly character of Greece (except Thessaly and Bœotia) was unsuited to its evolutions, and neither, as a rule, were the horses good nor the men of Greece used to riding. The constant employment of chariots is all the more curious. From these two or four horse two-wheeled vehicles the warrior descended to fight, the driver meanwhile remaining near at hand. At best they were cumbrous and of doubtful value, except as a moral stimulant.

In the tradition of the Seven against Thebes, to assert Polynices' claims as king, there are some traces of organization suggested. The city was besieged by posting a separate detachment opposite each of its gates, and by relying on hunger as an ally. But the Thebans made a sortie, slew the seven kings, and drove their forces away. Ten years later the sons of these kings captured Thebes, and placed Polynices' son upon the throne.

At the siege of Troy (1193–
1184 B. C.) we find clear evidences of organization. Aga-
memnon evidently had the legal
power to compel the reluctant
Greek monarchs to join him in
an expedition based on a mere
personal quarrel. Achilles had
twenty-five hundred men, divided
into five regiments of five hundred men each. The Greeks advanced to battle in a phalanx or
deep body, shield to shield, and
in silence, so that the orders of
the leaders might be heard. But

Greek Soldier, in Linen Cuirass.

in front of the lines of the armies there always took place
a series of duels between
the doughtiest champions,
— as it were a prolonged
and very important com-
bat of skirmishers before
the closing of the heavy
lines. But coupled with
an admirable idea of dis-
cipline was the habit of
plundering the slain, for
which purpose ranks
would be broken and
often a decisive advan-
tage lost. Prisoners were
treated with awful inhu-
manity.

Ancient Greek Soldier.

Camps were regular, and often fortified. The men used

no tents, but camped in the open, building huts if long in one place. At Troy the Greek camp had a broad and deep ditch, palisades, or a wall made of the earth thrown up from the ditch, and wooden towers on the wall. Behind this the army camped in huts.

Fortification had advanced but little beyond the roughest work. The art of sieges was all but unknown. The ten

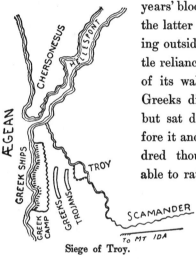

years' blockade of Troy amply shows the latter fact, as the constant fighting outside the town proves that little reliance was placed on the value of its walls by the Trojans. The Greeks did not surround the city, but sat down on the sea-coast before it and blockaded it, some hundred thousand strong. Troy was able to ration itself from the Mount Ida region. The Greeks were sadly put to it for victuals, and were compelled to detail half the army to the Chersonesus

Siege of Troy.

in order to raise breadstuffs. For nine years there was naught but insignificant small-war.

After the Greeks had wasted their time in isolated attacks on the Trojan territory until both sides were well-nigh exhausted, Nestor counseled concentration and the division of the army into bodies by race and families, in order to produce a spirit of rivalry and due ambition. It is evident that the troops knew how to deploy, for they filed out of the gates of their camps and then formed line of battle. The army had a right, centre and left. The infantry stood in several ranks, — in front the least brave, in the rear the most brave,

on the plan suggested by Nestor. And the army was marshaled on occasion in several lines; as, for instance, the
chariots in first, and the foot in second line. To attack the
Greek intrenchments, Hector divided the Trojans into five
troops, so that success should not depend on one attack alone.
Here is the crude idea of a reserve, as it were. Aristides
names Palamedes, who was at Troy, as the inventor of tactics; but Nestor must evidently share the honor. The one
thing which interfered with the successful use of tactics was
the prolonged dueling part of the fray between the heroes of
both sides. Of art in their warfare there was barely a trace.
It was only in the tenth year, after heavy fighting, that Troy
was taken, and it was without a siege, in the sense we understand it.

From the time of the Trojan war till the sixth century
B. C. the Grecian states made gradual advances in military
organization. The warrior's was the highest duty in the state,
as well as the precious privilege of the freeman. Religion,
education and public games combined to train the youth to
war. Religion taught that heroes became demi-gods; education was almost entirely confined to athletic and warlike
exercises, training in patience and endurance, the inculcation
of respect for superiors and elders and the love of country;
public games afforded the bravest, strongest and most expert
an occasion of exhibiting their skill and prowess, and of earning honor and repute. Chariot and horse races and athletic
games monopolized these ceremonies. The latter comprised
running, leaping obstacles, wrestling, throwing the lance and
discus, boxing, the pancratium or boxing and wrestling
mixed, and the pentathlium or an exercise combining all the
others. The prizes were as a rule mere evidences of honor,
but these were held to be far beyond material reward. A
noted victor had statues erected, inscriptions cut and hymns

sung in his honor, and was often maintained at the public expense.

The right and duty of war existed from the eighteenth to the sixtieth year, varying somewhat in different states. When

Hoplite (from a vase). Hoplite (from a vase).

war occurred, a draft of the requisite number was made by lot, or rote, or age. A given number of years' honorable service yielded a citizen many privileges, and opened to him every civil office. Warriors crippled in battle were cared for by the state and highly honored.

About the sixth century B. C. the Greeks fought almost exclusively on foot. The hoplites or phal-angites were the heavy, the psiloi the light, infantry. The former came from the best classes, and were armed with pikes up to ten feet long, short swords and large shields, and wore both helmet and breastplate, and some-times greaves. The breastplate was often of leather, and everything being provided by each hoplite for himself made the arms and

Leather Cuirass (iron plates).

equipments as various as the tastes of the individuals. The

psiloi had no defensive armor, and carried only bows and slings. Recruited from the poorer classes, they were of far less value in action than the hoplites, but some psiloi, like the Cretan bowmen, were celebrated for their accurate aim and the penetration of their arrows.

Chariots fell into disuse after the Trojan war. They were found to be unavailable among the rugged hills and vales of Greece. But cavalry began to take their place, at just what period is uncertain. Xenophon mentions cavalry in the time of Lycurgus. It was undoubtedly employed in the Messenian war, a century later. As an arm it was not good, excepting possibly the Bœotian horse, and especially that from Thessaly, on whose broad meadows had been bred an excellent race of stout, serviceable cobs.

The tactical disposition of troops was very various, but generally in earliest times was based on a decimal system like that of the East. The light troops covered the front and flanks of the army; and the hoplites were formed in a dense body, uniformly called a phalanx, which, however, at that time had no absolute rule of formation or numbers. Xenophon states that the unit of the then phalanx was a taxis (or lochos or century) of one hundred men, commanded by a captain, and ranged in four files twenty-four men deep, plus four officers, each file having four sections of six men each. Ten taxes made a chiliarchia, under a chiliarch, and four chiliarchias a phalanx. The names of the units of service were very various. Attacks were made in parallel order, but it was infrequently sought to lean the flanks and rear on obstacles which might prevent their being turned. Camps were pitched where they were secure from the nature of their location, and were rarely much fortified. The soldier carried no great burden, and the Greek armies were very nimble. The right flank was the post of honor. Marches were almost invariably by the right, and the flanks of the column of march were covered by the psiloi.

Engineering, as applied to fortification and sieges, still remained singularly crude. The latter were wont to be of long duration. They scarcely amounted even to blockades. Ithome was besieged eight years ; Ira, eleven ; Crissa, nine.

To the government, whatever it might be, was intrusted the care of all things pertaining to the military establishment ; but the right to declare war and to make treaties was reserved by the people, which expressed itself in public gatherings. The weak feature of the Greek military organization

Greek Strategos.

was the lack of unity of command. The armies were as a rule commanded alternately, for a given period, — often but a day, — by one of several leaders, elected by the people, who jointly made a council of war, and who were apt to be under the control of other non-military officials sent by the government to watch them. This system very naturally arose from the history and tendencies towards liberty of the various states, but was coupled with very difficult problems, and often resulted in disaster.

The Greek served his country without pay. To receive money for a duty was in early days considered an indignity. Plunder, however, made up for this lack of remuneration. After a victory, the booty was collected ; part was vowed to the gods and placed in their temples, and the rest was divided according to rank and merit, — the leaders being usually entitled to the lion's share.

Punishment for military crimes involved loss of honor, sometimes of civil rights, — the penalties most dreaded by the patriotic Greek. Rewards were embodied in an increased share of plunder, promotion, gifts of weapons and marks of honor, and in civil advancement or public support.

The Greek soldier was a curious mixture of virtues and vices. He possessed courage, discipline and self-abnegating patriotism in the highest measure, but was prejudiced, superstitious and monstrously cruel. The Greek states were characterized by similar tendencies. The individual merely reflected the state *in petto.*

Sparta. — Among all the Greek states, Sparta in the ninth century B. C., and Athens in the sixth, were distinguished for the perfection of their military organization. The main object of the laws of Lycurgus (820 B. C.) was to form a military power out of a mass of free citizens, and to impress on the individual soldier those qualities of courage, endurance, obedience and skill which would make him irresistible. This they did by banishing arts and sciences, — civilization almost, — and by reducing life down to its lowest limits of simplicity and self-denial. This method fully accomplished its aim; soldiers have rarely, perhaps never, been animated by so single a martial spirit as the Spartans. Love of country, and willingness to sacrifice to it self and all which lends life worth, has never been more fully exemplified than in the Pass of Thermopylæ. But what was gained in one sense was lost in another. A state cannot become great in its best sense by its soldierly qualities and achievements alone.

Greek Hoplite.

The Spartan youth belonged, not to the parent, but to the state. They were educated in common, and drilled in gymnastics and the use of arms from earliest childhood. They were compelled to undergo extraordinary fatigues, and this on slender rations; and were taught the simpler virtues of respect for age and obedience to superiors. From twenty to sixty all men were under arms. War was to them the only

art; death in battle the highest good. As a consequence, the Spartan army, for centuries, was considered invincible.

But Sparta's success in war led her into too frequent wars, and her disregard of the arts and sciences advanced other nations beyond her in the intellectual grasp of war. Sparta was forbidden by Lycurgus to possess either fortress or fleet; the army alone must suffice as

Greek Psilos (from a vase).

breastwork of the land. Still more curiously, the army was prohibited from pursuing a beaten enemy. Not conquest, but defense of the fatherland was sought. Such mistaken policy eventually gave Sparta's opponents the upper hand.

Heavy infantry was the main reliance of Sparta. The soldier wore full armor; he held it a duty to the state to preserve intact his body for the state, but he did not seek safety by the method of Hudibras. He deemed it dishonor to lose, or to fight without, his shield. Not to have it with him implied that in his haste to run away he had cast it aside, so as to run the faster. He bore a heavy pike, generally a lighter lance, and a short double-edged sword. There was little light infantry, and the cavalry was mediocre. It was formed in eight ranks, and generally got beaten.

There is some conflict of statement between Xenophon and Thucydides as to the organization of the Spartan troops into bodies. This is probably due to the changes in such organization from time to time. But rank and command were well settled. In a mora, or regiment of four hundred, and later of nine hundred men — Thucydides says five hundred and twelve men — were one polemarch, or colonel; four lochagoi, or majors; eight pentekosteroi, or captains; and sixteen enomotarchoi, or lieutenants. It had four lochoi, divided into sections of twenty-five and fifty men, each under a sort of sergeant. The word lochos, like taxis, or like our word division, is often applied to various bodies. Each mora had

Back of Hoplite's helmet.

added to it a body of one hundred horsemen or less.

Greek Hoplite.

The kings were the commanders-in-chief. In peace their power was limited; it was unlimited in war. But they were strictly accountable to the people for their use of the army. If there were two armies, each king commanded one. If but one, the people decided who should command and who remain at the head of the home government. In the field the king had a species of staff and body-guard, consisting of one or two polemarchs, several of the victors at the public games and a number of younger mounted warriors. Later the kings were accompanied by the ephors (of whom there were five), who acted as a species of council of war. These ephors were civil officials, whose duty was to watch lest the kings should exceed their legal powers.

The Spartans knew nothing of strategy. Their tactics was simple. They moved out to meet the enemy, drew up in a deep, heavy phalanx, and decided the day by one stout blow.

If the enemy was superior in numbers, they sometimes tried ruse. They marched to battle in cadenced step and in silence, to the sound of the flute. If they won, they might not pursue ; if beaten, they were generally able to withdraw slowly and in good order. A mounted vanguard accompanied the army on the march. In camp they had a police-guard under a provost-marshal, and they appear to have developed a system of pickets and patrols. They rarely fortified their camp, which was round in shape, if they could place it where its location made it reasonably secure.

Peace to the Spartans was a season of unremitting labor in preparing for war. War was their sole relaxation. The only duty then was to fight. The intervals between marches and battles were filled by games and gymnastic sports. They had none of the tasks of peace ; a campaign was a holiday. All fatigue-duties were performed by helots, who accompanied the army for that purpose only, but were in later years utilized in the ranks of fighting men. They carried abundant supplies on pack-animals, and the general meal, in peace a most coarse though ample mess, was in war rich and nutritious. The soldiers prepared for

Hoplite (from a vase).

battle as for a feast, wore their best garments, and plucked flowers wherewith to adorn their persons and their arms.

The Spartans never opened a campaign before the full moon. This was a religious custom, but occasionally, as at Marathon, far from auspicious. The gods were propitiated by tiresome but invariable ceremonials and offerings before every military movement.

Being allowed by law no fortresses, the Spartan territory was not only open to invasion, but the nation was ignorant of fortification. Nor did they understand how to lay siege to a strong place.

Athens. — From the abolition of the kings down to the days of Solon (1068–594 B. C.), owing to the internal discords and external conflicts of Athens, the war-establishment was uncertain. Solon's laws aimed at producing a form of government which should keep the aristocratic element within bounds, and at the same time not run into pure democracy. He divided the citizens into four classes (or phylæ), according to wealth, — the pentakosiomedimnoi, the hippeis, or knights, the zeugitoi, and the thetes. The first were the richest, the last the poorest. Every citizen was bound to service. Though Athens was a democracy, the citizens were often in a small minority. There were at one time but ninety thousand of them to forty-five thousand foreigners and three hundred and sixty thousand slaves. Another census, taken under Demetrius, showed twenty-one thousand citizens, ten thousand metics, and four hundred thousand slaves. The members of the first two classes above named were obliged on requisition to keep each a horse and serve as cavalry, but were then free from infantry duty in all but exceptional cases. The third class furnished the heavy infantry, in which each man must supply himself with arms. Of the fourth class, those who could furnish the proper arms might serve in the heavy foot; the others were the light troops.

Heroic Horseman
(from a vase).

Every Athenian freeman was held to pursue a certain

gymnastic and military training in the public schools. At eighteen years of age he took a solemn oath of fealty to the state, and entered upon his military du-
ties. From twenty to forty he was bound to serve, whenever drawn, within or beyond the At- tic territory. After twenty years' service the citizen was discharged, and entered upon civil pursuits. But up to his sixtieth year he must be ready at all times to fall into the ranks to resist invasion. Towards the end of the sixth cen- tury B. C., the classes were in- creased to ten.

Homeric Warrior.

The heavy infantry was the strong arm of Athens, as of Sparta. The hoplite still bore the Homeric arms, consisting of large shield, long lance and short sword. The Homeric armor remained substantially the same among the Greeks ever after. The warrior wore a tunic. He first put on his greaves ; then his cuirass in two parts, the mitre underneath, the zone above ; then he hung his sword on the left side in the socket of a belt which went over the right shoulder ; he next assumed his shield, hung in similar manner ; then his helmet ; then his spears. The hoplite fought in closed pha- lanx eight or more deep. The cavalry was weak ; the light troops (psiloi) insignificant. The army was apt to be set up in one or two lines, with the heavy foot in the centre, the light foot in the wings, and the cavalry on the flanks. But this was not invariable.

The organization of the troops at this time is not accu- rately known. It appears to have been much the same as the Spartan, — the names merely differing. Each of the ten phylæ furnished a body of one thousand or more hoplites, under command of a chiliarch, or colonel. The phylæ selected each a commander, called strategos, who was the equivalent of the Spartan polemarch. Of the ten strategoi, each in turn took command of the entire army ; all together they constituted the council of war.

The Athenian was equally brave, more fiery in his courage, but less constant and enduring than the Spartan, and the discipline to which he was subjected was somewhat less strict, as accorded with the national character.

Wars. — Immediately after the Trojan war came the invasions of the Heraclidæ (1104 B. C.), who subjugated the Peloponnesus. Except these, the wars of the Greeks, down to 750 B. C., were much what the quarrels of small semi-civilized tribes are wont to bring about, *i. e.*, wars quite without system. When Sparta and Athens had grown to be substantial nations, military movements came to be more noticeable. But they were still mostly confined to small-war and sieges. The territory of Greece, cut up by natural and political divisions into limited domains, narrowed operations down to this species of warfare. Larger evolutions were out of the question. But small-war was conducted with much intelligence. Sieges were more properly blockades ; fortification relied upon situation rather than art.

The first Messenian War (743–724 B. C.) is worthy of note for nothing so much as the long and excellent defense against the Spartans by Euphaës, king of Messenia. His maintaining himself in his capital during five years of preparation for war, his holding his own against the so-called invincible Spartans in the bloody but undecided battle of Amphæa, and the defense of Ithome, mark Euphaës as a great man. At

Ithome, in a rocky fastness, for eight years, Euphaës kept the best troops of the Spartans at bay, and in the last year beat them in the second battle of Amphæa, but at the cost of his own life.

At this battle of Amphæa (730 B. C.) Euphaës showed a fine conception of battle tactics. The Spartan kings, Theopompus and Polydorus, met the Messenian array in parallel order. The contest was severe. The right wing of each army was defeated. It was anybody's victory. But Euphaës

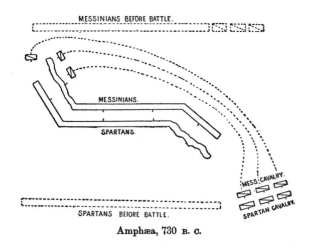

Amphæa, 730 B. C.

snatched it by a masterly stroke conceived on the instant and in the turmoil of battle. The cavalry on his left had defeated the Spartans in their front and driven them off the field. Speedily recalling them from pursuit, — always a difficult thing to do, — Euphaës led them behind his line of battle over to the succor of his retiring right. Thus supported the right was enabled to rally, and a few bold charges by the Messenian horse decided the day. Euphaës did not profit by the victory ; he fell in his moment of triumph.

Aristodemus, who succeeded him, kept up a constant small-war for five years, in which he maintained his superiority, and finally again beat the Spartans at Ithome, this time so badly that only the excellent discipline of the latter enabled them to regain Laconia with the relics of their army.

But the Spartans, with abundant population and resources, could easily recover themselves, while the Messenians were totally exhausted by their gallant struggle. On the death of Aristodemus the Spartans were able to take advantage of their superior strength and reduce Messenia to a tributary condition.

The second Messenian war (645–628 B. C.) was illustrated by the valor and ability of Aristomenes, under whose leadership the Messenians again rose to cast off the yoke of Sparta, invaded Laconia, beat their oppressors so badly as almost to recover their lost liberties and devastated large parts of the Spartan territory. After two years of disaster the Spartans were more successful, and by taking advantage of the treachery of their allies gained a marked advantage over the Messenians. Aristomenes retired to Ira, a fortress which he could victual from the near-by sea, for Sparta had no fleet. The same conditions had existed at Ithome. In Ira, for eleven years, Aristomenes held himself against the Spartans by able diversions outside the walls and stanch defense within. These long sieges exhibit as nothing else does the lack of engineering facilities of the day. But finally the Spartans, again by treachery, gained entrance into the fortress. Aristomenes was allowed to withdraw, but Messenia was subdued and parceled out by the Spartans.

V.

CYRUS AND DARIUS. B. C. 558–485.

THE great warriors preceding Cyrus are mere traditions. The first to leave lessons for us was the founder of the Persian Empire. The greatest conqueror may not be a great captain. It is *what* the former does which makes him great; it is *how* the latter does it which gives him rank. Cyrus began his campaigns by attacking Crœsus, and was the first to employ a strategic surprise. At Thymbra his battle tactics were novel. Crœsus vastly outnumbered and outflanked him. Cyrus formed his troops in five lines, so marshaled that when Crœsus' wings wheeled in on his flanks he could take these very wings in reverse, and at the same time poured into a gap in Crœsus' line and defeated him. He then turned on Babylon and captured it by diverting the water of the Euphrates, a gigantic work, and following its bed under the walls into the city. Cyrus left the local or civil governments of the peoples he conquered unchanged in the hands of the old satraps, merely retaining the military control himself, a plan later followed with great success by Alexander. Cyrus conquered Asia as far as Scythia beyond the Jaxartes, the natural limit to a kingdom. After him, Darius bridged the Bosphorus and Danube, and moved with seven hundred thousand men against the Scythians of Europe. These, by exceptionally able and interesting natural strategy, forced him to retire.

PRIOR to the age of Cyrus, in the sixth century before Christ, there is to be found nothing in the history of war which yields lessons to the soldier of to-day. Although among the nations of remote antiquity existence was a constant interchange of armed invasion, as famine or the lust of plunder induced one or other to prey upon the territory of its neighbor, yet in their wars we see no principle whatever governing military conduct, except the rule of numbers. Neither the Egyptians, Jews, Persians, Babylonians, Assyrians, nor Indians show anything like a defined military standard of campaign or battle. The conduct of war lacked every

element of system. Great conquerors there no doubt were.
Nimrod, the reputed builder of the tower of Babel and of
Nineveh, or whoever was his prototype, was no doubt justly
regarded by the Jews as the exemplification of temporal
power with all its attendant evil. Though we must now
admit that both he and his widow, the wonderful Semiramis,
were little more than mere names for explaining the traditions of successful wars and the founding of powerful cities,
to which condition of nonentity modern research has finally
reduced them, still both must be held to represent a line of
distinguished predecessors ; and though Sesostris' great conquests, even to Ethiopia, the Ganges and Scythia, as related
by the Greek historians, may have been the work of a whole
dynasty instead of an individual, there remains the skeleton
of a long series of able wars. Whether these famous names of
prehistoric times were those of real monarchs or not, no doubt
in all ages great warriors have existed and many more been
born to blush unseen. For opportunity is the coefficient of
genius. But however mighty the deeds of these and other
conquerors may have been, great captains in the sense of captains helpful to the military student of our times cannot be
found in tradition. From the legends of the conquests of
Ninus, Semiramis, Sesostris, we can gather nothing which
lends aid to modern war. This is so partly because victory in
those ages leaned to the side, not of the heaviest battalions,
but of the greatest mob ; partly because history gives us no
details of these movements, and tradition is picturesque rather
than reliable. It is perhaps indisputable that the actual conquerors whose deeds have been handed down to us under these
names were instinct with the same divine afflatus which inspired the conduct of later, and to us greater, captains. No
doubt they illustrated all the qualities which go to make up
the pattern army-leader. But prior to the time of Cyrus we

search in vain for something akin to the military science of to-day, something which has added to the art of war.

The same thing can be said of most historical conquerors. The greatest of these may by no means rank as a great captain. To overrun vast regions, devastate well-peopled countries, reduce to servitude brave tribes, may constitute a great conqueror. But it is the method with which this is done which makes a great captain. A lesser actor in the world's drama may well be a greater captain. Alexander was a type of both the great conqueror and the great captain. He had transcendent genius; he had fit opportunity to give scope to his genius. He was the greatest of conquerors, because he overran and subdued the largest territory and the most peoples; he was a great captain because he did this with a method which teaches us lessons of incalculable value. It is the purpose of this work to narrate the deeds of those great captains who have peculiarly influenced the art of war, as we understand it to-day. However great men may have been as generals, however valuable their life's work in the world's economy, unless they have made an essential contribution to the science of war, they find no place within the scope of this and succeeding volumes.

Cyrus is not only a historical verity, but we know from the Greek historians what he did, and to a certain extent how he did it. All histories vary, — often to a material degree; nor is this wonderful of the ancients, when we read the conflicting accounts in vogue to-day relating to the wars of the last hundred — the last twenty-five — years. But from the ancient histories we can generally arrive at something like the truth. No one historian can be relied upon in all things. But by diligent comparison of the statements of all, the study of the topography of the campaigns or battlefields, and the estimate of probability as between conflicting statements, a reasonably exact narrative is possible. Military critics of every age are wont to disagree in many things; but their variations are rarely fatal. The same lessons can be learned from any of them.

Cyrus, of the family of the Acheminidæ, was the founder of the great Persian empire (B. C. 558–529). Persia had been subject to the Medes, and was grievously oppressed. Cyrus deposed Astyages, the Median king, and united Persia and Media under his own sceptre. Alarmed for his safety, Crœsus, king of Lydia, which then comprised almost all Asia Minor west of the Halys, entered the lists against Cyrus, and advanced across the Halys into Cappadocia, the most westerly of the Persia-Median provinces, and devastated the rich lands and cities of Pteria. He had as allies the Babylonians, and the Egyptians and even Sparta had promised him support. Crœsus was preparing to advance still farther into Persia, when Cyrus, by a rapid march, anticipated him, and met him on the scene of his devastations. An indecisive, wild and bloody battle was fought here, and ended only by night (B. C. 554), after which Crœsus retired to his capital, Sardis, not expecting that Cyrus would undertake a winter campaign. Here he endeavored to strengthen

Conquests of Cyrus.

for the succeeding year his bonds with his allies, and procure material assistance.

But Cyrus, full of the ardor which brooks not delay, and acting on that oldest and soundest of military principles, to do that which your enemy least expects, gave his adversary no breathing spell. Winter was at hand. Crœsus, anticipating no further present activity on the part of Cyrus, had unwisely allowed his army to disperse on reaching Sardis. Taking advantage of this error, Cyrus, by forced and difficult marches, came upon him unawares at Thymbra, on the plains not far from Sardis, and utterly defeated him. This is perhaps the first instance on record of those strategic surprises with which the history of great captains is filled, and of which the campaign of Ulm is so notable an example. The capital, Sardis, was besieged fourteen days, and then taken by storm. Lydia was subjected. But, with that politic generosity which great soldiers have so often known how to employ, — unusual in those days, — Cyrus made Crœsus his friend and adviser, and profited much by the latter's knowledge and influence.

One of the earliest instances of excellent battle tactics has been described by Xenophon. It was at this same battle of Thymbra in which Cyrus destroyed the Lydian kingdom. Crœsus is reputed to have had four hundred and twenty thousand men and three hundred chariots ; Cyrus, one hundred and ninety-six thousand men, three hundred chariots, and three hundred war camels. Xenophon states that Cyrus had shown great skill in organizing and in victualing his army. The rival forces met on the plain of Thymbra, not far from Sardis. It has been suggested that Xenophon improved in his description upon the actual manœuvres. But if the relation is not a true account of what Cyrus actually did, it describes what Xenophon actually knew how to do, and is equally interesting from this standpoint.

Crœsus proposed to utilize his great numerical superiority, by extending his line far beyond the flanks of Cyrus, and by wheeling in upon these so as to encompass him on all sides. Crœsus' army was in one long line, some say in two, with the cavalry on the flanks. The depth of the line was thirty men, except in the centre, where the Egyptian allies kept their national formation of ploying each ten thousand men into a huge square block of one hundred files of one hundred men each.

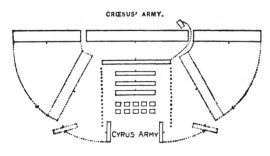

Battle of Thymbra.

The chariots were in front. Cyrus, aware of his opponent's great numerical superiority, and expecting this inclosing manœuvre, — an almost invariable one at that day, — drew up his army so as best to meet it. He reduced his files to a depth of twelve men, but arrayed his troops in five lines, so as to give the army, with the intervals between the lines, exceptional depth. In his first line were the heavy infantry-men in armor ; in the second, the acontists, or dart-throwers ; in the third, the archers, who were to shoot over the heads of the other lines ; in the fourth line the infantry *d'élite;* and in the fifth, the tower-bearing wagons, — a species of movable tower filled with armed men. Behind all this was the wagon train, in a huge square, within which all the non-combatants were placed. His chariots Cyrus placed, one hundred in front, and one hundred along each flank, and at the rearward end of the line of chariots he posted a chosen body of one thousand foot and one thousand horse. The camel-corps — archers mounted on camels — was with the latter body on the left.

Cyrus' idea in forming the line so deep was to oblige Crœsus to make a very extensive inward wheel if he expected to inclose his flanks. Such a wheel must of necessity open gaps in the Lydian line, of which Cyrus hoped to be able to take advantage. The wagon-towers made a sort of fortified camp to which he could retire if defeated. Cyrus awaited the onset of Crœsus.

When the Lydian monarch came within proper distance, his centre halted, and his wings began the anticipated turning wheel. As can be well understood, so vast a body could not make this manœuvre without losing touch in many places. When the wheel was about completed, the chariots on the flanks of Cyrus' army charged upon the somewhat disordered wings of Crœsus in front, while the reserves dashed in on their flanks. In a brief time these wings were entirely broken. Meanwhile gaps had also been made between the centre and the wings of Crœsus' army, seeing which Cyrus quickly gathered his best horse and attacked the flanks and rear of Crœsus' centre. This, too, was soon beaten, though the Egyptians fought so stanchly that Cyrus was compelled to make terms with them by which they entered his service.

After the battle of Thymbra, Cyrus left his lieutenants to subjugate the Greek cities on the coast of the Ægean, while he himself undertook the larger task of reducing Parthia, Sogdiana, Bactria, Arachosia, and the neighboring principalities. In this expedition he overran almost as large a territory as did subsequently Alexander the Great. The Sacæ gave him the greatest trouble.

He then turned upon Babylon, and in a two years' siege

(B. C. 539–538) reduced that city and incorporated the Babylonian with the Persian kingdom. It was not properly a siege, scarcely a blockade. The Babylonians were very confident in the strength of their huge walls and derided the besiegers. Cyrus had no battering-rams or catapults; nor does he appear to have understood the undermining of walls. He had to confine himself to erecting walls or mounds and towers higher than and commanding those of the city. But by this means alone he was able to accomplish nothing. Finally, by one of those audacious conceptions which cause the great captain to loom up above his fellows, Cyrus, hearing from deserters that an annual five days' religious festival was about to take place, during which the population would abandon itself to rejoicing and pay less heed to his proceedings, made preparation to divert the water of the Euphrates from its bed. He had shortly before drained the Gyndes; the experience so gained led him to the present idea; and the vast horde of Asiatics which always seeks for crumbs from the table of an army, afforded him the means of executing his plan, by widening the canal which Sesostris had dug for carrying the overflow of the river into the Chaldean Lake. He increased the vigor of the usual operations to divert the attention of the Babylonians, which he succeeded in doing; and, while the population was engaged in revelry, the water of the Euphrates was, in the course of a few hours, so far lowered as to yield a footing to his men under the wall and into the city. The king's son, Belshazzar, left in charge of the capital while King Na-bu-nahid took the field, was surprised in his palace and surrendered; or, according to other authorities, died sword in hand, surrounded by his ministers and attendants. Cyrus' stratagem had succeeded perfectly. Then, with both natural humanity and that supreme appreciation of policy which has always been the complement of the martial virtue of great

soldiers, Cyrus at once arrested the slaughter and promised unqualified amnesty to all who should surrender.

In all his conquests Cyrus was wont to leave the civil government in the hands of the ancient officials of each people, under his own supreme control, keeping a military hold upon the country by suitable garrisons. He was the first to show a broad conception of the best manner in which the elements of a new empire may firmly be consolidated.

Later on (B. C. 538–529), Cyrus extended his conquests to the Scythians, in the territories east of the Caspian Sea. He is said to have thrown a bridge over the Jaxartes, and to have built boats surmounted by towers to aid him in driving away the barbarians from the farther bank, and thus enable him to put over his army.

According to the legend, the Massagetæ were as frank and loyal as they were independent and warlike. They first tried to dissuade Cyrus from his purposed invasion of their land; but failing in their negotiations, they offered to withdraw from the river three days' journey and await Cyrus' approach; or Cyrus might do the like and they would cross to meet him. Cyrus accepted the first proposition, crossed, marched onward three days and camped, spreading out a vast store of provisions, wines and Persian luxuries. He then left a rear-guard in the camp and simulated retreat. The Massagetæ attacked the camp, routed the few men left there, and fell to enjoying the unwonted good cheer. Hereupon Cyrus returned by a speedy and secret march, fell upon them in the midst of their revelries, and utterly defeated them. The legend may have no value except as indicating the sort of stratagem on a large scale which a general then might be able to practice. It is not very different in principle from some stratagems of modern times. Not long after, it is said, Cyrus fell in battle with these same Massagetæ, and his army was totally annihilated.

Darius, son of Hystaspes, the consolidator of the Persian empire (B. C. 521–485), was so great a king that his mere military talent has been overshadowed by his statecraft. Among his great deeds of war is an expedition against the European Scythians north of the Danube. He bridged the Bosphorus, or rather the Greek Mandrocles did it for him, brought his fleet up the Danube from the Ægean, and bridged

Darius' Campaign against the Scythians.

the Danube as well. No doubt both these bridges were laid on boats. His army is said to have numbered seven hundred thousand men. He advanced into the steppes between the Danube and the Dniester. In meeting this gigantic invasion the barbarians showed consummate skill in their defensive scheme. Perhaps no savage nation ever exhibited sounder natural strategy. They were good horsemen and skillful archers, and were brave and warlike. They declined to meet the Persians in open battle, but in lieu thereof kept up a harassing system of partial attacks on the Persian flanks; they made constant threats on the Persian rear and line of retreat; they planned numberless attempts to seize the bridges on the Danube; they destroyed the crops and filled up the springs. These acts were not done in an irrational manner, but with the greatest forethought. They never so entirely devastated a province as to cause the Persians to turn back, for they desired to lure them on to their ruin. They retired from before Darius through the territory, not of friends, but of lukewarm tribes, so that these, irritated by the burden of war, should be compelled to cast in their lot with the others. They retired in three bodies by three eccentric lines, thus preventing Darius, who desired to bring them to battle, from overwhelming them at one blow, and by this means led him astray. This policy utterly exhausted the vast host of the Persian king in the course of a few weeks and compelled its withdrawal.

It was fortunate for Darius that the Greeks who were left to guard the bridge decided to remain faithful. Miltiades was among them, and advised its destruction so as to deal a fatal blow to the Persians. His counsel did not prevail. The *coup de grace* was reserved for him to give at Marathon. So hot was the pursuit of the barbarians, so constantly and effectively did they harass his rear, that Darius was obliged to resort to a ruse and make a sudden night march to withdraw from their front. The ruse was the leaving of the sick and non-combatants behind with the pack-train, while Darius marched away with all his effective troops. The Scythians saw the campfires and heard the braying of the asses, and naturally supposed the Persians still in camp. This was a barbarous but typical stratagem of the day.

So soon as the Scythians discovered Darius' retreat, they set out by the shortest route for the bridges, purposing to destroy them, or to head off Darius in his attempt to reach them. Darius, ignorant of the way, had retired by the circuitous route of his advance. The Scythians, having as they supposed induced the Greeks to destroy the bridge, for these custodians did in fact take up that part nearest the north bank as a matter of safety to themselves, were confident that they could intercept the Persians in their retreat. But happily Darius was able to secure his communications with the bridge, and was fortunate indeed to get his army over to the south bank in safety. He had lost eighty thousand men in seventy days. This campaign suggests in many features the Russian campaign of Napoleon, though the latter by no means failed for lack of careful preparation. But the method of the Scythians was in its intelligence somewhat similar to that of the Russians, while Darius had failed from lack of study of his problem, and because he believed that numbers alone sufficed in war. He had made no preparations for victual, nor provided a means of forestalling such opposition as the Scythians exhibited. But though Darius failed in this campaign, he subdued Thrace, and extended his empire to the confines of the Indus. His failure leaves him still with a large reputation as a soldier, added to a still greater one as a king.

Scythian Warriors.

VI.

ARMIES IN THE FIFTH CENTURY B. C.

THE Persian army was divided into active and garrison troops. The whole population was parceled out on a decimal basis, and from this the army was drawn. The body-guard of the king, "The Immortals," was ten thousand strong. The satraps gradually acquired more and more power, grew careless of war and lived in their harems. Mercenary troops were engaged, many from Greece. Cavalry was the most effective of the Persian arms; the foot was numerous but unreliable. Chariots remained in use. Wide, open plains were chosen as battlefields. Tactics underwent no improvement. The Persians were sliding backward in war. In Greece mercenary troops also appeared, and though citizens were still held to service, substitutes were allowed. The best Greek soldiers became professionals and sold their services abroad to whomsoever paid the most. Despite which there was always a kernel left of good native troops. Such was the Theban Sacred Band. The lance of the hoplite grew in length. A new body of light troops, peltasts, was created, much better than the irregular psiloi. The cavalry grew in numbers, but was still far from good. The phalanx was improved in drill and battle-tactics. It was a body perfect for one blow on level ground, or for defense, but was easily disorganized by rough ground, and if broken it was gone. Greek armies were small and carried little baggage. They marched far and stood hardship and rough usage with wonderful constancy. There were several orders of battle, but the parallel was still generally employed. Troops were now paid. After the Peloponnesian war discipline declined. There continued to be much religious ceremonial connected with the movements of armies, and the burial of the dead was demanded by custom. The Greeks were barbarous to prisoners. There was no field fortification, but cities were well fortified. These were usually taken by storm or stratagem. Rams and other siege machinery gradually came into use, with mines, mounds, towers, etc. War on land and war at sea were not so different as they are to-day. The hoplite served on the fleet as readily as on land. Ships were small and put into shore every night. The numerous rowers left small room for soldiers aboard. War ships sought to ram their opponents and then to board them. Naval tactics was simple. In Sparta, Laconians, freedmen, helots and mercenaries crept into the army. In Athens, the list of citizens freed from personal service grew large. The people allowed small scope to the strategoi; they were under a civil officer's control, to the great loss of ability to act. Cavalry began to improve somewhat in numbers and effectiveness. Athens looked at war more intelligently than Sparta. The latter never saw beyond its material side.

Persians. — The Persian kingdom founded by Cyrus first received a regular military organization from Darius, son of Hystaspes (B. C. 521–485). This monarch divided his territory into twenty satrapies, confided to each satrap only the

Persian Body-Guards.

civil power, while himself appointed and controlled the commander of the military forces. These troops were fed from the taxes collected in each satrapy. There were active and garrison troops. The former were divided into bodies of one thousand men each, and did duty on the borders and along the great highways which traversed the kingdom. They were rigidly inspected, and a grand review of them held each year. The whole kingdom was divided into military districts, with central assembling points in each. The garrison troops were kept under separate control for the protection of the city fortresses, and were not obliged to assemble for the annual inspection. Their organization was quite apart from the active army, though resembling it in minor detail.

Several corps, each ten thousand strong, served at court. The most noble and brave of the Persians served in a *corps d'élite*, which was kept always at ten thousand men, and was known as the Immortals. These held the first place of honor in the army. The second belonged to a somewhat similar corps of Medes. The satraps and great officials each had his own body-guard, which he regulated himself.

The whole population, like the Jews, was divided into tens, hundreds, thousands and ten thousands, and in case of war fresh corps or reinforcements could be raised quickly and effectively. These levies, when made, were apt to be commanded by the large land-owners of the districts where raised, thus preserving the national character of the force. Sometimes, as in Darius' expedition against the Scythians, or Xerxes' against Greece, a general draft of the entire people was made, and the king determined how much each province should furnish in men, material, horses, ships and so forth. Herodotus gives an extended and interesting description of the fifty-six tribes and peoples represented under Xerxes, and reviewed by him in Thrace at the time of his invasion of Greece.

The troops were not paid. During active service they were fed by simply seizing and gathering in supplies wherever found. Provinces through which a Persian army passed were eaten up as by a plague of grasshoppers.

Rank and command were well settled. The chiliarchs, or colonels, who commanded one thousand men, and the myriarchs, or division-generals, who commanded ten thousand, were held in honor. The higher commands were filled by the rel-

atives and favorites of the king. Though the Persians became a luxurious people and lost much of their warlike quality,
they were in early days simple, soldierly and
brave. They received an excellent training
for war. It was only cohesion which the Persian army lacked. But after the days of
Xerxes I. († 465 B. C.) they began to fall
backwards. The great nobles lived in their
harems and more rarely assumed command
in person. Mercenary troops were gradually
introduced, and to the best of these the safety
of the kingdom was confided. This labor-
saving system grew fast when it was found
easy to raise mercenaries. Asiatics and
Greeks were both enlisted. The former made
the bulk, the latter the kernel of the Persian
armies. The Greek phalangites received pay

Persian Officer.

at the rate of one daricus (a ducat) per head per month,
between four and five dollars, in addition to which sum, it is
probable, they received an equal amount for rations.

A great source of weakness of the central military power
arose when the satraps became more independent and gradually got possession of the armed, as well as the civil control of
their satrapies. It was not long thereafter before these satraps became practically independent monarchs, assuming all
the power and most of the attributes which properly belonged
to the sovereign, and yielding but a nominal fealty. But the
Great King retained the power of assembling the army.
Thus at the time of the Græco-Persian wars, the bulk of the
Persian forces was by the king's orders concentrated in
Thrace, Asia Minor and Egypt.

The most effective part of the Asiatic armies was cavalry.
In this the Orientals have always excelled. The horse was

in the East then, as now, the constant companion of man, and cavalry was the natural arm. The best heavy cavalry was the Persian; then followed the Median, that of Asia Minor, the Parthian. The nomad tribes furnished an excellent light cavalry, much like the Cossacks of to-day.

The foot was more numerous but less good. The light troops, slingers, darters and archers, were abundant, but had little discipline. The Greek mercenaries furnished the stanchest of the heavy troops. There were as high as fifty thousand in the Persian service at one time. Bodies of native troops were organized in like fashion. Some of the Persians were accoutred in the most splendid manner; wore scaled armor and carried weapons of the finest description. Chariots, plain and scythed, were in vogue, and camels bearing archers and darters were not uncommon.

There had been no progress in tactics since the elder Cyrus. Organization and discipline in the field were wretched. On the march there was no order. The army camped near water and pasturage, and surrounded the camps with wagons, stockades and earthworks, — sometimes using their shields as a capping to the latter. The higher generals had tents; the commonalty slept in huts in permanent camps, or without shelter in daily camps. In battle, the Persians, relying on their bravery, preferred to advance straight on the enemy, without resort to stratagem or tactical manœuvres. Wide, open plains were their usual choice for battlefields, on which their numbers, and especially the cavalry and chariots, could act to the best advantage. They formed in a long line so as to lap the enemy's flanks, the cavalry on the wings, the chariots in front. The centre was the place of honor. Here the king took his stand surrounded by his body-guard. On either side were placed the chosen troops, in great squares, always thirty, often one hundred deep, with light troops stationed all about them and in the intervals. The king gave the war-cry for the day, and at a signal the whole mass moved forward. The Persian army was full of gallant men ; it had for generations been a terror to the Greeks, who feared to face it ; but it was unwieldly from too vast a bulk and from lack of homogeneity and discipline, and was subject to speedy and unreasoning panics. After a defeat a Persian army was bound to lose heavily from lack of ability to rally for defense, and would often disperse so as absolutely to vanish. Destined to act in the plain, the chariots and horsemen and the huge squares were utterly unsuited to hilly countries, and were sure to fall into disorder when subjected to unusual tests.

Regular sieges were unknown. Cities were captured by ruse, treachery, or, on rare occasions, by storm. Sieges were still apt to be very long drawn out.

In campaigns against barbarians, the Persian method accomplished good results. But their mountain tribes always gave them much trouble, and the civilized discipline of the Greeks they could by no means withstand.

In declaring war, the Persian habit was to demand, through heralds, earth and water as a token of submission.

Greeks. — Down to the battle of Platæa (479 B. C.) there was small change in the organization of the Greeks. From that time on, many alterations came gradually about. A number of slaves appeared in the ranks. The first instance of a standing army was the occasion when the Greek cities, during the Persian wars, mutually agreed to keep under arms ten thousand foot, one thousand horse, and one hundred warships. Wars beyond the borders of Greece called for larger forces than had been necessary, and in addition to the citizen-soldier, who had so far been the glory as well as guardian of Greece, large forces of freedmen, slaves, and particularly mercenary troops, were created. In the Peloponnesian war, and during the period of her greatest splendor (465–429 B. C.), Athens made use extensively of mercenary troops, and other Greek states soon followed suit.

Down to the Peloponnesian war the Athenians had retained their civil and military virtues in full force. But this internecine struggle ruined the population, devastated Greece, and familiarized the Greeks with serving for gold. Pericles found it necessary to pay the troops. The hoplites had nothing left to subsist upon. They had already served for pay in Asia, on a limited scale ; but after the Peloponnesian war, the Oriental princes or satraps, Carthage, or indeed any other people or prince who needed them, had no difficulty in collecting large bodies of Greek mercenaries. From this paid foreign service it was but a step to the point where the Greeks were willing to serve in preference him who paid the most. The pay varied from five to twenty cents a day. The best of the Greek population embraced arms as a profession, engaged mostly abroad, and left the poorer material at home. Greek cities themselves had to hire soldiers. The better citizens would no longer serve. They procured substitutes, and the armies, often kept standing, were filled up with wretched stuff. But in most of the Greek cities there remained a better nucleus, a *corps d'élite*, in which alone the highest citizens had a place. Though this was small, it was a leaven. Such was the Theban Sacred Band, or Band of Lovers, which was bound together by ties of affection and oaths of fidelity, and, but three hundred strong, so often saved the day for Thebes. This gallant body was finally cut to pieces at Chæronæa. It would not yield a foot. Every man fell where he stood, sword in hand.

While the armies of Greece were thus degenerating, the schools, in which, in addition to gymnastics, were taught mathematics and the art of war as then understood, continued to grow in excellence. There was never a lack of well-trained leaders. It was the free-born rank and file which was degenerating, or allowing hirelings to do the duty it should do itself. The bone and sinew of the Greek republics had disappeared.

The hoplites continued to be the favorite troops. Only they were looked on as warriors. Their armament remained the same, except that their shields grew smaller, — from four to two and a half feet in height, while the pike grew longer, — from ten to as much as twenty-one feet, or, as some

Full-Armed Greek Archer.

state, twenty-four feet, which was the sarissa of Macedon. The psiloi served to protect the hoplites as well as to open the battle. The best archers and slingers came from Crete, Rhodes, Acarnania, Ægina, and Achaia. The psiloi came from a poor class as of yore, were illy armed and of little consideration. It was reserved for Iphicrates of Athens to

better their discipline and condition, and prove their utility in service. After the Peloponnesian war he created a new body, armed with well-poised spears for casting, light but good linen armor, and a small, round shield (peltē), from

Peltast.

which they were called peltasts. These troops had in a degree the lightness of the psiloi and the steadfastness of the hoplites. This new arm proved useful, and was shortly imitated by the other Greek cities. Scarlet or crimson were the favorite colors of the warrior.

The Greek cavalry was either heavy, — cataphracti, bearing long double-ended lances, sword and axe, small shield, and fully armored, as was also the horse; or light, — acrobolisti, far-shooters, — who were merely light-armed riders and like nomads in their methods. The force of cavalry had been somewhat increased by the time of the Persian invasion to about one tenth the foot. Agesilaus, in Asia Minor, made it for a time one fourth the foot. But the Greek cavalry was essentially poor, though certain leaders, like Epaminondas, managed to get good work out of it. The Greeks were not a nation of horsemen.

Cataphractos.

The relative numbers of heavy and light foot and cavalry were very various. At Marathon (Herodotus) were ten thousand hoplites, a few psiloi, no cavalry. At Platæa served thirty-eight thousand seven hundred heavy, seventy-one thousand three hundred light foot, and no cavalry. At the opening of the Peloponnesian war Athens had (Thucydides) thirteen thousand heavy, sixteen hundred light foot, and twelve hundred horse, not counting sixteen thousand hoplites to defend the city. Epaminondas had at Leuctra (Diodorus) six thousand heavy foot, fifteen hundred light foot, five hundred horse; at Mantinæa thirty thousand heavy and light, and three thousand horse.

The phalanx had proven so good a formation during the Persian wars that the Greeks sought to improve rather than to change it. The Peloponnesian war furnished the opportunity to do this, and the Greeks had by nature exceptional capacity as drill-masters and organizers. The unit was no longer decimal, but founded on the powers of the number *two*. The

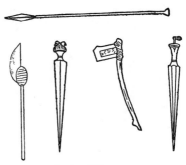

Ancient Weapons.

depth of the phalanx was rarely less than eight or more than sixteen men, though it was on rare occasions made so light as four or so heavy as twenty-four. Epaminondas made a column forty-eight men deep at Leuctra and Mantinæa, but this was not the phalanx proper. Generally the eight, twelve, or sixteen deep file was in use. Xenophon puts the average at twelve. By employing any given number of files under a

Ancient Helmets.

leader, any convenient unit of organization could be made, or detachment formed. The leader stood in front, and there were a number of file closers to keep order in the ranks. The larger divisions of the phalanx had their ensigns and trumpeters, and each leader had near him one or two men to convey or repeat his orders.   The right flank of the phalanx was

called the head, the left the tail, for the phalanx usually marched by the right, and on the right the commander of the phalanx had his station. Small intervals were left between the divisions to allow the light troops to pass through to front or rear.   There were many tactical formations of the phalanx for battle known to the Greeks, such as a refusal of the right or left wing and various forms of columns and wedges. Columns of attack were of later origin. Manœuvres were made in measured step to the sound of fifes.   The cadenced step was essential to preserve order in a

Swords.

phalanx with twelve-foot pikes.   The pike was practically the only weapon used so long as the phalanx held together. The foremost ranks protended their pikes; the rear ranks leaned them forward on the shoulders of their leaders to break the flight of arrows, or held them erect.

The psiloi, peltasts and horse were set up and employed in many fashions.   The psiloi never came to close quarters ; the peltasts often did so. The cavalry did not improve much.   But the Greeks recognized the uselessness of too great a depth, — such as the Spartans had had, — and the horse was formed in ilēs of files four deep and of a convenient length of rank.   If the ilēs were oc-

Holding Shield.

casionally formed deeper, only the first four ranks attacked ;

the balance remained for the moment in reserve. The intervals between ilēs were greater than those in the phalanx. Some of the Thracian and Thessalian and other semi-nomad horse was wont to form in wedge and rhomboid, or lozenge columns for a charge.

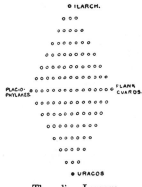

Thessalian Lozenge.

The phalanx, as the nucleus, occupied the centre. The light troops might be on the flanks, in front, in the intervals, in the rear, according as the demand was for protection to front or flanks, or for shooting missiles over the heads of the phalanx. Small bodies of psiloi often accompanied the cavalry. They were so active as to be able to follow its evolutions. Their general duties were to cover the phalanx and patrol the camp, seize heights, tear down obstacles, open the battle, follow the beaten enemy with the horse, or cover a retreat. The peltasts in battle were generally on the flanks. The horse was on one or both flanks. The acrobolisti skirmished; the cataphracti were held back for a final effort.

The advantages of the phalanx lay in its cohesion and weight. It was difficult to withstand its impact when the blow was delivered from a short distance and on level ground, or under such circumstances that the formation could remain intact. To break through it by an attack was practically impossible. Only its flanks and rear were weak. But if the phalanx was on rough and uneven ground, or had to march over a distance to the assault, gaps were apt to be rent in the mass, and into these a skillful enemy could pour and destroy the body. There was but one line. The phalanx had no re-

serve to reëstablish a failing battle. Neither the rear ranks
of the hoplites could perform this duty, for they were fatigued
by the march and battle, and if demoralization supervened,
they all the more partook it; nor could the psiloi, as they
were not stanch enough, nor armed with hand-to-hand weapons. Though the peltasts might have been so employed, it
never seemed to occur to the Greeks to put them to such a
use. A reserve was the conception of an individual, not a
principle of tactics, with them.

Thus the value of the phalanx lay in the defensive, or in an
offensive blow given from a short distance and always in close
order. The Greek wars, like the phalanx, generally partook
of a defensive character; or rather, from the defensive character of Greek wars very naturally arose the phalangial idea.

The Greek armies were usually small; their baggage-train
limited. Their marches were, as a rule, in one column, by
the right of the order of battle. Thus the head of column
consisted of psiloi, who also acted as flankers. Then came the
cavalry and the peltasts of the right wing; then the phalanx.
Behind this was apt to be placed the train of wagons and
pack-animals, and then came the peltasts and cavalry of the
left wing, then again psiloi. Hampered with little trains and
small in number, the armies of the Greeks could and did
often perform wonderful marches, and sometimes at once went
into battle. Fifteen miles was the average march; but the
Spartans marched to Marathon, one hundred and fifty miles,
in three days, and arrived ready for immediate action, but too
late. The theory of marches was not as generally understood
and practiced as the theory of fighting. Marches were often
carelessly conducted; but some of the Greek generals marched
their armies with consummate intelligence. There were no
such set rules for the route as for the battlefield.

The Greek orders of battle were: 1. The parallel. In this

the lines marched against each other, front to front, aiming to strike "all along the line" at the same moment. The advantage of this was an equal strength at every point; its weakness that it was liable to be broken in some place by valor or numbers, or by the occurrence of gaps; or that the shorter line could be outflanked by the longer. 2. The parallel, with one or other or both wings reinforced. The wing, strengthened by a line or column in its front, made direct or obliquely for the enemy, and the rest of the line, less advanced than the troops reinforcing the wing, was covered by light troops. The object was either to crush or surround the enemy's wing, or drive it in upon the centre so as to take advantage of the resulting confusion. Some-

Parallel Order, wing reinforced.

Parallel Order.

times both wings were reinforced and the centre withheld in similar manner, and other methods of strengthening one or both wings were employed. The weakness of this formation was the possible sundering of wings and centre, which would then lie open to being beaten in detail. 3. The oblique. This in its simple form was a mere variation from the parallel order due to accidents of ground or tactical difficulties; in its best form it was the invention of Epaminondas. One wing was materially strengthened, and fell first on the enemy's wing opposite, in front or flank. The other wing was refused (held back) or advanced more slowly, and from the nature of things in a sort of echeloned order, and thus the line became oblique. As used by Epaminondas, this was the greatest advance in battle tactics ever made at one step. The advantage of this order was that the strengthened wing

Oblique Order, simple form.

was sure to crush the enemy's flank, and while the whole enemy's army would partake of its demoralization, the centre and other wing which had been refused would remain in good condition for a further blow or for pursuit. It is perhaps the order which has in all ages proven the most effective. It will be described more fully in the battle of Leuctra. All other orders were mere variations of these, and up to Epaminondas' day the parallel was practically the only one used. There was much perfection of detail, but tactical originality was absent.

Rank and command remained the same as at an earlier period. The Thebans had from four to eleven leaders, bœotarchs, who commanded in rotation, and all laid down their office with the year. As already noted, until Platæa the Greek troops served without remuneration. The Athenians first began to pay the troops. The amount varied. It averaged ten drachmas (two dollars) per month for a foot soldier. The cavalry received two, three, and four times as much, according to its grading. The officers were paid twice to five times as much as the men. Thucydides says the soldier received as much for rations as for pay. Pay ceased with war, but the horseman received something for forage during peace, being held to keep his mount available on call.

The troops lived on the country they traversed. With small armies this was no great hardship within the national territory. Victual for several days was not infrequently carried in the baggage-train, or brought by sea to given points. When practicable, armies hugged the sea, to have the support of their fleet. Rations in bulk were sometimes contracted for by the state for delivery at times and places stated.

At their best the Greeks stood hardship perhaps better than any men have ever done. What other has ever marched so far as Alexander's tireless soldier? What retreat can

compare to that of the Ten Thousand ? Cæsar's legions came
closest to them. In one quality alone is the modern soldier
their equal, or superior. The soldier of the last two hundred
years has been called on to stand greater decimation on the
battlefield, and has cheerfully stood it. But in the other
qualifications of the soldier, especially the ability to march far
and fast on slender rations, the Greek is incomparable.

Discipline varied much at different times and with different nations, being naturally a reflection of the character of
the people, or of the leaders. Down to the Peloponnesian
war, discipline and the feeling of honor among the troops was
markedly good in almost all Greek
states. Military faults were severely
punished, grave ones by death, or,
what to the Greeks was worse, open
branding with dishonor. Rewards
were equally pronounced. The com-
monest citizen might rise to distinction by a signal act of bravery. The
leader who won a victory became the
worshiped hero of the people. But
great rewards were jealously given.
Miltiades was not awarded the crown
of laurel because he had not won
alone. The army must have the first
reward, the general the next. Booty
was largely distributed to both; and
booty included prisoners of war, who
were ransomed at high prices or sold

Victorious Greek.

into slavery. The place of victory was marked by trophies,
or piles of weapons, or weapons hung on masts, and by columns with inscriptions reciting the event. Sometimes all
Greece would join in recognizing the services of some state,

as in the case of Athens after Marathon, or of Platæa after the battle of that name. But after the Peloponnesian war, the better instincts of the Greeks appear to have been lost, and their military spirit slackened. Disorder and mutinies were not infrequent. Leaders were compelled to purchase the good conduct of the troops by largesses; awful punishments for base or scandalous actions grew in frequency. This showed a slackening in the soldierly bearing. Civil war not infrequently results thus.

Trophy.

The herald was an universally known and respected official among all the ancients. War was declared by a formal accusation of and demand for reparation for certain acts, by a herald. On refusal, a bloody lance and a firebrand were cast by him upon the enemy's soil as a declaration of war and a threat of revenge by fire and sword. Before war or battle many and tedious ceremonials and vows to the gods were universal. The priests and augurs divined from the sacrificial entrails. The practical application of these proceedings lay in the hold it gave the leader on the superstitious feelings of his army. If the victims were pronounced favorable, enthusiasm rose, the warriors took a light meal, and then, to the singing of the pæan and the playing of flutes, marched to battle. A battle-cry, as the phalanx closed with the enemy, was common. At certain periods the phalanx marched to battle in silence, so as the more distinctly to hear the orders, and chanted the pæan when near the enemy, clashing their lances upon their shields and raising the battle-cry when they closed in upon him. The Greeks were a talkative, almost a garrulous people; but under discipline they could be singularly quiet. As fighters they were quiet and determined.

Religion demanded the burial of those slain in battle. For this purpose a truce was usual after victory. The fear of the anger of the gods for refusal of this rite often forestalled the grasping of the fruits of victory. It was the victors who erected their trophies and buried their dead. The vanquished were compelled to sue for the rite of burial. Such a request was, of itself, an acknowledgment of defeat. The bodies or ashes of fallen warriors were sent to their homes, and were there received with solemn ceremonial and given due sepulture.

The Greeks were utterly barbarous in many things. As a rule, among the captives, the men were slain and the women and children sold into slavery. Not infrequently these last also were killed, or even burned, in numbers at a time. Enemies might be annihilated, tortured or used in the most inhuman or indecorous manner, without a suspicion that such an act was reprehensible.

The Greeks did not usually fortify their camps, but relied on situation for defense. The troops were often sheltered in tents, made of hides and carried by the men. The Greek soldier always carried a large blanket-wrap for protection from the weather. This was capable — as the cloak has been in all ages — of being used on occasion for defense.

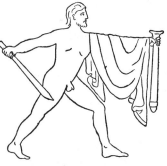

Use of Cloak as Shield (from a vase).

The field fortifications of the Greeks, or fortified lines for the protection of given places, or to protect the access from harbor to town (as of the Piræus to Athens), were constructed of earthen walls with ditch, palisades or hurdlework, abatis, or sometimes stone. The Spartans, in 429 B. C., surrounded Platæa with a double wall of intricate construction and great strength, which will be described elsewhere. But works were rarely so elaborate.

The Greek cities were generally provided with thick and high stone walls, the idea of which they borrowed from the East. On these walls, at the angles, or at arrow-shot distance, stood stone towers. Along the top of the wall ran a

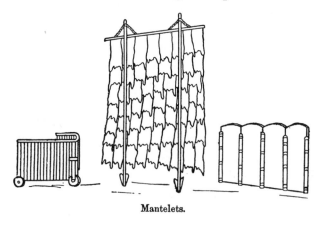

Mantelets.

road, protected outwardly by overhanging battlements, so castellated and perforated that the foot of the fortifications and the surrounding country could be reached by missiles. A wide and deep, dry or wet moat lay outside. Inside were one or more citadels in the places most capable of defense, and similarly but more stoutly fortified. In Athens such was the Acropolis; in Thebes, the Cadmæa.

The Greeks took fortified cities by ruse whenever possible. If storm was resorted to, the light troops drove the defenders from the walls with their missiles, while picked heavy troops mounted the walls by ladders, or on the upraised and interlocked shields of the rest (this was called a testudo or tortoise), or broke into the gates. They blockaded cities by

walls of contravallation around and facing the town; sometimes by additional walls of circumvallation built outside
and at a suitable distance from the first and facing away from
the town, to hold an army of relief in check. In regular
sieges they first established camps at appropriate intervals
and joined them with works; then cleared the walls of their
defenders with catapults or ballistas, built covered ways
towards the wall, threw up huge sloping mounds to command
it, filled the ditch, which they approached under cover of movable screens and sheds, and undermined the wall, or broke
it down with rams. A breach made, it was stormed. But
catapults and ballistas were apparently not known until the
Peloponnesian war. The catapult — or cannon of the ancients
— was a species of huge bow, capable of throwing pikes
weighing from ten to three hundred pounds over half a mile.
The ballista — or mortar — threw heavy stones, or flights of
arrows, or other substances, with accurate aim to a considerable distance.

Rams were at first mere iron-pointed beams handled by
men. They were later swung
in heavy framework, and hung
on ropes or chains. They were
generally placed in covered
buildings mounted on wheels,
which were then slowly pushed
up against the walls by men
with levers.

Mines were commonly opened

Hand Ram.

from a distance and dug to a point under the walls, and
were there sustained by wooden piles. The chambers were
filled with combustibles, and being set on fire, they baked,
crumbled and dropped the earth, and thus the heavy wall
above it.

tunnel + blow up earth
under wall

breaching towers

Movable towers of several stories set on wheels came into use as an easier means of overriding the walls than mounds. They were built at a distance beyond range of missiles, and rolled up by men. The lower story often held the ram.

The besieged used converse means of defense. They constructed wooden shields against the besiegers' fire, threw down the ladders of the storming parties, poured hot water or boiling oil or pitch upon them, and rolled heavy stones from the walls. They made sorties to destroy the besiegers' works, to reëstablish communications with the outside world, or to cut

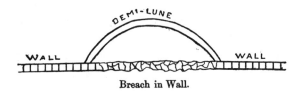

Breach in Wall.

their way out. They raised the walls, built curtains or half-moons inside a breach, countermined to destroy the enemy's mines, and set his works on fire by arrows tipped with tarred tow, or by fire-pots cast by the catapults, or by other similar means.

Sieges were very laborious. The defense was apt to be desperate, for the capture of a city resulted in the slaying or selling into slavery of all the inhabitants. Terms were rarely made, or if made were often violated. Sieges were therefore long in duration, and cost enormously in men and treasure. Good faith in ancient war was not universal. A pledge was by no means sacred. Heralds alone were inviolate, and not always they.

Fleets. — War at sea and war on land were much less different in olden times than to-day. All Greek soldiers were more or less sailors; all generals were equally admirals.

In the heroic days fleets were used merely for piracy. As commerce grew, piracy decreased. The best period of the Greek marine was from the Persian wars to Alexander's day. Themistocles was the founder of the Athenian navy. Until the fall of Syracuse, Athens was preëminent at sea. The Greek fleets always played a great part in war.

The irregular and rocky coast, as well as the sharp and sudden storms of Greece, necessitated the use of small craft. Ships of war were propelled by oars, using sails only as an auxiliary means. They were long and shoal, with one, two or three and more banks of oars. There was but small space except for rowers and soldiers. They could carry little victual and water, and had to be accompanied by transports or else keep close to shore. They landed, as a rule, every night, and the troops disembarked and camped. During storms the ships ran great danger of shipwreck, or the fleets of dispersion. Transports and merchantmen used sails more than oars, and were in shape very much like tubs. They were called *round*, as men of war were denominated *long*, ships. Each term was descriptive of the craft.

As the best citizens preferred service as hoplites or horsemen, only the lower classes, freedmen or slaves, were left for the fleet. But in times of danger much of the infantry served aboard the vessels. The duties were simple and could be easily learned. The triremes had from one hundred and fifty rowers upwards, and carried forty to fifty and more hoplites. Sea-fights were apt to occur near shore. Fleets were mobile and could readily manœuvre. In order of battle they kept as close together as ease of rowing would permit. The great effort was to ram the enemy's vessels amidships, for which purpose each Greek trireme had an iron prow. Or if its rudder could be broken, a vessel was at the mercy of the adversary. Boarding was the common resort, in which both warriors and oarsmen took a hand.

The methods at sea and on land were much the same. Fleets and armies were wont to sustain each other, even to the extent of using their men and artillery in common; *i. e.,* the fleet would come close in shore, disembark its quota and take part in the action. In sieges of cities on the seaboard, which were common, both worked together.

Sparta. — Sparta's system remained substantially the same from the time of Lycurgus down to the Peloponnesian war. But rivalry with Athens and the necessity of possessing a fleet, if Sparta would arrest her competitor's preponderance in Greece, changed the habits of centuries. Money became essential to conduct war against wealthy Athens, and money brought into Sparta those things which soon drove out the ancient national simplicity. And this all the more speedily from its novelty. The armies now no longer contained citizens alone, though these were still the kernel; but the Laconians, freedmen, helots and mercenary troops composed a large part of it. The free population was divided into five classes, from which the ephors called into service in war as many as were needed, according to age. Cleombrotus, at Leuctra, had in the ranks the citizens from twenty to thirty-five; after Leuctra, those up to forty were called in. The number of freedmen who gradually crept into service was large. Agesilaus had three thousand in Asia. The helots were called in only in cases of grave danger, as before Mantinæa. The kings still held the command, but came more and more under the control of the ephors. The latter held the real power, and went on occasion so far as to displace the kings from command. The troops were not yet on a paid basis, excepting the helots and mercenaries; but the kings and their staff or suite were victualed. Up to the close of the Peloponnesian war the Spartans were sparing of their rewards, and retained the severity of their punishments, such as death and loss of honor; while some criminals were clad and treated like slaves, and had half their head and beard shaven; and burial was refused to cowards. After the Peloponnesian war, discipline declined and the state was often forced to resort to largesses to encourage the troops to those exertions they had been in the habit of yielding as of course.

The citizens still formed the body of the hoplites. Each of the five classes put on foot one or more mores or regiments of five hundred to one thousand men. Each hoplite had one or more psiloi under his control and often several helots or servants. The Laconians, freedmen and sometimes the helots served as light troops. These became more and more numerous. At Plataea they outnumbered the citizens seven to one.

The cavalry remained poor. Citizens disqualified from service in the heavy foot entered the cavalry, which was used mostly for scouts and patrols. Agesilaus somewhat increased its numbers and efficiency. One mora or ilē from Scirus and vicinity, where horses were abundant, was of markedly better character, and was not infrequently used in battle, where it more than once decided the day. And there was a body of three hundred hippeis selected by the ephors, who were a cavalry *corps d'élite*. The horse now rode in four ranks, a great improvement over the former eight.

The Spartan foot stood in from eight to twelve ranks. The manœuvres were performed in cadenced step to the sound of fifes, and though very simple, were excellently devised. But by neglecting the arts and sciences, the Spartans remained stationary, and did nothing toward improving the art of war in a theoretical sense. They could not look beyond courage and the details of tactics. They still employed the manœuvres enumerated in a former chapter. But the wedge, pincers, and such other tactical movements were useful rather on the drill-ground than on the battlefield.

Athens. — Athens, after Marathon, which redounded to her greatest honor, rose rapidly in power, and the tendency towards democracy brought about many changes. Citizens from twenty to forty were still subject to military duty, but were permitted to procure substitutes. The list of citizens freed from military duty grew large. Aliens, freedmen and even slaves gradually crept into the ranks, the latter mostly in the fleet. Auxiliary troops from allied or tributary nations and mercenaries increased in proportion to the citizen-soldiers. The forces of Athens were large, especially at sea; and during the height of her power the conduct of her leading citizens and of the troops was uniformly patriotic and brilliant.

Greek Army Leader.

Ten strategoi commanded the forces, — one for each tribe (phylē), — and were selected by lot or vote. At the expiration of a year they laid down their command, and rendered an account of their doings to the people. They were often reëlected. Phocion served many successive terms. Such men as Themistocles and Aristides were constantly reelected. If the people were not satisfied (and the Athenians were singularly ungrateful and unreasonable) the strategos was mulcted in a fine; failing payment of which he and his children after him were cast into and kept in prison.

The proper men were often not the ones who were chosen strategoi. The ever-shifting command and the natural disagreements between the leaders frequently prevented Athens from securing the results of otherwise good management. Recognizing this difficulty, it was finally decreed that most of the strategoi should remain in Athens to attend to the victualing of the troops and the general business management, while one of the archons (polemarch) should accompany the army, and keep up communication between the strategoi at the rear and front, and preside at the council of war. The polemarch had also specific military duties, and commanded a wing of the army — usually the right. Sometimes, on occasions of great danger, the most celebrated general or citizen was chosen commander-in-chief with extraordinary powers. Alcibiades was thus honored. Under the ten strategoi were ten taxiarchs, who were a sort of aide-de-camp, but with specific duties and command. The taxiarchs looked after victual, camps, the order of march, weapons, and so forth. Each strategos also had one or more heralds.

Rewards and punishments were practically the same as with other states. Those who avoided military duty by false pretexts were dressed in women's clothes, and exhibited in public; cowards were excluded from religious ceremonials and conventions of the people. Culprits were forbidden to marry; even their families joined in disgracing them; and they were subjected to cuffs and insults in public, which they might not resent.

The Athenians, owing to their greater luxuries, were the first in Greece whose army fell into slackness and weak discipline. The Athenian army consisted of ten chiliarchias (or regiments), one for every tribe, of one thousand or more men each, commanded by a chiliarch or colonel, and under him captains and file leaders. Each hoplite had a servant or arms-bearer, who retired to the rear in action. Of cavalry there was, previous to the Persian invasions, a force of but ninety-six men, which number later grew to one thousand or twelve hundred, about one tenth the foot, and was divided into two

Hoplite.

hipparchias (regiments) under two hipparchs and ten phylarchs. The richest and best fitted citizens served in the cavalry. Rigid examinations of physical strength and financial ability to support the cost of cavalry service were required. But this arm none the less remained very mediocre. The Athenians were seamen, not horsemen.

Cataphractos (from a vase).

To the Athenians belongs the credit of first making war something more than a mere physical science. The keen wit of Athens elevated all which it touched, and among the other arts war gained something of value from her brain tissue. This gain took the form of marked improvements in tactics and in fortification and sieges; and still more of a broader intelligence in the conduct of war, and an appreciation of its intellectual character.

A more detailed account will be found in a later chapter of the military organization of Macedon. The Greek and Macedonian systems were analogous, and much of what is said of the one applies to the other.

Armor of Greek Chieftain.

VII.

MILTIADES. — MARATHON.   B. C. 490.

DURING the Persian invasion of Greece, at the battle of Marathon, occurred one of the early tactical variations from the parallel order.   Miltiades had but eleven thousand men; the Persians had ten times as many.   They lay on the seashore in front of their fleet.   To reach and lean his flanks on two brooks running to the sea, Miltiades made his centre thin, his wings strong, and advanced sharply on the enemy.   With his wings he scattered the Persian array; as was inevitable, the deep Persian line easily broke through his weakened centre.   But Miltiades had either anticipated and prepared his army for this, or else seized the occasion by a very stroke of genius.   There was no symptom of demoralization.   The Persian troops followed hard after the defeated centre. Miltiades caused each wing to wheel inwards, and fell upon both flanks of the Persian advance, absolutely overwhelming it, and throwing it back upon the main line in such confusion as to lead to complete victory.

NOT many years after his Scythian expedition Darius, son of Hystaspes, invaded Greece, and his army was defeated at Marathon.   On this occasion we find one of the first and most marked illustrations in a pitched battle of what to-day we call grand tactics.   From now on we shall see something akin to an advance in the art of handling troops.   Battle tactics would naturally come into existence before strategy. The latter, as a science, was not yet dreamed of.   Many great captains had to show the world what strategy was before its maxims could be guessed.

At Marathon Miltiades acted on a sensible and definite tactical plan of battle.   He was one of the ten strategoi, and his turn had come to take sole command.   But the others were equally divided in opinion as to the advisability of fighting. Miltiades pleaded with the polemarch Callimachus to give the casting vote in its favor. This was done, and, with the ardor not uncommon to great souls, Miltiades resolved to stake the fate of Athens — which was then the fate of the civilized world — on the issue of this one battle. He was to fight on historic ground, sacred to Hercules, the scene of the exploits of Theseus, and the rout of the invader Eurystheus, near the fountain of Macaria. There can be no doubt, though his words have not been preserved to us, that this large-hearted man made use of all these, by the Greeks, religiously credited traditions in a manner to inflame every man with the valor which conquers or dies. For at this time the Greek soldier

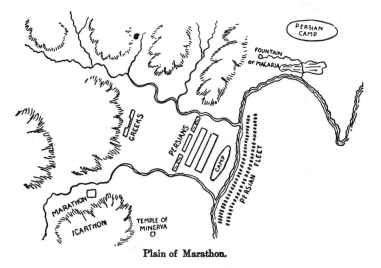

Plain of Marathon.

harbored a hearty dread of the Persian, and by no means understood his own strength. Miltiades had but eleven thousand men, of whom one thousand were Platæans. Datis and Artaphernes — the former was the real chief — had more than ten times the number. But the Greeks were more heavily armed and well disciplined, and they had the highest of all motives to bear themselves as men; the Persians were lightly armed, and though the better classes of the army were personally brave, the bulk of the rank and file had small notion of fighting except under the influence of the lash.

They were, moreover, recruited from every part of the huge Persian empire, and had none of the *esprit de corps* so strong among the Athenians. There was no cohesion in the Persian army; a panic would be surely fatal. But the Greeks did not know all this. To them the outlook was desperate.

The Persian hosts were drawn up in a deep body on the plain extending upward from the seashore. Their heavy baggage camp was farther up the coast. Their fleet had partly been beached in their rear. It is probable that at the moment of attack a portion of the Persian force had been reëmbarked for a projected attack on Athens.

Soldier of Marathon.

The Athenians were on the slope of the hills a mile or so away, having protected their flanks by leaning them on natural obstacles, and by some abatis or palisades. They had lain here nine days, awaiting the Persian initiative. Miltiades had concluded that safety lay in taking the offensive himself, and finally Callimachus' vote came in to decide in favor of his opinion. In the attack on the enemy, which Miltiades had determined upon, the Greeks ran the most imminent risk from the enemy's cavalry, of which they themselves had none; for this, if skillfully handled, might fatally turn their flanks. Miltiades saw that he must act with the greatest speed when the moment arrived, and take the Persians, if possible, unawares. He had not enough troops properly to fill a front by any means as wide as that of the Persians, and was thus compelled to alter his usual formation. He made his centre thin, — probably four men deep, — and thus gained in length of line, while he kept his phalanx of the usual depth of eight men in both the wings. In his advance upon the Persian line he was able to rest both his flanks on two brooks which ran down towards the sea.

This use of obstacles was very uncommon, if not quite unknown, at his day; and its employment here shows that quality in which the great captain always excels, — the adaptation of means to end; the ability to utilize his resources to the very best advantage.

Themistocles and Aristides commanded the centre. If the troops here were sparse, they were yet well led. The Platæans were on the extreme left. In this order, and choosing a moment when the enemy was apparently not anticipating an attack, Miltiades moved down upon the Persians. His men were all in good training, and though the distance between the lines was the best part of a mile, Miltiades had concluded that by an advance at the double quick he would run a lesser risk, even if he brought his men into action a trifle winded, than he would by advancing slowly and giving the enemy time to bring his cavalry into action. Moreover, the phalanx would be a much shorter time under the fire of the Persian archers and slingers. This course, then, he took, and in a few moments from giving the command to move forward at a run, the Greek army, still in good alignment, struck the Persian first line, which on seeing the attack had rapidly formed, but which was, no doubt, much startled by the audacity of the manœuvre.

Miltiades had calculated rightly. He had forestalled the use of the cavalry by the Persians upon his flanks, and had the strong moral advantage of the offensive. On the wings, where the phalanx was in files eight men deep, the struggle was decisive. The enemy, after a brilliant resistance, went to pieces under the Grecian spears, beyond the hope of rallying. But in the centre, which was strung out and weak, the Persians and Sacæ, despite a brave opposition, broke through and drove the hoplites back. The Greeks fought for every inch under their splendid leadership, but the mass of the enemy had too much momentum. Slowly but surely they were

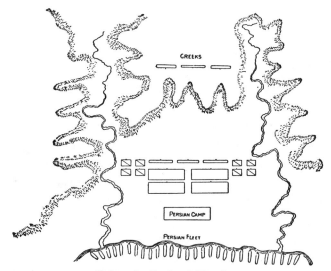

GREEKS

PERSIAN CAMP

PERSIAN FLEET

Before the Battle of Marathon.

pushed to the rear, nor could they be steadied and a new line formed until the foot of the hill was reached whence they had started. Here a stand was made, and here too came Miltiades' opportunity. He had no doubt foreseen the probability of just this turn in the battle; or if not, he seized it with the genius of the born captain. With true military *coup d'œil* he gauged the proper moment. The preconcerted or a well-known signal was given by the trumpets, and the two Greek wings, having routed the Persians opposed to them, without losing their steadiness, wheeled their serried ranks

right and left in upon the mass of struggling Oriental soldiery which had driven back the centre and was following
hard upon. This splendid manœuvre not only disconcerted
the enemy, but put him at the mercy of the Greek phalanx.
The Persian van, thus taken on either flank, was compromised. Only the efforts of isolated bodies were possible, and

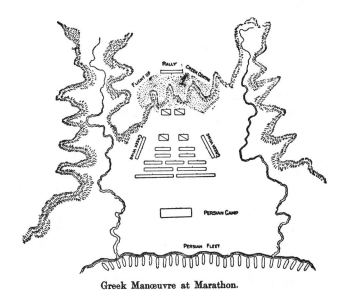

Greek Manœuvre at Marathon.

these could effectuate nothing. Demoralization spread. The
victory was complete. The enemy was followed to his ships.
Here the conflict was still more severe and the slaughter
enormous. There fell six thousand four hundred Persians
and but one hundred and ninety-two Greeks. The battle had
been won by crisp tactical skill and discipline, against enormous odds and equal individual bravery.

Thucydides devotes small space to the battle of Marathon.
He states that the centre was defeated and followed up by the
enemy; that the wings won a victory; and that then Milti-

ades, allowing the Persians to fly, united both wings and fought with those who had broken the centre. No other conceivable manœuvre than the one narrated seems to coincide with and satisfy these statements and those of other authorities. In order to unite the wings the victorious Persian centre must first be defeated. There is little doubt that what has been described is what occurred.

The great disproportion in losses which we constantly meet with in ancient battles can best be vouched for by pointing to the well-known losses at such battles as Crécy and Agincourt, in later days. The same thing is always found in the conflicts of disciplined with undisciplined troops, and in ancient times — and often in the Middle Ages — the defeated army suffered terribly after ranks were broken and during the pursuit. Annihilation was wont to follow a defeat.

Miltiades capped his work by marching speedily back to Athens, which he divined from certain signs to be the destination of the Persians. They had naturally guessed the city to be disgarnished of troops, and had at once set sail thither. He reached Athens just in time to forestall its capture.

The Spartans, whose religious rules would not allow them to open a campaign before the full moon, started too late, and by three successive marches of fifty miles a day arrived at Marathon the day after the battle had been won. Grievously chagrined, they returned to Sparta.

This victory shows, prior to the days of Epaminondas, the most brilliant of the variations from the parallel order of armies then uniformly in vogue. The battle exhibited a set and well-digested manœuvre promptly and intelligently executed in the heat of action. Whether Miltiades prepared for the manœuvre, or conceived and used it on the spur of the moment, it equally redounds to his honor.

This and the succeeding battles and campaigns herein nar-

rated by no means purport to describe all the instances of
military skill which are worthy of notice prior to Alexander's
day. They are rather types which show how the art of war
gradually advanced, and what its condition was when the
great conqueror began his wonderful career. Many noteworthy events have of necessity to be omitted.

Xenophon.

VIII.

BRASIDAS. B. C. 424–422.

THE Peloponnesian was not a great war. It was a war of exhaustion and of small operations. There were but half a dozen battles in twenty-seven years. But it shows instances of far-seeing strategy. Such was the seizure of Pylos, whence the threat of incursions on Sparta's rear obliged her to relax her hold on the throat of Athens. The siege of Platæa is peculiarly interesting as affording us the first detailed glimpse into ancient siege-methods; and it was one of the earliest instances of a complete, though crude wall of contravallation and circumvallation, and of something like systematic operations. This war bred some good generals. At the battle of Olpæ Demosthenes cleverly made use of an ambuscade to win an otherwise lost battle. Brasidas was the man who came nearest to showing the moral and intellectual combination of the great soldier. His speech to his troops when confronted by untold numbers of barbarians is a model. It has the true ring of the captain. His marches through Thessaly and Illyria and his defeat of Cleon at Amphipolis were admirable. He it was who first marched in a hollow square with baggage in the centre, and showed what fighting in retreat should be. In this he was the prototype of Xenophon. The siege of Syracuse, too, among its long and intricate details, furnishes us with two of the best known and wisest maxims of war.

IN the century succeeding Marathon there can be traced a constant if not rapid growth of the military art. This is shown not so much in the rise of distinguished captains as in the ability of the lesser lights to govern themselves by the success or failure of their predecessors, and thus gradually aid in shaping warfare into a system. In the far-seeing wisdom of Themistocles preceding the battle of Salamis (B. C. 480), we recognize the broad and self-poised reasoning of which is bred the soundest strategy. In the operations of the several campaigns of the Peloponnesian war, although the Greeks then practiced almost exclusively a defensive system, there

may be found an occasional lesson.   But many such must be
passed over unnoticed throughout all history.   The Peloponnesian was not a great war.   There were but a half-dozen battles in twenty-seven years, and only one decisive one, Ægospotami.   It was a war of exhaustion.

The siege of Platæa (B. C. 429–427) is interesting in that we
have in its story the first detailed account of any siege of antiquity, and can therefrom learn the methods practiced.   In

Pylos, B. C. 425.

this light it is more important to us than because a mere handful of men held the Spartans at bay for nearly two years.
Thucydides tells us that the besiegers began by surrounding
the town with a line of palisades; but that when the siege
operations showed no signs of success, they resorted to a careful blockade and built two walls sixteen feet apart, one facing
toward the town, one outward.   The detail on duty held this
double line; the bulk of the forces camped outside.   The
space between the walls was roofed in to protect the troops

against the fire of the enemy and the weather. Thus the two walls became one, with a double parapet. Towers surmounted the wall at intervals, and commanded both sides. Large ditches were dug on either side with drawbridges thrown across them. Previous to this we find no methodical plan of siege works.

The Peloponnesian war bred some good generals. Of these probably Brasidas, the Spartan, should hold the first place as a military man, though Athens developed the greatest statesmen. Pericles' conception of the plan on which Athens should work, — a defensive war on land, an aggressive war at sea, — and the words Thucydides puts into his mouth, are full of·wisdom. The foresight of Demosthenes in seizing Pylos (B. C. 425), by which he threatened so dangerous an incursion on the rear of Sparta that he at once compelled her not only to relax her hold on the throat of Athens, but sue for peace, is part and parcel of the very best of strategic ability. Demosthenes also won the battle of Olpæ (B. C. 425) by

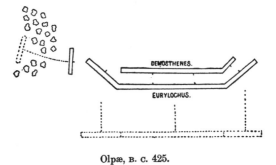

Olpæ, B. C. 425.

the clever use of an ambuscade. He hid in a wooded valley a force of four hundred hoplites and light troops, beyond his own right, hoping by a surprise to demoralize the Lacedæmonian left, which outflanked him, in case it should gain the advantage. What he anticipated occurred. Eurylochus turned his right, but at the proper moment the men in ambush debouched from hiding and fell upon Eurylochus' rear. So effective was this diversion, that although the right of Eurylochus' army won a decided success, it became compromised by the defeat of the left, and Demosthenes scored a victory.

The siege of Syracuse also furnishes us numerous lessons for which there is no space, as well as two of the best maxims known to the science of war: "The most certain means of conquering is to fall unexpectedly on your enemy;" and, "No greater damage can be inflicted on the enemy than by pressing him there where you have become certain he dreads it the most." There is space to do no more than instance a march and a battle of Brasidas, in illustration of what was best in the warfare of that century.

Perdiccas, king of Macedonia, together with some revolted Thracian cities and Sparta, had joined in a treaty against Athens, which city had long held the supremacy in the north. The march of Brasidas through Thessaly to join Perdiccas in Macedonia (B. C. 424) gives proof of a man with the moral element singularly and beautifully developed. Brasidas had none of the narrowness of the Spartan. He was not only a clear-headed soldier, but he was a clean man, who accomplished his tasks as openly and honorably as he fought his way bravely. The population of Thessaly was allied to Athens and inimical to Sparta. Brasidas must march through Thessaly to reach Macedonia. At the head of his four thousand men he made a series of forced marches with such rapidity and skill that he forestalled opposition. Before the people of any one section had met and determined to oppose him, Brasidas would have already passed by their land ; and when he was once arrested on the march by armed resistance at a defile through which he must pass, he persuaded his would-be adversaries that his mission was peaceful and advantageous to them in a manner, and with an eloquence, which illustrates

one of the happiest faculties of the soldier, and one most rarely possessed.

In his retreat from Illyria, whither he had undertaken a campaign with the Macedonians, Brasidas showed remarkable skill. Perdiccas had deserted him, decamping suddenly by night with his entire force, in abject terror at the compromised situation in which he and Brasidas found themselves, leaving Brasidas with but a handful of men to encounter a vast host of barbarians who were following up his retreat. The position was one to try men's souls; but such was the influence of Brasidas over his men that not the remotest demoralization was shown, nor loss of discipline. His speech to them, pointing out their superiority over the barbarians, despite their small numbers, both in courage, discipline and every manly quality, and the certainty of beating them if they but stood together, is a model for every soldier. Here first we find a general telling his men that the civilized warrior need have no fear from untold numbers of barbarians, trite as the saying is to-day. On the march the hoplites were formed in a hollow square or oblong, the light-armed troops and baggage in the centre. This appears to have been a new device with Brasidas. A number of active and brave young soldiers were selected and stationed in an outer rank, or where

March of Brasidas, B. C. 424.

they could quickly quit their places without disorganizing the body, so as to act as flankers, sally out and fall upon the barbarians whenever they came forward to the attack. Brasidas himself, with three hundred chosen hoplites, formed the rearguard. So soon as the command to march was given, the barbarians would begin their attacks. But there was not the slightest breach of discipline. At each onset the column halted, the flankers came out and they and the rear-guard made short work of the Illyrians. The march was then resumed. After two or three attacks the barbarians found that their losses were so severe that they had best be cautious, and a little additional punishment induced them to desist entirely from direct attack. But they only shifted their ground to ambuscade. On one occasion they stole a march ahead of the Greek column toward a height at the mouth of a defile which the phalanx was obliged to pass, proposing there to fight the Greeks at a disadvantage. But Brasidas was constantly on the alert. He saw the purpose of the enemy. Taking his rear-guard quickly in hand, he put it at a double-quick, and headed straight for the height; and though the Illyrians reached the place before him, they could not form readily enough to resist the onset of the hoplites. Brasidas drove them away, killing a number, and seized the mouth of the defile. The Illyrians, throughout the entire retreat, had been so roughly handled that they now gave over the pursuit entirely. In his ascendancy over his men, and his conduct under most trying circumstances, Brasidas may fairly be called the prototype of Xenophon.

The defeat of Cleon by Brasidas at Amphipolis (B. C. 422) further illustrates the rare qualities of this soldier. After his march to Macedonia and his campaign in and retreat from Illyria, he returned to the vicinity of this city, which he had taken some time before. Amphipolis is on the river Stry-

mon, situated on a hill, round three sides of which the river
flows, necessitating a wall on but one, the east side. Brasidas had his camp on Mt. Kerdyllium on the other bank of
the Strymon, connected with the city by a bridge. Cleon

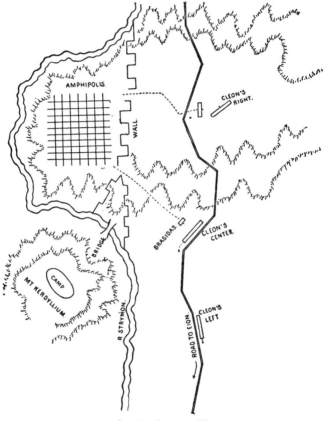

Amphipolis, B. C. 422.

had been sent by Athens to oppose Brasidas, and had landed
at Eion on the seacoast a few miles below. Desiring to reconnoitre the town, he advanced along the road, right flank
in front, to a position on the heights east of Amphipolis. He
had no idea whatever that Brasidas would attack him, for he

could plainly see his camp on the other bank of the river, as well as the city on the hill, and was advancing in loose and careless order. But Brasidas had made up his mind to attack the Athenian, whose heedless formation he had been watching to good advantage. Cleon perceived the march of Brasidas from his camp into the town, but still anticipated no attack. By and by a commotion was visible within the gates, and Cleon became aware that he was in danger. Still he supposed that Brasidas would do what was usual in those days, emerge from the gates, form in the regular order in front of them, and advance his phalanx to the attack. Though he was in much larger force and vastly better equipped than Brasidas, Cleon determined to retire, and faced his column about, so as to march it back left in front, but still was not careful to ploy his column into close order. The left wing was marching somewhat ahead, the centre and right at intervals behind. Brasidas, who had a perfectly clear idea of the advantage of doing what your enemy least expects, and had no thought of merely doing the usual thing, had been quietly waiting with a picked force of one hundred and fifty men under his own command behind the gates. He had pointed out to his men the careless formation of the enemy. He addressed to them words of glowing encouragement, and fired them to their task. Then in serried ranks, this small but determined body, not a man of whom but was worth a host, suddenly rushed from the gates, fell upon the flank of Cleon's centre, which was marching quietly along the road, and threw it into the utmost confusion. The left in the advance, instead of turning to the assistance of the centre, was so taken by surprise that it at once fled towards Eion. The right retired to a position on the hill. At the same moment another and larger body emerged from an upper gate, and advanced against the right, taking it in reverse. Cleon himself fled, but was slain in his flight.

The right resisted manfully, but uselessly.   Over six hundred Athenian hoplites were slain, and the whole army utterly demoralized.   The Spartans lost but seven men killed. Brasidas was fatally wounded.   The contrast between the two commanders in character as well as in ability is noteworthy.

There are many things in the career of Lysander, the victor of Ægospotami, which stamp him second only to Brasidas, but his exploits, like those of many other able men, must be omitted here.

The Peloponnesian war was limited in its military scope. Political means were as much employed as warlike.   To seduce an ally from the enemy or rouse sedition in his capital was as important as to win a battle.   Statesmanship overrode military ability.   Campaigns were usually raids, having some side-issue for object.   The war was conducted more at sea than on land.   Small war and sieges covered all the land operations.   The Peloponnesian war was essentially a little war, though on a large scale and over a large territory and with mighty interests at stake ; and it was characterized by unusual cruelty and unnecessary devastation.   It produced great men, dishonest men, and weak men, and the influence of all was marked in its conduct.   Pericles, Demosthenes, Brasidas, Gylippus, Lysander, Cleon, Alcibiades, Nicias, each impressed his own character for good or for ill on some part of this long-drawn-out conflict.   Had it not come to a close when it did, Greece might have gone to pieces as a factor in civilization.

IX.

XENOPHON. — AGESILAUS. B. C. 401-394.

The soldier of greatest use to us preceding Alexander was unquestionably Xenophon. After participating in the defeat of Cyrus the Younger by Artaxerxes at Cunaxa, in which battle the Greek phalanx had held its own against twenty times its force, Xenophon was chosen to command the rear-guard of the phalanx in the Retreat of the Ten Thousand to the Sea; and it is he who has shown the world what should be the tactics of retreat, — how to command a rear-guard. No chieftain ever possessed a grander moral ascendant over his men. More tactical originality has come from the Anabasis than from any dozen other books. For instance, Xenophon describes accurately a charge over bad ground in which, so to speak, he broke forward by the right of companies, — one of the most useful minor manœuvres. He established a reserve in rear of the phalanx from which to feed weak parts of the line, — a superb first conception. He systematically devastated the country traversed to arrest pursuit. The whole retreat is full of originality in the operations of every day. After the lapse of twenty-three centuries there is no better military text-book than the Anabasis.

Alexander had a predecessor in the invasion of Asia. Agesilaus, king of Sparta, went to the assistance of the Greek cities of Asia Minor, unjustly oppressed by the satrap Tissaphernes. He set sail with eight thousand men, landed at Ephesus, adjusted the difficulties of these cities, and, having, with consummate ability, conducted two successful campaigns in Phrygia and Caria, returned to Lacedemon overland, — a long, toilsome and dangerous march. On the way he won the battle of Coronæa by an admirable display of tactical ability.

CYRUS the Younger, second son of Darius II., proposed to dispute the kingdom with his brother Artaxerxes. He invaded Persia (B. C. 401) with an army of Asiatics and thirteen thousand Greek auxiliaries. The latter were a fine body of men, much above the ordinary class of mercenaries, of whom Greece had furnished vast numbers for many years.

They marched from Myriandrus to Thapsacus in twelve days, at the rate of nineteen miles a day. Their commander was Clearchus. The battle of Cunaxa, fought by Cyrus against Artaxerxes, is interesting as showing the discipline of which a Greek phalanx was capable, when compared with the heterogeneous troops of Persia, and as being the initiation of the Retreat of the Ten Thousand. Artaxerxes had an army said to be nine hundred thousand strong — probably an exaggeration; while Cyrus had, including the Greeks, nearly one hundred thousand. These two armies were marching toward each other, and came together near the river Euphrates.

On learning of the approach of the enemy Cyrus drew up his army. The phalanx was on the right, leaning on the river, some distance in front of the camp. A small body of one thousand horse supported it. Cyrus, with a body-guard of six hundred horse, was in the centre. The Asiatics were on the left. Artaxerxes advanced in order of battle. His enormous force, with its left on the river, so far overlapped the line of Cyrus that its centre was beyond the latter's left flank. As the Persians marched on in silence and with measured tread Cyrus rode his lines, encouraged his men, and bade Clearchus attack the centre, where Artaxerxes, with his six thousand cavalry, had stationed himself, knowing that success at that place meant certain victory. But Clearchus was loath to leave his position near the river, as this protected his unshielded side; for the shield was carried on the left arm, and a phalanx always felt more concern for its right than its left flank. He therefore practically disobeyed orders, but he promised Cyrus to hold firm.

As the Persian army came within about half a mile, the phalanx advanced, striking their pikes upon their shields, and shouting their martial pæan. So redoubtable did they appear that the cavalry and chariots in front of Artaxerxes' left wing

did not even await their attack, but melted away before the
Greeks came within an arrow flight. The phalanx, instinct
with ardor, advanced in good order upon the main body of
the left wing, defeated it and pursued it some two miles.

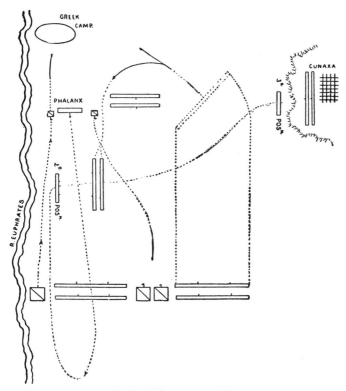

Battle of Cunaxa, B. C. 401.

Meanwhile Artaxerxes, seeing how far he overlapped Cyrus'
left, ordered his right wing to wheel round upon it and take
it in reverse; and the cavalry on the Persian left had attacked
the cavalry which had supported the phalanx, had driven it
back, and had made its way to the camp.

Cyrus had held his body-guard in hand watching developments; but when he saw the success of the phalanx, he desired to do something worthy to rival it, and projected his horse with so much *élan* upon the large body surrounding Artaxerxes that he dispersed it at a blow. Unfortunately his horsemen followed on in pursuit, leaving Cyrus with but a few of his intimates, or "table companions," around him. With these he charged on Artaxerxes in person, and wounded him indeed, but himself fell in the onset. The right wing of the Persians had meanwhile manœuvred round upon Cyrus' left, which, thus compromised and learning of the death of its leader, sought safety in flight. Both the Persian right wing and the cavalry set to pillaging the camp. Artaxerxes, seeing the rout of his left wing, rallied his right wing, which had thus made a complete wheel to the rear, and led it against the phalanx.

Clearchus had now completed the destruction of the Persian left wing, and had faced about to attack whatever other part of the enemy might be in his front; and as in moving back near the river he saw the new array of the Persians, he backed up against it, and obliged Artaxerxes to file to the left to face him. The phalanx then once more advanced on the enemy, and drove them off the field and to the hill on which is situated the town of Cunaxa. From here Clearchus retired to his camp. Not till then did the Greeks hear of the death of Cyrus. But one phalangite was wounded, though this body of thirteen thousand men had defeated an army at least a score of times greater. This battle illustrates the superiority of the phalanx over the no doubt brave but undisciplined soldiers of Oriental nations. But its success and meagre loss must not be taken as a measure of what was usual.

The Greeks were now compelled to make their way out of the country as best they might. Clearchus and some of the other generals having been treacherously murdered in a parley under safe conduct with the enemy, new ones were chosen in their stead, and to the lot of Xenophon fell the rearguard, while to Cheirisophus fell the van. Nothing like this famous retreat is known in the world's history. Xenophon is the father of the system of retreat, the originator of all that appertains to the science of rear-guard fighting. He reduced its management to a perfect method. More originality in tactics has come from the Anabasis than from any dozen other books. Every system of war looks to this as to the

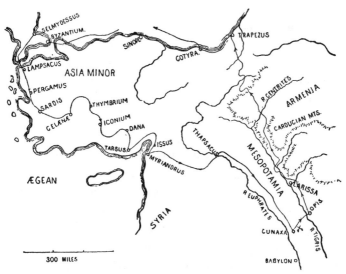

March of the Ten Thousand, 401 B. C.

fountain-head when it comes to rearward movements, as it looks to Alexander for a pattern of resistless and intelligent advance.

Necessity to Xenophon was truly the mother of invention, but the centuries since have devised nothing to surpass the genius of this warrior. No general ever possessed a grander moral ascendant over his men. None ever worked for the safety of his soldiers with greater ardor or to better effect. In this retreat a number of entirely new schemes were put into practice by him. The building of a bridge on goat-skins stuffed with hay or stubble and sewed up so as to be watertight is here first mentioned, though Xenophon does not claim its invention, and we shall see Alexander using this device constantly. Xenophon originated the advance by breaking forward by the right of regiments or companies instead of in line, in order to overcome bad ground or to maintain a better alignment, — one of the most useful of minor manœuvres. But it is in the method he displayed that he principally instructs us.

Parts of the Retreat of the Ten Thousand were a running fight for days. Xenophon began by organizing a small cavalry force and a body of slingers, both essential to meet the similar arms of the enemy. He was always at the proper point. The Greek order of march was apt to be careless and much strung out. Xenophon taught his men that a column of march well closed up could not only more easily force its way through the enemy, but that it was far safer in retreat because occupying so much less space. His opponents had no missile-throwing engines, and could not attack from a distance. So when the pursuing forces reached his rear, he had with his dense column to waste no time in concentrating before he was strong enough to attack; meanwhile by a slight skirmishing resistance, or a smart onset with his rear-guard, Xenophon enabled the main column and baggage to gain much ground, and could then quickly rejoin it. In well-closed order he reduced to a minimum the danger of flank attack. Across plains Xenophon marched, like Brasidas, in hollow square, with baggage and non-combatants in the centre, but in passing through the mountains — a succession of defiles — he changed the formation to one more compact, and always kept his rear-guard posted on some convenient eminence to protect the filing by of the phalanx. Before allowing the head of his column to enter a defile, he threw forward his light troops to seize the heights commanding its mouth, and these he held until the column had filed by. On this retreat also was first shown the necessary, if cruel, means of arresting a pursuing enemy by the systematic devastation of the country traversed and the destruction of its villages to deprive him of food and shelter. And Xenophon is moreover the first who established in rear of the phalanx a reserve from which he could at will feed weak parts of his line. This was a superb first conception. Something like reserves had been theretofore known; but nothing so nearly approaching our modern idea. These things all seem simple now, but we have been twenty-three centuries learning them, and to-day Xenophon's Anabasis is one of the best of military text-books. On this retreat it was first demonstrated how much the Persian empire lacked homogeneity and hence strength. What Xenophon actually did showed Alexander what he might, by persistent and intelligent activity, even with a meagre force, accomplish.

It is impossible to convey an adequate idea of the fertile and ingenious schemes of Xenophon by the mere relation of one or two incidents. But even this brief narrative of earlier exploits will serve its end after a fashion, by exhibiting the status of military science when Alexander ascended the throne of Macedon. Very many instances of able tactical battle manœuvres existed before his day, and one or two affairs of Xenophon's will give a partial idea of the resources, activity, good judgment and courage of which the Anabasis is full. To read Alexander's campaigns in the light of the Anabasis explains many obscure details.

The Greeks, about midway on the march, had just emerged,

after much danger and many wounds, from a defile in the
Carducian mountains, through which they had been obliged
to fight their way, and through which the van under Cheirisophus had hurried so rapidly that it had left Xenophon almost in the lurch with the rear-guard, when they saw, as they
descended into the valley, another defile in their front, the

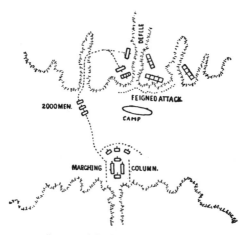

Capture of Carducian Defile, 401 B. C.

heights commanding which were held by the enemy in force.
The Carducians were brave, alert and well-armed.   Their
bows were nearly a man's height in length, with arrows over
three feet long,   To advance seemed a hopeless task; but
the native guides, of whom they always had several, informed
them that there was no other road across the range.   Perhaps
there is no greater test of a general's capacity, as there is certainly none of his patience, than to procure suitable guides
through an enemy's country, and to decide whether these
guides are leading him aright or astray.   Xenophon had, in
a combat in the defile just passed, captured two Carducians,
who, he was convinced, must be more familiar with this particular region than his other guides.   He interrogated them,

at first separately. The one obstinately denied the existence of any other pass. Xenophon put him to death in the presence of the other. This one then confessed that there was another equally good pass, which, being little known, would probably not be held in force. By means of this pass the position of the barbarians at the main gap could be turned, and it contained but one position which might have to be forced.

Towards night Xenophon dispatched two thousand volunteers to surprise the newly-discovered pass, under conduct of this guide, whom he bound, and who saw reward or death facing him on either hand. A heavy rain then falling tended to conceal this manœuvre from observation. In order still further to divert attention from it, Xenophon made a feigned attack in the front of the defile held by the enemy, with his main body. The Carducians received him with confidence in their ability to destroy his army. They felt certain that they had him entrapped. One of their means of defense was the rolling down the mountain slope of huge stones upon the Greeks. This they continued to do all night. Xenophon left a small party at this point, with orders to keep up active demonstrations, and retired with the bulk of his force to camp, to allow his men to rest. Meanwhile the two thousand volunteers reached the side pass, and had no great difficulty in driving from it the small body of barbarians who held it; and having made their way to the rear of the main pass, at daylight, under cover of the morning mist, they boldly pushed in upon the astonished Carducians. The blare of their many trumpets gave notice of their successful détour to Xenophon, as well as added to the confusion of the enemy. The main army at once joined in the attack from the valley side, and the Carducians were driven from their stronghold.

The army entered the hills through both passes, — Xeno-

phon through the second one, which the two thousand had
forced. The enemy, however, still had a considerable body
of troops in the defile, where they successively occupied each
commanding eminence; and at three of these the Greeks
were obliged to halt and to assault in regular form in order
to force a passage. They were always careful to so attack
as to leave the barbarians a means of retreat; they were not
strong enough to risk a battle à outrance. Each captured
height was then occupied by a suitable force and held until
the long column of troops, baggage, wounded and women (for
a large number accompanied the army, as was not unusual in
ancient and mediæval warfare) could file by. In retiring from
each position the Carducians were sure to harass the rear of
the defenders, who, at intervals, were obliged to face about
and drive them away. The enemy kept at the heels of the
Greeks every mile of the way. Xenophon was the soul of
every encounter, at the front as much as at the rear.

On approaching the river Centrites Xenophon found that
the satrap of Armenia had occupied its farther bank, while
the Carducians were still pressing upon his rear. The road
on which they were marching crossed the river at a ford, but
the water was high and the bottom full of rolling and slippery stones, so that in crossing the men could not hold their
shields in such a manner as to protect themselves from the
showers of arrows and darts shot by the Armenians. The
attempt was made, but, owing to the large force opposing
them, was abandoned. Xenophon with the rear-guard was
out, holding the Carducians in check. The situation was
desperate, and the army passed the night in grave anxiety.
But Xenophon, whose spirit was elastic and hopeful, had a
dream — or pretended to have it — as of shackles falling
from off his hands, and at daybreak bade his comrades not
despair. And true enough, early in the morning, some men

discovered another and better ford higher up the river by about half a mile. To this the army marched. But the Carducians, as well as the Armenians on the other bank, followed up the movement.

Arrived at the upper ford, Xenophon, who always was the

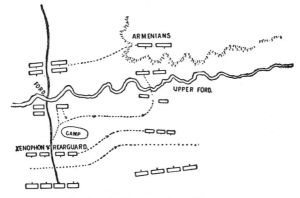

Crossing of River Centrites, 401 B. C.

most daring, discreet and therefore controlling spirit, though only equal in command with the others, arranged to have Cheirisophus pass over first. He kept himself in fighting trim, and with a sufficient body to hold the Carducians in check. In order to relieve Cheirisophus from the opposition of the Armenians on the other bank, Xenophon, with a large body, made a feint to move down again to the lower ford, as if the Greeks were about to give up the attempt to cross at the upper one. The Armenians, fearing lest they should be taken between two fires if Xenophon crossed below, as well as be cut off from the main road, set out in haste for the lower ford, leaving only such a body of troops opposite Cheirisophus as he could readily force. Thus disengaged, Cheirisophus was enabled to cross and gain a foothold on the other shore. Here he drew up his troops in phalangial order, for there was a large body of Armenians on the hills somewhat back from

the river.   Seeing that Cheirisophus had secured a foothold,
Xenophon speedily retraced his steps, and made preparations
to follow.

The Carducians, now perceiving their opportunity, began
to press in upon the Greeks very seriously and in vast numbers.   To meet this attack Xenophon sent word to Cheirisophus to order his archers and slingers to return part way
across the ford, and remain in the water where they could
cover the crossing.   Then, instructing the troops to make
their way over as rapidly as possible, he put himself at the
head of a few chosen hoplites and advanced out to meet and
impose upon the Carducians.   These, who were never able to
stand the attack of the Greeks, kept at a respectful distance,
but used their missiles freely.   When nearly all the troops
were over, Xenophon, in order to clear his front, sounded the
charge, moved upon the Carducians at a run, and dispersed
them in terror.   Then, before they could recover themselves,
he turned about, retired quickly to the river and crossed.
The archers and slingers remained to see the heavy-armed
well over.

After this admirable fashion was conducted the entire retreat.   The army as an army was saved.   But out of thirteen
thousand Greeks who fought at Cunaxa, only six thousand
lived to see the Euxine, and to cry, " The Sea!   The Sea ! "
In fourteen months these men had marched upwards of four
thousand miles in two hundred and fifteen marches, or about
eighteen and a half miles a day when afoot.

The Persians had degenerated.   " The empire of the great
king is powerful from extent of territory and sum of population ; the great distances and dispersion of forces make it
feeble to whomever conducts war with promptitude."   " Persia," said Xenophon, " belongs to the man who has the courage to attack it."   No doubt Alexander had read and pondered this remark.

Agesilaus. — Alexander the Great had a predecessor in the invasion of Asia. Agesilaus, king of Sparta, in what is called the Sparto-Persian war (B. C. 399–394), went to the assistance of the Greek cities of Asia Minor, which had been unjustly oppressed by Tissaphernes, the Persian satrap, for their share in the expedition of the younger Cyrus. Circumstances prevented Agesilaus from finishing his labors, but he showed the way, conceived the project, and no doubt Alexander's own more gigantic imagination benefited by what he did, as his spirit of rivalry urged him on to exceed even Cyrus in his conquests.

Route of Agesilaus, B. C. 396–394.

Agesilaus left Sparta by sea with eighty-three hundred men and six months' victual, and landed at Ephesus. Having adjusted, with commendable discretion, the troubles of the Greek cities, he apparently prepared to march into Caria, where Tissaphernes had advanced to the plains of the Mæander to meet him. But Agesilaus had no cavalry, and did not propose to accommodate Tissaphernes with a battle on a *terrain* which was particularly suited to this arm; and in lieu of advancing to Caria he directed his march into Phrygia. His manœuvres here were much to the purpose, but finding that horse was indispensable in a campaign in Asia, he returned to Ephesus for winter quarters, and while here raised and equipped an excellent cavalry brigade. When spring came Tissaphernes made every effort to divine the purpose of Agesilaus. The Spartan king gave out that he should march again into Phrygia. Tissaphernes understood this to be an effort to lead him away from Caria, and remained on the Mæander plains, as before. But Agesilaus, having thus misled his adversary, was as good as his word, and advanced toward the Pactolus, where he met and defeated a large body of cavalry. Such methods of misleading an enemy have been most successfully practiced by all great leaders.

Tissaphernes followed him to Sardis; but so frightened were his followers at the successes of Agesilaus that they assassinated the satrap, and paid the Spartan king thirty talents to march out of this satrapy into Phrygia. This he did, devastating the province, and wintering at Dascyllium. Here he made large preparations for a campaign into Persia. But Persian money excited intestine troubles in Greece, and Agesilaus was constrained to march towards home. He chose the overland route which Xerxes had followed. He was obliged to fight his way through Thessaly, and gave signs of great ability by the manner in which he handled his cavalry, to him a new arm, against the Thessalian horse, then the best in Greece. In Thessaly Agesilaus heard of the defeat of the Spartan fleet at Cindus. With consummate prudence, in order to prevent demoralization in his ranks, he announced to his army a brilliant victory. He then attacked the Thebans and their allies, and under the influence of the enthusiasm which prevailed he beat them at Coronæa (B. C. 394). In this battle he showed a marked capacity for tactical direction. When the lines met, Agesilaus on the right of the Spartans drove in the enemy's left, while the Theban right defeated Agesilaus' left, and advanced as far as the baggage camp. Agesilaus, so soon as his hands were free, wheeled the wing under his command sharply

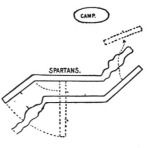

Coronæa, B. C. 394.

against the Thebans, and according to Xenophon, who was with him, the most terrific combat known in Greek history then took place. The Thebans, ployed into a square, were able, though with heavy loss, to cut their way through the Spartan ranks and join their defeated comrades; but they left the battlefield and victory to Agesilaus. The study of these and other campaigns of Agesilaus furnishes excellent matter for the military man. He is selected rather as a type of the best generals of the time than because he was prominent beyond all others. Agesilaus reigned forty-one years, to the glory of Sparta. All his campaigns were noteworthy.

X.

EPAMINONDAS. B. C. 371–362.

ASSOCIATED with one of the most notable tactical manœuvres — the oblique order of battle — is the immortal name of Epaminondas. This great soldier originated what all skillful generals have used frequently and to effect, and what Frederick the Great showed in its highest perfection at Leuthen. As already observed, armies up to that time had with rare exceptions attacked in parallel order and fought until one or other gave way. At Leuctra Epaminondas had six thousand men against eleven thousand of the invincible Spartans. The Thebans were dispirited by many failures; the Lacedæmonians in good heart. The Spartan king was on the right of his army. Epaminondas tried a daring innovation. He saw that if he could break the Spartan right, he would probably drive the enemy from the field. He therefore quadrupled the depth of his own left, making it a heavy column, led it sharply forward, and ordered his centre and right to advance more slowly, so as not seriously to engage. The effect was never doubtful. While the Spartan centre and left was held in place by the threatening attack of the Theban centre and right, as well as by the combat of the cavalry between the lines, their right was overpowered and crushed; having defeated which, Epaminondas wheeled around on the flank of the Spartan centre and swept it and the left wing from the field. The genius of a great tactician had prevailed over numbers, prestige and confidence. At Mantinæa, nine years later, Epaminondas practiced the same manœuvre with equal success, but himself fell in the hour of victory.

THIS great Theban, above almost all others, has stamped his name upon the military art as one of the world's early tacticians. To him is due the invention of a manœuvre to the use of which many generals, and Alexander and Frederick peculiarly, owe a number of their victories, — the well-known oblique order of battle. Up to his day, as already noted, all battles had been fought in parallel order, or in some variation of the parallel. The " two fair daughters " Epaminondas left behind him were the brilliant victories of Leuctra and Mantinæa, in both of which he put this manœuvre into use.

At Leuctra (B. C. 371) Epaminondas had a force of about six thousand men. By some it is stated as high as eight thousand. The Thebans were in a dispirited condition. Fortune had not smiled upon them. They lacked self-confidence. The Spartan army was about eleven thousand strong, and in the best of heart and

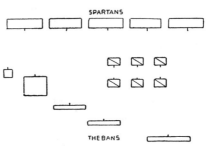

Battle of Leuctra, B. C. 371.

discipline. When the armies came into presence of each other, Cleombrotus, the Spartan king, drew up the Lacedæmonians in the usual phalangial shape prescribed by generations of usage and success, of twelve men in depth, and with the cavalry in front. He expected, as usual, to fight in parallel order and all along the line. Cleombrotus was not a man of force or originality. His own position, with his chief officers, was at the post of honor, the right. The Spartan idea was to swing round its wings into concave order when the battle should have been engaged, and thus inclose the Theban flanks. The fact that Cleombrotus was on the Spartan right Epaminondas well knew, and he determined to make up for his numerical weakness by a daring innovation.

We do not know whether Epaminondas had long ago thought out this manœuvre, or whether it was the inspiration of the moment. His phalanx on the right and centre consisted probably of eight men in a file. But thirty-two of the files in his left wing he made forty-eight men deep, thus forming the first narrow, deep column of attack of which we have any knowledge. On the left of this column and in a line with it marched the Theban Sacred Band under Pelopidas. Here again was a master's conception in thus protecting the weak point of a novel formation. His centre and right were instructed to advance more slowly, and were thus thrown back, refused, so as to make practically an oblique angle with the Spartan line. Like all inventions, the first oblique order of battle fell far short of its perfect echeloned formation at Leuthen under the masterly tactical dispositions of Frederick. But the conception was there, distinct, unquestioned, and it is probable that the line had a certain echeloned character. The position implies as much.

We can scarcely avoid assuming that the refused wing of Epaminondas advanced in a sort of echeloned order. It is stated that at first that entire part of the line which was refused was brought into an oblique position by a short right wheel, while the column on the left advanced straight forward. This would certainly bring the army-front into the proposed position; but in order to continue its advance towards the enemy the refused line must then march obliquely to the front. It could not strike the enemy effectively when thus advancing, and the natural thing was to allow successive syntagmas or morēs to move into a line parallel to the enemy before they approached too closely. This would naturally echelon the line. Epaminondas' merit lay not in the details, but in the masterly conception of the effect he could produce by an oblique order. Frederick's attack at Leuthen is celebrated for the brilliant and precise execution of the oblique order. As with all inventions, the one originated, the other perfected, the idea. But quite apart from the details of the manœuvres, the main fact remains that for the first time in the history of war an enemy's line was to be struck on one flank by a formation oblique to itself, and by a deep column of attack.

All the effect desired was produced. No amount of tactical nicety could have improved upon what Epaminondas did on this field. His small body of horse was, like the Spartan, in front, but only covering the centre and partly the right. It was less in number, but as soon as the battle opened it at once proved superior to the Spartan horse, and drove this force back in great disorder on the line of battle, in which it created no little confusion. Under cover of this wavering in the Spartan line, Epaminondas pushed forward his column towards the Spartan right, ordering the horse to keep up a hearty skirmishing along their front. The column he led in person, and we can imagine the tremendous momentum with which this compact body of fifty men deep, with their long spears and heavy shields and armor, struck the Spartan line. The fighting was desperate. The Lacedæmonians, surprised at the unusual Theban formation, instead of completing their concave manœuvre, extended their right to receive Epaminondas' column. This, if anything, weakened their line at the key-point. But they had not been familiar with defeat, and offered their wonted stubborn resistance. They would not yield.

Epaminondas, after heroic efforts, proved too strong for even Spartans. Cleombrotus was killed, together with a number of his lieutenants. The Sacred Band took the confused mass of the Spartan right in flank, and completed its destruction. Meanwhile on the Spartan centre and left there had been little or no fighting. Not ordered forward, because the right could not advance, and not being attacked by the Theban centre and right, which, thus refused, was practically in reserve, this portion of the Spartan army was at a loss what to do. Finally, when the right had been entirely annihilated, and the Theban column, elate with victory, wheeled and opened an attack upon its flank, it melted away in its uncertainty, and the whole Lacedæmonian army sought safety in flight to its camp. Only the hoplites of the right and the cavalry had been engaged, and yet the pride of generations of victories, the vaunted irresistibility of the Spartan phalanx, had been blown to the winds. The genius of a great tactician had prevailed over numbers, prestige and confidence. Xenophon's saying was here well illustrated, — " Especially in war, a surprise may turn into terror, even with the stoutest."

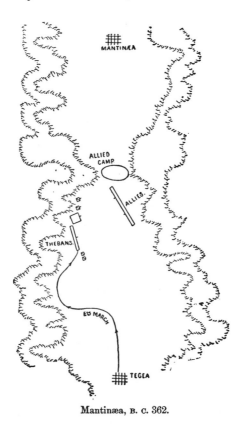

Mantinæa, B. C. 362.

At Mantinæa Epaminondas put the same brilliant manœuvre into practice. On this field the forces were larger, between twenty thousand and thirty thousand men on each side. It is possible that Epaminondas somewhat outnumbered the

Spartans and allies, but this is not certainly known. His army was at this time in most excellent condition and spirits, though partly composed of confederates not entirely reliable. The Spartans and allies lay in the valley of Mantinæa. This valley lies substantially north and south, is about twelve miles long and seven or eight wide in parts, but at the centre it narrows down to about a mile. Opposite this narrow place the Spartans had camped and drawn up their line. Epaminondas was at Tegea at the southern outlet. He proposed to march upon the enemy, who apparently were waiting for him.

This time it is quite apparent that Epaminondas had his battle plan as crisply wrought out in his own mind as Frederick had his, modeled upon it, at Leuthen. He left Tegea, marching left in front, with his best troops leading and the least reliable in the rear. He marched at first straight towards the Spartan camp. The enemy drew up in line to meet him. When within two or three miles, he filed off to the left and skirted the foothills, marching along them as if to get in upon the Spartan right flank. His purpose was to mislead the enemy as to his intentions. The Spartans stood in line of battle, watching his every movement. The histories do not state that they made a right wheel in order to face the new position of Epaminondas, but there can be little doubt that this was what they did. It was the natural thing to do. They expected an attack, and no other theory conforms with the rest of the relation. One is often called on thus to fill a hiatus in the inconsistencies or omissions of the ancient authors.

The Theban Sacred Band headed the march. Epaminondas had the rest of the Thebans and Bœotians, who were behind the Sacred Band in the column and thus formed the left wing, so ranked by lochoi that by a simple file to the

right there would be formed on the left of the line the same
deep column which had given him the victory at Leuctra.
The lochagos or captain remained at the head of his file, and
special officers stood in the front rank, each noted for his bravery. The rest of the line was marching, so that a simple face
to the right, or at all events a very similar manœuvre, would
bring them into the usual phalangial formation. The right
flank of the allies was held by the Mantinæans and Arcadians;
the centre by the Lacedæmonians, Ælæans and Achæans; the
left by the Athenians. Their cavalry was on both wings.

Epaminondas proposed to surprise his enemy. It is altogether probable that the allies were not aware of just how
they had been defeated at Leuctra. It has always taken
much time for the average general to grasp the keen devices
of the great captain. This is one reason why the success of
great captains is so marked. They cannot readily be copied.
At all events the allies were not cautious. Epaminondas,
having got into the position he purposed to occupy, now put
into practice a clever ruse. He ordered his men to ground
arms, as if for camping, and took such other steps as convinced the enemy that no attack would be made by Epaminondas on that day. The men in the allied army were
allowed to disperse; and though the semblance of the line
of battle was preserved, many of the soldiers took off their
armor, and the cavalry unbridled their horses. While this
was going on Epaminondas completed his dispositions, still
ostensibly going into camp. The ruse was carried out with
consummate skill. Opposite the allied horse he placed on
his left a body of his own horse, mixed with light infantry to
give it stability. Opposite the Athenian cavalry on the other
flank he also placed some squadrons. And fearing that the
Athenians might fall upon the right and weak flank of his
column as he advanced, he stationed a small but chosen force

near his right upon a hill, in such a position that they could take the Athenians in rear if they attempted such a manœuvre. His heavy column he proposed to drive through the enemy's right as at Leuctra. The rest of the army was ordered, when the signal was given, to advance more slowly, the right last of all ; in other words, in a sort of echelon.

Having thus quietly completed his preparations, issued instructions and no doubt encouraged his men by the promise of speedy victory, Epaminondas gave the order quickly to

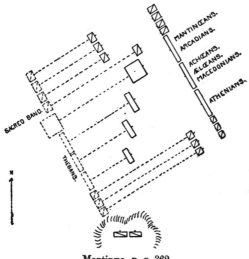

Mantinæa, B. C. 362.

take arms. The sight of this unexpected intention to give immediate battle took the allies absolutely by surprise. The battle signals were sounded, the men armed and rushed into their ranks and the line was speedily formed. But it could not have had the firm consistency of that of Epaminondas, so carefully and steadily marshaled by its wonderful leader. It must have lacked the confidence engendered of the captain's cheering words to prepare the men for combat; the strong tension of expected battle.

Meanwhile the Theban column bore down upon the allies with intuned pæan, serried files and hearts of oak. On its left, formed also in deeper column, charged the horse. This struck the allied cavalry first and bore it back. Immediately after, the remorseless column, headed by the Sacred Band, struck the allied right like the shaft from a catapult. The blow pierced the line, but the stern resistance of the Mantinæan hoplite was not so quickly overcome. The column, like a ship plowing into a head-sea, all but reeled in its onward motion. But the soul of the impetus was there. Epaminondas headed the column again, pike in hand, and fiercely led it against the still resisting foe, determined to crush his line. The struggle was sharp but decisive. The deep column of the Thebans pressed on. The Mantinæans, in firm opposition, fell in their tracks, but the column still made headway. The Theban centre and right advanced in due order, but found no serious resistance when it reached the allied line. The victory was won, but at a heavy price. In the charge headed by the brave Epaminondas, this great captain was wounded by a spear in the breast, of which, shortly after, he died. The victory was less decisive than it would have been had he lived; but it yielded peace with honor.

The manner in which the cavalry was used both at Leuctra and Mantinæa to sustain his oblique order shows that Epaminondas' conception of the value of this arm was clear, as his ability to use it was marked.

XI.

PHILIP AND MACEDON. B. C. 359–336.

THE kings of Macedon had long been vassals of the Great King, but after the Persian wars the country began to approach Greece in its tendencies. The government was not unlike a modern constitutional monarchy. Philip, Alexander's father, was a man second only to his son in ability. He found Macedon a small kingdom, and made it the most important and the most thriving state in Hellas. He married Olympias, princess of Epirus, and from her Alexander inherited his imagination and superstitious habit, as from his father his crisp common sense. Alexander was manly and precocious, and when eighteen commanded the left wing of the Macedonian army at Chæronæa, — the Grecian Waterloo, — where by obstinate charges at the head of the Thessalian horse he destroyed the theretofore invincible Theban Sacred Band. Philip was in consequence of this victory elected autocrator of Greece, and made preparations himself to invade Asia ; but he was murdered, and Alexander took up his work, having secured the throne by vigorous and rapid assertion of his rights, and by putting out of the way all possible claimants.

ALEXANDER I. of Macedon had been a Persian vassal. But the country had regained its freedom on the final retreat of the Persians (B. C. 478), and thenceforward began to approach Greece in its tendencies rather than the East. This Alexander was called by Pindar the Philhellenic. Archelaus († B. C. 399) was the next king of note. He did much to raise the country's prosperity by building roads, fostering commerce, instituting public games like those of Greece, and by copying whatever a more advanced civilization could teach him. He was pronounced by his contemporaries the richest and happiest of men.

After Archelaus, the Macedonian throne passed through several kings, there being considerable difficulty in determining their respective rights ; might and popular suffrage being always factors in the election. Three sons of Amyntas II. († B. C. 376) successively occupied the throne: Alexander II., Perdiccas III., and Philip II., who is commonly known as Philip of Macedon, and was father of Alexander the Great. Philip had been regent during the minority of his nephew Amyntas, son of Perdiccas III., but the dangerous wars in which Macedonia was involved with the surrounding barbarians called him to the throne, or at least gave him the opportunity of ascending it (B. C. 359).

Philip of Macedon, thus invested with the crown at the age of twenty-three, was in every sense a worthy progenitor of Alexander the Great. He had, during a three years' life as hostage in Thebes, received the best Greek education and training, and had studied the tactics of Epaminondas, as well as caught, by personal intercourse, the inspiration of this great man's genius for war. He had become thoroughly familiar with the Greek methods, and was intelligent enough to recognize both their strength and weaknesses. He was a strict disciplinarian, but more than a mere martinet. He copied from the army of Cyrus, and profited well by what had been done by Epaminondas and Iphicrates of Athens, as well as what had been taught him by the experience of his own numberless campaigns; and by improving on the Greek organization and armament, he introduced and perfected a disciplined and steady body of men such as the world had not yet seen. As the creator of an army organization he has perhaps never had an equal. His most prominent idea was embodied in the Macedonian phalanx. By means of his admirable army, and the aid of able and equally well-trained generals, among whom Parmenio held the chief rank, he subjugated Illyria, Pæonia and part of Thrace, captured many towns, and made constant encroachments in the direction of Greece; seized on the mines of Thrace, from which every

year he took considerable money, and showed a clear conception of the rôle of conqueror. Out of a petty country of uncertain boundaries, Philip created a kingdom extending from
the Euxine to the Adriatic. He was constantly at war with
Athens. Not the least of his merits is the debt literature
owes to his restless pertinacity and greed of power in the
Philippics of Demosthenes.

Philip married Olympias, daughter of the king of the Mo-
lossi. Olympias was of the royal house of Epirus, which
claimed descent from Achilles, while Philip traced his lineage
to Hercules. Philip had met Olympias at the Samothracian
mysteries. She was a woman of a high-strung nature, superstitious, semi-barbarous in her cast of mind, and is said to
have been fond of tame snakes and of magic incantations.
She became later in life repulsive to Philip. The night before her marriage it is related that she dreamed that the light-
ning fell upon her and kindled in her a mighty fire, which
broke forth and consumed everything within reach. Despite
the unintelligent nature of her character, Olympias always
retained a large measure of influence over her son.

Three lucky things happened to be reported to Philip, who
was at the siege of Potidæa, upon the same day: that Alexander was born; that Parmenio had beaten the Illyrians;
that his horses had won the chariot race at the Olympic
games. As it happened, the temple of Diana of Ephesus
was burned on that day also.

It was of Philip's marriage with Olympias that was born
Alexander, the third Macedonian king of his name (July,
B. C. 356). He was precocious in physique and in intellect,
and had so early advanced in manliness that, when he was but
sixteen years old, and Philip had left him at Pella, the capital,
as regent while he was absent besieging Byzantium, Alexander not only conducted the business of the state discreetly,

but put down the revolt of a tribe of the Thracians and took one of their towns, which he rechristened Alexandria, — the first of a long series so called.

Philip had gradually insinuated himself into Greek politics. He got himself elected to the Amphictyonic council, and finally chief of the Amphictyons, Sparta alone dissenting. As captain-general of the Greeks he proposed to invade Asia, as his son did later. This claim to universal leadership was, however, demurred to by the Athenians, under the powerful eloquence of Demosthenes, and by the Thebans, both of whom feared Philip's dangerous encroachments in Bœotia. War ensued. The Athenians and Thebans advanced to Chæronæa, in Bœotia, fifty thousand strong. Philip met them with thirty thousand foot and two thousand horse.

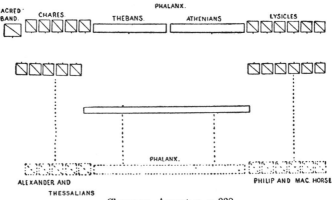

Chæronæa, August, B. C. 338.

Chares and Lysicles commanded the combined Athenian-Theban army. The former was ignorant, the latter rash. Philip had brought with him his son Alexander, then a youth of eighteen, and had intrusted him with the command of the left wing, aided by older generals, while he himself commanded the right. For many hours the event of the battle was doubtful.

Philip's horse was defeated early in the day by the vigorous onset of the Athenians. Lysicles rashly ventured to follow up this yet dubious advantage by a pursuit conducted in the visionary belief that victory had thereby been won. But Philip retrieved his loss by the vigorous use of the phalanx. The long spears of the Macedonians bore down everything. The battle was reëstablished at this point, and the splendid energy of young Alexander, shown in his determined charges at the head of the Thessalian horse, — in which he proved already that power to use cavalry which was always one of his strongest points, — enabled the Macedonians at this moment to overcome the enemy's right, where in the van of the allied array fought the Theban Sacred Band, so long the right arm of brave Epaminondas. This band of lovers, bound together by oaths of fidelity and ties of personal affection, died to the last man where they stood. Philip was enabled to break the ranks of the enemy on the right. The left took to flight before enthusiastic Alexander. Sharply advancing his centre at this juncture, Philip completed the defeat. The allies were irretrievably beaten. It was the Grecian Waterloo. The loss of the Athenians was one thousand killed; of the Thebans an equal number. Placing the lowest estimate on the wounded of eight to one, — twelve to one would be nearer the truth, — the loss in killed and wounded was thirty-six per cent. Philip's loss is not given. It has been suggested that Philip had designed to try the oblique order by the right, but that the impetuous ardor of Alexander in throwing forward the left, which was intended to be refused, had prevented his carrying out the manœuvre he had learned from Epaminondas. This assumption, however, rests on but a slender basis.

Philip was extremely moderate after this victory to all but the Thebans. He wisely approached the rest of the Greeks with an open as well as a strong hand. He had abundant common-sense, and found no difficulty in being elected Hegemōn, or autocrator of Greece. This was immediately proclaimed at Corinth.

The spirit of the victory at Chæronæa grew by what it fed on. Philip now saw his way clear to Oriental conquests, and sent a large force to Asia, which he intended later to follow in person. His generals, Parmenio and Attalus, were already on the ground, fomenting among the Grecian colonies revolt against the Great King. But his preparations were thrown away. Philip did not long enjoy the distinction of autocrator of Greece. His reign came suddenly and lamentably to an end.

Philip had married several wives, having repudiated Olympias on the allegation of infidelity. Olympias retired to the protection of her brother, the king of Epirus. Alexander sided against Philip. He always clung with respectful love to his mother, though recognizing her peculiar weakness. Quarrels ensued. At the marriage banquet of Cleopatra, the last wife, a toast was proposed by Attalus, Cleopatra's uncle, with the hope expressed for a speedy and legitimate issue. " Dost thou then call me a bastard?" quoth Alexander, and hurled a goblet at him. Philip started up in rage, drew his sword and rushed at his son; but intoxication, wrath and his Chæronæa wounds rendered him unsteady, and he fell prone. "Here is the man who proposes to cross to Asia, and he cannot cross from one couch to another!" was the sneering comment of his son.

Alexander conducted his mother to Epirus and thence went to the court of Illyrium. Attalus was promoted and loaded with honors. Alexander's young friends, among them Harpalus, Nearchus, Erigyius and Laomedon, Ptolemy, son of Lagus, Philotas and others, whom we shall see later among his celebrated generals, had either been before or were now banished. But a reconciliation was finally brought about between father and son through Demaratus of Corinth, who was bold enough to tax Philip with desiring peace in Hellas and making war in his own family. To conciliate Alexander, the brother of Olympias, Philip gave him his daughter Cleopatra, Alexander's sister, to wife. At this marriage-feast Philip was treacherously murdered (B. C. 336) by Pausanias, in revenge, it is said, for a grievous personal injury at the hands of Attalus, which Philip had refused to redress; but the act was no doubt secretly instigated by Olympias. Though often suggested in the modern crusade against Alexander, the crime is in no wise traceable to this prince.

Of the known accomplices, the Lyncestian Alexander was the first to salute Alexander, son of Philip, as king. This promptness secured him his pardon; for by such timely aid our Alexander was enabled to forestall the arts of the partisans of the young prince who had been born to Philip and Cleopatra, and to take possession of the throne.

At the moment of Philip's murder, Olympias, as if in anticipation of the event, was near at hand. The sympathizers of Philip against Alexander naturally held him too to have been cognizant of the conspiracy. Some believed that he could not have been legitimate; that this alone could account for his father's hate and new marriage. Others were of opinion that Philip's young son by Cleopatra should be king. Others again held that Amyntas, son of Perdiccas III., was the rightful heir. But while all these factions argued, Alexander acted. The partisans of Cleopatra's son were distant and not alert; Amyntas was a quiet, unknown lad. Alexander had already stamped himself upon the pride of the nation. The people sympathized with his persecution; the army, proud of the youthful hero, was his to a man. Facts

as well as acts were all in favor of our Alexander. His Lyncestian namesake, as before said, saluted him king, and he
was readily accepted by all but the usual crowd of grumblers
and malcontents ; and these speedily subsided or were suppressed. For there was in Macedon no rule of succession
definite enough to be respected. Attalus and Cleopatra and
her son, as well as the murderers of Philip, were put to death.
This apparent — so-called inexcusable — cruelty was a matter
of necessary personal safety with Alexander. That such an
act was in the regular course of proceeding in those days explains, if it does not palliate it. Indeed the act was no worse
than Macchiavelli advocates in " The Prince," as the *duty* of
a ruler who wishes to secure his throne. Alexander was no
worse, he was better than his times; but there is no claim
that he in any sense approached perfection, except as a soldier. Amyntas had perhaps a prior right to the throne, had
he been in a position to assert it and to do justice to the
growth and power of Macedonia; he also was put to death,
ostensibly for conspiring against Alexander. The simple facts,
rather than the discussion of the right or wrong of these political executions, — murders, if you will, — concern us here.

Though but twenty years old, Alexander was both mature
and self-poised. No sooner seated than he proved himself
every inch a king. He began by reviewing the army.
" Though the name has changed, the king remains," quoth
he, and the power, order and aspirations of the king and
country were kept intact.

Philip had found Macedonia a small state ; he had raised
it to be the greatest nation of the world, excepting only Persia ; and as the centre of civilized power Macedonia was the
more important factor in the world's economy.

Neither Philip nor Alexander were Greeks. The Macedonian stood midway, as it were, between the despot-ridden

Persian and the free and equal Hellene. He was a rugged peasant, owning the land he tilled, and no doubt exercising many rights of local self-government of which we do not hear. But he was liable to military duty. It is under Philip that we find the condition of the peasantry rising to marked excellence, and the fact that the Macedonian army was, in its civil capacity, a sort of popular assembly, shows that the instinct of liberty was supreme. The Macedonian kingdom seems more nearly to approach a constitutional monarchy than any other of the day.

All Philip's surroundings had grown step by step with his power. Their dignity may have been sometimes marred by excessive drinking, a habit which was hereditary in the land ; but no part of Greece had so superb or polite a court, such magnificent feasts and games. Except in Athens in the age of Pericles, the world had as yet exhibited nothing which of itself was so complete in intelligent and solid splendor, combined with perfectly managed business-methods, as Philip's court and country. Pella is said to have astonished even the Athenian envoys. Looking at his every side, Philip was one of the broadest-minded, strongest and most able monarchs who ever reigned. It is only by his own son, before whose all but superhuman successes everything shrinks into insignificance, that Philip is surpassed. Says Theopompus, " Take him for all in all, never has Europe borne such a man as the son of Amyntas."

XII.

PHILIP AND HIS ARMY. B. C. 359–336.

ALEXANDER found ready to hand the standing army, unequaled in excellence, which his father had created. Philip had seen what he had to encounter and had armed his hoplites with the sarissa, a pike twenty-one feet long, so that the Grecian phalangite could not reach his line. The Macedonian phalanx was the ideal of shock tactics. Its unit was a lochos or file of sixteen men with its sergeants at the head and rear. Sixteen files made a syntagma or battalion of two hundred and fifty-six men under a xenagos or major. This was the fighting unit. Four of these were a taxis under a strategos or colonel. Sixteen taxes made a simple phalanx of four thousand and ninety-six men. The grand phalanx contained four of the latter, and was carefully officered, much in the style of a modern army-corps. The hoplites were pezetæri, the sarissa-armed, and hypaspists, a more select body, armed with one-handed pike, sword and shield. Slaves accompanied the phalanx, and carried arms and rations for the heavy troops. Half as many peltasts or light infantry were attached to each phalanx, a quarter as much horse and a quarter as much irregular foot, — psiloi. These numbers varied. A grand phalanx all told had some thirty thousand men. In parade order a man occupied six feet square; in battle order three feet; in close order one and a half feet. The phalanx drilled much as we do to-day. Discipline was rigid. The heavy cavalry was Macedonian, Thessalian and Greek; there was abundance of light cavalry drawn from barbarian allies. The cavalry unit was an ilē of sixteen files of four men each. Eight ilēs made a hipparchy, under a hipparch, the equal of a strategos. The drill and discipline of the cavalry was perfect. One choice ilē of cavalry and one choice taxis of hypaspists were each called the agema, or body-guard of the king. The Macedonian heavy horse (cavalry Companions) was a splendid body, and on it Alexander relied for his stanchest work. The Thessalians stood all but as high. In line of battle the phalanx held the centre; the cavalry was on the wings; the light troops in front of the line, or in rear or on the wings as dictated by circumstances. The right was the post of honor. Here Alexander took his station with the Companions. The army was capable of making enormous marches, and stood unheard-of hardships. Philip and Alexander organized and used batteries of ballistas and catapults, which were, within their limits, as effective as modern artillery, and more easily moved. There is evidence that the quartermaster's and commissary departments were very skillfully organized and managed. The Greek camp was round or elliptical, and picket-duty was regularly performed. There was military music, and insignia were carried in lieu of colors. On the march, which was usually right in front, a van and rear guard and flankers were employed. Minor tactics was highly developed, but battles were wont to be decided by a single shock. One line of battle was usual, but Alexander constantly made use of reserves. Level ground was essential to the phalanx, and therefore always chosen for battle; but Alexander got exceptional work out of his phalanx on any ground. Philip organized a corps of pages, young men of family who lived near the king's person, and learned the profession of arms in camp. This was practically a military school, — a movable West Point. The word of the king was supreme law; but the Macedonians had apparently the right to demand that they should be consulted with regard to many matters; and councils of war were common.

THE heritage of Alexander the Great from his father, Philip of Macedon, was the same which came to Frederick the Great from his father Frederick William, to wit: an army organized, armed, equipped and disciplined in a better fashion than any which existed at that day.

It was Philip who first gave shape to the army, transforming what was a mere manhood duty of service, or obligatory militia system, into a standing army, which rose under him to number forty thousand men. This was the first instance in which a free people subordinated itself to a military autocracy whose head was the king. It was this which made Macedonia the superior of Greece, which had lost its old habits of personal service, and now depended largely upon mercenary soldiers, or upon volunteer service and substitutes. Personal service, unless coupled with the discipline and methods of a standing force, makes an army of volunteers rather than of regulars. In former days the Greeks had had what came very close to the best discipline attained by a standing army. But the phalanx had gradually lost its cohesion. One might compare the Greek troops of the days of Philip to our own volunteers in the early stages of the Civil

War, as against troops like the Prussian infantry of our own times. Later in the war many of our American volunteers had been hardened into a perfect equivalent of the best regulars. No doubt the Greek habit of relying on voluntary service made for true freedom, as our own organization rather than that of the Prussians yields the greatest good to the greatest number; but as a military machine Macedonia with its standing forces was far ahead of the rest of Greece.

When Philip was elected to the throne (B. C. 359) to succeed his brother, Perdiccas III., the Macedonian infantry was composed of raw and ragged material, mostly hide-clad shepherds, armed with wicker shields and ill-assorted weapons. It was a rabble rather than an army. The cavalry was better, in fact the best in Greece, where horse had not been much in vogue, and had been drilled to charge in compact order, and with a short thrusting pike as weapon. Still it could not be pronounced satisfactory.

Philip saw that cavalry would not suffice; he must have infantry to meet the solid ranks of the Theban, Athenian and Spartan phalanx. The foot-soldier, with whom he had by his Theban education become familiar, was the one who, under Epaminondas' skillful tactics, had broken the theretofore invincible array of the Lacedæmonians. Philip must build up an infantry which could break the Theban formation. The Greek hoplite had been armed with a large oblong shield, a sword and a one-handed pike, perhaps six to eight, rarely ten feet long. In close combat he pushed his enemy as well as defended himself with his shield, which was sometimes provided with a knob or spike, and used his pike or sword as occasion demanded. Philip invented the sarissa or long two-handed pike, which protruded so far beyond the front rank that the Greek hoplite could not reach his enemy so as to use his shorter weapons; and by this device he overcame the Grecian phalanx. At the battle of Chæronæa the front rank of the Theban hoplites fell to the last man. With his phalanx thus armed, Philip brought Greece to his feet, and enabled his son Alexander to reap from the start the fruit of his wonderful military genius.

The army for war was raised : first, from the Macedonian people, as a kernel ; second, from tributary tribes, — Thessalians, Thracians, Pæonians, Triballians, Odryssians, Illyrians and others ; third, from allied nations, such as the Greeks ; fourth, from mercenary troops, Greeks and others. The Thessalians were really allies ; but they were under a Macedonian chief, as were also the Greek allies.

We have no details as to the formation of the Greek phalanx until Thucydides and Xenophon, the latter of whom first describes it with satisfactory accuracy. There was considerable difference between the phalanx of Xenophon and that of Alexander. In fact, at all periods there were material variations in the formation, arms and drill of the phalanx, but a detailed description of the Macedonian phalanx will suffice to explain that of the other states.

To Philip is due the credit of organizing the whole Macedonian military establishment ; Alexander in no material manner changed what he inherited, but only expanded the system, so as to make room for the introduction of new elements in the East, and to create *cadres* of sufficient size to treble the strength of the army. He was wise enough to recognize that he could not better the results of his father's wonderful capacity for organization. But he used the army in a fashion his father had never dreamed of doing.

The Spartan and the Athenian phalanxes have already been described in a partial way ; they were superb of their kind ; but the Macedonian phalanx will always remain in history as the ideal of shock tactics. It was numerically much larger than the Greek phalanx. Its weight can be gauged by a simple comparison. In the French tactics of 1887 about seven men, including reserves, go to every metre of front line. In the Macedonian phalanx, including light troops, twenty-eight men went to about every metre, and close together from front to rear. This depth made its impact in good order irresistible.

Lochos.

The unit of the phalanx was a lochos or file of sixteen heavy infantry men, hoplites, whose chief, the lochagos (sergeant), was the front-rank man. The second man was one who received double pay, and the third and last men extra pay for gallantry. The last man, or file-closer, was a sort of second sergeant, called uragos. Each lochos was numbered from right to left.

These hoplites were either hypaspists (shield-bearing guards) or pezetæri (foot-companions) ; the former held the right, or post of honor, of the phalanx, though apt to be used as a separate body and placed in other parts of the line; the latter, being the ordinary rank and file, had the left of the phalanx. The hypaspists were of a better class, served voluntarily, and the most valorous of their number were the agema (royal footguards), always under a noted chief. The rest were called "the other hypaspists," and were organized in bodies of five hundred men, later of one thousand, each under a chiliarch. The hypaspists were trained for hand-to-hand fighting and quick evolutions, and though wearing full suits of armor were more lightly armed than the pezetæri. They car-

Hypaspist.

ried the one-handed pike (xyston), sword and large shield. They are sometimes called agyraspides, though this name is also given to another body of peltasts.

Kausia.

In the early armies what might be called the aristocracy had served as hetairai, companions, comrades-in-arms, already known in the times of Homer. They were the descendants of the few who had clustered about the original conqueror, and were more properly a class bred of wealth acquired by ancient service near the court than one of hereditary title; and in Philip's army included probably many of those families which had been reigning ones in their own uplands until subjugated

Greek Helmets.

by Macedonia. The pezetæri, or "*foot* companions," had originally been the infantry body-guard of the king, but had gradually been expanded into a much more extensive body and had become, under Philip, the ordinary heavy infantry. In similar fashion the word "guard" is in many countries still applied to ordinary infantry regiments. The pezetæri are

Coat of Scale Armor.

said by some authorities to have worn the hereditary kausia, or broad-brimmed felt hat; but by others the kausia is stated to have been later adopted by the king as a distinguishing headgear. At all events the pezetæri wore in battle a helmet, a cuirass or breastpiece and greaves or leggings.

Little is said about foot-gear. It was probably the usual sandal or boot. They bore a spear, the sarissa, which, according to Polybius, was fourteen cubits, or twenty-one feet, long (the drilling spear being two cubits longer, thus making the enormous length of twenty-four feet), a shield of such size as to cover the entire

Greaves.

person of a kneeling soldier, fixed to hang over the shoulder so as not to monopolize the left arm, and a short, straight, cut-and-thrust sword. The shield was apt to be decorated; often with some bird or beast or emblem of the soldier's natal city. The sarissa was held six feet from the butt, which was loaded so as to balance, and thus protruded fifteen feet in front of the

Sandal.

soldier. The first five ranks couched their spears, the others held them erect, or else leaned them on the shoulders of the rank before them. Only great individual strength, suppled by constant practice in the gymnasium, and steady

Boots.

drill could render the phalangite able to execute the manœuvres called for. Some of the best military critics have doubted the accuracy of Polybius in this particular, and have sought to read *feet* for *cubits;* but there is no good reason to doubt the

Sarissa Bearer.

fact as stated, particularly in view of the length of spear carried by other nations and of the results attained by the sarissa-armed phalanx.
Grote has discussed this point at length.

Shields.

Four of the above-described files, or lochoi, made a tetrarchia of sixty-four men, a platoon as it were, with a tetrarch or lieutenant, who also stood in front of the right-hand file. Two tetrarchias made a taxiarchia, or company of one hundred and twenty-eight men, under a taxiarch or captain. This body was sometimes called a taxis. The best men, it will be seen, were in front and in rear and the least reliable in the centre of this company.

TAXIARCH

Taxiarchia (close order).

The rank of sergeants in the front of the company was like the tempered steel edge of the axe. Two taxiarchias or companies made a syntagma, or xenagia, or battalion of two hundred and fifty-six men. This was a body sixteen men square, the Macedonian tactical unit; and its chief, the xenagos, or syntagmatarch (major), had an uragos (there seems some duplication of terms in the name) or second major, whose position was in the rear; an adjutant; a color-bearer, who also gave certain orders by raising or lowering the ensign; a herald, who had other besides the usual work attached to his office, and a trumpeter. These various officers provided an abundant number of file-leaders and file-closers, and each had specific and well-defined duties.

Four syntagmas formed a chiliarchia, or a taxis, under a chiliarch, or strategos (colonel), making a force of one thousand and twenty-four men, equivalent to one of our regiments. "Taxis," like our own word "division," is a much misused term. It is not infrequently employed by the old historians as an equivalent of "detachment," of whatever size. The numbers of all these bodies were of necessity very elastic and fluctuating, and, as in all armies in active service, the taxes were frequently all but destroyed. Sixteen syntagmas, or four chiliarchias, constituted a simple phalanx, which was thus

SYNTAC MARCH ♂
ENSICN ♂   ♂ TRUMPETER
HERALD ♂   ADJUTANT ♂

♂ ♂ ♂ ♂ ♂ ♂ ♂ ♂ ♂ ♂ ♂ ♂ ♂ ♂ ♂ ♂
♂ ♂ ♂ ♂ ♂ ♂ ♂ ♂ ♂ ♂ ♂ ♂ ♂ ♂ ♂ ♂
♂ ♂ ♂ ♂ ♂ ♂ ♂ ♂ ♂ ♂ ♂ ♂ ♂ ♂ ♂ ♂
♂ ♂ ♂ ♂ ♂ ♂ ♂ ♂ ♂ ♂ ♂ ♂ ♂ ♂ ♂ ♂
♂ ♂ ♂ ♂ ♂ ♂ ♂ ♂ ♂ ♂ ♂ ♂ ♂ ♂ ♂ ♂
♂ ♂ ♂ ♂ ♂ ♂ ♂ ♂ ♂ ♂ ♂ ♂ ♂ ♂ ♂ ♂
♂ ♂ ♂ ♂ ♂ ♂ ♂ ♂ ♂ ♂ ♂ ♂ ♂ ♂ ♂ ♂
♂ ♂ ♂ ♂ ♂ ♂ ♂ ♂ ♂ ♂ ♂ ♂ ♂ ♂ ♂ ♂
♂ ♂ ♂ ♂ ♂ ♂ ♂ ♂ ♂ ♂ ♂ ♂ ♂ ♂ ♂ ♂
♂ ♂ ♂ ♂ ♂ ♂ ♂ ♂ ♂ ♂ ♂ ♂ ♂ ♂ ♂ ♂
♂ ♂ ♂ ♂ ♂ ♂ ♂ ♂ ♂ ♂ ♂ ♂ ♂ ♂ ♂ ♂
♂ ♂ ♂ ♂ ♂ ♂ ♂ ♂ ♂ ♂ ♂ ♂ ♂ ♂ ♂ ♂
♂ ♂ ♂ ♂ ♂ ♂ ♂ ♂ ♂ ♂ ♂ ♂ ♂ ♂ ♂ ♂
♂ ♂ ♂ ♂ ♂ ♂ ♂ ♂ ♂ ♂ ♂ ♂ ♂ ♂ ♂ ♂
                                    URACOS ♂

Syntagma (open order).

made up of four thousand and ninety-six hoplites; in addition to which there were attached to it a regular complement of cavalry and light troops. It was our modern brigade, so to speak, and was under command of a phalangiarch, or brigadier-general. There was also a double phalanx (division)

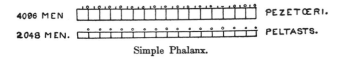

4096 MEN   PEZETŒRI.
2048 MEN.   PELTASTS.
Simple Phalanx.

of eight thousand one hundred and ninety-two men, and a "grand" or quadruple phalanx (army-corps) of sixteen thousand three hundred and eighty-four infantry. Each had its peculiar chief, the diphalangiarch and tetraphalangiarch. But these names are rarely used. The term "strategos" covered a multitude of titles; and Arrian, whose Anabasis is generally followed in this work, like the other historians, gen-

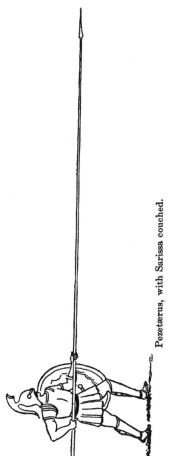

Pezetærus, with Sarissa couched.

erally refers to bodies by the proper name of their command-ers, — a much more convenient term.

Slaves, who accompanied the phalanx in great numbers, car-ried the rations, and often arms, of the heavy cavalry and infantry, which weighed from sixty pounds upwards ; though at times these camp followers must have been vastly reduced in number by incidents of the service, as they now and then were by direct orders, in which case the hoplite was remitted to carrying his own arms and ra-tions.

Behind this heavy sarissa-armed infantry (pezetæri) there were ranked, as a rule, half the number of peltasts, in files eight deep, thus occupying the same front space. The reader shall be spared the names of the peltast subdivisions and com-manders. The organization re-sembled that of the phalanx. The peltast was a light in-fantryman, half way between the psilos and the hoplite, originated by Iphicrates of Ath-ens, bearing a small shield (peltē), short pike and sword, and wearing a broad metal belt, which protected the abdominal region. The hypaspists are sometimes classed as peltasts, but they were more properly an integral part of the phalanx. At all periods there appear to have been differences in the arming and discipline of portions of the light troops, but they remained substantially the same. The peltasts are commonly called targeteers. The Agrianians, who were among the very best of Alexander's troops, came near to being peltasts, though usually classed with the light troops.

That part of the hypaspists or shield‑bearing guards

known as the agema was essentially a *corps d'élite*, — the infantry bodyguard of the king. The hypaspists generally were more available for some services than the pezetæri,

Casting a Javelin with a Twist. quicker and handier than these and yet steadier than the bulk of the peltasts or light troops. They were good for attacking and holding heights, forcing fords, supporting cavalry and in important night-watches and attacks. They could do the duty of either grade, as called on. The hypaspists in Alexander's army were under command of Nicanor, son of Parmenio, of whom we shall see more.

In front of the taxes of hoplites in a simple phalanx were one thousand and twenty-four psiloi, — slingers, archers or darters (acontists or javelin-throwers), who acted as skirmishers. On the wings were, under drill-regulations, two groups

of heavy horsemen (cataphracti), with sword and lance, sometimes javelin and battle-axe, and a small round shield, helmet, greaves and spurred boots. But

Greek Sandal and Spur. Alexander varied their position according to circumstances. The numbers of cavalry and light troops were elastic.

The normal strength of the grand phalanx all told was: —

Hoplites or heavy infantry . . . . 16,384 men
Peltasts and psiloi, say . . . . 8,192 men
Horse, heavy and light . . . . 4,096 men
                                          ─────────
                                          28,672 men

Or with officers, etc., about 30,000 men, having all classes of troops.

There were other subdivisions of the phalanx, each with its appropriate chief. But like the smaller details of tactics, the minutiæ of rank and command do not here concern us.

To summarize, the grand phalanx was divided and officered as follows: —

Lochos or section of 16 hoplites under a lochagos or sergeant.

Tetrarchia or platoon of 64 hoplites under a tetrarch or lieutenant.

Taxiarchia or company of 128 hoplites under a taxiarch or captain.

Syntagma or battalion of 256 hoplites under a syntagmatarch or xenagos or major.

Taxis or chiliarchia or regiment of 1,024 hoplites under a chiliarch or strategos or colonel.

Simple phalanx or brigade of 4,094 hoplites under a phalangiarch or brigadier-general.

Double phalanx or division of 8,192 hoplites under a diphalangiarch or major-general.

Quadruple or grand phalanx or army corps of 16,384 hoplites under a tetraphalangiarch or lieutenant-general.

With cavalry and light troops this made an army of 28,672 men under the king or commander-in-chief, or especially thereto commissioned officer, generally one of the somatophylaxes or intimates of the king.

It goes without saying that this was only the organization of the phalanx. In the field both numbers and subdivisions were constantly changed by losses or for convenience of handling. And it will be also noticed hereafter that when Alexander reached Asia, and incorporated Oriental soldiers into his army, he made changes not always consistent, as they are narrated, with this technical organization. But Philip's army remained practically unchanged.

In parade or open order each phalangite occupied a space
of about six feet square, with sarissa erect.   In close or battle

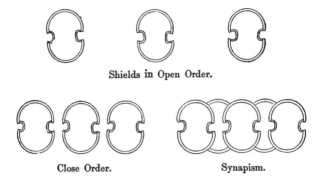

Shields in Open Order.

Close Order.   Synapism.

order — the usual field formation — each occupied a space
of three feet square, left foot advanced, so that the interval
on his left was to a certain extent covered with his shield.
The first five ranks advanced their sarissas, the eleven others

Syntagma in Perspective.

held them erect or leaned them on the shoulders of their file-
leaders, in which position they arrested many missiles.   The

Syntagma in Perspective.

front rank sarissas thus protruded fifteen feet; the second
rank, twelve feet; the third, nine feet; the fourth, six feet;

feet; the fifth, three feet beyond the front alignment. With
the drill-sarissa of twenty-four feet in length, those of six
ranks would protend in front of the alignment. The points
were slightly depressed. In defensive order, or to attack intrenchments, a tortoise, or synapism, was formed. The men

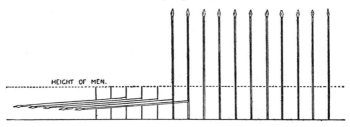

Position of the Sarissas of a Lochos.

stood close together, each occupying but one and a half feet
square, the front rank covering their bodies with their shields,
the other ranks using them to form a roof over the heads of
all. This synapism, or tortoise, was so strong that archers
and slingers could march over it to shoot their missiles, and
we shall see heavy wagons rolling over the formation without
harm to the soldiers. To repel an attack the hoplites kneeled
on the right knee and leaned the shield against the left knee,
the edge on the ground. This was a device of Chabrias, the
Athenian.

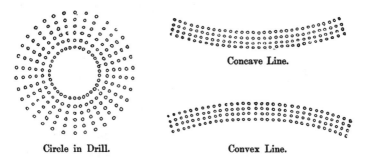

Circle in Drill.

Concave Line.

Convex Line.

It is probable that Epaminondas had brought the drill of

the heavy infantryman to a high state of perfection; while Iphicrates had done an equal duty by the peltasts. But this was still improved upon by Philip and Alexander. In their drill the Macedonian phalangites were taught to form a circle, small or large, for the same purpose as infantry to-day forms

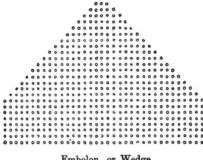

Embolon, or Wedge.

a square; to advance the wings so as to make a concave line to envelop the enemy's flank; to refuse the wings so as to make a convex line to resist front and flank attacks at the same time; to form a wedge or boar's head, which had but three men in the front rank and then gradually widened to thirty-six men in the sixteenth rank, and with eight ranks of an equal number of files as a base; and to form pincers, so-called, to receive and check the wedge formation. This was the exact converse of the wedge, and was a forma-

Koilembolon, or Pincers.

tion whose centre was withdrawn in wedge form. A column of any kind more deep than wide was also apt to be called a wedge.

The phalanx could wheel and half-wheel to the right and left, or wheel completely to the rear. Countermarches were made by files and by ranks. Ranks were doubled from open order by the even number man of each file stepping into the interval on the left of his file-leader.

Ground was taken to the right and left on the centre. Files were broken in two and the rear half marched into the intervals. The men broke by sections to the right and left to take order of march. The infantry was also drilled in a certain manual of arms, and in facing and marching to either flank, and to the rear, at different paces. There were numbers of other manœuvres and formations.

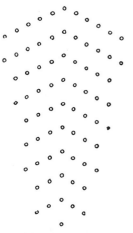

Formation with Broken Ranks and Files.

A lochos was forty-eight feet deep, in common or battle order. When each one occupied three feet front, a taxiarchia would take up twenty-four feet, a syntagma forty-eight feet front, or say fifty feet. This would give two hundred feet to the chiliarchia or regiment, not counting intervals, about which the information is very contradictory. A simple phalanx of infantry, without its cavalry, and placing the psiloi and peltasts in front and rear, would thus cover a front of eight hundred feet, and a grand phalanx three thousand two hundred feet, say three fifths of a mile.

Commands were given by the voice, by trumpets, and by signals of a standard, sword or spear. A raised standard meant advance; a lowered standard meant retreat; a lance held erect and still was a demand for parley. There appears to have been a code of signals by smoke, which Polybius says were not at all uncertain.

Philip introduced the strictest discipline. Punishments were summary. In 338 B. C., two officers of high rank were cashiered for introducing a female lute-player into camp against standing orders. This exclusion of women was not common, however, in ancient armies, nor could it be continued by Alexander when in the East.

Alexander employed more cavalry than any one up to his day, and handled it better. No one has ever surpassed his cavalry tactics. Epaminondas had but one tenth of his force mounted. Alexander had one sixth to one quarter. This he found essential in order to cope with the great and admirable force of cavalry in the Persian army. For cavalry was the choice arm of the Asiatics, and it was very skillful.

The cavalry, as a rule, was composed of Macedonians and Thessalians, who were heavy horse, and Thracians and Ætolians, who were light horse. Its unit was the ilē, or company of sixty-four men, in sixteen files, four deep, which was the equivalent of the syntagma ; eight ilēs were a hipparchy, under a hipparch, who ranked with a strategos ; two hipparchies an ephipparchy, the equivalent of the small phalanx ; two ephipparchies a wing, the equivalent of the double phalanx. When sixty-four ilē or two wings were

ILARCH 0

0 00 0000000 00 0000
0000000000000000
0000000000000000
0000000000000000

Ilē of Sixty-four Horse
(close order).

Deep Square.   Thracian Wedge.   Reverse Wedge.

together, they formed an epitagma of four thousand and ninety-six men, which was the allowance for the grand phalanx. But so much was not always present, nor always kept in one body. This was the technical formation; but there were exceptions. The iles of Companion cavalry numbered up to two hundred and fifty men each, and the chiefs held a peculiar rank. The changes in the cavalry made by Alexander in the East were also on a different basis. The army here described is Philip's army. This Alexander modified without changing substantially that in it which made it so efficient. It was a disciplined army, and discipline cannot be described in words; it is only shown in deeds.

Square.

Rhomboid with Mixed Files.

Alexander vastly improved his cavalry over what was theretofore known. It marched in columns of fours; it formed a solid square of eight men front to charge in small bodies; it formed in wedge or triangular bodies, charging apex or base in front as occasion demanded; it charged occasionally in rhomboid or lozenge form. This was the Thessalian column, and had the advantage of facing readily in four directions. The cavalry is frequently spoken of as charging " squadron by squadron " when fighting superior forces, but the exact tactical meaning of the phrase is not apparent. Perhaps it was an echeloned order. As a rule, the cavalry was on the flanks of the phalanx, to protect these weak points.

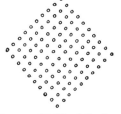

Square with Mixed Ranks.

Cavalry Companion.

The cavalry was of three classes. First came the heavy Macedonian horsemen, each of whom was accompanied by a mounted servant or squire, and originally by two or three slaves, though Philip, and again later Alexander, found it necessary to cut down this number to one. They were volunteers, the best men of the nation.

It was Philip who had formed this body of young nobles, and taken the greatest pride in giving them the highest military as well as the most enlightened polite education and training. They thus became fit both for command and for statesmanship and diplomatic service. They wore helmet and complete scale-armor, and carried a shield, thrusting-pike and sword. The horse had head-piece and breastplate, also of scale-armor. These were the so-called cavalry hetairai, Companions or brothers-in-arms. The first squadron constituted the royal body-guard. The hetairai were constantly competing under the eye of the king for glory and reputation. They were his right hand. No Asiatic cavalry could ever stand their shock, no infantry resist their onset. Alexander's battles were uniformly decided by them. The marches they could execute were well exemplified in the pursuit of Darius, when they made three thousand three hundred stades — three hundred and sixty-six miles — in eleven days, under a burning sun, and part way across a desert country without water. The cavalry Companions were under Philotas, the hipparch, son of Parmenio and brother of Nicanor, who commanded the hypaspists. Eight of these ilē accompanied Alexander into Asia, severally under Clitus, Glaucias, Ariston, Sopolis, Heracleides, Demetrius, Meleager, and Hegelochus, each some two hundred or more strong. Clitus' ilē was the agema of cavalry, which Alexander was wont to lead in person.

There appear to have been sixteen ilē in all, from sixteen districts, each varying from one hundred and fifty to two hundred and fifty men. The value of this body in action, like

Ilē of Hetairai of 225 Men.

the Theban Sacred Band, was, owing to its wonderful martial qualities, out of all proportion to its limited number.

From these " Companions," or from the " Pages," were, as a rule, selected all the officers for promotion or detail or civil dignities. The Companions also constituted a sort of tribunal for the trial of certain military offenses, as well as a species of council of war. Whether this was confined to the agema, or not, is not known. But the Companions were a strong power in both army and state, as well as unquestionably the social leaders in the society of the court.

The Thessalian horse was also heavy, and in efficiency ranked all but with the Macedonian. Some of its iles contained the aristocrats of Thessaly. Calas, son of Harpalus, commanded this body. Good throughout, the ile of Pharsalus had the most repute. In company with the Thessalians generally fought the Grecian auxiliary cavalry under Philip, son of Menelaus, but as separate corps.

Next to the Companions and Thessalians came light cavalry carrying sword and javelin. These were mostly mercenary troops. Later Alexander made a special body of sarissophori or lancers. Just wherein they differed from other pike-carrying horsemen, unless that the lance was longer, is not known.

Third were the dimachias (two - fashioned fighters), light dragoons, who could engage either on foot or mounted. They had light defensive armor and shields, swords and a lance which they could use for thrusting or casting. They opened the combat and pursued the broken enemy. These

Light Horseman.

were a sort of mounted peltast, midway between heavy and irregular cavalry. They seem to have fought much as our own cavalry did in the civil war. Some of the dimachias carried bows.

The light cavalry was especially recruited among the allies. Alexander used to mix archers and sometimes targeteers, *i. e.*, peltasts, or sometimes even shield-bearing guards with his horse. These footmen proved useful in checking disorder, and the archers were so active as to be able to keep up with the horse in all their marches and evolutions.

Greek Headstall.

Greek Headstall.

The cavalryman had no stirrups, nor were the horses shod. The manner in which the horses got through the long winter and mountain marches proves that their feet were very sound and the animals extremely hardy. The rider sat on a blanket held by a circingle. Some of these blankets look like a species of saddle-tree. The drill was largely adapted to give the man the strength of seat which the modern saddle with stirrups lends. Of course he could not stand in his stirrups to cut and thrust as the modern cavalryman

Rider from Frieze of Parthenon.

does; and was accordingly somewhat handicapped. But so was the enemy, and the drill made him strong and active. Despite, or perhaps by reason of, these drawbacks, the cav-

alryman had a good seat. There is nothing as perfect in
equestrianism as the seat of the riders on the frieze of the
Parthenon. There must have been perfect riders or this
piece of art could not have been produced.

Philip had kept a reserve of veterans, a sort of "Old
Guard," the early pezetæri, ready to act at the decisive moment. By some authorities many of the members of the agema
which went over to Asia are said to have been veterans of sixty
to seventy years. Alexander preferred to use his Companion
cavalry as an old guard. This, composed of the sons of the
first families of the land, drilled and exercised from their
youth up in all the habits of war, always responded to his
demand. The agema was more richly and fully armed than
the rest, and each individual enjoyed the king's confidence.

Alexander's cavalry does not appear to have ridden boot to
boot. The men were ranked slightly apart, but nevertheless
kept good alignment. Just how much space man and horse
occupied in the ranks cannot be given. Usually a cavalryman occupies ten feet by forty inches. The depth of the ilē
of four to a file was probably not far from the same as the
lochos, say fifty feet. How much front it occupied is not certain. Given six inches between horses, the ilē would take

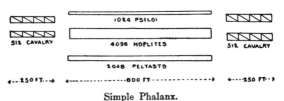

Simple Phalanx.

up some sixty feet, the hipparchy four hundred and eighty
feet. With its full complement of cavalry, one hipparchy
on each flank, in say two lines, the simple phalanx would
cover something like a quarter of a mile, the seven thousand
foot occupying less than two thirds the space; the one thou-

sand horse one third. It was, however, rare that the phalanx was worked in this fashion.

The light horse comprised Macedonians, Pæonians under Aristo, and Odryssians, who won great credit for efficiency with Agatho as their leader. The Macedonian lancers were under Amyntas, the Lyncestian. All these were called prodromari, — fighters in front, skirmishers. Finally, there were in Asia numerous bodies of irregular light troops, both foot and horse, slingers, archers and javelin-throwers. These were used much as the Austrians used Pandours in the Seven Years' War, or as the German Uhlanen or the Russian Cossacks are to-day. Of the light foot the Agrianians, who were javelin-throwers from the Mount Hæmus region, under command of Attalus, were the most important and numerous; and the Thracian javelin-throwers, Sitalces commanding, were equally useful and steady on all occasions. These were the flankers of the army. Famous archers came from Crete. Clearchus was their commander at the outset; but the chiefs mentioned were often subject to change on account of death or wounds. The archers thrice lost their chief in battle.

There were, to resume, four classes of infantry. First, the pezetæri, or foot companions, who bore the sarissa. Second, the hypaspists, or shield-bearing guards, with sword and xyston, or one-handed pike. Third, the peltasts, a well-organized and substantially armed light infantry. Fourth, the psiloi, or irregular lightly-armed foot, archers, slingers and darters. Of cavalry there were, first, the cavalry Companions and the Thessalians and some Greeks, all heavy armed. Second, the light-cavalry, well-armed mercenary troops. Third, lancers and dimachias, or horse-bowmen. Fourth, irregular nomads, armed in any manner.

Light troops had, until Philip's day, been of little use or repute in Greece. They had been raised from the poorer population, and being illy armed and not subjected to much discipline, were never apt to be steady or reliable. It remained for Alexander to put them under strict discipline, use them on the service to which they were peculiarly adapted, and thus make their worth apparent.

There is nothing definite known as to the rate of pay. Cyrus paid the hoplites under Clearchus a daric, about four dollars, a month. Demosthenes, in the Philippics, refers to the pay of a foot soldier as being ten drachmas (= two dollars) a month. There was an arrangement between the Athenians and the Argives to pay a drachma of Ægina a day to each horseman, and three oboli for a foot-soldier, twenty-seven and thirteen cents respectively. A man who lost a limb in war received an obol (four cents +) a day. Sinope and Heraclea offered Xenophon's men one stater of Cyzicus a month. Seuthes offered them the same sum, which is five dollars and fifty cents. Others offered a daric (four dollars) a month per man. Droysen makes a detailed calculation, suggesting that the monthly pay of the Macedonian horseman was three hundred drachmas, about sixty dollars; of the allied horseman two hundred and fifty drachmas, about fifty dollars; of the pezetæri one hundred drachmas, about twenty dollars; of the light-infantryman eighty-four drachmas, about seventeen dollars; and adds a similar amount to each for rations. From olden time it was the habit among the Greeks to give the soldier a sum equal to his pay for rations. But these sums are manifestly too high. Alexander may have distributed largesses to his men to this extent or more; but that the regular compensation was anything like so much appears doubtful. The daric a month seems nearer the truth; or perhaps Droysen's figures are intended for the annual stipend.

When the entire army was drawn up in line of battle, though indeed the order was much varied in the field, according as the conditions varied, the phalanx occupied the centre, the several taxes or brigades by rote from right to left, under their respective chiefs. It was a precedent that these brigades should change their order in line by a certain rule from day to day, or at other short periods. On the right of the phalanx were the hypaspists, the agema holding the right of their line. Again, on the right of these were the eight squadrons of Macedonian cavalry, changing order in similar fashion from day to day. Then came the light troops, lancers, Pæonians, Agrianians and archers, of the right wing, to act as flankers and skirmishers and to cover the right flank as well as to open the attack. On the left of the phalanx, if not on duty to protect the camp, were apt to come the Thracian javelin-throwers, in the place corresponding to that of the hypaspists of the right, farther on the Grecian contingent of horse, then the Thessalian horse, then light troops such as Agatho's Odryssian cavalry. The demarcation between the right and left wings was the junction of the third and fourth brigades of pezetæri.

This order was by no means a cut-and-dried rule. Alexander was peculiarly happy in tactical formations, and shifted his troops according to the work to be done. In line of battle the phalanx was sometimes divided into right wing, left wing and centre. Each wing was in two sections, with intervals through which the skirmishers who opened the combat could retire. But there appear to have been other intervals in active service. The post of honor of the phalanx was the right. Here the general took his stand, not merely to direct, but to lead the battle as the most valiant of the combatants.

Philip, and after him Alexander, thus greatly improved the organization and discipline of the phalanx, which was based on the Greek model. For the purpose of opposing what it then had to oppose, it was as nearly perfect as possible. It was taught before all things to attack, never to wait attack. The heavy foot and peltasts were drilled to fight by shocks, and the several bodies or brigades moved independently and with intervals of twenty to forty feet between small phalanxes, mutually supporting each other, and thus making up for the want of reserves. The cavalry especially attacked with extraordinary speed and *élan*, — Alexander was Frederick's model in this, — relying upon impetus just as the phalanx did on weight, and when broken was always able to rally and renew the charge again and again. The light foot and horse had no special place, but filled up the intervals between the heavy bodies and protected detachments and the exposed flanks of the phalanx by restless activity.

The marches were conducted with a rare appreciation of *terrain* and troops, and the distances continuously covered were often enormous.

The entire grand phalanx rarely fought as a body, but usually the several sections or divisions fought separately, each being called a phalanx. Occasionally one section was placed by Alexander behind another as reserve, or to deepen the column. A section or sections could be in reserve, faced to the rear, or to right or left, as at Arbela. One of Alexander's most prominent qualities was the ability to make quick dispositions suitable to the occasion and quite outside ordinary tactical usage. For instance, on Pelium plain in Illyria, in a narrow and mountainous region, he formed the phalanx one hundred and twenty men deep. Arrian calls this *cuneus* or wedge. After crossing the Danube Alexander formed square, with archers and slingers in the centre, much as Brasidas and Xenophon had done. No doubt he borrowed the idea ; but what Alexander borrowed he bettered. At Arbela he formed two flying wings with consummate skill and effect. At the Hydaspes he detached a cavalry force about Porus' right flank with equal foresight and results.

The artillery of those days was much improved by Philip and later by Alexander, who was the first to construct the machines, and to mount them on wagons in such a manner as to be able to march them in company with the army as our field artillery does to-day. Up to this time these military machines had only been used in sieges. Having them at hand, Alexander made constant use of them at defiles, against field-works, in crossing rivers, and in many sudden emergencies. Philip and Alexander consolidated the artillery into batteries, and Philip had one hundred and fifty companies on foot and twenty-five reserve batteries in his arsenals.

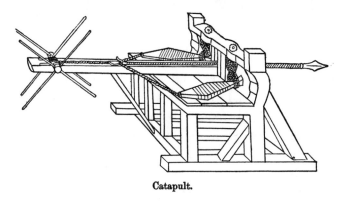

Catapult.

The catapult was the invention of the Syrians, according to Pliny. It was a species of huge bow, mounted on a platform. The propelling force was usually a twisted cord or gut applied to the arms of the bow. The bowstring was tightened by a windlass and released by a spring. The catapult shot huge iron-pointed arrows or pikes weighing from ten to three hundred pounds, which had considerable penetration. It may be called the cannon of the ancients. It was capable of carrying nearly one half mile, and was accurate up to five hundred paces. Some were so arranged as to hurl a flight of leaden bullets instead of an arrow.

The ballista originated with the Phœnicians. It threw stones up to fifty pounds weight and over, and was the mortar of the ancients. The missile could be cast about half a mile. The ballista consisted of a stout beam or arm of wood whose

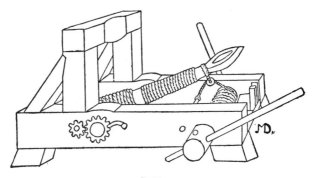

Ballista.

one end bore a spoon or bowl in which was held the stone, while the other end was secured in a twisted cord or gut mounted in a timber frame. Being brought backward against the twist to a nearly horizontal position by a windlass, and the stone or other projectile placed in the spoon or bowl, the arm was suddenly released and flew upward with great power. Its motion was suddenly arrested by an upper transverse beam, or by cords fastened to the frame-work. The projectile left the spoon at this point and could be directed with considerable accuracy. Red-hot balls and fire-pots were also hurled by the ballista, and sometimes infected corpses were thrown into a city to spread disease. These engines were really very effective; in some respects as much so as our modern artillery. In the hands of Alexander, the Macedonian engines were frequently of as great use as a battery is to-day. In transporting these machines the Macedonians carried only the essential parts, for the heavy timbers could be cut and fitted in any place where trees were accessible. A horse or mule could transport the essentials of one ballista or catapult such as they were when perfected by Alexander's engineers.

We know nothing about the baggage or wagon train, but it must have been much what it is to-day, except that pack-animals were more common than wagons. Horses had to have forage and soldiers rations then as now, and we do not hear that Alexander's men carried twenty days' victual, like Cæsar's legionaries, on their persons. They had basket-work haversacks, and their rations consisted of salt meat, cheese, olives, onions and corn. At one time there was, according to Philip's orders, a porter for every ten phalangites, and the hetairai or cavalry Companions always had servants. Philip is said to have first taken from the infantry their baggage-wagons and cut down the horseman's servants to one, and he often marched his men with full complement of equipment, baggage and provision, even in summer heat, thirty miles a day as a mere matter of training. Headquarters must necessarily have had certain facilities for doing business. That there were provost-marshals we know, and there are one or two references which sound as if there was a regular field-hospital service. All this demanded transportation.

The quartermaster's and commissary's as well as engineer departments we read little about. But there is evidence of their wonderful efficiency in everything which Alexander did. The system was the creation of Philip. Pella, at Philip's accession, was a place of small pretensions. At his death it had become a great capital, whose war department must have been as carefully managed as the best of to-day. Such a military machine was an entire novelty in the then world, as wonderful in that era as to-day Prussia's perfect organization would be if it were the only regular army and the rest of the world had but militia, such as is possessed by our own States in America.

The Greek camp was constructed with great care. It was

Greek Camp.

usually round or elliptical in shape. It had streets which met in the centre, where also was placed the headquarters. Slaves, of whom, as we have seen, a great number always accompanied the army, were set to work to dig a trench about the camp so soon as it had been located, and threw the earth up into a rampart about six feet high. This wall was usually defended by entanglements, *trous-de-loup*, crow's feet, and a species of abatis.

Picket duty was strictly performed, but the guards were not placed at the distance of our pickets from camp. Posts of fifty hoplites each surrounded the camp, from which a line of sentinels was sent out. These sentinels passed from hand to hand a bell to show that they were on the alert. Officers, accompanied by torch-bearers, made prescribed rounds, also ringing a bell. Sentinels appear to have challenged this officer much in the same manner which obtains with us. A password, apt to be the name of a god, was exchanged between patrols and sentinels.

On the march the phalanx moved, with few exceptions, right in front. Martial music, mostly pipes, was usual. Each syntagma had its own trumpeter, but just what a Macedonian band may have been like we are left to conjecture. The cadenced step was practiced more than nowadays. With the sarissa, a cadenced step was a *sine qua non* to keep the ranks unbroken.

In the face of the enemy the soldiers were wont to chant

the pæan. At certain times the phalanx advanced in silence, so as the better to give heed to orders, then intuned the pæan as they neared the foe, and closed with him shouting the battle-cry. Every old soldier remembers the inspiriting nature of a battlefield cheer. It will ring in his ears throughout life. Alexander's men raised so terrifying a shout, as they advanced to the attack, that its effect upon the enemy was sometimes prodigious.

A vanguard and rearguard of light troops, infantry and cavalry, were usual on the march, often sustained by the heavier hypaspists. The artillery, baggage and elephants, if any, marched in rear of the phalanx. Rations in bulk were carried on beasts of burden or by slaves in the train. The trains must have been very extended. But the East was densely populated, and Alexander habitually lived on the country, much as Napoleon did, though we do not note the consequent loss of discipline in the Macedonian ranks which was prevalent in the French armies under Bonaparte.

Many of the most usual and effective manœuvres on the battlefield of to-day have come down to us from the Greeks. As we have seen, Epaminondas showed us the value of the oblique order and the value of the column of attack, and Xenophon distinctly describes an advance in columns by the right of companies (or regiments) to overcome ground which would be apt to break the solidity of a line of battle. There are numberless others. The tactical works about the Greek armies are quite detailed and intricate, and show as great intelligence in grand and minor tactics as appears in the treatises of any age. It remains, however, a fact that most battles were fought in simple parallel order. The Greek tacticians knew more than their generals could apply.

Battles were intended to be, and were usually, won by a single shock. For an impact, or as a line of defense, on level ground the phalanx was irresistible. The habit in attacking the enemy was first to throw forward the archers and slingers in skirmishing order, sustained by the light cavalry, perhaps on the flanks. This attack was followed up by putting in the targeteers and hypaspists, and last the phalanx and heavy cavalry. But Alexander often gave his first blow with the Companions. After the light troops had opened the combat they filed off to the left and right, or passed through the intervals and uncovered the phalanx. The music then sounded, the pæan was chanted, and to its inspiriting strains the phalanx advanced in cadenced step.

In each phalangial subdivision there was apt to be an insensible movement to the right because each man had his own left side protected by his shield and endeavored to hug the protection afforded by the shield of his right-hand man. This naturally resulted in the right flank often becoming somewhat advanced; and, no doubt, one reason why the commander's station was on the right was the desire to control this edging tendency. Some authors have ascribed to it the origin of the oblique order, which was so valuable to Alexander in nearly all his battles. We shall recur to this question of the oblique order frequently. We know that Alexander was familiar with Leuctra and Mantinæa, where the manœuvre was by no means dependent on this tendency.

As a rule, but one line of battle was formed. The depth of the phalanx rendered a second one impracticable, and moreover there were rarely enough troops, with the great depth, to make a line of sufficient length, if many were to be left in reserve. Especially was this so in Alexander's case, who fought such greatly superior forces, which could readily extend beyond and turn his either flank. Still Alexander frequently had reserves. Arbela, for instance, is an exception to the general rule, dictated by the peculiar circumstances. Here Alexander had a partial first line of light troops, a second of the phalanx, and placed a third in reserve to protect the rear, and to wheel to right and left to cover the flanks. The cavalry on the right and the troops on the left were likewise in three lines. As a habit Alexander placed the bulk of his horse where he proposed to make his most serious attack, and not by any hard and fast rule.

It was usual at this early period for level ground to be selected as a battlefield, and on such ground each army was formally marshaled and marched against the other. But by Alexander's time the art of war had advanced beyond this simple array, and a few other tactical manœuvres had come in to take their place. We shall see how much Alexander himself taught the world in this branch of the art, as well as how he gave it the first lessons in the passing of rivers at the Granicus, the Pinarus and most memorably at the river Hydaspes. What he showed the world of strategy was, however, lost on all but such captains as Hannibal and Cæsar.

In retreat, in presence of the enemy, the Greeks were wont to march in a circle or square, with the slaves, women, booty and baggage in the centre. A vanguard, rearguard and flankers were thrown out.

The Greeks usually constructed on a field of victory, from the spoils of the enemy, a monument to commemorate the victory. This was a religious rite due to the manes of the slain.

The Macedonians had an excellent system of signals, by beacons at night and standards by day. They appear to have been able to convey information with accuracy and great speed.

The corps of "pages" was perhaps the first institution which may be said to have been an embryo military school, — a by no means incomplete West Point. From these pages came eventually all the higher officers. They were youths of high extraction, who surrounded the person of the king, waited upon him, brought him his horse, stood watch at his bedside at night, did his confidential errands, sat at his table, studied the art of war while thus serving at court or at head-quarters in the field and became personally known to him. They underwent the same kind of training which is usual at modern military schools, and their places were far from being sinecures. They were so hard-worked in Asia that many of them died. Alexander usually pushed his subordinates hard. He himself was capable of unremitting labor, and he required it of others. These pages, after a certain number of years' training, were gradually appointed, according to their merit or the confidence of the monarch, to moderate commands, and from these positions were in the way of success as their ability and courage won it. They might rise to be chosen somatophylaxes, of whom there usually were seven, and who were like adjutants-general, or prominent aides of the king, or army leaders ; they might fail and never gain promotion beyond a modest rank. In line of battle these pages served as a part of the hypaspists. In Asia they were under command of Seleucus.

In the army of Alexander, the following may be given as the successive ranks from the king down. Philip had introduced the graduated system of rank and command, and of advancement strictly according to merit.

1. Alexander, king and commander-in-chief.
2. Parmenio and Antipater, army commanders immediately under Alexander. Among the noble families clustering about Philip, two were prominent. Of one of these Parmenio, Philip's (and later Alexander's) oldest and most trusted lieutenant, was the head ; of the other, Antipater. The first, in the Macedonian economy of Alexander's reign, represented the military, the other the civil government.

Antipater was left in Macedonia as quasi-regent; Parmenio accompanied the army to Asia. He stood to Alexander somewhat in the same relation as Meade to Grant in 1864. But Alexander habitually commanded the right, Parmenio the left wing in person.

3. The seven somatophylaxes (confidential body-guards), general officers who were placed in command of large detachments for special service, or who held important commands to which they might be appointed by the king, or acted as *aides-de-camp*.

4. Tetraphalangiarch, or commander of a quadruple phalanx.

5. Diphalangiarch, or commander of a double phalanx.

6. Phalangiarch, or commander of a simple phalanx of four thousand and ninety-six hoplites.

These three titles were more descriptive of command temporarily enjoyed than of a rank as distinct as lieutenant-general, major-general or brigadier-general of to-day.

7. Chiliarch or taxiarch or strategos, colonel of infantry, and hipparch, colonel of cavalry.

8. Xenagos, syntagmatarch, major of foot. Just how high in rank the uragos, or second major of the syntagma was, is not clear.

9. Taxiarch, captain.

10. Tetrarch, lieutenant.

11. Lochagos, sergeant.

There were officers of cavalry, whose rank was assimilated to the last four; and the light troops were similarly officered throughout.

The word of the king was supreme law. But it was common to summon councils of war from time to time to decide matters of great moment. Just how far these were required by law or precedent does not appear, but they were constantly called as if a matter of rote. In such councils the officers of given rank, whether of Macedonians or Greeks, auxiliary or mercenary, Thracians or Agrianians, Odryssians, or Pæonians, were all present and had equal right to be heard and considered. But it is probable that the Macedonians had higher rank and more influence in such councils, and the opinion of the somatophylaxes, for instance, would be apt to bear greater weight. But Alexander invariably, excepting at the Hyphasis, carried his point. His persuasiveness was always equal to the respect and affection of his subordinates.

Philip of Macedon, from a coin.

XIII.

THE ART OF FORTIFICATION AND SIEGES.

THUCYDIDES' account of the siege of Platæa gives us the first insight into ancient methods. The art of sieges was less developed than that of fortification. The earliest means of attacking walls was by scaling ladders, or by mounting on a tortoise of shields. Then came walls of circumvallation and contravallation, mounds to override the walls, towers, sheds and mantelets, rams and engines to cast heavy missiles and break down the walls, and mines. The mounds and towers were often of extraordinary size. The besieged used converse means. They made sorties, shot burning missiles to fire the siege works, built half moons behind breaches in the walls, and countermined. The various devices exhibited great ingenuity. Field fortifications were rare.

PRIOR to the Peloponnesian war the art of attacking cities had not risen to any great height. Thucydides' relation of the siege of Platæa gives us the first detailed account of the operations then usual. Alexander gave to the art a marked impetus. Of all acts of war sieges allow the military art to approach most closely to the other arts and sciences; that is, call for the employment of more of the arts which chiefly are of use in peace. The methods of a siege, if the garrison cannot be starved out, are either to scale the walls or to make breaches in them which can be carried by assault; and it is essential to do the latter with as little exposure to the enemy's fire as possible. The besieged, on the other hand, must seek to destroy the besiegers' means of accomplishing this, and to inflict what loss they can on them as a means of driving them from their purpose.

The earliest means of attacking walls was by scaling-ladders. These were first used at the siege of the Seven against

Thebes, and Campaneus, one of the kings and their inventor, is said to have lost his life in falling from one of his own ladders. A later means was the tortoise, made, as has been already described, by joining together bucklers, or shields, above the heads of a massed force, on which a second party could

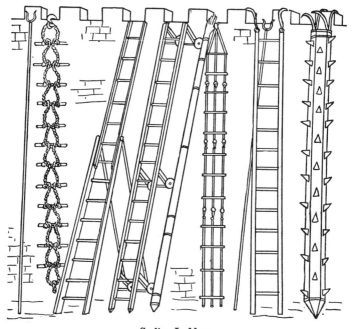

Scaling-Ladders.

stand to scale the walls or form a second tortoise for the scalers. But these crude methods soon gave way to more regular means, which aimed at making a defense against sorties from within and against relief from without, at erecting a shelter from the enemy's fire and at organizing vigorous measures of attack.

A wall of contravallation to inclose the town or fortress and keep the garrison within its defenses was first built; then outside this a wall of circumvallation at a suitable distance and facing outward to prevent a relieving army from interfering with the operations of the besiegers.

In front of the wall of contravallation mounds were erected, from which the walls of the town could be attacked. These were gradually thrown up under the protection of movable screens or sheds, or, as they also were sometimes called, tortoises. One common form of shed was a roof built of and sustained by heavy beams, covered with clay or tiles and fresh skins and other materials calculated to resist fire, and mounted on wheels. Two lines of sheds were sometimes built on a slightly converging angle up to a certain distance from the wall, and then the lines united. The front of these sheds towards the enemy was protected by hanging on them blankets made of rawhides and twisted ropes.

Tortoise.

The mound itself was constructed of earth, stones, trees, sometimes trestlework, the whole filled in with earth and stones or any material which could be quickest got together and would bear the weight of the towers which were to be advanced. The mound had a gradual slant upwards towards the wall, but as erect a face as possible at the ditch. Upon or beside this mound, during erection, smaller towers were placed from which the besiegers could be attacked with arrows, darts and stones, and prevented from interrupting the

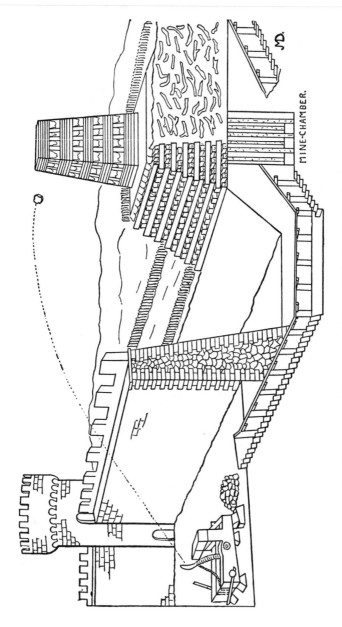

MINE-CHAMBER.

JD.

Fort, Tower, Mound, Mantelets and Mine, with Section showing Construction.

work. From this mound, when completed, the ditch could be
filled up and the walls could be demolished with battering
rams and other devices. The besiegers had the advantage
of the mound for their engines, whereas the engines of the
enemy were usually on the ground inside the walls of the
town, whence their aim was by no means so accurate. But
often mounds of equal size were built inside by the besieged
to get a better chance for their fire. The rapidity with which
these mounds could be thrown up to an extraordinary height
is most astonishing, even when we consider that the whole
army worked at them, and that often the entire population of
the surrounding district was pressed into the service. Cæsar
made a mound at Avaricum in twenty-four days, which was
eighty feet high and three hundred and thirty feet wide, and
had towers at each side. Sylla is said, at the siege of Ma-
sada, to have made a mound two hundred and eighty-six feet
high, and to have surmounted it by structures one hundred
and fifty-five feet higher. These figures may possibly fail
somewhat of accuracy. They sound exaggerated even when
we remember the walls of Babylon. But the enormous size
of these structures is well established.

Instead of mounds, towers alone were often built, as they
could be more quickly constructed. The size of these seems
equally fabulous. They are said to have been sometimes
twenty stories in height, and the ordinary towers had ten
stories. The carpentry in them must have been wonderful.
Each story was filled with armed men, and had loopholes
from which these could shoot missiles at the besieged on the
walls. These towers rested on a number of wheels, very
broad and solid, and required many hundred men to move
them. Demetrius Poliorcetes, at Rhodes, according to Diodorus, had one made by Epimachus of Athens, which was
seventy-five feet square, one hundred and fifty feet high, and

Tower with Drawbridge and Ram.

rested on eight wheels whose felloes were six feet wide **and**
heavily ironed, as was also the tower. It took three **thou-**
sand four hundred men to move it, working no doubt **in**
relays. These towers were of course pushed forward **very**
slowly and probably by levers applied to the wheels from **the**
inside. Plutarch says that it took a month to move a **big**
tower two hundred and fifty paces. Diodorus states that **they**
could be moved one thousand paces in less time. The **raising**
and moving of buildings to-day explains to a certain **extent**
how all this was done. The towers contained reservoirs **of**

water to quench fires which the besieged might set. Generally
the battering-rams were slung in the lower story; the engines
stood in the middle ones; the soldiers occupied the upper
stories. While the tower was being advanced, the men in
the several stories kept up a constant fire of arrows, javelins
and other missiles upon the besieged who occupied the walls,
to prevent their interference with the operations of the siege;
and from this tower, when near enough, bridges hinged
thereto, and sometimes concealed, were dropped upon the walls.
Over these bridges the besiegers marched to the assault.
Towers were often made on permanent foundations, and not
infrequently of brick.

Rams were at first long bars of iron, or beams pointed with
iron, which were handled by the soldiers. Pliny recognizes
the ram in the story of the horse of Troy. Thucydides clearly
describes one at the siege of Samos in the Peloponnesian
war. Next came the idea of suspending the rams in a frame-
work and moving them to and fro by manned ropes, thus
getting the advantage of impetus. Later they were mounted
on wheels running in tracks. This latter kind averaged fifty
feet long. Demetrius is said to have had two, each one hundred and twenty feet long. They were often loaded at both
ends so as to deliver a heavier blow. They needed many men
to operate them, as they often weighed hundreds of tons. To
transport one mentioned by Diodorus required three hundred
pairs of horses; to operate it fifteen hundred men, including
the relays.

While the besiegers were engaged at undermining the walls
of the town, the besieged were busy undermining the terrace
or mound and the towers of the besiegers. Having no explosives, they were obliged to make chambers large enough
to weaken the entire structure. The roofs of these chambers
were sustained by beams, and when completed, they were

filled with combustibles and fired. This consumed the supporting beams, further weakened the earth, walls or terrace, and dropped the structures erected above.

Mining and countermining were extensively carried on. Subterranean fights were not unusual. Certain means of discovering the position of mines by the sound of metal vessels in their vicinity were practiced, and great ingenuity and no little scientific ability were displayed in both attack and defense.

To shelter the men who protected the works in front of the  walls, or who advanced to the assault of a breach, the Greeks used mantelets, both portable and mounted on wheels, as well as the rolling galleries or sheds above described.

Mantelets.

Alexander's engineer, Diades, was the inventor of a huge hook or "crow," swung upon a high vertical frame, by which the upper stones of a wall could be seized and pulled down. He also invented the telenon, which consisted of a huge upright mast, across which was hung a yard or boom, and on one end of this a basket or car capable of containing a number of soldiers. This car was raised or lowered by means of ropes attached to the other end of the boom. By this device, a party or forlorn hope could be raised to the height of the wall, clamber upon it and attack its defenders.

In defending a town, the besieged adopted every means by which the access of the enemy's soldiers could be prevented. They had forked poles with which to push away the ladders which the besiegers placed in position; they were supplied with vessels which they could speedily heat so as to pour boiling oil, or pitch, or red-hot sand upon the scalers; or else materials which rendered the air impure were thrown down upon the besiegers' works. The mound was often undermined as fast as built. A second wall, or curtain, or half-moon, was sometimes built behind the place selected by the enemy for operating a breach, so that he found himself confronted with new labors so soon as he had completed the first. Towers were raised on the walls to dominate those of the besiegers. Efforts were unremitting to set the work of the

Telenon and Mural Hook.

besiegers on fire, by casting inflammable arrows with the catapults and fire-pots with the ballista. Walls were protected against the rams by aprons calculated to deaden the blow. These were made of wool mattresses, ropes and other soft material. The rams were seized and picked up by huge tongs operated from the wall, or were broken or unhinged by weights dropped on them from above.

Sorties were constantly made to endeavor to burn the works and disturb the besiegers. Apparently the ancients were as fertile in resources as we are to-day in the matter of sieges, and if their artillery was less powerful than our own, their machines nevertheless were capable of doing remarkably efficient work.

Field fortifications were rarely employed by the Greeks. These were usually confined to the defense of defiles, and, except to surround the camps, were never used in the plains.

Pent-House and Ram picked up by Tongs.

Indeed, the Greek camps were by no means so admirably fortified as they were in later centuries by the Romans. Still, the Greeks in front of Troy fortified their camp, and on one occasion it saved them from disaster, and there are many later instances of temporary intrenchments. But their use, as we understand them to-day, was unknown.

XIV.

ALEXANDER AND GREECE. B. C. 336.

PHILIP had for years harbored designs of an expedition against the Persian monarchy, but did not live to carry them out. Alexander succeeded him at the age of twenty. He had been educated under Aristotle. No monarch of his years was ever so well equipped in heart and head. Like Frederick, he was master from the start. "Though the name has changed, the king remains," quoth he. His arms he found ready to hand, tempered in his father's forge. But it was his own strength and skill which wielded them. The Greeks considered themselves absolved from Macedonian jurisdiction by the death of Philip. Not so thought Alexander. He marched against them, turning the passes of Tempē and Callipeukē by hewing a path along the slopes of Mount Ossa, and made himself master of Thessaly. The Amphyctionic Council deemed it wise to submit, and elected him autocrator in place of his father.

IT was in the midst of such a circle and such a government that the youth of Alexander was spent. From his infancy the superstitious blood of his mother coined in his mind the stories of Hercules and Achilles and Bacchus, while the practical sense of his father led him to look upon the earth and water which his ancestors had been compelled to bring to the Persian king as injuries to be avenged. The glorious story of Marathon and Salamis taught him that the few with soul-stirring common purpose are stronger than the many who lack cohesion or leaders ; and the destruction of the holy temples and tombs of Asia Minor by the ruthless servants of the Great King roused his righteous indignation to the highest pitch. The boy's shoulders bore a man's head, and his father's splendid exploits, coupled with what Philip looked forward to accomplish in the future, made Alexander fear that there would be nothing left for him to conquer. His mind was alert and inquisitive beyond his years. So, when Persian ambassadors once came to the Macedonian court, it was natural that this boy should inquire of them about the armies and topography of Asia, the resources and wealth, the laws and customs, the government and the life of the peoples; but the ambassadors were none the less astounded. No wonder Philip was proud of his son and heir.

Alexander's early education was presided over by Leonidas, a relative of his mother, and an austere man. His special pedagogue was Lysimachus, who indulged in superstitious lore and in unwise flattery, and bred in the youth a half belief in the divine origin of Peleus and of Achilles, from whom he claimed descent. He was afterwards more fortunate; for "Aristotle, who conquered the world of thought, gave instruction to him who should conquer the world itself" (B. C. 345–4). From this great man Alexander gained all that was wisest and best; and what he thus learned never forsook him. It was well that the teaching of this philosopher should fall on such fruitful soil. It was sad that the pupil should, later in life, lose his trust in his great preceptor and friend.

Alexander inherited his enthusiastic nature, his deep wealth of sentiment, his truly heroic soul, from his mother. From his father he took his physique, his power of reasoning, his cool judgment, his infallible penetration. Vigor and quickness of movement, a bright and intelligent look and a full, round, strong voice distinguished him in action. At rest he was gentle and pleasing, and possessed a peculiarly moist, expressive eye. He wore long and curly hair. He is said to have had a trick of habitually inclining his head over the left shoulder, a thing at one time much imitated by the dandies of Greece. He was agreeable in person, and very temperate in his pleasures. In sports and gymnastics he easily excelled all, but cared little for professional athletes. The story of Bucephalus is probably no myth. No one, from Plutarch's narration, had apparently been able to control the high-strung beast, mainly because he had been treated with indiscretion. Alexander, however, observant of the animal's peculiarities, by intelligent kindness and fearlessness bestrode and managed him with ease. Bucephalus served him stanchly and affectionately from that day till the battle of the Hydaspes, where he died, gamely pursuing Porus.

Bucephalus had been brought to Philip for sale. The price was thirteen talents. He must have been a celebrated horse at that time to command so much. But no one was able to mount him on account of his rearing and plunging. He was being led away, when Alexander asked for leave to try him. The lad was laughed at, but his entreaties finally prevailed.

"Alexander immediately ran to the horse, and taking hold of the bridle, turned him directly towards the sun, having, it seems, observed that he was disturbed at and afraid of the motion of his own shadow; then letting him go forward a little, still keeping the reins in his hand, and stroking him gently when he found him begin to grow eager and fiery, he let fall his upper garment softly, and with one nimble leap securely mounted him, and when he was seated, by little and little drew in the bridle, and curbed him without either striking or spurring him. Presently when he found him free from all rebelliousness and only impatient for the course, he let him go at full speed, inciting him now with a commanding voice, and urging him also with his heels." (Plutarch.)

In his mental equipment Alexander was equally strong; he enjoyed all manner of intellectual friction. In strength of character few in the world's history have been his equals, none his superior.

It was thus that Alexander the Great grew to manhood. We have seen how he came to the throne. Once fairly seated, he speedily showed that though his father had forged the tools he found ready to his hand, he himself could wield them with a suddenness, boldness and decision of which Philip was probably never capable. No man was ever in so full a sense the leader of an army. He fought with it, commanded it, and handled it in an almost superhuman way. Always an absolute example to men and officers, he asked nothing from high or low that he was not able to do far better himself, and willing to undertake.

He made no mistake in his political beginnings. He continued his father's ministers in power, and committed none of the blunders associated with youth. But his position was critical. On the death of Philip the Greeks claimed to be absolved from Macedonian jurisdiction. Athens at once prepared for war and built herself a fleet. Thebes attempted to eject the Macedonian garrison from the Cadmæa. The smaller cities were in a ferment. Sparta, as we know, had never submitted. Philip, anticipating nothing of the kind, had divided his army, and Parmenio was in Asia with a large part of it. The northern tribes were becoming unruly. In fact, the Illyrians rose in active revolt. Thus from north, east, west, south, danger stared Alexander in the face. Moreover, as we have seen, Attalus, uncle of Cleopatra, under pretense of getting the kingdom for her son by Philip, was really conspiring to seat himself upon it, and being, with Parmenio, in joint command of the army of Asia, he relied on his influence with the troops to accomplish his design. Everything looked desperate. Alexander's friends advised him to compromise with Greece and seek for peace with Attalus. But Alexander was made of no such stuff. He had already waded through much blood; security could be had by no other path, nor had he been taught to recognize a better. He at once sent to Asia and caused Attalus to be executed for treason.

This was safely accomplished by his general and intimate, Hecatæus, who, with a fresh and faithful body of troops, passed over to Asia and joined Parmenio.

This gravest of his dangers put aside, within two months from the death of his father Alexander marched on Thessaly, with a force said to have been equal to that which Philip commanded at Chæronæa. He determined to exhibit his power to those who believed that there was no more Philip. His route lay along the coast towards the Penæan passes. The main defile of Tempē as well as the minor one of Callipeukē was strongly held. To attack them was more than hazardous; it would plainly be futile. Ossa rises in steep rocky masses south of the pass of Tempē. From the sea, however, the slope of Ossa is more gradual than

March into Thessaly.

along the Penæus. With that fertility of resource and active embracing of difficulty which was always his marked characteristic, Alexander, unknown to the enemy, hewed himself a never-yet-trodden path along the slopes of Ossa on the seaside, blasting a foothold for his army where it could not otherwise make its way, and turned the Thessalian force in the passes. He was thus master of the situation, and his bold intelligence had made him master of Thessaly. But he desired to keep this country friendly, for the Thessalian horsemen made the best cavalry in Greece, and he needed above all things horse in his projected Persian war. With the plausible generosity which he could so well display, — and Alexander's promise was always sacredly redeemed, — on convening an assembly, he persuaded the Thessalians to give him all they had granted Philip, and if necessary to help him as against the rest of Hellas. Not only Thessaly, but other tribes which had Amphictyonic votes Alexander thus gained, and speedily made his way unopposed through the pass of Thermopylæ.

Here he convened the Amphictyonic council and was declared Hegemōn (captain-general) of Greece, as had been Philip before him. Thebes and Athens sent no representatives; but on Alexander's moving on Thebes, both cities hastened to agree to the terms of the Amphictyonic decision. Alexander was glad to accept this tardy acknowledgment. He caused the vote to be repeated at Corinth, where implacable Sparta alone was absent, preferring the isolation of independence. Alexander continued his march into the Peloponnesus to exhibit his strength, but undertook no operations there. Autonomy was assured to each Greek state.

Alexander had ascertained the mood of Greece, and had for the moment calmed it. All the wealth, intellect and power of Greece had joined to simulate honor to the bold young king. Diogenes alone waited for Alexander to come to him, and then requested as his only desire that Alexander would stand a trifle out of his sunlight. "By Jupiter, were I not Alexander, I would wish to be Diogenes!" said the king. The danger from east and south had been overcome, at least for the moment. Alexander returned before winter to Pella.

It is clear, says Freeman, that both the great Macedonians really loved and revered Greece, — Athens above all. To humble her politically was an unavoidable part of their policy; but they always kept themselves from doing her any wrong beyond what their policy called for. They felt as Greeks, and they had no temptation to destroy what they claimed as their mother-country. They had clearly no wish to swallow up Greece in Macedonia, but rather to make Macedonia, as a Greek state, the ruling power of Greece. Such was undoubtedly the aim of Philip, and it was that of Alexander too, till, from the throne of the Great King, he may have learned to look on both Greece and Macedonia as little more than corners of his empire, nurseries of his most valiant soldiers.

Matters being thus smoothed over, Alexander could foresee the possibility of carrying out his Persian project. Parmenio had so far not accomplished much in Asia Minor; but his presence and position there had forestalled any invasion of Macedonia by the Persians, and might be said to cover Alexander's flank in any campaign he should be compelled to make against the Thracians. This was at least a negative gain. There remained but to be secure of lasting quiet at home.

Macedon was well equipped. The people, as we have said, enjoyed equal rights, and were to a man liable to military service when called on. The soldier was citizen; the citizen, soldier; the soldier a regular. There was no conflicting interest. If a king was no general, his Macedonians could exercise suitable control over him. If the king was a Philip or an Alexander, the respect and admiration of his citizen-soldiers gave him a power all the more worth having. And the courage and discipline of such a body, combining the virtues of both the volunteer and regular, was on a plane much higher than that of the soldier of the rest of Greece; immeasurably higher than that of the soldier of Persia.

XV.

THE DANUBE. B. C. 335.

THERE remained the task of quieting the northern and western borders, a work Philip had ably begun but had not lived to finish. The tribes along the Danube had risen *en masse*, and those in the mountains of Illyria had banded together. They had heard of the death of Philip, and knew not Alexander. The king headed for Mount Hæmus. Here the barbarians had drawn up in front of the only available defile, and had disposed their wagons in such fashion as to roll them down upon the phalanx. By so arranging his men that they could form lanes through the ranks to allow some of the wagons to pass, and by ordering the rest to form a tortoise and permit the wagons to roll across it, this singular danger was averted. The enemy was then attacked and dispersed. Beyond Mount Hæmus the Triballians endeavored to get around to his rear, but Alexander turned on them, and in a sharply contested battle at the Lyginus signally defeated them. At the Danube he met his fleet, which had been ordered from Byzantium to and up the river. Most of the tribes had taken refuge on an island in the river. Alexander sought to drive them out; but the steep banks and rapid current prevented his so doing. He then crossed the Danube — an able performance — and inflicted due chastisement on the Getæ. This was followed by the surrender of all the rest, including the refugees on the island. Alexander's borders to the Danube could be deemed secure.

BEFORE Alexander could start on his expedition against Persia, he saw that he must reduce to subjection some of the savage tribes on his own borders. These tribes had been in part subdued by Philip, in part received as allies, in part punished whenever they attempted inroads on Macedonia, and thus held in temporary check. Now the Illyrians, under Clitus, whom Philip had in bloody conflict pushed back of Lake Lychnitis, and the Taulantinians from the coast near Appolonia and Dyrracchium, under their chief Glaucias, and the Autariatians from the valleys to the north of these latter, all rose *en masse*. But even more dangerous were

the Thracian Triballians on the Danube, with whom Philip
had had a far from successful bout, in which he had been
wounded. And beyond these tribes lay others, "fearful robbers even to robbers themselves," all of whom were liable to
join in any insurrection or raid which might be begun by
those nearest the Macedonian frontier. These tribes had
been quelled, but not thoroughly subdued, by Philip. And
now, in a second uprising, no halfway measures would do,
if Alexander expected to absent himself from Macedon for
years.

Greece was tranquil; spring afforded suitable conditions
for mountain warfare; the time was rife. Parmenio had been
recalled from Asia, where a lieutenant still remained, and was
left in Macedonia to guard it against Illyrian incursions, while
Alexander set forth to teach these Danube barbarians the
lesson which Philip's wound had prevented his giving them
au fond. Antipater, meanwhile, was given the civil government at Pella in charge.

There were two roads open to Alexander: following the
course of the Axius up its passes through the land of the
faithful Agrianians; or easterly along the coast through
the domain of the free Thracians, up towards the valley of
the Hebrus and across Mount Hæmus range to attack the
Triballian question from the east. He chose the latter route,
as it led through the land of the uncertain-minded Odryssians,
whom he could probably conciliate on the way. He ordered
a fleet from Byzantium to repair to its mouths ready to ascend
the Danube, on which river he proposed in due time to meet
it. Early in the spring he started along the route with the
purpose of settling the troubles at the Danube and afterward
those on the Illyrian borders once for all.

From Amphipolis he marched to Philippi and northward
along the Nessus and over the Rhodope mountains toward

Mount Hæmus, — now the Balkans. The foot of the range he reached in a march of ten days. Here the Thracians had prepared to meet him on the southerly slope at the entrance to its passes. The defile he attacked we can probably identify

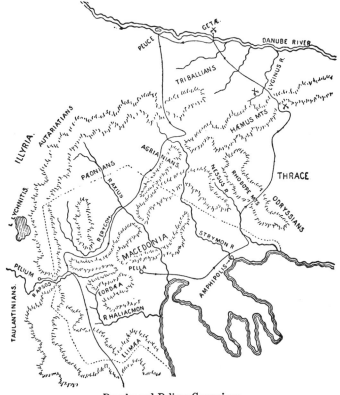

Danube and Pelium Campaigns.

as the principal pass in the Balkans, north of Adrianople, later known as Porta Trajani.

The barbarians had adopted a very intelligent means of meeting the phalanx, whose power they had good cause to dread. Armed only with dagger or hunting-spear, and with a fox or wolf-skin for headgear and covering, they could not

for a moment resist the Macedonian close array of pikes.
But they had collected all their wagons and chariots, and
formed them as a rampart in their front in such manner that,
as the phalanx advanced to the attack, the wagons could be
rolled down upon them, and by breaking the ranks enable
them to attack the Macedonians in individual combat with
some chance of success. The denser the phalanx, the more
dangerous the wagons, they rightly argued. But Alexander
was equal to the occasion. He knew that this was the only
available pass, and seeing what the barbarians were proposing

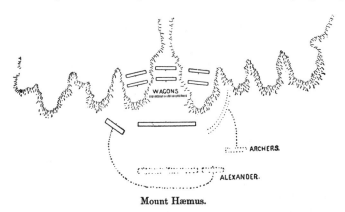

Mount Hæmus.

to do, he ordered the phalangites, where the ground would
permit, to open lanes at the proper time by closing files to
right and left, and thus allow the descending wagons to pass,
when possible. Those who could not thus step aside to avoid
them he bade to lie down, and, by holding their shields above
them and locking them together tortoise-fashion, to allow the
wagons to roll over the thus improvised bridges. This defense, as strange and ingenious as the means of attack, the
Macedonians put into practice as they marched up toward
the foe; nor was a single man killed by the rolling wagons.

When this really dangerous attack was happily avoided,

the phalangites advanced, with loud cries, upon the enemy, already disconcerted by the failure of his well-laid scheme. Alexander detailed his archers forward from the right wing to fall upon the flank of the Thracians as they moved down upon the forward-marching phalanx, while he himself, with his own body-guard, the hypaspists and some Agrianians, moved by a circuit about their right. Aided by the diversion of the archers, the phalangites reached the enemy's line and made quick work of the half-armed barbarians. Even before Alexander could finish his circuit, the battle was over, and all who had not fled had fallen. Some fifteen hundred were killed, and the balance dispersed in the woods and ravines of the mountains. All their women, children and baggage were captured, and sent to the markets of the seacoast under Lysanias and Philotas, son of Parmenio, to be sold for booty.

Alexander crossed Mount Hæmus in safety and moved down the easier northern slopes into the valley of the Triballians, and across the Lyginus, now Jantra (or it may have been, as claimed by some authorities, the Oscius), about three marches from the Danube. Syrmus, their king, in anticipation of Alexander's arrival, had sent the women and children for refuge to an island in the Danube, called Peucē, not easily identified but probably near and below modern Widdin, to which the Thracians had also fled and King Syrmus had himself repaired. When Alexander had crossed the Lyginus and was moving toward the barbarians on the Danube, he found that the main body of the Triballians was marching back on the former river as with intent to seize the passes in his rear. By a sudden countermarch, Alexander surprised them at eventide as they were going into camp.

The Triballians retired into a woody glen near the river, difficult of access. Alexander marshaled his army for attack.

He led the phalanx in person, but took the precaution to throw
out a curtain of archers and slingers, hoping to draw the barbarians from their retreat into the open. These light troops
advanced and gallantly forced the attack. The over-eager
Triballians could not be restrained from rushing out to engage in a hand-to-hand conflict, and had small difficulty in

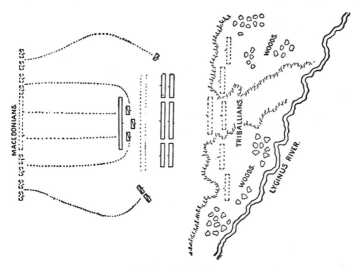

Battle at the Lyginus.

pushing the light troops back. This easy success induced them
to advance still farther, and gave Alexander the opportunity
of sending Philotas with an ilē of cavalry to charge in on
their naked right wing, which had advanced beyond their
main line. Heraclides and Sopolis he sent with other two
ilēs of horse to attack their left, while he himself, with the phalanx, preceded by cavalry, advanced straight upon the barbarians. So long as the attack was confined to skirmishing
the Triballians were not to be overcome, but when the dense
phalanx pushed in upon them, and the horse came to close
quarters, riding them down bodily by mere weight, they were

broken and driven back, with a loss of three thousand killed, into the ravine. The uncertainty of night prevented the Macedonians from pursuing. The rest of the Triballians fled in all directions. About fifty of Alexander's men were killed. The wounded are rarely mentioned in ancient narratives. They averaged eight to twelve for one killed.

Alexander turned again to pursue his former track. Three days after, the army reached the Danube, probably some way below the island of Peucē. Here he was joined by the fleet which he had caused to be sent with provisions from Byzantium to meet him. Filling the vessels with archers and heavy troops, he sailed up to the island, which Syrmus had put in a state of defense. But though he essayed a landing he found that he could make no headway, for the ships were small and could hold but few armed men beside the rowers; the banks were high and well patrolled, the current, penned in by the narrows, was very rapid and hard to stem, and the defense was stout. Alexander was obliged to withdraw, for the moment foiled.

But on the other side of the Danube were the Getæ, who had assembled to the number of four thousand horse and over ten thousand foot to oppose his crossing, and appeared to be ready to make common cause with the island forces (mid-May, B. C. 335). Alexander determined to dispose of the Getæ first. The barbarians naturally believed that if Alexander attempted to cross it would be only after many days' preparation, and that they could attack the successive parties as they reached the northern bank. Alexander's obstinacy always rose with opposition, and he determined to cross at once, foreseeing that if he beat the Getæ the island would probably surrender at discretion. He utilized the fleet; he collected a number of boats made of hollow logs, " dug-outs," so to speak, which the inhabitants used for fishing, trading, moving to and fro, and for occasional bits of piracy, and which were found in numbers all along the river; he filled the hides which the soldiers used for tent-coverings with hay,

Method of Using Skins.

tied them closely together and upon these either constructed rafts, or used them to float the men in swimming. The latter was an ancient custom. By means of all these devices and an activity which with Alexander was always abnormal, he

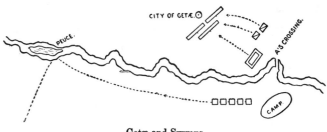

Getæ and Syrmus.

managed to put over during a single short summer night fifteen hundred cavalry and four thousand infantry. Whoever has seen the width and rapid current of the Danube can the better gauge the extraordinary nature of this feat.

The Macedonians landed unobserved at a place where the

growing corn stood high, which in a measure concealed their movements; and here, too, the enemy had no outpost. Through this field they advanced at daylight, pressing down the high thick corn with sarissas held transversely, the infantry leading, followed by the horse, which, says Arrian, could not well make its way until the corn was trampled down. So soon as they came to open ground the infantry, under Nicanor, son of Parmenio, formed square and advanced, leaning its left on the river, while its right was sustained by the horse under Alexander. The Getæ were so utterly dumbfounded at this crossing of the greatest of rivers in a few hours by so large a force that they were ill-prepared to oppose the Macedonians, and fled, at the first attack of the cavalry, towards their city, which was about four miles from the river. Lest there should be an ambush, Alexander continued to march his phalanx in a square, with the left flank leaning upon the river bank; but he vigorously pushed the cavalry on in pursuit of the retreating Getæ. The latter, their city being poorly fortified, attempted no defense, but fled, with as many of their women and children as they could carry upon their horses, to the steppes leading upward from the river. Alexander razed the city to the ground, took the booty, which he appointed Meleager, son of Neoptolemus, and Philip, son of Machatas, to collect and carry away, offered sacrifice to Jupiter, Hercules and the Danube, and recrossed the same day to his camp. He did not care to advance his borders beyond this great natural boundary, for, particularly as the Getæ had been taught to respect his power and prowess, the Danube itself was the best of defenses to his kingdom.

Alexander now received ambassadors from Syrmus and other near-by tribes, asking for the young king's friendship. This was cheerfully granted with mutual pledges. One of these tribes, Celts from the Adriatic region, of gigantic stature and reputed for bravery, came also to beg Alexander's friendship, having heard of his great deeds. Alexander, among other things, asked them what they especially dreaded, expecting they would confess that they most feared his anger. But his astonishment and chagrin were marked when they replied that they were afraid of no one, and feared nothing except that the sky might some day fall upon them.

Alexander.
(From a Statue in the Dresden Museum.)

XVI.

PELIUM. B. C. 335.

ALEXANDER now marched southwesterly towards Pelium, where the Illyrians
had rendezvoused. This town lay in the only gap in the range which bounded
Macedon on the west, and was an outpost necessary to the security of the land.
Unless held, Macedon was never safe from attack, and now the enemy had seized
it. Alexander feared that he might be cut off from the nearest road to Greece,
— where trouble was again brewing, — as well as from Pella, and be forced
to make a long circuit in retreat. But he reached the gap in season to forestall
these dangers. In the gap he was, however, cut off from rations, and so vastly
outnumbered that he was unable to make headway against the barbarians, who
surrounded him and threatened his communications. By an equally ingenious
and brilliant stratagem Alexander reëstablished himself, and awaiting a suitable opportunity he fell on the enemy, unprepared, and inflicted a stinging
defeat upon him. This resulted in the recapture of Pelium, and the Illyrians
were glad to sue for peace. His barbarian neighbors on all sides were now
well checked.

HAVING by the victories over the Getæ and the Triballians
rendered innocuous the tribes along the course of the Danube,
the Macedonians now turned southward toward the land of
the friendly Agrianians and Pæonians. Here Alexander first
learned the revolt of the Illyrian tribes under Clitus and
Glaucias, already referred to. He heard that they were holding the passes of Pelium and had taken this city. He also
heard that the Autariatians proposed to attack him on his
way through the mountains towards Pelium, they having
made common cause with the other barbarians.

Alexander's situation was far from bright. The pass of
Pelium, through which flowed the Aordaicus or Apsos (De-
vol) River, was the one available gap through the range which
divided Illyria from upper Macedonia. Its possession was

the sole means of keeping the western tribes back of the watershed. He himself was heading for this locality along the Erygon. Should the Autariatians fall upon his flank on the march, as they threatened to do, their diversion might retard him so much that the Illyrians would find time to invade and inflict immense damage on southern Macedonia before he could reach the scene of action. Or in fact, as he had already advanced too far between the mountain ranges readily to return, the Illyrians might cut him off from Greece (which rumor said was again becoming restless) by seizing the passes on the line of the Erygon, while keeping open their own communications and their entrance to Macedon by way of Pelium. This would be a most serious check, perhaps a fatal one, to his Grecian affairs, by giving Thebes and Athens time for preparation, not to speak of the danger to his own territory from the uncivilized but brave and skillful Illyrians. Philotas, to be sure, held the Cadmæa at Thebes ; Parmenio, at home, had a goodly force of troops on hand, but even these two were scarcely equal to so large an undertaking as another uprising in Greece, coupled with an incursion into Macedon by Clitus and Glaucias.

The gap of Pelium had been seized by Philip as the result of many wars. It lies southeast of Lake Lychnitis (Ochrida), and is long and narrow, but widens out at intervals into larger valleys. Through its entire length flows the Apsos to the west into the Adriatic. Whoever holds the gap commands not only this river but the headwaters of the Erygon (Tzerna), which from this point flows northeasterly, and of the Haliacmon (Jendje Karasu), which flows through southern Macedonia, as well. Pelium was a mountain fastness of the greatest importance; and the town had considerable strength. In the heart of the mountains, it was for the Macedonians an outwork which protected the road running along the valleys of the Erygon and the Haliacmon, and one which must at any cost be held as a barrier against the restless barbarians of Illyria. The town lay in a wide plain in the mountains, and fully commanded the road through the gap. This road most of the way ran along the rocky precipices bordering the Apsos, and in places was so narrow that but four men could march abreast. The game was really a serious one for Alexander. A slight failure, and he would forfeit the western security of his kingdom, conquered by Philip with so much bloodshed; and as he was already engaged in the mountain ranges, the Illyrians could now readily interpose between him and Pella, which Alexander could then only reach by a countermarch and circuit of many days; and even this march in retreat might be cut off by the Autariatians. A serious backset would forfeit perhaps the control he now held in Greece. The king's Persian expedition looked far off indeed.

The danger from the Autariatians, however, was happily disposed of. Langarus, king of the Agrianians, of old a faithful personal friend of Alexander, and whose contingent in the late campaign on the Danube had behaved with splendid hardihood, now came to meet the king with his best troops and volunteered himself to keep the Autariatians busy by attacking them and making inroads into their country. This service he performed in so workmanlike a manner that the Autariatians, not a very warlike race, were fain to keep to their hills. For this kindly and efficient service Langarus was rewarded by Alexander with many proofs of friendship, and the promise of his half-sister Cyna's hand, — which, however, Langarus did not live to claim. We shall constantly refer to the gallant Agrianians who accompanied Alexander to Asia. They were among the bravest and most efficient of his light troops.

This initial danger put one side, Alexander advanced on

Pelium by forced marches up the Erygon and towards the gap. Clitus had already seized Pelium, and there he was awaiting the arrival of Glaucias, king of the Taulantians. Alexander hoped to recapture the town before the arrival of Glaucias, but Clitus held all the heights in the vicinity, intending to fall upon Alexander's rear if he advanced near enough to make an assault on the city.

Alexander camped on the Apsos and prepared for immediate attack. According to the barbarian custom of his tribe, as Arrian relates, Clitus, before meeting the Macedonians, offered up in sacrifice three boys, three girls and three black rams, and then made disposition to fall upon them. Despite the difficulties, Alexander was by no means to be deterred

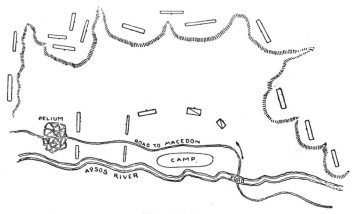

Plain of Pelium.

from his purpose, and opened the action by an advance upon the heights held by the Illyrians. This was made with such vigor that they were unable to stand their ground. The assault resulted in their retiring into the town and shutting themselves up within its walls. Alexander, having failed to capture the town by first assault, then began to erect lines of contravallation and circumvallation. But this was next day interrupted by the arrival of Glaucias with an overwhelming force, who seized and occupied the heights around the eastern side of the valley in which Alexander was camped, so that should he again assault the town they could take him in rear and perhaps seize his line of retreat.

Alexander was seriously involved, for the enemy outnumbered him many times. Victory was essential to him in his situation here. He could not afford the slightest check. Not only time but supplies were scant. He was in great stress for both rations and forage. Sending Philotas one day, with some horsemen and pack-animals, on a foraging excursion, the latter was followed and surrounded by Glaucias, who took possession of the hills about the plains where he was collecting corn. Philotas was with the utmost difficulty rescued by Alexander, who hurried to his assistance with the hypaspists, Agrianians and bowmen, sustained by some four hundred cavalry, and by a timely diversion enabled him to cut his way out. The king was neither strong enough to cope with the barbarians, unless he could lure them into a pitched battle, nor had he food sufficient to last until he could procure reinforcements.

Clitus and Glaucias, on the contrary, could afford to sit still and wait. They held the key of the situation. They had their breadstuffs available and their communications open, and had no other business on hand than to hold the pass. They were wise enough to be shy of battle. They congratulated themselves that Alexander was so seriously compromised that they would by and by have him at their mercy. They held all the heights about Pelium, the garrison of which could debouch on Alexander's rear as they upon his flanks should he retreat from the plain where he was camped. Moreover, his only line of retreat lay through the narrow defile by which he had come, between the precipices and the river, where but four men could march abreast. The army must ford the river on its way towards the gap, which gave the barbarians a still greater advantage; for they held the heights which commanded the ford as well as the entire valley, and had sent detachments along the hills to command the road on which lay the Macedonian line of retreat. They were a warlike and well-armed people, and their confidence was so high that they were apt to do stanch fighting. The heavy woods on all hands offered them a chance for ambuscade whenever any part of the army was sent out in search of provisions. Alexander's position was well-nigh desperate. And yet he must have Pelium.

The young king had no idea of retreat. Neither would he wait for reinforcements. His natural impatience stood him in good stead. This problem must be worked out successfully, or he could not attempt to leave Greece for Asia; and quickly, or the Greek insurrection would gain too much headway to be handled without vast trouble. The first step in the problem was to make secure his line of retreat, now dangerously threatened. He conceived one of those brilliant ideas which only emanate from the brain of a man of genius. He resolved to impose on the enemy by a display of military manœuvring, a battlefield drill, as it were; and having thus made him uncertain of how he might be about to attack him, seek to fall on him at a disadvantage. While the horse and light foot were thrown out towards the town, the king accordingly drew up his phalanx with files one hundred and twenty men deep, placed some cavalry on each wing to protect the manœuvres, and began, in the middle of the plain, in full sight of the enemy, who was also drawn up in battle array on the heights surrounding the plain and at the town, a series of those incomparable evolutions which only a Macedonian phalanx could execute. Imagine the splendor of this hostile

review, with its holiday aspect and its deadly intent; the hills
and the walls of the town crowded with myriads of wonder-
ing barbarians; the Macedonian soldiers in equal wonder as
to what their chief was about to do, but trusting with blind
confidence that this young king, of whom they were so proud,
would wield their skill and courage as he could his own good
sword. Never was so curious, so magnificent a ruse employed
in war before; never since.

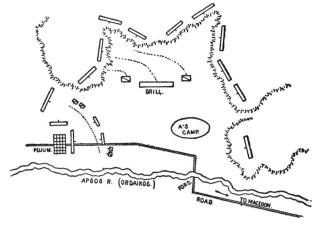

Pelium Manœuvre.

The phalangites drilled in perfect quiet, with set teeth and
purpose, listening intently for the commands which the bugles
rang out sharp and clear. First they smartly couched their
spears at the word of command, and then as smartly shoul-
dered them, each with the thud of a perfect manual; going
through their times and motions with the precision of an inspection at Pella. Next they faced to the right, and couched
their spears as if to attack the enemy on that front; but
instead of so doing were again made to rehearse the manual.
Again the phalanx was faced to the left as if for similar purpose, and on each occasion the enemy on the threatened side

made ready to resist or fly should the phalanx advance. Then Alexander marched and countermarched the body by either flank, going through the complicated drill of which Philip's phalanx was supreme master.

The enemy, who had been watching this parade with amazement almost amounting to awe, and whose uncertainty as to what it all meant gradually made him careless of his own formation, was quite unprepared for a real attack, for this drill must have lasted some time. Suddenly, as it were a part of this wonderful review, Alexander ployed his phalanx into a wedge and launched it at a *pas de charge* by the left flank at that part of the enemy's army which was nearest him and most open to attack. The barbarians made not even a pretense of sustaining the shock, but at once fled from the lower mountain ridges. Hereupon Alexander gave the Macedonians the order to raise their war-cry and clash their spears upon their shields. Still more alarmed, the Triballians, who had so far been outside the gates, retired precipitately into the town.

A small force still remained on one of the ridges which especially commanded Alexander's line of retreat and the river-ford over which he must cross. To dislodge this he hurried the Companion cavalry and some light horse towards the ridge, with orders for half of them to dismount and fight on foot if the enemy remained to defend the place. For mounted men alone might not suffice. It will be seen that Alexander found useful, as we did in 1861–65, that species of cavalry which could fight on foot as well as mounted. Traversing, as he often did, a rugged country, to perform this double duty made his horse doubly valuable. This same cavalry we shall see doing as splendid work in the saddle as the most exacting *beau sabreur* could demand; in fact, work never surpassed in the world's history, despite the idea so often expressed that to dismount a cavalryman spoils him. No defense was attempted by the enemy to this last attack, but he withdrew in disorder right and left and made for the mountains. Alexander took possession of the hill which was the key to the ford, and posted the Agrianians and archers upon it, some two thousand strong.

This dispersion of the enemy afforded him means of safely passing the river, where he could be more secure from sudden attack, to which he had laid himself open from there being but one ford. The hypaspists and the heavy infantry were ordered to wade the river first and form at once into phalanx towards the left so as to present as imposing an array as possible, and the king gave instructions to set the artillery in battery for the moral effect of its novelty on the Illyrians. He himself remained on the hill to observe the operations. The barbarians, perceiving that their foe was about to escape, came down from the surrounding heights to which they had again returned when they saw the Macedonians, as they thought, taking to flight by the ford. They hoped to be able to attack their rear. But Alexander was closely scanning their movements. As they drew near he headed against them his own brigade — the companion agema — with an impetuous rush and its terrible battle-cry, and the phalanx made motion as if to advance again across the river. This attack and simulated advance drove the barbarians back, and the pause enabled Alexander to get the Agrianians and archers over the ford.

To sustain this operation the military engines (of which he had brought an ample number from the arsenal at Pella) showered projectiles of all kinds upon the enemy. This is the first record of the use of artillery in battle. The archers also from mid-river turned and sent their flights of arrows at the barbarians, who, under Glaucias' incitement, constantly returned to the attack By these means, Glaucias being unable to breast the storm of missiles, Alexander with the whole army gained the other side in safety.

The first step was successfully taken. The line of retreat was secure. Alexander had fought in the van, as all through his life he did, and had been wounded by a sling-stone upon the head and by the blow of a club upon the neck. Not a man, however, was killed during this well-managed manœuvre. Numbers were wounded, but the excellent armor of the Macedonians saved them from fatal casualties as much as the weaker weapons of the barbarians. It is to be noted that the killed among the light troops were not generally deemed of sufficient moment to record.

Alexander had gained a place of safety. His late position in front of Pelium had been untenable, for he was surrounded by multitudes and was cut off from victual. But he was far from content. He was unwilling to retire without inflicting a signal defeat on the barbarians and recovering Pelium. He was now placed so that he could collect corn and await reinforcements. The enemy could not cut him off from the supplies in his rear. But a retreat, happily, was not made necessary, for time was of the utmost consequence. Three days after the crossing, Alexander's scouts, whom he always kept briskly at work, reported to him that Clitus and Glaucias, who no doubt flattered themselves that he had retired from fear and who were becoming careless accordingly, lay in a negligent position in front of Pelium, with no outposts, ditch or rampart, and in much too extended an order. This was the opportunity Alexander had been watching for. As night came on he crossed the ford with his shield-bearing guards, the Agrianians, archers and the brigades of Perdiccas, son of Orontes, and Cœnus, son-in-law of Parmenio, as vanguard. So soon as he arrived on the ground, without waiting for the rest of the troops, which had been ordered to follow rapidly on his heels, he launched the Agrianians and archers, formed in phalangial order, upon the flank of the barbarians' camp and took them *en flagrant délit.* Many were caught in their beds; all were taken by surprise. The rout was complete. Numbers were slaughtered, numbers captured. Those who escaped lost their weapons. Alexander pursued the relics of this force as far as the Taulantian Mountains. Clitus fled into the city, but finding that he could not hold it, set it on fire and withdrew to join Glaucias, near the Adriatic coast.

Thus Alexander regained Pelium and reëstablished the outpost which was so essential to the security of Macedonia. Clitus and Glaucias were glad to accept terms and again swear fealty to Alexander. The position was put into such a state of defense that no fear remained of its falling again into Illyrian hands. The barbarian neighbors of Macedonia had received a series of salutary lessons, and recognized that a greater than Philip now sat upon the throne.

Tetradrachma in Louvre.
(Head of Alexander, idealized as Hercules.)

XVII.

THEBES. B. C. 335.

THE Persian monarch had foreseen the threatening danger to his kingdom from restless Alexander. He began to distribute money among the anti-Macedonians of Greece. The rumor of the death of Alexander before Pelium determined Thebes to revolt and eject the Macedonian garrison from the Cadmæa. Athens and other cities promised active aid. So soon as Pelium was taken Alexander marched rapidly southward. In two weeks he covered three hundred miles over a mountain road, and appeared suddenly before Thebes. He was anxious to save the city, but the misguided Thebans pronounced their own doom. The town was stormed, sacked and razed to the ground, and the Theban territory added to that of its neighbors, late its vassals. Athens begged off. In one year this young king of twenty had firmly seated himself on his throne, had made himself master of Greece, had utterly defeated the Danube barbarians, had reduced the Illyrians to obedience and had welded the shackles on Hellas. He was now ready for Persia.

THE king of Persia, foreseeing grave danger to himself and his kingdom from this youthful but vigorous monarch, who on his side made small secret of his intentions, in addition to sending Memnon the Rhodian, his most able general, to Asia Minor to oppose the Macedonians there, began to distribute money in Greece to induce the cities to take up arms against Macedon and their new autocrat. The long absence of Alexander on his Illyrian expedition and the lack of news from him had given rise to rumors that he and his army had been destroyed by the barbarians. A man, in fact, is said to have reached Athens, — at all events Demosthenes produced such an one, — who pretended to show a wound received before Pelium, and who stated that he saw Alexander receive his death-blow. The man may have had a fair basis for his story.

Some of the Theban exiles in Athens deemed the occasion good for throwing off the Macedonian yoke. The Cadmæa or citadel of Thebes, situated on an eminence in the town, had, since the battle of Chæronæa, been held by a Macedonian garrison. These exiles proceeded to Thebes, hoping to surprise the Cadmæa, and, being admitted to the city at night by friends, they met and slew two Macedonian officers who, in no expectation of mutiny, had descended from the citadel, incited the national assembly to revolt, and persuaded the populace to reinstate the Bœotarchs and again proclaim the independence of Thebes. Several of the neighboring cities declared themselves ready to do the like, and Thebes was promised help from many quarters. Her plausible excuse was that she believed Alexander to be dead, and her allegiance *ipso facto* at an end.

So soon as the news of the event reached Alexander, he foresaw grave danger to his standing in Greece unless the revolt was summarily nipped in the bud. The vote creating him Hegemōn had been passed under the pressure of an army on the spot. Sparta had been constant in her enmity. Athens was half-hearted. It would be easy to raise a powerful coalition against him. The Illyrian question had just been happily settled. It was here that began the remarkable series of fortunate events which always seemed to run in Alexander's favor, which always, when the sky was most threatening, blew away the clouds.

Fortune is said to be and is generally of a man's own making. So long as he will not allow circumstances to dictate to him, fortune is apt to be constant. When he begins to heed adverse facts, we see what is generally called bad luck step in. This is undeniably true. But it is equally true that the utmost ability sometimes runs foul of uncontrollable circumstances. No one can study the careers of Alexander and of

Hannibal without acknowledging that, with equal capacity, equal determination to control circumstances, the former had fortune uniformly in his favor, the latter misfortune as constantly staring him in the face. If a skillful general wins

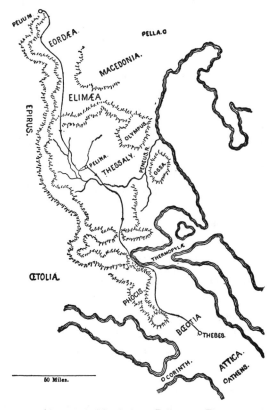

Alexander's March from Pelium to Thebes.

because he is opposed by crass stupidity, must it not be set down to good luck that he did not happen to be matched by talent equal to his own? It is in this sense that Alexander's luck is referred to, and in such a sense only can luck be said to exist for the captain. Fortune is and should be almost uniformly of his own creation.

Alexander at once started by rapid marches for Greece. His route lay through Eordæa and Elimæa in Macedon, and along the uplands — the peaks, says Arrian — of the Pindus range. Alexander probably selected the higher foot-hills because along these the rivers were smaller than in the plains. It was a choice of evils he had to make between mountain roads and unfordable rivers. In seven days he reached Pelina, on the Peneus, in Thessaly. Thence in six days he entered Bœotia. Alexander's celerity of movement in this case was undoubtedly supplemented by good fortune; but the gods help those who help themselves, and the king never failed to put his own shoulder to the wheel. No character in history ever exceeded him in constant personal endeavor. So speedy was this march that the Thebans did not even know of his passing Thermopylæ until he reached Onchestus, fifty stades, less than six miles, northwest of their city. Even then his enemies continued to maintain that the son of Philip was dead, and that Antipater commanded the army, or else the Lyncestian Alexander. For Alexander, as narrated, had really been wounded by a club and a stone in the last battle, and the belief in the fatal nature of these wounds was universal. If the Danube and Illyrian campaigns leave one full of astonishment at their rapidity, energy and able management, this march of over three hundred miles, through a rugged mountain country, in a fortnight, with a considerable army of foot and horse, the equivalent of our artillery, and no doubt some trains, worthily caps the climax.

Alexander's appearance at once caused all her allies again to fall away from Thebes. Even Athens preferred to await events. Thebes stood alone.

Alexander desired to be just as well as to save his men.
He moved slowly on the city, so as to afford the Thebans time
to send an embassy and
crave pardon (August, 335
B. C.). He camped north of
and over against the city,
and waited. Diodorus and
Curtius place his force at
thirty thousand foot and
three thousand horse. But
far from acting on a peaceful policy, the Thebans
boastingly sent out their
cavalry and light troops
and made a determined
attack on Alexander's outposts. This attack was
repulsed by a body of
archers and heavy foot at
the moment it had all but
reached the Macedonian
camp. Alexander now

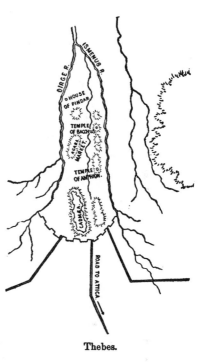

Thebes.

moved around the city and encamped opposite the gate which
led to Attica, thus cutting the Thebans off from Athens, as
well as placing himself in view of the Cadmæa, and close to
it, for here the Cadmæa touched the city wall. The Thebans
inside had blockaded the Macedonian garrison in the citadel,
and had fortified their position with an outer stockade besides,
in order to forestall assistance. They now began to push the
siege. Alexander was still patient. He sent to demand the
two ringleaders, Phœnix and Prothytes, but promised the
status quo ante to all others who might surrender. The bulk
of the citizens were for giving in, but the exiles, with whom

it was neck or nothing, left no stone unturned to hold them up to their work. The demand was refused. Still Alexander was unwilling to attack. His moderation certainly savors of a kindly motive, for it was unusual with him. He wished to save the splendid city, as well, no doubt, as loss in his own ranks.

The Thebans, however, by this obstinate perversity, sealed their own doom. Alexander, says Diodorus, made all his plans for an assault; but, according to Ptolemy, he still put off his action. The delay was, however, brought to an end by Perdiccas with the first brigade, who, without distinct orders, but seeing a favorable chance, assaulted the Theban lines. After breaking the outer stockade, or city wall, with his engines, he mounted the breach and fell upon the siege lines of the Thebans. Amyntas, whose brigade was next to that of Perdiccas, followed close on his heels with his own troops. Alexander, seeing that Perdiccas and Amyntas had made a lodgment, and, lest their isolated brigades should become compromised, threw forward the entire force of light troops, archers, and Agrianians, which had been held close by as supports, giving them instructions to press on after Perdiccas and Amyntas, and held the agema and the other hypaspists for the nonce farther in the rear and on the outside, as a reserve.

Perdiccas was severely wounded in carrying the second stockade; but his men drove the enemy into a hollow way leading to the temple of Hercules, and followed them as far as the temple itself. Here the Thebans rallied, and with a desperate onslaught pushed back the two Macedonian brigades and the light troops. The latter lost their chief and fell into some disorder upon the reserves. The Thebans followed hard upon. Alexander was well prepared to receive them; and as he moved upon them, somewhat disorganized by their success, in regular phalangial order, he drove them back into the gates and entered with them. A sally from the Cadmæan garrison was made at the same moment towards the temple of Amphion. The walls were swept by a force taking their defenders in flank right and left, and were captured. Connection with the garrison of the Cadmæa was reëstablished. A stand was attempted by the Thebans in the market-place as well as opposite the temple of Amphion, but Alexander's phalanxes quickly routed the few who awaited their onset.

The Theban cavalry fled from the city, while the infantry dispersed wherever it could find an outlet, fighting for their lives in isolated bodies, but bravely as of yore. Numbers were slaughtered, more by the Bœotians, Phocians, and Platæans than by the Macedonians, who, says Curtius, did not join in the massacre. For the former had an old score to settle with Thebes for many years' oppressions. Even women and children did not escape. Nor was house or temple or altar a protection. There fell that day five hundred Macedonians. Adding the wounded, this was a loss of about seventeen per cent., — a high average. Six thousand Thebans were slain; thirty thousand were sold into slavery. These latter are said to have brought about five hundred and thirty-five thousand dollars, not quite eighteen dollars each. This is an interesting gauge of values at that time, though the number probably glutted the market. In later days Alexander repented of the cruelty perpetrated at Thebes, believing that he had offended Bacchus, its tutelary deity, who therefore looked with unfavoring eyes upon some of his subsequent exploits.

The celerity and power of Alexander's blow made a deep impression throughout Greece. Athens was in no condition to oppose the conqueror. Sparta was amazed to see the city which under Epaminondas had humbled her at Leuctra and Mantinæa, broken to pieces as if by the arm of a demigod. The Thebans were believed to be under the ban of the gods, and Alexander the favored of Olympus.

The king allowed his allies, whom Thebes had for years oppressed, to settle the affairs of the city. Thebes was razed to the ground. Only those connected with Philip and Alexander by ties of hospitality, and the house of Pindar the poet, were spared. The Cadmæa was again occupied by a Macedonian garrison. Theban territory was parceled out among the allies. Thus miserably perished the proud city of Epaminondas (September, 335 B. C.). Its fate, when we remember this splendid chief, evokes our compassion. Orchomenus and Platæa, which Thebes had destroyed, were rebuilt.

The Athenians had gone so far towards aiding Thebes as to send forward troops to join her. These they speedily recalled on hearing of her fate. The Ætolians and Elæans had also erred, but all hastened to send ambassadors to crave forgiveness. This was universally granted, no doubt quite as much because Alexander was anxious to set out on his expedition to Asia as from generous motives. Though he by no means lacked these, Alexander always knew when and how to supplement punishment with clemency as mere political expediency. Athens likewise sent an embassy to deprecate the king's wrath. Alexander at first demanded the surrender of nine men who had particularly inveighed against him, including Demosthenes; but, on an urgent appeal from the city, wisely consented to forego this demand. He insisted only on Charidemus being exiled. This was done, and Charidemus went into the service of King Darius, to be later executed by his new master, as we shall see. Alexander returned to Macedon in the fall.

For the coming dozen years, until Alexander's death, the history of Greece is practically a blank. The land of heroes became a mere appanage of Alexander's great empire in the East. Internal broils and constantly recurring ebullitions of opposition to Macedon monopolized Hellenic politics.

Thus in one brief year Alexander had settled himself firmly upon his throne, had made himself secure against his barbarian neighbors, had nullified his Grecian brethren, and could safely turn to the Asiatic problem which was to be his life's work, as it was his life's ambition. Surely a wonderful first twelvemonth for a monarch of twenty years. The coming weeks were full of restless business in assembling his army, equipping his ships, and in studying out the vast problem before him, — the most vast ever attacked by man. The more important part of his military life now begins.

Alexander.
(From Bust in Louvre.)

XVIII.

OFF FOR ASIA. B. C. 334.

ALEXANDER probably possessed all the existing information with regard to the topography and resources of Persia; but this only reached as far as the Euphrates. Beyond this all was guess-work or dream. On what he knew he founded careful calculations. He was heavily in debt, but he started with thirty thousand infantry, five thousand cavalry and a month's supplies. He had no fleet worth the mention. Antipater was left at home with twelve thousand foot and fifteen hundred horse to keep order in Hellas. The Persian kingdom was enormous in extent, population and wealth; but it lacked cohesion. Each satrap was a sort of independent monarch, and jealous of all his neighbors. This condition greatly facilitated Alexander's plans. Persia was ripe for a fall. The army marched along the coast, in twenty days reached the Hellespont, and crossed to Asia Minor in safety. Alexander visited Troy and offered due sacrifices to the manes of Homeric heroes.

IN narrating the life of Alexander two extreme theories have been enunciated. The expedition against Persia has been treated as the act of a half-mad adventurer, a soldier of fortune, whose erratic visions were moulded into action by a wild, unreasoning will and absolute power over his small monarchy, and whose success was due to hairbrained courage and proverbial good luck. It has been treated as a deliberate, well-digested scheme, having as a basis a profound knowledge of all the countries, governments, resources, geographical limitations and military power he was to encounter; about such knowledge, in fact, as Napoleon possessed himself of before entering on the Russian campaign. Each of these extreme theories is far from being exact; but granting the abnormal good fortune which was pleased to wait on Alexander's intelligence, and on his courage, moral and physical, there is no doubt that the latter is the more reasonable point of view. What the ancient world had so far learned Alexander had by heart. Why should he not, with Aristotle for a tutor?

We know comparatively little about the extent of Alexander's information respecting the Persian kingdom. Asia Minor had long been full of Greeks with whom there was constant intercourse. This portion of the Great King's dominions was no doubt familiar to him. Beyond this point, Alexander had perhaps nothing but Xenophon's Anabasis and the unsatisfactory Cyropædia to guide him. Travelers then, as in modern times, lied by authority. Greek mercenaries who had been in Persian pay might have observed but partially. The Persian history of Ctesias he may never have seen. Artabazus and Memnon, distinguished men both, had been refugees at the court of Pella, and could have told much. Persian ambassadors could be interrogated. How carefully these sources of information had been used cannot be said. We know that Alexander's habit in all his campaigns was to gather information with scrupulous care; we can imagine that he had got together a fair nucleus of facts to serve him as guide so far as the Euphrates, though the actual obstacles and enormous distances to be encountered could scarcely have been fully comprehended, even by him. Beyond the Euphrates was a blank or a dream.

But Alexander had one peculiarly marked power. He could generalize from specific facts with astonishing accuracy; he could gauge the exact value in a problem of one or two isolated facts. There is no mark of the perfect military grasp so positive as the power of seeing the whole without being misled by the parts; of never allowing detail to obscure the main purpose; of properly interpreting partial signs. All Alexander's campaigns exhibit this ability in an exceptional degree, and it is fair to infer that from even the paucity of

detail he may have possessed on the to him all-important subject, he had been able to construct the skeleton of his plan, at
least as far as the great river on which lies Babylon.

That his imagination carried him beyond this there can be
no doubt. All great captains have possessed an abundant
share of imagination, or its complement, enthusiasm. But
they have kept it well under control. In this quality Alexander was preëminent. We know that Philip had long cher-
ished the plan of an invasion of Asia, and Alexander had
grown up with this plan as a part of his daily food. All
things tend to show that preparations were for years constantly and persistently made tending towards this object.
Few things tell historical truths better than the coinage of the
ancient countries. And in the coinage of Macedon, and of
the cities of Asia Minor, during the reign of Philip, and constantly and for many years succeeding Alexander's campaigns, one may read the early purpose of conquest of both
father and son.

The policy of Macedon so far had not demanded of Greece
the aid of a fleet. With such assistance as Greece could have
given Alexander might have seized the Ægean, and placed
his projected campaign on a much more certain basis. But
it was now too late to do this. He must rely on his land
forces alone. Fleets then were more readily equipped and
got to sea than they are to-day, but still it would have caused
some months of delay to prepare a suitable squadron. Alexander was impatient of every moment; and it is moreover
probable that even he did not entirely recognize its value.
His finest quality was the power of quickly and thoroughly
learning from experience. He often divined, almost, long
before the event. But the full advantages of a fleet had probably not as yet gained access to his mind. Alexander had
until now seen war only on land. He had but one hundred
and sixty triremes.

Wise preparations were duly made to leave Macedonia in safety. The chiefs of most of the allied nations were to accompany the king, with their contingents generally officered by the more prominent citizens, thus insuring the good behavior of their respective countries. Antipater was to be left as regent, with a sufficient force of Macedonians to command respect. Entreated by Antipater and Parmenio to marry and await the arrival of an heir before going forth, Alexander rejected the advice as unworthy when Persia stood all ready for the fray. Should he await the arrival of the fleet of the Great King on the shores of Macedon, or the crossing of the Taurus by his army? If he expected to utilize Asia Minor as a base, there was not a moment to be lost. He must seize it before it was still more strongly occupied by the enemy. The Persian dependencies in Phœnicia and Cyprus, which furnished the best mariners of the day, could put four hundred vessels into commission at the first call. All Greece could not equal this complement. The Persian armies were numberless, and day by day might inundate Asia Minor. How would he then be able even to open his campaign? He must do so now before the road was blocked.

So complete were Alexander's preparations for a long, even permanent, absence that he is said to have given away all his personal possessions and effects, — mostly to his friends to aid them to defray the heavy expenses of equipment, — leaving himself, as he laughingly said, only his "hopes." His conduct roused his Companions to the highest pitch of enthusiasm, and many of the rich ones among them did the like. This anecdote is probably exaggerated. But it shows the spirit which prevailed, the birth of which lay in Alexander's enthusiasm.

Philip had died owing five hundred talents for money spent in perfecting the army. Before leaving Macedon Alexander

borrowed eight hundred talents more. He started heavily
handicapped, with but sixty talents of ready money left. He
needed his " hopes."

The monarchy of Persia was ripe for a fall. Its overgrown
body had long been diseased. If it did not die of one, it
must of another cause. Its one protection against the restless
efforts of Greece had long been money, which, judiciously
disbursed among the several cities, kept them at odds with
one another, and prevented their joining hands in an attack
on Persia. But Macedon had risen superior to the effects of
this pusillanimous policy, and now stood knocking at its gates.

Darius had, as we have seen, sent Memnon, the Rhodian, to
oppose Parmenio and Attalus in Asia Minor. These generals
had conducted a campaign of no particular moment in Mysia.
Attalus had been executed for treason by Alexander's command, and his troops, after momentary hesitation, had returned to their fidelity and were again concentrated under
Parmenio, the ever faithful. The campaign was not prolific
of results, but the points essential to protect Alexander's
crossing had been secured and held, as it were, by bridge-
heads. Memnon was an excellent soldier, and it looks to us
strange that he did not succeed in brushing away the Macedonian force here, particularly after Parmenio was recalled to
the capital, just before the Danube and Pelium campaign ; but
we may look for an explanation in the fact that the jealousy
of the Persian satraps so constantly broke forth against every
Greek in authority, that he was usually prevented from anything like vigorous action by the reduction of the means at
his disposal and the consequent tying of his hands. All this
again was Alexander's luck. Memnon unfettered might have
stemmed the tide setting against Persia.

Persia had recently reconquered Egypt and Phœnicia, principally through the aid of Greek mercenaries under Mentor,

the Rhodian. Mentor had afterwards become commander-in-chief of the entire Hellespontine region, and had placed under him Memnon, who was his brother, and Artabazus, his brother-in-law. But Mentor was now dead, and the work had devolved on Memnon. The Persian royal line of Ochus had been poisoned wholesale by the eunuch Bagoas, and Darius Codomanus of the line of Artaxerxes Mnemon had been placed upon the throne. On the death of Philip, Darius, who came into power about this time, imagined the youthful Alexander to be unequal to the invasion of Asia, and became careless of defense, deeming a distribution of money among the anti-Macedonians of Greece a sufficient means of keeping him at home. Memnon was better informed, and advised the king wisely; but he was not listened to. Darius possessed qualities which, under less unfavorable auspices, might have made him a successful, as he was a wise and just king. Nothing short of the overwhelming career of such a man as Alexander, whose onward course seemed to be irresistible, can explain the hebetude and inaction into which Darius now fell.

The kingdom of Persia was a disjointed mass, whose several parts were under dissatisfied satraps having no longer a binding tie to the ruling sovereign. They were, on the contrary, by no means disinclined to welcome any new conqueror. Though nominally one empire, it was really a host of minor kingdoms, with little or no interdependence. No doubt Alexander was as well acquainted with the political and geographical status of western Persia as he was with all which was then known of the art of war. The mutual jealousies and constant bickerings, almost rising to a condition of warfare, between neighboring satraps, opened the door to easy success for Alexander if he but took advantage of the situation. This he was prepared to do. His army was not only passionately attached to its young commander, but was eager for the spoils of the richest of countries, which it knew would be, and which in fact were, most lavishly distributed to all by Alexander. The generals, as we shall see, became greater than princes; even the private soldier grew to untold wealth, compared to what he had possessed at home, in recompense for his bravery and toils.

Having completed his preparations for home rule and foreign warfare, Alexander felt that he could safely leave Macedon. His expedition against Persia, ostensibly to free the Greek colonies under Persian rule, was so popular throughout Greece, despite the secret cabals of malcontents, always more or less pronounced, that a force stated at seven thousand Greek allies and five thousand mercenaries was put at his disposal. As an assumed descendant of Achilles, he could claim an inherited right to lead such an expedition. After his return from his Theban expedition to Macedonia, he had spent the winter in the hard labors of preparation, alternating with sacrifices and games in honor of the gods. Of his two most trusted lieutenants, he planned to take Parmenio with him, and leave Antipater behind, who, though the queen-mother, Olympias, and he were always at odds, was the only man on whom he could rely to carry on the government wisely and firmly during his probably extended absence.

Early in the spring of 334 B. C., leaving with Antipater a force of twelve thousand foot and fifteen hundred horse, with which he was charged to keep Greece in subjection, resist Persian fleets, and hold Macedonia against the malcontents or aspirants to the throne; and assuring Antipater's fidelity by taking with him the latter's three sons, Alexander marched towards the Hellespont. He had about thirty thousand foot and five thousand horse, — a small force indeed with which to attack the myriads of the Great King, to undertake an invasion destined to change the current of the world's history, — and only the paltry remnants of such moneys in his camp-chest as he had been able to borrow.

He was about to invade the land of Xerxes, of Cyrus, a land of untold resources and wealth, full of brave and able men, but a land rotten to the core. The weakness of Persia, though it exceeded his own territorial limit thirty to one, was its lack of homogeneity. Composed of many kingdoms, as it were, each success of Alexander's would place under his control (so long as he continued to be victorious) such territory as the victory was won upon. Alexander was aware of, and proposed to rely upon, this, for him, fortunate set of conditions, together with a free-handed policy of rewards to his officers and men, as well as to such of Darius' servants as should volunteer to join his cause. He intended to forage on the country as he advanced.

Following was the organization of his army: —

1. CAVALRY.

Heavy :

Macedonian hetairai, Companions, under Philotas, 8 Ilē, 150 @ 300 each		. 1,800	
Thessalians, next in reputation, under	Calas, 8 Ilē .	. 1,200	
Greek auxiliaries "	Philip, 8 " .	. 400	3,400

Light :

Macedonian lancers, Prodromoi, under	Amyntas, 4 Ilē	. 600	
Pæonians, " "	Ariston, 4 "	600	
Odryssians, "	Agatho, 8 "	. 600	1,800
Total cavalry			5,200

2. INFANTRY.

Phalangites :

Macedonian pezetæri, companions, in six small brigades or taxes, in each of which were, say, six syntagmas of 250 men, or three moras of 500 men, under	⎧ Perdiccas, ⎪ Cœnus, ⎨ Amyntas, ⎪ Meleager, ⎪ Philip, later Polysperchon, ⎩ Craterus . . .	. 9,000
Greek Auxiliaries, Antigonus commanding, 6 brigades		. 4,000
Greek mercenaries, Menandrus commanding, 6 brigades		. 6,000 19,000

Peltasts :

Macedonian hypaspists (companions), Nicanor comd'g, 5 taxes.

   (These might properly be classed with the phalangites) . 3,000

Greek auxiliaries, commander not named, 5 taxes   .   . 1,000

Greek mercenaries, commander not named, 5 taxes   .   . 1,000

Thracian acontists (javelin men), Sitalces comd'g, 4 taxes . 4,000 9,000

   Light armed :

Macedonian archers,	Clearchus comd'g	.	.	.	.	{ 500
Cretan archers,						500

Agrianian acontists (javelin-men), Attalos comd'g   .   . 1,000 2,000

Total Infantry	30,000
Add Cavalry	5,200
Total	35,200

It will be noticed that the proportions of the troops are not those set down in the organization details above given. No army in active service corresponds strictly to its technical organization. Alexander took with him what he had left after leaving Macedon secure.

No artillery officers are mentioned. The engines no doubt had specially drilled men to work them, but these apparently were not recognized in the specific organization of the army. The same low estimate of artillery officers was apparent in the Middle Ages.

The above named were the original commanders. But active service produced many changes. Later in the war, as will be seen by the list of officers, fourteen others are also mentioned as commanding infantry brigades. Commanders of other corps were also often replaced, and the army, largely by Oriental accretions, grew to be one hundred and forty thousand strong in India.

The Macedonians, Greeks and allies were generally recruited in localities and kept together as much as possible, so as to breed rivalry and a proper *esprit de corps*. Whether the Thracians, Agrianians, Odryssians and Pæonians were all allies, or partly mercenary, is not known. The allies enlisted "for the war," as it were; the mercenaries for set terms. The aristocrats owed service with their fealty; the regulars served very long terms. The Greek auxiliaries and mercenaries were often mixed with the Macedonian troops in actual service — so many lochoi or syntagmas of one to an equal number of the other.

We are obliged to draw largely on guess-work for the size of the baggage-train which accompanied Alexander's army. The artillery — it is surely proper so to call the missile-throwing engines — needed horses, though nothing like the number called for by our guns; for many of the heavier parts of the engines, the beams, etc., and of the larger missiles, were not transported, but cut on the spot. Ammunition was always readily procured. Still, rations had to be carried, and forage. Philip had cut down the several slaves a mounted man had been allowed to one. This one was probably also mounted, and if he had to carry forage for his master's as well as his own animal, he would need a pack-horse. This alone would multiply the cavalry contingent by three. Each ten phalangites were, at the time of the strictest reduction, allowed one slave, and probably a pack-horse. Headquarters must have considerable transportation. On the whole, the train of the Macedonian army could not have fallen very much short of ours, especially when booty and women were allowed to be carried by the soldiers.

Following are such of Alexander's officers as deserve mention, numbering sixty-eight. Changes in some commands were constant. In others one man retained office for years. It is impossible to give an exact list of generals as they stood at any one date. The old authorities vary. But the following one is as accurate as may be: —

1. Parmenio, general-in-chief, under the king, usually commanding the left wing of the army, while Alexander commanded the right.

2–9. The Somatophylaxes, specially trusted officers, always near the king, unless put in command of detachments. They acted as general officers, chiefs of staff or aides-de-camp, and were the king's military family. They were, according to Arrian, though two or three more are added by other authorities: —

   2. Hephæstion, the king's bosom friend, son of Amyntas, from Pella.

   3. Leonnatus, son of Anteas, from Pella.

   4. Lysimachus, son of Agathocles, from Pella.

   5. Perdiccas, son of Orontes, who also commanded a brigade of pezetæri, from Orestis.

   6. Aristonus, son of Pisæus, from Pella.

   7. Ptolemy, son of Lagus (succeeded Demetrius), from Æordæa.

   8. Peithon, son of Crateas, from Æordæa.

   9. Peucestas, later appointed in Carmania, B. C. 325.

10. Philotas, son of Parmenio, commanding the Companion cavalry.

11. Nicanor, son of Parmenio, commanding the hypaspists.

12. Clitus (the "black" one), son of Dropidas, commanding the cavalry agema.

13. Glaucias, commanding a squadron of Companion cavalry.

14. Aristo, commanding a squadron of Companion cavalry.

15. Sopolis, commanding a squadron of Companion cavalry.

16. Heraclides, commanding a squadron of Companion cavalry.

17. Demetrius, commanding a squadron of Companion cavalry.

18. Meleager, commanding a squadron of Companion cavalry.

19. Hegelochus, commanding a squadron of Companion cavalry.

20. Cœnus, son-in-law of Parmenio, commanding brigade of pezetæri and later agema of cavalry.

21. Amyntas, son of Andromenes, commanding brigade of pezetæri.

22. Meleager, 2d, commanding brigade of pezetæri.

23. Philip, son of Amyntas, commanding brigade of pezetæri.

24. Craterus, commanding brigade of pezetæri.

25. Polysperchon succeeded Ptolemy and Craterus in command of brigade of pezetæri.

26. Calas, son of Harpalus, commanding Thessalian heavy horse.

27. Philip, 2d, son of Menelaus, commanding Greek heavy horse.

28. Philip, 3d, son of Machatas, commanding brigade of infantry.

29. Sitalces, commanding Thracian acontists.
30. Clearchus, commanding Macedonian and Cretan archers and later Greek auxiliaries.
31. Cleander succeeded Clearchus, commanding Macedonian and Cretan archers.
32. Antiochus succeeded Cleander, commanding Macedonian and Cretan archers.
33. Ombrion succeeded Antiochus, commanding Macedonian and Cretan archers.
34. Antiochus, 2d, commanding a brigade of infantry.
35. Attalus, commanding Agrianians, later an infantry brigade.
36. Admetus in temporary command of hypaspists at Tyre.
37. Amyntas, 2d, son of Arrhabæus (the Lyncestian), commanding Macedonian lancers.
38. Amyntas, 3d, commanding infantry brigade.
39. Aristo, commanding Pæonian light horse.
40. Agatho, Parmenio's brother, commanding Odryssian light horse.
41. Antigonus, son of Philip, a Macedonian, commanding Greek auxiliary phalangites.
42. Balacrus, son of Amyntas, vice Antigonus, commanding Greek auxiliary phalangites.
43. Balacrus, son of Nicanor, sometimes mentioned as a Somatophylax.
44. Menandrus, son of Nicanor, commanding Greek mercenary phalangites.
45. Seleucus, in command of royal pages.
46. Ptolemy, 2d, son of Seleucus, commanding infantry brigade.
47. Sitalces, commanding Thracians.
48. Ptolemy, 3d, son of Philip, temporarily commanding a squadron of Companion cavalry.
49. Philotas, commanding an infantry brigade.
50. Calanus succeeded Balacrus in command of Greek auxiliaries.
51. Alcestas, commanding an infantry brigade.
52. Ptolemy, 4th, commanding an infantry brigade.
53. Gorgias, commanding an infantry brigade.
54. Aristobulus, a minor officer, who wrote a history of Alexander.
55. Clitus (the white one), commanding an infantry brigade.
56. Peithon, 2d, son of Sosocles, an infantry officer.
57. Peithon, 3d, son of Agenor, commanding an infantry brigade.
58. Neoptolemus, commanding an infantry brigade.

59. Antigenes, commanding an infantry brigade.

60. Cassander, commanding an infantry brigade.

61. Alexander, son of Aëropus, the Lyncestian, commanding Thessalian horse, vice Calas.

62. Erigyius, commanding Greek allied cavalry.

63. Simmias, commanding infantry brigade.

64. Artabazus, commanding Darius' Greek mercenaries, later with Alexander.

65. Nearchus, an infantry officer and later the distinguished admiral.

66. Eumenes, the secretary.

67. Diades, the engineer.

68. Laomedon, provost marshal.

Others there were but of lesser importance. Some of the above generals are constantly mentioned in all accounts of Alexander's campaigns. They usually retained their commands, as given, but wounds, death, detail on other service, promotion, and sometimes unbecoming conduct, wrought changes.

At the head of these generals, and in a sense which no captain has ever since reached, stood Alexander, the king, the master, the first and in every respect the leader of his army ; its pattern, its hardest worked, most untiring, most energetic, bravest, most splendid member. What he did, and the way in which he did it, roused the emulation of his lieutenants to an unexampled pitch. With Alexander it was never "Go!" but "Come!" The hardest task he invariably selected for his own personal performance. The greatest danger he always entered first. Despite his better armor, he could show more wounds than the most reckless of his men. None could vie with him in courage, bodily strength, expert use of arms, or endurance. And in every detail of the service, from hurling the Agrianian javelin to manœuvring the phalanx, from the sarissa-drill of the heavy pezetærus to the supreme command of the army, he stood absolutely without

a peer. In his every word and deed he was easily master;
not from his royal birth, but from his qualities of body, head
and heart.

Alexander's route lay between the coast and Lake Cercini-
tis, via Amphipolis, and passed Abdera and Maroneia. Crossing the Hebrus, he continued along the coast, passed the
Melas, and pushing down the peninsula, arrived at Sestos,
some three hundred and fifty miles from Pella, in twenty

Pella to Asia Minor.

days. This was a rapid march. It is said that the fleet accompanied the army along the shore, and that they rendezvoused every night. This was the usual habit when army
and fleet had the same destination.

Parmenio was charged with conveying the cavalry and
nearly all the infantry from Sestos to Abydos, for which service he had the aid of the one hundred and sixty triremes,
and of many trading vessels which had already been assembled in the Hellespont. This transit was easily accomplished,
for there was practically no opposition from the Persians or
the Greek mercenaries under Memnon. Alexander himself,
with a few of his troops, — the hypaspists and Companions, —
is said to have sailed from Elæus, where he offered sacrifices
at the tomb of Protesilaus, the first Homeric Greek who per-

ished on the Trojan shore, steered the vessel with his own hand, and landed on Cape Sigeum, not far from the tombs of Ajax, Achilles, and Patroclus. Having in mid-channel again sacrificed to Poseidon and the Nereids, he was himself the first man to step, in full armor, upon the coast of Asia, having from the bows of his boat first cast his spear as a symbol of conquest upon the land of the Persian foe.

Troy was then visited, Alexander heading the chosen troops he had brought with him, and due sacrifices were made to the gods and to the shade of Priam. Especially to Achilles did the king make sacrifice, while Hephæstion, his bosom friend, poured libations to Patroclus. From the temple of Athenē, on the heights of Ilium, Alexander took certain arms, said to have been carried by the Homeric heroes, — perhaps even by Achilles, — leaving his own panoply in their place. These historic arms were thereafter always carried near him in battle by some specially selected brave man. Here also games and feasts were held. The multiplicity of these sacrifices was in accordance with the customs of the Greeks, and was, moreover, in unison with Alexander's somewhat superstitious nature. The landing was marked by the erection of altars and memorials, and by the founding of a new Troy.

In all such matters Alexander gives us an index to his character. We may better liken him to an Homeric Greek than to an ordinary mortal. Great in love and hate, in common sense and superstition, in generosity and savage rage, he was Achilles come to life. The Æacidæ had indeed a fit representative in Alexander. But grafted on this heroic character was all that Greek intelligence could lend it; and this it was which enabled him to grow into the greatest soldier whom perhaps the world has ever seen.

The army was here reviewed, and, according to Diodorus, was as follows : —

Infantry.

Macedonian phalanx	12,000
Allied hoplites, 7,000 ; mercenaries, 5,000 . .	12,000
Thracians and Illyrians	5,000
Agrianian javelin-men and archers	1,000 30,000

Cavalry.

Macedonian heavy, under Philotas	1,500
Thessalian heavy, under Calas	1,500
Greek mercenary, under Erigyius	600
Thracian and Pæonian light, under Cassander .	900 4,500

                                                          34,500

These figures vary not materially from those already given. To these must be added some five thousand men already in Asia Minor, the remnant left by Parmenio. But the effective force was speedily reduced by the garrisons left behind in Asia Minor.

Head of Alexander.

(From the Equestrian Statuette found at Herculaneum.)

XIX.

BATTLE OF THE GRANICUS. MAY, B. C. 334.

THE Persian chiefs were awaiting Alexander on the line of the Granicus. Memnon had advised them to retire and devastate the country behind them. But overweening courage and jealousy of this wise Rhodian made them reject his counsel. Advancing to the river, Alexander found the Persian cavalry drawn up on its banks to dispute his crossing, with the infantry in its rear. The order should have been reversed. Foot could better defend the fords. Of this faulty disposition the king took immediate advantage, and determined on attack. He placed his phalanx in the centre with the Companions on the right and the Thessalians on the left. Parmenio, commanding the left wing, operated independently, and sought to force a crossing below the Persian right; while Alexander, on the Macedonian right, endeavored to break the Persian array at the main ford. The vehemence of the king's attack on the Persian left advanced the Macedonian right so as to give the line the aspect of an oblique order. It was solely a cavalry battle, in which Alexander had four to one against him. The fighting was stubborn; splendidly gallant on the Persian side, many princes, nobles, and generals being killed; bold, pertinacious, heroic on Alexander's. Finally, after great personal risk and true Homeric daring, the king succeeded in forcing a passage opposite the Persian left. The phalanx began to follow. Parmenio crossed below and came in on the Persian right. Thus compromised, the Persian cavalry was dispersed. The Persian infantry, which had not lifted hand, took to flight. The Greek mercenaries fought for existence, but without avail. The victory was decisive. No army could again oppose Alexander in the open field in Asia Minor.

ALEXANDER joined his army at Arisbe, and next day advanced to Percote. The passes of Mount Ida were found to be defended, and the Persian army lay on the plains of Zeleia. Alexander headed northward along the coast. He could thus turn the Mount Ida positions as well as seek the enemy. Orders were issued against devastation or injury to the people. Passing Lampsacus, he threw forward as scouts

a cavalry force consisting of one ilē of Companions and four
of lancers, all under the Lyncestian Amyntas, and sent Pane-
gorus with another body of Companion cavalry to take Pri-
apus, a town lying at the mouth of the Granicus, in a position
to command the plains through which it flowed. The place
was readily surrendered.

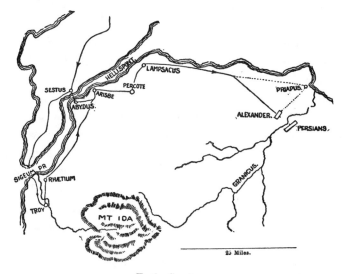

To the Granicus.

The Persian fleet was ready at hand, and commanded the
Ægean. The army lay in the plains behind the Granicus.
It consisted of twenty thousand cavalry, — Persian, Bactrian,
Median, Hyrcanian, Paphlagonian, — and not quite an equal
number of Greek mercenaries. The figures of Diodorus, —
one hundred thousand foot and ten thousand horse, — are
unquestionably inaccurate. But the force was ample, if employed with intelligence.

The Persians were under a sort of joint command of Spithridates, satrap of Lydia and Ionia, and of Arsites, viceroy of
Phrygia in Hellespont, aided by many noted and brave chiefs,

among whom were the Persian Omares, Mithrobarzanes, hipparch of Cappadocia, Arsames, Rheomithres, Petines, Niphates, Atizyes, satrap of Greater Phrygia, and others, near relatives of the Great King, and nobles of high degree. The Greek mercenaries were part of the command of Memnon. This was a very respectable force, which, well led, was capable of delaying and embarrassing, if not arresting, the Macedonian army.

Memnon, though having only a subordinate command, volunteered to the Persian officers the very sensible advice to avoid a decisive battle, to retire and to lay waste the country by burning crops, farms and villages, if need be, so as to cut Alexander off from supplies. For Memnon kept his eyes open, had his own sources of information, and knew that Alexander was but scantily provisioned and had little money. He offered to lead a large land force into Macedonia, and suggested that this should be coupled with a naval expedition; for the fleet was ready at hand. This admirable advice was rejected, the Persian generals being jealously suspicious of Memnon, not only as a Greek, but as a favorite of the king. They were conscious of their own personal bravery, and deemed courage enough to make short work of the invader. Particularly Arsites refused to allow a single house to be burned in his satrapy. It was well for Alexander that Memnon's opinion was overridden. Having deliberated and agreed that to give immediate battle was the one thing to be done, the Persians advanced, determined to dispute the further passage of Alexander on the line of the Granicus.

Instructed that the Persian force was in that vicinity, and always going straight for his objective, Alexander forged ahead with his heavy-armed troops in two columns consisting of right and left wing, the Macedonian cavalry on the right, the Thessalian and Greek on the left flank, the baggage and bulk of the light troops in the rear. Hegelochus with the lancers and some five hundred light troops curtained his front. Not far from the river came galloping back couriers with the news that the Persians had occupied the other bank, and stood there in order of battle.

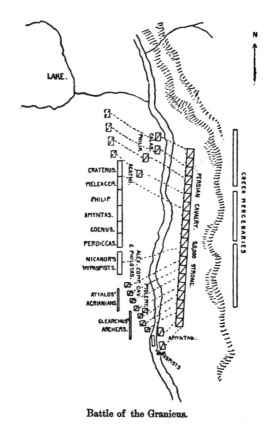

Battle of the Granicus.

The Granicus was fordable in many places; in others it was deep and rapid. Its farther bank was steep, and it was far from easy to cross in face of opposition. The troops would be obliged to ford the stream in column, and thus not only present a meagre front to the enemy, but also be liable to be taken in flank by the Persian cavalry. Parmenio advised to camp for the night, — the day being already far spent, — hoping that the sight of such a considerable force would constrain the enemy to retire, and fearing that a first check, which was not improbable under the existing conditions, might produce a bad effect on the *morale* of the army. But Alexander always believed in the moral effect bred of a bold offensive, and having reconnoitred and ascertained that the disposition of the Persians was faulty, he determined to force the passage at once. This he believed he could do, and preferred the attempt even to a resort to ruse, for he would not have the Persians think that he would for an instant pause at even so considerable an obstacle, and thereby give them confidence in their ability to oppose Macedonians. The quality of Alexander's moral courage was always equal to his personal daring. At this his first encounter, it is hard to say that daring, even to the verge of foolhardiness, was not a better policy than prudence.

The Persian chiefs had employed their cavalry, which had for generations ranked as the best in existence for attack, to defend the passage of a river which the Greek mercenary infantry, with their long spears, could vastly better have held, while the latter, on account of native jealousy of Memnon, had been placed in the rear, where it was distinctly useless, and could only be spectator of the fray. This error Alexander had at once recognized. The Macedonian columns were filed right and left into line. Parmenio was placed in command of the left; Alexander himself took command of the right wing. There was no centre.

In the right wing, counting from the right, were first Philotas with the cavalry Companions, sustained by the archers and the Agrianian acontists. To Ptolemy, son of Philip, had that day come by rote the honor of leading the van of the heavy horse with, as Arrian says, the ilē of Socrates. Amyntas, with the lancers, the Pæonians, and one taxis of hypaspists to give them stability, was thrown out in front on the right. Alexander was behind Ptolemy with the rest of the hetairai. Nicanor, with the other shield-bearing guards, was on the left of the heavy cavalry; then came the taxes of Perdiccas, Cœnus, and Amyntas, the infantry officer; and finally the taxis of Philip, son of Amyntas.

Alexander proposed to make a diversion on the Persian left with the light troops under Amyntas; to have this followed up by Ptolemy with his squadron of heavy horse; while himself, with seven squadrons of the hetairai, backed up by the phalanx on his left, would deal the heavy blow, advancing on the enemy with the right wing. This operation would throw this wing into an oblique line, left refused. The left wing, under Parmenio, was, if necessary, to act independently. In the latter wing, counting from the left, came the Thessalian cavalry, under Calas; then the allied Greek cavalry, under Philip, son of Menelaus, and the Thracian cavalry, under Agatho. Then came the infantry taxes under Craterus and Meleager, which adjoined Philip. The artillery was posted on this flank to throw missiles across the river at the enemy, and thus aid Parmenio, who was to advance also in oblique order, on the Persian right. It is not stated how efficient service the engines may have rendered. In the *mêlée* beyond the river they might be equally dangerous to friend or foe. It is the novelty of their use, not their effectiveness, which is of interest in this connection, for engines had until Alexander's day been used exclusively in sieges.

The Persians had four to one of Alexander's force of cavalry. They made no use of their infantry. The battle was almost solely decided by the use of horse. The phalanx merely capped the stroke. The Persian horse was extended in long phalangial order along the bank of the river. Their foot, as stated, was in its rear, on the higher ground which gradually ascended from the water-side. This was a fatal mistake. The heavy infantrymen with their thrusting pikes were peculiarly adapted to defend the crossing, while the cavalry, by attacking the Macedonians after they had crossed and were somewhat in disorder, would be in their very element. The order should have been reversed; but no doubt excess of gallantry in the Persian chiefs led them to open the first and heaviest fighting in their own persons, as leaders of their choicest cavalry. Memnon, with his sons, and Arsames were on the left with the mass of the cavalry; the Medes and Bactrians were on their right; the Phrygians, Paphlagonians, Hyrcanians and Lydians were under Arsites and Spithridates in the centre; Rheomithres was on the right. More than forty Persian chiefs of high rank and princes were prominent in the battle.

The Persians, so soon as they perceived the Macedonian formation, concentrated the bulk and flower of their horse upon their left, opposite the place where they recognized Alexander, who was always conspicuous in action by his two white plumes, resplendent arms, and commanding presence. And this Macedonian wing, too, was somewhat advanced by the accidents of the ground. While Alexander was marshaling his array, the Persians were doing the like. When this was completed, for a brief period both armies stood facing each other in profound silence. The Persians were waiting to take the Macedonians at a disadvantage as they crossed. Alexander was assuring himself that each brigade was in place and ready for action. To do this he rode the lines, and calling on all to show themselves men, he ordered Amyntas, the cavalryman, forward with his lancers, and the Pæonians and hypaspists. Ptolemy followed upon his heels.

The pæan was intoned, the trumpets blared, the war-cry, "Enyalius!" an Homeric name for Mars, was shouted, and the attack was begun with true Macedonian *élan*. In the order given the army entered the fords with the confidence bred of many victories. But they had never yet encountered such foes as the splendid Persian horse.

Alexander was leaning his right on Ptolemy and his left on the phalanx. This whole wing, by the advance of the extreme right, was, as stated, thrown into a sort of oblique order, and the right still kept on edging to the right, partly on account of the way the main ford ran, and partly so as to prevent the enemy from outflanking it in that quarter. The left wing, under Parmenio, was operating lower down, so as to fall on the Persian right. The two wings were separated, — not the error then which it now would be. The phalanx of the right wing was to make its way across the ford when the horse under Alexander had opened the way by its vigorous onset; the phalanx of the left to follow Parmenio.

The oblique order of the right wing was thus partly intentional, partly owing to the greater rapidity of onset of the hetairai and light horse, and the inability of the phalanx to get over the fords as soon as they did. But it was none the less effective. Alexander's excessive ardor, and the fact that he always commanded the right, gives the appearance in all his battles of a premeditated oblique order. But, as will hereafter appear, it was sometimes accidental and due to his own tremendous energy. At the Hydaspes, no doubt, the oblique order was intended. Here it was not so. Many books on the history of war portray Alexander's battles with the troops as regularly echeloned in oblique order as Frederick's army at Leuthen; but the careful comparison of the original authorities by no means sustains this view. The regular order in echelon is of late creation, though Epaminondas certainly originated, and Alexander constantly used, a formation which had the quality and effect of the oblique order in the shape best adapted to the circumstances. It has been discussed above how far Epaminondas' formation at Leuctra or Mantinæa probably approached the echeloned. At the Granicus there could be no such regularity from the very nature of the case.

The Persians began the use of weapons by hurling their javelins from the high banks in all directions towards the fords, where Ptolemy, preceded by Amyntas, was struggling through the slippery clay towards the shore. The cavalry fell to, hand to hand. The Persians advanced boldly to the water's edge to force the enemy back. They cast their spears; the Macedonians used theirs to thrust, and could thus repeat their blows many times with the same weapon. The Macedonian cavalry was much inferior in number; the men suffered severely from the missiles showered down from the high bank above them, where were posted the best-armed Persian horsemen, commanded and encouraged by renowned and valiant chiefs. The leading Macedonians fought with valor, but they were quickly cut down and the line was driven back. The king, leading the agema of cavalry, came to the rescue with Philotas and the remainder of the Companions, and fiercely attacked that portion of the Persian line where he saw that the flower of the horse and the leaders stood. Holding himself here by efforts worthy of his ancestor Hercules, he enabled squadron after squadron of his cavalry to essay the crossing under protection of his stanch attack. The fight was unlike the cavalry skirmishing of that day, which was by short and repeated shocks; it was more like an ancient tussle of heroes, man to man, horse to horse; each one trying to force the other back by the momentum of weight, as well as by valor and sturdy blows. The Persians were determined to drive the Macedonians back into the river ; the Macedonians to win a footing on the bank. Having cast all their javelins, the Orientals fell to with their curved swords. The fighting was furious. The bravest and stoutest bit the dust. The white plumes waved everywhere. " Enyalius ! " resounded above the din. Finally, under the king's magnificent gallantry, the cornel-wood spears of the Macedonians bore down the lighter weapons of the Persians, and the landing of Alexander's immediate command was effected.

Alexander ran great personal risk in the combat at this point. He broke his own spear in the conflict, borrowed another from a Companion, and slew Mithridates, son-in-law of Darius, who was rushing at him with a chosen body formed like a wedge. He received at the same time a blow with a scimitar in the hands of Rhoisakes, brother of Mithridates, which cut away part of his helmet, but he slew the prince with his spear. He was always in the thickest of the fray. Spithridates, from behind, rushed upon him with uplifted weapon, and but for the aid of swarthy Clitus, whose sword severed the Persian's arm, he would not have escaped a grievous wound or death. He was the centre for all to rally on. Nothing but Alexander's irrepressible courage could have held the Companions to their work. According to Diodorus, he received two body-wounds and one in the head.

Having thus pushed his van forward, the rest of the right wing was gradually enabled to cross. The cavalry of the left had forced a passage below, where the opposition was less determined, and was getting in on the Persian right flank. The Macedonians struck at the faces of the foe with their spears, and at their horses. The light-armed troops, mixed with the cavalry, did great execution upon the Persians. The enemy broke first where the king fought in the right wing.

Instantly seizing this opening and pouring into the gap with the Companions, the Persian cavalry was borne back in a body ; a few more doughty blows and it was dispersed.

What Asiatic infantry there was decamped at once. The twenty thousand Greek mercenaries, under Omares, alone stood firm. They fought for their reputation as Greeks as well as for their lives. Drawn up in close order, they refused to stir. They begged for quarter, but Alexander refused it. They had been inactively watching a battle they might perhaps have saved, and had no orders which could apply to this unforeseen, incredible result. They fought like Greeks. But they were surrounded by the phalanx ; the cavalry of the right closed in on their left ; the Thessalians rode around their right ; they were cut to pieces where they stood, two thousand alone being captured. In this last attack, Alexander had his horse killed under him.

About one thousand Persian horsemen were slain, but a fearful percentage of the chief officers fell, for they had recklessly exposed their persons. Among these were the viceroy of Lydia, the governor of Cappadocia, the son, the son-in-law, and the brother-in-law of Darius, and many other princes. On the Macedonian side some twenty-five Companions of the van were killed, and sixty of the other cavalry. Many hundreds were wounded. Less than three thousand horse had been engaged on the right. Some thirty footmen were killed in the attack on the Greek phalanx. It seems as if this statement must be below the truth. The query naturally arises, the latter being well armed, placed where they must fight for their lives, and in the open field, how could the Macedonians slay so many thousands of them with a loss of only thirty infantry ? This question is always cropping up in ancient and mediæval warfare. The only explanation is that the beaten, broken army becomes a mere mob, — demoralized, panic-stricken, incapable of any resistance, collectively or individually. There was in ancient days no artillery with which to cover the retreat of a beaten force. In this case the Macedonians bore the twenty-one foot sarissa, the Greeks but a twelve-foot pike; and the cavalry attacked them on both flanks. Look at battles so late as Crécy (1346) and Agincourt (1415). At the former, the English loss is stated to have been one squire, three knights, and very few soldiers; while the French are said to have lost eleven princes, twenty-eight hundred knights and nobles, and thirty thousand soldiers. At the latter, the English lost sixteen hundred men to twenty thousand French. The experience of nineteenth century warfare makes it all but impossible to comprehend this; but the numberless examples of history vouch fully for its truth. It has been claimed that Macedonian losses were understated as a matter of braggadocio. But even gross exaggeration will not alter the vast excess of losses by the vanquished, nor would the many enemies of Alexander in Greece have failed to record the truth.

There are few things more curious than the comparison of losses in given battles in all ages with their military and political results. At Cunaxa, in the Greek phalanx, not one man was killed, and but one man wounded. At the Granicus there were one hundred and fifteen killed; at Issus, four hundred and fifty; at Arbela, five hundred. These three battles decided the fate of Persia. At the battle of Megalopolis, however, Antipater, with forty thousand men, defeated Agis, with twenty thousand, the Macedonians losing thirty-five hundred killed, and the Spartans fifty-three hundred. Important as the battle was, it is the fierceness of the fighting, especially on the Spartan side, which is the noteworthy fact.

We are wont to imagine a greater gallantry in olden times than in our own so-called degenerate days. Courage is said to decline into stoicism when long-range weapons supplant hand-to-hand combat. But it is a question whether the latter in the soldier is not the greater virtue. Since the days when the lines of battle had to close in order to decide the day, troops have been forced to stand, and have stood, far greater decimation. Let us go no farther back than a few brilliant examples in our own day and generation.

To take small bodies : —

At Balaclava, the Light Brigade, out of 673 men, lost 113 killed, or 16.8 per cent.

At Mars la Tour, the 16th Infantry (Westphalian), out of 3,000 men, lost 509 killed, or 16.9 per cent.

At Metz, the Garde Schützen, out of 1,000 men, lost 162 killed, or 16.2 per cent.

These are the heaviest percentages of killed shown by these two nations within recollection.

During our Civil War, each of sixty-six Union regiments, *in some one battle*, lost a higher percentage in killed than this. Of these, one lost 28 per cent. in killed ; one, 26 per cent. ; one, 24 per cent. ; four, 23 per cent. ; five, 22 per cent. ; five, 21 per cent. ; seven, 20 per cent.

Or, to take somewhat larger bodies : —

At Gettysburg, the First Corps, out of 9,000 men, lost 593 killed, or 6.6 per cent. ; the Second Corps, out of 10,500 men, lost 796 killed, or 7.6 per cent. ; the Third Corps, out of 11,000 men, lost 578 killed, or 5.3 per cent.

At Antietam, the Second Corps, out of 15,000 men, lost 883 killed, or 5.9 per cent.

At Chickamauga, the Fourteenth Corps, out of 20,000 men, lost 664 killed, or 3.3 per cent. ; McCook's Division, out of 12,500 men, lost 423 killed, or 3.4 per cent.

At Stone River, the Twenty-first Corps, out of 13,000 men, lost 650 killed, or 5 per cent.

At Gettysburg, Gibbon's Brigade, out of 3,773 men, lost 344 killed, or

9.1 per cent. ; the Iowa Brigade, out of 1,883 men, lost 162 killed, or 8.6 per cent.

At the Wilderness, the Vermont Brigade, out of 2,800 men, lost 195 killed, or 7 per cent.

Or, to take some large armies of this century : —

At Borodino, the French, out of 133,000 men, are reckoned to have lost 4,400 killed, or 3.3 per cent. ; the Russians, out of 132,000 men, are reckoned to have lost 4,500 killed, or 3.4 per cent.

At Waterloo, the Allies, out of 72,000 men, are reckoned to have lost 3,600 killed, or 5 per cent. ; the French, out of 80,000 men, are reckoned to have lost 4,100 killed, or 5 per cent.

At Gettysburg, the Federals, out of 82,000 men, actually lost 3,063 killed, or 3.8 per cent. ; the Confederates, out of 60,000 men, actually lost 2,665 killed, or 4.4 per cent.

At Gravelotte, the Germans, out of 146,000 men, actually lost 4,449 killed, or 3 per cent.

The term " killed " does not include those who die of their wounds. The men, for instance, in the Federal army at Gettysburg, who were killed *and* died of their wounds (most of them within a week) numbered five thousand two hundred and ninety-one men or 6.4 per cent. But to keep the same method of figuring for all cases, only those killed in the battle are counted, viz. : three thousand and sixty-three. The figures of killed at Borodino and Waterloo cannot be vouched for, but they are not far from the truth.

The following deductions can be made from the above figures. The larger the force the less the *percentage* of killed ; principally because a smaller percentage of men can be actually got into fighting contact. In bodies exceeding sixty thousand men, the loss in *killed, in a very stubbornly contested battle,* may be some four per cent. ; in bodies of from ten thousand to twenty thousand men, five per cent. ; in bodies of from two thousand to five thousand men, seven and a half per cent. ; in regiments of from one thousand to two thousand men, seventeen per cent.; in battalions of five hundred men, twenty-two per cent. This makes no account of wounds whatever, even mortal ones. These percentages apply only to very stubbornly fought battles. The average battle, even if severe, falls far short of these losses.

Among the Greeks only the losses of the victors can fairly be counted. The vanquished were invariably massacred. Should we count both, the Greek losses in killed would be many times those of our battles. But, in an occasional battle of ancient days, the losses in killed, quite apart from the massacre following defeat, were far higher than anything shown in modern warfare. At Megalopolis the Macedonian victors lost nine per cent. in killed, twice the loss at Waterloo, two and a half times that at Gettysburg. In the average Greek battle, the killed were usually fewer than in modern actions. Hand-weapons were less deadly than musket-balls; and the men wore armor and carried shields, which were a reasonably good protection against spears, arrows and stones. The wounded were numerous. In Alexander's combats they average ten or twelve to one of killed, often twenty. Nowadays, about seven to one is the ratio. On the basis of killed alone, Alexander's battles were not so deadly as ours; on the basis of killed and wounded, they were not far from the same.

If we take a general casualty-list composed of the killed *and* wounded in celebrated battles, we shall find that

Napoleon, in nine battles, lost, in each, about . . . . . 22 per cent.
Frederick, in eight battles, lost, in each, about . . . . 18½ per cent.
The Confederates, in eleven battles, lost, in each, about . 14 per cent.
The Unionists, in eleven battles, lost, in each, about . . 13 per cent.
The Germans, in eight battles, lost, in each, about . . . 11½ per cent.
The English, in four battles, lost, in each, about . . . . 10 per cent.
The Austrians, in nine battles, lost, in each, about . . . 10 per cent.
The French, in nine battles, lost, in each, about . . . . 9 per cent.

These figures are a good gauge to measure by.

The loss then, in killed, at the Granicus, of the three thousand horse headed by Alexander, was less than three per cent. Cavalry never loses as heavily as infantry; the organization of mounted troops does not enable them to stand up to decimation so well as foot. The fighting ranks high as a combat of cavalry, and victory was won against vast odds. If we estimate the wounded at ten to one, the loss was thirty-one per cent., exceptionally high for cavalry, high for any body of men. We shall recur to these statistics often. It is well to bear the percentages in mind.

These first Macedonian brave to perish at the Granicus had statues by Lysippus erected in their memory; they were buried in full armor and with the greatest honors, and their families were relieved from taxes and handsomely provided for. The wounded were treated with the highest consideration. Alexander personally visited each and listened to the story of his prowess. The Persians and Greek mercenaries were also buried, and plundering was prohibited; but the Greek prisoners were sent to Macedonia in chain-gangs, to till the soil, for having, contrary to the decision of the associated cities at Corinth, entered the service of the Persian king and made war on Greeks. Such Thebans as happened to be among them, the king let off scot-free. Three hundred panoplies were sent to Athens to be dedicated in the Acropolis with this inscription: "Alexander, son of Philip, and the Greeks, *except the Lacedæmonians*, present these spoils of the foreigner inhabiting Asia." Booty was freely distributed to all the soldiers to whet their appetite for more.

The battle of the Granicus was courageously but unintelligently fought by the Persians, who relied upon courage instead of tactics, and put their infantry to no use whatever. And yet this infantry was one of the largest and best bodies of foot the Persian army had so far had, and capable of doing, if led by a man like Memnon, the very best of work.

Calas, son of Harpalus, who was familiar with this territory, having been here with Parmenio during the preceding two years, was made satrap of Hellespontine Phrygia. His instructions were to make no internal changes, to administer the government with the ancient officials, but subject to Alexander's control, and to collect taxes as usual. These now flowed into the Macedonian army-chest.

This victory was well calculated to give Alexander a great repute and abundant success in Asia. His personal prowess, the exceptional slaughter of noble Persians, not unlike the fall of heroes in the Iliad, must have impressed itself with wonderful force on the Persian imagination. The moral effect of the victory at the Granicus, and the loss of so many of the governors and chiefs of this section in that battle, so completely broke up the power of the Persian satraps, that no army thereafter was found to face Alexander in the open field in Asia Minor.

The road to the heart of Persia lay open to Alexander. He could march straight on Gordium and down towards Cilicia. The direct route lay that way. But he clearly saw that this path could not yet be trodden. The Persian fleet was in the Ægean. His advance across the Taurus mountains would not be safe till all the cities of the coast were in his possession, so as to neutralize the one power of Persia — her ships — in which he was not prepared to measure arms with her. And he must have control of these cities to protect his own rear and flanks as he advanced. Full of Greeks and democrats, these towns, not unwilling before, stood all the more ready now, after this unexpected triumph, to yield themselves and their treasures and fortunes to the conqueror. And the possession of these towns would have yet another effect, and one of the most to be desired. It would tend to forestall the far from improbable invasion of Macedonia by the Persians. This was a danger Alexander knew he was constantly running, and one to be delivered from which was equivalent to a second army.

To fully complete his victory, the king dispatched Parmenio to reduce Dascylium on the Propontis, the residence of the satrap of Phrygia, a measure necessary properly to protect his rear while he advanced, as he now proposed to do, southerly along the coast.

Bronze Statuette of Alexander.

(Found at Herculaneum in 1751, and thought to be a copy of the statue known to have been made of him by Lysippus after the battle of the Granicus.)

XX.

SARDIS, MILETUS, HALICARNASSUS. FALL, B. C. 334.

ALEXANDER now marched on Sardis, whose rocky citadel might have kept him indefinitely at bay. Luckily, the commandant concluded to surrender the place, and was handsomely rewarded by the king. Ephesus opened its gates, and many other cities sent deputations tendering submission. All such places Alexander treated with distinguished generosity, reduced their taxes, made public improvements, and restored ancient laws and customs. Miletus elected to hold out. Alexander seized the island of Ladē, commanding its harbor, and by clever management of his small fleet and land forces, neutralized the Persian squadron, which attempted to succor the city. Finally Miletus fell, and after an unsuccessful minor sea-fight, the Persians sailed to Samos. Alexander now disbanded his fleet, as he needed the men for land service, and had scarcely funds enough to sustain it. This was, perhaps, a mistake. From Miletus the army moved on Halicarnassus, capturing many cities on the way. To this place had retired Memnon and a number of able Greeks and Persians, determined on stanch defense. The king attempted to capture Myndus, west of the town, as a point of vantage, but failed. He then sat down on the northeast side, and began regular siege-operations. These were long and exhausting; but finally Macedonian persistency succeeded, and Halicarnassus fell and was destroyed. Memnon and others retired to one of the citadels, and the king left a force behind to besiege this, and provided for the government of the land.

SARDIS, the capital of Lydia, was the first city of importance which the programme of Alexander required him to take, and he lost no time in advancing on this ancient residence of Crœsus. Judging from the modern routes, and the general topography, he marched by the east of Mount Ida; though some authorities make him retrace his steps by way of Ilium. Parmenio had easily taken possession of Dascylium, and shortly rejoined his chief. Sardis was noted for its citadel, which, built on an isolated, high and precipitous rock, and surrounded by a triple wall, might have bidden defiance

to almost any force. If held, it might lend efficient aid to
the Persian fleet; and its treasure might again summon an
army into existence. Time, at this juncture, was very precious. But when the army came within a short march of
Sardis, the terror produced by the recent victory became

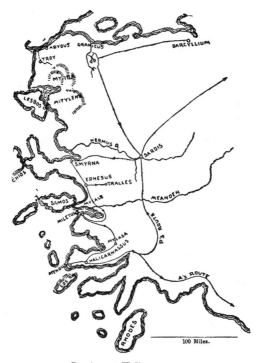

Granicus to Halicarnassus.

manifest. Alexander was met by a deputation headed by
Mithrines, the Persian commandant, who, proving recreant
to his trust, surrendered the city, the Acropolis and the vast
treasure lying therein. Alexander camped on the Hermus,
a couple of miles off, and sent Amyntas, son of Andromenes,
with his infantry brigade to take possession of the citadel.

He gave to Mithrines an important place near his own person, to show the world how he could reward such signal service rendered to his cause. He had little fear of similar treachery to himself. He granted freedom to the city, and guaranteed its ancient privileges under the old Lydian laws, of which, for two hundred years, it had been deprived by its conquerors. He thus won its good - will, and insured its fidelity. Parmenio's brother, Asandros, was appointed viceroy; Nicias, collector of customs; and in the citadel was left a garrison of Argives under Pausanias. Both the latter were Companions — probably of the agema. Alexander also laid the cornerstone of a temple to Zeus on the Acropolis. Being the first great city to succumb to his arms, he was anxious to show his friendly animus towards all who should submit without a conflict. Moreover Sardis was a cross-roads of great importance in Asia Minor. It could not be held too securely, and the king employed both force and favor to strengthen its fealty.

From here Alexander detached the rest of the Greek auxiliaries under Calas, the new viceroy, and Alexander, son of Aëropus, the Lyncestian, who had succeeded Calas in command of the Thessalian horse, on an expedition into the Hellespontine region, where Memnon had for some time commanded for Darius, to work up a friendly feeling for his cause. If expertly done, this would protect his left as he advanced south, as well as hold the great roads running inland through Gordium towards the Taurus, which by and by he expected to use as he moved farther into Asia. Nicanor, placed in charge of the fleet (no special training was deemed essential for command at sea), was ordered to Lesbos and Miletus to impose upon the coast cities, and thus aid in their eventual capture. It was his appearance which won over Mitylene to the Macedonian cause — a gain of greatest value.

The easy success at Sardis was an enviable piece of good

fortune for Alexander. Its citadel might possibly have kept him as long at bay as Tyre did subsequently; and a delay now, in the moment when his victorious advance was beginning to make a marked impression on the susceptible Asiatic mind, would have been a grievous check to his prestige. The king showed his appreciation of these facts in his conduct towards the city. Sardis and the satrapy of Lydia, in addition to many privileges, were held but to pay the same tribute to Alexander which it had been usual to pay to Darius.

From Sardis, Alexander marched in four days to Ephesus, the queen of the Ionian cities. This place also opened its gates, and the king broke up the tyrannical oligarchy there regnant, and established in its stead a democratic form of government. Wherever the democratic feeling was strong, there was opposition to Persian tyranny, and Alexander was naturally received with open arms. He here ordered the tribute, hitherto payable to Darius, to be contributed to the temple of Diana, and himself paid the highest honors at her shrine, which he commanded to be rebuilt in the most superb manner by his engineer, Denocrates. It will be remembered that this temple was burned on the day of Alexander's birth. His liberal treatment of this city, and especially of its tutelary divinity, gave to his name immense popularity.

It was here that the great painter Apelles lived, and doubtless the picture by him of Alexander holding thunderbolts in his hand, which is known long to have been an ornament of the temple of Diana, dates from the time of this visit. At this place Alexander also received deputations from Tralles and Magnesia, and from some other Carian cities, tendering submission. Parmenio, with five thousand foot and two hundred horse, was sent to Caria to receive the surrenders; and Antimachus, brother of the Somatophylax Lysimachus, with an equal force, to the Æolic and Ionic cities which were under

Persian rule, twenty-four in number. The king's instructions were to overturn the oligarchies in every case, reëstablish democratic government, restore the old laws, and remit the tribute paid to Darius, collecting but the ancient smaller contributions for his own uses.

In every Greek city which he visited, Alexander began some public improvement in commemoration of his setting it free from the Persian yoke. Smyrna had been practically destroyed; its Greek character had been quite lost; Alexander began its reconstruction. At Clasomenæ he laid the foundation of a mole, and opened a canal to improve its harbor. Moneys for these works were easily forthcoming from the superabundant taxes heretofore collected by the Persian king; Alexander diverted a considerable portion of these to the public good. He thus made firm his hold on the territory he conquered, not only by the best measures for military occupation, but by fostering political good-will in the cities. These are the beginnings of those extensive improvements which prove Alexander to have looked on his conquests as possessions to be benefited, not oppressed; which show that greed of territory was but one incentive to his restless forward march.

After sacrificing at the temple of Diana and conducting a procession in her honor, with his army in full parade order and gala-dress, Alexander set out for Miletus. The commandant, the Greek Hegistratus, had lately been anxious to surrender, and had so written to the king more than once, no doubt expecting rewards and honor like Mithrines; but news that the Persian fleet was coming to his rescue changed his determination, and he resolved to hold the place for Darius and to defend its citadel. For Persia had not oppressed Miletus, but rather utilized its commercial importance as it had that of Phœnicia, allowing it to retain its own government, and not a few exceptional privileges.

Miletus was of the utmost consequence to the Persians, if they proposed to hold the Ægean, now that the season was growing late. It was built on a cape south of, and protected by, the jutting headland of Mycale, fifteen miles distant;

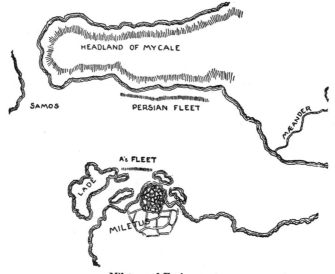

Miletus and Environments.

while twenty miles seaward lay the island of Samos. Divided into outer and inner towns, the latter surrounded with strong walls and a deep ditch; with one large harbor on the island of Ladē opposite, and three smaller ones formed by islands on the coast, it could both shelter the largest fleet and offer road-ways to vast numbers of merchantmen. More than once in the past history of Asia Minor its possession had determined victory.

Alexander with small effort captured the outer city, which, practically defenseless, was quickly evacuated, and set to work to blockade the inner one with a line of circumvallation. His fleet of one hundred and sixty ships, under Nicanor, was fortunate enough to arrive three days before the Persian squadron, and he was enabled to seize the island of Ladē, and thus insure by land and sea the complete blockade of the inner city. Alexander sent the Thracians and some four thousand mercenaries to the island to place it in a state of defense beyond danger. He had with him, after his several detachments, some twelve thousand phalangians and hypaspists, the Agrianians and bowmen, four squadrons of Macedonian horse and the Thracian light cavalry.

Many of Alexander's generals, even cautious old Parmenio, advised Alexander to attack the Persian fleet, consisting of four hundred vessels, which had arrived and now rode at anchor near the headland of Mycale. A naval battle seemed indeed inevitable, and the *morale* of the Macedonians was high; and, said Parmenio, it was well to keep up its tension by a constant offensive. But Alexander decided that a present victory at sea could bring him no advantage commensurate with the risk, while the loss of a naval battle would carry with it a dangerous fall in prestige which might encourage to revolt his enemies in Greece. He declined to make venture of his fortunes on an element where he was not only not so strong as on land, but an element so far not his own. Despite that the Greeks had always defeated the Persians on the water, his ships were not as well manned as those of the Cyprians and Phœnicians, and were only one hundred and sixty to four hundred. His intelligence overrode his natural antagonism. He was right, for there were reasons why he could not repose the greatest confidence in the fidelity of his Greek mariners.

Parmenio looked at the matter from another standpoint. An eagle had been seen sitting on the rocks near the ships, an omen which Parmenio construed as favorable. So did Alexander. But the king maintained that the eagle being on land signified that he would be victorious on land and not at sea. And he acted on this interpretation. It seems strange indeed to think of these two generals, men of exceptional ability, intelligence and common sense, disputing over so trivial a thing as this. That they should seriously argue such a matter is as curious as the apparent pliancy of the omen. And yet is it more strange than the intellect and acrimony wasted in our day on the quite as trivial question of the damnation of the heathen?

The Milesians now sent a deputation to the king, and offered to make their port and city equally open to the Persians and Greeks if Alexander would raise the siege. But Alexander rejected their offer with scorn. He came not to Asia, said he, to take a half, but the whole. He determined to assault the walls the next day at daybreak, and dismissed the deputation with a threat so to do. The engines were at once set to work, speedily broke down the wall in several places, and Alexander led his troops to the breach at the time he had set. To prevent the Persian fleet from succoring the town, as well as to forestall the flight of the Milesian mercenaries to the ships, Nicanor ranged his galleys across the narrowest part of the harbor, side by side, with beaks towards the enemy. The Macedonians, pressing sharply in through the broken walls, easily drove the garrison from its defense, and slew vast numbers. Many of the Greek mercenaries attempted to escape in skiffs, and even by floating upon their hollow shields, to an island near the city. Of these the greatest number fell into the hands of the fleet, but some succeeded in reaching the island. When Alexander endeavored to capture this place of refuge the next day, approaching it in his triremes with ladders lashed to the prows so as to be able to scale the rocks, this handful of men, three hundred in number, made so brave a resistance that, out of simple admiration of their courage, he was fain to offer them a truce on condition of their taking service under himself. He also pardoned the surviving citizens of Miletus, and granted the city its freedom. The other inhabitants were sold as slaves.

The Persian fleet daily offered battle to Nicanor, which the latter as often declined. At night they returned to, and anchored near, Mount Mycale, whence they had to send to the Mæander, over ten miles distant, for water. Alexander tried a scheme to drive them from their position without battle. He sent Philotas, with some horse and three brigades of infantry, to occupy their landing-place, and to patrol the shore near by to prevent them from getting their usual supply, as well as keep them from foraging, and thus, as it were, besiege their fleet. The Persians were soon forced to sail for Samos, whence, after they had revictualed, they returned. Having exhausted every effort to bring the Macedonians to battle by parading each day in line at the mouth of the harbor, they essayed to cut out some of the Greek galleys, while the sailors were ashore gathering fuel and provisions — a daily necessity in olden times — and sent five ships into the roadstead between Ladē and the mainland to surprise the fleet unmanned. By thus sailing into the harbor, they believed they might get between the army and the fleet. They came close to being successful in their effort, for the Macedonian ships were nearly all, for the moment, without their crews. Perceiving this, Alexander, who happened to be on hand, hastily assembled what sailors were to be found, gave chase to these five galleys with ten of his own which he quickly manned, drove them off, and captured one. The Persians, chagrined by this slight disaster, and seeing no chance of disturbing Alexander's hold on the place, decided to leave the vicinity of Miletus. This they soon did, sailing for Samos, and having accomplished no result whatever, despite their superior numbers and better condition. Alexander's waiting tactics had been efficient to a degree.

Alexander now saw that his fleet was no longer of distinct use to him in what he had undertaken to do, and especially so if it must keep to the defensive. It had already accomplished its greatest aim in protecting him in the initial steps. It was no match for that of the Persians in open fight, for the Phœnicians and Cyprians in the Persian service were by long odds the best sailors then known. The king felt that he could better neutralize the enemy's fleet by capturing, and thus excluding them from, the principal seaports, than by provoking a naval engagement; whereas by an unfortunate defeat at sea, which he might suffer at any moment, he would lose much ground difficult to recover. The Persian fleet could in no sense compromise his land operations as it was, though it might give him trouble. His own fleet was expensive, costing fifty talents a month for pay alone and an equal amount for rations, — as much indeed as the army and without making conquests, as the latter did. His treasure was small, for he could not plunder the cities he had come to befriend, and was in the habit, as we have seen, of collecting only reasonable taxes. He needed for land duty such of the men in the fleet as were available. It took nearly thirty thousand men all told — sailors, rowers and soldiers — for the one hundred and sixty triremes. He would be able again to assemble a fleet when he could better afford one. He therefore took steps to disband the seamen and lay up the ships, excepting a few transports and the twenty ships Athens had contributed. These latter he preferred to keep in commission as a sort of hostage for their city's good behavior. Diodorus says that Alexander disbanded his fleet to show his army that they had no means of retreat, and must win or perish. But this is a shallow reason. Alexander's men could always fight without bolstering of such a nature.

The king then marched along the coast to Halicarnassus, taking, one by one — usually by surrender — the cities from Miletus down, and leaving a garrison in each. It had become doubly important to secure every town upon his route. Only by such a land blockade could he drive the Persian fleet from the Ægean. This conception of Alexander's, of forcing the enemy's fleet from the sea by occupying all the coast towns, was as noteworthy as the execution was excellent. It was, on an enormous scale, what he had done at Miletus on a limited one. The towns relied for subsistence upon the interior; the fleet could do them no harm except by interfering with their commerce; and the king felt that he could best restore their trade at sea by starving out the Persian fleet. The longer its naval operations were kept up in the Ægean, the longer the trade of these towns would droop; the sooner he drove the fleet to other waters, the better for his friends.

Halicarnassus was the last great Persian stronghold on the Ægean. Here had collected a large force of Persians and Greek auxiliaries, under Memnon, who, after the defeat at the Granicus, unable to save Ephesus and Miletus, had retired hither, by a circuit, with some fragments of his army, accompanied by Ephialtes, an Athenian exile, and Orontobates. The place was very strong by nature, and Memnon, who had now been appointed governor of Lower Asia and chief admiral of Darius, — for if he could not save what remained, no one else could do so, — having sent his wife and children to the Persian court as voluntary hostages for his truth and fidelity, had added all that art could supply. The mighty walls and a newly-made ditch, exceeding wide and deep, encompassed it upon three sides. On the other, the south side, was the sea. It contained three citadels, — the Acropolis, on the heights of its north side; the Salmakis, on the southwest corner near the sea, on the neck of the cape which forms the western boundary of the harbor; the royal citadel, on an island at the entrance of the harbor. The island of Arconnesus had been fortified, and garrisons put in the surrounding towns as outposts to divert Alexander's attention from the city. The city had been provisioned for a long

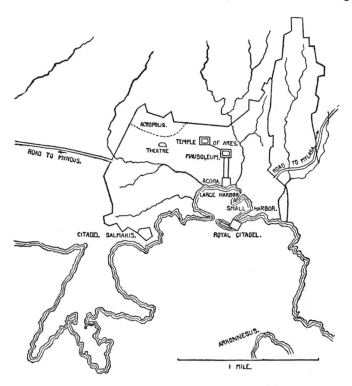

Halicarnassus.

siege. A number of war ships were in the harbor to hold it against the Macedonians, and to use in procuring supplies, which latter proceeding Alexander could not prevent without a fleet. Meanwhile, the sailors were mostly told off for land duty. Many noted refugees were in the city, among them the Lyncestian Neoptolemus, brother of Arrhabæus, who was mixed up in the murder of Philip; Amyntas, son of Antiochus, who fled from Alexander's anger, though it would seem that his flight was uncalled for; Thrasybulus and others.

A siege of Halicarnassus became necessary. On the day of Alexander's approach, as he was leading his men up to the gate opening towards Mylasa in the northeast, and was still about a thousand paces distant, a sortie was made by the garrison, and a sharp skirmish ensued, in which the Macedonians proved too strong for the Halicarnassians, and drove them back into the city. The king then opened his operations with vigor.

There was a town on the western extremity of the peninsula named Myndus. Alexander thought that if he could take this town, it might materially aid in the siege by furnishing him a convenient depot, and accordingly moved a considerable part of his forces — the hypaspists, the cavalry Companions, the brigades of Amyntas, Perdiccas, and Meleager, and the archers and Agrianians — around Halicarnassus by the north to that point. In addition to the above purpose, Alexander intended this movement to be a general reconnoissance to ascertain if there might not possibly be a better chance of assault on the Myndus side of the city wall. Some of the Myndians had offered to surrender the place if he would come under cover of night; but when he reached the spot his friends had probably been overpowered, and he was received with arms. Angered with this outcome of the affair, though not having brought ladders or engines, Alexander none the less resolved on an offensive; and in the darkness of night attacked and undermined the walls, and threw down one of the towers. But this did not effect a practicable breach, and the Halicarnassian garrison, informed early next morning of the danger in which Myndus lay, hurried reinforcements by sea to the succor of the place.

Alexander was reluctantly compelled to give up the prospect of capturing Myndus, returned to his old location, and again sat down to besiege Halicarnassus.

He elected to remain on the northeast side, not having found a more promising position. He first covered his men with pent-houses (tortoises) and filled up the ditch, which was forty-five feet wide and twenty-three deep, in convenient places so that he might advance his towers to override the

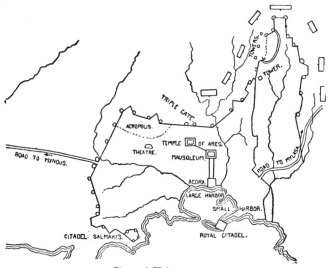

Siege of Halicarnassus.

wall, drive away its defenders, and bring up his battering rams to open a breach. While he was getting the towers in place, the garrison was by no means neglectful. Their engineers not only erected on their side a tower one hundred and fifty feet high, from which they could dominate Alexander's, but made a night sally to destroy the works so laboriously constructed by the besiegers. The Macedonians were alert, the outposts were quickly reinforced, and all combined met the attack with vigor; they repulsed the sortie with a loss of one hundred and seventy of the enemy killed (Neop-tolemus among them), and sixteen of Alexander's men killed and three hundred wounded. The excessive number of wounds was the result of the surprise, and of the fact that at night the men could not so well protect themselves from the missiles with their shields and the mantelets.

Shortly after, an attack was brought about by two of the Macedonian phalangites who, as a matter of braggadocio and rivalry in courage, armed themselves, and went forward, sin-gle-handed, to assault the wall at the point nearest the citadel. A few of the defenders, half in sport, made a sortie upon the reckless couple, who, however, killed and wounded a number of their assailants. This led to others joining the fray from both sides and to a pretty general fight and sortie in force of the garrison. A somewhat similar case occurred in the Gallic War in the land of the Nervii, and is mentioned by Cæsar. The sortie was repulsed, and had the assault been regularly planned and followed up, it might have been successful; for the walls were not well guarded, and two towers on this side (towards Mylasa), with all the wall between them, had fallen. A third tower had also been undermined, and was ready to fall, but the garrison sustained it by an interior wall or demi-lune. Next day Alexander brought up his engines against this new wall, and the garrison made another sortie in an attempt to destroy them. In this they were partially success-ful, for they managed to set fire to some wicker-work sheds covering the engines and to part of one tower; but Philotas preserved the rest from injury, and Alexander, leading up his Macedonians in person, drove the enemy back with loss. Still Alexander had to ask a truce to recover his dead, — the only time he ever made this confession of defeat; for this new defense was difficult to approach, inasmuch as from the old wall the garrison could throw their darts upon the rear and flank of any party assaulting the demi-lune.

But the Halicarnassians were none the less in parlous case. They foresaw a speedy prospect of surrender unless they could fully destroy the besiegers' works, and resolved upon another general and desperate sortie. This was made from two places at one and the same time, the breach, and what was called the triple gate. The former was under charge of Ephialtes, and was so sharp and unexpected that the young Macedonian troops, who were on guard at the demi-lune works, were at first driven in, and it was with some effort that the heavy fire from the towers, and Philip's veterans, under the personal lead of the king, reëstablished the matter. Here Ephialtes was killed. The Halicarnassians were well provided with torches and combustibles of all kinds, and came near to accomplishing their purpose. But they tried to fire the towers and engines at the place where Alexander was himself superintending the work, and had, as usual, some of the best troops. They were met fiercely and hustled back. The breach was narrow, and the defeated enemy could not easily make his way through the débris. His loss was heavy. The second party issued from the so-called triple gate, where one of the Ptolemies (not the son of Lagus) was posted. This sortie was also driven back; and as the Halicarnassians in crowds were retiring over a bridge which they had thrown across the ditch, it broke under the excess of weight, and many fell in, and were there slain. Seeing the rout of their comrades, the garrison shut the gates lest the besiegers should enter pell-mell with them; and the Macedonians cut to pieces a number who remained outside without weapons, horror-struck and incapable of defense. The city could doubtless have been taken, had not the king ordered the recall to be blown, for he hoped now for surrender, and desired to avoid delivering up the ancient city to plunder. About one thousand of the garrison were killed, and of the Macedonians some forty, including one of the Ptolemies, Clearchus, chief of the archers, and many noted Macedonians.

The wall of the town was now so far destroyed and weakened, and so many of the garrison had been killed or wounded, that Orontobates and Memnon decided to withdraw to the fortress called Salmakis, and to the royal citadel, on an island in the harbor. This they did in the second watch of the night, after setting fire to their big tower and other works, and to the houses near the walls. The fire spread rapidly. The Macedonians speedily moved in, did their best to arrest its progress, and measurably succeeded. Some booty was secured. The city could, however, not well be abandoned to Memnon, and it was essential that Alexander should continue his advance. He deemed it best to raze what was left of Halicarnassus to the ground.

Alexander was unable from lack of time personally to carry on a siege of the strongholds to which Orontobates and Memnon had retired, but he left a garrison of three thousand foot and two hundred horse, under another of the Ptolemies, to reduce them and then finish the capture of the remaining coast cities. His siege train he sent to Tralles. The political charge of Caria, as vice-regent, he left to Queen Ada, who had once ruled over the land, but had been displaced. She was a woman of strong character and noted virtues, and Alexander paid her singular honors. Her influence had weighed much in bringing the Carian cities to Alexander's side. Garrisons were left in the several cities under Macedonian officers. Harpalus was placed in receipt of custom.

With the fall of Halicarnassus, Alexander could consider the west coast of Asia Minor entirely under his control, and permanently. He had done a good summer's and autumn's work since the battle of the Granicus.

XXI.

TO THE TAURUS. WINTER, B. C. 334–333.

ALEXANDER now headed for the interior of Asia Minor. He divided his army into two columns. The heavy trains and the bulk of the heavy troops were sent under Parmenio towards Gordium by way of Sardis, with orders to winter there. The king retained the lighter part of the army, and marched along the coast to where the Taurus range comes down to the sea. On the way he captured or received in surrender all the important towns. At Phaselis he performed the unheard-of feat of marching his army along the tide-washed beach at the foot of Mount Climax, — a matter of cool calculation with the king, but by all others ascribed to the divinity of his character. From Sidē he turned northward, reducing many places and masking such as he could not readily take. In the Termessian defile he was fain to resort to a ruse to obtain the upper-hand, which he got only then by a hard fight. At Sagalassus he had a still more bitter combat and some loss; but victory here opened his way to the upland plateau of Asia Minor. Thence he advanced, *via* Selænæ, to Gordium, where Parmenio's column duly reached him, and some recruits from Macedonia.

ALEXANDER'S plans now pointed towards the interior of Asia Minor. The renewed freedom given to the Greek cities so far captured had placed their allegiance on a basis secure beyond a peradventure. The Macedonian garrisons, holding all the important places of the Ægean coast, rendered the ground already gone over comparatively safe against any incursions by the Persian fleet, while the Persian army had practically evacuated Asia Minor. Alexander now rightly estimated that the thereby weakened means of resistance of the cities of the southern coast, and their lessened hope of aid from either the fleet or the army of their suzerain, would enable him to make more or less easy capture of them all. And this with but a small part of his forces. But he would need recruits for the next campaign.

It was approaching winter. A considerable number of the men in the Macedonian army had been newly married before starting from home. The king furloughed these men and sent them back to their homes to stay with their wives till spring, under charge of Ptolemy, son of Seleucus, Cœnus, Parmenio's son-in-law, and Meleager, who were also married men. This act added greatly to the good-will of his soldiers, and on their return the furloughed men brought with them many comrades. He likewise detailed Cleander to the Peloponnesus to recruit.

Alexander then divided his effectives into two columns.

Halicarnassus to Gordium.

Parmenio with part of the Macedonian and all the Thessalian heavy horse, the Greek auxiliaries, the siege material and the wagon train, was headed for Sardis, which was to be an intermediary base as it were, *en route* to Phrygia. He was to winter here, and, as spring opened, march to Gordium, which was to be the rendezvous of all the forces. Alexander had cut out for himself a winter campaign. He never intrusted the dangerous or important work to the hands of others. With the second column, consisting of the rest of the troops, — some Companions, the hypaspists, phalanx, Agrianians, archers and Thracian prodromoi (dragoons) — in light marching order, he proposed, despite the inclement season and rugged country, to move by way of Lycia and Pamphylia, capture and garrison the coast cities, and thus finish the work of neutralizing the Persian fleet. For without a port on the mainland it must soon leave the Ægean. Thence his route would lie across the mountains through Pisidia into Phrygia, due north to Gordium.

The columns separated. Parmenio, whose task was easy, carried out his programme with discretion, and in due time

Halicarnassus to Gordium.

turned up at Gordium with the troops in excellent discipline and heart. We shall find him there by and by. Alexander started along the coast. Having taken Hyparna, where the Greek mercenaries surrendered the citadel on promise of safe conduct, Alexander invaded Lycia, and captured Telmessus, Pinara, Xanthus, Patara, and some thirty other towns. This was the more easy, as Lycia had retained under the Persian king a sort of semi-independence. Of all the cities, Marmara alone defended itself desperately. But naught availed it. When the engines had effected such a breach that all chances were cut off, these brave people organized themselves into a forlorn hope, fired their city and household treasures, and actually made their way by stealth through the Macedonian camp, and escaped to the mountains. With whatsoever pride and admiration we watch our hero's progress, it gives us pleasure to see an occasional act of signal bravery like this one meet with a less bitter than the usual fate.

Though the mid-winter season was very unfavorable, Alexander pursued his advance — probably up the Xanthus, and marched into Milyas on the headwaters of this river. To him here came embassies from Phaselis and nearly all the coast towns, offering, in token of surrender and greeting, golden crowns and presents, for the news of his liberal treatment of those who did not oppose him had preceded him, and acted as an open sesame. These embassies Alexander received with honor, and bade each accept the regent he should send to represent him.

As a rule, in all the important towns which the king captured, or which submitted to his arms, a few Macedonians were left behind as the nucleus of a garrison, generally wounded or disabled or invalided men who had earned a right to easier duties than those in the field, but who were still able to leaven the lump by their skill and fidelity. If the town was important or the population hostile, a larger garrison was left; but even a few Macedonians, under a good chief, in possession of the citadel of a town, could hold their own with the aid of the mercenaries, with whom they increased their force up to a figure sufficiently high.

From Milyas Alexander proceeded to Phaselis, perhaps the most important of those cities which had surrendered to him. It lay at the foot of Mount Climax, and possessed three fine harbors and an ample roadway. It was powerful and wealthy. From Phaselis there ran over the mountain ranges the principal road into the interior, leading direct to Pergē. On this road a Pisidian tribe had built a fortress, from which they made frequent descents on Phaselian territory to gather booty. Alexander at once came to the rescue of his new subjects, and lent them armed assistance in reducing this den of robbers, for it was little more. Moreover as he must use the road himself, it was essential that it should be opened.

In Phaselis the king spent the rest of the winter. He was well pleased with his prosperous campaign, and indulged in feasts and games. His enjoyment of such occasions was keen. No man ever worked harder when at work; his periods of relaxation, comparatively rare, sometimes partook of the same exuberance of strength. It is related that on one occasion here he headed a procession through the streets after a feast, and decorated with wreaths the statue of the poet Theodectes, who had once been at Philip's court, and left a savory reputation.

Nearchus of Amphipolis, a Cretan, whose affiliations made him acceptable to the population, was made satrap of Lycia.

It was here that occurred the unfortunate treason of the Lyncestian Alexander. This man, we remember, had been implicated in the murder of Philip, but had been pardoned for being the first to salute Alexander as king, and had been rewarded with honors and brilliant commands. When, however, Amyntas had fled from Macedonia to Darius, this Alexander, fearing lest his pardon should not be lasting, had made overtures through Amyntas to the Persian king. He was not of those who believed in Alexander's star. Darius, under another pretext, dispatched a messenger to convey his answer, which was to the effect that if this Alexander would kill the king, he himself should be king of Macedon, and should receive one thousand talents of gold ($1,250,000) as a present. The messenger was captured by Parmenio, and compelled to reveal the plot. The Lyncestian Alexander was at the time commander of the Thessalian horse, a position second to none in the army, and was also one of the Companions. To this body the king confided the facts. The Companions had long mistrusted the man, and feared that the king's confidence was misplaced. The traitor, who was with Parmenio at Sardis, was deprived of his rank and ordered under guard. The Companions would have sentenced him to death; but the king still strove to spare him despite his treachery; he never forgot a benefit. This Alexander was eventually executed three years later on the occasion of the conspiracy of Philotas.

When the weather became more auspicious, Alexander moved from Phaselis, sending a part of his light troops over the mountain road, which he had caused to be repaired by the Thracians after he had driven the robber tribe from its all but inaccessible fastnesses, to Pergē. This was stragetically the most important town of this part of the country, because the key to the passage of the mountains on the north. The king himself, with the cavalry Companions and phalanx, marched along the seashore. This march was a very risky one to make. A narrow beach, shut in between Mount Climax, which rose in bold outlines to the height of seven thousand feet, and the sea, was generally covered by water a number of feet deep, or by marshes, for a distance of many miles. Only at those very rare intervals, when the north wind, blowing with unusual violence, beat back the tides, could the beach be used at all, and this but for a few hours at a time. The idea of marching an army along this beach was almost as bold as the conception of Hannibal's march through the Arnus swamps, though not undertaken with the crisp strategic purpose of the latter. Still, if it could be done, Alexander might surprise the position of Pergē, whose inhabitants would not expect him from this direction, and the moral effect of such a march would not be inconsiderable.

It happened with Alexander's usual good fortune that about the time when to make this march would be desirable, the elements conspired in his favor, and the periodical north wind blew with exceptional fury. That luck attended him cannot be gainsaid, but Alexander deserves none the less credit for seizing the proper moment to enable him to secure a prosperous passage of this treacherous route. In places the troops waded to the middle, but the transit was safely accomplished. His success gave still further voice to the superstitious notion that Alexander was under the direct favor of the gods. The whole expedition was no doubt well calculated by Alexander in all its details, and what generally was a most hazardous feat may have been at that time a safe one. Not a man was lost, but his soldiers, gazing back on their perilous passage for miles through the waves of the sea at the foot of a perpendicular rock, shuddered indeed, but all the more gained confidence in their king, and gloried in his skill and courage, as they did in his youth and beauty. While the wonderful good luck which always followed this great conqueror was a marked factor in his success, it must not be forgotten that at his headquarters the king always had the very best scientific and professional talent; that he was indefatigable in studying up the questions which bore upon every step he took; and that what often appears to be crass luck was the result of close calculation. Moreover, Alexander never gave Fortune a chance to desert him; whenever she stood ready to help him, he always helped himself. The Peripatetic, Kallisthenes, who accompanied the king's headquarters, and first wrote a history of his campaigns, related the march with his usual unction, and claimed that the sea was fain to bow to the power of this godlike youth. But Alexander simply wrote home that "he had made a path along the Pamphylian Ladders, and had marched over it."

Pergē, which was the key to the mountain passes, north and west, surrendered; whether on account of this march or not, does not appear. The town of Aspendus was willing to do the like, but demurred at admitting a garrison; and Alexander agreed to accept, in lieu thereof, a tribute from this city of fifty talents — pay for his army — and certain horses which it had been in the habit of rearing annually for Darius. Thence he marched to Sidē, and here he put the usual garrison. The city was the last place of importance on the hither side of the Taurus, and was situated near the point where the range comes to an abrupt end on the seashore.

Alexander could now turn safely northward, and subdue the interior provinces; for he had under his control practically the entire coast line of Asia Minor. There were but a few isolated and not important points left behind in a state of blockade. He was preparing to besiege Syllium, a place about five miles from the sea between Aspendus and Sidē, when news reached him from Aspendus that the promised tribute had been denied. Syllium was an exceptionally strong place, and was held by Greek mercenaries in Persian pay, — men of a different stamp to the ordinary Asiatic soldier; so that Alexander deemed it wise to turn from this fortress for the moment, and march back upon Aspendus. The king was fond of hard tasks for their own sake. He was obstinate to a degree in his resolution; but he had a strong enough grasp of his general problem not to allow this natural antagonism to lead him astray. There was method in his stubbornness. There can scarcely be pointed out an occasion when it misled him. And on this occasion he concluded that he would not waste time in besieging Syllium, but made arrangements to observe it instead.

Aspendus was built mainly upon a very high rock, at the foot of which ran the Eurymedon; but a part of the inhabitants lived in a village which nestled at its foot, and was protected by a wall. This the citizens deserted on the approach of the Macedonian army, and the empty houses afforded Alexander an opportunity to quarter his army to good advantage. The place was of extraordinary strength, and might well have held out an indefinite time, for all Alexander's siege material was with the column under Parmenio; but the garrison, doubtless influenced by the current rumors of Alexander's divine powers, — which superstition Alexander was by no means loath to foster, for its political value as well as, be it frankly confessed, the gratification it yielded to his personal vanity, — agreed to surrender on terms harder than the former ones, namely, double tribute and hostages; and the king, having no desire to devote his time to minor exploits with the world open to his arms, settled the matter in this form, and made haste to march on Phrygia by way of Pergē.

Alexander had no intention of halting long on his way to subdue the mountain tribes of the Taurus. He had altogether too much work cut out ahead. It sufficed if, in passing through, he personally taught them a salutary lesson. He could then leave the eventual settlement of the country to whatever lieutenant he might commission to represent him. Alexander invariably kept the main object in view, and did not allow unessential matters to call his attention from the more important ones. His hope now was speedily to measure swords with the Great King.

The only road to Phrygia lay west of Pergē, skirting the foot of the mountain and then running through the defiles of Termessus, where the mountains had been torn asunder into a gap with sides so precipitous that a handful of doughty men could readily obstruct the passage of a host. The road was hewn in the rock along one side of the steep wall, and was commanded by yet higher rocks on both sides of the gorge, and within arrow-shot. Beyond the defile lay a strongly fortified town. On reaching the defile, Alexander found that the rocks on both sides commanding the road had been occupied by a considerable body of mountaineers. He at once made preparations to go into camp, rightly arguing that this act would lead the barbarians to suppose that he would not attack the defile that night. The ruse had its natural effect. It was the same Epaminondas had practiced at Mantinæa. The bulk of the enemy retired to the city which lay beyond, leaving but a slender guard on duty in the gorge, which in its turn became somewhat careless of its work. The king, watching his opportunity with his wonted restless eye, no sooner ascertained this fact than he took his archers, javelin throwers and hypaspists, marched with the utmost caution to that part of the defile which the enemy had chosen for defense, and fell with great audacity upon this guard. Surprised and unable to withstand the heavier missiles of the Macedonians, the enemy was driven headlong from his foothold. This opened the pass. The king at once moved up his army and went actually into camp near the city gates. Here he received an embassy from Selgē, a town whose inhabitants were at enmity with the Termessians, and were accordingly glad to assist the Greeks. Alexander made a treaty with Selgē, to which that city remained steadily faithful. But as Termessus promised to give trouble and waste much time in its capture, he blockaded and passed it by, as he had Syllium and several other places, and, no doubt leaving a suitable detachment to hold the defile, marched on to Sagalassus.

This was a city whose inhabitants were called the most warlike of all the Pisidians, themselves a race of marked courage

and determination. Sagalassus lay at the foot of the highest
terrace of the mountains, and beyond it opened the uplands of
Phrygia. The king found this people drawn up on the rocks
on the south front of their city, which rocks formed, as it
were, a natural rampart. And here, too, a considerable force
of Termessians had joined them to oppose the Macedonian
advance. Alexander could make no use of his cavalry on
this rugged ground, but he prepared at once to assault the
position with his foot. He drew up these troops with the
shield-bearing guards under his own command on the right,
and the phalangites on the left, each brigade placed according to the day's roster, the whole under Lyncestian Amyntas,
son of Arrhabœus, and so marshaled as that each commander
of rank should have an occasion to display his personal valor.
The archers and Agrianians covered the right, the Thracian
acontists, under Sitalces, the left. The light troops in front

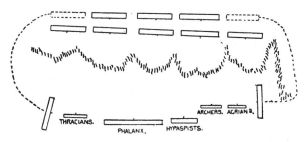

Combat near Sagalassus.

of the right advanced boldly up the heights, followed closely
by the line, and fell upon the Pisidians with a fierceness which
deserved to encompass a victory, But both wings were suddenly taken in flank by an ambuscade, easily prepared on such
a field. The archers being light-armed, and having lost their
leader, gave way in disorder ; but the always gallant Agrianians, better armed, held their ground with great tenacity,
and enabled the phalangites to come to their rescue, headed

by Alexander in person. Undismayed at the formidable array of the phalanx, the mountaineers showed wonderful devotion, rushing in crowds upon the line of sarissas, in front of which they fell by hundreds in a vain effort to break it down. But they found the Macedonians as immovable as their own native rocks, and confessing the hopelessness of their task, but hoping to try conclusions again, dispersed all over the surrounding country in places where the Macedonians, heavily armed and ignorant of the ground, did not deem it wise to attempt to follow. About five hundred of the barbarians had been slain. This dispersion, however, worked them no good. It was at once taken advantage of by the king, who advanced on and stormed the town, capturing it without difficulty in its half-deserted condition. There had fallen in this combat about twenty Macedonians, including Cleander, the general of the archers, — the second chief of this gallant body killed in action.

At this point Alexander made a halt, and undertook a number of expeditions against the rest of the strongholds of Pisidia. By taking some by storm, and by granting terms to others, he managed in no great time, and without any single case of noteworthy opposition, to reduce the entire country to his control, so far as it was essential to protect himself in his onward march. The road to the upland plains beyond this range was open to him, without leaving danger in his rear.

The king now marched into Phrygia, leaving Lake Ascania on his left, and reached Celænæ in five marches. This city lay in the mountains at the headwaters of the Mæander, and had been constructed by Xerxes, after his defeat by the Greeks, as a bulwark against their expected advance. It was built on an inaccessible rock and could have made an interminable defense; but the garrison, consisting of one thousand Carians and one hundred Greek mercenaries, headed by the viceroy of Phrygia, after listening to Alexander's proposals, agreed to surrender in a given period — Curtius says in sixty days — if not succored by that time. Alexander accepted these terms, knowing that his own advance on Gordium would cut off any reinforcements which they might be expecting; left fifteen hundred men under Antigonus, son of Philip, to see that the treaty was duly carried out; placed Balacrus, son of Amyntas, in command of the Greek allies, a position which Antigonus had hitherto held, and after a rest of ten days marched to Gordium, the ancient capital of the Phrygian kings. Parmenio shortly arrived, and the married men who had been on furlough likewise joined at this point, bringing thirty-six hundred and fifty recruits with them, namely, three thousand phalangites, three hundred Macedonian and two hundred Thessalian heavy horse, and one hundred and fifty Æleans.

To Gordium also, Athens sent an embassy praying for the release of the Athenian prisoners captured at the Granicus and sent to Macedonia in chain-gangs. Alexander saw fit to deny the request, with intent to show that he was able to hold Greece in subjection; but he promised to consider the matter when the present expedition should be happily accomplished. He was now again on the high road from the Hellespont through Cappadocia and Cilicia to the heart of the Persian kingdom, which he might have taken after the Granicus victory. His extensive circuit along the coast had been wisely and advisedly made. It had rendered safe his base in Asia Minor, which less than this could not have done.

The king had finished his first year's campaign, the last part of it during the winter season, among the mountains. There are few things which show the wonderful capacity of Alexander to face, and his men to endure, hardship so well as the fact that the difficulties of a winter or a mountain cam-

paign are never dwelt upon by the ancient historians. Neither
is credit given for overcoming the unusual labors of such
campaigning, nor are these deemed an excuse for delay or
failure.

In a certain sense Alexander's success had not been so
splendid as to overawe the Greek opposition at home. It
must not be supposed that tongues wagged any less noisily
two thousand years ago than they do to-day. To be sure he
had captured all the coast cities of Asia Minor as the result
of his victory at the Granicus, but there were many who
alleged that Memnon, whose ability was well recognized, had
only permitted this apparent gain so that he himself might
more securely occupy the islands of the Ægean in force, and
make ready to cut Alexander off from his base by invading
Macedon. Then indeed, said Alexander's opponents, he
would soon show the Macedonians how slender had been their
hold on all this territory. And it was openly prophesied in
Athens that Alexander would not dare advance further inland. Nor were these arguments without a substratum of
reason. Memnon was capable, and the one man who was so,
of giving Alexander a vast amount of trouble ; and no one
as yet appreciated the full extent of Alexander's resources
and ability. This was natural enough.

But Alexander's political *nous* was no less strong than his
military sense. As we have seen, he gave back their freedom
and old laws to all the Greek cities he had captured or which
had surrendered to him. This meant not that he had merely
stepped into the shoes of the Persian king ; not that these
cities had but exchanged one tyrant for another ; they had
made so substantial a gain — and they recognized the fact —
that Alexander could rely almost certainly on their remaining
faithful to the end to him who had dealt thus generously
by them. And it will be noticed that the king had already

begun to put in practice his uniform rule of treating with marked generosity places or parties which helped his cause, with exemplary severity those who resisted or rebelled. Nor did all this tend merely to give him the aid he needed for his invasion of the Persian monarchy; it added abundant strength to his home politics. For every city in Asia which accepted Alexander accepted also the fact that Macedonia was Greece. This reinforced him by just so much.

Meanwhile the Persian king was no whit abashed. He looked upon the defeat of his generals by the Greeks as a mere accident, due to bad management, which could be readily repaired by proper means. Asia Minor was at one of the distant ends of his dominions, and he did not comprehend what Alexander's progress meant. He did, however, see by how much Memnon's advice had been the best, and had, accordingly, placed him in supreme command of the theatre of operations, in the expectation of speedily retrieving the disasters which had followed Alexander's initial success.

Tetradrachma in Berlin Museum.
(Alexander idealized as Hercules.)

XXII.

CILICIA. SUMMER AND FALL, B. C. 333.

MEMNON, who had just been placed in sole command of the Ægean by Darius, and was preparing to invade Macedonia, now died. This relieved Alexander from grave danger, for Memnon had no worthy successor. Darius determined to collect an army and march to meet Alexander. The latter, after his late successes, was better able to sustain a fleet, and took measures to replace the one he had disbanded. At Gordium Alexander cut the Gordian knot, — or at least managed to impress upon all the idea that he had fulfilled the omen connected therewith, and would be lord of Asia. Master of all Asia Minor west of the Taurus, he marched towards the Cilician Gates. This defile Darius' satrap had failed to fortify. Alexander captured it, descended into Cilicia, and took Tarsus by a *coup de main*. Sending Parmenio forward to secure the Syrian Gates, he himself reduced Rugged Cilicia in a week's campaign, and overran the rest of the country. He here learned that the citadels of Halicarnassus and all the other important Carian cities had been taken by his lieutenants.

MEMNON, who was now in sole and unlimited command of the Ægean, having the design of carrying the war into Macedon, of instigating revolt against Alexander among his enemies in Greece, and of cutting him and his army off from Europe, managed to get possession of the island of Chios by the treachery of Apollonides, and reëstablished the oligarchy. Thence he sailed to Lesbos, landed, and took its four large towns, all, in fact, but the city of Mitylene. This city resisted his efforts for some time with the aid of its Macedonian garrison. But Memnon went systematically to work. He cut the city off from the land by double walls, and blockaded its port with his fleet. This soon reduced it to great straits. But no doubt very luckily for Alexander (for he was his one distinctly able opponent) Memnon shortly after died of a fever, leaving the temporary command to his nephew Pharnabazus. Memnon's plan had been to sail for the Hellespont, so soon as he had a suitable base in the Ægean, cut Alexander's communications at this point, and thence invade Macedonia. He was the one man in the service of Darius whose conception of the methods by which to meet Alexander's invasion had all along been clear, intelligent and practicable. His successor was, however, by no means equal to the task thus inherited.

Ægean.

Mitylene, hard pressed, was finally obliged to surrender its allegiance to Alexander, which it did on the promise by Pharnabazus and by Autophradates, who was serving with him, of certain favorable conditions ; but no sooner did the Persians obtain possession of the city than they violated all the agreements, and exacted heavy tribute from the citizens. They obtained possession of Tenedos in much the same manner. Memnon's vigor seemed to survive him for some months. The activity thus displayed by the Persian fleet, if put in practice a year sooner, might have seriously interfered with

Alexander's landing in Asia. But Memnon was not at that time fully trusted, and was unable to make his influence or his intelligence avail.

The death of Memnon was on a par with the uniform current of good fortune, which always seemed to set in Alexander's favor. It robbed Darius of the one man who could probably have made head against the Macedonians, who would have known how to utilize the vast resources of the Persian empire to advantage, and who would have restrained Darius from committing the irreparable errors of which he was guilty. With but a tithe of the forces Darius raised, he would, no doubt, have increased Alexander's task tenfold. His death disabled the management at sea so as to make it more probable that Alexander could again utilize a fleet. He felt able to cope with Memnon's successors, if he had not been with this admirable soldier himself.

After Memnon's death, Darius held a council of war to determine what action it were best to take to oppose the rash but dangerous invader of his dominions. Rejecting the advice of the Greeks about him, he placed his confidence, naturally enough, in the courage and intelligence of his Persian courtiers and generals, and determined to take the field himself, with a levy *en masse* of the kingdom. He sent to the Ægean to confirm Pharnabazus in his command, but at the same time withdrew from him all the Greek mercenaries serving in the fleet, purposing to use them in the army to be put on foot. This latter act handicapped the Persian admirals, and effectually put a stop to any chance of invading Macedon. But Datames, meanwhile, had taken Tenedos.

The Macedonian treasury was now in better condition to afford the expense of a fleet. This, happily, it was not difficult to create. Alexander sent Hegelochus to the Hellespontine region to seize all merchantmen coming home from the Euxine sea, and convert them into war-ships. Antipater raised vessels from Euboea and the Peloponnesus. Athens, angered at the seizure of some of her wheat-carrying craft, declined to furnish her contingent, but armed one hundred vessels, and entered into correspondence with the Persian king. Hegelochus, on hearing of this, deemed it wise to release the Athenian ships which he had seized; but he had on hand, without counting these, a goodly number suitable for the purpose.

It was as well that Alexander had decided to organize another fleet as it had perhaps been necessary to disband the first one. Not only was the ability of the Persian fleet to accomplish results still an open question, but some of the Greek cities were by no means beyond taking active side with Darius when it could be safely done. The fleet became useful from the very start. The first exploit of Proteas, whom Antipater put in command, was the capture of eight out of ten triremes which Datames, the Persian admiral, had at Siphnus, one of the Cyclades; and the appearance of a new squadron had a marked effect in forestalling an outbreak of hostility from Athens, if not a general Greek revolt.

It is natural to question Alexander's wisdom in disbanding his first fleet. It was perhaps an error. If Memnon had lived, it might have proved a fatal one. Alexander had apparently, by his want of ships, placed his rear in grave danger. The Persian fleet, unopposed, was sure, sooner or later, to make a descent on Macedon. But, on the other hand, it was not a direct threat to Alexander's standing in Asia Minor. His presence there was the rather dangerous to the Persian fleet, by closing all the coast harbors against its vessels, which, with the scant naval equipment of that age, must land daily for water and provisions. And though it would seem that a fleet was a matter almost of necessity, Alexander may have calculated that Antipater could hold head against any revolting Greek force which might grow dangerous to Macedonia (as indeed he proved his ability to do at Megalopolis), and meet a Persian invasion as well; he no doubt looked to the future for success enough on land to outweigh any losses in the Ægean; his operations imperatively called for many of the crews which manned the fleet for shore duty, let alone the fact that he had not funds enough to pay the men; and it was not difficult, as the coming year showed, again to make himself strong at sea, when the demand should become more urgent. If it was a mistake, it had happily not proven a disastrous one.

To Gordium, then, the various columns of the Macedonians converged, and here the army was reunited. The column which had made the winter campaign with Alexander from the south; the column from Sardis, under Parmenio, with the artillery and train and heavy cavalry; the newly married men, reporting on expiration of furlough, and bringing their contingent of recruits from Macedonia, all met and shook hands over the brilliant success of the first campaign; all looked forward to vastly greater victories and richer booty, as they penetrated deeper into the territory of the wealthy Persian king. Their implicit belief in their leader made success an article of faith. The recruits were a welcome arrival; their number all but compensated for the losses incurred, and the details on garrison duty in the various cities captured.

It was here in Gordium, in February or March, 333 B. C., that Alexander imposed upon the credulity of the Phrygians by cutting or otherwise unloosing the famous knot of King Midas, the performance of which feat was by the oracle said to betoken that the successful man should be king of Asia. However the feat was accomplished, there is no doubt that Alexander did succeed in making the populace believe that

he had fulfilled the requirements of the omen, and that he
would be the conqueror of the East. It makes, perhaps,
small odds how Alexander managed to impose upon the cred-
ulous by his actual deeds of wonder, or by his plausible way
of putting things. It is none the less true that his support
largely came from a popular belief that he was more than
human.

From Gordium, Alexander marched along the southerly
slope of the boundary range to Ancyra, where he received
the submission of the Paphlagonians, but granted their request that no Macedonian army should be quartered upon
their country. But he probably placed them under the super-
vision of Calas, satrap of Phrygia. Hence marching into
Cappadocia, he crossed the Halys and subdued the entire
region west of this river, which had been the boundary between Persia and Lydia before the days of Cyrus, and that
portion beyond the Halys as far as the Iris; and appointed
Sabictas viceroy. Here, too, he returned to the Greek cities
their ancient laws and customs; but not desiring to withdraw
too much time from his greater task of seeking Darius and
coming to a decisive encounter with him, he left the democratic party in each city with power sufficient to control the
oligarchical faction, without attempting entirely to extirpate
the latter party.

Alexander was now master of all Asia Minor west of the
Taurus, and could choose to remain on the defensive or cross
the range in offense. The latter course was the one which
was always the more consistent with his character. He, therefore, took up his march toward the chief pass in the Taurus
mountains, known as the Gates of Cilicia, Pylæ Ciliciæ (the
modern Golek Boghaz), a defile thirty-six hundred feet above
the sea, and well-nigh inexpugnable if held by a determined
party. When Cyrus the Younger had passed this defile, he

had expected to be unable to force it, and had made preparations to turn it by transporting a force of troops by sea to the
rear of the pass. Xenophon characterized the defile as beyond

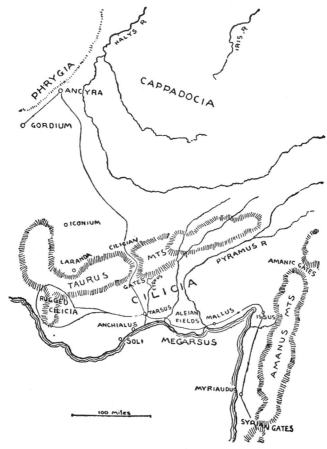

Gordium to Amanus.

human ability to take. In many places but four men can
march abreast between the perpendicular walls of stone. Alexander was unable, without a fleet, to resort to Cyrus' turning manoeuvre. The Persians, did they but know it, had the

power to block his path. He might possibly have turned the defile by way of Laranda, from which place were passes into western or Rugged Cilicia. But this was a difficult and dangerous route, to be avoided by all means if possible, and it is far from improbable that these passes were not then known to any but the native barbarians.

But Arsames, satrap of Cilicia, Darius' chief officer at this point, made no preparation to hold these Gates. He had probably received no specific orders on the subject. When the Macedonian army arrived in the vicinity, the Gates were found to be beset by but a slender force. Leaving Parmenio in camp with the heavy troops, Alexander took the shield-bearing guards, archers, and Agrianians, and after nightfall essayed an attack, almost against hope, upon this formidable defile. Why Arsames had not occupied this place in force, and why Darius had not so ordered, will ever remain a mystery. Alexander's very boldness in advancing to attack the defile succeeded; the small guard evidently considered itself left in the lurch, took to flight, and, next day, the pass having thus fallen into his hands, the entire army filed into Cilicia. Alexander, says Curtius, wondered at his good fortune.

Alexander learned on descending the mountain that Arsames, seeing that he must yield up Tarsus after having lost the Gates, intended to plunder the city before evacuating it. With his usual untiring activity, he led his cavalry and lightest foot by a forced march to Tarsus, and was fortunate enough not only to anticipate Arsames by his rapid manœuvre, but by a sudden and vigorous attack drove him into headlong retreat.

The invaders had thus passed the first great rampart of the heart of Persia. The second was the range of Mount Amanus, on the farther side of Cilicia.

It was at Tarsus that Alexander fell sick — from overwork, according to Aristobulus; it is said by others from bathing in the cold water of the Cydnus, on which river Tarsus is situated, when overheated by the hot mid-day march, and somewhat unstrung by the toil of the preceding week. A severe chill and fever set in; his life was despaired of by all his physicians except Philip, who was the medical attendant of his boyhood, and much beloved by the king. The position of a medical man who in those days attended a monarch or other great person was far from enviable. Perhaps the others were afraid of the penalties of failure. Later, when Hephæstion died, Alexander is said to have crucified his physician for malpractice, and it certainly required more than ordinary nerve to undertake a critical case in high quarters. Against this Philip, Alexander had been warned, by even cool-headed old Parmenio, as having been bribed by Darius with the promise of one thousand talents and the hand of his daughter in marriage, to poison this annoying intruder. The king, however, had abundant confidence in Philip's integrity. With one hand he gave him Parmenio's letter, while with the other he drank the potion Philip had prepared, eying his physician, meanwhile, with a look none could encounter but the innocent. Conscious of his fidelity, Philip's demeanor never changed. The potion worked; Alexander happily recovered. The king was an excellent judge of men. Perhaps no man ever reaches greatness who lacks this faculty. Bad servants can tear down more than able masters build. Alexander's capacity for selecting those who could do their work well was never at fault; and, save in the few abnormal instances by which his life is blemished, he requited those services handsomely.

From Tarsus Alexander sent Parmenio forward with the Greek auxiliaries and mercenaries, the Thessalian heavy horse

and Sitalces' Thracians, to capture the Syrian Gates and
hold the pass. With this defile, which cut through Mount
Amanus near the sea, he must have been intimately acquainted from the march of Cyrus, the details of which he
of course well knew; and by its possession he secured his
entrance into Syria and Phœnicia. With the rest of the
army Alexander advanced to Anchialus. Here was the gigantic statue of the Assyrian king, in the position of clapping its hands, with the remarkable inscription: " Sardan-
apalus built Anchialus and Tarsus in one day; do thou, O
stranger, eat, drink and love, naught else in life is worth
this!" meaning a clap of the hands. Upon Soli, which he
also captured, he levied a tribute of two hundred talents on
account of its tenacious fidelity to Darius, but later remitted
the fine.

Hence, with three brigades of Macedonians, the archers
and Agrianians, Alexander marched against those mountain
tribes of the western province, known as " Rugged Cilicia,"
who still held out. These tribes were a species of mountain
robbers who, though they could do no serious harm, might
easily interfere with his communications and cause considerable annoyance unless subdued. They possibly might make
their way through the passes to Laranda and Iconium, and
thus turn the Cilician Gates, though this indeed was not a
danger to be anticipated. They lived in fastnesses which
were all but unapproachable by reason of the rough nature
of the country. Despite the difficulties of the task, however,
in a short week's campaign Alexander reduced these robber-
hordes to reason and returned to Soli. Though we know
little of the details of the short campaigns of Alexander,
there is something in the mystery which surrounds them,
which, added to the certainty of the accomplished fact and
the known difficulties of the situation, clothes him not only

with a personal heroism beyond what we find in any other soldier, but shows rare strength, discipline and endurance, and a fidelity without equal in the men who followed in his footsteps. Success depended wholly on the wonderful physical and moral force of the man himself, and it was he alone who could evoke from his men such efforts as are implied in the conduct of some of the campaigns of which we possess but the baldest outlines.

At Soli, Alexander heard that Ptolemy and Asander, Parmenio's nephew, had won a great battle against the Persian Orontobates, in which seven hundred and fifty Persians had been killed, and had captured the Salmakis and royal citadel at Halicarnassus. Other Carian cities, — Myndus, Caunus, Thera, Calipolis, — as well as Cos and Triopium, had fallen, which happy events he celebrated with games and sacrifice; not forgetting Æsculapius in token of his recovery. Likely enough these celebrations had also for object the reclaiming of the Solians to Greek manners, customs and aspirations, which, in the course of many years' subjection to the Persians, had become but a tradition. He then marched to Tarsus and thence along the coast to Megarsus and Mallus, which two cities of Greek origin he also restored to their old status and abolished their tribute; and, after sacrificing to the deities of both, he sent Philotas with the horse across the Aleian field to the Pyramus to reduce the territory of that quarter.

The season of B. C. 333 had been expended in the advance through, and reduction of, the territory from Gordium to Mount Amanus.

XXIII.

ISSUS. NOVEMBER, B. C. 333.

ALEXANDER had learned that Darius was awaiting him on the plains of Sochi, beyond the Amanic range. He headed for the Syrian Gates, intending to seek him, but was ignorant of, or else forgot, the Amanic Gates farther north. Darius, tired of waiting for his coming, advanced through this latter defile to Issus, thus cutting the Macedonian communications. Alexander was compromised, but had the courage and ability to save his men from demoralization, and convince them that in the narrow pass of Issus, Darius had lost that superiority which on the plains of Sochi he would have retained. This was, in fact, true, as the result showed. Alexander countermarched through the Syrian Gates, and drew up in Darius' front, who lay behind the Pinarus with an army six hundred thousand strong, of whom two hundred thousand were effective, the balance a source of weakness. They were set up with his Greek mercenaries in the centre, where stood Darius, and the best of the cavalry on the right. The Persians proposed to turn the Macedonian left by breaking their line near the seashore. There was a bend in the river, which, after some preliminary manœuvring, enabled Alexander to advance his line back of the Persian left centre. Here he proposed to make his own stoutest attack. While the Thessalian horse held Darius' right, which crossed to the attack, in check, though outnumbered ten to one, Alexander with his Companions and the hypaspists on the right of the phalanx, followed somewhat more slowly by the rest of the hoplites, dashed into the river, and attacked the Persian line with fury. Where he fought, the Persians were soon broken. But the Greek mercenaries, by a splendid rush, checked the phalanx and threatened disaster. From his advanced position Alexander sharply wheeled upon and took the Greek mercenaries in flank, tearing open their formation. This not only relieved the pressure on the Macedonian brigades, but opened a gap through which he cut his way to the place where Darius stood in person. The Great King turned and fled. This was the signal of a *sauve qui peut*. The battle was won, and great slaughter of the Persians followed. Large treasure and the family of Darius fell into Alexander's hands. The latter he treated with magnanimity. In this battle was exploded in the East the reliance on mere numbers.

ALEXANDER, when in Mallus, learned that Darius was at Sochi, beyond the mountains in Assyria, two marches from the Syrian Gates. Hither the Persian king had come from the Euphrates, with an army of half a million men. Like Napoleon, perhaps like every one of the greatest soldiers, Alexander had lurking in his methods that touch of the reckless which has sometimes been described as the characteristic of the gambler, and never shrank, when the occasion came, from risking his all on one stroke. In the present instance this impulse proceeded equally from his self-confidence and enthusiasm, and from the situation into which his task had thrust him. He called together his Companions and other commanding officers who formed his usual council of war, to ascertain their views, and told them fully what he heard about the proximity and enormous size of Darius' army, concealing nothing of the difficulty or danger. He found them all eager to be led against the enemy. Alexander therefore determined to seek the Persians on the plains beyond Amanus, and advanced along the seacoast, by the route he knew from Xenophon. On the second day he passed the Syrian Gates, a

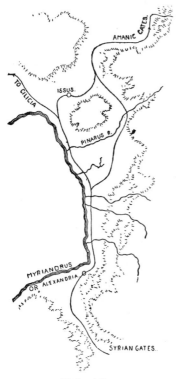

Plain of Issus.

second Thermopylæ lying between the coast and the mountains, with a difficult mountain-pass beyond, and camped near Myriandrus. He no doubt intended at once to march to the encounter of Darius, but was delayed a day or two by heavy stress of weather, for the early November storms had set in.

Alexander was apparently ignorant or oblivious that there was another pass farther north by which Darius could reach his rear; or else he was guilty of a serious lapse. There were two mountain gaps by which the Amanic range could be passed from Cilicia into the heart of the Persian empire. The more northerly one led to the Euphrates region; the other led into Syria, and was therefore known as the Syrian Gates. Alexander, after passing through these, had the intention of filing to the left, or northeast, and thus seeking Darius on the plains of Sochi. If Alexander knew of the northern pass, he may have been partially justified in calculating that Darius would remain where he was, in the broad plains of Assyria; and he may have dismissed the idea of the huge Persian army filing through a long mountain gap to seek the invaders on ground unfavorable to its numbers and arms, and where it could scarcely victual itself for two weeks, as too absurd even to make it worth while to detach a force thither to hold the defile. Alexander generally learned the topography of the country he traversed very thoroughly. He had able officers about him for this purpose, and he worked them hard. It seems as if he must have known of the Amanic Gates. In this case his leaving it absolutely open for Darius falls far short of his usual care. At least a small observation party to give him early notice of such a manœuvre as the Persians actually made was demanded by the circumstances.

Alexander may have little feared this danger in any event. That he did not anticipate it is clearly shown by his leaving no garrison at Issus to guard his hospitals there. But in case it should occur, he may have felt that his own and his army's activity would enable him so to manœuvre as by a few bold marches easily to escape from the clutches of his vast but sluggish and ill-led enemy, if not enable him the better to attack the Persians after disorganizing them by severe and rapid marches. One can conceive several things which an Alexander might do, other than fight the enemy; but it was none the less a lapse to leave open the Amanic Gates.

Darius had from the first abandoned the only true policy he could have adopted, namely, to utilize his navy, to carry the war into Macedon, to employ Greek mercenaries, and especially to defend the mountain passes, and thus keep the enemy from gaining a foothold in the interior of his kingdom. Memnon had clearly outlined this policy from the beginning. With a superior fleet in the Ægean, the Hellespont could have been made impassable. The line of Mount Taurus barred the entrance to Cilicia. The occupation of its passes would have all but absolutely prevented the Macedonian incursion. Behind these again was the pass between Mount Amanus and the sea — the Syrian Gates — and the more northerly pass, or Amanic Gates. Both mountain ranges could have been easily blocked against Alexander. For this purpose no troops were as good as his Greek mercenaries, and he had plenty of them. Such blindness is hardly to be understood. Alexander's good fortune was certainly the complement of Darius' folly.

It is not unusual to inveigh against luck as not being part and parcel of a man's success. And certainly fortune, not well used, will never remain constant. Success is won by using good fortune; by combating ill. But no act of Alexander's could have brought about the fatally absurd course of action of the Persian monarch. That Darius was so ill-advised, or ill-starred, was his own fatuity no doubt, but it was equally Alexander's good luck. Had the Taurus or Amanus been strongly barred to Alexander, it is hard to see how he would have carried out his scheme of conquest on this line of advance, unless we assume that he could have turned these defiles, as he later did the Persian Gates. It is in this sense that the Macedonian king's good fortune is so often referred to in these pages. When we come to Hannibal we shall see how, with equal ability, a constant run of bad luck — or untoward events, if that term be preferable — forestalled the success of perhaps the most wonderful military efforts the world has ever seen.

Darius, having crossed the Euphrates, had long lain in the open country awaiting Alexander. His army incumbered the plain from very numbers. A large body of Greek mercenaries had recently reached him under Bianor and Aristomedes, running the sum of his Greeks up to thirty thousand men. His heavy-armed men (Cardaces) and his armor-clad cavalry were of the best. Darius felt certain of success. He relied upon his numbers, his righteous cause, the past fame of his royal house, and the fear the Great King and his myriads must of necessity inspire ; and it is said was lulled into security by a dream which, before leaving Babylon, the Chaldeans had interpreted as promising speedy victory and decisive. On such a plain as Sochi the great multitude of his troops, and especially his cavalry, could manœuvre to advantage. Darius must have recognized the error of his past military conduct, but he was now correspondingly eager that Alexander should enter the broad levels of Persia, so that he might all the more easily surround and annihilate him by his countless hordes. The Persian army was accompanied by the usual vast train of attendants and harems. It is said that there was gold and silver enough to be loaded on six hundred mules and three hundred camels ; and that it took five days and nights to pass the bridge over the Euphrates with the army and trains.

Arsames, flying from the Cilician Gates, had first brought the news of Alexander's approach; and Darius anxiously looked for his coming. But when Alexander, on account of his sickness and the campaign in Rugged Cilicia, tarried so long at Tarsus and at Soli, Darius, once more misled by the bad native advisers who surrounded him, and who hated and therefore imputed doubtful motives to the Greek officers in the royal suite, gave up his excellent position, and, sending his harem, baggage, and treasures to Damascus, under Kophenes, advanced through the Amanic Gates, which were on the nearest road from Sochi to Issus.

Darius was by no means alone in his belief that he could crush the invaders. Demosthenes is said to have gone about the streets of Athens exhibiting letters from Persia to the effect that Alexander was cooped up in Cilicia, from which trap he would never live to escape. All Asia, says Josephus, was persuaded that Alexander would not even be able to come to battle with the Persians on account of their vast multitudes. On the other hand, Amyntas, who, we remember, had deserted from Alexander, advised Darius strongly against leaving Sochi, asserting that the Greeks would surely come to meet him. But Darius' Persian advisers, who prophesied smooth things unto him, prevailed. They assured him that Alexander was already losing courage, and would endeavor to make his escape; that only by speedy action could he catch and punish this impertinent upstart, and thus prevent future aggressions. Darius advanced towards his ruin. In a similar manner, the intrigues of Darius' courtiers had previously caused the execution of the Greek Charidemus, who foretold misfortune to the Persian king, if he hastily met the Macedonian army, relying only on numbers and the courage of his Persian officers; for art was essential to meet art, said this wise but unfortunate man. Charidemus had for a moment held Alexander's fate in his hands.

Having passed through the northerly or Amanic Gates, Darius had now placed himself in Alexander's rear. At Issus, which he reached on the same day that Alexander went into camp at Myriandrus, he found some of the Macedonian sick and wounded, left behind by Alexander. These he cruelly maimed and slew. He then moved forward to the Pinarus.

Alexander was loath to believe that Darius was at Issus. He sent some of the Companions by sea in a triaconteros, or fast sailing long boat, manned by one bank of fifteen rowers on each side, to reconnoitre, and these speedily ascertained the fact. Even Alexander's bold spirit must at first have been startled at the miscalculation which had thus resulted in compromising his safety. But he by no means allowed it to be known, and his powers of conception and action were never so great as when he was most hardly pushed. In this quality he has been equalled perhaps by no one except by Frederick. It is probable that his apprehensions soon disappeared in looking at the other side of the question, a habit of mind he strongly possessed. He knew his own power of manœuvring; he saw that the enemy, though standing athwart his path, had far from as good ground as on the Sochi plains; he knew that the vast host could not long subsist in Cilicia; he knew that they were not ably led, despite the undoubted individual bravery of their leaders and excellence of the men. Were he alone to be consulted he might have risked a good deal and resorted to any feasible stratagem to place Darius in this, to the Macedonians, really advantageous position, how ever threatening it may at first have appeared. Even Alexander, however, before the event, would scarcely have dreamed of trying to induce the Great King to cross the range to Issus.

But the effect on the troops was different and might easily have become alarming. To a surprise like this it is always difficult to reconcile even the best of soldiers. They had been looking forward to meeting the enemy on the plains beyond the mountains after the lapse of some days; and now they suddenly found him in their rear to be encountered on the morrow. No doubt there was much talk in the Macedonian camp of the surprising and incomprehensible situation. A soldier likes to feel that his retreat is safe. Here the phalangians looked back along the perilous path they had trod, and remembered the mountain ranges they had passed, the difficulties they had overcome. Were not these passes now occupied by the enemy? Must they not cut their way back to their homes through a sea of blood? Could they accomplish what alone Xenophon had done? The Macedonian soldiers were wont to speak their minds. They had a certain American independence in thought and word. They did not understand or like this situation, and they openly said as much. This very independence and intelligence was, however, what made them, like our own volunteers, such excellent material for an army called on to do long and arduous campaigning and to encounter dangers in which demoralization would mean destruction. This discussion was a safety valve; and it was coupled with unswerving faith in their king. Soldiers are quick to catch alarm. These Macedonians showed no sign of demoralization, but doubtless they were by no means lacking in that feeling of uncertainty which is akin to it. They needed the one touch to set them right.

Well aware of this feeling among the men, but by no means disconcerted by it, for he knew his phalangians well, Alexander held another council of war, calling in all his chief officers (the infantry strategoi, and cavalry ilarchs, both of the Macedonians and of the Greeks, of the light troops, mercenaries and allies), and exhorted them to do their bravest, promising them certain victory. He assured them that Darius had done the very thing he most ardently desired; that the gods had no doubt interfered in his behalf in placing the Persians where their enormous forces could not manœuvre, while they themselves could deepen their phalanx. They must not be misled, said he, by the idea that the enemy was in their rear. He showed them that they were the always victorious going out to fight the always vanquished; that they were vastly superior to the slaves in the ranks of Darius, who were driven into battle by the lash, while the Greek mercenaries who fought there for a miserable stipend were little better when contending with their countrymen; and that the coming battle would decide the fate of Asia; for this was not a satrap's army, but Darius and all his peoples with him. He praised every man who had shown valor and spoke modestly but confidently of his own ability to lead them. He bade them remember Xenophon and the glorious deeds of the Greeks in every age. He promised them rewards such as they had never dreamed of, and with that consummate art which a true leader must of necessity possess, Alexander roused his officers to the highest pitch of enthusiasm. All crowded around him eager to grasp the king's right hand and swear to do or die. No doubt also hundreds of Macedonian soldiers stood about the place of conference whence they could hear the echo of these stirring words, and the hot blood which the young monarch's own brave heart-throbs sent pulsating through the arteries of his listeners, soon bounded along those of every man in the command. The interview strikingly reminds one of the glowing words of Frederick before the battle of Leuthen, and the hearty response of his generals.

The coming night Alexander countermarched towards the seashore pass in the Syrian Gates, which he had promptly reoccupied with some cavalry and archers, and took up the road to Issus, the place he had left but two days before. Resting in the rock-bound pass and throwing out his outposts, he passed the night, and in the early morning red, he marched in column through the defile towards the plain.

This plain stretched from the Syrian Gates northward, gradually widening, but shut in on the west by the seashore and on the east by more or less rugged foot-hills for some twenty odd miles to Issus. Some smaller streams flowed at intervals from mountain to sea. A few miles south of Issus the plain is crossed by the larger mountain stream, Pinarus, in a southwesterly direction, and along the southern boundary of the stream the hills jut forward into the plain. Just beyond the Pinarus began the Persian encampment.

As the army debouched from the defile and the narrow pass began to widen, Alexander advanced the successive columns with manœuvring precision into phalangial order, on the centre forward into line. Alexander's habit was to keep his men in parade order when marching to battle. The drill steadied them and kept the lines closed up. The cavalry had been following the infantry; but when the plain was reached the cavalry rode up to the flanks and the king formed the whole army in order of battle. The phalanx was as usual sixteen deep. Next the mountain, in the right wing, he placed Nicanor with the agema and other hypaspists; next the brigades of Cœnus and Perdiccas. The left wing under Parmenio leaned on the sea, and counting the phalanx from the left came Amyntas, Ptolemy, Meleager; these infantry brigades being under the orders of Craterus, the position of whose brigade is not given. Parmenio had strict orders to allow no gap between his left and the sea, and the Greek allied infantry was sent him to strengthen it. The king's first idea was to keep the Macedonian and Thessalian heavy cavalry on the right, and they were ordered thither. The flanks were thus abundantly safe, for the plain beyond the defile as far as the Pinarus was, at that time, but about a mile and a half wide at most. The topography has materially changed since then.

Darius, who lay near Issus and south of it, on learning

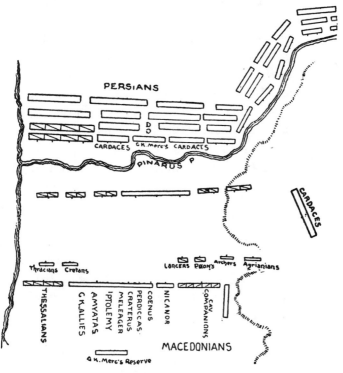

Issus before the Battle.

Alexander's whereabouts, had made ready for an advance. He had hoped to seize the Syrian Gates, but found that Alexander had anticipated him. He had then taken up a position behind the river Pinarus, and, on hearing of Alexander's proximity, threw out thirty thousand horse and twenty thousand light foot across the stream to make a curtain behind which he could form unobserved; ordering them, on being recalled,

to retire right and left around the flanks. He was well intrenched. The Pinarus formed his ditch; its northern bank,
which was high, his wall. He had in his army some thirty
thousand heavy armed Greek mercenaries under Thymondas,
son of Mentor. These he placed opposite the Macedonian
phalanx, which he could see from his position as it deployed
into line, and on both sides of this he placed double their
number of Cardaces (foreign mercenaries known by this name)
who were also heavy armed and trained to combat hand to
hand. There is some conflict of authorities as to the numbers
and positions of the Greeks and Cardaces. But the conflict is
not material. This part of the Persian force was in the centre and more than ample.

The Greeks and Cardaces appear to have formed the first
line. If ninety thousand strong, and in a phalanx sixteen
deep, they would occupy a breadth of over three miles. Cal-
isthenes states the then breadth of the valley at the Pinarus
as fourteen stadia. To crowd into this breadth (one and two
thirds miles), the Greeks and Cardaces would have to be
twenty-five deep. These questions are interesting, but by no
means material to that consideration of the subject on which
this work is intended to dwell. They may have been in two
or more lines.

Some twenty thousand men, perhaps the Cardaces in part,
were on the extreme left, near the mountains, on the left
bank of the Pinarus. They were intended as a threat to
Alexander's right. For, owing to the configuration of the
ground, which had once been a bay in the seacoast, part of
this latter force would extend beyond the rear of Alexander's
right flank, so soon as he advanced. This was a clever formation, and deserved success.

The rest of Darius' men were drawn up in rear of this
front line, by nations, in columns so ordered that they might,

it was thought, be successively brought into action, but really in equally unserviceable and dangerous masses. The whole, including probably camp-followers, was said to be six hundred thousand strong. The effective fighting force may have been two hundred thousand men, but it was decidedly weakened by the admixture of unreliable material. The very size of the army was its infirmity. Being assured that they were in pursuit of a flying enemy, their courage was by no means raised at the sight of the Macedonian army ready for attack.

Having completed his formation, Darius now withdrew his curtain of cavalry and light foot, which fell back right and left. But finding that it could do no service near the hills, he ordered the bulk of the horse over to his right, opposite Parmenio, where on the seashore sand was the only place it could find room to manœuvre. A few he ordered to the left. He relied on the hills to protect the latter flank, and proposed to make his main attack with the cavalry of the right, which was under Nabarzanes, and which he intended should break through the Macedonian left by mere weight, and take the line in reverse. Darius took up his own station in the usual place, the centre, in rear of the Greek mercenaries. The whole army extended from the mountains to the sea.

The Macedonians were in the highest spirits and full of confidence in their own valor. The king's words had roused their enthusiasm, and so soon as they came within sight of the enemy they grew eager for the fray. One can scarcely imagine a situation which, according to our notions, was worse compromised than that of Alexander at Issus. It might have proven so in his case. And we can only marvel at the cool daring and extraordinary ability which enabled him to keep his troops in heart and rescue a brilliant victory from such desperate danger.

When Alexander perceived that Darius' cavalry was filing

over to his right opposite Parmenio, he saw that his lieutenant
was apt to be overmatched, for only the Peloponnesian and
Greek horse was stationed on this wing. He therefore dispatched his own Thessalian cavalry, quietly but speedily, by
the rear of the phalanx, so as not to be seen, over to his left.
Of the horse which he retained on the right, the Companions
were in line; the lancers under Protomachus, and the Pæonians under Aristo, were in front of them; and of the infantry, the archers under Antiochus, and the Agrianians
under Attalus, were also on their right front. He threw
back a crochet of light foot and horse on the right to oppose
the body which was posted so as to take this flank in reverse;
but he saw the danger of this force so long as it remained *in
situ*, and before the battle attacked it with a body of light
troops, and though it had the advantage of being on higher
ground, drove it away to the top of the hill, and occupied
a position in its front by two ilē of Companion cavalry, some
three hundred men. The troops in the crotchet he was then
able to use to strengthen the right wing phalanx, which was
weak in places. The right of the phalanx, when the formation was completed, proved still to be rather thin, and he
filled it by two squadrons of Companion cavalry, named from
the districts from which they came, the Anthemusian and
Lugæan. In the left wing the Cretan archers and Thracians, under Sitalces, were in front of the infantry line; the
cavalry in their front, towards the left. The Greek mercenaries were in reserve. It will be noticed that Alexander
fully appreciated the value of a reserve, as only Xenophon
before him had done. He recognized that the one weak point
of the phalangial order was, as a rule, its lack of reserves,
and was wont to correct the defect by dispositions of his
troops, unusual in those days.

The formation was completed with masterly skill and in

perfect quiet, and each change was made after full reconnoitring of the enemy's position, which happily could be readily seen. There was no flurry, no apprehension. Everything was orderly and precise to the last degree. Some thirty thousand men stood in line.

The Pinarus, looking from Alexander's right towards the Persian left, made a northerly sweep such as to throw backward Darius' flank ; and by advancing the archers and Agrianians, and some Greek mercenaries, now that the Cardaces had been driven away, Alexander so thrust forward his right that it enveloped and extended beyond the left of the Persian first line. He had contrived just such a threat to Darius' left as Darius had sought to make to his right.

The position was a very good one for an inferior force. The flanks were protected, the ground well covered, and mere numbers ceased to be of the value they would possess in an open plain. Alexander now gave his men some rest, thinking that Darius might advance on him, and hoping to attack him as he crossed the river. But the Persians kept their ground, except that the cavalry of the Persian right began to cross the Pinarus to attack the Macedonian left. Alexander saw that Darius made a mistake to hold his centre, where he himself was, on the defensive behind the Pinarus, while advancing his right in offense across it, because if this centre was disabled, no efforts or success of the right could rectify it or retrieve a disaster which might happen to headquarters. Particularly, Oriental troops would be demoralized by a defeat of that part of the line which was held by the king in person. Alexander's problem then was how to break this centre, and he guessed that it could best be done by destroying the Persian left, and taking the centre in reverse. This he felt confident he could do if only Parmenio would hold the Macedonian left until he could make some headway.

Darius awaited the attack of the Greeks, confiding in his numbers, and intending, as above said, that his cavalry should, by defeating Alexander's, break the latter's left wing, and take the whole army in reverse. Thus the strong right flank of each army was opposed to the other's weaker left. Alexander's sending the Thessalian cavalry to his left had to a degree remedied this evil in the Macedonian army, for the Thessalians were wonderful fighters; but Darius had not corrected the corresponding weakness of his own left. His flying wing of Cardaces had disgracefully failed him.

The defensive attitude of the Persian king gave Alexander's troops the impression that Darius was lacking in courage, and this still more heightened their own. There was a general shout to be led to the attack, and Alexander gave the order to advance. The tone in which troops cheer is indicative of what breeds victory or defeat. Here it was unmistakably for victory. As the line slowly and with the steadiness of parade moved forward, Alexander rode in front of the line, calling on the men to do their duty, saluting each brigade of the phalanx by its name, individually addressing each chieftain, and rousing all to heroic tension. He was received with loud huzzas, and his noble presence and confident bearing acted as a stimulant on every soldier in the ranks.

The river had to be crossed, but this difficulty only raised the spirits of the men who had fought their way across the Granicus. The north bank of the Pinarus was in most parts steep; where it was low, Darius had caused a stockade to be erected. The water was everywhere fordable.

The battle was about to open. The enthusiasm of the Macedonians rose to boiling point. In order to keep the line intact and free from wavering, the phalangites advanced slowly to the sound of music, as they were wont to do on parade, with measured tread and soldierly bearing, until, reaching the zone of darts, at a preconcerted signal, and headed by Alexander and the agema, they took the double-quick, and dashed into the river with the shout which their enemies had always heard with dread, and which the hills sent reverberating back to the sea. This rapid attack both astonished the Persians and saved themselves from being long under the

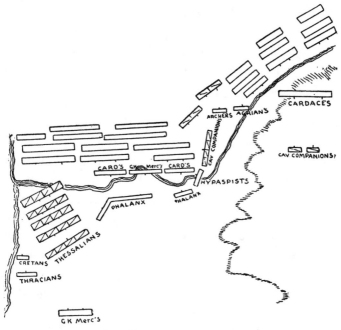

Issus (Alexander's manœuvre).

fire of missiles. Where Alexander fought in person, near the right, so soon as the troops came to close work, the Persians gave way in disorder, being, as we have shown, taken somewhat in reverse by the position which the bend in the river enabled him to give the line.

It will be seen that this bend in the river again resulted in the formation of what many have termed Alexander's favorite method, — an oblique order of battle, the left refused. It was again accidental, but none the less effective. It enabled him to force the attack on the Persian left centre, which he saw was the weak point of Darius' line.

The impact of the Companions and hypaspists was tremendous. There was but a brief resistance. No soldiers under Darius' standard could stand up under the blow. The Persian line reeled and weakened. The Macedonians pressed steadily on. So soon as Alexander had driven back that part of the Persian left wing which he had struck, he found himself on the left flank of the Greek mercenaries in the Persian centre, on whom Darius peculiarly relied, and who had so far held the Macedonian phalanx in check. Where Alexander led, fortune always followed. He had won a foothold of first importance. Success here made it certain that success by Darius' right could not be fatal; for Alexander cut Darius from his line of retreat by turning his left or strategic flank.

The discovery that the enemy has a strategic flank, that is, a flank the turning of which will cut him off from his line of retreat, has often been ascribed to Napoleon, and it is no doubt true that no captain ever made use of this weak point on so grand a scale or so efficiently as the great Corsican. But here it is plain that Alexander saw the advantage of an attack on this flank; we shall see him make use of the idea again; and that Hannibal very clearly understood the matter is shown by the march through the Arnus marshes. It was the commentators of Napoleon's campaigns who explained to the world the value of that captain's methods. Napoleon himself repeatedly acknowledges his indebtedness to his predecessors in the art. But he carried what they taught him to its highest degree of perfection.

In the centre the Macedonian phalanx had not been so speedy or so successful as it had on the right where Alexander's irresistible spirit led the way, and the line was somewhat disordered and less advanced. The banks had been higher where they crossed; they were more heavily armed, and the king's impetuosity had carried him and his immediate surroundings ahead of the line. Darius' Greek mercenaries had attacked the phalanx with dangerous ardor. Not only had the Macedonian centre lost its alignment, but there had been opened a gap in the phalanx towards the right wing, owing to Alexander's forward rush which the brigades on the right of the phalanx were trying their best to follow up. The Greeks and Macedonians were rivals in courage, and this gap boded evil. Ancient hatred made the combat all the more bloody. The fray covered both banks of the river and the main ford itself. Both fought desperately; the Greek mercenaries to reëstablish the battle and earn the praise of the Great King and their promised reward; the Macedonians not to be behind their own king in conduct, nor lose the name of invincible for the phalanx. To yield their ground meant destruction to the Macedonian army. The lines came to close quarters, where darts were useless and swords were the only weapon. Here fell Ptolemy, son of Seleucus, and one hundred and twenty Macedonians of no mean rank. Despite utmost gallantry, the phalanx was in grave danger.

But as usual Alexander came to the rescue. His wing had by this time driven the Persian left well away from its position near the river. For the moment he was hand free. Heading the hypaspists and the right brigades, while the Companions followed up the initial success, and thus sustained his right, he wheeled about and took the Greek mercenaries in flank, tearing open their formation with a terrific blow, and immediately relieved the pressure on the failing brigades. The danger was averted. Renewing the struggle under better auspices, the phalanx at once regained its ground and alignment, and thenceforward held its own.

On the left the Persian cavalry had crossed the river, and attacked the Thessalian horse with fury. A fierce combat ensued in which the enemy began by winning a marked advantage. Indeed, Parmenio was getting so decidedly the worst of the fight at this part of the line that, but for the effect of Alexander's wonderful impetuosity on the right, serious results might have followed. Yet this was traceable rather to the Persian numbers and splendid conduct, than to any fault of Parmenio's, who had carried out his orders with zeal and discretion. The multitude of the Persian cavalry kept it in one mass, so heavy and irresistible that it threatened to sweep the field like an avalanche. Only by constantly repeated isolated attacks at different points, and by their perfect discipline, could the Thessalians with all their gallantry hold their ground. But though vastly outnumbered and all but crushed, they would not yield, but clung desperately to their ground, rallying and returning again and again to the charge. The Companions themselves could not have done more noble work. Thus they kept up their blows as best they might.

Darius, as was the rule with Persian kings, occupied in the centre the position of greatest prominence. In a gorgeous chariot drawn by four horses abreast, and surrounded by his military family, including all the grandees of the court, under command of his brother Oxathres, he must have been the centre of all attraction. It was not long after the phalanx had been reëstablished before Alexander had hewn his path clear through the Persian masses, and had headed for the very kernel of the Persian centre. It was straight for this royal group that the king at once began to carve his way. Here it was, as at Cunaxa, that the battle was to be lost or won ; and Alexander, with his usual directness, made straight for the centre point of opposition. Darius was defended by his crowd of nobles ; Alexander led his Companions. The Great

King was soon surrounded by wounds and slaughter. His
horses became unmanageable; only by a charge, under his
brother Oxathres, could he be extricated from a position
where he must quickly have fallen a victim. For Darius had
ceased to be a hero; and it was the godlike fury of Hercules
and Achilles which swept like a whirlwind about him.

When Darius saw that the left of his army had been
broken, that Alexander was getting between the Amanic
Gates and his army, and that he himself was in danger of
capture or death, he lost all sense of self-control, and summarily took to flight in a fresh and lighter chariot which had
been brought up for him. But a chariot could not convey
him far. The ground was rough, and the mass of fugitives
quickly became enormous. Darius had had in readiness, as
if contemplating flight, a high-bred mare whose foal had been
left behind on the road through the Amanic Gates. He soon
left his chariot, mounted this mare and galloped from the
field. The flight of the king was followed by the immediate
dissolution of all discipline in the Persian ranks at the left
and centre, where his movements were within the ken of all.
The reserve troops in the rear, who might have now come
forward, at once melted away and followed in the footsteps
of Darius. The Pæonians, archers, Agrianians, mercenaries,
and the two ilē of cavalry pushed in on the extreme Macedonian right, and cut down all who could not escape with speed.
The victorious cavalry on the Persian right became aware of
the rout of the left, and soon heard the cry, "The king
flees!" They also lost courage and began to waver; then,
seeing that no efforts could now avail, they turned and fled.
They were pursued by the Thessalians, who not only slew
great numbers of them, but so hampered their movements
that they trampled each other down in flight.

Alexander could not begin his pursuit until he was sure of

his centre and left; nor was he able to pursue to any great distance, owing to the approaching darkness. This facilitated Darius' escape, but Alexander captured the Great King's chariot, in which were his Median mantle, bow and shield. Darius did not halt till he placed the Euphrates, which he crossed at Thapsacus, between himself and Alexander. He was here able to assemble but four thousand Greek mercenaries out of all his vast host. Of the infantry, such as were not cut to pieces took refuge in the foot-hills; the cavalry followed the coast until they could cross to the upper Amanic pass. A body of eight thousand Greeks, under Amyntas, is said to have cut its way out to the south along the beach, and to have reached Phœnicia, where, seizing Lesbian vessels and burning such as they did not need, they sailed to Cyprus, and thence to Egypt. Accompanying Amyntas were Thymodes, son of Mentor, Aristodemus of Phares, Bianor of Acarnania, and other refugees.

Arsames, Rheomithres, and Atizyes, who escaped at the Granicus, fell here. Vast numbers of the Persians were slain. The sum of killed is stated at one hundred thousand, including ten thousand of the cavalry. In the pursuit, Ptolemy, son of Lagus, asserts that the men who followed him filled up a deep ravine with dead bodies in order to bridge and cross it. The loss in Persian generals was heavy. They had, as usual, exposed themselves most bravely. The Macedonian loss was four hundred and fifty killed, — three hundred foot, and one hundred and fifty horse, or one and a half per cent. of the number engaged. Curtius gives one hundred and eighty-two, Justin two hundred and eighty, as the number killed. The wounded are given at various figures. The average of ten to one of killed is probably not far from correct. Taking the killed and wounded at five thousand men, the loss, not counting "missing," was not far from seventeen per cent., which is much higher than the average of modern battles. The killed and wounded alone rarely overrun ten per cent.

The number of men who died of their wounds in Alexander's army we have no clew to enable us to guess. It was no doubt large, for though wounds were not so severe in the days of javelins, stones and arrows as they are to-day, yet medical attendance was inefficient. That there were very many permanently disabled, we know, and the total number who disappeared from the rolls of the army was so great, that we must conclude that the battle mortality was by no means measured in the figures given of those killed.

Prisoners were never lost by the victorious army. Hence the item of " missing " in the tabulated losses of modern battles, — and it is a very big one, — must be eliminated before we can institute a comparison between these and ancient battles as regards casualties.

The Persian treasure on the field was barely three thousand talents ($3,600,000), but vast stores of gold were got in Damascus, whence they were being conveyed away, when, through the treachery of the Syrian satrap, they were stopped by Parmenio, whom Alexander ordered up the Orontes valley after the battle to collect the booty Darius had sent to that place. It was then stored in Damascus.

Next day Alexander, though himself disabled by a sword-cut in his thigh, went among the Macedonian wounded, commended and rewarded with money all who had distinguished themselves, and saw to the burial of the dead with military honors, the army marching to the funeral as to battle.

The family of Darius had been left behind in the Persian camp. They were treated with great respect and dignity. If, as is sometimes alleged, Alexander was not really generous, he assuredly curbed his passions to policy in a manner unusual in men so young. It is pleasanter to believe what

Plutarch, Arrian, and others tell us of his real magnanimity. We cannot equitably debit his account with all the ill which can be discovered in his character, unless we credit it with what was noble. It is related that when Alexander returned from the chase of Darius, and was supping with his Companions in the Great King's pavilion in the Persian camp, he heard in the adjoining tent the sobs of women. Inquiring the cause, he was informed that the queen-mother, Sisygambis, and the queen, Statira, were lamenting the death of their son and husband. He at once sent Leonnatus to assure them that Darius still lived, and that they themselves had nothing to fear. He was as good as his word, for not only did he take no advantage of the acknowledged right of the conqueror of those days, but forbade the beauty and accomplishments of Statira to be mentioned in his presence. For Statira passed for the most lovely woman of her times. The royal ladies were surrounded by their accustomed Eastern state, and were treated as queens, and in no respect as captives. Perhaps Alexander was the only Greek of his time who would have done this; and his forbearance does as great honor to his heart as the keeping of his royal captives on this scale redounds to his knowledge of state craft. For all his contemporaries praised him; it became the more easy to handle Darius, and the Persians acquired as high a regard for his character as they already had for his skill. When, the next day, the king and Hephæstion paid a visit to the queens, Sisygambis fell at the feet of the latter, thinking him the monarch, for Alexander was in no wise more richly habited, and Hephæstion was the taller of the two. And when she discovered her error, and in fear for the result fell at the feet of the conqueror, Alexander at once raised her from the ground, and assured her that it was no mistake, for Hephæstion was also an Alexander. Then, taking up the little son of Darius, he fondled him.

The entire army of Darius (except the small force of Greek mercenaries which joined him at the Euphrates, and that which escaped to Egypt) disappeared at Issus — how we cannot say. Parts held together and made for inner Persia; parts for the Cilician mountains. Many, grouped in smaller or larger bodies, wandered for a while, and then deserted to their homes. Squads or companies of the army reappeared at intervals in Asia Minor, — Cappadocia, Paphlagonia, Lucania, — to be overcome by the Macedonian viceroys. Antigonus in Phrygia and Calas in smaller Phrygia dispersed many such, but no serious opposition to Alexander could be organized for two years to come. The approach of winter saved Darius from sharp pursuit.

The battlefield of Issus is said to have been much changed by the deposits of the streams which crossed the ancient plains. A large part of the coast is now a continuous marsh. The Syrian Gates have been blocked up by land slides, and disuse. The road across the range is now by the Amanic Gates alone. The other is a mere path.

Thus was exploded, even in Persia, the reliance on simple numbers. So trite a maxim is it to-day that numbers without skill cannot avail, that it is perhaps difficult to place ourselves in the position of the peoples who at this time knew nothing but numbers. Napoleon's saying that God is on the side of the heaviest battalions, and his calculation on the equality of thousands, implies that these battalions and thousands are drilled and disciplined substantially on the same methods, and, saving only the genius of the commander, are substantially similar bodies. Mere hordes of men are not covered by his dictum or his theory. Darius had boasted that he would trample Alexander under foot by the weight of his magnificent army; and but for his personal weakness here, and later at Arbela, perchance he might have done so. The misconduct of the Great King is another instance of the good fortune of Alexander. The Persians, as a rule (especially the grandees and generals), were brave and faithful; but the mass was easily to be demoralized. Nor did Darius by nature lack heart; but when he saw that the Greeks, whose meagre numbers he had been led to despise and underrate, really dared oppose him, he lost his head. In contrast to this, Alexander's splendid conduct stands out in highest relief. The keen eye which grasped the situation, and discovered the weak point in his adversary's position, and the courage which faced vast odds with such calm skill, are alike admirable. And as no doubt it was just these qualities put into action which produced the effect from which Darius weakened, in so far was Alexander the arbiter of his own fortune on this field.

Perhaps Issus was the most far-reaching of all Alexander's victories. In consequence of the event the name of Alexander became the synonym of god. The usual games, feasts and sacrifices were held, and the town of Alexandria at the Syrian Passes was built as memorial of the victory. Three huge altars at the Pinarus were erected as a monument to the slain.

Alexander appointed Balacrus, son of Nicanor, one of the royal body-guards, viceroy of Cilicia. This was the most important military territory which he had as yet taken, and must be in the best of hands. He put Menes in Balacrus' place among the body-guards. Polysperschon succeeded to the command of Ptolemy, son of Seleucus. Menon, son of Cerdimmas, was made satrap over northern Syria, as far as Parmenio had taken it, and left with a force of Greek allied cavalry to hold the land.

XXIV.

TYRE. NOVEMBER, B. C. 333, TO AUGUST, B. C. 332.

Issus did as much to weaken the Persian fleet by fostering desertion in the Phœnician and Cyprian contingents as to exalt Alexander's name. The king now moved down into Phœnicia, proposing to reduce the coast line before venturing inland. All the towns received him with open gates until he came to Tyre, queen city of the coast. Here he was denied admittance, and resorted to a siege. He began a mole from the mainland to the island on which new Tyre was built, using the forests of Lebanon and the old city of Tyre for material. This mole was two hundred feet wide and half a mile long. On it were built towers and sheds to protect the workmen. The Tyrians showed wonderful skill in their efforts to break up the work and once set the towers on fire with a fire-ship, consuming the labor of months. Alexander went to Sidon and there got together a fleet larger than the Tyrians', returning with which he was able to coop them up in their two harbors. He now built his mole wider and stronger and reached the city walls. But he was eventually forced to operate a breach on the seaward side, where the walls were not so strong. After a sea-fight, in which he was victorious, Alexander made a breach in the wall, stormed the city, captured and sacked it, hung two thousand men and sold thirty thousand into slavery. The city was practically destroyed. Darius now approached Alexander with an offer of ten thousand talents, all the territory west of the Euphrates, and his daughter in marriage; but Alexander declined the offer, claiming a right to the whole of Asia.

AFTER the battle of Issus the Persian admirals made an effort to save what might yet perchance be snatched from the burning. Pharnabazus sailed with twelve triremes and fifteen hundred mercenaries to Chios, fearing its defection. But the cause had suffered disastrous blows in the death of Memnon, and the defeat at Issus. There soon appeared threatening signs of falling off among the Phœnician and Cyprian allies which still more materially weakened the Persian cause at sea. For when Alexander headed towards Phœnicia, instead of the Euphrates as he had been expected to do, the kings of the coast cities serving with the Persian admiral at once caught alarm for their domains and markedly weakened in their allegiance. Memnon's strong influence was no longer felt.

The Persian admirals, having garrisoned Chios and sent ships to Cos and Halicarnassus, themselves made for Syphnus. Hither came Agis, king of Lacedæmon, still restlessly opposing Alexander, and endeavored to persuade them to send a force to the Peloponnesus which the Spartans might join in active opposition to the galling Macedonian supremacy. Agis had great schemes in his head and urged them warmly. But the news of the defeat of the Persians at Issus which now came in effectually arrested such a movement. Pharnabazus returned to Chios, lest the place should revolt from Persian rule, as seemed not unlikely. Agis secured from the Persians only thirty talents in money and ten triremes. With these he dispatched his brother Agesilaus on a cruise to foment discord in Crete and neighboring islands of the Ægean, and himself joined Autophradates, who had finally sailed to Halicarnassus.

By his victory at Issus, Alexander had not properly forced the entrance to Persia, for the Euphrates still lay before him, but rather that to Phœnicia. To reduce the cities of this seacoast country would neutralize all opposition as far as Egypt. It was part of his general plan to make sure of the coast before moving inland. Whether this plan was already matured before the king left Pella, or whether the full grasp of his problem grew with its growing size as he advanced farther towards the heart of Asia, cannot be said. It is doubtful whether Alexander knew enough of the geography of the regions he invaded to construct a completed plan at the outset. But none the less was the strategy of his entire

movement so fully perfected that it bore the stamp of distinct homogeneity as it was gradually developed. He had, as above said, already sent Parmenio with the Thessalian horse up the Orontes valley to overcome Syria, as well as take possession of the treasures and camp-belongings which had been sent to Damascus by Darius, from Sochi, before he crossed the range to Issus.
He himself, having suitably arranged for the conduct of the affairs of Cilicia, marched towards Phœnicia.

This country had not been so utterly tyrant-ridden as the other parts of the sea-coast controlled by the Great King. The skill of its mariners and the dependence of Persia upon the cities of Phœnicia for its fleet, as well as for an outlet for commerce, made the Persian authorities favor these marts beyond all others. They occupied a position not unlike the free cities of Germany. They had not that insular position which is essential to perfect independence, but they were shut in between the range of Mount Libanus and the sea, and the cities were many of them built on coast islands, or in such a way as to be inaccessible from land or sea alike.

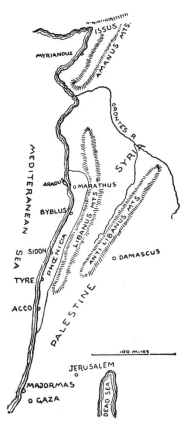

Syria and Phœnicia.

Each city controlled a greater or less extent of territory in-land. The enormous trade and the clever handicrafts of these cities did not fall away as they did in other towns which became weakened by Oriental rule, but were cultivated by Persia to the utmost.

The ships of these Phœnician cities were on duty with the Persian fleet, the squadron of each generally under command of its king. But the battle of Issus, as above stated, materially altered their footing. The home governments saw the necessity of going over to Alexander. Had these cities worked in unison they could have cut out for Alexander a very serious task. But each one harbored some petty spite against one or more of the others, and their mutual jealousies, added to Alexander's clever manipulations, forestalled such action. The possession of Phœnicia was a condition precedent to Alexander's success. If Darius could retain his control or influence over, or even the merely formal coöperation of these Phœnician towns, he could always be sure of a fleet. If these towns deserted their allegiance, the power of his right arm would be transferred to his opponent.

Moving towards Phœnicia, Alexander was first met by Strato, son of Gerostratus, king of the territory of Aradus. The latter was serving with Autophradates; but Strato volunteered the surrender of Marathus, his great and prosperous capital city, and of the island of Aradus, near by, of Sigon, of Mariamme, and all the other territory subject to himself and his father. This was a first and marked gain for Alexander, as will be seen. In token of his submission, Strato had come with kingly gifts, and, in accordance with custom, he placed a golden crown on Alexander's head.

At Marathus, where he tarried a few days, Alexander received a letter and embassy from Darius, entreating that his mother, wife and children be restored to him, and proposing friendship and alliance. Alexander's victory he ascribed in the message to the favor of some one of the gods. He recalled the ancient amity of Persia and Macedon, and, himself, a king, begged of a king the return of his family. To this letter Alexander replied. He sent his missive by an equal embassy. His letter recited the injuries of Persia to Greece; the beginning of hostilities by Darius; the instigation of his father's murder by the Persian court; it asserted his right as conqueror to the whole of Asia; it demanded that Darius should address him as his lord, and not as an equal; and threatened to follow him up wherever he should go till he had accomplished his mission by destroying the Persian sovereignty. As a touch in Alexander's portrait, his very words are of interest: "I am lord of Asia. Come to me, and thou shalt receive all that thou canst ask. But if thou deniest my right as thy lord, stand and fight for thy kingdom. I will seek thee wherever thou art." The letter was addressed, perhaps, as much to the Greek world as to the Persian king.

Here, too, at Marathus, Alexander caused to be sent to him from Damascus certain Greeks who were at Darius' court as ambassadors from Sparta, Thebes and Athens. These men he treated with exceptional generosity, in view of their position. He released the Thebans, and but temporarily confined the Spartan. The son of Iphicrates of Athens, the general and originator of the light troops known as peltasts, who was one of them, he appointed to a position of honor near his own person.

Alexander next advanced on, and occupied Byblus by terms of capitulation. King Enylus was with his squadron in the Persian fleet. This, says Arrian, was called the oldest city in the world, and possessed a considerable territory. Sidon opened her gates, from hatred of the Persians engendered of ancient wrongs and from bitter jealousy of Tyre. Tyre, queen city of the coast, also sent ambassadors, headed by the son of King Azemilcus, who himself was also with Autophradates, tendering submission, provided, however, Alexander would not enter the city. Alexander replied that he desired to come and sacrifice to the Tyrian Hercules. To this the Tyrians made objection, because at Ephesus Alexander had marshaled his whole army at the gates of the temple of Diana; and such an entry meant absolute surrrender of all their liberties. For Alexander, once in possession, might not be willing to vacate. They had not so admitted Persia, and would not Alexander. They were open to be persuaded to transfer their allegiance and fleet to Alexander's service, but not their life, liberty and pursuit of happiness. They no doubt wished to keep their city free to join whichever king might eventually prove the victor. They knew their importance both to Darius and to Alexander, and did not propose to yield it up in exchange for mere uncertainties. If Darius won — as still seemed far from unlikely — they would profit by being the only Phœnician city which had retained its loyalty. If Darius should be again beaten, they could still offer a stanch resistance, and perhaps make their own terms. Their argument was natural and sensible. But they did not know Alexander. The city therefore refused the Macedonian overtures. The citizens shut their gates, and their king returned home to defend the city.

Alexander had matured a sensible sequence in his plan of campaign: first, an expedition to Egypt, to complete the conquest of all the maritime cities of the Eastern Mediterranean, so as to neutralize the Persian power at sea; and second, an advance on Babylon, which he could undertake if Macedon and faithful Greece were, by the possession of the seacoast, put beyond the danger of harm from Sparta and her Persian

allies. But he could accomplish neither of these things till
he held Tyre, for he could not safely advance on Egypt or on
Babylon, with Tyre, the chief of the naval stations of Phœnicia — all but of the world — in his rear. He therefore called
the usual, perhaps legally required council of Companions,
strategoi, ilarchs, taxiarchs, and officers of the allies, and put
the case to them. Tyre, they agreed, must be taken; but
how? The thing seemed impossible. But, said Alexander,

General Map showing Alexander's Base-line.

what must be done is never impossible to you and me. Relying
on the fertility of resource of the king, it was determined to
isolate the city, and then operate against it. This decision,
when matters eventuated in so long a siege, was one which
would have been working directly into Persian hands, if but
such a spirit as Memnon's were still in control. But Darius
had no master-mind to oppose the ability of Alexander.
Time, usually of the essence in war, did not now run against
him.

Many critics have inquired why Alexander, immediately

after the battle of Issus, did not sharply follow Darius, and penetrate to Babylon and Susa, seek to control the Persian kingdom from its centre, and prevent Darius from accumulating another army. A similar criticism has been passed on Gustavus for not advancing on Vienna after crossing the Lech. But the truth was that Alexander had vastly more grave fears for his rear and for Macedon than dread of any force in his front. The Persian fleet still commanded the Ægean, though it was fast being neutralized; King Agis' brother had got control of Crete; the Greek states, though quieted for the nonce by the late victory, were easily capable of again breaking out into revolt; and until the entire coast from the Hellespont to the Nile was in his hands, it would be but a thrust in the dark to venture his all on an expedition into the interior. If his objective was the conquest of the whole then known world, his base of operations must be the entire coast-line of the then known sea. The prize won at Issus was not his objective, but his base. This coast-line was the least he needed as a base for so gigantic an undertaking as he had planned, and that his schemes of conquest were broad and sensible, is by nothing so well shown as by his patient waiting and working here on the coast before he ventured beyond the Euphrates.

On reaching Tyre, Alexander found the old city on the mainland vacated. The citizens had retired to the so-called new city. This was situated on an island two miles long, less wide, and separated from the coast by a passage half a mile wide, some eighteen feet deep near the town, shallow and swampy near the shore. It was surrounded by very lofty walls. It had two harbors, one the harbor of Sidon on the north, and one the harbor of Egypt on the south, both partly facing the mainland. The old town, vastly less strong, had stood a siege of thirteen years by Nebuchadnezzar. It was well provided with arms, and had a brave population, — a garrison stated by some at thirty thousand men, though this figure may refer to arms-bearing inhabitants, — all manner of machines suitable to resist a siege, and a number of war-ships, which were brought back by King Azemilcus just before the

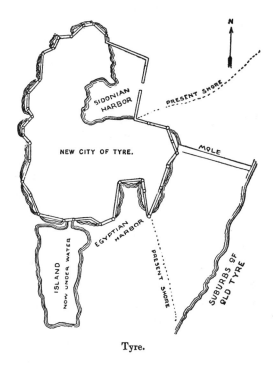

Tyre.

investment was completed. It was provisioned for a long period. Alexander hoped to get the assistance of the Phœnician fleet. The Tyrians still trusted that their old associates might join them, rather than help Alexander crush an ancient ally.

As the king had for the moment no vessels, and was reduced to attacking the city from the shore, he made up his mind to build a mole across the channel from the mainland. The mole was designed to be two hundred feet wide, and was built by driving piles into the bottom, and filling in with stones, earth and wood. Work was begun at once. Laborers were procured from every part of the neighboring country. The piles were cedars brought from Mount Libanus, and these were easily driven into the swampy soil; the stones came from the old town on the coast, abandoned by its citizens, and now demolished and used against them. The rushes from the swampy land made excellent binding. To prevent the edges of the mole from washing away by the attrition of the waves, whole trees, leaves and all, were cast into the sea to still the water which the southwest wind usually kept in heavy motion. A city and a forest were exhausted to build this wonderful mole.

Alexander oversaw every part of the work, and constantly encouraged the Macedonians and other workmen who labored at it day and night, with cheering words and substantial presents. The work progressed rapidly; but as they approached the deeper water near the city and within reach of missiles, it not only became difficult, but hazardous. The Tyrians mounted engines on the walls, and employed all manner of expedients to break up the work. They attacked the workmen on the mole with vessels of war at all times and places. They sent expert divers to undermine it. Their devices were beyond telling clever and unexpected. Diodorus details many of them, for which we have no space. They were bound to show their old skill to these impertinent Macedonian upstarts. Alexander was soon forced to build two towers on the end of the mole to keep the Tyrians at a distance. These he manned with soldiers and engines, and covered the front with skins to keep them from being set on fire by missiles from the walls. He made movable breastworks of wicker-work and skins, and erected palisades and mantelets for the workmen so as to protect them from such assaults. Under cover of these the work made worthy progress.

The Tyrians saw that they must destroy these towers. From an old horse-transport provided with two masts and a wide deck, with room to carry a bulky burden, they constructed a fire-ship and loaded it with a quantity of bitumen, dry twigs, and other inflammable material. From the yard-arms or booms, which stood out like antennæ, they hung cauldrons filled with sulphur, naphtha, chemical oils and similar substances. They towed this fire-ship between two triremes, one blustering day when the wind set well inland, towards the end of the mole, and leaving the men who were put aboard to kindle the fires to swim back to the city as best they might, retired to a safe distance for hurling missiles to keep off the Macedonians from quenching the flames. The headway it acquired carried the fire-ship towards the mole in a few minutes. The poop was ballasted so as to throw the bows out of water and allow it to run up on the mole where it could be anchored firmly in place. The towers, breastworks and engines of war caught fire; the yard-arm cauldrons emptied their inflammables; the wind lent its aid; despite manful fighting of the flames, all were destroyed. For the northwest wind was very fresh and the missiles from the soldiers on the Tyrian vessels and from the garrison on the town walls, made it all but impossible for the Macedonians to work at extinguishing the flames, which were blown directly in their faces. Boats from the city also brought out many Tyrians who, landing on the wind side of the conflagration, aided in pulling down the breastworks and burning up the engines of war. Not only were the towers lost, but the end of the mole was cracked and weakened so as later to be washed away by the waves. The work of months and multitudes had been destroyed in a short hour.

But this disaster by no means discouraged Alexander. He was by nature incapable of taking a backward step. Curtius and Diodorus suggest that he now contemplated a treaty with Tyre. But it nowhere appears that he took any steps in that direction; nor was such an act consonant with his moods. He at once set to work to construct a wider mole on which he could build more than two towers, and to replace the burned military engines. The new mole is said to have been headed more end on to the prevailing wash of the sea. The old one had taken the heavy water at the side and been weakened accordingly. He had plenty of able engineers and good machinists. Diades and Chairias from the school of Polycides were at their head.

It was early spring. Alexander was convinced that he could not accomplish much so long as the Tyrians held the sea. He went to Sidon to collect triremes, leaving Perdiccas and Craterus in command, and taking with him the hypaspists and Agrianians. His mission was soon accomplished. Gerostratus, king of Aradus, and Enylus, king of Byblus, who, as we have seen, had been serving with Autophradates and the Persian fleet, so soon as they ascertained that their cities had surrendered to Alexander, had deemed it wise to desert the Persian navy and now placed all their vessels at the service of Alexander. These, with the Sidonian contingent of triremes, made up eighty ships. Rhodes concluded to send its ship of state and nine others. Vessels from other places also joined the new fleet, induced thereto by the victory at Issus, and still later Cyprus sent one hundred and twenty ships under Pnytagoras. Among the ships were many with four or five rows of oars. This was a crowning triumph of Alexander's persuasive arts, and the conqueror was glad to overlook in present zeal past opposition wherever it had existed.

While this naval force was being put into condition for battle, and the engines were being built, Alexander, with a few ilēs of cavalry, the hypaspists, Agrianians and archers, conducted a ten days' campaign against the mountain tribes of Anti-Libanus, who were in control of the roads which led from the Orontes Valley to the coast, as well as of the valley itself, and gave much trouble. This campaign he made as thorough as the one in Rugged Cilicia, storming a number of mountain fastnesses, and sweeping like a whirlwind through the uplands. We have no information as to the details of this expedition, and can only judge by other similar feats of this untiring monarch how thoroughly he did his work, and by a knowledge of the difficulties of the region how huge was the task to be accomplished in so brief a space. The mere marching to and from his objective was apparently enough to do within the time. Plutarch mentions, on the authority of Chares, many acts of personal valor by the king during this expedition. But heroism was Alexander's daily habit. We cease to notice it. On his return to Sidon he found there a reinforcement of four thousand Greek mercenaries under Cleander, and the fleet well on the road towards completion.

When his fleet was ready, Alexander embarked on the vessels as many of his shield-bearing guards as he deemed to suffice for boarding and for close conflict, and by the first fair wind — for, though the vessels depended mostly on oars, they did not willingly encounter head-seas — sailed in order of battle towards Tyre, intending without delay to come to pitched battle with the enemy. He himself, with the Cyprians and Phœnicians, was on the right. Craterus and Pnytagoras commanded the left wing. As this imposing array approached the city, Alexander stayed the advance to rectify the line, much as he had slowed up the impetuous forward march of the phalanx at Issus. When the slower vessels had come up, the king again gave the order to advance. The Tyrians, who had previously resolved to fight, and were noted for their prowess, especially at sea, were so astonished at the number of vessels — thrice their own force — which Alexander had collected, so disheartened that their allies had deserted them, and so taken aback by Alexander's audacity in offering battle, which he did with unquestioned confidence, that they declined to come out into the open, but contented themselves with blockading the mouth of the north or Sidonian harbor by a row of as many triremes as could be put in, which they disposed bows on for fear of capture. Seeing this, Alexander did not seek to force the entrance. The Phœnicians, however, by some skillful manœuvring, managed to cut out three triremes which had ventured beyond the harbor, and destroyed them. The sailors swam to shore. Alexander moored his fleet along the coast on both sides of his mole, where there was shelter from the winds. Andromachus and the Cyprians moored opposite the Sidonian harbor, and the Phœnicians opposite the Egyptian harbor. Alexander's headquarters were established on the latter side. The reduction of Tyre was now only a question of time.

A vast number of missile-throwing and other machines had now been collected from Cyprus and Phœnicia, or built on the ground. All that the science of the day afforded and much in new invention was put to use. Of these engines, some were mounted on the mole and others on flat-boats or merchantmen, and on the slowest-sailing triremes. Towers were built on some of these vessels, provided with bridges to be thrown over to the walls. Rams were mounted on others. These floating engines were moored opposite the city. They were now brought into play, but were speedily and skillfully opposed by the Tyrians, who erected towers on the walls opposite the mole and opposite the ships. This prevented the bridges from being dropped upon them, and enabled them to discharge missiles from their own excellent artillery. They shot fire-tipped arrows against the vessels which approached and cast fire-pots from their ballistas. The walls of Tyre were one hundred and fifty feet high and correspondingly broad, and were built with the utmost skill and care of square hewn stone, laid in gypsum in a fashion of which the secret seems to have been lost. It was almost impossible for engines to be got near enough to work at undermining these walls, not only on account of the missiles from the walls, but because the water at their base was filled with loose stones, purposely cast in there to impede such approach. These stones Alexander now proceeded to fish up and remove, a work requiring no little skill and patience. The vessels which were moored and set at this work were soon interfered with by triremes which the enemy clad in mail, and from which, with long-handled, sickle-shaped knives, they cut the stone dredges adrift. This manœuvre Alexander met by mailing vessels in the same manner and placing them in front of the dredges, to prevent the cables of the latter from being cut. Then the Tyrians resorted to divers — this was the mart for sponges, and divers were many and expert — who cut the cables under water. Alexander nullified this scheme by using chains. The stones were then laboriously seized with slip-knots, taken out by cranes, carried away and thrown into deep water. In this manner, one part of the wall previously selected was gradually made accessible to the engineers for undermining.

The Tyrians had naturally hoped for aid from Carthage, which was its most flourishing colony, and whither they had sent their families out of harm's way when Alexander's mole had become a threatening matter; and they were no doubt grievously disappointed at the unfilial conduct of this eldest

daughter; for Carthage volunteered no assistance whatsoever.
To be sure she was at war herself, but, as she did later in the
days of Hannibal, Carthage pursued a thoroughly selfish
policy.

The Tyrian fleet was divided into two sections, one in each
harbor.   The Macedonian fleet rode near the mouth of the
harbors, and prevented all egress, so that they could not join
forces for attack.   Together they were too weak to expect to
do much; singly they were impotent.   But the harassed
Tyrians felt called on to undertake some sharp offense, and
determined to attack the Cyprian ships moored on the north
side of Alexander's mole.

Under cover of sails spread as for drying across the mouth
of the harbor, and thus unknown to Alexander, they placed
expert rowers and their bravest soldiers on board thirteen
ships of war, — three quinquiremes, three quadriremes and
seven triremes; and, towards the middle of the day, when
Alexander's sailors were scattered in quest of victuals, and
Alexander was in his tent on the farther or Egyptian side of
the mole, where headquarters had been located, the Tyrians
rowed out of the harbor.   At first they moved with as little
commotion as possible; but when well under way, they raised
their battle-cry, and sharply made for the Cyprian fleet.   So
sudden was the attack that at first they had things their own
way, and drove on shore, sank or damaged a number of these
allied vessels.   Some of Alexander's outposts had, however,
conveyed to him speeedy information of the attack, or, as
others relate, he had happened to leave his tent earlier than
usual this day.   He at once manned as many of the vessels
on the south side of the mole as he could get together, posted
some of the half-manned ones at the mouth of the southern
harbor, to prevent the exit of more Tyrian ships while he was
absent, and with the rest — all the quinquiremes and five tri-

remes — started for the scene of action. The mole had now so nearly reached the city walls that he was compelled to make the entire circuit of the island in order to reach the place opposite the Sidonian harbor, where the Tyrian ships were committing such dangerous havoc. His direction would, however, enable him to take them in the rear. Seeing the danger of their vessels from Alexander's manœuvre, — and his men rowed fast, as fast as an average steamer of to-day, — the Tyrians signaled from the walls to their vessels to return; but before these, deafened with the noise of battle and excited with unwonted success, understood the meaning of these signals and essayed to escape, Alexander was upon them. The Tyrian vessels at once made off, but the king damaged many beyond use and captured two, one with five and one with four rows of oars. The mariners mostly escaped by swimming. Alexander had shown himself to be an admiral.

This victory was the beginning of the end. The loss of the sea was to the Tyrians much like the loss of the glacis of a fort. Alexander blockaded the harbors so as to confine the Tyrian fleet within them, and was thus at liberty to try his engines upon the walls.

Alexander had accomplished a goodly part of his labors. He had advanced his mole to a point from which he could attack the walls; he had secured a safe anchorage for his vessels; he had cleared the channel so as to enable his engine-bearing ships to reach the walls; he had driven the Tyrian fleet into its harbors, and held it there. Nothing remained to be done but to break down and carry by assault the city walls. But just this was the gravest task of all. The desperation of the Tyrians grew with the danger.

Despite all his trouble, Alexander found that he was unable to make any impression on the wall next to the mole, it being too solid for any engines he had constructed. Nor could the floating engines make any impression upon the side nearest Sidon. Still, though he was much disappointed, all this did not discourage the king. After long efforts and trials on every part of it, the floating engines finally succeeded in greatly weakening the wall on the side toward Egypt and seaward, where the Tyrians, expecting no attack, had constructed a masonry less solid, and in breaking down a portion.

The besieged had shown themselves to be easily masters in their inventiveness and mechanical skill; and Alexander's engineers had needed all their ingenuity to match them. The impatience of the army had been growing, and confidence began to weaken in the possibility of capturing this extraordinary fortress. But the opening of a breach kindled fresh courage in the hearts of all. Into this breach Alexander now threw a bridge and a storming party, but the Tyrians, with showers of missiles, fire-pots and other devices, drove this partial assault back, and repaired the breach by a half-moon. Alexander waited for a better chance. It is asserted that he was again tempted to observe the place, and proceed upon his way. But there is no act of his to support this theory, and it is scarcely compatible with Alexander's characteristic persistency.

Three days after this failure, the sea being calm, Alexander made preparations for a new attack in force. It was the end of July. He assembled his battering engines at the most assailable place, which was on the southwest front, and ordered some of his vessels carrying catapults and other missile-throwing engines as well as slingers and archers to skirmish around the island on all sides, in order to make the garrison uncertain as to where the stoutest attack was to come, and stationed others near the breach so as to overawe the enemy by the violence of the assault and the multitude of missiles. Upon still other vessels he placed his best troops, the shield-bearing guards under Admetus, and the phalangial brigade of Cœnus. He proposed to lead the assault in person. He sent parts of his fleet to the mouths of both harbors to endeavor to force an entrance, by breaking the chains which barred them. All the rest were put to use to assist in the final struggle. After some hours' effort, he succeeded in opening a still wider breach, the battering vessels were withdrawn, and the two which had been fitted with bridges were brought up; the bridges were thrown, and the shield-bearing guards, under the personal eye of Alexander, mounted to the assault. The affair was sustained in the most courageous manner by the Tyrians; but when the Macedonians had once got a footing upon the wall, they pushed back the enemy with their accustomed gallantry. Admetus was the first to fall, pierced by a spear. Alexander with Cœnus and the phalangians followed up this success, and having taken several towers and the wall between them, advanced fighting along the battlements towards the royal citadel. For this was an easier means of approach than to descend to the level of the city streets. The citadel was taken.

Meanwhile, the fleet at both harbors — the Phœnicians at the Egyptian, and the Cyprians at the Sidonian — had found its way in, and, making short work of the Tyrian vessels, captured the north and south fronts of the city, erected ladders and soon forced an entrance. Being thus taken between two fires, the stronger force of Tyrians opposite Alexander deserted the walls and rallied near the temple of Agenor. But Alexander, who, after the death of Admetus, had headed the shield-bearing guards, emerged from the citadel and soon broke down all opposition; and the enemy being attacked from all sides by Cœnus and by the men of the fleet, a fearful slaughter ensued. For the Macedonians were enraged at the obstinacy of the city's defense and the cruelties practiced on Macedonian prisoners captured by the Tyrians, who had tortured and put them to death on the walls in full sight of the army, and thrown the bodies into the sea, thus depriving them of the rights of burial. They had even cast Alexander's heralds into the sea from the top of the walls. Over eight thousand men were slain. Two thousand Tyrians, say Curtius and Diodorus, were hung or nailed to gibbets on the seashore. Of the population, Alexander pardoned all who had fled into the temple of Hercules, among whom were the king and many prominent officials; but sold into slavery the rest of the Tyrians and mercenary troops, some thirty thousand men. The women, children and old men had mostly been previously sent to Carthage, their, as it proved, ungrateful colony. In the assault, but twenty of the shield-bearing guards were killed. During the siege, four hundred Macedonians had lost their lives. No doubt between three and four thousand had been wounded, — a somewhat higher rate of loss than that of Grant at Vicksburg. Grote deems this number much too small. A part of the population is said to have escaped by connivance with the Phœnicians on the fleet, and to have later returned to Tyre. Curtius says fifteen thousand were thus saved.

The cruel fate of Tyre was but the usual outcome of the sieges of antiquity. Inexcusable, if you like, but readily matched by the similar horror at Magdeburg in the Thirty Years' War. If, after sixteen centuries of Christianity, thirty thousand men, women and children, out of a population of thirty-six thousand, could be butchered in the name of religion, the less criticism passed on the so-called cruelties of Alexander the better. Masses have no soul. The armies of olden times demanded such holocausts. Even such a king as

Alexander, had he so desired to do, could scarcely have prudently stood in their way. To deny his men their rights in this particular would have forfeited much of his influence. And Alexander, no doubt, was at times as revengeful as the basest of his phalangians.

Alexander now offered the proposed sacrifice to Hercules with military honors, his army parading at the very gates of the temple, and dedicated the particular engine which had opened the breach, to the god, as a thank-offering. The fleet was drawn up in battle order, and passed in review; and the Tyrian ship, sacred to Hercules, which had been captured, was likewise dedicated, and a suitable inscription placed upon it. Games and gymnastic sports were celebrated within the precincts of the temple.

Thus fell Tyre, after a siege of seven months, and no doubt its extraordinary resistance and awful doom made as deep an impression upon the world as had the battle of Issus. The pride of centuries had been humbled by the persistent courage, ability and military skill of Alexander.

The place was retained as a naval station, but Tyre was entirely destroyed, though Strabo says that it again became a flourishing city. The building of the mole altered the flowing tides in such a manner that the ancient harbors have been filled up with deposits of mud, and the island has become a peninsula, nature's monument to the almost superhuman labors of this greatest of captains.

While besieging Tyre, Alexander received from Darius a second letter, tendering him ten thousand talents for the release of his mother, wife and children, and offering him his daughter Statira in marriage and all the territory west of the Euphrates. Alexander submitted this letter to the Companions, and Parmenio is said to have advised its acceptance. "If I were Alexander, I would accept." "If I were Parmenio, so would I; but being Alexander, I will not," — are the words said to have been exchanged. Alexander replied to Darius that the whole of Persia was his, and that he would marry his daughter, if he so wished, without his consent; as for the money, he was in no need of it. Thus rebuffed, Darius prepared for a further contest.

It is related by Josephus that Alexander now (some put the event after the capture of Gaza) marched towards Jerusalem, which had refused him supplies, feeling bound to honor its oath of allegiance to Darius. But at the gates he was met by a procession of citizens headed by the high priests. These he treated with the highest respect; and having been shown in the prophecy of Daniel that he was the Greek foretold as the one who should overcome the Persian king, he not only abstained from injuring the city, but granted it every seventh year immunity from taxation. If this be not strictly true in all its details, it is nevertheless certain that Alexander would not have left in his rear so prominent a city as Jerusalem unvisited and unsubdued. No doubt the relation is substantially exact. Sanballat, satrap of Samaria, cast in his lot with Alexander. Acco made no resistance.

Alexander.

(From Cameo in Zanetti Museum.)

XXV.

GAZA AND EGYPT. SEPTEMBER, B. C. 332, TO SPRING, B. C. 331.

FROM Tyre Alexander marched to Gaza on the way to Egypt. This town, the outpost protecting the road to Egypt, under Batis, made stern resistance to the conqueror. It was captured only after a two months' siege, and by the erection of mounds and works of remarkable extent. The garrison was exterminated, and Batis treated with unnecessary cruelty. From here Alexander went to Egypt, which he found no difficulty in reducing. He laid out Alexandria, and visited the temple of Jupiter Ammon. He might have kept on to Carthage, but learning of Darius' new army, he turned back. The Ægean fleet had completed its work, and Alexander had possession of the whole Mediterranean and its coast. He could advance into the interior with safety.

IT was early September. All Syria except Gaza had submitted to Alexander. But Gaza must be reduced. This city was situated near the edge of the desert on higher ground than the level of the plain and on an artificial eminence sixty feet high, and was by far the most formidable place in southern Syria, a bulwark, as it were, which dominated the road from Damascus to Egypt, from the Red Sea to Tyre, and had been the fortress from which the restless population of that country had been controlled by Persia. It had been intrusted by Darius to one of his most faithful servants, and victualed for a long siege by the Eunuch Batis, its commander, who, with a eye single to his master's interest and honor, believed that he could hold the fort with his Persian garrison and Arab contingent, and thereby keep the Egyptians in subjection until Darius could again gather a new army, and come in his might to chase this overbearing adventurer from the sacred soil of Asia. Batis knew that Alexander had captured Tyre

with his fleet. Vessels could not approach his fortress. Gaza
was some two miles inland, — Strabo says but seven stades ;
the coast was marshy and bad for landing ; the fleet here was
useless. Batis was satisfied that he was safe.

Alexander, on his arrival, camped near the weakest-looking
part of the wall on the south side, and ordered suitable engines to be built for its reduction. The engineers were of
opinion that no towers could be erected from which the walls

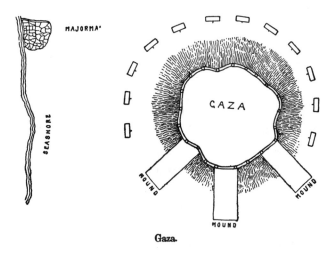

Gaza.

could be successfully reached and battered down, owing to the
height of the ground on which they were built above the level
of the plain. But Alexander would consider no difficulty
whatever. After Tyre, was there any city which could resist
him ? He began the construction of a mound around the
city, beginning on the south side where the walls seemed least
stout ; and here, too, the mound was largest. In an almost
incredibly short time this mound had — probably only in
places — risen to a height such that the engines could be set
at work upon the walls. It is not improbable that there were
several of these mounds.

When the battering was about to begin, and Alexander was, according to custom, sacrificing to the gods, a bird of prey flew above him, and let fall a pebble which smote Alexander on the head. But the bird then alighted on one of the machines, and was caught in some of its ropes. The soothsayer Aristander, from this event, prophesied that Alexander should indeed capture the town, but must in the assault have a care of himself. Alexander, therefore, kept somewhat more than usual in shelter, taking up post near the batteries instead of near the walls. But one day, when a sortie was made by the garrison, the works erected with so much toil were near to being fired, and the Macedonians from their lower position were in danger of being driven from the towers and engines, Alexander, seeing the imminent danger of defeat and unable longer to contain himself, seized his arms, and heading his shield-bearing guards, came quickly to the rescue. The sortie was repulsed, though the Macedonians had lost some ground; but Alexander was wounded by a shaft from a catapult which pierced through the shield and corselet, and entered the shoulder. The wound was a serious one, and came close to being worse. According to Curtius, the king received two wounds in this siege.

The engines from Tyre which had been sent for now arrived by way of Majormas, a neighboring small harbor, and the mound was completed all around the city, though possibly the expression " all around " may mean concentric with the wall. Part of it — Arrian leads one to infer that all of it — was twelve hundred feet wide, and two hundred and fifty feet high (that is, near the wall); and as the sand from this plain could not be used, materials were brought from a distance. If such figures as these were not abundantly vouched for, they would be incredible; but we know from Ethiopia and Egypt, and Nineveh and Babylon, what gigantic works can be erected by the forced labor of the entire population of a district. The fact that to build such a mound all around the city would be a vast expenditure of unnecessary labor (for the mound was of use only for the towers and rams, and these were erected but at one or two of the most available spots, and the rest of the wall of contravallation need be but comparatively small), leads us to construe the passage as above, whatever the dictionary meaning of the words. If opposite but a small part of the wall, the performance is sufficiently magnificent.

From this mound the Macedonian engines could easily operate. A large part of the city wall was speedily undermined or battered down, and much more made full of breaches. But though Alexander thus commanded the walls, and could drive the defenders from the parapet and embrasures, the defense was very stubborn, the garrison forcing back three assaults, though these were made with true Macedonian élan, and the garrison lost heavily. The fourth was delivered in greater force, and from several sides, after enlarging the breaches and making use of all the ladders and tools which their previous ill success had shown to be necessary. There was the greatest emulation as to who should first scale the wall. Neoptolemus, one of the Companions, was the man who outstripped all the rest. Being closely followed by other leaders, on whose heels pressed the balance of the troops, the wall was surmounted, and a chosen body made for each gate. These were soon opened, and the Macedonians passed into the city. The most bloody contest raged through its entire extent. The brave Gazeans fell to a man sword in hand, where each had been posted. The women and children were sold into slavery. It is said that ten thousand men were slain at Gaza, and that Alexander took barbarous revenge on Batis, the commander, dragging him around the walls lashed to the back of his chariot — as his ancestor Achilles had done to Hector. Unusual vengeance, and one which, however much in accordance with the spirit of the age, we can wish untrue of Alexander. The siege had lasted two months.

Enormous stores of spices were captured here at Gaza, which was the chief market for such goods. Alexander is said to have sent Leonidas, his ancient tutor, five hundred talents' weight of frankincense and one hundred of myrrh, in memory of a reproof once given him. When as a boy he was, at a sacrifice, throwing incense by the handful into the fire, Leonidas had said to him that until he had conquered the land of spices he must be more sparing. Alexander now accompanied his gift with the hope that Leonidas would no longer be a churl to the gods.

The study of numismatics furnishes us with many of our historical facts. The coinage of Asia Minor and Syria shows us that, while Alexander restored to the territories west of the Taurus their liberties, the cities being left on the same footing as those of Greece, those east and south of the Taurus were treated as possessions of his own. The coins of the latter countries bear the impress of Alexander as king; those of the former are not so issued. Syria and Phœnicia were accordingly left under a strong government, and Alexander headed for the country of the Nile.

It was early December, just a year after the battle of Issus, when Alexander started on his Egyptian expedition. In seven days he reached Pelusium, whither he had ordered his fleet under command of Hephæstion, so that it might meet him on his arrival. Though recently conquered, Egypt had no bond whatsoever with its Persian masters, nor was there any desire for an armed conflict with the Macedonians. The Egyptians were a peaceful folk. The occupation of a new conqueror seemed quite immaterial to population and rulers alike. The Persian Satrap Mazaces, in lieu of receiving as friends the Greek mercenaries who had fled from Issus under the renegade Amyntas, and thus being able to use them for the defense of the country, as they had anticipated he would do, had attacked and dispersed the force, and massacred most of them. This left him no means of offering resistance, and being moreover at odds with the population, Alexander gained easy admittance to all the cities of Egypt, besides enriching himself with some eight hundred talents in money. He placed a garrison in Pelusium, sent his fleet up the east branch of the river to Memphis, and marched on the east side of the

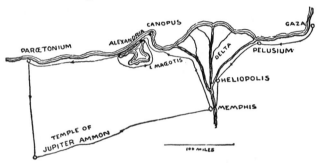

Egypt.

Nile to Heliopolis through the desert, taking possession by voluntary surrender of all the towns upon the way. He then advanced towards Memphis, crossed the Nile at this point and sacrificed to Apis, the Sacred Bull, with Greek feasts and gymnastic contests. Alexander was always careful to treat the religion of the countries he conquered with respect instead of contumely and outrage, and on this occasion desired to see what could be done to merge the feelings of his old and new subjects by mixing the Macedonian religious customs with those of Egypt.

From Memphis he sent his army down the Nile to the coast, the agema of cavalry, hypaspists, Agrianians and archers on vessels down the west branch, and turning towards the west he arrived at Canopus. He sailed round Lake Mareotis, and foreseeing that a city might become very prosperous at this location as an *entrepôt* of trade, he chose the site of Alexandria and founded this famous mart. His first selection was the Pharos as the site of the city, but its extent being too small, he drew the outline of the city on the mainland. The harbor is one of the best, and Alexander's calculations as to the future value of this, his first Alexandria since crossing the Hellespont, were not disappointed. In making the plans, there being nothing on hand wherewith to mark the lines proposed for walls, Alexander resorted to the use of the soldier's barley, which he scattered along the ground. Numerous birds were thus attracted to the spot, and the future great prosperity of the place was prophesied from this sign by Aristander and other soothsayers present.

At this point Alexander was joined by Hegelochus, his admiral in the Ægean, who reported that Tenedos had revolted from the Persian yoke forced on them against their will and had come over to him; that Chios had taken a similar step; that the fleet had captured Mitylene, and brought over other cities of Lesbos; and that Amphoterus, his vice-admiral, had captured Cos. He brought with him a number of the chief men of these places who were opposed to Alexander, as prisoners. These men the king sent back to their several cities to be judged by those, now holding power under himself, who were cognizant of the facts and better able to convict or acquit. By these victories, added to the closing against the fleet of their usual harbors, the Persian power at sea had been paralyzed, and Alexander had gained possession of the whole Mediterranean coast.

Alexander was now seized with a desire to visit the temple of Jupiter Ammon in the Libyan desert. Perseus and Hercules, his ancestors, were said to have consulted this oracle,

and Alexander not only wished to tread in the footsteps of
these heroes, but desired to learn certainty concerning his
own origin and future, or, as Arrian says, "that he might be
able to say he had learned it." Both Plutarch and Arrian
agree that Alexander claimed descent from Jupiter only in
order to impose on the credulity of the populations he
conquered. He did so, according to Curtius, "because he
either believed Jupiter to be his father, or had a mind the
world should think so, not being satisfied with his mortal grandeur." While admitting the truth of many of the
allegations against this monarch, it must be allowed that folly
was not one of his characteristics. His intelligence ranged
far beyond that of most of the wisest men of his day. And
he was much more capable of pretending a belief in his own
divine origin for political effect, or because it administered to
his personal vanity, than of really harboring it.

Accompanied by a considerable body of horse and foot,
Alexander advanced along the seacoast to Parætonium, nearly
two hundred miles from Alexandria, thence south an equal
distance to the oasis where the temple lay. Aristobulus
states that on this occasion rain fell in this always arid region
as a sign that the gods were propitious, and that the march
of the army was led by two, Curtius says great flocks of,
ravens (Ptolemy, son of Lagus, says two snakes, uttering
a voice), which moved on before them the entire distance.
The voyage was certainly prosperous.

The oasis was five miles long by three wide. It was well
inhabited and tilled, and full of olives and palms. Dew fell
there, and the fertility of the spot was in wonderful contrast
to the ocean of sand which surrounded it. Justin says Alexander gave the priests instructions as to what answers should
be given to his queries, and particularly ordered them to
salute him as son of Jupiter. "Now, whoever would judge

sagely of the sincerity and credit of the oracle, might easily have perceived by its answers that it was all imposture," says Curtius. Having, at all events, consulted the oracle to his satisfaction, though his queries and their answers are not divulged by history, Alexander returned by the same route to Alexandria, and thence to Memphis, as narrated by Aris-tobulus; or straight across the desert to Memphis, according to Ptolemy. Possibly, a part returned by the former, and Alexander, with the hardier part of his force, by the latter route. Had Alexander not heard of Darius' new levies, he might have moved farther along the coast towards Carthage. But this important news beckoned him in the other direction. Carthage was isolated and entirely innocuous. Alexander remitted it to the future.

At Memphis many embassies from Greece came to the king, each with its own request. Always expert in his policy, Alexander was able to send all these embassies back with a feeling of satisfaction. He also received a small reinforcement from Antipater. This consisted of four hundred Greek mercenaries under Menidas, five hundred Thracian cavalry under Asclepiodorus, and several thousand phalangites.

In providing for the future government of Egypt, Alexander returned, as was his habit with all conquered peoples, to its ancient and beloved customs. The king had a fine sense of how to mix civil and military rule among peoples used to a central government. He kept the civil entirely distinct from the military control. The former was invested with no power except that of levying taxes and carrying forward the old and well considered laws and customs then prevailing, which Alexander was wise enough not to upset; the latter was removed from the temptations of finance, from the danger of handling moneys. Native ministers were continued in office, but carefully watched; only the head of the state was changed ; thus the people had no chance of organizing resistance. The citadel of every town was put in charge of a trusted band of his own Macedonians. In addition to this a general commanded outside, with a sufficient Macedonian force to act as a leaven for the native levies he was directed to make, and command and drill in the Macedonian manner. Alexander was generally readily accepted as king, because the people knew of the change only by a general lightening of their burdens, and a less oppressive method in the collection of taxes.

In this instance Alexander appointed an Egyptian, Doloaspis, governor of Egypt ; but placed the military command in Macedonian hands. He left two Companions, Pantaleon in Memphis and Polemo in Pelusium, in command of garrisons. Some Greek auxiliaries, which he also left in Egypt, he intrusted to Lycidas. Peucestas and Balacrus were commissioned generals in command of the Egyptian army, which, including the above garrisons and auxiliaries, consisted of four thousand men ; Polemo was also admiral of the navy of thirty triremes. Charge of Lybia he gave to Apollonius ; of part of Arabia to Cleomenes. Calanus succeeded Balacrus in command of the Greek auxiliaries who kept on with the army. Ombrion succeeded Antiochus, who had died, in command of the archers. Leonnatus became one of the somatophylaxes. Alexander, says Arrian, was induced to leave the country under many governors on account of its distance from his probable future campaigning grounds, and because he deemed it unsafe to intrust a country so large and full of resources to the command of any one person. The lists of viceroys, governors and commanders left in the various countries often vary in the different authors. Changes in command account for this. It is not important to us.

XXVI.

ON TO BABYLON. SPRING TO SEPTEMBER, B. C. 331.

ALEXANDER now marched to Tyre and thence to Thapsacus, where he crossed the Euphrates. The Persians expected him to move straight on Babylon and had devastated the district in his path. But Alexander turned northerly and marching to the Tigris crossed this river, likewise unopposed. Darius's evident plan was to let him reach the very bowels of the land and then crush him on the level plain by numbers. Moving down the left bank, Alexander ran across the Persians drawn up on the plains of Gaugamela. He camped and gave his men four days' rest. Parmenio advised a night attack, but Alexander refused to "steal a victory." Darius had forces estimated between a quarter million and one million one hundred thousand. Alexander had forty-seven thousand men. Alexander left his impedimenta in a stockaded camp in the rear, so as to go into action unfettered, and addressed words of noble encouragement to his men, who were at the highest pitch of enthusiasm.

So soon as spring opened, Alexander, having bridged the Nile, crossed with his army and marched to Tyre, where he found his fleet already riding at anchor. Passing through Samaria, he deemed it necessary to chastise the inhabitants for having assassinated his deputy Andromachus, whom he replaced by Memnon. In Tyre he again celebrated rites and games at the temple of Hercules, with great splendor and pomp. Here the Athenians once more sent an embassy asking that their fellow citizens, captured at the Granicus, be released, to which request, in view of the better tone of the Athenian political atmosphere, Alexander, according to Curtius, now acceded with gracious generosity. It is said that Demosthenes, on this occasion, sent a letter to Alexander craving pardon for his virulent opposition. Alexander also dispatched a fleet to the Peloponnesus to counteract the Spartan influence still being exerted against him, with all the national stanchness of that wonderful people.

The king placed trusted men in charge of the receipt of custom. Cœranus was appointed to Phœnicia and Philoxenus to the Cis-Taurus region. Harpalus, just returned from desertion, Alexander made treasurer of the army chest, he not being rugged enough for field service. Harpalus had been among the small crowd of Alexander's intimates who were expatriated when he himself fell under his father's displeasure. Alexander never forgot his friends. Harpalus had been in favor, but, guilty of some misdemeanor, had fled, just before Issus. He was now recalled and put in charge of the moneys. A remarkable judge of men, Alexander sometimes went too far in relying on his intimates. It was once a friend, always a friend with Alexander. Unqualified treachery alone could warp his affection. Nearchus, later the admiral, was made viceroy of Lycia as far as Mount Taurus; Asclepiodorus was appointed viceroy of Syria, vice Menon, removed for negligence. Menander was given office in Lydia. Clearchus succeeded the latter in command of part of the Greek auxiliaries; Erigyius was made chief of the Greek allied cavalry; Laomedon was appointed provost marshal, as he was well acquainted with the Persian language.

Having made sundry other changes in the command of his troops, he marched on Thapsacus, no doubt drawing in some of the Asia Minor garrisons to reinforce his ranks. His route was by way of the Orontes Valley to Antioch and thence easterly; and from Phœnicia he reached the Euphrates by a march of eleven days. From Myriandrus to Thapsacus the ten thousand Greeks had marched in twelve. This was close upon twenty miles a day. It was early summer. Thapsacus had a much used ford and was the place formerly chosen by Cyrus for crossing the Euphrates. Here Alexander's engineers, whom he had sent out with a vanguard, had undertaken to build two bridges of boats. They had not completed them to the farther bank, for Mazæus with five thousand cavalry and two thousand Greek mercenaries, under orders from Darius, was guarding the river. But they had the work substantially done. This force under Mazæus was the farthest outpost of the new army which Darius had raised to defend his kingdom. On hearing of Alexander's arrival, Mazæus at once decamped. He could do no good in disputing the passage, for Darius was already prepared to meet the invader, and anxious for the encounter. The military theory under which the Persians seemed to be acting, was that of allowing Alexander to come into the very heart of the kingdom, where, presumably, if beaten, he could be more utterly destroyed. And in this view Mazæus' orders were confined to reconnoitring and reporting Alexander's movements. Delay was the last thing Darius wished. The bridges were completed, and one other which Mazæus had broken down was repaired.

Alexander laid the foundation of a city, Nicephonium, at this spot, before he crossed into Mesopotamia, a work which consumed some weeks. This constant founding of cities was in pursuance of a clearly defined policy. It had three objects, — one, to provide an asylum for the wounded or invalided Macedonian soldiers who were no longer fitted for the field ; again, to form a chain of military posts on the line of communications ; and the third, to build up in the country a knowledge of Hellenic arts and methods. In so founding a city its outline was first drawn up by the engineers upon the site selected, then the location for a citadel was chosen and protected by a ditch and rampart, and gradually made strong ; then the inhabitants of the surrounding country were invited to come in and settle under the protection of the garrison, and were no doubt secured certain privileges. The population of Asia, then very considerable, soon produced a thriving city in each of these locations. The choice of sites was generally excellent and no doubt, as to-day, corner lots were sold at a premium. Moreover, the advantage, in a military sense, of having a series of garrisoned towns at no great intervals all along his line of operations was pronounced. For there was a constant movement to and fro along this line of couriers, reinforcements, material of war, and impedimenta of all kinds. We shall see how effective these posts were.

Having founded Nicephonium, Alexander crossed and marched into Mesopotamia, "having the Euphrates River and the mountains of Armenia on his left," says Arrian, — that is, his route was northerly as if towards Armida. He took this course, which was not an unusual one, on account of its being an easier region to march over and having greater abundance of forage and victuals. The country between him and Babylon on the direct road down the Euphrates, which was the one pursued by the Ten Thousand, had been wasted by the Persians to impede his advance by that route on the capital; they having calculated that he would attempt to march the same way. Moreover the heat was much more excessive along the plains of the Euphrates than on the uplands of the Tigris. The route down the Euphrates was, Xenophon tells us, naturally an exceedingly poor one for an army to pass over, being arid and without a sufficient supply of breadstuffs. It may be suggested that Darius ordered the devastation to bring Alexander towards the position he had selected for the *coup de grace.* There is no doubt that the Great King was eager for battle, and was pleased when the Macedonians headed in his direction. He had this time no fear for the result.

Alexander had intended to march to the point now called

Eski Mosul, near ancient Nineveh ; but having heard from captured Persian scouts that Darius lay on the Tigris with a large army, he feared that he intended to dispute his crossing. He did not deem it wise to try to force the passage of so great a river in the teeth of Darius' enormous army, though indeed the army of Darius was his objective ; but preferring an open battlefield for the final conflict, he altered his direction to a point above, where, when he reached the Tigris, he would be apt to find no opposition. The army had none the less great difficulty in crossing the river on account of the swiftness of its current, the ford being up to the armpits of the men. Indeed, the name of the river in Persian signifies " arrow." It flows to-day quite six miles an hour. It may be worth while to state that the limit of depth for cavalry is generally assumed to be less than four feet, and for infantry less than three. A line of horse was stationed above, to break the current ; and one below to catch those who might be carried away. Alexander crossed on foot, first of all, carrying his arms above his head, to encourage the infantry. Some of the men joined hands, and not a soul was lost. This is in some respects one of the most interesting cases of fording a difficult river by a large army in history. The place of crossing was most probably near Bezabde, — which better fits Arrian's relation, — though some modern authorities put it near Eski Mosul. The point need not detain us.

While resting here after crossing, there occurred a total eclipse of the moon (September 20), usually an ominous portent ; but Aristander, the soothsayer (probably under instructions from Alexander, who well knew how to sway the superstitions of his men), construed the startling event as a favorable omen. It was not the sun, Apollo, the deity of the Greeks, but the moon, Astarte, the goddess worshiped by so many nations under Persian rule, which was obscured. Alex-

ander's tact always rose superior to his superstition. No
doubt this eclipse produced a profound impression also upon
him; but his uppermost thought was always his scheme of
conquest, and nothing which could affect his only means of
carrying this on — his army — ever failed to engross his whole
intelligence. There is nothing more marked in the character
of Alexander than the way he browbeat his own often intol-
erant superstition by the exercise of his superior intelligence.

Having crossed the Tigris, the army moved down the left
bank of the stream with the Gordyæan Mountains (the Carducian Mountains of Xenophon) on his left, and on the
fourth day ran across the immediate outposts of Darius'
army, — a force of one thousand cavalry. Darius had wasted
the land, and there was scarcity of breadstuffs.

Extensive as Alexander's conquests had been, Darius had
in reality lost but a small part of his immense kingdom.
Asia Minor, Syria, Egypt were as nothing compared to the
vast territory from the sources of the Euphrates to the Indus
and Jaxartes, with its brave and loyal peoples. But the Great
King had done practically nothing for two years except to
recruit another army. This he had accomplished by a general draft of the entire population of his empire. He had
neither attempted to prevent Alexander from overrunning his
distant provinces, nor interfered with his sieges, nor blockaded the mountain passes he must cross, nor — most near-
sighted of all — sought to aid his own fleet in the Ægean.
Not only had Darius failed to defend the mountain passes,
but he had allowed Alexander to cross the last two broad and
difficult rivers unopposed. He might easily have made the
country a desert, and have thus rendered all but impossible
Alexander's advance. The result of his system, or lack of it,
was that the Macedonians had marched through a country
rich in supplies, had accumulated vast treasures, and had

arrived in Assyria in the best of condition and *morale*. Instead of the numberless chances he had neglected of crushing the Macedonians, he was reduced to a single chance. A lost battle now meant a kingdom lost for good.

No doubt all these points had been fully discussed by the Persian strategists, who in their way were able and intelligent, though wont to be divided in counsel; but still confident that on a plain their enormous numbers, especially in horse, must beyond a peradventure crush Alexander's small army out of existence, they deemed it their best policy to allow him to reach Mesopotamia, and there give him, far from any possibility of retreat, the final blow. And they had preferred to let him cross the Tigris as well as the Euphrates, for on their theory, the farther from home, the more dangerous his situation. Moreover, behind the Tigris, should Alexander be defeated, he would be thrown back on the mountains of Armenia, or on Mesopotamia, where he could be easily followed up and destroyed; while, should Darius again suffer a reverse, his road was open to Babylon.

Alexander had now been on the throne five years. He had made himself master of Greece. He had conducted a successful campaign against the Danube barbarians; had chastised the Illyrians; had taught Greece, by the fate of Thebes, what his anger could do. He had conquered Asia Minor; had crossed the mightiest mountain ranges and rivers; had defeated Darius in a great pitched battle, and destroyed his army, root and branch; he had carried through to a successful issue the greatest siege of antiquity; had overrun Syria, Phœnicia and Egypt, and had captured an hundred fortified cities, and built others. He had driven the Persians from the Ægean, and reduced to control the entire coast-line of the Mediterranean; he had advanced into the heart of the Persian empire, and had placed behind him its two great river bulwarks. He had marched over six thousand miles, despite the delays of sieges and the difficulty of establishing new governments in every section he traversed. And all this, no doubt, with as large trains and as much in the way of impedimenta as a modern army boasts. Yet he had but begun his work. The final struggle for the mastery had yet to come.

Darius appeared to have lost the character for strength which he was thought at one time to possess. An excellent ruler in peace, he was his own worst enemy in war. He was to all appearances paralyzed by the loss of his family, since Issus, as we remember, in Alexander's hands. These acted, as it were, as hostages for Darius' good behavior. It is not unlikely that Alexander's treatment of them, so noble from one aspect, was dictated by a motive to keep their value as hostages up to the very highest point, both as regarded Darius and his own army as well. In case of a serious reverse, these royal persons might prove of incalculable value. There was more than one reason why Alexander should keep Darius' family with his army instead of sending them to some city in the rear. Their own safety was nowhere so secure as in the midst of the Macedonian soldiery. This the royal captives knew full well, and showed in the coming battle. Turned adrift, where could they go when Darius himself was all but a fugitive? Moreover, by keeping them near him and giving them royal state, Alexander was increasing his own importance and standing in the eyes of all ancient friends and subjects of the Persian king; and multiplied his power of dictating terms a hundred-fold. At some period antedating the battle of Arbela, Queen Statira, the wife of Darius, sickened and died. It is said by some historians to have been in child-birth. It may have been later than such a cause would place the sad event, and was perhaps from the toils of the way, perhaps from humiliation and homesickness. Alexander is reported to have done everything which was possible to show his respect for the deceased queen, and to have exhibited genuine good feeling. All this is presumably true. He had enough enemies to record the facts if they were not as stated.

Darius had now assembled a much larger army than had been on foot in Cilicia, and had armed it with swords and longer spears, thinking thus to meet the Macedonian sarissa. But he had not probably been able to alter its drill and discipline to correspond. This required time and experience not at his command, though he is said to have been assiduous in practicing the men in their new manœuvres. That he should have committed the imprudence of not defending the passage of the Euphrates and the Tigris can be partly accounted for on the supposition that he still hoped for a peaceful accommodation, by which he might recover his family. It may have been for the purpose of further negotiation to this end, that, instead of risking his battle in Mesopotamia, where the ground was quite as favorable to his numbers, and whither he had marched from Babylon,

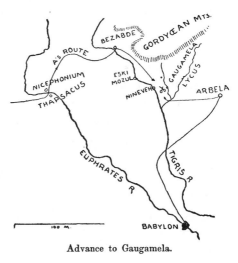

Advance to Gaugamela.

he turned eastward from this province and himself crossed the Tigris. Having done this, he stayed his march at Arbela, where he established his magazines, harems, and treasury, subsequently moving his army forward across the Lycus (modern Great Zab) to Gaugamela, on the Bumodus, seventy miles westerly from Arbela.

Darius appears to have here again renewed his offer of half his kingdom, his daughter's hand, and thirty thousand talents of gold to Alexander for peace and the surrender of his family. He is said to have been deeply touched, not only by Alexander's respectful treatment of his wife, — so unusual in a conqueror, — but quite as much by Alexander's generosity to the queen during her fatal sickness, and to his mother and his children. On learning these facts, he is represented as having implored the deity, that if he could no longer sit upon the Persian throne, the crown might rest on the head of the Macedonian monarch, his bitterest foe, his greatest benefactor. Alexander submitted the proposal of Darius to the Council as a matter of usual routine ; but himself eventually decided that Darius was endeavoring to corrupt his friends, and sent away the ambassadors with contumely.

When Alexander's scouts had reported a Persian force in his front, he had at once put the army in order of battle, and continued his advance ; but further scouts ascertaining the force to be only a small body of perhaps one thousand cavalry, he took an ilē of horse-guards, the royal squadron and Pæonian dragoons, and himself led the van forward. The army followed in two columns, with cavalry on the flanks and the baggage in the rear, every man on the *qui vive* for what might soon be coming. The Persian outpost decamped ; a few were slain, some captured. From these latter the king learned the composition of Darius' army. There were assembled all the nationalities under the Persian sceptre. In numbers the army is stated by different authorities at from two hundred thousand infantry and forty-five thousand horse to a million infantry and one hundred thousand horse. There were two hundred scythed chariots which had scythes on the axles and yokes and a spear on the pole, and fifteen elephants brought by the Indian contingent, and now for the first time introduced into warfare against Europeans. The troops were commanded as follows : Bessus, viceroy of Bactria, commanded the Bactrians, Indians, and Sogdianians ; Mavaces commanded the Sacians, who were mostly horse-bowmen ; Barsaëntes, satrap of Arachotia, led the Arachotians and Mountain Indians ; Satibarzanes, satrap of Aria, led a large body of Arians ; Phrataphernes led the Parthian, Hyrcanian, and Tarpurian contingents, all horsemen ; Atropates led the Medes, Cadusians, Albanians, and Sacessinians ; Orontobates, Ariobarzanes, and Otanes led the divisions raised near the Red Sea ; Oxathres commanded the Uxians and Susianians ; Boupares commanded the Babylonians, Carians, and Sitacenians ; Orontes and Mithraustes commanded the Armenians ; Ariaces led the Cappadocians ; Mazæus led the Cœle-Syrians and Mesopotamians.

The places in line of some of these troops are not given by any of the authorities ; and there is as considerable variation in chiefs and nations as in numbers. As usual, unless manifestly wrong, Arrian has been followed. The discrepancies are readily to be explained by the assumption that, when deployed in line of battle, the commands of many of the important chiefs were enlarged.

Darius' position was well chosen. It was on a large plain, near Gaugamela, and the ground had been carefully leveled, all obstacles had been removed, and the brush cut down, to allow the free evolutions of the chariots and horse.

Alexander gave his army four days' rest. We can imagine the Macedonian soldiers repairing and sharpening their weapons and polishing their shields and armor with unusual care.

The camp, which was but seven miles from Darius' army, was fortified with a ditch and stockade; the utmost circumspection on all hands was ordered. Here Alexander intended to leave all his heavy baggage and hospitals, so as to be able to go into battle with his troops bearing nothing but their arms. From all indications he judged that Darius proposed to choose his own ground on this occasion, and not allow his impatience to lure him to a battlefield where he could not employ his masses.

After the four days' rest and preparation, Alexander broke up about the second watch, and made his march towards the enemy under cover of darkness (September 29–30), hoping to reach and attack the Persians by daybreak. But he was delayed on the way. The Arbela plain is full of huge conical mounds to-day, the burial places of ancient cities; perhaps many existed then. A ridge of rolling ground lay between the armies, so that Alexander came within four miles of the Persian host before he caught sight, as he finally did through the morning mists, of their huge masses darkening the plain. Darius had them already drawn up in battle array, " in enormous squares of prodigious depth " of cavalry and infantry mixed. From the top of the last of the hills Mazæus and his cavalry had just retired, and Alexander, who halted his phalanx on this high ground, reconnoitred the situation from a distance, and called together his Companions and officers of rank for the usual council of war. Many of the younger ones advised at once to attack, for the troops were in high spirits and eager for battle; but Parmenio and the older officers advised by all means to delay until the ground could be examined, so as to discover if pit-falls and such like obstructions had not been dug in front of the enemy's army; and until the enemy's tactical arrangements could be learned. Though Alexander's councils of war, unlike the proverbial ones, were not slow to fight, under his casting vote, this advice prevailed. A new camp and stockade were here made on the hill-slope near modern Börtela. The army lay on their arms in order of battle, while Alexander with some light infantry and Companion horse busied himself in thoroughly reconnoitring the ground.

On his return from this important duty, he again called together his Companions and officers, and addressed them. We can readily imagine, if we do not know, his soul-stirring words. Arrian but gives us the summary of them, most likely from the relation of Ptolemy, son of Lagus, one of his most interested auditors. He knew, said the king, that he could rely on their so often proved valor, but it was essential for them to infuse their ardor into every man of the command. In the approaching battle they were to fight for the whole of Asia, as well as for existence. Discipline must be maintained with an exactness never before demanded. Instead of chanting the pæan as usual, the men were to advance in perfect silence and order, so as not only to hear the trumpet calls the better, but so that their battle-cry, when given at the word of command, should strike an unwonted terror in the breasts of the enemy. Orders must be quickly transmitted and absolutely obeyed. Each man must remember that on his own individual courage depended largely victory or defeat. The council responded to his stirring words by a demand to be at once led against the enemy, that they might prove their obedience and valor. But Alexander bade them rest and refresh themselves by food, so as to go into action strong and vigorous the next day.

Late that evening Parmenio visited Alexander in his tent, and urged a night attack, as the Persians would be more liable to panic and confusion in the dark. They had the habit of unsaddling their horses and hobbling them, and of

taking off their own armor, so that they would be helpless
and more easily overcome. But Alexander replied, partly for
effect, — for there happened to be others listening to the conversation, — that it was more worthy to conquer without artifice, and not to steal a victory. He fully understood, moreover, the dangers which beset the attacking party at night, in
the midst of a hostile population full of the enemy's spies;
and knew not only that unless he defeated Darius in open
battle he could not morally conquer Asia, for Darius would
be able again to explain away his defeat, but also that if he
were not certainly victorious, retreat would be all but impossible in the night, from a foe who perfectly knew the *terrain*
of which the Macedonians were ignorant, — except merely
the path they had just pursued. He rejected the proposal.

Alexander.

(From Cameo in Zacharia Sagrado Collection.)

XXVII.

ARBELA. OCTOBER 1, B. C. 331.

DARIUS anticipated a night attack and continued his troops under arms all night. Having stood thus all through the previous day, they became tired and unstrung. Early in the morning the Macedonians deployed into line, Alexander and the Companions on the right, Parmenio and the Thessalians on the left. The Persians had leveled the plain for their cavalry and chariots. They far outflanked Alexander, who, to meet this threat, made two flying columns of reserve, one behind each wing, with orders to wheel outward and stand against any outflanking force, or to the rear, or to reinforce the phalanx, as needed. The battle opened by Alexander's taking ground to the right to avoid entanglements in his front. Darius launched his chariots against him and hurried Bessus with a cavalry force to fall upon his right flank. The chariots proved useless; Bessus was checked by Alexander's right flying column. Alexander sharply advanced against the Persian left centre. Here was a gap made by the Persian first line edging to the left, to follow Alexander when he edged to the right. Perceiving this, the king formed a wedge and drove it sharply at this gap and at Darius, whose station was near by. Meanwhile Alexander's taking ground to the right had rent a gap in his own line, as Parmenio could not follow him, because Mazæus had smartly attacked his left. The Thessalians held head against Mazæus, but a column of Persian cavalry rode down through the gap and penetrated to the camp at the rear. Again the army was saved by the wisely disposed left flying wing, which attacked this Persian column. Parmenio feeling sore pressed sent to Alexander for aid. The king had just driven his wedge into the Persian line, and again Darius, as at Issus, terrified by the dangers which beset his person, and unmindful of his duty as a king, had taken to flight. This gave rise to a headlong flight in the whole centre and left. Alexander was about to pursue when he heard of the danger to his left. Turning rapidly from pursuit, he headed the Companions and galloped back to strike the cavalry which had ridden through his lines. He met them just as they were coming back with the left flying column at their heels. Here occurred the stoutest fighting of the day. The Companions outdid themselves. The Persian column was annihilated. Bessus had been driven off; Mazæus had been defeated; the Persian centre and left were broken; the right now followed them in flight. The battle for the kingdom of Persia was won. Alexander pursued sharply, reaching Arbela, seventy miles distant, next day. The Persian loss was from forty to ninety thousand men, the Macedonian killed were five hundred. As at Issus, the Persian army was dispersed. Darius took with him but nine thousand men and fled to the interior.

THE Persian army at early dawn had watched the small array which had ventured within the wrath of the Great King, gathering on the heights west of the Gaugamela plain. They had anticipated a speedy attack and had come into battle order. But Alexander had spent the day in preparation and reconnoitring. Having no stockade, and fearing an attack after night-fall, Darius gave orders for the troops to remain under arms all night. (September 30–October 1.) This made a long twenty-four hours that the Persians had so stood. Their *morale*, already weakened by Issus, was probably far from heightened by this fatigue; and still less by the dread thus instilled of the Macedonian prowess. Darius rode his lines at night to show the royal countenance and to inspirit his men.

A document containing the arrangement of the Persian army was captured among the archives after the battle. This showed not only the formation of Darius' army, but also made mention of the above facts. No doubt it was a species of order of the day. The marshaling of the Persians was as follows: In the left wing from the left stood the Bactrian cavalry under Bessus with the Daans and Arachotians; the Persians, horse and foot; the Susians and Cadusians. In the right wing from the right were arrayed under Mazæus the Cœle - Syrians and Mesopotamians; the Medes; the Parthians and Sacians; the Tarpurians and Hyrcanians; the Albanians and Sacessinians. All these were in three lines and in large squares or in deep masses. In the centre was King Darius, surrounded by his "kinsmen" soldiers or body guards, fifteen thousand strong; the Persian guards with spears butted with golden apples, the Indians, Carians and Mardian archers. The Uxians, Babylonians and Red Sea men, and the Sitacenians were behind the centre in a deep column as reserve to the body surrounding the Great King. The Scythian cavalry was in front on the left, and near it one hundred scythed chariots. In front of Darius stood the fifteen elephants, and beside them other fifty scythed chariots. In front of the right were drawn up the Armenian and Cappadocian cavalry, and still other fifty scythed chariots. The Greek mercenaries, on whose skill and courage Darius relied to meet Alexander's phalanx, but whose fidelity at the same time he needlessly suspected, were stationed in two divisions, one on each side of the king and his body-guards. Bessus commanded the left wing; Mazæus the right.

Darius had likewise encouraged his army by a stirring address. He bade them not be disheartened by the partial defeat at the Granicus or by the defeat at Issus, where the mountains and the sea so shut them in that the Macedonian fighting force was as large as their own. He bade them do battle for their families and hearthstones. "It has become a contest for existence, and what is dearer still, the liberty of your wives and children, who must fall like mine into the hands of the enemy, unless your bodies become a rampart to save them from captivity." He conjured them by the splendor of the sun, the fire on their altars, and the immortal memory of Cyrus, to preserve the Empire and its glory.

The Macedonians filed out of their camp on the hills at early morn, after a hearty sleep and breakfast (October 1). They moved forward in order of battle which was marshaled thus: The right was held by the cavalry Companions, the royal squadron leading under Clitus, accompanied by Alexander in person. Then to the left, the squadrons of Glaucias, Aristo, Sopolis, Heraclides, Demetrius, Meleager, Hege-

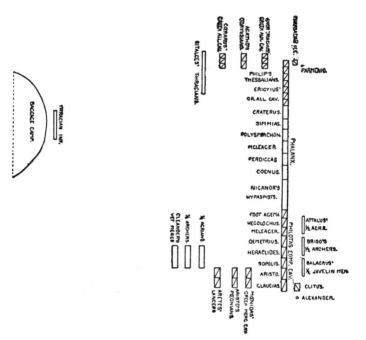

Position of Troops before the opening of the Battle of Arbela.

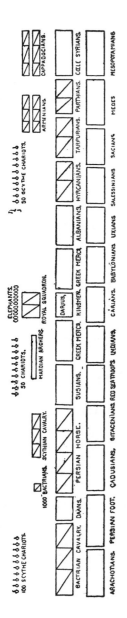

lochus. The whole body of cavalry
Companions was as usual under
supreme command of Philotas, son
of Parmenio. Then came the
Macedonian phalanx, according to
Curtius in two lines, meaning probably hoplites and peltasts ; first the
agema of hypaspists, then the other
hypaspists under Nicanor, son of
Parmenio ; then the phalangites under Cœnus, Perdiccas, Meleager,
Polysperchon, Simmias (commanding Amyntas' brigade), Craterus.
The latter was in command of the
left wing of the infantry. Then
came the allied Greek cavalry under Erigyius, and the Thessalian
cavalry under Philip, which body at
Issus had shown itself to be the
peers of the Companions, and was
therefore posted on the left, as the
Companions were upon the right.
Parmenio with the Pharsalian
horse, the best ilē of the Thessalians, as body - guard, commanded
the left wing, as was the rule.

The Persian army far overlapped
the Macedonian flanks. This was
unavoidable, if the king was not to
jeopardize the solidity essential for
attack. To provide against this
danger, Alexander for the first time
formed a second or reserve line,

or rather a column in rear of each flank, so placed that it
could face about or wheel to the right or left, and fight to the
rear or on the flanks if needful to resist attack from these
directions. It was a flying column behind each flank. He
naturally feared that he might be surrounded by the immense
number of the enemy, for to attempt this was the one usual
manœuvre. This disposition has been called a grand hollow
square, but it was more than that. The arrangement was
such as to insure greater mobility than a square is capable of
possessing. For the flying columns were so organized and
disposed that they could face in any direction, and were prepared to meet attack from front, flank or rear. Indeed, the
left flying column met an attack from within, and beat it off.
" In fine," says Curtius, " he had so disposed his army that it
fronted every way " — he should have said could front every
way — " and was ready to engage on all sides, if attempted
to be encompassed; thus the front was not better secured
than the flanks, nor the flanks better provided than the rear."

In this second line, in his right wing, Alexander had disposed the cavalry at intervals, so that it could wheel into line
at such an angle to the front line as to be able to take in
flank any body which might advance on Alexander's right;
and this force had orders, if need be, to close in like a sort of
rear or reserve line so as to form a huge square; or if called
for to reinforce the first line or phalanx for a front attack
by filing in behind it. In the right flying wing were half
the Agrianians under Attalus, and the Macedonian archers
under Briso; next the veteran Macedonians under Cleander.
In front of these were the light cavalry, and the Pæonians
under Aretes and Aristo. In front of these again were the
newly arrived Greek mercenary cavalry under Menidas, placed
where they might win their spurs. And covering the agema
and Companion cavalry were half the Agrianians and archers

and Balacrus' javelin-men, the latter opposite the chariots in the centre of Darius' army. The special duty impressed on Menidas was to ride round and take the Persians in flank if they tried to surround this Macedonian wing.

On the left was a similar flying wing in which were the Thracians under Sitalces, the Greek auxiliary cavalry under Cœranus, the Odryssian cavalry under Agatho. In front of all these stood the cavalry of the Greek mercenaries under Andromachus. The exact description of this formation, excepting that of the main line, is difficult to decipher from Arrian, and impossible from the other ancient authorities. Diodorus calls it a semicircle. We know better what these reserve troops, or part of them did during the battle, and this suffices. The accompanying chart satisfies quite closely the statements of the several authorities, and suits Alexander's manœuvres as developed by Arrian from Ptolemy and Aristobulus with reasonable accuracy. It is moreover consistent with itself, and the successive manœuvres as shown by the charts accord with all the ancient authorities.

The baggage, prisoners and camp followers had been left in the stockade in charge of the Thracian infantry. Here also was the family of Darius. The heavier part of the train was in the first camp seven miles to the rear. Alexander's whole force numbered seven thousand cavalry and forty thousand infantry, plus some few Asiatics. The latter were useless. They were not engaged, nor do they appear in line.

Alexander had passed the night in unusually careful discussion of plans for the morrow's battle. He is represented by some historians as having been exceedingly apprehensive as to the situation, by Curtius as alternately haunted by fear and hope. This is not Alexander. It is more probable that the king did not become in any degree anxious. It was not characteristic of him. He belonged to the type of man a

large part of whose strength lies in a constant, almost audacious, hopefulness. This, however, never clouded Alexander's
intellect, which remained open to a full comprehension of all
factors on which he must act. It is just this exceptional
combination of character and intellect which goes to make up
the great captain, and no less suffices. It is related that, late
at night, after fully completing his battle plan, he fell into a
deep sleep, out of which he was awakened by Parmenio long
after dawn. He was so confident of victory that he could
sleep. This does not look like nervous anxiety. He arrayed
himself with care, and appeared in his most glittering armor
and with a face which presaged certain success to the army.
The ilēs and taxes had in due order filed out of the camp and
into line. The stockade which had been erected to protect
the camp was left intact to protect the non-combatants and
prisoners, and the army stood forth ready for battle. After
riding the line, the advance at slow step was ordered, and the
Macedonians strode forward, as proud a force as ever relied
on its courage and discipline to wrest victory from so vast a
foe, or perish sword in hand.

Nothing leads one to rely upon Arrian rather than Quintus
Curtius more than their respective descriptions of this battle.
Arrian's portrait of Alexander is uniform, and commends
itself to one's judgment; his description of the battle enables
the careful student to place and manœuvre the troops. There
may be some variance as to details, but the main facts are
there, clear and crisp. The relation of Curtius of all battles
and sieges is obscure, and inconsistent in most parts; while
his sketch of the king makes him alternately a demigod and a
milksop — never an Alexander.

Darius, though he proposed to fight upon his own prepared
ground, was ready to open the battle by a charge of chariots.
Anticipating this, and to receive such a charge, Alexander

had ordered the phalangites to be ready — as at Mount
Hæmus — to open spaces for the chariots to pass through,
and, as we have seen, had detailed javelin-throwers in their
front to wound or frighten the horses as they came by. Alexander proposed to open by a charge of his cavalry *d'élite* on
the left of the Persian centre, opposite which his own right
stood arrayed. As he was about to advance, he learned by a
deserter that caltrops had been scattered in certain parts of
the field. He took some ground to the right to avoid these,
probably by a right half wheel and an advance by ilēs in
echelon. It was moreover natural for him to manœuvre in
this direction lest the much longer Persian line should overwhelm his right flank.

It is not improbable that Alexander anticipated that this
obliquing manœuvre might induce the Persian left to follow
in a parallel line, and thus open a gap between the Persian
left wing and centre, or at least unsteady the line. Whatever
his intentions, his movement had this effect. For, perceiving
this manœuvre, and fearing that Alexander might get his
whole army beyond the leveled ground where alone the
scythed chariots could operate to advantage or the cavalry act
effectively, Darius impatiently launched the chariots against
him, followed up by an advance of his centre, and at the
same time ordered forward the leading squadrons of his cavalry, one thousand Bactrians and some of the Scythians, to
envelop the Macedonian right and prevent any further obliquing. Alexander ordered out Menidas to oppose this charge.
But the Scythians and Bactrians so largely outnumbered
Menidas that they bore him back. Aristo with his Pæonians
was then launched on the enemy, and drove him back some
distance, till the rest of the Bactrians under Bessus, fourteen
thousand in all, they and the Scythians wearing more and
heavier armor than the Macedonians, reëstablished the Per-

sian diversion, and seriously threatened the Macedonian right. A sharp and for some time indecisive cavalry battle was here fought. But finally, when Alexander put in an appearance,

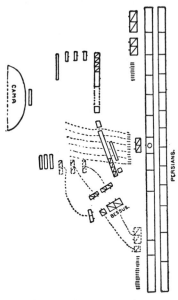

Arbela (second phase).

cheered and rallied the troops, and Aretes, at the king's order, charged in on the left of the Bactrians and Scythians with the splendid discipline for which his corps was noted, he enabled the Macedonians to score an advantage; and the entire body of cavalry continued to charge upon the enemy "squadron by squadron," with the peculiar tenaciousness which this tactical manœuvre called forth, and which Alexander's cavalry always so markedly exhibited.

Nothing is stated in the old histories as to what orders were given to Parmenio on the left when Alexander began to take ground to the right. No doubt he was instructed to follow the manœuvre. But he was not able to do so with equal speed; and his movement in support of Alexander was roughly interrupted, as we shall see. The ardor which Alexander had put into the work of his right wing, and the fact that the left Macedonian wing was prevented from keeping pace with him, again transferred what began as a parallel order into a semblance of oblique order, left refused. Inasmuch as Alexander always intended that the right, where he commanded, should take precedence in attack, which was indeed the usual thing among the Greeks, this fact, coupled with his natural aggressiveness offset by Parmenio's always more deliberate though courageous onset on the left, gave to this as to other battles, as has been already observed, the appearance and effect of an attack in oblique order, which came about partly by intention and partly by the operation of other causes.

While the cavalry forces on the right flank were gallantly stemming the tide of overwhelming numbers, the charge of chariots against the Macedonian phalanx, from which so much was expected on the one side and which was so much dreaded on the other, had been made, — and had failed, like the charges of elephants and so many other abnormal schemes of warfare have often done. For as the chariots galloped rapidly over the leveled surface towards the phalanx, the hoplites frightened the horses by clashing their spears upon their shields ; the Agrianians, archers and acontists received them with a formidable shower of arrows, stones and javelins ; they stopped some of the horses from simple fear ; they wounded others. Habituated to manœuvre with cavalry, they were quick of foot as we can scarce imagine ; they leaped at and seized the horses' reins ; they cut the traces ; they killed the drivers and warriors ; and while many forced their way to the rear through the purposely opened ranks of the Macedonian army, many others rushed on the protended sarissas, and fell or turned from the bristling array. Those who reached the rear were nearly all captured by the non-combatants, or broken up by the peltasts of the second line. The result was that the vaunted chariots accomplished little good commensurate with expectation or dread, and many charged back on the Persian lines, where they did vastly more damage than they had inflicted on the Macedonians, on account of the Persian greater depth. They had but unsteadied Alexander's line, and good discipline would repair this evil.

Chagrined by the failure of the charge of the chariots, Darius gave orders to set his entire centre phalanx in motion forward. This required some time. But the cavalry of the Persian first line, — Bactrians and Scythians, — in moving away from its post to join the columns which were threatening Alexander's right flank, had to a certain extent been followed by the infantry line, which had also edged to its left as Alexander had to his right. This had produced a marked gap in the Persian front, which the second line should have moved up to fill, but lacking orders, did not. Alexander, who had not only been leading his Companion cavalry, but also directing and personally rallying the dangerous and still doubtful combat on the right flank, when Aretes began to hold head against Bessus again turned to the front. His eye on the battlefield was like the hawk's for keenness; he instantly perceived the opening gap in the Persian line, and seized with quick apprehension this coveted chance. With a speed which no troops could then rival, — if, indeed, any have rivaled since, — he formed from that part of the Macedonian phalanx which was on the right — hypaspists, Cœnus and Perdiccas — a deep column or wedge; and heading it by his cavalry Companions in serried ranks, he wheeled round obliquely to his left towards this gap, and for the first time on this day raising that battle-cry by which the Macedonians never failed to shake the courage of their foes, he thrust this wedge at the double-quick, with the impetus of a battering-ram, into the Persian line, straight at the place occupied by Darius in person. Here, if anywhere, as at Issus, victory was to be snatched by boldness.

The Macedonian wedge struck the Persian line as a thunder-bolt rives an oak. Hand-to-hand the bravest hearts of

Macedon and Persia for a brief instant contended for the mastery; but nothing could resist the impetuosity of the Companions, who, headed by their gallant king, and instinct with the glories of the Granicus and of Issus, thrust at the faces of the foe and hewed their way through living masses; nothing could stand against the sarissa of the phalanx, which had never yet found its match. Darius was once more seized with alarm. Not waiting for support or for reinforcements, without personal effort to retrieve what might have been but a temporary disadvantage, but full of terror, especially when his own charioteer fell transfixed by a spear, he turned and fled. The splendid array of Oriental legions has lost its leader. Will no one fill his place and call into action the myriads of brave souls eagerly waiting to do the Great King service?

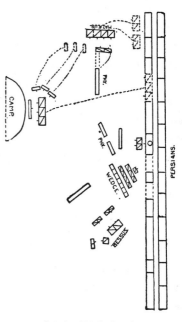

Arbela (third phase).

The cavalry of the Persian left had by this time also broken and was being driven back by Aretes upon the second line, which should but did not advance to its support, throwing it into quick confusion. The flight of the Great King put an end to any idea of resistance by the Persian centre and left. The vast mass began to melt to the rear, and but a few charges of the Macedonian right were needed to send them, as at Issus, ebbing in consternation from the battlefield.

While Alexander was heading his wedge for the Persian centre, and the cavalry of the right was charging home upon the Bactrians and Scythians of Bessus, the Macedonian left had been almost fatally compromised. Into the king's wedge had been thrust the brigades of Cœnus and Perdiccas, and the rest of the phalanx as far as the right of Simmias had tried to follow the movement to protect its flank. The latter brigade and that of Craterus, however, could not join in the king's forward movement, for Parmenio was hard pressed, and needed every man he could collect. The scythed chariots here may have won more success than on the right. It is not stated. But the cavalry on the Persian right was already moving out to attack the Macedonian left, and the troops in the Persian right centre were moving forward. These causes had operated to keep Parmenio from seconding the king. He had remained *in situ* to resist these threatening attacks. Thus Alexander's manœuvre, as masterly as it was pregnant with promised victory, had produced a gap in his own line which Parmenio, occupied with the serious onslaught of Mazæus, had been unable to fill.

Here was a grievous danger. There was no lack of able generals on the other side, and perceiving the chance, a part of the cavalry of the Persian right wing (said to be Parthians and Indians, together with some Persians, though these are not elsewhere mentioned as being in this part of the field) had left the line and headed straight for the gap, had ridden clean through the opening, had thrown the Macedonian left into the utmost confusion, and had actually reached the camp and baggage in the rear, before any means to arrest their swinging charge could be devised. The Thracian foot fought stubbornly at the gate of the stockaded camp, but many of the prisoners rose and attacked them in the rear. The enemy's cavalry released many others, who at once flew to their assistance, and they all but rescued the family of Darius. These, however, wisely refused to be carried off, feeling no manner of personal safety in the wild turmoil outside the camp.

The second line, which Alexander had posted in rear of the left wing with orders to face to the rear if necessary, now came into play. Sitalces, Cœranus, Agatho, Andromachus were not the men to stand about idle. So soon as they saw the danger, wheeling about their squadrons, they galloped to the rescue, fell sharply on the rear of the enemy and drove him off in wild confusion, killing and capturing men wholesale. What was left of these squadrons rode back the way they had come. This special danger seemed to be averted.

But a more threatening danger was at hand. At the time this irruption was at its height, Mazæus, commanding the Persian right, with the Armenian and Cappadocian cavalry of that wing, perceiving the effect of the charge through the Macedonian centre, and thinking to clinch the matter here and now, ployed his men into a heavy column and rode down upon the Macedonian left flank with a concentrated energy which threatened to overwhelm the entire force under Parmenio. Happily Alexander's Thessalians were here. As proud of their record and as stanch as the Companions themselves, these splendid squadrons, anxious not to be left out of the fray, wheeled to the left, received Mazæus half way with a counter charge, and as at Issus, by dint of hard knocks and clean-cut purpose, held the gallant Persian, despite his utmost efforts, from passing the limit they drew to his advance.

The situation was curious. On the Macedonian right Menidas, Aristo and Aretes were still struggling manfully to save the army from the furious and constantly repeated assaults of Bessus. Alexander's wedge had just aimed its mighty thrust at the heart of the Persian centre. The Thessalians were holding gallant head against Mazæus' overwhelming numbers. The Parthians, Indians and Persians were about to be taken in the rear by the reserves of the Macedonian left. An instant might change the current of the fray. The battle was anybody's, — were it not for Alexander.

Parmenio, unaware of Alexander's success on the right, felt, from the utter confusion in which the squadrons which had ridden through his lines, and Mazæus' thundering charge, had left his wing, that the case was desperate. He sent to Alexander urgently begging for reinforcements. This word reached the king at the moment he saw victory fairly wavering in the balance. He sent back answer to fight it out to the death. " Tell Parmenio," spake the king, " that if victorious, we shall regain all; if defeated, we shall die blade in hand. Let him fight as becomes Philip and Alexander!"

But victory sometimes marches fast. " Le sort d' une bataille est le résultat d' un instant, d' une pensée. On s' approche avec des combinaisons diverses, on se mêle, on se bat un certain temps; le moment décisif se présente; une étincelle morale prononce, et la plus petite réserve accomplit " (Napoleon). No sooner had the columns near Darius become aware of the flight of the Great King than they melted away once more, as they had done at Issus. There was no head, no purpose. The enormous columns of gallant men ready and eager for the fray if but some one would direct, were so many inert masses — dangerous to each other from their very numbers. A few more vigorous blows and the tide set back; nothing could retard its ebb. The retreat of the centre quickly became rout; Bessus perceiving the fatal effect of Alexander's charge, withdrew his cavalry; the splendid wedge of the Macedonian right had won the victory, — the Persian centre and left were in full retreat.

But danger still lurked in the situation of the left. Reluctantly yielding up immediate pursuit, and leaving his infantry to hold what he had won, the king wheeled his Companion cavalry to the left, and galloped to the aid of his embarrassed lieutenant. Just as the Parthian, Indian and Persian cavalry, driven from the camp by the reserves of the left, were retiring through the lines, Alexander struck this body in full swing. Here occurred the most stubborn fighting of the day. The enemy's horse must cut its way out or perish; the Com-

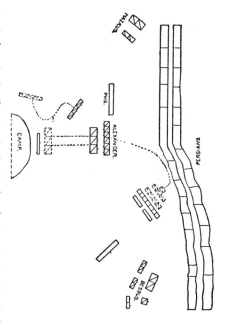

Arbela (fourth phase).

panions, furious at delayed pursuit, determined to give no quarter. It was hand to hand work. The fighting was close and quick and bitter. Some sixty Companions bit the dust within a few brief minutes; many, including Hephæstion, Cœnus and Menidas, were severely wounded. Few of the enemy cut their way through; nearly all remained upon the field. For, taken in the rear by the reserves as well as met in front by Alexander, they had no outlet but with sword in hand; and it was the Companions who barred the way.

The Thessalian cavalry had, during this interval, completed the defeat of Mazæus despite this officer's splendid struggle, and, aided by the fast spreading demoralization, had driven back the Persian right. Alexander's strong arm had not really been required. Seeing that Parmenio could now attend to this part of the field, Alexander once again turned to the pursuit of Darius, too long delayed. It is said that the fugitives made a cloud of dust so thick that only the sound of the whips urging on the horses were his guide in following up the enemy. Parmenio easily completed the destruction of the Persian right, which had not only been checked, but, on learning of the flight of their king, at once yielded up the struggle. Mazæus, with a body of troops, escaped around the left of the army, crossed the Tigris, and made for Babylon.

Alexander advanced across the Lycus, in which thousands had been drowned in trying to escape, and camped to give his men and horses a little rest. Parmenio seized the Persian camp at Gaugamela with all the elephants and camels. At midnight, the moon having risen, Alexander again set out in pursuit towards Arbela, hoping to capture Darius, the treasure and royal property, and reached the town, seventy miles distant, the next day. But Darius had kept well ahead. He could not be caught, though, as at Issus, Alexander took his spear and bow and chariot, and a large amount of gold.

In the battle and pursuit Alexander lost one thousand horses from wounds or from fatigue; and, according to Diodorus, whose figures here seem most reliable, five hundred in Macedonian killed. Taking the usual ratio of wounded, the loss of the Macedonians fell little short of twelve per cent. Of the Persians the slain are estimated by Curtius at forty thousand; by Diodorus at ninety thousand. " There were said to have been three hundred thousand slain," relates Arrian, this time manifestly quoting an error.

Arrian's Anabasis generally contains internal evidence of accuracy. From what he says you can plan out what Alexander did. But in quoting losses he is sometimes less correct.

He may allow himself to exaggerate here as a harmless species of flattery to his hero, whom at other times he is not wont
to overpraise. But the loss was enormous. The rule in
all old battles is the same. The victors lose little; the vanquished are cut to pieces. The elephants and chariots were
all captured. Whatever the relative losses may have been, it
is certain that the Persian army was dispersed, as it had been
at Issus. Doubtless the various detachments made their way
to their several homes, there being no head to keep them together. Darius collected some three thousand cavalry and
six thousand foot, and made for the interior.

This battle is remarkable for the valor and skill of the
commander of the victorious army, to whose constancy and
intelligence the success was clearly due, as well as for the
vacillation and cowardliness of the defeated monarch, despite
some most excellent work by his subordinates. Never were
dispositions better taken to resist the attacks of the enemy at
all points; never on the field were openings more quickly
seized; never threatening disaster more skillfully retrieved
than here. However great the advance in battle tactics as
the ages roll on, the world will never see more splendid tactics than the day of Arbela affords us. Even had Darius
stood his ground, his lines would scarcely have resisted Alexander's able combinations. Mere inert masses would have
availed nothing. The Persians still relied on multitudes.
Alexander was introducing new tactics. As Frederick taught
the modern world how to march, and Napoleon showed that
not masses but masses properly directed were of avail, so Alexander first of all men taught that a battle was not to be
won by weight of masses, but by striking at the right place
and right time. Macdonald's column at Wagram was scarcely
comparable to Alexander's wedge at Arbela. For this was
the first of its kind.

Parmenio may, by comparison with his chief, be found wanting; and some historians have laid much at his door, even going so far as to charge him with sluggishness from envy of the king's success. This seems overdrawn. Parmenio was none the less a good soldier, in view of his age a remarkable one. Mazæus' attack was made in grand style and was not easy to beat off, and it was Alexander's very success which opened the gap for the Indian, Persian and Parthian column to ride down through the centre of the Macedonian host. No wonder Parmenio felt that his case was desperate, ignorant as he was of the king's advantage. The wonder lies in Alexander's rescuing victory from so desperate a strait.

Only the Persian cavalry was engaged *au fond*. But this force behaved with valor, and in seizing the opportunity of the gap in Alexander's left to ride through the Macedonian army, showed clearly that it was led by able men. The near-by Persian infantry was routed by Alexander's wedge so soon as it struck the line, and Darius' flight completed the disaster for the remainder. The value of discipline cannot be better shown than by the fact that the gap in the Persian line produced demoralization which proved irretrievably fatal; the gap in the Macedonian line but a temporary disturbance by no means affecting the temper of the troops. The Macedonians were quickly rallied, and were at once again ready for work; the Persian army went to pieces.

XXVIII.

ALEXANDER marched on Babylon, fearing a second Tyre. With walls three hundred feet high, it could well have delayed him as long as did the queen city of Phœnicia. But Mazæus, who, after his gallant efforts at Gaugamela, had retreated on the capital, deemed it wise to surrender the city. He received his due reward. Here Alexander gave his men a long and well-earned rest, and distributed to them a handsome gratuity out of the treasures taken from the Great King, and here, too, Alexander made a number of army changes, fitting the organization to its new conditions. Babylon became a secondary base. Susa had also been surrendered, with its vast treasures, to an advance column, which Alexander had sent thither from Arbela. The next objective was Persepolis. To reach this home of the Persian monarchs, Alexander had to cross several rivers and an Alpine range; but, though it was now winter, he set out. The first opposition he encountered on the way was at the defile of the Uxians, who had for generations compelled a tribute for passage even from the Great King. This defile Alexander captured by a clever manœuvre, and reduced the Uxians to submission.

FROM Arbela the fugitive king fled through the mountains of Armenia towards Media, with the remnants of the Bactrian cavalry under Bessus, the "kinsmen," a few applebearers, and a handful of Greek mercenaries, all told some six thousand infantry and three thousand cavalry. Ariobarzanes, one of his generals, who had commanded part of the Red Sea troops, rescued from the turmoil a force stated at from twenty-five to forty thousand men, and retired to defend the Persian Gates. Anticipating that Alexander would march on Babylon and Susa, the great prizes of the campaign, Darius retired in a quite opposite direction towards Ecbatana, where it would have been difficult for an army to follow. He seemed to forget that it was possible for him still to make a successful defense of his kingdom at the entrance to Persis, which was covered by one of the most difficult mountain barriers in the world, and inhabited by a hardy population ready to do sterling service for the defense of their master. He fled as if his life were the only thing worth saving. His desertion left no head to the state. Ariobarzanes had probably no idea that Darius would abandon Persis. He saw that Babylon, in the open plain, was scarcely to be saved. Susa was equally accessible. But Persepolis was behind the mountains, and afforded abundant chances for defense.

Alexander was obliged quickly to leave Arbela, lest the stench of corpses should breed a pestilence. The army advanced on Babylon by the main road, and crossed the Tigris at Opis. With his usual care to leave no danger in his rear, and to make sure of his booty, Alexander neither followed Darius in his flight to the mountains, nor Ariobarzanes in his retreat to the Persian Gates. He preferred to take immediate possession of Babylon, before any one could organize for its defense. He naturally expected opposition here. He knew its history and had heard of its mighty walls. Perhaps the sieges of Halicarnassus, Tyre and Gaza were to be repeated. He could not tarry an instant.

The extent of the power of Persia can, to a small degree, be measured by its capital. It must be remembered that although Greece was the actual seat of the intellect and liberties of the world, Persia represented its material prosperity. Many of the now desert regions of the vast empire were, in Alexander's day, covered with smiling fields and a contented people ; and the vast structures and illimitable luxuries of the Persian kings do not point alone to a selfish centralized power, and a yet more selfish and cruel system of serfdom, but also to rich as well as vast dominions from which these yet unapproached creations of kings could emanate.

Babylon, within its outer fortifications, was superficially about seven times as big as Paris within hers, being not far from fourteen miles square. Of this enormous territory of nearly two hundred square miles, but a small third was covered with buildings like a city. The rest was open country, as it were, where farms, tilled to the highest limit of productiveness, were capable of feeding the population almost indefinitely. The Euphrates cut the city into two parts, and on one side was the royal quarter, with its hanging gardens and palaces; on the other the work-a-day world. Fifty main streets, one hundred and fifty feet wide, and four boulevards divided up this territory. The walls of the city in its prime were two hundred cubits (three hundred feet) high and seventy feet wide, and were surmounted by towers. One hundred gates of brass offered access to the country beyond. Perhaps ancient Babylon in its glory was never approached by any other city. And though conquerors antedating Alexander had destroyed many of its features, these had, no doubt, been replaced so that it was still the most wonderful of cities, and to the plain Macedonian of double wonder.

Alexander had heard that Mazæus, who had fought so bravely on the Persian right at Gaugamela, had posesssion of the city. Nearing its walls he marched slowly and in battle array. But instead of being saluted with closed gates and ramparts manned, he saw to his surprise and delight the portals open, and the population with wreaths and presents, led by the Chaldæans and elders and Persian officials, emerge to do him honor and bid him welcome. Mazæus, the servant, surrendered to Alexander, the conqueror and new master, as was the Oriental custom, and the Macedonian king entered without a blow into the impregnable city of Semiramis.

The surrender was duly rewarded. Alexander appointed Mazæus viceroy. No doubt Mazæus counted on this result, for Alexander's reputed generosity had preceded him. Apollodorus was made commanding officer of the city, and Agatho chief of the garrison in the citadel. Asclepiodorus was appointed collector of customs. Mithrines, who had surrendered Sardis, Alexander made satrap of Armenia. Menes was made hyparch of Cilicia, Phœnicia and Syria, and given the duty of keeping the roads on the line of operations free from predatory bands, of which, since the dispersion of the Persian arms at Issus and Arbela, there were many and troublesome. It will be noticed how scrupulous Alexander always was, while leaving the civil authority in the old channels, to place the military control in the hands of his own soldiers. This, as we remember, was Cyrus' plan, and Alexander ably carried it out.

To his army Alexander gave a long rest, richly deserved. No doubt these rough Macedonians enjoyed to their full this gorgeous city of the East, with all its luxurious habits, palaces and temples. From the vast treasures captured here, according to Curtius and Diodorus, Alexander distributed gratuities to his men. He gave each Macedonian cavalryman six minæ or six hundred drachmas, a sum equal to one hundred and twenty dollars; each Greek and light horseman five minæ or one hundred dollars; each Macedonian infantryman forty dollars; and the allied infantry and peltasts two months' extra pay. These sums at that day had many times greater purchasing value than now. Alexander sacrificed to Belus according to the Babylonian rites, adding games and races in the Macedonian manner. His ideas of merging races were being matured. Babylon now became a secondary base from which Alexander could proceed on his march of conquest, and where he could accumulate his stores and material of war.

Susa was the more central capital of the Persian Empire, and had been the winter residence. This city now became the next objective, and Alexander was wont to be restless, and anxious to be on the road, as long as there was work to be done or danger to be encountered. After the stay of a month in Babylon to make his footing secure, — he may have feared too long delay for its effect on his Macedonians, — he moved on Susa, which he reached in a march of twenty days, probably in November. The weather was auspicious. During the hot season the march could hardly have been made. The country then was rich and fertile, now it is a desert. But the geological conditions are still the same; the meteorological ones have not materially changed. On the way Alexander learned that Philoxenus, whom he had dispatched to Susa with a light advance-corps, immediately after the late battle, had received its surrender with all its treasures. These amounted to from fifty to eighty millions of our money, part ingots and part Darics. There was besides endless wealth in jewels, stuffs and other valuables, and the statues of Harmodius and Aristogiton, carried away by Xerxes, were found in the treasure house and restored to Athens. At Susa, too, Alexander offered sacrifices and celebrated games.

As an almost uniform rule, Alexander rewarded what was really treachery to Darius, though a common Oriental habit. Arbulites, the commander of the city, had welcomed Philoxenus. His son had come to meet Alexander with a procession of camels and elephants, laden with treasures as presents to the conqueror. Alexander made Arbulites, in consequence of this service, viceroy of the province; but Mazarus, a Companion, was associated with him as commander of the garrison in the citadel, and Archelaüs as general of the force of three thousand men left in the city. The treasure at Susa came in good stead. Alexander was enabled to send, through

Menes, to Antipater three thousand talents to carry on the war with the Spartans, a much needed remittance.

In Susa Alexander domiciled the family of Darius, and surrounded it with royal state.

Here were received considerable reinforcements, brought by Amyntas, son of Andromenes, from Macedonia. These are stated by Curtius to have been fifteen thousand men, including fifty pages. Alexander found it desirable to make some changes in his army organization. We are told that the mora or battalion (two syntagmas) up to this time had been five hundred strong. Alexander increased it to one thousand. The chiliarch or colonel, one of the most important of officers, because commanding the unit of service, given above as a taxis of one thousand and twenty-four men, was ordered to be chosen by certain judges appointed by Alexander, who were obliged to give their reasons for their selection, so that every soldier might see that the best man had been promoted. The king, like all others, had his favorites; but beyond favoritism was the desire to keep an army on which he could rely. The earliest promotions numbered Adarchias for gallantry in retrieving a failing assault at Halicarnassus, Antigenes, Philotas, Amyntas, Antigonus, Lyncestes, Theodotus, Hellanicus, each to the command of a new mora. This statement does not accord with what we have given of Philip's organization, but it shows that Alexander, under his new conditions, was compelled to make changes, to assimilate the new material entering the army. It is not impossible that the old historians have, in reporting the changes made, used misleading phrases, or employed Greek rather than Macedonian terms. But the matter is not of the essence. Alexander's changes were all of a similar and excellent kind. All distinctions in the foreign cavalry were abolished. He doubled up his cavalry organization by dividing each ilē or squadron into two companies, and placed reliable Companions in command, supplementing the small offices with the old pages, who had already learned something of war. This gave him a larger *cadre* which he could fill by drafts from the Oriental nations. Up to this time the Macedonians had always broken camp to the sound of the trumpet. Alexander now introduced a system of signals, partly by torches at night and smoke by day, given from a masthead erected near his headquarters. He thus evaded giving the enemy notice of his intentions, and made them clearer to his men. Prior to Arbela, the Macedonians and Greeks always marched to battle chanting the pæan. At that battle Alexander, it will be remembered, gave orders that the troops should not raise the battle-cry until instructed to do so, when it would have all the more effect. This was noted and acted on in after days. The reinforcements which Alexander received consisted of men, all of whom knew their trade, and could at once fall into the ranks. But they had to learn discipline. Alexander could teach them that better than any one alive. It is always hard to impose new rules on old and successful soldiers. Alexander wisely chose a time when reinforcements were arriving, and new elements were being introduced into the army to inaugurate his changes.

Xenophon, speaking of certain officers, says : " Proxenes of Bœotia was made to command honest people ; he had not that which is essential to inspire adventurers with respect or fear. Clearchus, on the other hand, always hard and cruel, could obtain from his soldiers only that sort of sentiment which children have for a schoolmaster." This is a crisp distinction, which every man in service has noticed. Alexander was of a different stamp. In his treatment of his army or of conquered peoples he was alike happy. " I have not come to Asia," said he, " to destroy nations; I have come here that those who are subdued by my arms shall have naught to complain of my victories." And he accomplished what he set out to do by the singular ability to control all classes of men, and to fuse discordant elements into a homogeneous mass.

Alexander now set out from Susa. His next objective was Persepolis, the capital of Persis, the place of origin of the Persian conquerors. The possession of Persepolis would mean to the superstitious population the possession of the kingdom. It was important, not only to reach the treasures

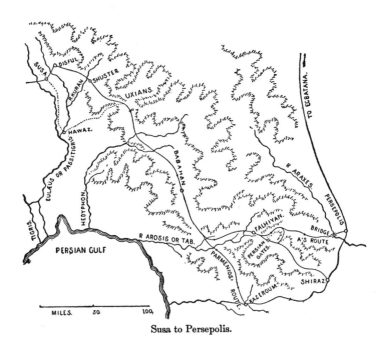

Susa to Persepolis.

in the cities of Persis, but to reach them before Darius had time to get together another army for their protection. For Alexander was as yet unaware of Darius' plans and purpose. He merely knew that he had fled from Arbela. Between him

and Persepolis lay a rugged Alpine country, traversed by but
a single practicable road, and with defiles easily held by a
handful. But the Greeks were always good mountain fighters. They were mountaineers by birth, and had had training
in mountain warfare from their earliest campaigns. It is
doubtful if any modern nation has ever come near to equal-
ing the mountain tactics of Xenophon or Alexander. Mountains had no terrors for the Macedonian army.

It is perhaps difficult to give an adequate idea of the tremendous difficulties to be surmounted in this march from
Susa to Persepolis, which some of the ancient historians dismiss with a sentence. There is to-day a plentiful lack of information about this rarely visited region. From the lowlands where stood Susa, to the uplands of Persepolis five
thousand feet higher, Alexander had to cross a mountain
range as well as several large and rapid rivers. The Coprates
and Kuran or the Passitigris, the Heduphon, the Arosis, the
Araxes were among these, not to mention scores of good-sized
affluents. The ancient names of some of these rivers are
uncertain, but they stood in his path then as now. The mountain chain which separates Susiana from Persis was so high
and rugged as to make the march much like a passage of the
Alps. Perhaps no mountains with which we are familiar can
convey the idea of these snow-clad heights except the Alps,
no passes show the difficulties of the road he had to follow so
well. This is no figure of speech. It was winter, and while
on the plains a winter campaign might be preferable to one
under the midsummer sun, in these mountains even summer
scarcely mitigated the severities of the march.

It has been claimed by excellent authority that this mountain barrier is the worst which any army has ever crossed.
This is probably inexact. The passage of the Parapamisus
must have been more difficult. And no similar feat will ever

equal Hannibal's passage of the Alps. But it was none the less a wonderful undertaking. The mountain chain rises in eight or nine successive terraces and water-sheds, to an altitude of fourteen thousand feet. It is a labyrinth of rocks, precipices, torrents, valleys, passes. Through this snow-clad range ran the one usual road. The first serious obstacle to be encountered, not to speak of the enormous difficulties of the route, was the defile of the Uxii, the next that known as the Persian Gates. These latter could be avoided by a more southerly route, along the plain from modern Babahan by way of Kaizeroum to Shiraz, though, indeed, this also is described as " a bad rock-bound road up and down."

Among the most remarkable qualities of Alexander as a general was his ability to get hold of geography, topography, climate, and the other factors of the problem of each country he was about to invade. No doubt he had all the means of knowledge at hand, in the presence of numerous professional and scientific men, Greek and Persian, who crowded about his headquarters; but the knowledge he acquired was nevertheless wonderful. That he never forged ahead until he knew all that was to be ascertained about his route is abundantly demonstrated by the results of his marches.

On his way towards Persepolis, Alexander must first reduce the land of the mountain Uxians. He started early in December. He is said by some geographers to have made a détour to avoid the Coprates (Dizful), and to have crossed the Passitigris above modern Ahwaz. Others put his route *via* modern Dizful and Shuster. The fact is not material. The tribes of the plains, which had always been subject to the king of Persia, had at once tendered their submission on learning of the capture of Susa; but the mountaineers, who had not only held out against Persian conquests, but had actually compelled the payment of tribute by the Great King for a passage through their defiles, headed by Madates, sent word to Alexander that he could not march over their mountains into Persis, without paying the same tribute which the late monarch had been wont to pay.

These mountains are to-day equally full of brigands, as intractable now as then. Alexander received their ambassadors with courtesy, and sent them back with word to be at

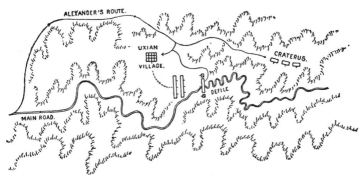

Uxian Campaign.

the entrance of their passes on a given day, when he would come with toll in his hand, and they should receive their just due. The Uxians naturally expected Alexander by the usual road, and he did in fact dispatch the bulk of the army that way. But having ascertained that there was another but very difficult road, he took his royal body-guards, the hypaspists, and eight thousand other troops, and marched at night with great toil, and led by native Susian guides, over mountain roads, to a position near by the Uxian villages.

The Uxians had built walls across the defile which they proposed to hold. The king dispatched Craterus by a circuit to occupy high ground to which the barbarians would be apt to retire if he could drive them from the wall. At daylight the next morning the king fell suddenly and unexpectedly upon these barbarians, destroyed their villages, and captured much booty. And having demoralized them, so that they were unprepared to act, he anticipated them by a forced march to the defile they had proposed to defend, reaching the place well ahead of any considerable body of the Uxians. When the Uxian warriors put in their appearance they found the defile occupied, and the Macedonians drawn up in order and ready to advance upon them. Utterly nonplussed by Alexander's celerity, and by the surrounding of their chosen position, the Uxians did not pretend to sustain themselves, but fled. Many were slain; many in their flight were thrust over the precipices; many sought refuge in the mountains, and were captured or killed by Craterus. Their defeat was total.

This is Arrian's account, who mentions no particularly hard fighting; but Quintus Curtius and some other authorities state that the Macedonians laid regular siege to the Uxian stronghold, while the light troops took it in the rear. There was such stanch defense that the siege threatened to be a failure. On one occasion, in fact, the shower of arrows and darts was so heavy that the troops were on the point of falling back, and had formed a tortoise, under the protection of which they were seeking to force even the king to fall to the rear. For a moment Alexander was helpless to control his men. He was reduced to shaming them into their usual vigor by recalling their past deeds. Stung by his vigorous reproaches, the phalangites recovered their courage. The ladders and engines were got into position, and Craterus now appearing in the rear of the barbarians, the works were eventually carried. Only the bald details of this interesting manœuvre are narrated by the old historians.

Alexander founded his course on the well-known habit of many barbarians to fight and prepare for action only by day.

They had by no means anticipated that Alexander would
come upon them, over all but impassable mountain roads, by
night. This very thing Alexander seized and acted on, — as
he was wont to do ; and by putting into execution the unexpected, he won with a handful in a few hours, and with slight
loss, what all Persia had not been able to win in many generations and with unlimited forces. Alexander's capacity for
doing the apt thing was always equaled by his utter con-
tempt of difficulty, and both together gave to his efforts such
uniform success.

The Uxians at once sued for peace. Alexander proposed
to extirpate this tribe, but Sisygambis, the queen-mother,
pleaded for them, and, after some hesitation, Alexander
granted her prayer, and gave them permission to retain their
territory by delivering as tribute one hundred horses, five
hundred beeves, and thirty thousand sheep a year, — they
being shepherds, and never having money or other treasure.
The Uxian territory was added to the Susian satrapy.

Alexander.

(From a broken Cameo in the Louvre, thought to be by Pyrgoteles.)

XXIX.

THE PERSIAN GATES. DECEMBER, B. C. 331, TO MARCH, B. C. 330.

FROM the Uxian mountains Alexander sent Parmenio with the train and heavy troops towards Persis, by the road south of the range; with the lighter and picked troops he advanced through the mountains, where at the Persian Gates Ariobarzanes and forty thousand men now held the defile. Reaching the position, Alexander essayed to force it, hoping for the same success he had met with at the Cilician Gates. But he found the task impossible, and was driven back with much loss. He was at a standstill. The pass could not be carried. Yet he must not leave this force behind him in his advance on Persepolis; it could create a dangerous diversion in his rear. Luckily, among his prisoners, Alexander found a Lycian slave who had been shepherd here for many years. This man pointed out to Alexander paths by which he could turn the defile. Leaving Craterus behind to hold the attention of the Persians, Alexander set out along these paths with a picked force. His exertions were incredible, but they were rewarded with success; on the second night he reached Ariobarzanes' rear, and attacked him at daylight. Craterus joined in, and between them the position was carried. Alexander then moved towards the Araxes, which he had sent forward to bridge, and reached Persepolis in season to prevent the despoiling of its treasury. But in revenge for the burning of Athens, Alexander gave the city up to pillage, and set fire to the palace. Here he gave his men a four months' rest, but he himself spent the time in reducing the mountain tribes of Persis, and especially the Mardians to the south.

FROM the Uxian mountains Alexander advanced in two columns. He sent Parmenio by the road along the foot-hills to the south, with the baggage and siege train, the Thessalian cavalry, the Greek allies and mercenaries, and the heavier part of the phalanx, while he himself, with the lighter part, the Companion cavalry, the lancers and horse-bowmen, the Agrianians and archers, pushed on by forced marches over the nearer but more difficult mountain road. Having marched one hundred and thirteen miles, probably reckoned from near modern Babahan, which is at the outlet of the Uxian mountains, on the fifth day he reached the vicinity of the Persian or Susian Gates, also called the Susiad Rocks, or Pylæ Persicæ or Susæ. Alexander hoped to surprise the pass as he had once done the Cilician Gates; but the satrap of Persis, Ariobarzanes, had occupied, and had built a wall across this defile, which is now called Kal-eh-Sefid, and begins to narrow four miles east of modern Falhiyan, and held it with a force of forty thousand foot and seven hundred horse, all Persians and good, reliable troops. Kal-eh-Sefid means "white fortress," and is "a mountain of one piece of rock, inaccessible on all sides, and battlemented at the top like a castle." It is the key and entrance to the plateau of Iran, and all travelers agree as to the difficulty of its approach.

Alexander might have reached Persepolis by the longer but easier road over which he sent Parmenio, which skirted the range along the southern foot-hills, but he could not leave so dangerous a force in his rear. Ariobarzanes had an army in number equal to the total of his own, and might at once have marched on Susa so soon as he saw Persepolis wrested from his grasp. And while Susa was left abundantly garrisoned, and could probably take care of itself, the moral effect of such a diversion would have nullified much of Alexander's work already done. It was no part of Alexander's plan to pass by any well-posted armed force, unless he could completely neutralize it. The distance from Babahan to Shiraz, *via* Kal-eh-Sefid is reckoned by La Gravière at one hundred and seventy-three miles; *via* Kaizeroum at two hundred and thirty-eight miles.

Having gone into camp, Alexander reconnoitred the position, and next day made a determined effort to take the walls by direct assault. The description in Arrian reads somewhat as if the king had stumbled into a species of ambuscade. Even Alexander was not beyond committing an occasional blunder. He had before him no common antagonist, nor indeed an ordinary line of defense. The rapidity of his

Operations at Persian Gates.

marches, which had so often snatched the prize of victory from the grasp of his unsuspecting enemies, was here of no avail. Ariobarzanes had fully anticipated him, and lay prepared at every point to dispute his passage, in the best chosen position, fortified by nature and by art as no obstacle Alexander had yet encountered had been. He allowed the Macedonians to march up the defile, which some modern travelers liken to the St. Gothard, without making the least demonstration. Barely three men could march abreast through this contracted path. When the head of column had reached the narrowest and most dangerous part, before it had got near the wall, while the Macedonians were marching between two perpendicular walls, suddenly they were startled by a bitter shower of sling-stones and arrows, by the shouts of the enemy and by heavy rocks being cast down upon them, in such a manner as to crush whole files of men. Against the ordinary missiles they could use their shields, but nothing could resist the immense boulders which the enemy rolled upon them — an enemy unseen and out of reach. It is asserted that Ariobarzanes had collected a number of missile-throwing engines at the wall ready for use if an assaulting party should reach so far.

Not to be easily discouraged, the Macedonians tried their best to scale these walls of granite. They helped each other up; they formed a tortoise; they pulled themselves up by the bushes; they clung to the rocks like flies. The men who later scaled the rock of Chorienes were among them. They essayed every avenue of approach; took advantage of every crevice. But all was of no avail. Alexander was compelled to sound the retreat, a rare thing with him. After the loss of many men — the casualties are not given, though Diodorus says a great number were killed and wounded — he returned to the camp at the mouth of the defile, some four miles from the wall — for the moment foiled. Napoleon, stopped by the Fort of Bard, comes strongly to mind, when we see Alexander for the moment reduced to helplessness at the foot of these unassailable defenses. But the Fort of Bard was a trifle compared to this. Here were defenses held by forty thousand men.

Alexander had captured some prisoners. From these at first he learned nothing; but finally a shepherd, who had been a slave, and for many years had fed flocks in these mountains, told him that by certain other, but unknown and difficult foot-paths, he could reach the farther end of the defile, or in other words, the rear of the position of Ariobarzanes. Alexander was always prolific of his gifts for services rendered. This guide was a native Lycian who had been sold into slavery, and while pasturing herds here had learned the lay of the land. Alexander well knew that a camel laden with gold was of no value compared to the life of one of his men; of less than want of immediate success; that rewards were of more effect here than many batteries of catapults. He promised this Lycian untold wealth if he led him aright, and gave him assurance of summary death if he betrayed him. In the event Alexander gave him thirty-three thousand dollars, — an enormous sum in those days. In his gifts Alexander always acted on the superb theory; " It is not what Parmenio should receive, but what Alexander should give " was his motive.

Alexander always undertook the most difficult work in person. Perhaps this was personally the most hazardous enterprise he ever carried through. He left Craterus with his own and Meleager's brigades, and some archers and cavalry in the camp in front of the wall, charging him to keep up the appearance of being still present in force by lighting many camp-fires at night, and by keeping up by day a series of minor demonstrations, so as to attract the enemy's attention and keep him on the alert, and finally to attack briskly when he should hear Alexander's trumpets call the charge from the farther side. Taking with himself his best troops, the shield-bearing guards, the taxes of Perdiccas, Amyntas and Cœnus, the lightest-armed archers, the Agrianians, the royal squadrons of Companions and four other cavalry ilēs — sure footed-horses they must have had indeed to scramble along these mountain cattle-paths over the December snows — he set out at night with three days' rations carried by the men. A distance of nearly a dozen miles was made with great speed considering the road. It was stormy, and the toil must have been great. But Alexander's physical endurance was abnormal, and he always managed to get wonderful feats of marching out of his men. He had made half the distance. The balance could probably have been made during the remainder of the long winter night, had not his path been cut by a deep and apparently impassable ravine which he had to wait till daylight to find a means of crossing. He then ascertained that it was readily got around.

He was now on the north slope of the range. Before him lay stretched out the plain, across which beyond the Araxes was Persepolis; behind him the range he must cross to reach Ariobarzanes' rear. He was in perilous case. His own army was cut up into small detachments, by the circumstances of the march and check; the barbarians were all in one body. Nothing but good fortune and a complete surprise of the enemy could save him from annihilation. The least failure, or what elsewhere would be but a small disaster, must prove utter ruin. But in this direction lay his only chance. Nothing except retreat or this was left. He might have held the mouth of the defile against Ariobarzanes with a small force; have returned down the mountain; have followed Parmenio, and thus taken the Persians in a trap. Or he could march on this side the range, direct to Persepolis, but only by bridging the Araxes. Time was precious. If Ariobarzanes should guess his intention, and either manœuvre was perhaps a matter of several days, he might speedily retire to Persepolis, which he could reach by the main road long before Alexander. And the thing the king most wanted was to reach this city before its treasury could be rifled, or its walls put into a state of defense. Moreover, either of these plans would necessitate the leaving the bodies of the men slain in front of the defile to lie without burial, a thing Alexander was loath to do.

With his usual grit he embraced the danger. He had marched all night in single file where there were no roads, over treacherous snow. The men strode on, hushed into silence by the unusual excitement and the great exertion. From where he stood led a path to Ariobarzanes' camp. He must avoid this road, for along it lay not only certain detection, but failure of his plan, for he would strike the enemy from a direction enabling him to escape.

It was now morning. From the point he had reached, with his usual foresight, a part of the detachment under Amyntas, Philotas, Cœnus, was sent forward, along the northern foothills, to the Araxes, with instructions to bridge the river. As this was a swift torrent with high and rocky banks, to bridge it rapidly argues no small engineering abilities at Alexander's command. The bridge was constructed from materials taken from adjoining villages demolished for the purpose. The king with the rest of his party waited again till night should cover his march, and then set forth, marching with rapidity, but circumspection. The exertion called for was extraordinary, but cheerfully borne. He reached the vicinity of the rear of the barbarians before daylight of this second night. His vanguard soon ran upon their outposts in the passes, and by very clever devices he successively surprised and captured two and dispersed a third. He reached the rear of the main camp unperceived. For the pickets had not only been cut off; they had been so demoralized that they had fled into the mountains rather than towards the camp.

Ariobarzanes' camp was as usual long and narrow, and Alexander first reached a position near the left flank of it. The weather had as stated been stormy. Ariobarzanes' outposts had observed by day Craterus' detachment still in place, and had counted its watchfires by night. The Persians kept quietly to their camp, satisfied that the bold conqueror had at last met his match. They were expecting nothing less than attack, when suddenly the blare of many trumpets roused them from their fancied security. So sudden was Alexander's appearance on the scene, that Ariobarzanes had barely time to range his army in two lines in front of his camp. Alexander drew up in parallel order, but reinforced his left with all his cavalry, sending it around Ariobarzanes' right to turn it, and, if possible, take possession of his camp, while Ariobarzanes was busy with Alexander's assault on his own front. He had already sent Ptolemy with three thousand infantry forward from his right, to the road above mentioned as leading to the Persian camp, to a position where he could make a sudden onslaught on the camp while Ariobarzanes was being kept engaged in front and on his right. There were thus three attacks on Ariobarzanes' rear. However questionable such a division of forces might be to-day, it was here not only justifiable, but demanded by the circumstances. Alexander's main force, or Ptolemy, could either of them hold head against anything Ariobarzanes could probably bring forward, and Alexander calculated especially on the demoralization these several attacks would breed.

It was just dawn when Alexander's cavalry fell upon the camp from the left, while Craterus, who had been holding his men in readiness and happy indeed to hear the sound of the king's bugles, assaulted the fortifications in the defile in its front. The diversion of Alexander's cavalry enabled Ptolemy to seize the camp by a *coup de main* with his three thousand infantry. Craterus, the enemy in his front being weakened by fear and by the sudden call of Ariobarzanes for more troops, scaled the wall, drove the defenders back, and took the Persians at the camp in reverse. These operations were nearly simultaneous — a rare and happy conjunction — and they were followed by complete success. Thus attacked on all sides, and utterly unprepared (for Ariobarzanes, even if he knew them, had believed the mountain roads to be impassable), the enemy was cut to pieces at close quarters; many in their escape threw themselves headlong down the precipices. "A great many fell on both sides," says Curtius. Ariobarzanes forced his way through to the rear with a small body-guard, or, as Curtius states, forty horse and five thousand foot, but found himself cut off from Persepolis by Philotas, who had crossed at the bridge.

Not waiting a moment for rest, lest the treasury of Persepolis should be plundered, as he had heard was the intention in case of reverse, and leaving Craterus to follow, Alexander marched with his Companions to the bridge, the completion of which was due to his brilliant forethought, forty miles in one night, over the snow, crossed the Araxes, and by hurrying ahead with these wonderful squadrons anticipated Ariobarzanes, who had escaped along the usual turnpike by way of Shiraz, and reached Persepolis before any damage had been done. For Tiridates had joined Philotas in preventing Ariobarzanes from pillage, hoping to earn Alexander's good will. Ariobarzanes was slain in his efforts to resist. For this service Tiridates was made viceroy of Susa.

Here and at Passargadæ Alexander found over one hundred and fifty million dollars of our money, plus other treasures in fabulous amount. Nothing like it has been known except to the Spaniards in America. The bulk of the treasure he deposited for the nonce at Susa. This wealth was later sent to Ecbatana, whither it was said to have been conveyed by ten thousand two-mule carts and five thousand camels.

As he approached Persis there came to meet him eight hundred (Curtius says four thousand) mutilated Greek captives, — mutilation has always been common in the East as a penal infliction, — who greatly excited his ire and sympathy. These men he pensioned off by giving them lands with slaves to cultivate them, in a colony by themselves. To each one he presented a sum equal to six hundred dollars' weight in gold, ten complete changes of raiment, two yoke of oxen and fifty sheep.

Alexander was now in the home of Persia. Here in the valley of Passargadæ, Cyrus had overthrown the Median power, and in memory of his victory had established his court, erected his palaces, built his mausoleum. This was the place to which all vassals and dependents of the Great King looked as the home of the monarchy, as the Mecca of the kingdom. Cyrus and his successors had made this valley a wonder of beauty as it was by nature healthful. Palaces, temples, the king's gate of the "Forty Pillars," the rocky hillsides cut into terraces, huge sculptured oxen and horses at the entrances of the temples; the noblest and most colossal architecture on the grandest plan and most enormous scale adorned the entire valley of the Araxes and the Medus.

Alexander had penetrated to the very heart of the empire of the arch-enemy of Greece. The Persian king had burned and desecrated Athens. The hegemōn of Hellas could now inflict the same hardship on Persepolis. The two nations would be quits. Against his usual habit, which was to preserve and not to destroy what he conquered with so much toil and danger, and it may be alleged equally against policy, Alexander — perhaps unable to resist the demands of his Macedonians — not only gave the city up to plunder, but caused to be burned the magnificent palace of the Persian kings.

This act is stated by Diodorus, Curtius and Plutarch to have been the result of a drunken orgy, and done at the instigation of the Athenian courtesan Laïs, the mistress of Ptolemy. But the account of Arrian, coupled with what is said about the massacre by Plutarch, establishes the act as one of deliberate purpose committed in retaliation for the destruction of Athens and its sacred temples by the Persians. Parmenio strongly advised against the act for many excellent reasons. Not unlikely the burning of the palace may have occurred at the same time as the feast spoken of by Diodorus, Curtius and Plutarch. Such periods of revelry always and naturally succeeded the hard work of Alexander's successful campaigns. It is not agreed how much plundering and pillaging there was. As in all such cases the desolation was no doubt extensive and cruel beyond our modern conception, though it is said that the king gave orders to spare women and their jewels.

It is no doubt true that Alexander was beginning to show more markedly that intemperance which was his inheritance, personal and national. The Macedonians were always hard drinkers; his father — probably all his ancestors were such. This is not adduced to excuse or palliate the vice; it barely explains it. From this time on, the habit became more pronounced, and was more than once followed by lamentable consequences. But this must be borne in mind. Alexander at work was always Alexander. It was only when off duty, so to speak, and these periods were rare indeed, that temptation proved too strong. To insinuate, as has been done, that this monarch was a drunkard, in the usual acceptation of the term, is worse than absurd. It is puerile.

With reference to the pillage of Persepolis, it must be remembered that in Alexander's era war was not so near to being a mathematical calculation as it is to-day, when regiments and squadrons are mere masses of given value, but that the soldiers were assumed to need an occasional taste of blood. Unless there was a certain ferocity to the soldier of that age, he lacked in part the qualities most essential in battle. *Virtus* to-day means a very different thing from the *virtus* of Alexander's phalangites, who were wont not infre-

quently to demand in their acts, if not in words, the chance
to satiate their thirst for blood and other horrors.

The army had reached Persepolis late in the year, and
here Alexander quartered his troops four months in order to
escape the rigors and losses of a winter march in the mountainous regions of Persia. In this he exhibited his usual wisdom and the care he always lavished on his men. But he
himself, heedless of the pleasures of the gay capital, and
leaving Parmenio and Craterus in command, started in three
weeks, and made various excursions against the neighboring
tribes, so as to reduce the provinces of Persis to complete subjugation once for all.

The Mardians in the mountains to the south, between
Shiraz and the Persian Gulf, had, much like the Uxians, been
almost independ-
ent. These Mar-
dians were hun-
ters only, who had
never sowed a
seed. They dwelt
in caves. The men
and women did
equal work, and
both fought in bat-
tle. The women
were said to be the
fiercer. It was es-
sential to subdue
these tribes, in or-

Mardian Campaign.

der to secure the roads from Persis to the sea, which by and
by Alexander proposed to use.

To conduct a campaign at this midwinter season, in the
snow-clad hills held by these tribes, was very difficult and

exhausting; but with his usual sharp and skillful measures Alexander in thirty days subdued them. No man ever had such a record for fighting mountaineers.

Curtius states that the land of the Mardians was snow-covered and full of difficult and precipitous localities. The weather was misty, rainy and chilling. There were no roads, and the men felt that they had reached the end of the world, and that daylight would soon cease altogether. On one occasion, when the troops murmured at the toils of the way, the king dismounted and marched on foot, and his example was followed by all the horsemen. This act at once quelled the dissatisfaction. Difficulties of all kinds had to be overcome. A frozen slope which lay athwart the path was surmounted by cutting steps in the ice. Roads had to be hewn through the woods. But finally the Mardians were reached, and by mingled severity and generosity subdued; or, if not subdued, thoroughly quieted. The king had advanced to a point near Carmania, and its satrap, Aspastes, made haste to offer his submission. Alexander confirmed him in authority under himself, and then returned to Persis. Phrasaortes, son of Rheomithres, who nobly fell at Issus, was made satrap of Persis, and it is said that a force of three thousand men was left in garrison in the capital.

Alexander had now in four years (March, 334, to March, 330) conquered his way to the heart of the Persian empire, and reduced to possession all the territory between himself and Greece. He had accomplished the converse of the task which Xerxes had set himself a century and a half before; in lieu of incorporating Greece as a mere province into the great Persian empire, Alexander had stamped the intelligence of Greece upon the Eastern world. That more of this Western civilization did not last is largely due to Alexander's short life, which ended with his conquests, leaving him no

years in which to consolidate his work and impress it with
an element of permanency.

Additional treasure was found in Passargadæ, the original
city founded by Cyrus, where also was his grave. Persepolis
had later taken the place of Passargadæ in importance.
There were two cities of the name. The Passargadæ in which
Cyrus' remains were buried is now thought to be the one
north of Persis, instead of east.

Alexander.

(From a Statue in the Capitoline Museum.)

XXX.

DARIUS. MARCH TO JULY, B. C. 330.

ALEXANDER followed Darius to Ecbatana, but the Great King retired to the Caspian Gates. At Ecbatana Alexander established his treasury, and deposited here some four hundred million dollars. This city was a central strategic point of great value, and Parmenio was left in command with a strong garrison. Darius still had money, weapons, officers, troops. He could at the Caspian Gates easily bar to Alexander the entrance to the eastern quarter of his kingdom. But there was treason in his camp. From Ecbatana Alexander headed his column and pushed on to Rhagæ, at the rate of twenty miles a day. Here he ascertained that Bessus and others had seized Darius, and held him prisoner, purposing to enjoy their several satrapies as kings. Taking the cavalry, and mounting a few phalangites, he pushed on ahead with but two days' provisions. Marching three nights and two days, with a rest of but a few hours, he came to a village where Bessus had camped the day before. He had exhausted men and horses. From here, selecting five hundred officers and men, — the best and strongest apart from rank, — he marched across a desert tract of fifty miles during the afternoon and night, and at daybreak came upon the enemy. Only sixty men had been able to keep up with him when he reached and charged in upon their thousands. But the very fact that he was Alexander saved him. The enemy dispersed. He had marched four hundred miles in eleven days. Alexander came too late. Darius had been murdered by the conspirators, and these had fled, each to his own satrapy.

DARIUS had fled to Ecbatana, in Media, five hundred miles from Persepolis, and remained there awaiting events. The exact position of this ancient city, where the kings of Persia were wont to spend part of the summer months (the spring was passed at Susa, and the rest of the year at Babylon), is disputed. It has been identified as Hamadan, and also as some fifty miles to the west of this place. Questions of topography constantly present the same difficulty. Its situation was at all events at the foot of Mount Orontes, six thousand feet above the sea level, in a lovely plain, where for eight months the climate was delightful. It had seven walls, each inner one higher than the next outside it, and each of a different color, the last two being covered with silver and gold plates. The citadel was a treasury, and the palace a marvel of beauty.

In Media Darius proposed to watch events, perhaps to fight again in case Alexander followed him up; perhaps to retire into Parthia and Hyrcania, or even as far as Bactria, laying waste the land, to prevent pursuit. He seemed intent only on personal safety. He had sent his baggage train, the women, and what treasures he had still preserved, to the Caspian Gates, a defile through the Elburz or Caspian Mountains, while he for months remained at Ecbatana, awaiting what Alexander might do. He had taken no military steps to meet his antagonist, but he had not been idle in other directions. By the present of three hundred talents he had induced the Lacedæmonians and Athenians to join in an attack on Macedonia.

Alexander now had all the treasure he needed to carry on the war to the confines of the known world, as well as to protect himself at home. He proposed to follow up Darius, wherever he might turn.

The Great King still had a kernel of strength about him, and possessed the ability to do much to defend the eastern quarter of his kingdom. Nabarzanes, general of the royal horse-guards, Atropates the Mede, Autophradates of Tarpuria, Phrataphernes, who controlled the satrapies of Hyrcania and Parthia, Satibarzanes of Aria, Barsaëntes, the ruler of Arachosia and Drangiana, Bessus, viceroy of Bactria and Darius' cousin, his brother Oxathres, and, most worthy of all, Artabazus, "the first nobleman of Persia," commander of the Greek mercenaries, with his sons, still surrounded him.

There were brave souls and wise heads enough were they but
controlled. Here, too, he was joined by Ariobarzanes, from
the Persian Gates, who gave him what news there was, as to
what Alexander had been doing. Nor was there any lack of
troops or weapons. Curtius gives him thirty-seven thousand
men. Nearly as well-appointed an army could still be collected at Ecbatana as Darius had yet commanded. And the
Caspian Gates furnished a position which could be defended
against almost any force. Here, perchance, he might finally
make peace with the Macedonians, and at least recover his
family and retain quiet enjoyment of his eastern possessions,
by yielding up the legal title to what he had already irretrievably lost. Greece might still give such a turn to affairs as
to compel Alexander to make some such trade. Or the Macedonian might tire of conquest. Perhaps the unfortunate career of the Great King would yet flow into a more prosperous
channel.

Alexander left Persepolis, by a northerly route, about the
close of winter, 330 B. C. The month in which he set out

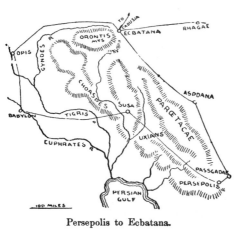

Persepolis to Ecbatana.

is not certain. He
left the train to fol-
low, and marched,
in hope and anti-
cipation of battle,
along the foothills
of the great moun-
tain barrier. Alex-
ander was travers-
ing a country in
those days popu-
lous and peaceful.
To-day the land is

savage compared to its then condition. But the geological

status was the same, and in places the population, which always more or less partakes of a geological flavor, was as wild as now. Heat and cold were then as fierce as now. The wet season lasts from November to February; the rest of the year is dry and parched. The people live in earth-covered huts, where they remain during the heat of the day.

In twelve days Alexander reached Media. Here he learned that the Lacedæmonians had been defeated and King Agis slain by Antipater, in the bloody battle of Megalopolis, and that the Cadusians and Scythians had therefore refused their aid to Darius. But he knew the Persian king to be still surrounded by many of his bravest nobles, and by an army by no means to be despised, one indeed which, ably led, might do better work than the numberless hordes of Arbela. So long as Darius lived, he must remain the centre-point for all the enemies of Alexander to rally on. And beside the Caspian Gates, there were plenty of positions readily susceptible of defense.

On his way from Persepolis to Ecbatana Alexander subdued the Parætacæ, a tribe living on the eastern water-shed of the mountains between Persis and Media, back to back with the Uxians. We have no details of the campaign. Like all his mountain work, bare mention is made of it. He left as viceroy Oxathres, son of Abulites, satrap of Susa, and hurried forward in pursuit of Darius.

Ecbatana was a central strategic point which Alexander was naturally glad to seize upon. It was situated upon the more direct line of commerce with Macedon, distant about three hundred and fifty miles from Babylon, by the valley of the Gyndes, and an equal distance from Susa, by the valley of the Choaspes. Alexander had hoped that Darius would stand, and had been marching with circumspection though rapidly; but three days from Ecbatana he was met by Bisthanes, son of King Ochus, who had left Darius to seek shelter with Alexander, and learned that the Great King was once more retiring to the east, with but three thousand cavalry and six thousand infantry. The Cadusians and Scythians had not joined him, afraid of the paling of his star, and desertions from his ranks were multiplying.

At Ecbatana Alexander discharged the Thessalian and Greek allied cavalry, whose term of enlistment was up, paying them in full, and presenting them with two thousand talents besides. In the distribution of bounty the best horsemen received a sum in gold equal in weight to eleven hundred dollars of our money; the least footman about four hundred dollars; and the others their due share. He made proper arrangements (Menes being charged with the details) for their transportation back by sea. The Thessalians appear to have owned their horses, and to have sold them before leaving the army. But many voluntarily reënlisted and remained. The bounty to these men, probably including the pay for the new term, was some thirty-three hundred dollars each. Out of these statements we are unable to construct any definite basis of compensation.

Alexander was now to operate in a different country, and against different enemies. He could no longer expect to combat in large masses, but needed lighter and more active troops. The Thessalian heavy cavalry was therefore more readily to be spared as a body than when he anticipated battles in the open field. Moreover, of the heavy armed only his Companion cavalry would be willing to stand the hardships of mountain and desert he now expected to encounter. Clitus, who had been left behind at Susa, sick, was to follow, and on the way pick up invalids who had become reëstablished, and rejoin Alexander in Parthia, bringing with him some six thousand men from Ecbatana. Alexander also, says Curtius, received reinforcements here of six thousand Greek mercenaries, under Plato of Athens. That this small body of men could march from the Hellespont through conquered Persia to Media shows how entirely the country had accepted its new yoke.

To Ecbatana Alexander now brought his treasures gathered in the camps and cities captured from Darius. The sum total of the precious metal brought hither by Alexander is variously stated at from two hundred to four hundred and fifty millions of dollars. It was guarded on the road by Parmenio, and was placed in vaults in charge of Harpalus. Six thousand Macedonians, some cavalry and light troops garrisoned Ecbatana.

From Ecbatana Alexander ordered Parmenio forward to Hyrcania, through Cadusia, with the Greek mercenaries, the reënlisted Thessalians, and all the cavalry except what was with the king, in order to bring that region into subjection. But later on Parmenio was ordered back to Ecbatana in command. He had grown gray in the service, and unfitted for severe exertions.

Though the army had just completed its march from Persepolis to Ecbatana, its labors were not interrupted. Alexander must keep upon his way. He at once called on the phalanx to follow him over the dry and arid plains of Parthia, under the July sun, and scale the mountains of Hyrcania. Never was army so hard worked.

In the Caspian regions the rainfall is excessive, and the country is hot and damp, feverish and most unhealthy. On the upper table-lands it is fiercely cold in winter, and very hot in summer, but being a dry, clear heat, not as unbearable as in India. Spring and autumn are the pleasant seasons. The mountains are snow-clad, ten to twenty thousand feet high, and on these intense cold prevails at all times. From Bushahr, on the Persian Gulf, to Teheran and the Caspian, you go through parching heat, sand and barrenness in the south, a temperate climate, pastures and cultivation in the centre, and severe cold, with bare and ice-covered mountains in the north. Even the best part of the country, which is lauded by the Persians for its climate, can be extremely hot, and is subject to drought and scarcity. The soil is good when irrigated, but two thirds of the table-land remains sterile from lack of water. The country may be well described as a desert, with numberless oases; there are forests in the north and on the mountain slopes, but the table-lands are bare.

Having completed his work in Ecbatana, Alexander headed a column formed of the Companion cavalry, the light-armed and Greek mercenary cavalry of Erigyius, the phalanx except what was left in the garrison at Ecbatana, the archers and Agrianians, and set out on a forced march to overtake Darius. He proceeded with such speed that it exhausted many men and horses, but these were left behind, and in eleven days he reached Rhagæ, probably near the present Teheran, having averaged about twenty miles a day. This rate of speed under a midsummer sun in this country with heavy infantry is remarkably good.

He was now within one of his marches of the Caspian Gates. But Darius had already passed this defile towards Hyrcania on his way probably to Bactria. He had again neglected to bar the onward march of the Macedonians at this most available spot. So many deserters had straggled behind the Persian army that it had become more easy to ascertain its movements. Most of these made their way to their homes; others surrendered to Alexander. All but despairing of catching up with Darius by mere pursuit, and his army being much exhausted, says Arrian, but not unlikely because he was far from certain of the direction taken by the

Persian king, as well as because his rapid march had depleted the commissariat, Alexander here gave his troops five days' rest. He made Oxodates, a man whom Darius had imprisoned for life in Susa, viceroy of Media in place of Atropates. In his case Alexander thought his treatment by Darius would vouch for his fidelity. He then marched to the Caspian Gates, thirty miles from Rhagæ, in one day, passed through the defile, a march of three hours' distance, and learning that the country

Ecbatana to Zadracarta.

beyond was nothing but a desert, he sent Cœnus out to forage, in order to collect rations for a further advance.

Darius began to fear that even flight could not rid him of his terrible pursuer. The farther he fled, the more his army dwindled from desertion. Might it not be wiser to turn and face the Macedonians, who were exhausted with the pursuit? He called a council of his nobles, it is said, and advised one more resort to arms. But his companions had not only lost courage and their faith in Darius, — there was treason in the

camp. There occurred a stormy scene, in which his abdica-
tion was demanded, and Darius found that the ancient ma-
jesty no longer hedged the Great King's person. The dissen-
sion was, however, smoothed over. His nobles for the moment
curbed themselves, and craved their lord's forgiveness. But
the end of their fealty was near.

While pausing at the Caspian Gates, Alexander suddenly
learned from Bagistanes, a Babylonian, and Antibelus, son of
Mazæus, who came to him from Darius' camp, seeking amnesty, that a conspiracy headed by Bessus, Barsaëntes, and
Nabarzanes had seized the person of Darius. In vain Artabazus and his sons, who controlled the Greek mercenaries —
Patron was the immediate commander — had urged the king
to place himself in their hands; for Artabazus had foreseen this treachery. The fidelity of mercenary troops is
often remarkable. All Greek mercenaries had uniformly remained faithful to Darius. Like the Swiss guards of Louis
XVI., these hired troops would have died to the last man in
defending their master in his misfortune. But Darius, though
suspicious of his nobles, and willing enough to put himself in
Artabazus' hands, weakly delayed his action until the three
conspirators seized him. This they did one night, bound him,
as the fable goes, with golden chains, and placed him in a
covered chariot, or, as Curtius says, in a cart covered with
sordid skins, so that he might not be recognized. Upon his
seizure, Darius' army melted away like snow under the midday
sun; many chiefs dispersed with their troops to their respective homes; many more went over to Alexander with prayers
for mercy. Artabazus and the Greek mercenaries retired
north into the Tarpurian mountains.

This news spurred on Alexander to still greater speed.
He formed a *corps d'élite* of the cavalry Companions, the
horse-archers and lancers, and some phalangites selected for

courage and endurance. These he mounted on the best horses, and started at once, following the flying conspirators as well as might be — not even waiting for Cœnus to bring in his rations. He had but two days' provisions for his own party. He left Craterus to come on behind at a lesser speed. He marched all night and till noon next day, rested till evening, and marched again till daybreak, when he reached the camp at Thara, from which Bagistanes had deserted. Here Alexander found Darius' interpreter, Melon, left behind sick, and from him first got the actual facts. These were to the effect that Bessus had the command of the flying army, and that Artabazus and the Greek mercenaries had remained faithful to Darius as long as they could, but that the king had preferred his native legions, and by these been finally betrayed. Bessus had been put in command by the Bactrian cavalry and the rest of the troops, for he was related to Darius, and this was moreover his vice-regal province. He knew the king's importance to Alexander, and his plan was to surrender Darius, if he should be overtaken, in exchange for quiet ruling over his own dominions as sovereign; if not, to seek to gain the sovereignty of Persia for himself. And in this the other conspirators had concurred on receiving the usual fair promises from Bessus.

Alexander pushed on with incredible speed. He marched all the succeeding night and until noon, and reached a village (perhaps modern Bakschabad) where the enemy had encamped the day before. It was with great exertion and much loss in men and horses that he had thus got within one day's march of Bessus. Here he heard that Bessus was doing his marching by night, and on careful inquiry the people showed him how, by taking a short cut across a desert tract, he could probably catch up with the Bactrian army, which had kept to the main road. Infantry could not cross this waterless waste, nor indeed keep pace with Alexander's ever-increasing speed. Everything was exhausted except the king's tremendous purpose. This was inexorable. Alexander selected five hundred of the best horses, mounted on them five hundred of his best officers and men chosen irrespective of rank, but solely for their grit and bodily strength, and armed as they were, despite the terrible heat, set out on the indicated way. Nicanor with the hypaspists and Attalus with the Agrianians, who had come so far, were to follow on the route taken by Bessus, with the utmost speed and in light order; the rest of the column to keep on in the usual manner but by forced marches. Alexander started in the afternoon, and with his abnormal energy put forty-seven miles (four hundred stades) behind him during the night, and before daybreak came upon the barbarians by surprise. He had marched one hundred and seventy-five miles in four days; four hundred in eleven.

The king had hurried ahead of his small body of men with such speed that he reached the enemy with but sixty companions. It was in the gray of the morning. He waited for nothing, but at the head of this mere handful he made a sudden charge upon the thousands of the enemy, and as they were in loose order, and many of them unarmed, happily dispersed them, killing the very few who turned to resist. The mere sight of Alexander had paralyzed their arms. But all his exertions had proved of no avail, for, probably by a preconcerted understanding, Nabarzanes and Barsaëntes, those conspirators who had Darius in their immediate charge, seeing that they could no longer prevent his capture, and as he could be of no further use to them, purposing that he should be of none to Alexander, transfixed him with their spears and took to flight. The place of this murder is supposed to have been near modern Damghan. When Alexander reached the carriage in which Darius had been conveyed, he found but a corpse, and upon this he threw his purple mantle as a token of respect. This was probably in July.

Alexander must have been grievously disappointed, after his herculean efforts, at not taking Darius alive. By so doing, he would have made a much more easy conquest of the eastern provinces, and it would have satisfied his inordinate and naturally fast-growing vanity to have near his person in some capacity — as Cyrus kept Crœsus — this last of the Great Kings. Probably his remorseless pursuit of Bessus from now on proceeded largely from his feeling of disappointment, though it was to punish him for the crime of regicide that he ostensibly dealt. Alexander had no doubt succeeded beyond expectation and beyond what he had a right to expect. Yet he had deserved what he had got. His indefatigable pursuit was due to his own unrestrained, relentless will. It was almost superhuman in its energy. Had he not himself borne the heaviest load, it might well be laid up against him as despotic and reckless cruelty to his men. As it was, he himself, as always, bore heat and thirst, hunger and toil, danger and exhaustion best of all, and most cheerfully.

It was on this terrible march across the desert that some of his men brought to the king some water in a helmet. When about to drink, Alexander looked around, and saw the tired, famished look of his companions. " Why should I drink," said he, " when you have nothing? " and returned the water untasted. "Lead us where thou wilt," responded they, with shouts of hearty affection ; " we are no longer mortal, so long as thou art king."

Perhaps it was better for Alexander that Darius was dead. Alive, he might have been a constant rallying-point for malcontents. Now, Alexander had none of the blame, and might reap the benefit, if any, of his violent death. By pitilessly following up the murderers, he could appeal to the feelings of the Persians. No other had a perfect right to the Persian throne; Alexander had possession of it; and, except that he lacked the legal title, was the most promising monarch Persia had seen since Cyrus.

Alexander sent the body of Darius to Persepolis, — some say to his mother Sisygambis, who was at Susa, — and gave it most royal burial with all the pomp and circumstance usual with Persian kings. He continued to treat his family with the utmost distinction, for he felt honest commiseration for the misfortunes of his brother king.

Darius, last of the Achæmenidæ, was of a character to make a good king, but a poor soldier. He was personally brave. Diodorus tells us that, under King Ochus, Darius fought a Caducian champion in single combat, and killed him, thus earning the name of "Bravest of the Persians." But he lacked moral endurance and equipoise. He had brought his fate on himself. His reign had been unfortunate. Coming to the throne in B. C. 336, he was soon involved in war with Greece and Macedon, and his royal career opened almost with the defeat at the Granicus. Darius was about fifty when he died, — a fugitive among traitors, a king in chains.

Alexander appointed Amminaspes, a Parthian, who had surrendered with Mazaces in Egypt, viceroy over the Parthians and Hyrcanians, and associated with him Tlepolemus, a Companion, as general.

XXXI.

BESSUS. JULY TO FALL, B. C. 330.

THE murderers of Darius had retired, each to his own satrapy, to recruit, proposing to rendezvous in Bactria, there choose a king, and join in sustaining him. Bessus felt confident of being elected. Before following Bessus, Alexander crossed the Caspian range, and reduced the land of the Mardians and Hyrcanians. At the same time he captured the relics of Darius' Greek mercenaries. On the shores of the Caspian he determined, in the future, to create a fleet. Parmenio, from Ecbatana, had advanced along the north slope of the range to attack the Caspian tribes from the west, as Alexander did from the east. This territory subdued, and Sparta having been neutralized by its defeat at Megalopolis, Alexander could safely advance towards the Caucasus. He set out for Bactria. Having gone more than half way, he heard that Satibarzanes, left as satrap in Susia, had revolted. Alexander turned on him, and inflicted summary chastisement. This revolt showed the king that he must not cross the Caucasus until he had reduced all the territory north of the Gedrosian desert, and west of the Arachosian Mountains, to complete subjection, particularly as some of Darius' old officers held satrapies in these regions. He therefore headed south towards Drangiana instead of north towards Bactria, adding nearly one thousand miles to his task. Revenge on Bessus must wait.

IT had been understood by the conspirators who murdered Darius, that they should first disperse each to his satrapy, there raise forces, and finally join Bessus in Bactria, when they would elect a new Great King, and by their arms sustain him. No doubt Bessus, who was Darius' cousin and the most prominent among them, had good reason to feel that he would be the fortunate man. But no sooner separated than each of these conspirators began to distrust the others, and forget the common cause. Phrataphernes remained in Hyrcania, where Nabarzanes afterwards joined him. Satibarzanes fled to Aria, and Barsaëntes to Drangiana. This lack of unity was a happy circumstance for Alexander.

The army was exhausted, the divisions all strung out along the late line of march, at considerable intervals, in what, under other circumstances, might have been a highly dangerous condition. Indeed, had not Darius been in abject flight, the late pursuit would have been a foolhardy one. Alexander was absolutely incapacitated from continuing an immediate pursuit of the traitors. Indeed, he did not at the moment know their whereabouts. He concentrated and rested his army near Hecatompylus, north of which city the foothills of the Parachoathras or Caspian (modern Labuta or Elburz) mountains begin to rise. Thence he decided to invade Hyrcania. He not only desired to obtain a foothold on the Caspian Sea, but could not leave the restless tribes in and beyond the mountains upon his flank and rear as he advanced.

For the first time he here had some difficulty in inducing his men willingly to join in his project. They were tired of wandering, physically exhausted, and thought that by the death of Darius their work should be at an end, and that the homeward path should now be trod, or at least the road to Babylon. But the persuasiveness of Alexander was never overtaxed. By dint of appealing to their loyalty and affections, and by lavish promises for the future, well sustained by his generosity in the past, he overcame their scruples. Curtius says that the men were constantly in the habit of murmuring. To a certain extent this is true, and the more they did so, the higher it throws Alexander's ability into relief in the fact that he, as constantly, persuaded them to follow him and got from them such splendid efforts. His present object was not only to conquer Hyrcania, but also to find the Greek mercenaries, who had served under Darius, and punish them for fighting for pay against their compatriots. Moreover, he suspected that some of the Great King's fleeing nobles would have taken refuge in Hyrcania, and they, with the Greek troops as a nucleus, were too inflammable a matter to be passed by.

North of him lay the Caspian range, which divides Parthia from Hyrcania. On the south slope of the range dwelt the Tarpurians. The range was cut by comparatively few, but long and difficult, notches, and stood as a huge outpost to the Caspian Sea, with peaks of from twelve to twenty thousand feet above the level of the ocean. On the Caspian side, the multitude of mountain streams and the narrow stretch of land, often less than twenty miles in width, made the country all but one huge marsh. The forests were thick and easily defended; the vegetation was rank; it was parched in summer, overflowed in winter; the climate was that of the Pontine Marshes. In places, there were rich plains dotted with villages. But the roads were deep in mud, and a recent traveler found, in a journey of three hundred miles, no less than twenty rivers so large as to be rarely fordable. The Macedonians were remarkable soldiers. They passed from desert sands to mountain snows with equal unconcern, and their work on either was equally well done. Still more remarkable the leader, whose irrepressible energy and broad intelligence had made them what they were!

Leaving Bessus for further operations, — as of necessity he must, — Alexander advanced through the range in three columns, whose rendezvous was to be at Zadracarta, the capital of Hyrcania. He himself undertook the most difficult task along the route farthest to the west, with the largest column and the lightest troops. Craterus took a route farther to the east of him, and had his own and Amyntas' taxes, some six hundred archers and an equal force of cavalry. He was to attack the Tarpurians. Erigyius took the easier public thoroughfare to Zadracarta, with the Greek mercenaries and the rest of the cavalry, the baggage and the vast train of camp followers.

Alexander's advance had to be made with the utmost circumspection, for the barbarians beset every one of the many
and intricate passes, and were ready to fall upon any unprotected part of this column; but what Alexander had early
learned from Xenophon about doing this species of work,
had since been supplemented by a goodly amount of individual experience. Having with his column crossed the first
range of mountains, he learned that some of Darius' old officers were not far off. He pushed forward with the hypaspists, the lightest of the phalangites and some archers, over
very hard roads, and in the midst of threatened attacks and

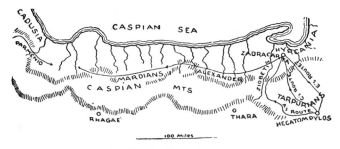

Caspian Campaign.

ambuscades. He was compelled to leave rear-guards at many
points, to protect the passage of his column. Pity, indeed,
that the details of his march have been lost! Reaching the
river Ziobetis, which cannot now be identified, he camped
four days, during which time many of these men came in
and surrendered. Among them were Nabarzanes and Phrataphernes. The latter and his sons did subsequent excellent
service for Alexander. Of Nabarzanes no further mention
is made. He was probably relegated to obscurity. By the
exercise of skill and care, Alexander drew in his rear-guards,
and completed his passage of the mountains without material
loss, though the Agrianians had a sharp rear-guard fight at

the very close of the operations. He then advanced to Zadra-carta, the capital, where his other columns rejoined him. Cra-terus had subdued the country of the Tarpurians as he traversed it, partly by force, partly by capitulation. Erigy-ius had found little or no opposition. Here, too, came Arta-bazus with three of his nine sons, among them Ariobarzanes, whom we remember at the Persian Gates, and Autophra-dates, viceroy of Tarpuria, and handed in their allegiance. To Autophradates Alexander gave back his viceregal office.

No conqueror ever understood how to attach ancient ene-mies to his own cause better than Alexander. His treatment of the faithful old satraps and servants of Darius always made them his own stanch adherents. He understood that fidelity to Darius meant future fidelity to himself. This by no means clashed with his often rewarding what was actually treachery to Darius in those who surrendered strong places or treasures to him. Alexander had no hard and fast rules. He took men as he found them, and punished and rewarded according to the conditions governing the acts of each. He rarely made mistakes. Those occasions when we find him at fault merely serve to remind us that he was human.

Artabazus, whom Alexander had known in Pella as a ref-ugee, with his brother-in-law Memnon, the Rhodian, and the sons of Artabazus, were rewarded by being kept on duty near Alexander's person. The Greek mercenaries, who were the survivors of those who fought at Issus and Arbela, begged for terms, but Alexander would accept nothing short of uncondi-tional surrender, threatening them with summary vengeance if they did not at once come in. They were fifteen hundred in number, and when they gave themselves up were, after due censure for their misconduct, pardoned and drafted into his own service. The Lacedæmonian ambassadors to Darius, who were with them, he confined.

Alexander had clearly recognized the importance of Hyrcania as the future home of a Caspian fleet, and, as above narrated, had ordered Parmenio to march from northern Media by way of Cadusia, along the coast through Hyrcania, and by that route join the army, so as further to reduce the country to subjection and open a road north of the Caspian range.

Alexander then turned back westerly from Zadracarta and marched towards Parmenio and against the Mardians, a poor but very warlike tribe, who were apt to interfere with this scheme of a Caspian fleet, unless thoroughly subdued. He took the shield-bearing guards, the archers, the Agrianians, the brigades of Cœnus and Amyntas, half the Companion cavalry, and a newly created body of horse darters; leaving the bulk of the army in camp at Zadracarta. Despite the difficult nature of the country, which, as above described, was without roads, heavily wooded, and affording no supplies (its very poverty, and the fact that Alexander had already passed beyond their territory, inducing the Mardians to believe themselves free from attack), the king overran their land.

His route lay probably between the mountain range and the marshy forest-covered coast-land, along the foothills. The Caspian used to be higher in elevation than it now is. How much this may have altered the topography of the coast cannot be said, but its then descriptions are much like those of modern travelers. Many of the Mardians fled back into the mountain recesses of the interior. But even here they were not safe. Alexander followed them up in the most systematic manner, sending detachments right and left, and allowing them no manner of rest. Parmenio, at the farther end of the Mardian land, gave the tribes no chance of exit. They were caught between two armies of good mountain fighters, and were thoroughly subdued. It is not stated whether the king and Parmenio at any time joined hands on this campaign. Alexander found of much use in these operations, the above named troop of horse darters. They were equipped like the Parthian cavalry, and for a mountainous terrain were all but unapproachable in efficiency. The king was not above learning even from his enemies, and adopted a number of the Oriental methods, especially in the light cavalry.

Mardia was added to the satrapy of Autophradates, who had lately been continued in office as satrap of Tarpuria. Having thus made secure the whole mountain chain, Alexander returned to Zadracarta, where he celebrated games and held feasts for two weeks. Parmenio was sent back to Ecbatana in command.

As Alexander had learned when in Media, the anti-Macedonian turmoils of Greece had been settled for some time by the defeat of Agis, king of Sparta, and his death in the bloody battle of Megalopolis. The losses in this battle have already been referred to, and these, as well as modern losses, have often been compared to the moderate list of killed in Alexander's battles. These losses have been already discussed and their relation to modern casualties shown. But it must not be forgotten that losses in action are but one of the measures of a soldier's tenacity and value, and the measure of but one of the qualities of a captain. It is methods and results which guage a general, not the capacity to kill or stand killing. The most splendid triumphs of history are not the hecatombs. Would Arbela have been tactically any more superb a battle, if Alexander had lost thrice the number killed? Rather the reverse is true. To accomplish great results with the least expenditure of life is one of the very highest tests of ability. Nor is this incompatible with the courage to sacrifice troops to the last man, for an object worthy of the sacrifice and under conditions demanding it. It is altogether probable that Alexander would have won the battle of Megalopolis with but a fraction of the loss sustained by Antipater; it is all but certain that only Alexander would have won Arbela. That Alexander did not always encounter picked troops, by no means reduces his rank. He showed the same great qualities when he did encounter them. He matriculated in war by destroying the Theban Sacred Band, which no troops in Greece had been able to stand against. He never encountered Spartans, but he beat the Thebans who had vanquished these; and the very Persians whom, at Platæa, Pausanias had declined to meet till he was forced into battle, were Alexander's constant opponents in Asia. Nor must it be forgotten that the Parthians whom Alexander was at this time encountering were the same who defeated and destroyed Crassus' seven Roman legions. Shall we say that Grant's Virginia campaign was more splendid than Vicksburg because in the one he lost 60,000 men and in the other only 8,000? Comparisons such as these are of absolutely no value, for the reputation of a great captain rests on an entirely different basis. But such comparisons have been made and it is well to dissect them. Alexander never gave way in battle; he fought until he won. That his wonderful impetus and skill combined enabled him to win quickly and without the severe losses of other battles, is the very highest praise. Nobody can deduce from Alexander's history any conclusion except that he would, against the best troops ably led, have won any battle within the range of human skill and the endurance of soldiers to win.

Alexander had constantly run great risk by the machinations of Sparta. But he had been content to trust to good fortune, the ability of Antipater, and what treasure he could send him to prosecute the war. He was never for an instant deterred by any danger in his rear from pushing his schemes of Asiatic conquest. He always provided against such danger, as far as in him lay, and then moved on ahead. Many have called this blind recklessness, but it is rather close calculation and a spirit of bold hopefulness. Certainly no one ever became a great captain without the courage to face just such risks, and the ability to gauge their degree. But Alexander was now reassured by the defeat of Sparta, and relying on his communications being amply protected by the numerous garrisons along his victorious line of operations, he felt that he could press into the interior with less risk. He would have done so in any event; but no doubt he advanced with a feeling of greater satisfaction at the lessened cares behind him. Fortunate for him that there was in his rear no one who was able to cope with him, — in other words, that he was Alexander.

Alexander's route to Susia lay along the northern slopes of the Parachoathras. The population of these regions was considerable, and when the season was auspicious, the roads, except in the mountains themselves, were no doubt excellent. We can scarcely otherwise explain the ease and expedition with which the extensive baggage trains were moved at the exceptional rate of speed of the Macedonian army. An enormous amount of baggage had accumulated. The men had been allowed to load up the heavy train with all manner of loot; women had accompanied the army, probably in considerable numbers; useless luxuries of all kinds had grown to a bulk beyond reason. All this had by no means interfered with the capacity of the troops to march ahead in light order and live upon the country; but it had made the trains cumbrous to a degree. In his projected advance into an almost unknown territory, all this must be changed. Alexander gave the example. He burned his own baggage to satisfy the men of the necessity of doing the like, and the trains were summarily brought down to the old Macedonian standard.

It is said to have been here that the king first assumed Oriental attire, probably in part only. We shall see what this change of costume led to. It is not to be supposed that, as captain, Alexander ever wore anything but his Macedonian armor and cloak. His white plumes had too often led the van to be now discarded for the luxurious habiliments of the Median monarch. It was as sovereign alone that he was induced to adopt the manners and costume of the East.

Alexander had recently learned from some Persians who had come over to him, that Bessus had assumed the rank of king of Asia, adopted the royal robes and tiara, and had changed his name or title to Artaxerxes. Many of the Persians had escaped into Bactria, and the Bactrian divisions were with him. This last act roused Alexander to the utmost degree. He determined that the murderer of Darius should keep not even his own kingdom, and made ready to march against Bessus without further delay. For this purpose he put an end to the festivities at Zadracarta, in which he had perhaps been overindulging, and prepared for the march.

The king took under his personal command about twenty thousand foot and three thousand horse — consisting of hypaspists, phalanx, Macedonian cavalry, Agrianians and archers. With this force he set out by way of Aria for Bactriana, his immediate objective. Satibarzanes had tendered his submission in Susia (modern Tus); and though he was one of Darius' murderers, Alexander saw fit to continue him in charge of his satrapy, associating with him Anaxippus, a Companion, and sixty horse acontists, which he was ordered so to station as to prevent depredations by the Macedonian army in its march through Aria, as well as show a semblance of authority. This Alexander thought would suffice to neutralize

Satibarzanes for the moment, and save causes of complaint.
Alexander hoped to reach Bactria before Bessus could be
joined by any of his associates. For Bessus expected the
aid of the Scythians, as well as had already many of the old

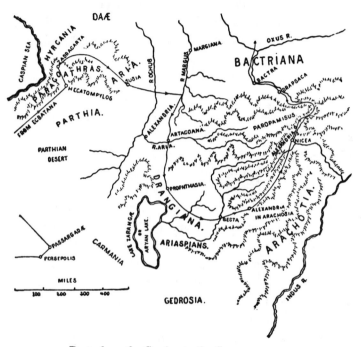

Route from the Caspian to the Caucasus.

adherents of Darius. At Susia, Nicanor, son of Parmenio,
commander of the shield-bearing guards, died, much to the
grief of the whole army. Alexander was unable to delay his
advance; but he left Philotas behind with twenty-six hundred
men to conduct the funeral rites with becoming splendor.

The plateau of Iran, as it stands to-day, has been described
as "sterile plains, separated by equally sterile mountains,"
where the temperature ranges from 0° to 120° Fahrenheit.
We know that the population was greater in Alexander's day

than now, and no doubt the country afforded vastly more to a marching army. But heat and cold must still be borne, though rations may be plenty, and the sun burned as fiercely then as now.

When the column had made a considerable part of the march towards Bactriana, Alexander learned that Satibarzanes, through whose satrapy he had just passed, had massacred the guard under Anaxippus which had been left with him, as well as that officer, had declared for Bessus, whom he proposed to join, and had established himself in Artacoana (at or near modern Herat), where many confederates were joining him. Here was a grave danger. Alexander could not leave such treachery behind him, for Barsaëntes from Drangiana was very apt to cast in his lot with Satibarzanes. Much of his cavalry from Ecbatana, viz.: the Greek mercenaries, the reënlisted Thessalians, and the men of Andromachus, had now joined him under Philip, son of Menelaus. The king at once stopped midway in his march towards Bactria (he was pursuing a route thither much easier than the one he later trod), left Craterus in command of the bulk of the army, and taking the Companion cavalry, horse lancers, archers, Agrianians, and the taxes of Amyntas and Cœnus, he headed for the scene of hostilities. By one of his splendid forced marches of seventy-five miles (six hundred stades) in two days, he fell upon Artacoana like a hurricane. Satibarzanes managed to escape with a few Arian horsemen, but Alexander slew three thousand of his officers and men, and sold many others into slavery. He then proclaimed the Persian Arsames viceroy, and called in the command of Craterus.

From Artacoana northward there were several excellent gaps by which the army could cross the Caucasus into Bactriana. At this point the mountains do not reach the rugged altitude of the Parapamisus. But Alexander was imperatively called southward, instead, into Zarangeia or Drangiana (so named from Lake Zarangæ or the Arian lake) where Barsaëntes, another of the murderers, was satrap. This way he accordingly headed. Conscious of his guilt and treachery, and not waiting for the vengeance he had invoked but dreaded none the less, Barsaëntes fled towards the Indus, or into Gedrosia. But he was taken by some adherents of the conqueror, and returned to Alexander, who put him to death.

Admiral La Gravière figures that Alexander's column marched from Hecatompylos to a given point in Aria, a good deal over five hundred miles, in one hundred and ninety-eight hours, actual marching time. At ten hours a day, or twenty days, this would be at the rate of over twenty-five miles a day. Accurate or not, the figures are interesting, and it is certain that the Macedonians were extraordinary marchers.

It is probable that it was these untoward events in Alexander's march towards Bactria and his consequent countermarch to Aria which proved to him the necessity of caution, and determined him to put into practice the clean-cut strategy which preceded and succeeded Issus and Arbela, and fully to protect his rear before he proceeded on his way. Aria was of the highest importance. In it were the cross-roads between Iran, Turan and Ariana. Where the Ochus or Arius suddenly turns north, the great army roads, from Hyrcania and Parthia, from Margiana and Bactria, from Arachotia and India and the upper Cophen, meet and cross. At this point, about one hundred miles west of Artacoana, Alexander founded a city, Alexandria in Aria, and to-day among the people of this section dwells the remembrance of this wonderful king.

No doubt Alexander had made a study of the topography of this region, as far as it could be made, and had located as well as may be the roads and rivers, mountains and defiles,

cities and peoples. He saw that he must positively not leave
so great a section in a questionable attitude upon his flank.
He therefore deferred his revenge upon Bessus for the moment, loath though he was to give him breathing spell in which
to accumulate power and troops, and planned to make a southerly sweep so as to reduce to submission all the tribes north
of the desert and west of the Arachotian ranges. This route
implied an extra march of nearly a thousand miles. Then,
and not till then, could he with safety advance over the great
water-shed of the Parapamisus (Hindu-Koosh). In accordance with this plan, so soon as Craterus arrived, he advanced
south to Prophthasia, meeting small opposition, except from
the tedium and difficulties of the route.

It is on this march that Alexander is related to have encountered an inimical tribe, which, on being pursued, retired
up the wooded slope of a mountain, the farther side of which
was a sheer precipice. As he had little time to delay, and as
the wind was blowing towards the mountain slope, Alexander
contented himself with setting the woods on fire, and thus
drove the barbarians over the precipitous cliffs. This is an
illustration of his fertility of resource, if it is at the same
time a demonstration of the cruelties of war.

Coin in the Bodleian Library, enlarged.

XXXII.

PHILOTAS. FALL, B. C. 330.

In Drangiana was discovered the so-called conspiracy of Philotas. There had been growing in the army a spirit of criticism which materially threatened its discipline. Philotas, among others, had been very outspoken. At this time a minor conspiracy, among obscure officials, to murder the king was discovered. Philotas knew of it and did not reveal it. He was tried by the Companions, and under torture confessed to what was treason, and implicated his father and others. True or not, he was found guilty and executed by the Companions. Parmenio, at Ecbatana, was also secretly executed. A number of others either fled, committed suicide, or were arrested and executed. Some were acquitted. The guilt of these so-called murders has been laid at Alexander's door. It is to-day difficult to decide the truth. But the effect was healthful to the discipline of the army, though Parmenio and Philotas were hardly to be spared.

It was in Prophthasia that Alexander discovered the so-called conspiracy of Philotas, son of Parmenio. This incident makes one of the saddest stories of his life. This was a matter intimately connected with the discipline of the army, and, as such, properly finds a place in our narrative. It should, perhaps, be mentioned that Alexander's plans, large and comprehensive beyond their grasp, were not generally understood by his Macedonians. Perhaps his *alter ego*, Hephæstion, was the only one to whom he unbosomed himself with perfect freedom. Some of the Macedonian generals, like Craterus, did their duty for duty's sake ; others were very outspoken and hypercritical. This was a right they reserved to themselves. Freedom of speech, almost as we understand it, seems to have been indulged in as one of their political rights. But Alexander had gradually become less patient of such talk, as the talk doubtless grew in volume and openness. Perhaps the Eastern notions of royalty had already begun to take root in his mind, by nature and character and success so essentially imbued with the idea of one man power. Perhaps his Macedonians were suffering from the same ideas, and thought this people, which they had crushed in war, only fit to be further trodden under foot in peace ; and the fact that Alexander had begun to adopt in part the dress and ceremonial of the East, — if you like, largely from excessive vanity, but no doubt also for its excellent political effect on his Eastern subjects, who needed to see their new lord habited like their ancient ones, — had already given rise to much discussion and no little fault-finding among the simple Macedonians, and likely enough envy among those who wished to emulate the king's example, but could not. This fault-finding had not been decreased by Alexander's giving Orientals equally high places with Macedonians in the government of conquered provinces and near his own person, — though this, indeed, was altogether a political necessity, if he would keep what he had won, by satisfying instead of oppressing these peoples. The Macedonians, however, could not see why even the greatest among the peoples they had fairly conquered should now be set over them in authority. They felt that the least of the Hellenes was better than the greatest of the Persians ; it seemed to them as if the king were forgetting what he owed to them ; and they feared that he would end by treating them like the Asiatics.

The king had been often warned against an outbreak of this feeling, but had paid little heed to it. His mother, who always exercised great influence over him, had constantly protested against his reckless manner of trusting men against whom there was cause of suspicion, but without result. Still, Alexander must have been well aware of the existence of this disaffection, for the expression of it was open. He had been used to advice and criticism from Parmenio, from youth up ; this was no novelty. But he felt that Philotas, though always brave in battle and constant in duty, had of late grown more and more antagonistic. Craterus, even, was not always like-minded with the king, though a pattern of what the soldier should be. Clitus was growing daily more estranged. In the war-councils these feelings had plainly come to the surface. All seemed to unite in desiring a cessation of conquest, a division of booty, a return home. Alexander stood alone with but Hephæstion by his side. So far the king had won his way with presents, without punishment. Now, largesses had lost their effect. Had the time come for other methods ?

This spirit of criticism, if left to grow, tended to the destruction of discipline, with its thousand accompanying dangers. It is scarcely possible to imagine success in an undertaking of so gigantic and difficult a nature, so far from home, and against such vast odds as the one Alexander had in hand, unless the very essence of discipline could be maintained. It was evident that on the first outbreak of disaffection an example must be made. If Alexander failed to maintain an unquestioned authority, he was no longer king.

Parmenio was seventy years old. His youngest son, Hector, had been drowned in the Nile in the Egyptian expedition ; the second son, Nicanor, who, as worthy chief of the hypaspists, had won the good will and admiration of all, had recently died. Philotas was the well-known leader of the Companion cavalry, distinctly the most brilliant command in the army. No family in Macedonia had earned the gratitude of the king in so high a degree.

The crime of Philotas appears to have been that he heard rumors of a certain conspiracy to murder Alexander, originating with some obscure members of the royal household, who were tired of the everlasting wanderings, and thought to relieve themselves by so bold an act; and that for two days, though constantly near the king, he neglected to speak of it. Unless there was some remarkable and easily stated excuse for this silence, it is very hard to explain. The plot came through other channels to Alexander's ears; the chief plotter, Dimnos, committed suicide at the moment of arrest. On being taxed with knowledge of the plot by the king, Philotas stated that he had considered it of so little import that it had made no impression upon him. This excuse Alexander apparently accepted, no doubt to be the more secure of arresting all the conspirators. Philotas was bidden as usual to supper. At midnight the king called together his most trusted officers, — Hephæstion, Craterus, Cœnus, Erigyius, Perdiccas, Leonatus, — and sent them out with suitable guards to arrest those to whom suspicion pointed — Philotas, chief of all.

Philotas had, in common with many other Macedonians, spoken in public with more or less acerbity of Alexander's growing Orientalism and vanity, and had also very naturally vaunted the services of his father and brothers and self, ascribing to his family in great measure Alexander's abnormal successes. More especially had he talked in this fashion to his mistress, whom Alexander, it is said, had suborned to reveal to him what Philotas had said in private. This espionage had been going on for over a year, and Philotas' doom was probably sealed long before the incident which was its immediate and alleged cause. Philotas was not without faults. He was overbearing as an officer, and is said to have been disliked by his men. He was no doubt open to criticism, if not censure, in many ways. But the fidelity to Alexander of the entire family had always been unquestioned till of late.

Next day a formal council of the generals was called, the king detailed the facts, and at once turned the matter over to the Companions for judgment, himself appearing as accuser.

To be so tried was probably Philotas' right, and appears to be a species of trial by his peers. But possibly the Companions inclined towards Alexander's behest in their action. They may have feared the king. They may have recognized that without discipline the whole army might be lost, — and discipline often means hardship, sometimes injustice to the individual. On the trial there was much testimony as to the conspiracy; according to many accounts, Alexander behaved without haste or prejudice; according to Plutarch, Curtius, Diodorus and Justin, Philotas was tortured to compel him to reveal who were his associates. Torture was a usual procedure, and need not be laid to Alexander's charge. It is alleged by some, one cannot but hope without truth, that Alexander witnessed this torture from behind a screen, and taunted the sufferer with cowardice. Brave though he was, Philotas succumbed under the ordeal, as many great souls have done, and perhaps untruly, and because he was tortured beyond endurance and the idea was then suggested to him, — implicated his father, and described a plot long subsisting, if not to assassinate the king, at least to take advantage of any accident to him to seize the reins of power. The confession was read to the army, which by a loud shout, immediate and unanimous, voted death to Philotas and Parmenio. Hereupon and at once, Philotas and all his confessed accomplices present with the army were put to death by the Companions with their javelins. Alexander sent an urgent messenger, Polydamus, to the generals commanding at Ecbatana, Cleander, Sitalces and Menidas, ordering that Parmenio suffer the same fate. Polydamus rode eight hundred and sixty miles in eleven days on camels, and reached Ecbatana long before the news of the trial.

Parmenio had written to his sons: "Care first for yourselves, then for your dear ones, thus we shall reach the end we aim at," — words of doubtful import. Alexander was either convinced that the father must have been aware of the son's plans, or deemed that Parmenio would be dangerous after Philotas' death, his influence being great. He was at the head of a large detachment — seven thousand men — and in possession of the treasures at Ecbatana. On either hypothesis he must be put aside. The order was executed, as it were, by assassination, and the worthy old man fell, one must hope unaware that the dagger was directed by the hand of the young king, to whom and to whose father his life's work had been given, and for whom his life had been so often risked. Perhaps it was impossible to successfully act aboveboard, but the details of this Asiatic method of inflicting death are too sad to relate. Despite all Alexander's care, it is said that the suppression of this conspiracy in this bloody manner was not accomplished without grave danger of mutiny, for the army to a man was devoted to Parmenio, and the king himself had always shown him the greatest respect and affection. Quintus Curtius ends his long account of the trial of Philotas thus: "It is certain that the king here ran a great risk both as to his safety and his life; for Parmenio and Philotas were so powerful and so well beloved, that unless it appeared plain they were guilty they could never have been condemned without the indignation of the whole army. For while Philotas denied the fact, he was looked upon to be very cruelly handled; but after his confession, there was not any, even of his friends, who pitied him." This, like much in Curtius, can be construed both ways, but inclines towards the exculpation of Alexander.

Amyntas, son of Andromenes, commander of one of the infantry brigades, and his three brothers (Polemo, a Companion, and Attalus and Simmias, brigade commanders), were likewise accused of being associated with the matter. They

had been on very intimate terms with Philotas. Polemo fled
to the enemy. The others, on trial before the Macedonians,
bravely defended themselves, and were acquitted. Polemo
was induced to return. It would seem that this acquittal of
Amyntas by the same judges who condemned Philotas runs
in Alexander's favor. Shortly after, Amyntas was killed in
action. The other brothers remained in honorable service,
and were entirely trusted by the king. Demetrius was also
discharged from his post as confidential body-guard, on suspicion of being accessory to the fact; and Ptolemy, son of
Lagus, was put in his place. Hephæstion and Clitus were
made commanders of the Companion cavalry, hitherto under
Philotas, which was divided into two regiments for this purpose. The king deemed it wise not to intrust his cavalry
d'élite to a single man — even Hephæstion. It was subsequently reorganized. A separate squadron was formed of the
sympathizers with Parmenio, and this squadron later greatly
distinguished itself.

The murder of Parmenio, the brutality to Batis at Gaza,
the treatment of Bessus and the murder of Clitus to be hereafter mentioned, are indeed black pages in the life of Alexander, though it may be more fair to characterize all these
things as rather unhappy than guilty incidents. It must be
remembered that Alexander dared run no risk, either personally or for the army, and that it was his peers and not his king
who had found Philotas guilty, who pronounced judgment
and conducted the execution. Some historians have doubted
the existence of any conspiracy whatsoever, and have ascribed
to Alexander's blood-thirstiness the whole disastrous drama;
but a number of supposed conspirators either resorted to
flight or self-destruction, which fact, so far as it goes, affords
ground for believing the conspiracy to have been real, and
not wanting in importance.

Perhaps no monarch has so much that is great and good to his credit, without being charged with more of evil, than Alexander. It is quite possible, by judicious extracts from all the ancient authorities, to prove Alexander a monster. It is equally possible to prove him superhuman in his virtues. He was neither. He had glaring vices, especially overweening vanity and often uncontrolled rashness of temper. But he had noble virtues as well, and a just estimate of all that is said of him by all the old historians, barring none, exhibits a personal character equal perhaps to any other man in history who enacted so eminent a rôle. But whatever the truth or the motives, that Parmenio and Philotas were grievous losses to the army, remains indisputable.

The Macedonians also demanded at this time the execution of the Lyncestian Alexander, whom the king had formerly shielded from death in Asia Minor, and who had since then been under arrest. This was carried out. Their zeal now outran their ancient spirit of antagonism. The king's danger had revived all their old enthusiasm for his person. The incident, terrible in its details, and much to be regretted, had none the less purified the atmosphere of discipline. The army was all the better for it.

Alexander.
(From a Medal struck at Apollonia.)

XXXIII.

THE CAUCASUS. FALL, B. C. 330, TO MAY, B. C. 329.

HAVING turned south, Alexander made a circuit through the land of the Ariaspians and Drangians, and the outskirts of Gedrosia, and then passed north, through Arachotia towards the Caucasus. All the peoples on this route he reduced to subjection and tribute, — detaching forces right and left to thoroughly overawe the population, and garrisoning the towns. He again made some changes in organization to get his army into lighter order, for from now on he had small war rather than pitched battles to anticipate. Bessus lay behind the mountain barrier of the Parapamisus (modern Hindu-Koosh), feeling safe in the protection of its mighty summits. From Aria, Alexander could have crossed by an easy pass; from the Cophen region, to which his long circuit had brought him, he had before him passes higher and more difficult than any in the Alps. He started so soon as winter was fairly over, and, after incredible suffering and great loss, in fifteen days reached the farther side. Bessus fled from before him. Bactria and Sogdiana were the seat of an ancient civilization, with plenty of resources; but when Bessus abandoned Bactria, the whole country surrendered to Alexander, who thence crossed the Oxus, and marched on Sogdiana. Bessus' confederates then surrendered this prince in hope of pardon. He was later executed. Alexander marched to Maracanda.

ALEXANDER now marched (very likely through the valley of the modern Adoreskan River) into the land of the Ariaspians, a nation of horse breeders, who had afforded much assistance to Cyrus in his invasion of Scythia. He had a number of rivers to cross in his path, but the army had grown expert in such work, and there is infrequent mention of these, unless very large. They were taken as a matter of course. He found the Ariaspians an agricultural people dwelling in a fertile oasis surrounded by mountains or deserts. They were independent and self-governing on a model not unlike the Greeks. The king treated them with especial favor and honor, and accorded to them additional territory, which they had long desired, but were unwilling to go to war to obtain. He left them without viceroy or garrison, relying solely on their good-will and character for fidelity. Having dwelt with them two months, he turned northeast and marched towards Bactria, reducing the rest of the Drangians, and some northerly tribes of the Gedrosians on the way. Gedrosia was the farthest province of Persia on the southeast. It is now part of Beloochistan. Here, four years later, on his homeward march, Alexander lost the greater part of his army crossing the desert.

The Arachotians also submitted without constraint. Their territory ran as far as the water-shed of the mountain range which separated Persia from India. Menon was given a force of four thousand foot and six hundred horse, and made viceroy over the Arachotians. Alexander here founded another city of his name (modern Kandasar), to hold head against possible irruptions across the mountains from India, over which there were several passes debouching near this point. He then continued his march onward towards the river Cophen, and the land inhabited by the Indian tribes known as the Parapamisians, who dwelt at the foot of the Indian Caucasus. On this march across the range from Arachotia, the weather was severe — it was November — and the army suffered much privation in toiling through the snow, especially as they were short of breadstuffs. But the tribes were friendly, and afforded help in lieu of hindrance. They had food in abundance for themselves, but the inroad of an army taxed them beyond their ability to supply.

Alexander now learned that the Arians had again revolted, induced thereto by Satibarzanes, who, at the time of Alexander's return to Artacoana, had fled to Bessus, and had received from him a force of two thousand cavalry, with

which Bessus hoped that Satibarzanes would create a sufficient diversion on Alexander's rear to keep him out of Bactria. The king dispatched against them the Persian Artabazus, with the Greek mercenaries, including those who had
served under Darius, some six thousand all told, accompanied
by Erigyius and Caranus, with six hundred Greek allied
horse; ordering Phrataphernes, the viceroy of the Parthians,
to afford them all aid within his power. Parmenio's veterans,
some eleven thousand men, had now joined the army, leaving
Cleander, with the new levies from Greece, in Ecbatana.
This reinforcement enabled Alexander the more easily to
make the necessary detachment. The officers mentioned,
basing on Prophthasia, did their work with energy and skill.
In an obstinately contested battle, Satibarzanes was killed,
and his forces dispersed. This task completed, Artabazus,
Erigyius and Caranus rejoined the army.

Alexander was now in the valley of the Cophen (modern
Cabul) River. This valley, near Nicea (modern Cabul), is
some six thousand three hundred feet above the sea. To the
north of him lay the Parapamisus. There are now, and were
probably then, among others, three principal passes through
the range, leading to the Oxus valley beyond, — up the affluents of the Cophen, and down those of the Oxus. The northeast road leads to Inderaub (ancient Drapsaca) up the Pandshir Valley and over the Khawak Pass, thirteen thousand two
hundred feet in altitude. The west road runs up the Kushan
Valley and over the Hindu-Koosh Pass to Ghori. This was
the one by which Alexander returned. The southwest road
goes up the Ghorband Valley over the Hajiyak Pass to Ba-
mian, by a road over three hundred miles from Cabul. Alexander camped nearest the easterly passes, which are by far
the most difficult ones. He recognized that Bessus would
probably expect him by the easier route, and make prepara-

tions to defend its defiles. By the most difficult one he could
scarcely travel at this early winter season, certainly not take
his horses with him. He was forced to wait.

During this interval Alexander founded a new city — Alexandria ad Caucasum — near modern Beghram, some twenty-
five miles northwest of Cabul. He chose the site with his

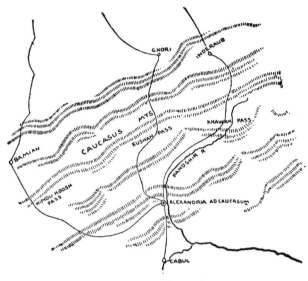

Routes over Caucasus.

usual discretion, at the point where the three roads branch
off to the different passes to Bactriana. The city was built to
keep his troops busy till the winter season had so far passed
that he might cross, and to enable him to hold the pass he proposed to use. For the inimical tribes he was about to encounter might as easily cut off his retreat in case of disaster as now
impede his advance. Alexander recognized, also, that beyond
this range he was going into a real *terra incognita*, where
varied and great and unknown perils certainly awaited him,
and he took his measures accordingly. Here in his new post

were left the Persian Proëxes, as viceroy, and Neiloxenus, a Companion, as his military associate.

By the experience of his late campaigns Alexander had learned that the fighting he would now be called upon to do would need much greater mobility in his troops than they had hitherto possessed. There was no more organized opposition to his sway on a large scale. There would be in the future no pitched battles to fight. What he would now have to encounter would be isolated bodies, such as that under Bessus, and much small war, demanding rapid marching and restless pursuit. He needed an army consisting of smaller units; he must have a greater percentage of light troops; he must utilize Oriental recruits in filling gaps, for sheer want of Macedonian reinforcements. For these reasons he was induced again to make sundry changes, partly, too, for that he had lost many of his old and trusted officers and must advance the younger to more responsible commands. From 329 B. C. dates the promotion of young lieutenants, and from now on his work was done with these.

Each of the eight iles of horse Companions had been already divided into two companies; and eight companies were now made into a hipparchy. Thus he had two hipparchies or regiments of eight companies each, instead of but one of eight iles. As before stated, Clitus was put in command of one; Hephæstion of the other. Later, again, when the army grew much larger, the Companion cavalry appears to have been extended to eight hipparchies, of say eight hundred men each. In the Indian campaign five hipparchs are named, — Hephæstion, Perdiccas, Demetrius, Clitus, Craterus and Cœnus with the agema.

The mercenary cavalry, which in 331 B. C. had reached Alexander four hundred strong under Menidas, was likewise increased to a hipparchy by additional recruits; it is not said

Oriental recruits, but that they were such is altogether probable; and a corps of mounted archers was organized. Important changes in the foot were made after the arrival of heavy reinforcements to the army in Bactria. Alexander recruited altogether a considerable amount of cavalry, — the Oriental soldier being, as a rule, better suited to this arm of the service than to infantry duty. The army was beginning to assume that new character which Alexander had always designed to give to his vast kingdom. It had consisted alone of Macedonians, Greeks and European barbarians. He now incorporated in it Orientals to a high percentage, and began to subject them to Greek training and habits. For war, Macedonian discipline was alone available.

In Alexander's army stood side by side both the civil and military administrations. We look with astonishment upon what this army did, and imagine that it could not have performed its extraordinary work, except by being divested of every superfluity, and brought down to the scant proportions of a mere fighting machine. And yet, with this army marched the Court, with all its ceremonial and trappings, the directory of the home and Persian governments, the treasury officials and other civil functionaries, as well as the ordnance equipments with their special officers, the engineers, the quartermaster and commissary departments and the hospital corps. These latter alone, with the changes of climate as the army passed over its extraordinary course, from the tropical heat of the desert plains to the arctic snows of the highest mountains, must have called for endless labor. Tradesmen and sutlers accompanied the army, speculators, men of science, litterateurs, philosophers, many guests of the Court, priests and augurs, and surely a great number of women. It was a moving capital. All the more wonder that the king could control this vast caravan, and from it choose, at a moment's notice, a force which could execute the wonderful marches and fight the splendid battles of which history gives us the details. How any one can look upon the man who could hold in his single hand such a huge aggregation of conflicting elements and make them useful, as a mere military adventurer, passes comprehension. Those who knew him in his own era and called him a demi-god came far more near the truth.

Alexander had now subdued all the tribes south of the Parapamisus, thus fully protecting his rear, and could safely cross the range to attack Bessus, whose main protection lay in this all but impassable mountain chain. He had received the bulk of the troops lately under Parmenio, which were largely replaced by reinforcements from the rear, and in addition some phalangites from Greece; and he had ordered thirty thousand selected Persian youths to be trained to fight Macedonian fashion, some of whom it is said he had already with him.

Bessus was the head-centre of all opposition. He had about him many of the fugitive chiefs from Darius' army, some relics of the Arbela infantry, about seven thousand cavalry from Bactria and Sogdiana, and several thousand Daäns; and had added to the difficulties which Alexander must encounter in the way of mountains and snow and lack of provisions all that he could by ravaging the land for several days' march on the north slope of the mountains. As already stated, he had sent Satibarzanes with two thousand cavalry to Aria, but with poor results. He had dispatched Barzanes to Parthia to foster insurrection in that province, but he was not yet heard from. He now collected his own forces, and for a while remained in Zariaspa. He hoped that Alexander might invade India rather than Bactria, or at all events fight shy of the terrible passage of the Caucasus. This would give him an opportunity of rising and operating in Alexander's rear.

The newly subdued countries could, he thought, be easily raised in rebellion. As a temporary expedient he sent out a number of small expeditions against Alexander's advance. Oxyartes of Bactria, Dataphernes, chief of the Daäns, Spitamenes of Sogdiana, and Catanes of Parætacenæ were in his company.

It is probable that Alexander's inquiring mind had possessed itself of all the information of the geographers of that day; was well aware of the extent and height of the mountain chain he was about to cross, and of the difficulties to be encountered in its passage; and that he knew something of the countries beyond the range. For the pursuit of knowledge, the love of adventure and the calls of trade had before his day carried an occasional Greek to distant points in India and Persia. He was intent on reëstablishing for his own benefit the ancient trade possessed by Phœnicia, which his own wars had tended to check. Silk, furs, iron and other merchandise had long been brought from here to the Mediterranean. There is clear evidence in the rapidity and certainty of his marches that his periods of inactivity were spent, not altogether in feasts and follies, as his severer critics would have it, but in studying up the countries he proposed to traverse. Moreover, he kept beside him, not only the philosophers, litterateurs and artists, but the engineers and scientists most celebrated in the world. No doubt he added to these the most available and best of native talent. And as Alexander was an enthusiast on the question of the fusion of races, he undoubtedly gave much time to the study of national as well as topographical characteristics. There is no disposition to deny Alexander's occasional, perhaps frequent overindulgence in the national vice of Macedon, any more than to veil some other of his failings, such as his inordinate vanity and greed of adulation. But altogether too much stress has been laid on these. So much attention has been called to Alexander's vices that the true perspective of his portrait is in danger of being lost. He had vices, but they became prominent only at intervals; his life was, with rare exceptions, one prolonged period of toil and danger. Perhaps no great man has ever had less of the mean or evil in proportion to the great and good than Alexander; and in sketching his character, it is certainly safer to draw our colors from the materials of the ancient authorities, rather than from the speculations of the modern critic.

Alexander started as soon as the severest weather was over, and before the snow was fairly off the ground. It was many weeks earlier than he should have started, but he could no longer constrain himself to wait. The army marched, with great suffering from cold, hunger and exertion, up the Pandshir Valley, and climbed to the height of the pass at modern Khawak. This is four thousand feet higher than the Stelvio, which is the highest pass in the Alps, and is within two thousand feet as high as the summit of Mont Blanc. Many soldiers had no force to follow the army, says Diodorus, and were abandoned on the way; some lost their sight from the effect of the sunlight on the snow. The villagers along the route were friendly, but had no provisions. A few cattle were their only wealth. Finally the column began the descent.

The ancient historians dismiss this remarkable march with a few words; but it has no parallel, except Hannibal's crossing the Alps, and it is the first undertaking of the kind of which we have any record. Hannibal, from unexpected delays, started too late in the fall; Alexander, from overeagerness, started too early in the spring. Both contended with heavy snows, and suffered from all their attendant trials.

The villagers had consumed or concealed all their winter

supplies, mainly wheat, but scant at best; there was no wood for camp-fires. The rocky mountains were covered solely with a scrub growth of turpentine bushes. The only obtainable food consisted of a few roots, an occasional fish, and the beef cattle of the trains, which latter were eaten raw or seasoned with silphium (asafœtida), growing here in abundance. The farther down the mountain the column got, following an affluent of the Oxus, the worse off the men were, for they ran into the devastated region, where all the houses had been burned and the flocks driven away. On the south side, which they had ascended, the snow-line was but ten to twelve miles below the summit; on the north side the march was nearly forty miles through deep and treacherous snow-banks. And we must not imagine that the roads approached the magnificence we see in the great military turnpikes of the Alps. Over the snow there were practically no roads.

On the fifteenth day, after incredible suffering, the army reached the first Bactrian town, Drapsaca (modern Inde-raub). Here the men were given a rest. We do not learn the loss in this terrible march. That the horses largely perished is stated. We are left to conjecture the loss in men. The more awful march through the Gedrosian desert, which the bulk of the army never lived to cross, has no losses given. Only those killed in battle were wont to be honored by mention, few indeed compared to the men who perished in exposures such as these. The route from Susia, before Alexander turned south to Drangiana, would have been in comparison easy. And this, as we have seen, was his first-chosen path; but the dangers from the southerly provinces forestalled his intention, and having reached the Caucasus at a point so far to the east, he had practically no choice but between passes in this part of the chain, and had selected this one for the reasons given.

Bactria and Sogdiana were the seat of an ancient and well-developed civilization, and had since their conquest been the eastern bulwark of Persia. Never entirely reduced to possession by the Great King, they had none the less joined his standard, while retaining their own liberties ; and, in the last

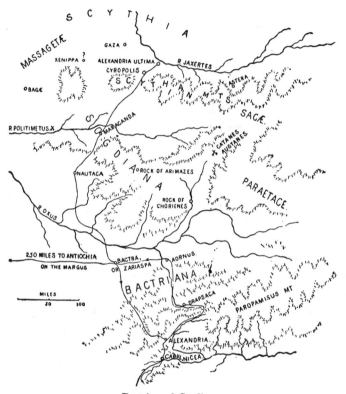

Bactria and Sogdiana.

campaigns, Bessus had been rather a confederate than a subordinate of Darius. That Bessus had brought the Scythian Sacæ to Arbela as "allies of the Great King" looked as if Alexander might have to encounter these wild peoples as well.

From Drapsaca, Alexander rapidly advanced over the passes in the lower ranges without opposition to Aornus, and thence over the fruit-bearing plains towards Bactra or Zariaspa. Bessus, who had believed himself well secured from invasion by the mountains and the devastated land on their northern slopes, awoke suddenly to his danger. On the first sign of Alexander's appearance he retired behind the Oxus (Jihoun or Amou), burned all the boats he used in crossing, and took refuge in Nautaca, in Sogdiana. When his Bactrian cavalry saw that he would not stay to defend his own satrapy, it dispersed, every man to his home. But the Sogdianians and Daäns still remained with him.

Reaching Zariaspa, Alexander took it at the first assault. Artabazus and Erigyius having returned from the Arian expedition, the king appointed the former viceroy over Bactria, and placed Archelaüs, a Companion, in command of a suitable garrison at Aornus, which, situated at the mouth of the defiles, was chosen as a depot. The apparent subjugation of the region between the Parapamisus and the Oxus had been as easy as the toil of crossing the mountains had been severe.

The spring of 329 B. C. saw Alexander ready to undertake the conquest of Sogdiana. This country was peculiarly adapted to offer easy and stanch resistance to the Macedonian advance. Maracanda, the capital, was situated in a populous and rich plain, protected on the west by deserts, on all other sides by mountain barriers, and was difficult of access. It could be easily defended, and Sogdiana was, besides, not only able to raise a considerable army, but was so placed as to enable a force to debouch into Aria, Parthia, and Hyrcania at will, and operate on Alexander's rear. The Daäns and Massagetans, and the Scythians beyond the Jaxartes, were always ready for plundering raids; and some of the Indian kings, indeed, are said to have promised to take part with Bessus, whom they could reach by passes leading from the headwaters of the Cophen affluents to the headwaters of the Oxus. With the mountains and the desert to afford temporary refuge, it was hard to see how Alexander could subjugate Sogdiana. It was the sort of task in which Napoleon failed in Spain.

From Bactra, whose vicinity is fertile, the route to the Oxus was over a barren tract, which made the marches more difficult. There was not a brook for fifty miles, and the weather was, for the season, extremely hot and dry. The difficulty of the march may not have been recognized beforehand, for a large percentage of the men fell in their tracks; but when the Oxus was reached, water was carried back to the sufferers, and many were thus rescued. It is said that Alexander never took off his armor, nor rested from personal endeavors until the last live man was thus brought in; but Diodorus puts the loss higher than that of any of his battles.

The Oxus was the largest river Alexander had yet encountered. It was deep, about three quarters of a mile wide, full and rapid, and with a sandy bottom that would not readily hold piles. There was little timber growing in the vicinity; it would take too long to collect materials for a bridge or for new boats, and Bessus had destroyed all the old boats on the river for a long distance up and down. But Alexander must cross by some means; and he again utilized his tent-skins, as he had done at the Danube. These he filled with straw and other light floating material, and stitched up so as to be watertight. Using them as floats for rafts, or a flying bridge, or as floats for the men themselves, he leisurely put his army over in five days. There was no opposition. This use of floats for men is both ancient and common. To-day, fishermen in these parts are said to cross rivers with earthern vessels as floats, and to fish on the way.

Before crossing, Alexander allowed a number of old and worn-out Macedonians, and the reënlisted Thessalians whose time was up, to return to Macedonia. Each horseman is said to have received a sum equivalent to two thousand two hundred dollars, each foot-soldier five hundred dollars. These bounties vary so considerably that no rule of distribution can be deduced from them. He also sent Stasanor, a Companion, into Aria, to displace Arsames, the viceroy, whom he thought disaffected; for Bessus had been tampering with him.

After crossing, Alexander made a forced march towards Bessus. The latter had quite lost the confidence of his associates by his constant retreats, and by his weak management since the murder of Darius. The king had gone but part way when he was met by messengers from Bessus' chief abettors, Spitamenes, Dataphernes, Catanes and Oxyartes, who, probably overawed by Alexander's evidently offensive intention in crossing the Oxus, and anxious to make their peace with the conqueror, had deemed any treachery justifiable, and had revolted from Bessus and seized his person, as he had done Darius. They now promised to surrender him if Alexander would send them a force to aid in the work. Alexander sent Ptolemy, son of Lagus, with three squadrons of the Companion cavalry, the lancers, the infantry of Philotas, one thousand shield-bearing guards, the Agrianians and half the archers, — some six thousand men all told, — by forced marches towards Sogdiana, he himself following more slowly to rest his men. This force seemed ample to compel the surrender if declined. Ptolemy made what is stated as a ten days' march in four (*i. e.* one hundred and fifty miles in four days, or thirty-seven miles a day) and reached the camp where the barbarians had been the day before. Spitamenes and Dataphernes were loath to make the surrender of their late companion themselves, but arranged the matter so as to isolate

Bessus in a village by himself, and then retired. Here Ptolemy seized Bessus. This wicked but unfortunate prince, when he was brought to Alexander, naked, confined in a wooden collar, and led by a halter, was ordered to be subjected to the indignity of scourging, and was then sent to Zariaspa. He was later executed. Spitamenes, Dataphernes, Catanes and Oxyartes appear to have been pardoned, for we are not told that Alexander put any viceroy over their heads.

In this province Alexander was able to remount a large part of his cavalry, a matter of prime necessity, for many horses had been lost in the crossing of the Caucasus. He then marched to Maracanda, the capital (modern Samarcand), where plentiful supplies could be got from the rich and fertile valley, known to-day as Al Sogd, and often called the Mohammedan paradise. Here again he left a garrison. The territory in the south had practically submitted. But as Alexander advanced north, he encountered more serious signs of opposition.

A Scythian Prince.

XXXIV.

THE JAXARTES. SUMMER, B. C. 329.

ALEXANDER now marched on Cyropolis, near the Jaxartes, the farthest point attained by Cyrus in his conquests. In one of his mountain battles he was again wounded, but still continued his activity, carried in a litter. Arrived at the Jaxartes, Alexander founded another namesake town on its banks. He was anxious to make this section of his kingdom self-governing, but his efforts in this direction were misunderstood, and an uprising ensued. Alexander took the matter sharply in hand, moved against and destroyed seven cities, to which the rebels had retired. But he was again wounded by a sling-stone. He then crossed the Jaxartes, and defeated the Scythians in so marked a manner that they were glad to make a permanent peace. This was a happy outcome, for all Sogdiana was now in open revolt in his rear, and Alexander had got himself into the most dangerous situation he ever occupied.

ALEXANDER marched on Cyropolis (not far from modern Khojend), the last city of the satrapy, and named after its celebrated founder. It was not far from the banks of the Jaxartes ("Great River"), which Alexander mistook for and called the Tanaïs, as it was the Araxes of Cyrus. Arrian, in his narrative, frequently strays off into geography. In this he is often and naturally inaccurate. But his own errors, though committed centuries later, help us to understand those into which Alexander still more naturally fell. His incomplete knowledge, however, by no means interfered with the king's taking advantage of every natural and artificial means for attack, defense and permanent occupation.

Hereabouts, in crossing some passes in the Scythian Mountains, through which ran the road from Maracanda to Cyropolis, one of the Macedonian foraging parties, having lost its way in the defiles, was ambushed and cut to pieces by the barbarians, who then escaped to a part of the chain in which were several fastnesses or easily defended positions, some thirty thousand armed men in number. Alexander determined at once to punish this act. He took his lightest troops, pursued the barbarians, and attacked them vigorously in their principal retreat. This was exceedingly strong, so much so that Alexander made many ineffectual assaults on them, though indeed these barbarians, like all the other tribes he met in arms in this region, rarely fought hand to hand, but relied mainly on missiles cast from a distance. Alexander himself — leading his men with his accustomed recklessness — received a wound in the leg from an arrow, which broke the fibula. This accident so inflamed the anger of the troops that nothing could resist their onset; a fresh assault resulted in the capture of the place. Many of the barbarians were massacred, more cast themselves down the rocks ; out of thirty thousand men not more than eight thousand escaped from the holocaust to tender their submission. Alexander was for some time obliged to travel in a litter, which the different bodies of cavalry and infantry alternately vied to escort. This enforced rest must have been irksome indeed to the king, especially as there was abundant call for all the activity, mental and physical, of which he was capable.

About this time also occurred the massacre by Alexander of the descendants of the Branchidæ, who had surrendered to Xerxes the treasures of the temple of Apollo at Miletus, and to escape the vengeance of the Greeks had accompanied the Great King into Persia, and been by him settled in Sogdiana. Here they had kept themselves free from mixture with the barbarians for one hundred and fifty years. Alexander deemed it wise to exterminate this people. Such an act, unpardonable according to our ideas, can be only explained by the natural inhumanity exercised in that age by every one to his enemies. Or perhaps, as the act was in the nature of a religious retribution, the massacres of the era of the Reformation make a parallel which better elucidates, if it does not palliate, the cruelty.

The territory (modern Ferghana) in which Alexander now stood, between the rugged range of the Scythian Caucasus and the wide and deep Jaxartes, had always been a marked boundary between the then so-called civilized world and the Scythians, as were named the wild and roaming tribes beyond, — now the Tartars; and in fact it plays to-day a somewhat similar rôle. On the south and east were difficult mountain ranges; on the north the rapid river; on the west alone was it open to assault. There was no present inducement to Alexander to move beyond this boundary, while the riches of India awaited his conquering progress. He desired but to establish a point from which he could in future proceed against the roving barbarians, if he so wished; which point would also have its commercial value in whatever intercourse could be had with them.

There had been from time immemorial a series of fortified towns or posts not very far apart along this border. There appear at this time to have been seven prominent ones, of which Cyropolis was the most important. Alexander garrisoned these towns, occupied the defiles in his rear so as to secure his line of retreat, and camped at the last narrows of the Jaxartes, where it turns northward into the flat, sandy plains of modern Tartary.

Alexander's desire to remain at peace with the Scythians seemed at first about to be realized. While near the Jaxartes an embassy came to the king from the so-called Scythians in Europe, and another from those in Asia, known as the Abian Scythians, which latter Homer lauds as the most just nation on earth, probably from their being poor and unambitious, and desiring nothing of their neighbors. With these embassies, on their return, Alexander sent Companions, with instructions, ostensibly to convey his friendly greetings, but really to observe the country, its topography, riches, strength and military conditions. To supplement these friendly advances, Alexander determined to found a city near the Jaxartes, as a base for future expeditions against the Scythians, should this be desirable, as a bulwark against their incursions, and because the city, he thought, would naturally grow to be an important one on account of the thickly-settled country, and his own royal patronage. This city, probably modern Khojend, though indeed its locality is in dispute, still remains to testify to Alexander's good judgment in selecting its location.

Alexander seems to have entertained different notions as to the best methods of governing this trans-Caucasian country, from what he had so far practiced with his Asiatic conquests. He had conceived the idea of giving this people a larger share in its own government, and thus attaching it the more firmly to his interests. For this purpose he called the Sogdianians together to a conference to decide upon the best interests of the country; but instead of conciliating them, this well-intentioned step and the planning of a fortified city gave rise to the suspicion that Alexander proposed to gather together all their chiefs, and by assassinating them, at one blow to deprive the country of its leaders as a first means of reducing it to servitude. With this idea they revolted, instigated, no doubt, by Bessus' treacherous associates, seized upon the Macedonian garrisons in the seven towns above named, and slew the soldiers. They then shut themselves up in these towns, all of which were fairly well fortified. Simultaneously with this occurred a revolt of Spitamenes in Maracanda, and several uprisings in Bactria, all apparently having the same suspicion at the root, or at all events community of action. It is not unlikely that in surrendering Bessus to Alexander, the conspirators imagined that Alexander would leave the region, — for the capture of Darius' murderers was the alleged object of his presence, — and that they would then be free to resume their sway; and when they saw that Alexander proposed to subdue the whole country, they fomented the revolt which now broke out. They were not slow to see that Alexander had placed himself in a dangerous position.

Alexander's general military situation was indeed more

" Seven Cities " Campaign.

perilous than at any other time. Farther from his base than ever before or after, with limited numbers, many unreasoning, inflammatory and warlike tribes at his back, and with an almost impassable mountain range in his rear, where his enemies could easily arrest his retreat; with the Scythian hordes ready to cross the river, intent on spoil, in fact eagerly watching this very chance, for with the details of the uprising they were probably familiar, — nothing but the utmost vigor and instant action could save him, coupled with the errors which would probably be committed by the natives.

Upon learning of the local uprising, Alexander took his measures on the minute. He had not yet heard of the insurrection in his rear, nor was he probably aware of the extent of the matter. But he determined to suppress the one in his front in short measure. He instructed each company to get ready its scaling ladders. He sent Craterus by a forced march to Cyropolis, the largest of the towns of the country, with instructions to blockade it with a stockade and ditch, to build siege engines on the ground, and to keep up such active demonstrations as to prevent any aid being rendered the other cities by this one. Cyropolis was surrounded by stone walls, and had a citadel with a large garrison.

The king himself marched to Gaza, the nearest city to the Macedonian camp. This was defended only by an earthen and conglomerate rampart. No sooner on the ground than he began operations. With his archers and slingers, and the smaller military engines he had brought with him, the walls were speedily cleared, and the phalangites then advanced to the assault with their ladders. It was but short work; the town was taken at the first rush, and every man put to the sword. The women and children were reserved as plunder, and distributed among the soldiers; the town was razed. The second city, probably at no great distance, was taken in like manner on the same day, and suffered the like fate. This was indeed a marvelous day's work, well exhibiting Alexander's tireless energy. The third city fell the next day.

While all this was going on, Alexander had established a cordon of cavalry around the two nearest other towns to prevent the population from taking to flight and reaching the uplands. When by the smoke from the burning cities and by the report of some who escaped, their fate was known, the inhabitants of the two other towns endeavored, as Alexander had anticipated, to secure safety by flight; but they were remorselessly cut down by the cavalry which was around them on every side, and nearly all perished. Thus five cities were taken and destroyed in two days. This fatal reverse was chiefly due to the fact that the barbarians had committed the imprudence of discontinuing the desultory warfare in which alone they were preëminent, and in taking to one in which they were no match whatever for the Macedonians.

Thence Alexander moved on Cyropolis, which Craterus had already blockaded. The stoutest hearted and most notable of the barbarians had gathered there, and the place was surrounded by so strong and high a wall, that it could not be taken by a *coup de main.* Some fifteen thousand soldiers, and many of the lesser chiefs, had rendezvoused there. While Alexander was preparing his engines to batter down the walls, a work of some days, as their heavy timbers were usually cut on the ground, he noticed that a small confluent of the Jaxartes, on which the city was built and which ran under the city wall, — or, according to Arrian, a small channel which was full only during the freshet season, — was dried up to such a degree as to afford a passage into the town. He sent the Companions, the shield-bearing guards, the archers and Agrianians to the nearest gates, and he himself headed a small party; and, while the attention of the inhabitants was taken up on the farther side of the city by the severity of the fire from the engines and light troops, which he ordered to be redoubled in vigor, he secretly made his way along the channel into the town, on the other side, and speedily forced the gates at the place where he had stationed his *corps d'élite.* Through these gates the expectant Macedonians rushed in, and captured the city. But the barbarians would yet not yield. Though they saw that the city was gone, they must fight for their lives. A fierce struggle ensued, in which Alexander was again wounded by a sling-stone on the head and neck, and Craterus by an arrow. The number of wounded was exceptionally large, including many officers. The barbarians were driven out of the market-place, where they had made their stand; the defenders of the walls were swept away, and the rest of the troops from the farther side joined Alexander. About eight thousand barbarians were slain; the rest, some seven thousand in number, fled into the citadel; but after one day's siege they were forced to surrender for lack of water. The seventh city was also taken at the first assault, and most of its inhabitants perished.

Many of the survivors were imprisoned in chains. Alexander proposed to transport those who were known as leaders out of the country, to prevent their encouraging future sedition. The cities were uniformly razed to the ground. Whether this course was justifiable or not will always be the subject of dispute. It seems unnecessary to go over the ground again. But it is to be noticed that Alexander invariably treated those who submitted with as marked and constant generosity as he did those who revolted after submission with the utmost, almost savage, severity. In his late situation, it had been with him a case of life and death, and not merely of present subjection and future submission of these tribes. He had been and still was in a *cul de sac* from which there was no escape if the plans of the barbarians were not utterly thwarted. But, by his rapid and vigorous measures, Alexander had now opened the road back to Sogdiana. This was a first but only a partial gain.

Meanwhile, the Scythians, quick to act on hearing of the uprising, arrived with an army on the other bank of the Jaxartes and camped, ready to take a hand if a favorable chance should occur, and, meanwhile, taunting the Macedonians from what they considered a safe distance. Alexander now first learned that Spitamenes had again risen, and had begun to besiege the garrison at Maracanda. The Massagetæ, the

Daäns, the Sacæ were reported to have joined in the insurrection; and Oxyartes, Catanes, Chorienes, Haustanes and

Scythian Archers.

many other noted chiefs were fostering it. Alexander understood that this was still part and parcel of the insurrection of the seven towns, and now fully comprehended the gravity of his situation. But he also saw that he must protect himself against an invasion of the Scythians before he could turn on Spitamenes. He was therefore fain to content himself with sending against the rebels a force under Andromachus, Menedemus, and Caranus, consisting of eight hundred Greek mercenary cavalry and fifteen hundred Greek mercenary infantry. To these he associated (Arrian says placed over them) an interpreter, Pharnuches, who had shown himself clever in dealing with the barbarians. For he believed the population in bulk to be more inclined to peace than war. This force, at all events, he felt could create a diversion sufficient to enable him to finish the Jaxartes problem before turning southward.

It was plain that the Scythian question must be settled before the Bactrian. Alexander could not turn back from the Jaxartes except distinctly as conqueror. The body of Scythians on the other shore was as yet small, but vast hordes were probably assembling on the desert in their rear. Should he retire without making them feel the weight of his hand, he would have the most troublesome of enemies on his heels, so soon as he retired. Now, as always, Alexander took the broadest views of the military problem before him. The details were secondary. To compel a favorable outcome to these he could take such action as the immediate circumstances warranted.

In three weeks Alexander had fortified his intended city on the Jaxartes, Alexandria Ultima, and settled therein some Greek mercenaries and Macedonians who had grown unfit for military service, such barbarians as chose to join the colony, and such of those who remained over from the seven destroyed towns as he deemed safe to leave behind. Among the denizens of the new city were some captives purchased by Alexander. These were drafted into the ranks to serve as garrison. The Hellenes must have felt much in the position of abandoned sentinels. Having celebrated the foundation of this most distant of his namesake cities by the usual games and sacrifices, Alexander turned his attention to the Scythians. These barbarians were growing restless and audacious, and had endeavored to interrupt his building operations from the other side. They assembled in groups and taunted him with fear to cross and attack the Scythians, whom he would find, they gave him to understand by unmistakable signals, different from the weaklings he had so far met; and generally acted in a manner showing their need of a salutary lesson.

Scythian.

In offering the sacrifices which always preceded an advance, the soothsayer Aristander pronounced the signs of the victims to be unfavorable to success. Alexander contented himself with waiting a while, which he was the less reluctant to do, as probably his wound was not yet quite healed. Again shortly sacrificing, with the purpose of crossing the river, the victims proved on this occasion to portend personal danger to himself; but the king declared that he had better incur grave risk than be a further laughing-stock to the barbarians, and resolved to delay no longer.

Alexander no doubt was superstitious. He came honestly by it. His mother was the triple essence of superstition. But he was far from being a bigot. His determination always overrode his belief in the portents. " We have not always in war a choice of circumstances," quoth he. " I could desire, no doubt, more propitious auguries to fight under ; but necessity goes before the counsels of reason. If we allow the Scythians to insult us unpunished we shall add courage to the Bactrians. Our rôle is attack. That day on which we put ourselves on the defensive will see us lost."

But despite these brave words, Alexander was, according to Quintus Curtius, far from easy. Unlike the night before Arbela, he could not sleep, but incessantly gazed at the many watch-fires on the farther bank. Nor is this unnatural. At Arbela he slept, conscious of his own ability, the courage of his handful of men, and of the fact that here was a fair field and no favor. At the Jaxartes he was caught in the meshes of a danger of unknown extent. He was absolutely compromised by the revolted provinces in his rear, and saw in his front a problem perhaps as awkward as any he had yet faced. But his conduct, as we shall see, partook in no sense of the weakness usually associated with overanxiety.

In dry seasons the Jaxartes was fordable here. But Alexander's only present means of crossing was skins, used, as at the Oxus, as floats for the light troops and to float rafts for the cavalrymen and phalangians. The horses were swum over. Alexander was just recovering of his wound. This was his first appearance in command, and he was greeted with affectionate enthusiasm. To protect the crossing he brought up his artillery, and trained it on the barbarians across the river. A number were shot down, and one of the killed, apparently their chief or champion, was shot by a shaft through his wicker shield and linen breastplate. Astonished

beyond measure at being struck by missiles from such an incredible distance, the Scythians retired to a more respectful
position back from the banks. This is the first record of the
use of artillery to protect the crossing of a river in offense.

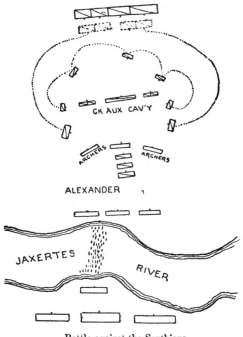

Battle against the Scythians.

Alexander led the way on the first raft, with the trumpets
sounding, while the men made breastworks or tortoises of
their interlaced shields, and used their missiles freely during
the passage. The archers and slingers were first got across,
and skirmishing gallantly with the Scythians, prevented their
approaching the river, while the phalangites and cavalrymen
were ferried over. The horses of each party swam behind the
boats.

Alexander now engaged the enemy by sending forward a

regiment of Greek auxiliary cavalry and four squadrons of  lancers, in all one thousand two hundred strong. These the Scythians smartly attacked, and by riding in circles around them, according to their method of attack, without coming to close quarters, wounded

Scythians.

many with their arrows and darts, and threatened them with defeat. Seeing his men close pressed, Alexander, covered by the archers, Agrianians and light troops under Balacrus, led forward the cavalry in one body, and compelled the Scythians to forsake their skirmishing tactics and form line. Then, throwing part of the light horse about their flank, he himself headed three squadrons of Companion cavalry and the horse lancers, and advanced sharply on the enemy in column. The Scythians, finding themselves unable to use their peculiar skirmishing tactics on account of the rapid manœuvres of Alexander's columns, lost head, and, unequal to the task of a clash with the Macedonians, were speedily dispersed, encountering a loss of one thousand slain. There were one hundred and fifty of them captured.

Pursuit was at once undertaken. The heat was very oppressive, the distance great, and the men, suffering from thirst, drank largely of stagnant water, there being no other to be had. Alexander did the like, and shortly after, while following up the enemy, he was seized with a grave sickness as a result, and thus the prophecy of the victims was fulfilled. The pursuit was arrested. The king was carried exhausted back to the camp, and his life for some days was in much danger. But his rugged constitution came to the rescue, and he recovered. The battle at the Jaxartes had cost one hundred and sixty killed, and one thousand wounded, a loss of nearly twenty per cent., for not exceeding six thousand men had been engaged. Much booty, including eighteen hundred camels, had been taken.

Alexander's victory over the Scythians had by good fortune the desired result. Not long after, envoys came from the Scythian king, with an apology for the conduct of the troops at the river, alleging that this was but a band of marauders and freebooters, with whose lawless acts the Scythian state had nothing to do. The king tendered his fealty, and undertook to perform whatever Alexander should prescribe. As Alexander had no desire or time to engage in operations beyond the Jaxartes (for he must turn at once on the Sogdianians, and moreover his vanity was satisfied with having advanced as far as Cyrus), he was pleased to give credit to the message of the ambassadors, and sent them back with a courteous answer, releasing without payment of ransom the prisoners he had taken. This generosity, coupled to the king's remarkable feats of war, which they had both seen and heard of, gave to his name among the Scythians the same halo with which their brethren beyond the Danube seven years before had surrounded it. This reputation was Alexander's surest defense against these tribes.

Alexander the Great.
(From a Mosaic in the Louvre.)

XXXV.

THE Scythian campaign had given the Sogdianians time for preparation. Spitamenes was the ruling spirit of the insurrection. He had unsuccessfully tried to seize Maracanda. Alexander dispatched a force against him. These men drove him into the desert, but being poorly led, Spitamenes turned upon them, surrounded them near the Polytimetus, and massacred them, to the number of over two thousand. Alexander, when he learned of this disaster, had just completed his Jaxartes programme. By a forced march, he reached the scene in four days. But Spitamenes fled. Alexander took bitter revenge by devastating the land. The winter was spent in Zariaspa with many feasts but more labor. A dozen new cities were started, and Sogdiana again colonized. Considerable and much needed reinforcements reached Alexander in Zariaspa, and embassies from many and distant nations came to him. He began to plan for his Indian campaign; but the Sogdianians again rose under Spitamenes, and intrenched themselves in the mountain strongholds. Another campaign became essential. Alexander divided his troops into five flying columns, and traversing the land in length and breadth, stamped out the insurrection once for all, and rendezvoused at Maracanda. Spitamenes, with a force of nomads, was still afoot and threatened much trouble, but between Craterus and Cœnus he was defeated, and finally murdered by his own allies. He was the last of the rebels.

ALEXANDER'S delay at the Jaxartes had given time for the Sogdianian revolt to make much headway. In part by threats, in part by cajolery, Spitamenes had induced the entire population to join the insurrection. They were like clay in the hands of the potter. The delay had been unavoidable; but so soon as the Scythian question was settled, Alexander lost no time in turning towards Maracanda.

Spitamenes with his immediate command had been able to make but small impression against the garrison of Maracanda. The Macedonians had not only held him at bay, but had made a successful sortie upon him, in which they had punished him severely, and had again retired to the citadel without loss. And when Spitamenes learned that the forces which Alexander had dispatched against him to Maracanda were near at hand, he retired from the vicinity of the capital in a westerly direction. The commanders of the relief party, on its arrival at the theatre of operations, not content with what had already been won, but anxious to distinguish themselves, followed Spitamenes up in the hope of punishing his audacity; and, in fact, they seriously harassed his rear during the retreat, which he now continued towards the desert. But emboldened by their success, they were unwise enough to advance well into the steppes, and to attack a body of nomad Scythians, whom they suspected of being Spitamenes' allies, or at all events of having given him aid and comfort. These people, angered by the act, did in reality join forces with the Sogdianians, and sent them a reinforcement of six hundred of their best horse.

Spitamenes, seeing that the Macedonians were illy led, determined to risk the offensive. Selecting a level plain near the Scythian desert where he could fight in open order, — a formation which allows the great individual bravery of the Oriental cavalry to have full play, — he declined to come to close quarters, in which the Macedonians were easily his superiors, but rode round and round the phalanx, discharging darts and arrows, and making feints at all points. His troops did not once attempt to stand their ground when the Macedonians charged home upon them. From the onsets of the Macedonian horse they continually fled, but again turned when the pursuit halted, and tired it out by unceasing activity, as with their great preponderance of force they could easily do. Their horses were fresh, while those of Andromachus were exhausted by their long march to Maracanda, and had been but half fed for many days. The Macedonians had got themselves where they could neither advance nor retreat; for the Scythians were constantly on the alert, and afforded them no rest. Many were killed and wounded in this desultory fighting.

Pharnuches, who was brought up to diplomacy rather than to arms, refused any longer to head the expedition; the other leaders declined the command of a matter already past cure. There was neither head nor purpose. The only recourse of the Macedonians was to form square, and march towards the river Polytimetus (modern Sogd-Kohik), where they saw a wooded glen which might afford them shelter. But there was lack of common action. Caranus, commanding part of the cavalry, attempted to cross the river, but failed to notify Andromachus of what he was about to do; the infantry followed Caranus heedlessly; the men became demoralized, missing the strong hand, and began to break ranks at the ford. Seeing this, the barbarians, who had kept close on their heels, and pressed in hard, waiting for just this chance, now attacked the force in front, flank and rear, and from both sides of the stream, crossing over above and below the Macedonians, and threw the phalanx into complete confusion. The retreat became a *sauve qui peut*. Most of the soldiers who had not been killed or fatally injured made their way to a small island in the river. Here they were surrounded at a safe distance by the barbarians, and all slain by arrows, except a few who were kept for trophies, subjected for a while to the bitterest slavery, and later killed. Some sixty horse and three hundred foot are all who are said to have got away.

In this pitiful campaign, the account of which varies but slightly in Arrian and Curtius, and which is so unlike what we are used to see under the Macedonian standard, two thousand men were lost to Alexander, — more than the entire number killed in the battles for the conquest of Persia. It is but one more proof that success in war depends not alone on men, but needs a man. Alexander was to blame in the selection of his commander. Spitamenes returned in high spirits to Maracanda, and prepared to besiege the citadel a second time, with far greater prospect of success.

On learning of this untoward event, Alexander, chagrined beyond measure at the disgraceful check, at once prepared to put his own shoulder to the wheel. He had finished the Jaxartes problem, and could leave this outpost safely now that the new city was fairly started. He took half the Companion cavalry, the shield-bearing guards, archers, Agrianians, and light phalangians, and headed towards the valley of the Polytimetus, leaving Craterus to follow with the bulk of the army. The king, who was never slow in his movements, this time marched one hundred and seventy miles in three days, and on the morning of the fourth day reached Maracanda. But Spitamenes, on the first notice of Alexander's presence, abandoned the siege of the city, and fled. Alexander pursued him well into the desert, where Spitamenes crossed the Polytimetus, but he could not overtake him. The king's path lay near the late battlefield. Here he buried, with as much ceremony as the time allowed, all the soldiers whose remains had not disappeared, and in retaliation for the loss of his men he laid the whole district waste. The miserable Sogdianians, suffering for another's guilt, had retired into every place of safety, and had fortified every town and hamlet. They could expect no mercy; nor did Alexander show any. He swept over the length and breadth of the land like a blizzard, burning and destroying villages and farms. He slew all the barbarians who had taken part in the campaign, most of whom had fled to the fortified places. These were each in turn reduced and razed. In this frightful retribution one hundred and twenty thousand men, not counting women and children, are said to have perished. Only Cæsar's massacres in Gaul exceed the frightful score of this devastation.

Alexander then left Peucolaus with three thousand men in Maracanda, and returned to Zariaspa, where he intended to remain for the coming winter. The people of Bactria, after the fate of Sogdiana, needed no further effort to reduce them to subjection. The revolt had not progressed far in this province. Little more is mentioned about it. Clemency succeeded cruelty, says Quintus Curtius, and had a good effect. But some of the leaders in the late insurrection had fled into mountain fastnesses, where they deemed themselves secure from pursuit.

During this winter Alexander had his headquarters and camp at Zariaspa. The reinforcements which reached him here were considerable. We know that there was quite an amount of trouble in the rear among the newly-appointed satraps and other civil governors; it could scarcely be otherwise; and the fact that these detachments were able to march through the length and breadth of the land, despite these turmoils, points conclusively to the excellence of the chain of military posts which Alexander had established in the succession of cities he had founded on the way.

Military activity at Zariaspa was shared with the toils of state, and both alternated with games and feasts. Alexander is said by Curtius to have founded six cities in Bactria and Sogdiana; by Justin, twelve. The general convention which had evoked the insurrection was now held. It was here that Bessus was tried before the assembly of notables, convicted and mutilated by cutting off his nose and ears. He was then sent to Ecbatana, probably exhibited as an example on the way, and was there executed. This was the Oriental method of procedure.

To show that modern critics have not been the first to

discover weaknesses in Alexander's character, the following extract from Arrian, his most accurate historian and chief laudator, is of interest: " I do not commend this excessive punishment; on the contrary, I consider that the mutilation of the prominent features of the body is a barbaric custom, and I agree with those who say that Alexander was induced to indulge his desire of emulating the Median and Persian wealth, and to treat his subjects as inferior beings, according to the custom of the foreign kings. Nor do I by any means commend him for changing the Macedonian style of dress, which his fathers had adopted, for the Median one, being, as he was, a descendant of Hercules. Besides, he was not ashamed to exchange the head-dress which the conqueror had so long worn for that of the conquered Persians. None of these things do I commend ; but I consider Alexander's great achievements prove, if anything can, that supposing a man to have a vigorous bodily constitution, to be illustrious in descent, and to be even more successful in war than Alexander himself ; even supposing that he could sail right round Libya as well as Asia, and hold them both in subjection as Alexander indeed designed to do ; even if he could add the possession of Europe to that of Asia and Libya ; all these things would be no furtherance to such a man's happiness, unless at the same time he possess the power of self-control, though he has performed the great deeds which have been supposed."

It cannot be denied that the Persian habit was constantly on the increase with Alexander, as how could it be otherwise if he was suitably to maintain the godlike character which these Eastern peoples would not believe in without their accustomed pomp and circumstance ? And was not this blind but most natural belief a great part of Alexander's stock in trade ? No doubt history would show us a more perfect man, if, with all his wonderful ability and native truth and generosity of character, Alexander had kept up his Macedonian simplicity. But Alexander, though a perfect captain, was by no means a perfect man. And was Macedonian simplicity either natural or politically wise? His ancient domain was but a small spot even on the map of the then world, the greater part of which he had already conquered. What more proper in almost every sense, than his adoption of the habits, dress and customs — in part, at least — of those peoples which made up all but a limited percentage of his empire, though, indeed, it was by his Macedonian simplicity, discipline, intelligence and superior skill that he had attained his extraordinary preëminence.

The reinforcements above referred to, which reached Zariaspa during this winter from Greece, were under Nearchus, satrap of Lycia, and Asandrus, satrap of Caria, Asclepiodorus, viceroy of Syria, and Menes, his deputy, Epolicus, Menidas, and Ptolemy, the Thracian strategos, and amounted in all to seventeen thousand foot and twenty-six hundred horse. This accession of troops was sadly needed to repair the gaps rent by the last campaigns. For north of the Parapamisus, the warlike tribes of herdsmen and mountaineers, of whom every one was a soldier, by no means succumbed to one or two battles, as did the peaceable inhabitants of the more western countries, who were accustomed to be ruled and to pay tribute; of whom but a few bore arms, and the rest were artisans and farmers. In fact, without these reinforcements, the king would shortly have been·in an untenable position. They were the leaven of a considerable lump of new troops. "When," says Admiral La Gravière, "the Emperor Napoleon camped under the walls of Moscow, there is no strategist but what would pronounce his position very hazardous, and would be tempted to accuse it of adventurous temerity; the temerity was much greater on the part of Alexander the day when

he came and established himself between the Oxus and Jaxartes. Never had the king of Macedon manœuvred on a theatre so perilous." But Alexander's temerity was forced on
him. To penetrate into Russia so far as Moscow was an op-
tional proceeding with Napoleon. The conquest of Bactria
and Sogdiana was a prerequisite to Alexander's holding the
plateau of Iran. And once on the borders of Scythia, there
was no alternative. From the Jaxartes it was a question of
successful withdrawal without losing what was already won
or of absolute destruction. His temerity was rather exceptional boldness of action.

Phrataphernes, satrap of Parthia, and Stasanor, satrap of
Aria, now arrived and brought in chains Arsames, late satrap
of Aria, Barzanes, an adherent of Bessus, to whom the latter
had assigned Parthia, and some others. These were the last
of the ringleaders who had betrayed Darius. With them in
arrest, opposition in the rear might well be said to have been
crushed out.

The Companions whom Alexander had sent to the European Scythians now returned with another embassy, for the
old king was dead and his brother was reigning in his stead.
The latter desired to make a friend of Alexander. He
sent such presents as the Scythians deemed of the highest
value, and invited him and his officers to unite in marriage
with his own family. No doubt he looked on this as an equal
alliance. He offered to come to receive Alexander's orders,
if the king so desired. Alexander also received a deputation
from the Chorasmians, who dwelt between the Caspian and
Ural seas, headed by their king, Pharasmenes, and fifteen
hundred horse-guards, asking for a treaty, and offering him
guidance and provision in case he wished to make a campaign
against the Amazons, whose land they said was next beyond
their own. Pharasmenes feared lest Alexander should think

he also had abetted Spitamenes. Alexander received both these embassies with courtesy and sent them away satisfied, having made friendship between them and Artabazus, whom he had appointed viceroy of Bactria.

Alexander had early imagined that the Caspian Sea was a part of the ocean, and that as such he must eventually subdue its borders in order to complete the boundaries of his ideal empire. But he had now learned from the reports of his own officers and from those of the barbarians that the ocean was nowhere near the Caspian, and that untold stretches of country beyond were inhabited by the people he called Scythians. He was therefore content to make alliances with and to erect obstacles against these tribes rather than seek to extend his conquests into their territory. His limitation of his own borders was always conceived on a scale full of common sense. He told Pharasmenes that he must first conquer India; but once lord of all Asia he would return to Greece, and thence advance through the Hellespont, the Bosphorus and Euxine Sea. He would then gladly ask his alliance and aid. Alexander was very anxious to get matters to rights in Bactria and Sogdiana, for his mind was set on the conquest of India, and he was impatient of these seemingly never-ending delays.

Alexander's plan of conquest was well matured; its scheme was compact and intelligent. Few things show Alexander's grasp of his gigantic problem better than the fact that he limited the boundary of his conquest of Persia by the water-shed of the upper Euphrates and Tigris, of Ariana by the Oxus and Jaxartes, and made his eastern limit the Indus and Hydaspes, fortifying these rivers with suitable cities, or military posts, as a barrier against the tribes beyond, and erecting a yet better barrier against them by his control over the bordering nations.

But the campaign against India was destined to be delayed.

While Alexander was preparing for this campaign, the Sogdianians again rose against Peucolaus, the satrap Alexander had appointed over them. Their late punishment had made them desperate rather than tamed them, and many bands had taken refuge in the uplands, whither some of their chiefs had previously fled, and had there intrenched themselves in strongholds of every nature, — the castles of their chiefs, villages, defiles, mountain heights, forests. A new problem, and a worse than ever, seemed to have been thrust upon Alexander. The more desperate the people the more dangerous the situation. Peucolaus, with his three thousand men, could not even attempt to reduce this insurrection ; he could scarcely protect the valley of Maracanda ; and Alexander himself, after leaving suitable garrisons in Alexandria Arachotia, ad Caucasum, Ultima, had kept not exceeding ten thousand men with him, of which he could dispose for a campaign against these people. He was handicapped. Happily Spitamenes was in the land of the Massagetæ, and not on hand to head the insurrection. And it may be characterized as another instance of "Alexander's luck" that about this time, mid-winter, the reinforcements above mentioned reached him.

It was in the early part of the year that the army broke up from Zariaspa, where were left in garrison some convalescent Companions, eighty mercenary cavalrymen and a few pages. Alexander sent the brigades of Polysperchon, Attalus, Gorgias and Meleager, now reinforced, in several detachments among the Bactrians to hold them in subjection, and to reduce to control that part of the land which was still in questionable humor ; and in order to cover as much ground in as short a space as possible, and have done with the matter once for all, divided the entire rest of his army into five flying columns, under Hephæstion, Ptolemy, son of Lagus, Perdiccas, Artabazus and Cœnus, and himself. There being

none but isolated bodies to contend with, this was a safe
enough proceeding. As the king approached the Oxus and
camped, a spring of water and oil (no doubt petroleum)
sprang up or was discovered beside his tent. From this circumstance the soothsayer, Aristander, foretold that victory,
but dearly bought, would be his meed in the present undertaking.

There are unfortunately few details of this campaign preserved to us. The Sogdianians had again committed the fatal

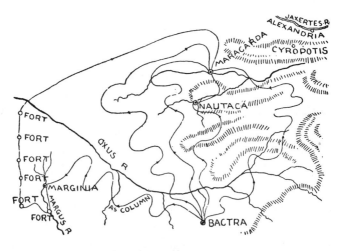

Five Column Campaign.

imprudence of taking to their fortified towns instead of relying on their usual desultory warfare, which it would have
puzzled the Macedonians infinitely more to meet. These five
columns swept to and fro across their land, very likely up and
down the Oxus and the Polytimetus and their affluents, reducing place after place, some by force and some by terms of
surrender, going as far as the Margus River and beyond,
and finally rendezvoused at Maracanda. According to Quintus Curtius, Alexander's column moved down the Oxus, and

thence up the Margus, as far as Marginia or Antiochia (modern Merv). Here he built six fortresses, two facing south and four west, to hold in check the Daäns from the vicinity of the Caspian Sea.

These several insurrections followed by their frightful retribution must have brought the Sogdianian land to the very verge of ruin. It had been essential that Alexander should subdue it thoroughly; it became essential that he should again populate it ; for the wars had transformed what had been a garden to the semblance of a desert. This duty Alexander committed to Hephæstion, who founded new cities, moved fresh inhabitants into them, and built up and fostered the agriculture of the land in every possible way. But it must have taken many years to bring back the thrifty condition of Sogdiana.

Although occurring some months later, the fate of Spitamenes may as well be detailed here.

Many places in the mountains on the north and east still remained unsubdued, and Alexander naturally feared that Spitamenes might again appear to fan the flame. Only a leader was wanting. From Maracanda, therefore, Alexander sent the column of Artabazus and Cœnus into Massagetan Scythia, whither he had heard that Spitamenes had fled, and assuming personal direction of the others, marched on the rebellious towns in Sogdiana, which were as yet unsubdued. After a campaign of marvelous marches, he reduced them to a full sense of their helplessness, and again returned to Maracanda. No details of this campaign exist.

Spitamenes had collected a force of six hundred Massagetan horsemen in addition to some of his old troops, and with these he made a descent on an outlying fort in Bactriana, garrisoned by Macedonians. This chieftain by no means lacked ability. He manœuvred so as to induce the garrison

to leave the fort, waylaid it by a cunning ambush, captured
the place, and slew every man. Emboldened by his success,
he advanced, burning and ravaging, to Zariaspa. He had
collected much booty, but declined to attack the town. A
few convalescent Companions, as above stated, constituted

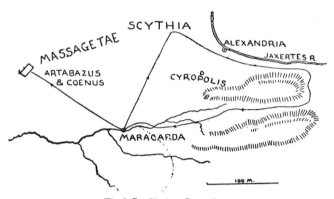

Final Sogdianian Campaign.

the paltry force at Zariaspa with a few attendants; but with
them was Peithon, son of Sosides, Aristonicus, eighty Greek
mercenary horsemen, and a few pages. These, though a
mere handful, were not to be dismayed. They sallied out,
fell opportunely upon the Scythians, gave them a sound beating, took away their booty, and slew a large number of them;
after which handsome work they were returning to Zariaspa,
supposing themselves beyond danger, and probably in loose
order, when they fell into an ambuscade, and lost seven Companions and sixty mercenary cavalrymen. Aristonicus was
killed. Peithon, wounded, fell into the enemy's hands. The
city barely escaped capture. Spitamenes threatened to make
trouble, when Craterus (where he was at the moment does
not appear), hearing of the situation by couriers, marched
against this chieftain, and he, conscious that he could not
meet regular troops, fled towards the desert with about one

thousand horsemen in his company. Craterus overtook him, and defeated him with a loss of one hundred and fifty men. The rest escaped.

About this time Amyntas was made viceroy of Bactria in place of Artabazus, who, ninety-seven years old, felt compelled to retire for age. This place had been intended for Clitus, whose unhappy fate will be detailed in the next chapter. Cœnus was left in Sogdiana for the winter with his own brigade and Meleager's taxis, four hundred Companions, the horse archers, and Amyntas' old command of Bactrians and Sogdianians. It was made the peculiar duty of Cœnus to watch for Spitamenes, who, finding Bactria too hot to hold him, was now wandering about the outskirts of Sogdiana.

While Hephæstion returned to Bactria to make arrangements for provisioning the troops during the coming winter, Alexander moved across the Polytimetus to Xenippa in pursuit of a number of the Bactrian and Sogdianian rebels. The Xenippians, fearing to be mixed up in the matter, refused their countrymen the usual hospitality. Some two thousand in number, these were compelled to turn and defend themselves, and after a severe struggle, in which they lost eight hundred men, they were obliged to sue for peace.

After this success, Alexander moved on the rock fortress of Sisimithres, the location of which is undetermined, but by some authorities is put at a distance of several hundred miles from Maracanda; and after much toil and danger — the march to the fort being as severe as the work of taking it — this also succumbed by capitulation.

Meanwhile, Spitamenes determined to make one last effort in Sogdiana. In addition to his own renegades, he had collected a force of three thousand Scythian horsemen eager for booty. These people, having no homes or cities, and ground

down by poverty, were always ready for raids in which there
was a prospect of profit. With this force, Spitamenes advanced to Bagæ, near the boundary of the Massagetans and
of Sogdiana. Cœnus, always ready for duty, marched out to
meet him, and in a sharp combat defeated him with eight
hundred killed to his own thirty-seven. The Bactrians and
Sogdianians with Spitamenes, recognizing the helplessness of
their cause, and out of patience with this luckless leader, surrendered in a body. The Scythians, after plundering their
baggage, fled with Spitamenes toward the desert. But many
returned to Cœnus, and gave themselves up. Learning shortly
after that Alexander was on the march toward them, these
same Scythians slew Spitamenes, and sent his head to the
king as a matter of conciliation. Quintus Curtius says that
his wife murdered Spitamenes, and brought his head to Alexander. The death of this persistent, treacherous and wily
foe gave final promise of peace to this territory. Only Dataphernes was left of all the conspirators, and him the Daäns
surrendered. Alexander was able to undertake substantial
measures towards replanting a country which has been called
the Garden of the Orient, but which had been absolutely des-
olated by the war.

Alexander.
(From a Coin in the British Museum.)

XXXVI.

CLITUS. WINTER, B. C. 329–328.

At Maracanda there was an attempt by some of the Greeks and Persians, much to the annoyance of the Macedonians, to introduce the custom of prostration on approaching Alexander, who had already begun largely to imitate the dress and manners of the Persian monarchs. This was partly a political desideratum, partly a very natural growth of vanity on Alexander's part. At a feast here, when much fulsome flattery had been indulged in, Clitus, excited with wine, let his natural repugnance to such servility get the better of him, and indulged in insulting and treasonable language. Alexander, at first patient and cool, finally allowed his anger to control him, and, seizing a spear, ran Clitus through the body. Repentance, however sincere, came too late. This same mood gave rise to a conspiracy of the pages, which was discovered and suppressed; and to the execution of the philosopher Callisthenes, for indulging in too much free speech. The discussion of this subject is not properly part of this volume.

It was at Maracanda, as Curtius informs us, during the winter preceding the death of Spitamenes, that the habit of intemperance to which Alexander, in his hours of leisure, was becoming too much addicted, began to produce its most lamentable results. The murder of Clitus at a drunken bout, for words spoken in the heat of wine, can be traced only to a lapse in self-control due to excess of vanity, and to rage largely the effect of overdrinking. The fact that such lapses were rare, and that they did not interfere with work to be done, cannot be warped into an excuse. This incident, unlike the conspiracy of Philotas, has properly nothing to do with the military history of Alexander; but it has been given so great prominence by most historians that it cannot well be skipped, especially as Clitus was one of the most distinguished of the

Macedonian leaders. The devotion of some pages to the matter will therefore be pardoned. As a touch in Alexander's portrait, the story is perhaps essential.

Alexander's assuming some portions of the Oriental dress and manners, and encouraging, or at least allowing, the Eastern custom of prostration on approaching his person, was no doubt partly another symptom of weakness as derogatory to his character as his occasional fits of intemperance; although the latter had no connection with political requirements, the former had. It was such lapses from moderation which gave rise, also, to the conspiracy of the pages and the execution of Callisthenes, the philosopher, and of Hermolaus.

Alexander had no doubt begun to suffer in personal character from his almost superhuman successes. His moral force had in nowise declined; but some of the petty traits of human nature had struggled through to the surface. This was natural enough. We have seen how violent were the passions and how strong the superstition he inherited from his mother. These had been increased by his career of victory to a very material extent. The priests of the oracle of Jupiter Ammon had deemed it wise to declare him descended from a god, and though it is improbable that Alexander actually gave credit to such an idea, he saw fit to use the oracle for political effect. His remarkable campaigns might well have inflated his ideas to the point of real belief in this oracular dictum; but there are many hints to the effect that among his friends he laughed at the proposition. He had begun to adopt the Eastern dress and customs for perfectly valid political reasons, but he had gone beyond the necessary or advisable, and had recently come to require a servility which his liberty-loving Macedonians gravely resented. To those who remembered the honest greatness of Philip, Alexander's claim to be descended from other loins than his had always been a distasteful morsel. And at an unhappy feast in Maracanda, on the day sacred to Bacchus, but when Alexander chose rather to sacrifice to Castor and Pollux, when the Macedonian habit of overdrinking had no doubt been indulged in by all to a much too great an extent, the first serious outbreak of this change of mood occurred.

Flatterers had been extolling Alexander, singing his Æacic lineage, and comparing him to the demi-gods. Clitus, son of Dropidas, the "black" one, commander of the agema of cavalry, no doubt strongly under the influence of liquor, but retaining sufficiently his ancient Macedonian manliness to be stung to the quick by this slur on his old and beloved king, harangued the party in the opposite strain, and told Alexander to his face that he owed his victories to the army Philip had created, and to the generals Philip had trained ; that Parmenio and Philotas, now dead by his hand, had done as much as — more than Alexander ; and that he, Clitus, had saved Alexander from death at the battle of the Granicus, — as was true. Of the two, Clitus was apparently the more heated by his drinking. It is alleged that Alexander stood these taunts with great patience and self-possession for some time, turning to a neighboring Greek with : " Do not you Greeks feel among us Macedonians like demi-gods among beasts ? " But if Clitus' words and manner were to the last degree insulting to the man, how much more to the king ? Nothing better illustrates the meaning of the word " Companion " than Alexander's tolerance of so much. No monarch of modern times ever allowed a subject so much laxity of tongue. At all times in the world's history, such intemperate language would be treason punishable with death. Finally, infuriated at the continued flow of such language, Alexander started to his feet. Clitus was removed by his friends. Harmony was about to be restored. But on Clitus returning into the hall with a

fresh taunt, Alexander, after vain attempts to restrain him
by his companions, seized a pike and ran Clitus through the
body. His subsequent grief was as violent as his fatal act,
but repentance, though creditable to his feelings, was no
excuse for his murderous transport of rage.

In this place it may be as well to say a word about the
alleged desire of Alexander that prostration should be practiced before him as was usual before Persian monarchs. The
Orientals at the court naturally continued to Alexander that
obeisance which they were habituated to practice to their own
sovereigns. It was not less naturally irksome to them to see
that the Greeks and Macedonians approached this humbler
of the Great King as if he were indeed but a companion.
Whatever the really strongest underlying motive may have
been, this difference led to difficulties which the wisest policy
might have been puzzled to remove. It is certain that many
of his nearest Macedonian friends had agreed that the Eastern
habit of prostration should be introduced among all. The
bulk of the Macedonians held this practice in abhorrence,
though some few Greeks and Macedonians had already
adopted it. At a banquet in Zariaspa, no doubt with Alexander's privity, there was an attempt made by a party of which
some noted Greek philosophers and literary men were members, to introduce the custom by a surprise, in the hope that
once adopted by the majority, under whatever circumstances,
the active opposition to it would cease. In the speeches at
this banquet, Alexander was compared by the philosopher
Anaxarchus to Bacchus and Hercules, and those who favored
the plan, joined in this fulsome adulation, as well as actually
prostrated themselves. Most of the Macedonians were dis-
gusted at both speech and act, but remembering the fate of
Clitus, deemed it prudent to abstain from criticism.

Especially two philosophers were prominent in Alexander's

court: Callisthenes, who told Alexander that not his descent from Zeus, but what he himself should write in history would make him famous or the reverse ; and Anaxarchus of Abdera, who was of quite another mould, a man of the world, practiced in flattery, and wont to eulogize to over-satiety. It was he who, after the murder of Clitus, told the king in the way of comfort that the son of Zeus could do no wrong. The philosopher Callisthenes was bold enough to take this matter of prostration up. He was the pupil and nephew of Aristotle, at whose request indeed he had accompanied Alexander, as witness of his deeds, and their future historian. There was always a large number of artists, historians, philosophers and actors among other professional men in the suite of Alexander, who delighted to have those about him who could record and illustrate his deeds, and sincerely enjoyed their society. Callisthenes on this occasion, though invited by Hephæstion to join the rest in performing the act of worship, refused, and gave publicly the reasons of his refusal. Nothing was said or done at the time. This act was imprudent, no doubt, but full of moral courage. Callisthenes became a marked man.

About this same time there was a plot among the pages, led by Hermolaus, son of Sopolis, whom the king had punished for misbehavior with stripes and dismounting, probably aware that Hermolaus was imbued with too much of the extreme Macedonian spirit. Hermolaus and Sostratos, son of Amyntas, plotted to murder Alexander the next time the turn came to them to watch at his bedside. Four others joined the conspiracy. But on that night, as it happened, Alexander sat late at supper, induced thereto, it is said, by the advice of a female soothsayer who followed the camp, and the plot fell through. Before the next opportunity arrived, the plot was divulged. The guilty pages were seized, and implicated Callisthenes. The army, as usual, judged and executed the pages. Callisthenes, not a Macedonian, was kept imprisoned, and is said by Aristobulus, to have died in prison; by Ptolemy, to have been hanged. The antagonism of Callisthenes, Alexander is said to have ascribed to his old teacher, Aristotle, whom he now remembered with feelings of not unmixed affection. These are among the pages which are well quickly shut. So restless under freedom of speech had Alexander become, it has been observed, that it is hard to say whether his periods of rest were not more dangerous to his friends than his marches and campaigns to his enemies.

Perhaps all this is out of place in a volume which makes no pretense to being a history of the man or king Alexander or of his times, but is merely a narration of the deeds of the soldier, as illustrative of the growth of the art of war. It is difficult, however, to pass over such grave personal incidents, or to divorce the man with his weaknesses from the captain with his glorious achievements.

Alexander.
(From a Coin in the British Museum.)

XXXVII.

ROXANA. WINTER, B. C. 328–327.

HEADQUARTERS for the winter were at Nautaca. Complaints of mismanagement began to come in, and a number of changes were found to be necessary among the satraps of the provinces in the rear. Bactria and Sogdiana were now definitely reduced, except a few rocky fastnesses to which some of the unreconstructed chiefs had retired. Oxyartes had fortified himself in the Rock of Arimazes. The march thither was very laborious, and the place seemed beyond capture; but it was taken by the bold feat of some Macedonian mountaineers, who escaladed the perpendicular sides of the rock, and terrified the garrison into surrender. Here Roxana, daughter of Oxyartes, was captured; her beauty and grace led Alexander an equal captive, and he soon after married her. Thence Alexander moved by an equally toilsome and longer march to the Rock of Chorienes on the upper Oxus. This was also surrendered after the bold bridging of a difficult ravine. Both Oxyartes and Chorienes Alexander made his friends and viceroys. Craterus finished the remaining work by defeating in battle both Catanes and Austanes. Sogdiana was completely subdued, and the entire region beyond the Oxus was left under a freer form of government, the rulers and people being given a species of independence.

WINTER was approaching. The various detachments under Cœnus and Craterus now rejoined Alexander at Nautaca, where he had finally taken up winter-quarters. Phrataphernes, from Parthia, and Stasanor, from Aria, likewise reported. A number of changes were made in the command of the satrapies. Phrataphernes was sent to replace and arrest Autophradates, satrap of Mardia and Tarpuria, who had neglected to repair to headquarters when ordered so to do. Stasanor was sent to Drangia in command. Atropates replaced Oxydates in Media. Stamenes was made satrap of Babylonia, vice Mazæus, deceased. Sopolis, Menedas, and Epocillus were sent to Macedonia to recruit.

Arrangements looking to an Indian campaign were seriously begun. It was hoped that this might be undertaken early in the coming summer, so soon, in fact, as the melting of the snows should have sufficiently opened the mountain passes.

Bactria was quiet. Sogdiana had been reduced to submission, and thenceforth remained so. The exceptions were only one or two strongholds, where the last relics of opposition had collected. But these in nowise affected the general sentiment of the country. Oxyartes, an influential Bactrian, had conveyed his family for safety to the Sogdian Rock, or Rock of Arimazes, in Sogdiana, a fastness which was supposed to be quite impregnable, and was victualed for a long siege. The snow furnished abundance of water.

Alexander opened operations early. The march was full of difficulties. Storms were very severe. One is mentioned by Quintus Curtius in which one thousand men perished from cold and exposure; and Diodorus details the energy and courage displayed by Alexander in cheering his men to those exertions by which alone they could save themselves. The severity of the climate corresponds with what travelers tell us of this trans-Caucasian region to-day.

The snow was not yet off the ground when Alexander appeared before the place. This rock was very high; its sides were almost perpendicular, and an assault promised utter failure. It was absurd to attempt one. How to begin siege operations was a question no one could answer. There seemed to be no approach; the one road up the rock could be held by a dozen men. The snow made treacherous footing for the Macedonians if they attempted to climb the rock. But the difficulty of the situation made the king all the more determined; "for," says Arrian, "a certain overweening and insolent boast uttered by the barbarians had thrown him into a state of ambitious pertinacity." On being summoned to surrender, with promise of free exit and safety, the garrison laughingly replied that they feared only winged soldiers. This whetted Alexander's ambition.

The fortress was probably built on a rock jutting out from the side of a mountain, — for there was a precipice overhanging the fortress. But its sides were perpendicular. If

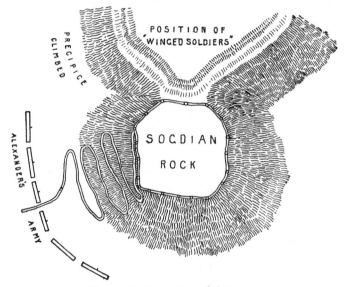

Sogdian Rock, or Rock of Arimazes.

this precipice could be gained, it would dominate the enemy's position. Alexander sent a herald through the camp, offering prizes to such men as would essay to scale the rocks; twelve talents (fourteen thousand five hundred dollars) to the first who succeeded, nine to the second, and so on, down to three hundred Darics (eleven hundred dollars); and excited the ambition of many. Of those who were expert climbers, having learned in sieges and mountain training how to scale walls and cliffs, three hundred in number volunteered.

They provided themselves with ropes, took their iron tent pegs, and selecting the most dangerous, because least watched, spot, began the ascent at midnight, by driving the pegs into the crevices of the rocks, or into the ice or frozen ground. The operation was hazardous in the extreme, and thirty of the climbers fell and were killed. The inaccessibility of the ledges is shown by the fact that none of the bodies could be recovered for burial. But by dawn the heights were occupied, and the men made great parade of themselves, waving their white scarfs in token of success.

Alexander now pointed out his "winged soldiers" to the garrison, sent a herald towards the gate, and again called on Oxyartes to surrender. The position gained may not have had any peculiar value in compelling this; but, astonished beyond measure at being thus outdone, and imagining the men on the rocks above to be much more numerous than they actually were, and fully armed, the whole thing savoring, moreover, of the supernatural, with which Alexander's name was uniformly connected, the demand was complied with.

Among the many captives, male and female, was the daughter of Oxyartes, Roxana, said by the Macedonians who saw her to be the most beautiful woman of the East, since Statira, wife of Darius, was dead. She fell as captive to Alexander. But the king is stated to have fallen an equal and honest captive to her charms. He treated her with all becoming dignity, — as he had Statira, — and shortly afterwards married her. This side of Alexander's character is wholly admirable. Oxyartes was not only forgiven, but received into highest favor.

One other place remained, the Rock of Chorienes, in the land of the Parætacians, which was the mountainous region of the upper Oxus. Here Chorienes himself, and many other chiefs, had retired for refuge. There is a great deal of disagreement as to where the Rock of Cho001enes was situated. It has not been any more positively located than hosts of other places where Alexander performed his remarkable exploits. Though its conformation is carefully described by the ancient authors, its whereabouts are not given. This region, indeed, is not well known to geographers. Colonel Chesney locates this rock, or the " Rock of Oxyartes," near the southeast shore of the Caspian Sea. Droysen puts it on the upper waters of the Oxus, seven hundred miles farther east. There is no means of reconciling this extraordinary disagreement, nor object in trying so to do, but probably the rock was to the east rather than to the west of the Sogdo-Bactrian country.

The march to this fortress was, in any event, over snow-clad mountains, and was a most severe one. The men suffered terribly from cold storms and lack of food. Many were frozen, many died of exposure. The king, as usual, shared the labors of his men in every sense, but could not lessen their sufferings. It seems that a march to the westward, where the land was less in altitude, would not have been so severe at this time of year. For it was early spring.

These mountain marches of Alexander are all in the highest degree remarkable. He appeared able to surmount any and all difficulties. The pity is that we know so little about their details. Anecdotes survive when important details have failed of record. It is related that one day on this march, when the king was warming himself at the camp-fire, a Macedonian, almost frozen stiff, was brought in. The king himself helped to take off his armor and gave him his own place at the fire, where the man revived. Coming to consciousness, the soldier was wonder-struck and frightened to find himself in the king's place. " Look you, comrade," quoth Alexander, "among the Persians, to sit on the king's seat entails death. To you, a Macedonian, it has brought life."

This remarkable rock of Chorienes is described as about seven miles (sixty stades) in circumference at the base. A difficult, narrow, winding road, artificially made, easily defended, and something over two miles (twenty stades) long, was its sole outlet. This was not easy of ascent, which must be made in single file, even when no one barred the way. The only height near by, from which the rock

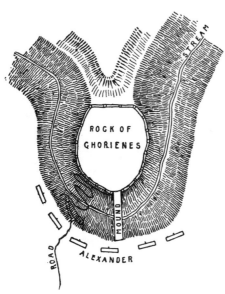

Rock of Chorienes.

could be approached, was separated from it by a deep ravine through which rushed a violent mountain torrent. This must be bridged by a causeway in order to get near the walls. Arrian says the ravine ran all round the rock. The place in question was probably the only spot high enough to operate from. Though it was deemed entirely impracticable, Alexander nevertheless undertook the task. From the height mentioned, the soldiers were obliged to use ladders to descend into the ravine, the walls of which were very steep. These ladders were made by cutting down the pine-trees, which were here abundant and lofty.

Once in the ravine, Alexander began to build up a sort of

trestle-work of covered galleries, the whole army working at it, one half by day, under superintendence of Alexander, and the other half in three watches by night, under the somato-phylaxes Perdiccas, Leonnatus, and Ptolemy, son of Lagus. With all their efforts, but thirty feet could be built during the day; at night the stint was less. In the narrowest part of the ravine they drove piles, close enough to sustain great weight. On these they constructed a sort of bridge of hur-dles, woven of willows and osiers, and this was covered with earth. The barbarians began by deriding these efforts; but when they saw the structure rise, and covered in such a man-ner with screens and roofs, that, although below them, they could not harm the Macedonians; while these, from engines and with bows and slings, covered them with missiles, — which, being of better material and construction, killed and wounded many, — they changed their tone. Chorienes sent to Alexander, asking that he might see and consult his an-cient ally, Oxyartes. This was granted, and Oxyartes, quot-ing his own case as example, so entirely impressed Chori-enes with the idea of Alexander's justice, as well as his ability to do anything he set his hand to, that Chorienes concluded to surrender. He came to Alexander, who received him with the utmost kindness, entertained him in his own tent, and sent messengers to receive the surrender. Next day the king, accompanied by five hundred hypaspists, inspected the rock and fortress. So large a store of victuals had Chorienes in this fastness, that he was able for a period of two months to ration Alexander's entire army, giving them corn, salt meat, and wine; and this consumed but a tenth part of the stores laid up in the rock. The aid was opportune, for Alexander was sadly lacking in supplies, and during the siege much snow had fallen, making the hardships of the operation ex-cessive. Alexander made Chorienes his friend, and continued him in command as his viceroy of all he had ruled before.

Alexander now returned to Bactra, and dispatched Craterus with six hundred Companions and four brigades, his own and those of Polysperchon, Attalus and Alcestas, against the only two remaining rebels in this Parætacenian mountain district, Catanes and Austanes. Craterus did his work well. He was growing to be one of Alexander's best generals. These chiefs were defeated in a bloody battle, in which Catanes and sixteen hundred men were killed, and Austanes was captured. This event ended the subjugation of the territory. Craterus returned to Bactra. Spring had now come.

For two years Alexander had been laboring to reduce this trans-Caucasian territory to a condition something like submission. He had found the people of an entirely different stamp from the inhabitants of the plains. In this most eastern land he had encountered the fiercest opposition ever made to him, and he had all but reduced a flourishing land to a desert — to a condition which only the care of years could improve — before he could call it his own. He found, too, that different measures were desirable to keep this land in subjection from those employed elsewhere. Alexander endeavored to leave the trans-Oxian region under a sort of dependent king. There are few details given of just what was done, or who was left in power. Sogdiana, filled with newly grounded Greek cities, and having Bactria and Margiana as a sort of reserve force in its rear, made a perfect bulwark against the incursions of the roving Scythians. Alexander carried with him no less than thirty thousand youths from Bactria and Sogdiana to serve not only as soldiers, but equally as hostages for the good behavior of their native land. It is far from improbable that the marriage with Roxana was as much a bold stroke of policy as it was a case of love at first sight. For her father's great influence could perhaps accomplish more towards keeping the population quiet than his own arms. By his union with Roxana he began in his own person that blending of the Occident and the Orient which was his favorite scheme. It was also from this idea that grew his assumption of a part Eastern dress and habits and the public insistence upon his descent from the gods. But this, however essential for the Eastern ear, he was, it is said by many, wont to scoff at with his closest friends.

The Macedonian soldier had changed too, in these six years' campaigns. From the independent but simple and well-disciplined shepherd-soldier, he had grown to be, as it were, one of the owners of the boundless wealth and luxury of the mighty East. As such he had acquired a self-esteem, an overweening sense of his own importance, which under any other commander would have been fraught with grave danger; but underlying this feeling was a still stronger sentiment, which may indeed be said to have been his one impulse, — a passionate love for his godlike young king, for the chief who was foremost in all dangers; superior to all in his personal gallantry, his superhuman endurance of fatigue, hunger, thirst; who was kinsman of the common soldier while he was easily lord of the phalangiarch; who, from his personal beauty to the gigantic grasp of his intellect, from his heroic daring to his divine military genius, was distinctly the first of soldiers — the first of men. No wonder, indeed. And while these Macedonians might criticise and bluster and browbeat, there was yet never a moment during Alexander's whole reign when, from the least to the greatest, each and every man in his army would not without thought or hesitation have laid his life at the feet of his beloved chief. This wonderful superiority, indeed, is the reason why Alexander's lieutenants have themselves less personal prominence; their own individ-

ual rays were swallowed up in the greater refulgence of the
central light. " Thus the noble Craterus, who, as it is said,
loved the king; the gentle Hephæstion who loved Alexander;
thus the ever reliable and duty-doing Ptolemy, son of Lagus;
the quiet, through and through faithful Cœnus; the calculating Lysimachus." The Macedonian hoplite, the artist, poet,
philosopher who followed the camp-court, the Persian noble,
each stands out in history in bolder personal relief than the
most efficient of Alexander's generals. It is wont to be thus
with all great captains.

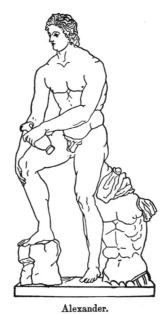

Alexander.

(From a Statue in the Glyptothek in Munich.)

XXXVIII.

THE COPHEN COUNTRY. MAY, B. C. 327, TO WINTER.

DURING the spring of B. C. 327, Alexander set out for India, a sort of fairy-land to all Greeks. From some Indian princes who had come to him with embassies of peace he had discovered that the Cophen cuts its passage through the mountain ranges to the Indus, in a narrow defile which formed, as it were, the Gates of India. With some hundred thousand men he left Zariaspa, and crossed the Caucasus to Alexandria. Thence, in two columns he advanced down the Cophen. The lesser column marched down the south bank, subduing the narrow strip of land between the river and the mountains, with orders to meet the king at the Indus. With his own column he moved along the north bank, and by sending detachments up each valley, and holding its outlet, he subdued the peoples of these mountains. This campaign in the mountain snows was very severe on the men, and cost much toil. A number of minor battles and sieges were among its features, and Alexander showed again and again how remarkable he was as a mountain fighter. He was twice wounded during this campaign. At Massaga, especially, he had a difficult problem, being repeatedly repulsed by Indian mercenary troops from the walls of the city. Finally all the barbarians abandoned the cities, and fled for refuge to the Rock of Aornus.

SPRING being well advanced, Alexander began to make definite arrangements for his expedition to India. Only Bacchus and Hercules had preceded him on this route. This country had always been a species of fairyland to the western nations. Shut out from access on the north and west by the greatest of mountain chains, it was a rare person, in the days of Alexander, who had ever reached the land of Brahma. Its wealth and glories were known only from the tales of merchants. Probably then at the height of its glory, these reports had been enough to excite the cupidity as well as the curiosity of Alexander, beyond any other land, and having got so near, he was bound to tread its sacred soil. He had discovered by good fortune, added to his native keenness, the best gate through the protecting mountain chain from Persia to the Indian plains, viz., the roadbed of the river Cophen, which plows between walls of rock through a narrow precipitous valley, from the parched uplands of Central Asia to the smiling levels of India. As Strabo expresses it, Alexander discovered India, and in view of the ignorance of geography at that day, the phrase is not inappropriate. At the outlet of the Cophen valley, the Five Rivers make a fresh boundary to the interior, and beyond them, Alexander knew, lay the head waters of the Ganges, the holy stream of India. Of the Ganges, Alexander had no doubt heard more than of any other feature of the country, and he believed that he could easily reach this river, which, as he heard, would conduct him to the great ocean, the confines of the world.

The Aryans had wandered from the upland plains, where they originated, through this very pass. Some had gone as far as the Ganges; some no farther than the Cophen valley. When Assyria grew strong, she conquered the Aryan uplands, still inhabited by a part of the race, but "Semiramis saw," it is related, "the camels of the Western steppes fly from before the elephants of the Indian East at the bridge over the Indus." The Medes came after the Assyrians, then the Persians. Cyrus claimed fealty from Gandara; Darius sent a Greek to the Indus, who sailed down the river to the sea, and then returned through the Arabian Gulf. A few Indians served at Gaugamela under Bessus and Barsaëntes; but beyond the Indus the Great King had never pretended to extend his grasp. There was a patchwork of independent states along the borders of the Five Rivers down to the sea and eastward to the desert. Kingdoms and republics vied in making a turmoil of political divisions.

Alexander had practically finished his military expedition, when he reached the limits of the Persian Empire. But several things, added to his restless ambition, combined to carry him onward. His reasons are not usually given in the authorities ; the event tells the story. The king of Taxila, who was at war with Porus, lord of the region beyond the Hydaspes, had invited Alexander to come to his help. And Sisicottus, king of a land near the Indus, had joined Alexander after the fall of Bessus, and had since been faithful to him. From such persons as these Alexander not only received much information concerning India, but from intercourse with them had drunk in a deep longing to invade it.

Alexander's force at this moment is hard to calculate. Plutarch gives it as one hundred and thirty-five thousand men in the campaign down the Indus. It is probable that despite his losses, the large accessions of recruits from Macedonia, probably those classes owing military service whose turn had come for active duty, soldiers of fortune from Greece, Thrace, Agriania and other sources — about one hundred and fifty thousand men in all reached him from home — had at the present moment more than doubled the small army of thirty-five thousand men with which he crossed the Hellespont. Added to these, were large numbers of Oriental recruits embodied in the cavalry and phalanx. Many troops were drawn from the satrapies in the rear, which, in their turn, drew fresh men from home to replace the lost. Thus were repaired the enormous losses in battle, by severity of climate and the heavy marching of six long years. But there must be taken into consideration the very heavy garrisons Alexander was obliged to leave behind. In Bactria alone, as a sample, ten thousand foot and thirty-five hundred horse had been stationed. We know that he replaced these garrisons largely by levies from the warlike tribes he had just conquered ; that Phœnicia, Cyprus,

Egypt each furnished its contingent; and Curtius says that
his total effective, a year later, on the Indus, was one hundred and twenty thousand under the colors. In this army
were all manner of soldiers, horse and foot from Arachotia,
the Parapamisus, Bactria, Sogdiana, Scythians and Daäns,
all showing a marked fealty to the conqueror, if furnishing
elements perhaps difficult to control.

The force was no longer an Hellenic army. It was an
army of Orientals with but a leaven of the old Macedonian
element, moulded into the Macedonian organization and
curbed by the Macedonian discipline. That Alexander was
able to weld these diverse elements into a shape which gave
the results he thereafter obtained from it; that he dared to
trust himself and his work to a body so largely alien ; that he
was able to fight such a battle as the one against Porus and
win it, speaks more than volumes for this wonderful man's
organizing ability and self-confidence. But Alexander never
for a moment doubted his ability to do anything to which he
put his hand. If his vanity was overstrained, he possessed
the complementary virtue of self-reliance as perhaps no other
man has ever had it.

The force left with Amyntas in Bactria, was, in the present condition of the land, abundantly able to hold the restless
tribes north of the Caucasus in subjection. Alexander himself set out from Zariaspa at the end of spring, with perhaps
something over one hundred thousand men. The roads were
now better than when the army toiled over the mountains two
years back, and provisions had been accumulated in abundance. A ten days' march, it is probable by the shorter pass
of Kushan, took him across the mountains to Alexandria ad
Caucasum. Here he found good cause to be disappointed at
the management of affairs, and deemed it essential to make
sundry changes in government. Neiloxinus, the commander

of the garrison, as well as Proëxes, the satrap of the region, were both removed. The king left a number of invalided Macedonians as colonists, settled some of the native tribes in the place, and appointed Tyriaspes viceroy of Parapamisus, and Nicanor military governor of the city. He then marched to Nicea, where he offered sacrifice to Athena as was his wont at the beginning of every new campaign, and began his advance towards the Indus, down the Cophen and through the gate of rock at the easterly boundary of the Parapamisus level.

On the south side of the Cophen (modern Cabul) River lie the outpost ranges of the Sufeid-Kuh, which make one side of a narrow valley two hundred and fifty miles long, as the crow flies, from Nicea to the Indus, and dwindling to a defile forty miles long from Dhaka to Peshawur. To the north bank, mountains come down in huge scallops from Kafiristan. The Choës or Choaspes, the Euaspla and the Guræus with numerous tributaries here descend in narrow valleys from the Caucasus or western Himalayas. The whole course of the Cophen is through a huge but well defined gorge, with immense masses of mountains on either hand.

Alexander sent heralds ahead to the chiefs of the Indian tribes living along the Cophen, ordering them to report to him with hostages in proof of their submission. The king of Taxila, whom Curtius calls Omphis, and a number of native princes came to headquarters in royal state, accompanied by elephants, which they placed at the king's disposal, and bearing splendid and unusual presents in token of their readiness to serve him. Alexander informed these princes that he expected to exhaust the summer and autumn months in reducing the country between him and the Indus, to winter on that river, and the next year to cross over and chastise the nations beyond, enemies of his new associates. As it turned out, the following winter was consumed in mountain campaigning along the Cophen. He had illy gauged the size of his task in this alpine region.

At Nicea Alexander divided his army into two columns. He detached Hephæstion and Perdiccas along the right bank of the Cophen, through the land of Gandara, towards Peucelaotis on the direct road to the Indus, with the three brigades

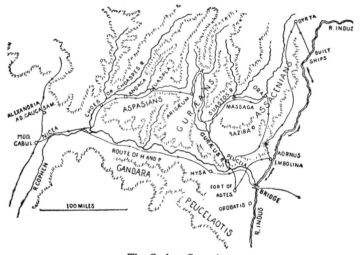

The Cophen Campaign.

of Gorgias, Clitus (the white one) and Meleager, half the Companion and all the Greek mercenary cavalry. They had orders to reduce the towns on the route, and when they reached the Indus to make preparations for bridging it. The king of Taxila and some other chiefs were to be their guides. This corps was to be a flying wing, as it were, of the army of the king, who, taking a more northerly route, proposed to reduce all the strongholds in the mountain passes on the north bank of the Cophen, which region was full of warlike native tribes, marching from pass to pass, and completing his work thoroughly as he advanced. The two columns would prevent the tribes north and south of the river from combining to assist each other, and either column could retire upon the other in case of disaster.

On the way Hephæstion and Perdiccas were delayed a month by the so-called revolt of Astes, king of Peucelaotis, who retired into his fortified city. This it became necessary to besiege, but the place was captured and Astes was killed during the hostilities. Sangæus, who had deserted Astes, was left as viceroy. Beyond this Hephæstion and Perdiccas had little trouble. They easily pacified the country, whose inhabitants were evidently far from warlike, marched to the Indus, which they reached while the king was still struggling through the mountains, and made all due preparation against his arrival, by collecting provision and materials for a bridge. The land they protected by garrisoning the fortress of Astes and Orobatis.

The king meanwhile led the bulk of the army over the much more difficult northerly route on the other side of the Cophen. His task was to reduce such of the mountain tribes there dwelling as would be necessary to secure and make permanent his control of the valley of this river. He had with him the shield-bearing guards, the other half of the Companion cavalry, the phalanx, except what marched with Hephæstion and Perdiccas, the foot-agema, the archers, Agrianians, and horse lancers. With these he first marched into the land of the Aspasians, next to which was that of the Guræans and beyond them the domain of the Assacenians. On the river Choës or Choaspes (probably the modern Kama) — some geographers make these separate streams — which rises from the glaciers of the Caucasus, and flows through an almost inaccessible valley with towering mountain masses on either hand, Alexander learned that most of the neighboring barbarians had fled for refuge into the cities of that country, which were situated well up the valley. Their capital lay some days' march up stream. The Aspasians were herders, and very rich in flocks. From the upper end of the valley was a pass to the head waters of the Oxus, by way of which constant intercourse was kept up between these tribes and the Sogdianians. It was highly important to gain control of this capital, as the key of this section of country.

Anxious to settle the question quickly, Alexander crossed the river, and advanced along the farther bank with a van consisting of the cavalry and eight hundred Macedonian infantry mounted on horses, towards these strongholds. The chronology of Curtius is apt to be inaccurate, but he says that Alexander used pontoons in this campaign. "Now, as there were several rivers to pass, they so contrived the boats that they might be taken to pieces and carried in wagons, and put together again as occasion required." Other authors mention this first on the farther side of the Indus. In any event, the invention was made about this time. At the first town, whose name is not given us, the barbarians drew up outside the walls to oppose him; but without waiting to rest or for the balance of the troops to come up, Alexander attacked, quickly routed them, and drove them into the gates. He himself received a shot through the breastplate in the shoulder, and Ptolemy and Leonnatus were also wounded. This arrested further operations for that day. The army went into camp near the place where an assault seemed to promise the best results.

From the nature of Alexander's wounds, we can, after a fashion, judge what the usual wounds of the Macedonians in combat with the barbarians were apt to be. No doubt Alexander's armor was of finer make, and protected him better than that of the ordinary soldier. As a rule, his wounds were such as to heal readily; and, with his inflexible will and wonderful good health, he was not wont to be long laid up. The same rule will apply to the average of the soldiers. There were probably many wounded who scarcely went off duty; who certainly kept with their commands or with the train, even if relegated to easy work or none for a shorter or longer period.

The town in question had a double wall, and was stoutly defended. The next morning the rest of the troops arrived. An attack was made. The barbarians could not resist the Macedonian onset. The outer wall, not being very substantial, was at once taken. The inner wall was more difficult, but was defended only a few hours after the ladders were brought into use. As usual, the better weapons and good defensive armor of the Macedonian heavy troops gave the barbarians no chance. The Macedonians were comparatively safe from wounds, as well as under the best of discipline. The barbarians were wise enough to make their exit while they might by the rear gates, and fled to the mountains. Here they were followed up, and many of their number overtaken and slain. Alexander's men, in revenge for their leader's wound, razed the city to the ground. Marching to the next town, named Andaca, Alexander gained possession of it by capitulation, the inhabitants being appalled by the summary fate of their neighbor.

Alexander saw that by holding with suitable forts the outlets of these valleys, he could readily control the valleys themselves, and by carefully blockading them, reduce their inhabitants to terms in his own good time. He therefore left Craterus with an ample heavy infantry force to continue the reduction of the minor towns, place garrisons in them, and arrange the affairs of the country as best might seem to him, and then, by a lower pass over the mountains nearer the Cophen River, to join him in the valley of the Guræus (modern Pandj Kora).

Two marches then brought Alexander to Euaspla on the river of the same name, where dwelt the chief of the Aspasians. Learning of his approach, the Aspasians set fire to their city, and fled into the highlands. The king and his bodyguard led the flight, full of terror. Alexander followed sharply, and slew a great number of the fugitives. Hotly pushing the pursuit, and recognizing the Aspasian king a short distance ahead on an eminence, surrounded by his bodyguard, Ptolemy, the ground being steep, dismounted his men, rushed after with a few hypaspists, and brought him to bay. A hand to hand fight took place. The Indian king thrust his spear through Ptolemy's breastplate, but the weapon stopped there; Ptolemy's pike transfixed the Indian king through both thighs, inflicting a mortal wound. The others fled; but when Ptolemy was despoiling the Indian of his arms, the bodyguard, ashamed to desert their king, turned upon him. Alexander, having seized the hill on which the barbarians had stood, came to the rescue with his agema, and here Ptolemy and Alexander engaged in individual combat with the barbarians over the corpse of their leader in true Homeric fashion. The advantage remained with Alexander and Ptolemy. The barbarians beat a hasty retreat. Events such as this have perhaps no bearing on the military question, but they serve to show the individual nature of combats in that age, and in so far explain some of those characteristics of both soldier and leader which are otherwise difficult to understand. We cannot but regret that instead of these personal recollections, Ptolemy has not told us more about how this campaign was really conducted. Alexander was leading a large army; the narration of some of the operations sounds like the work of a bare brigade. What he accomplished was wonderful; all we can do is to trace his itinerary.

From this place Alexander advanced over the mountain

passes to Arigæum, which he found burned. Here Craterus joined him by the more southerly route mentioned, having left the region of Andaca well provided for. Him again Alexander put in charge of Arigæum, which was a convenient and promising place for a settlement, instructing him to rebuild and colonize the town afresh with some of the invalided Macedonians and with well-disposed natives, and to fortify it strongly. For this city and Andaca commanded the valley heads of the Choës, Guræus and many intervening rivers and streams; and the possession of strong places at these two points gave Alexander substantial control of nearly all the passes in the uplands, and thus left no opposition or danger between him and Sogdiana. But the thoroughness of this method of working consumed much time.

Some tribes north of Arigæum had rendezvoused with the fugitives from this vicinity at a point farther up the mountains, and threatened trouble to the new city. Alexander saw that he must leave the garrison he proposed to place in Arigæum free from risk of attack for some time, and took up his march against them. While on the way, Ptolemy, having preceded the army on a foraging and reconnoitring expedition, returned with news that a very large force of barbarians was near at hand, lying on a mountain side, with camp fires vastly outnumbering Alexander's. The barbarians of the whole adjoining territory had, it seems, joined forces, their spirits by no means cowed by the loss of their town. A part of his army Alexander left in reserve, encamped at the foot of the mountain, and marched with a force which he judged sufficient towards the barbarians.

When he had reached their vicinity, he divided his forces into three parts: under Ptolemy, who took a third of the hypaspists, the brigades of Philip and Philotas, two squadrons of horse-archers, the Agrianians and half the other cavalry;

Leonnatus, with his own, Attalus' and Balacrus' brigades; and himself, leading the phalanx and the cavalry Companions. Alexander advanced on what seemed to be the strongest part of the barbarians' line, sending Ptolemy and Leonnatus each by a hidden circuit, to take post where they could

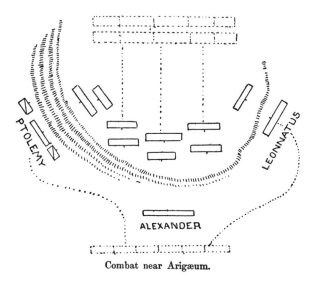

Combat near Arigæum.

attack on either flank when the barbarians should have placed themselves at a disadvantage; for the king designed to lure them into an ambush. Perceiving the small force of Macedonians under Alexander, and not aware of the flank detachments, the barbarians came down from their stronghold to the plain, expecting an easy victory over such a meagre body. But they had never yet encountered Macedonian discipline, and reaching Alexander's steady handful while in loose order from their hasty advance, they broke to pieces on the sarissas of the phalanx.

Ptolemy and Leonnatus now attacked opportunely on the flanks. Ptolemy was placed opposite a rugged ascent, and encountered heavy resistance. The barbarians perceived his advance, and met him with unusual vigor. The natives here, whom Arrian calls Indians because dwelling near the Indus, were strong, bold and active, and made a stanch defense. But Ptolemy formed column of assault, and, though checked, finally carried the hill by storm. Leonnatus won an easier success. Thus closed in on both their flanks, and sharply thrown back from their front attack, the Indians lost heart, threw down their arms, and were surrounded and captured to the number of forty thousand. This number is the one given by Ptolemy, though it seems exaggerated. The country, however, was thickly populated. All their cattle, said to be two hundred and thirty thousand in number, were also corralled. These were of such excellent quality for size, strength, activity and for easy fattening, that Alexander picked out the best, and sent them to Macedonia to breed from. This is the origin of the hump still seen on the cattle in parts of Greece.

Craterus now joined with the forces under his command and the military engines, after settling the affair of Arigæum, and, with the whole army, Alexander advanced down the Guræus, intending to move into the territory of the Assacenians, who, in the next adjoining valley of the Suastos, were said to have assembled twenty thousand cavalry, thirty thousand infantry and thirty elephants. Alexander hurried forward with the van, Craterus followed more slowly with the heavy train and engines.

The army had been campaigning in an alpine region. The entire route of the king's column from Alexandria ad Caucasum thus far towards the Indus had been through a mountainous and difficult country, entailing much exertion on the men, excessive hardships and frequent lack of rations. The present descent to the smiling lowlands must have been an agreeable change. The route lay along the right bank of

the Guræus. The barbarians attempted to defend this river
at a point where they might have given Alexander much
trouble, for it is swift and with a rocky bed, which afforded
a poor footing to troops crossing under fire; but overawed
by the firm front of the Macedonians, they retired, each
party to its own city, and decided to defend their homes in
lieu of risking a general battle in the open field.

It is curious that savage or semi-civilized nations so often
commit the mistake of standing a siege, or of delivering a battle, in lieu of resorting to small war. In the latter, especially
on their own soil, they are not unapt to be on a par with the
best troops; in the former, with equal bravery, they uniformly fail against the better weapons and discipline, or the
greater technical skill, of the civilized armies.

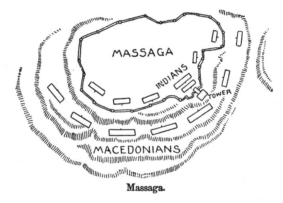

Massaga.

Alexander now marched on Massaga, the largest town and
capital of the Assacenians. The barbarians had hired a force
of seven thousand Indian mercenaries, and emboldened by
their presence, — for apparently these professional soldiers
were held in high repute, and deservedly, — they undertook
to make a sudden attack on Alexander's force when it had
reached their vicinity and was about to go into camp. In
order to throw them off their guard, and draw them away

from the town into the open, Alexander simulated retreat, and retired to a hill nearly a mile distant. The enemy followed. But when the barbarians were within arrow-flight a signal was given, and the Macedonians turned upon the Massagans and Indians, who were in loose order in anticipation of an easy victory. Their battle-shout and fierce front, as the light troops advanced, fired a volley, and opened right and left to uncover the heavy troops behind, surprised the barbarians beyond measure, and when the line, headed by Alexander, charged down in phalanx at a run, the enemy was utterly overthrown so soon as they came hand to hand. Some two hundred were killed, and the rest fled headlong to the city. Alexander at once pushed on to the wall, hoping to take the town by a *coup de main*. But he found this impracticable. The wall was well defended, and he himself, in reconnoitring for the morrow's attack, was slightly wounded in the calf of the leg. He drew out the arrow himself, ordered his horse to be brought, and went on with his work without stanching the blood. But by and by he was compelled to stop. " They may call me son of Jupiter," said he, laughing, " but I suffer none the less like a mortal. This is blood, not ichor ! "

This wound stopped proceedings for the moment. Next day Alexander, whose activity no wounds could abate, brought up his engines, and in a short while battered down a piece of the wall ; but the Indians proved themselves stanch and brave, and the Macedonians could not, despite their best efforts, on that day force an entrance through the gaps. As speedily as possible, a tower and terrace were built, — Curtius says it took nine days to build the terrace, — and on the day after their completion the tower was advanced to the wall. From this, missiles could be hurled by engines and shot by the archers and slingers, to keep the defenders at a distance ; but even this fire did not enable the Macedonians to force an entrance through the breach. Alexander had met with the stanchest troops he encountered in this region. The night was spent in preparation. These backsets would not do. The king was on his mettle. By the next morning he had got ready a bridge to throw from the tower to the wall, and had selected the shield-bearing guards, who had in similar fashion captured Tyre, to charge over it and drive the defenders from the breaches.

The preparations were duly completed; the bridge was thrown; the gallant hypaspists made the assault with all their usual dash, and with the confidence bred of a hundred victories thus snatched. But the bridge, hastily built and being overcharged by the ardor of the men, who crowded upon each other in their efforts to outdo themselves, broke, and a number of Macedonians were dumped pell-mell into the ditch. Perceiving their advantage, the eager barbarians not only showered stones, beams, fire-balls, and all manner of missiles upon the luckless wounded men below, but with a great shout of triumph made an immediate sortie from the side gates between the towers of the town, and inflicted much loss on the mass of struggling humanity in the ditch. Alexander was fain to sound the recall. He immediately ordered in fresh troops, and it was by the heroic efforts of Alcestas' taxis alone that the wounded and dead were rescued without still greater loss. Several detachments had got isolated in the general attack, had not heard the trumpet signal, and had to be withdrawn by the advance of other troops, which was done with some difficulty.

On the succeeding day another bridge was thrown in the like manner; but the Indians defended themselves with the utmost gallantry; Alexander still made no greater progress. It must have been a novelty to the Macedonians to find themselves thus matched. Nor, indeed, would the town have yielded at all until the last extreme, had not the leader of the Indian mercenaries haply been killed by a missile from a catapult. Many of the body had already been killed, and nearly all were wounded. Thus deprived of leadership, the gallant fellows sent a message to Alexander, who agreed to receive their capitulation if they (the Indian mercenaries) would enlist as a body in his service, and surrender as hostages the family of the king of Massaga. To this they agreed, marched out, and encamped on an adjoining hill. It is claimed that they refused to carry out their promise, lest they should, in Alexander's advance across the Indus, be obliged to fight against their fellow-citizens, and that they made an attempt to retreat at night. This may or may not be true; but Alexander surrounded the hill on which they were, intercepted their flight, if any was intended, and on one or other pretext the Macedonians got beyond control, attacked them, and cut them all to pieces.

Massaga was easily captured by storm after the Indians had withdrawn. The garrison was put to the sword as if there had been no capitulation, — apparently a quite indefensible act, if these are all the facts. It is alleged that an example was necessary in order to appall the adjoining tribes, and to prevent more Indian mercenaries from coming hither; but this is scarcely a palliation. Alexander's loss had been twenty - five killed, and an exceptionally large number wounded.

Alexander now sent a force under Attalus, Alcestas, and Demetrius, the cavalry leader, to Ora, with orders to blockade it until his arrival, which was done. He also dispatched another, under Cœnus, to Bazira (probably modern Bajour), hoping it would surrender on hearing of the fate of Massaga. This, however, was not the case. Bazira was situated on a lofty hill, and well fortified. Bad news soon came from both places. Alexander saw that he must undertake the task in person. He had intended to march first on Bazira, but from the reports he deemed it wise to make his earlier move on Ora, where Alcestas had with difficulty defeated a sortie of the garrison. He meanwhile instructed Cœnus to fortify a strong position near by to use in besieging the town of Bazira, and to cut off its supplies; then to leave a garrison in the works sufficient to keep the Bazirans within walls, and join him at Ora. For Abisares, king of Cashmir, northwest of this locality, was said to have sent large reinforcements to Ora.

All these orders were duly executed, but when the Bazirans saw Cœnus marching off with the bulk of his force, they imagined that they would now have matters their own way, and, emerging from their city, they attacked the garrison of the newly-built fort from the plain. In a sharp battle, however, they were worsted, with five hundred killed. This defeat had the effect to narrow the lines about Bazira, and all the more securely to coop up the inhabitants in the city. Ora proved an easy prey to Alexander, who took it on the first assault and there captured a number of elephants. And when the men of Bazira learned this, they evacuated their city in the night, and retreated to the rock of Aornus. All the barbarians were deserting their cities for this last refuge.

Hephæstion and Perdiccas had fully secured the south bank of the Cophen; had pacified all the tribes in the mountains which hug this bank all along its course; and had insured the land against revolt by garrisoning the forts of Astes and Orobatis. This duty had occupied but a fraction of the time consumed by the king's larger task. Alexander, on the north of the river, with everlasting snows always in sight, had successively reduced the valleys of the Choaspes, Guræus and Suastos; had subdued the territory of the tribes living on these rivers ; had driven the barbarians back into the mountains, and held the more important passes, as well as controlled the valleys at Andaca and Arigæum ; had fortified Massaga, Ora, Bazira, which controlled the land of the Assacenians, and shortly after took Peucela, which commanded the west bank of the Indus. The whole cis-Indus land was under Macedonian control. The Gates to India were firmly grasped. But one place still held out. The Macedonians called it Aornus — "a spot higher than the flight of birds."

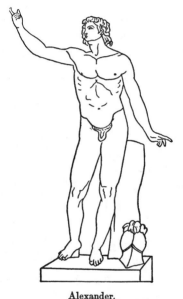

Alexander.

(From a Statue in Dresden.)

XXXIX.

AORNUS. LATE WINTER, B. C. 326.

THIS rock, the last stronghold of the Cophen barbarians, was said to have resisted Hercules. It contained arable land sufficient to sustain the garrison. Situated not far from the Indus, it was much larger than Gibraltar. Having garrisoned the strong places of the country, Alexander moved on Aornus. By promise of great rewards he procured native guides who showed him paths by which to gain a position commanding the fortress. To this he sent Ptolemy, and later with great exertion led the whole army. Between him and the fort was a deep ravine, as at the rock of Chorienes. Having tried escalade and failed, Alexander began to build a mound across the ravine, and in six days had so nearly reached the fort that the enemy asked for terms. These Alexander granted, but on their violation seized the place and slew most of the garrison. He then moved north to Dyrta, where there was an uprising; having subdued which he made his way to the Indus and descended on boats, which he built on the spot, to the mouth of the Cophen, and joined his second column. Alexander's self-imposed duty to Greece had ended when he had reduced to possession the kingdom of Darius. His right to invade India was mere lust of conquest. His *casus belli* against Porus, whom he first attacked, was enmity between Porus and the king of Taxila, with which latter prince Alexander had made an alliance.

THIS remarkable rock was the last stronghold of the barbarians between Zariaspa and the Indus, and was said to have resisted Hercules. It commanded the whole country between the Cophen, the Indus and the Suastos. From it a vast stretch of country could be observed. The more difficult of access this fortress, the more essential that Alexander should take it, not only on account of the moral effect, but in order to leave his rear secure. Such a threat to his communications, as this fort in the enemy's hands, could not be left behind, if he was to cross the Indus. No man ever looked more carefully to his communications. This was the military side of the question.

But the other aspect of the case was equally important. If Alexander could but do what Hercules had been unable to accomplish, was not his divine origin more surely made manifest to his Eastern subjects? And though this was always one of the strongest of motives with Alexander, it is very noteworthy that it was uniformly secondary to military common sense. This fact alone, and it is indisputable, silences much of the unreasoning criticism of Alexander's weaknesses.

Situated, as identified by Major Abbot (though its whereabouts cannot be surely determined), on the Indus about sixty miles from the Cophen, the last outpost of the mountain ranges, the rock of Aornus (Mount Mahabun) was some twenty-three miles

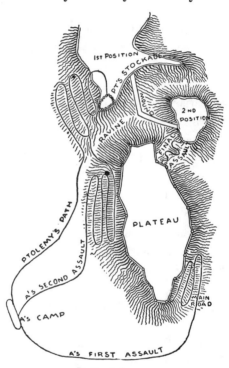

Rock of Aornus.

in circumference at the base, and stood up, it is said, five thousand feet at its summit above the plain. This made this fastness much larger and more formidable than Gibraltar, which is about six miles around the base, and but fourteen hundred feet high. According to General Cunningham, Aornus is the rock of Rani-gat, which is but twelve hundred feet in height, and some five miles round at the base. The exact spot is perhaps not material, though it would be highly interesting to know the locality. At the lowest place it was said to be a mile and a quarter in the ascent, which was artificially constructed, and very difficult. At the top of the rock was table-land well watered by an abundant spring; and there was timber and arable land enough to sustain one thousand men by tillage; or, as Arrian puts it, "for one thousand men to till," which means even more. There seems to be no reason to doubt the accuracy of this description. A large army could hold this rock year in year out, and the barbarians felt that they were entirely secure from the Macedonians.

Alexander saw that he could not avoid besieging this stronghold. He accordingly transformed Ora, Massaga and Bazira into Macedonian fortresses for the purpose of helping to keep the land in subjection, and Hephæstion and Perdiccas did the same with Orobatis, which controlled the land near the Indus. A number of such fortresses were essential to the full security of the army. Nicanor, one of the Companions, was made viceroy of the cis-Indus territory. Continuing his march towards the Cophen, Alexander, having taken Peucela, near by, garrisoned it under Philip. He also took possession of some other small towns, with the help of friendly chiefs, prominent among whom were Cophæus and Assagetes. Thence he marched to Embolina, near the rock of Aornus, where he left Craterus to establish an immediate base of operations and to gather victuals for a long siege of the rock, should it prove to be necessary. Then taking the bowmen, the Agrianians and the brigade of Cœnus, the lightest and best armed of the phalanx, two hundred Companion cavalry and one hundred horse-bowmen, he marched to the rock and camped. On the next day he reconnoitred the ground and shifted his camp nearer the rock.

Some of the natives now came to Alexander, no doubt attracted by his reputation for giving princely recompense, — the king had probably made inquiries and promises on all hands, — and offered to lead him to a part of the rock which they pointed out from below, and from which the citadel could be assailed, if at all. Particularly an old shepherd and his two sons were selected as guides, and the king offered a prize of eighty talents for success in this enterprise. Alexander sent Ptolemy, son of Lagus, with some of the Agrianians and other light troops, added to a body of picked hypaspists, with directions to occupy the place and signal to him when he had done so. Ptolemy, after a long and difficult march over narrow and dangerous footpaths, in conduct of the guides, reached the position undiscovered by the barbarians, and after fortifying it by a stockade and ditch, he fired a beacon where Alexander could see it.

Next morning at dawn the king led his men to assault the hill from the main approach, expecting that Ptolemy would be able to help him from his new position. But the main approach was so well defended by the Aornians that the king could make no headway, even with the aid of a well-meant but not vigorous diversion by Ptolemy on their rear. Finding that Alexander could be easily held in check by limited numbers, the barbarians fiercely turned on Ptolemy in force, and drove him back to his stockade; but, though with the utmost difficulty, this officer managed to hold his position there, and the enemy withdrew his troops at nightfall, having lost heavily by the fire of the Agrianians and archers. The next night Alexander managed, through a deserter familiar with the locality, to convey to Ptolemy the information that he would assault early next day from a point more nearly in his direction than at the main approach, and gave him orders, instead of holding his position, to move down the mountain, and attack the barbarians in the rear, whenever he saw them emerge from their defenses to repel the assault he should make. In this way Alexander would try to reunite the forces, whose division at this moment had proven to be unwise, for it had not resulted in surrender, as the ruse of the " winged soldiers " at the rock of Oxyartes had done. At the same time he hoped that the barbarians might afford him an opening by which he could surprise the fort.

At daybreak Alexander began the ascent of the mountain, prepared for an assault. The barbarians soon perceived his movement, and began to harass his men as they climbed one by one along the steep paths, with darts and arrows, to roll stones down upon them, and to embarrass them in every manner. But the Macedonians persevered, and by sharp persistent fighting and the protection of good armor made some headway. Ptolemy now fell upon the flank and rear of the barbarians, who had advanced between the two bodies, and threw them off their guard; and towards afternoon Alexander managed to make a junction with Ptolemy. At the same time the flying Indians led him to believe that he could capture the fort, and he endeavored to follow the enemy into their defenses, but was not speedy enough to do so. The gates were closed upon him, and the place was too narrow for an assault to promise success.

The army with Alexander now reached the eminence where Ptolemy had built his stockade, — a place lower than, and separated from, the top of the rock by a precipitous ravine. This he tried the same day to cross by escalading the rocks, but found that the task was an impossible one.

On this occasion he gave the pages a chance to distinguish themselves. He called for volunteers, and thirty of these royal youths presented themselves. Under two of their number, Charus and Alexander, this forlorn hope, suitably sustained by the Agrianians and archers, started on its mission to fray a path to the fortress. The Companions had prevailed on the king not to accompany them. But the gallant pages had not gone more than quarter way, when Alexander, impatient of any one gathering glory he might share, turned towards his body-guard, and inviting them to follow, sallied out after the pages. The barbarians were prepared. Huge blocks of stone were rolled down on the assailants; many fell. But still the pages pushed on. One by one they reached the crest but only to fall pierced by many missiles. The king and his guards were still too far to hope to assist them in season to be of any avail. The assault had failed. Another promised a like result.

Alexander, after due study of the problem, determined to build a mound across the ravine so as to bring his engines into a position from which he could use them against the walls. The whole army set to work with a will. The day's stint of each man was to collect and bring one hundred stakes. There was abundance of timber. Hurdles were made of the smaller wood. Stones, earth, stumps, every available thing was put to use to help the filling of the mound. On the first day, the work was so rapidly pushed, that the Macedonians had built the mound forward from their side, where the ravine was not so deep as farther on, nearly three hundred paces. The Indians at first contented themselves with collecting on the walls beyond bowshot, and deriding these efforts; but when their astonishment and alarm grew with the progress of the mound, they sought to harass the Macedonians in their work by a fire of arrows across the ravine. But the engines and archers and slingers with their better fire held them steadily in check.

It has already been noticed that only the more necessary parts of the catapults and ballistas were carried along.

Wherever there was timber, the rough frame-work could be put together in a few hours. It is evident that Alexander had mountain-batteries, so to speak, which could be carried even on the backs of men where pack animals could not go. And it is also evident that these engines were as effective against the defenses of that time as our modern guns are against those of to-day. Their utility was abundantly demonstrated in the passage of rivers as well as in sieges.

For three days Alexander continued this work, and made considerable progress in the mound. As usual the king was everywhere and harder at work than any of his men, directing, encouraging, reproving and lending a hand. On the fourth day a small party of Macedonians made their way over the mound and the rest of the ravine to an eminence which was on a level with the fortress, and drove the defenders from it. Some of the authorities state that the fight here was bitter, and that Alexander headed the agema in order to secure the eminence. Having done so, he now aimed the mound towards this height, which was for him the key point; for its elevation would enable him to use his fire to advantage. The height was reached on the sixth day from the start, after great effort and continuous labor.

The Indians, astonished before, were now dazed at the audacity and skill of the Macedonians and the manner in which they made vain all the natural obstacles of the mountains, driven on by the never-flagging energy and matchless skill of Alexander. They sent to the king, and asked for a truce, agreeing to surrender on stated terms. Their honesty Alexander mistrusted, but he accepted the terms. He soon discovered, however, that the barbarians proposed, by delaying the ratification, to gain time to scatter and escape in squads to the plain, and to their several cities, instead of surrendering themselves as agreed. He proposed to checkmate this scheme. He gave no sign of suspecting the treachery, but allowed the barbarians to begin their retreat, which they did at night. He then took seven hundred of his best men from the agema and hypaspists, and making his way across the ravine, himself was the first to scale the rock at a point where the rear-guard of the enemy had deserted it. By pulling each other up and by the use of ropes and poles, the force was, without great delay, and undiscovered by the barbarians, who were intent on collecting their valuables for flight, got upon the upper level of the rock, from whence, falling on the enemy at a concerted signal as they were just flying, they slew many; while others, in their panic-stricken endeavors to escape, threw themselves down the precipices right and left. A large number undoubtedly escaped, and made their way into the mountains; but the force was quite dispersed. Thus Alexander captured the inexpugnable rock of Aornus, against which, according to the legend, even Hercules had recoiled. Sacrifices were offered on the highest point of the rock, the works were strengthened, and a Macedonian garrison was left to defend it. Sissicottus, who had obtained Alexander's favor by his faithful and intelligent assistance, was made viceroy of the district.

Alexander now heard of a body of barbarians which had assembled in the northern country, and immediately made a retrograde movement to Dyrta, a fortified place in the land of the Assacenians. Here had been gathered, by the brother of the chief who died at Massaga, an army of twenty thousand men and fifteen elephants. This new chief hoped that the inaccessibility of Dyrta, which was well back in the recesses of the mountains, would deter Alexander from moving against him; and that when the Macedonians left, he might be able to reassert his authority, and by falling on Alexander's rear, accomplish something of importance.

Alexander was not slow in setting out to put an end to this scheme; but on reaching Dyrta after a long and arduous march, he found it deserted by the barbarians, who had been astonished and had their superstitious notions aroused by the extraordinary capture of Aornus. Alexander sent out parties in various directions under Nearchus and Antiochus, the two chiefs of the hypaspists, the former with the Agrianians and light troops, the latter with his own brigade and two others, to reconnoitre the country, and especially to search for the elephants; for the barbarians had conveyed away all these animals, of which Alexander desired to accumulate a number, either from motives of curiosity, or to be able to test for himself their value in war. He was enabled to get on their track by some natives whom he captured, and who showed him the way to the place where, near the Indus, these creatures had been sent to pasture in a spot deemed secure from discovery. The barbarians' army had fled into the pathless wilderness across the Indus, to seek the protection of Abisares, king of Cashmir; but some of the lesser chiefs had assassinated their leader, and brought his head to Alexander. This practically disorganized the force; and seeing no use in following the body into the thickets where roads had to be cut, Alexander determined to begin his move down the Indus. Of the elephants he captured all but two, which, in the pursuit, fell over precipices and were killed.

A part of the army had some time before been sent ahead to cut roads to reach the Indus. From the place to which Alexander had penetrated towards the Indus was a stretch of wilderness. On arriving at this river, Alexander discovered a supply of timber suitable for shipbuilding. He stayed here time sufficient to enable him to build a number of boats. This was a work at which many of his men were experts, and could be done rapidly; and on these, with the aid of native pilots, he carried the army down the river to the spot where Hephæstion and Perdiccas had long been busy in making preparations for a bridge. The last part of the way, near modern Attock, the men probably had to disembark and march, for the current there is very swift and dangerous. Attock is at the confluence of the Caboul and Indus.

Before crossing the Indus with his army, Alexander made a march to ivy-clad Nysa, a city said to have been founded by Bacchus, which, finding it well governed and friendly, he left in possession of its ancient freedom; and sacrificing to the god with feasts upon Mount Meros, he returned towards the Indus. Here he found that a substantial bridge of boats had been thrown, and a large number of vessels constructed; and here he gave his army a thirty days' — or perhaps longer — rest, much needed, for a large part of the men had undergone the fatigues of a most harassing winter campaign, and required not only recuperation, but some reorganization.

It was late in the winter when he broke up. On leaving Zariaspa, Alexander had expected to be able to finish the Cophen campaign before the arrival of winter, so as to rest his army in winter-quarters; but he was so long delayed that, before he actually got to work on this region, winter had overtaken him. His anxiety to cross the Indus was so great, however, that he had carried through this winter campaign rather than defer the Indian matter to another season.

The Taxiles, or king of this region, had, as we know, long ago solicited Alexander's protection; had guided the column of Hephæstion and Perdiccas to the Indus, and now came to headquarters with a present of two hundred talents of silver, three thousand beeves, ten thousand sheep, and thirty war elephants. He brought, moreover, seven hundred Indian horsemen as a reinforcement, and agreed to surrender to Alexander his flourishing and beautiful capital city of Taxila, the largest between the Indus and the Hydaspes, whose ruins to-day cover six square miles, on consideration that Alexander would help him against his enemy Porus, king of the region beyond that river.

Alexander had always placed the limit of his intended conquests and wanderings at the river Indus. His claim as Hegemōn of the Greeks was a right to the kingdom of Darius, and this only in revenge for wrongs done by Persia to Greece. But now came in this new alliance with Taxiles which gave him a pretext for crossing the boundary he had set, and of venturing into the unknown land of India. His place of crossing was probably at modern Attock near the mouth of the Cophen or Caboul River, which he had been descending from Bactriana. His bridge, according to Diodorus, was made of boats. This, and numerous craft of all sizes and kinds built or found in the neighborhood, together with what he had brought down the Indus, made the crossing a simple matter, as he was advancing into the land of friends. The king and his suite crossed on two thirty-oared galleys, with suitable ceremony. The movement was not only propitiated by the usual numerous sacrifices, but also celebrated, when accomplished, by games and feasts. The pomp and circumstance of these splendid pageants finds its proper place in the pages of many authors. It does not belong here.

On the farther side he was joined by an army of native troops twenty thousand strong, and with fifteen elephants. This force had murdered its king, Aphrices, and now joined Alexander, with a request that it might serve under his banner. At Taxila he was received with befitting splendor. Here friendly embassies came to him from many adjoining tribes, among them Doxaris, a neighboring potentate, and one from Abisares of Cashmir, headed by his brother, who strenuously denied having afforded aid to the Assacenians. As had now become all the more the custom with Alexander, during the remainder of the season which he spent here, he made his sojourn a series of festivities in the Macedonian manner, but without neglecting the demands of the army, whose mixture of nationalities called for much time in discipline and organization. Then leaving a garrison, mostly of invalided men, under Philip, son of Machatas, as a sort of viceroy, but clothing Taxiles with practical authority, he advanced towards the line of the Hydaspes, which he was informed was held by Porus, king of the region beyond the river.

No doubt the readiness with which Taxiles placed himself under Alexander's command was due to the enmity existing between himself and this Porus, whose kingdom was too strong to attack single-handed, and of whom he stood in constant dread. For Porus was certainly the most able chieftain of this country, possessed a rich and flourishing kingdom, said to contain one hundred large cities, and had Cashmir as an ally. Porus was not only at odds with Taxiles and the Himalayan tribes, but also with the " kingless " peoples of the Five Rivers.

In order to be able to bridge the Hydaspes, Alexander sent Cœnus back to the Indus to bring forward the boats which had been used there. This Cœnus did by cutting them in two, or, in case of the thirty-oared galleys, in three parts, and conveying them on wagons. This is probably the first instance of anything resembling a pontoon bridge being transported, though, as above stated, this is alleged to have been done in the Cophen campaign. The army then moved forward towards the Hydaspes. Alexander had from Taxila sent his herald Cleochares to Porus, commanding him to bring in his submission. To this high-handed call Porus replied that he himself owned his country, owed allegiance to no man, and that he would come to the river which was his boundary with his whole force, and there dispute Alexander's right or power to enter his domains. Alexander therefore moved against him, and, in addition to his own troops, took with him some five thousand Indian auxiliaries. But the elephants he left in Taxila. The Macedonian horses had not become used to these beasts, nor were the tactics of the Macedonians suited to their employment.

Alexander.
(From a Statue in the Louvre.)

XL.

PORUS. MARCH TO MAY, B. C. 326.

IT was the rainy season when Alexander advanced to the Hydaspes. Reaching the river, he found it half a mile wide, swollen and rapid. He could see Porus with his splendid army and many elephants on the farther side. He could not force a passage in his teeth; he must steal one. He went into camp and by ostensible preparations, rumors and other means, induced Porus to believe that he would not try to cross till the dry season. To further confuse and tire out Porus, he made constant feints at partial crossings by night and day. Porus began to meet these feints by keeping his troops under arms, but when they got exhausted from overmuch toil, and Alexander never actually attempted a passage, Porus grew careless and paid less heed to what the Macedonians were doing. Then came Alexander's time. He selected a point some miles up stream and made all his preparations for a real crossing, leaving Craterus in camp and posting many other parties at convenient stations along the bank. Finally, at night and with great care and skill, he put over fourteen thousand men to the south side. Porus was quite deceived. He could see Craterus and the other troops on the right bank, and did not know what this force of Alexander's was. He sent his son with a small body to oppose it. This Alexander defeated, and then advanced towards Porus' main army. The latter came to meet him. This passage of the Hydaspes is the pattern of all that is best in the crossing of rivers in the face of the enemy.

THE rainy season had just set in. To-day it is said to begin in July. Unless the ancient chronology is at fault, it began earlier two thousand years ago. Thunder-storms and hurricanes were frequent. The men suffered much from the weather. Marching was hard and progress was slow on account of the roads, often cut by swollen streams, and everywhere deep and heavy. As the army passed the southern boundary of Taxila and neared the Hydaspes, it was obliged to march through a narrow pass in the kingdom of Spitakes, a relative and ally of Porus. This pass was held in force.

The hills on either side were occupied and much delay was threatened. But Alexander, by a brilliant cavalry manœuvre under his own leadership, the details of which we do not possess, surprised and drove Spitakes out of his position, crowded him back into the recesses of the defile where he had hard work to find an exit, and obliged him after considerable loss to fly to Porus for safety. The army thence moved in two marches to the river and camped.

In summer the Hydaspes is nowhere fordable, though it is so at many places during the dry season of winter, when the frosts seal up the ice and snow in the mountain ranges. On the other side of the stream, now over half a mile wide, owing to the rains, though in the dry season relatively small and clear, could be seen Porus with his superbly accoutred army drawn up in battle array before his camp and with his three hundred elephants ranged in front, ready to dispute the passage. According to Diodorus, Porus had more than fifty thousand infantry, three thousand cavalry, one thousand chariots and one hundred and thirty elephants; according to Curtius, he had thirty thousand foot, three hundred chariots and eighty-five elephants. The Indians

were tall, athletic and agile. The infantry were armed with bows five feet long, shot arrows of three feet, and bore a long two-handed sword. Their shields were raw hide. The horsemen had two javelins and a shield, presumably also a sword. Porus, like other Eastern leaders, relied mainly on his elephants; then

War Elephant.

on his chariots; next on camels when he had them; last on cavalry. Such was the value placed on these several arms. Porus' infantry did not accomplish much in the coming battle, though the Indian mercenaries in the Cophen region had fought more desperately than any troops Alexander encountered east of Babylon. Alexander's tactics made it useless.

Porus had sent strong detachments under experienced captains to guard every fordable part of the river and keep a line

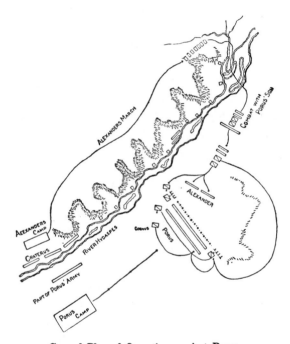

General Plan of Operations against Porus.

of posts along it up and down from his camp. The possession by Porus of war chariots and elephants, and of so large and apparently well disciplined an army made Alexander cautious about attempting to force a passage in the teeth of the enemy, and induced him to manœuvre for a chance to cross in safety. Here was the most splendid force which had faced him since Arbela. From mountain fighting he was getting back to level plains and pitched battles. He had gained much respect for the fighting qualities of the Indians from what he had seen of them at Massaga, and had been given to understand that Porus was a man of no common order. He was reduced to stratagem, and, happily for us, his masterly manœuvres on this occasion have furnished the world with a manual of all which is most valuable in the passage of rivers in the face of the enemy.

It was now May. The Hydaspes was full of sand banks and rapids, and was turbid and swollen with the melting of the Himalayan snows and the rainfall of the season. Diligently guarded by Porus, it presented the most difficult natural and artificial obstacle Alexander had as yet encountered. It had come to a trial of wits between the two kings. Alexander first took measures to convince Porus that he intended to wait until the river fell. This he did by devastating the country of Porus' ally, Spitakes, by accumulating the vast stores of corn so gathered in his camp on the western bank, and by settling his troops in comfortable quarters, all of which operations were conducted where they could be overseen or were sure to reach Porus' ears. At the same time, perceiving that Porus remained active in scouting the river so as to prevent himself from being taken unawares, Alexander sought to tire him out by constant activity on his own part. He desired to confuse Porus as well as exhaust his troops. He kept part of his army afoot in numberless detachments moving to and fro along the bank, began the preparation of rafts by stuffing skins with hay and accumulating beams and boards on the river bank, and sent his boats, which had been joined and launched again, up and down the river so as to distract the attention of the enemy. Parties were sent over to the islands in the river where they had many skirmishes with the Indian patrols — and thus learned to know their new enemy. He made feint after feint, often by night and with great clamor. He got his phalanx under arms in the light of the camp-fires; the signal to move was blown in the camp; the horse trotted rapidly and with much noise up and down; the boats were got ready and loaded as if to cross. All this was done *en évidence.* The troops worked incessantly, though it took comparatively few of the Macedonians to make a very lively feint. To offset these apparently threatening attacks, Porus would bring out his elephants and march them down to the bank where he heard the most noise; place his whole force under arms and wait till daylight at the spot where he supposed Alexander was attempting to make a crossing.

After some time Porus began to weary his troops by marching them to and fro, in answer to anticipated attempts to cross, and finding that the attempts were never actually made, he grew more careless. He disliked to expose his troops to the bad weather of the season. Alexander could make a deal of commotion with a small part of his forces; Porus felt safe with no less than his whole army in line. He was exhausting his men faster than Alexander his. He evidently came to believe that Alexander would wait for a low state of water, and that all these attempts argued a fear to cross. For Alexander had purposely spread a report to this effect which had reached Porus. Yet he had kept his troops well in hand, and proposed to steal a passage whenever it was possible, despite the bad condition of weather and water.

Alexander of course saw how inexpedient it would be to attempt a passage opposite the enemy's camp. His horse could probably not be made to face the elephants if these beasts were brought near the shore. To the unusual smell of the huge animals as well as their aspect they had as yet not become accustomed; and they showed the utmost dread of the trumpeting of the creatures. Alexander feared that the horses would not remain quiet on the rafts during the passage if they saw the elephants on the farther bank; and he knew that he could never get them to land. Even his infantry was unused to them. Alexander had also ascertained that Abisares, king of Cashmir, far from remaining faithful to his promises, was preparing to send his entire force to the assistance of Porus. This made it all the more important to cross the river before the junction of these armies. But he could not force, he must seize a passage by stealth.

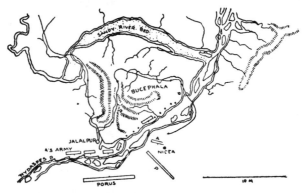

Topography of the Hydaspes, after Cunningham.

The right bank of the river, where Alexander had his camp, for a distance of many miles up and down, was high and hilly. The bank on which Porus stood was a wide fertile plain. This afforded Alexander the marked advantage of hiding his own movements while those of Porus were easily observable.

When Alexander saw that he had confused Porus as to his intentions, and that the Indian king had ceased to march out to meet his feigned crossings, but remained in camp, merely occupying the places where crossings were most likely to be attempted, he made his preparations for a real crossing, meanwhile keeping up his feints with intermittent regularity. He selected for his crossing a spot in the river seventeen miles up the stream from his camp, where there was a headland formed by a considerable bend in the river and a small affluent. This headland was wooded, and was ample to conceal a large force. It was itself curtained by a wooded and uninhabited island in its front. This place Alexander connected with the camp by a line of posts along the river bank, which was the nearest road. These were so close together that orders could be quickly signaled or conveyed from one end of the line to the other. These posts, moreover, with the sentinels calling from one to the other, the many camp-fires and the bustle and stir could be used as feints to harass the enemy, who had lost all belief in any present attempt to cross, but was still alive to the possibility of such a movement. For many nights the Macedonians made noisy demonstrations at every place between camp and island, and lighted fires at intervals in open places as if considerable bodies of troops were present.

Having made all his secret preparations, and these were particularly hastened, because Abisares was reported within three marches, Alexander openly planned a feint at crossing in force on boats in Porus' front, where there was a dry-season ford. Craterus was left here in the main camp, with instructions not actually to cross, unless Porus was beaten, or unless he moved away the bulk of his army, and especially the elephants, towards the island up the river. In no case was Craterus to attempt to face the elephants; but if they were moved off, he was to cross in reality. The king left with Craterus the latter's own division of cavalry and some Arachotian and Parapamisadian horse, the brigades of Alcestas and Polysperchon and five thousand Indians. Attalus, who resembled the king, was arrayed in armor much like his, and instructed to counterfeit his presence.

Between the main camp and island, where was another dry-season ford, Alexander posted in one body the brigades of Meleager, Attalus and Gorgias, supported by the Greek mercenaries, cavalry and infantry, with instructions to cross in successive columns when the expected battle should have been engaged. He himself took the agema of Companion cavalry and the regiments of Hephæstion, Perdiccas and Demetrius, the horse from Bactria, Sogdiana and Scythia, and the Daän horse-archers, the shield-bearing guards, the taxes of Clitus and Cœnus, and the archers and Agrianians, and marched by a route well back from the river, so as not to be seen by the enemy — and happily, there was no dust to betray him — to the selected place. His route is thought to have been along the streams, now dry, known as the Kandar-Nullah and Kasi. Hither the hay wherewith to fill the tent skins had been brought; these were speedily stuffed, and everything made ready for the crossing which at the chosen place was perhaps more difficult, but had the great advantage of being hidden.

The night was tempestuous, and the thunder and rain, usual during the southwest monsoon, drowned the noise of the workmen unavoidable in such preparations, while the woods and ravines concealed the Macedonian camp-fires. Most of the boats, including the thirty-oared galleys, had again been cut apart and conveyed hither, and lay concealed in the woods after being put together. Beams and plank had been carefully prepared. Everything was made ready for use at a moment's warning. At the approach of daylight the storm abated, and the army crossed to the island unobserved by Porus' sentinels; nor were they detected until they had passed the island, when the scouts of Porus observed the movement, and gave the alarm. The infantry crossed in the boats, Alexander leading in a thirty-oared galley accompanied by Perdiccas, Lysimachus and Seleucus, " the cavalry mounting upon the skins," which by some is held to mean that the cavalrymen, while swimming beside their horses, used these skins, as boys learning to swim use bladders, so as not to burden their horses; but which, to judge from the context and other passages, more probably means that the skins were used to help float rafts, and on these latter the horses were conveyed. Perhaps the stream was too swollen and rapid and wide to make it safe to swim the horses, especially as severe duty was to be expected from them immediately on landing.

So soon as the enemy's guards made up their minds that this crossing was real and not a feint, they galloped off at full speed to Porus to convey the news. The cavalry was ordered to land first; and as they reached the bank, they were ranged in column of march by Alexander and his officers. Two or three taxes of the phalanx were left on the right bank to observe the road from Cashmir, which comes in here to the crossing of the river. Three of the taxes mentioned in Bactriana and Sogdiana fail of mention at the Hydaspes — Philotas', Balacrus', Philip's. It may have been these which were detached on this duty.

It soon appeared that Alexander, from ignorance of the locality, had not landed on the south shore, but on another large island separated from the mainland by water generally so low as to be easily passed over, but now grown quite high and rapid from the great storm just past, which had fairly dug out the bend in the river. Here was a serious dilemma. There was no time to bring the boats around, but the troops must be got over at once, lest the enemy should gain opportunity to bring up a heavy column and perhaps some elephants, and oppose the crossing. The great advantage already won was threatened to be lost; but after some delay and a good many accidents, the most fordable place was found, and the troops, wading to their breasts, were safely got over.

As the cavalry emerged from the water, Alexander brought the agema and the best of the other horse forward into line for the right wing, throwing out the horse-archers in their front, and placing the royal shield-bearing guards, under Seleucus, in front of the other infantry. Next the agema came the other hypaspists, and on each side of the phalanx he stationed the archers, Agrianians, and javelin-throwers.

The body of infantry which he had with him, some six thousand strong, he ordered to follow slowly and in regular order; with his five thousand cavalry, which he knew to be his right arm, he set out towards Porus, ordering Tauron to follow with the archers, — there may have been three or four thousand light troops, — and keep up with the cavalry as best he might. Alexander was confident that, even if Porus should attack with his whole force, he would be able to hold him till the infantry came up, if not worst him with the cavalry force in hand; and he knew that if Porus retired, he ought to be on hand with his cavalry to follow him up and harass his retreat. He therefore started in the direction of the Indian camp at a sharp trot, hazardous though an advance with so small a force undoubtedly was.

Porus, who had been watching Craterus' feints, at first imagined that the troops which his scouts reported as crossing above might be those of Abisares, his ally; but he was speedily undeceived. As he could see the large body of Macedonians under Craterus, and the detachments under Meleager and the others still on the farther side, he must have known that the body in his front was but a part of Alexander's army, and he ought unquestionably to have gone in person with a substantial part of his force to cut it out, particularly as some elephants, backed by infantry, could readily protect the fords for the time being. But Porus seems to have wished to put off a decisive battle until Abisares joined him, and contented himself with sending a small body to meet Alexander's advance, whose force he probably quite underestimated, or may have looked upon as a venturesome patrol. He imagined the king himself to be still on the other side.

Not long after Alexander had landed, therefore, the son of Porus put in an appearance, with two thousand horse and one hundred and twenty chariots. He had been put in command of the force and sent by his father to hold the approaching Macedonians in check. The king shortly ran across him. He at first thought that Porus was upon him with his entire army, of which this was but the van, and sent the horse-archers forward to skirmish with the Indians, while he paused to give instructions for hurrying up the other troops. But when, on reconnoitring, he could see no troops coming up behind the Indian column, he recognized that he had to do merely with a small force, and at once rode in upon them at the head of his Companions, and while the light horse skirmished about their flanks, the Macedonian cavalry charged home. It was rather a combat than a battle. The Macedonians charged in on the enemy " squadron by squadron," a term not unfrequently used by Arrian, whose meaning has already been discussed.

The charge at once broke the enemy's formation, and in the *mêlée* the son of Porus was killed and four hundred men were cut to pieces. The chariots were captured; for, being very heavy, — they contained each six men, — their movements were hampered by the deep mud in this agricultural lowland. The survivors fled; the Macedonians followed hard upon. Porus soon learned the presence of Alexander. He saw that the enemy had outwitted him, had crossed a river he ought to have been able to hold, or, at least, in the passage of which he could have inflicted heavy losses on the enemy. He must now fight on the plain instead of at the river fords.

The Indian king was much taken aback, and uncertain what to do. Alexander's manœuvre had been intended to deceive, and had completely deceived him. He could see Craterus actually preparing to cross, and could count a large body of troops with him. Yet he knew Alexander to be by far the more dangerous foe, though he had no idea of which had the bulk of the troops. He very clearly recognized his error in sending only two thousand men against Alexander, and determined now to repair it by crushing him by numbers before he could be joined by reinforcements from across the river. He therefore marched directly towards the king, leaving a few elephants and an adequate force opposite the camp to prevent Craterus from crossing.

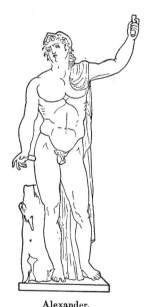

Alexander.

(From a Statue in the Louvre.)

XLI.

BATTLE OF THE HYDASPES. MAY, B. C. 326.

Porus had set up his two hundred elephants in one line, one hundred feet apart, sustained by his thirty thousand infantry; one hundred and fifty chariots and two thousand cavalry were on each flank. His ideas were limited to a parallel order, and he chose a defensive battle. Alexander had his phalanx of six thousand men; some three thousand light troops, and, above all, five thousand splendid cavalry. Eliminating the elephants and the chariots, Alexander had a good chance to win. But could these be neutralized? The Macedonian horse could not be got to approach the elephants; nor was the infantry steady in their vicinity. Alexander saw that he could not advance direct on Porus. He chose rather to attack his left flank; and sending Cœnus with part of his cavalry by a hidden circuit to turn and demoralize the Indian right, he moved his phalanx, left somewhat refused, up towards the Indian left wing, while with his cavalry he rode around the left flank and attacked it smartly. Porus, though brave and with brave men, knew nothing of grand tactics, and was unequal to opposing this oblique attack, except by detaching the cavalry of his right over to his left to meet Alexander. This enabled Cœnus to throw the right into vast confusion by a sharp attack, and then to ride, in rear of Porus' line, over to the Indian left, and take in rear the cavalry opposing Alexander. Between them, Alexander and Cœnus used up the Indian cavalry; the chariots proved useless; the elephants, at first effective, were courageously met by the Macedonians and driven back on Porus' line; the infantry, having nothing in its front and unused to manœuvring, proved useless. After eight hours of hard fighting and the heaviest loss he ever incurred in battle, — one man in every fifteen was killed, and the majority were wounded, — Alexander was completely victorious — a result he owed to splendid management and the very best of fighting. Porus, captured, was every inch a king. Alexander made him his friend and viceroy.

Porus had with him all his cavalry, four thousand strong, three hundred chariots, two hundred elephants, each with a tower filled with well-armed men, and some thirty thousand infantry. When he came to a place back of the river lowlands, where the ground was level, harder than near the river, and fit for manœuvring elephants, chariots and cavalry, he halted, and drew up his army in line of battle.

In this he showed considerable skill. In first line were the elephants, one hundred feet apart, covering the entire infantry body, which thus presented a front of about four miles. Porus expected by means of these animals to intimidate the horses of Alexander's cavalry, and prevent them from attacking with any kind of *vim ;* while the elephant-drivers could wheel their animals right and left and trample down the Macedonian infantry which might push into the intervals. The Indian infantry was in second line close behind the line of elephants, in companies of one hundred and fifty strong supporting each one, ready to fill the gaps between them when necessary, and to attack the Macedonian foot if it should advance so far. Small columns of foot flanked the elephants. Two thousand Indian cavalry was on each extreme flank, and in the front of the cavalry of each flank one hundred and fifty chariots. This was the Indian fashion, as it was much the usual habit elsewhere in the East. The chariots were drawn by four horses, and contained each two mailed drivers, two heavily armed men, and two archers carrying the long bows of the country. The infantry carried this long bow as well, and shot three-foot arrows ; but having to rest the end of the bow on the ground as they shot, they were not rapid in their fire.

When Alexander arrived near the place where Porus' army was drawn up in line, he found that he must hold himself by manœuvring with his cavalry while he waited for his infantry to come up. His position was precarious in the extreme. An immediate advance by Porus might have seriously compromised him, with only his cavalry and no supports. It was Alexander's good luck that Porus declined to attack, and the phalanx came on at a rapid gait. Alexander gave it a breathing spell while he inspected the line, reconnoitred the position of the enemy, and continued to keep him busy by small demonstrations, pushing a few squadrons at a time up towards the Indian front, but not so far as to provoke attack. He could not help admiring the ability which Porus had exhibited in drawing up his army, under the conditions presented. His strength lay in his line of elephants, which the Macedonian horse would not face, and Porus knew it ; and knew, moreover, that this horse was the body on which Alexander chiefly relied. The elephants were the unknown quantity of the problem. Of the chariots Alexander had less fear. He had met them at Arbela.

Alexander had advanced so as to be able to lean his right flank constantly upon the river or the river bottom-lands. He did not propose to lose touch with his lieutenants on the other side. He saw that he must mould his own tactics to correspond to Porus' dispositions. He was stronger in cavalry than the enemy, but vastly weaker in infantry. He could not attack in front, for it was certain that his cavalry would not face the elephants. The horses could not be driven or coaxed up to them. Nor could he resist the onset of these and the chariots, if made in a parallel order. But as Porus was evidently bent on fighting a defensive battle, Alexander had the choice of when and where he should attack, and how he should attack. The enemy promised to be a more or less stationary mass compared with his own rapidly moving Macedonians. This was a first and great gain.

With the rapidity of clear conceptions, Alexander determined to attack the Indian flanks, the left flank in force, and to seek to grasp some advantage before any tactical manœuvre could be undertaken or change of formation made by the enemy. He knew full well that his army could work with thrice

the rapidity of the enemy; and he was as always conscious
that he himself could think and act more quickly.   He therefore sent Cœnus with his own — the agema — and Demetrius'
cavalry by a circuit, and hidden by the rolling ground, against
the enemy's right, with instructions, should the horse on Porus'
right attempt to ride to the assistance of the horse on his left,

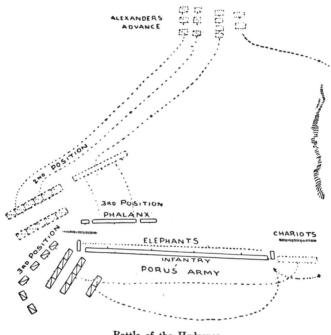

Battle of the Hydaspes.

to fall, if possible, upon the rear of the infantry.   Alexander himself, with the bulk of the cavalry, followed at sustaining distance by the infantry, made an oblique movement
against the enemy's left where Porus had but two thousand
cavalry and the chariots — these latter a doubtful support.
He chose this flank for his own attack, partly because he had
been hugging the river and the protection of his forces on the

other side, and partly from his usual habit of himself leading his own right wing, where he felt the most at home. He made this movement in such a way as to lead Porus to suppose that he was merely uncovering his infantry, so that this might then advance to a front attack, the very thing Porus desired.

Porus' attention was first called to the movement of the king ; he failed to perceive Cœnus' flanking march ; and as Alexander had shrewdly guessed, sent his two thousand cavalry of the right wing by the rear of his line to join the cavalry on the left, where he saw that he must oppose Alexander's attack.

Seleucus with the pages and hypaspists was on the right of the infantry, Antigenes with the phalangites was in the centre, and Tauron with the light troops was on the left. This whole body was ordered by Alexander to follow his own movement at a proper interval, and advance on the enemy, but not to engage until it saw that the enemy's wings had been thrown into confusion by the proposed cavalry charges. This Alexander thought would neutralize the value of the Indian elephants and chariots, and so far demoralize the infantry line as to lay it open to a fatal assault. It would appear that the phalanx had been formed in open order, so as to cover more ground, as well as better resist the elephants.

With his overwhelming force, and outflanking the Macedonians as he did with his greater length of line, Porus should by all means and at once have advanced to the attack with his elephants, which were protected by infantry much as our modern batteries are. Had he done this without giving Alexander time to manœuvre, pushing forward the elephants so as to render Alexander's cavalry ineffective, and ordering the chariots to charge from each wing and by an inward half wheel take the phalanx in flank, it would seem as if such action must have been fatal to Alexander. And Porus had sufficient horse for pursuit, and excellent for such purpose, though some part of it had been demoralized by the defeat under Porus' son. But Porus awaited the attack which Alexander was always glad to make, for no one more than he knew the advantage of the offensive. This defensive attitude of Porus was not only a piece of good luck; it was Alexander's salvation.

Thus Alexander's decision to strike the enemy in one place, the left flank, with substantially his whole force, brought him again into the oblique order of Epaminondas — this time clearly by design.

Riding forward then towards the right, Alexander opened the battle at bow-shot distance by sending the Daän horse-archers upon the Indian left to engage them in front, while he, by a wheel to the right into column and marching in their rear, could get round to the enemy's flank with Hephæstion's and Perdiccas' heavy horse, and haply strike it before it could make dispositions to meet him. The Indian cavalry leaders do not appear to have comprehended this manœuvre — as Alexander did not intend they should — for they did not hold their men well in hand, and advanced far out of support of their infantry line. Cœnus had now finished his circuit to the Indian right, and in the absence of the cavalry of that wing, fell smartly upon the right and rear of Porus' infantry, which he threw into grave confusion, and rendered useless for the day. It is evident that he struck a hearty blow, for Porus' right rendered absolutely no service during the battle. Then, completing his gallant ride, with the true instinct of the *beau sabreur*, Cœnus galloped along the Indian rear, and rode up to join in the cavalry battle already engaged on the enemy's left.

To oppose this new danger as well as Alexander's attack;

the Indian cavalry was obliged to make a double front, but the largest body remained facing Alexander. It was while they were wheeling into this front and rear formation, that Alexander drove his own stoutest charge home upon the Indian horse. The latter at once gave ground, and retired upon the elephants, "as to a friendly wall, for refuge," says Arrian. A number of these monsters were made to wheel about to the left to sustain the cavalry by charging upon Alexander's body of horse. As anticipated, Alexander's horse could by no means be made to approach them. But the elephants, by facing Alexander, were exposing themselves, and the Macedonian infantry, by now advancing, was enabled to take in flank those elephants which had wheeled to sustain the Indian horse. This they did with a will, wounded many, and slew a number of the drivers, so that the animals were without control, and rushed purposeless to and fro, equally dangerous to friend and foe. But some of them again wheeled about to the right, and urged forward by their drivers threatened to tread the phalangites under foot. Luckily the men stood in open order, so that they could the more readily avoid these creatures, and drive them back with wounds.

The Indian cavalry rallied somewhat under the diversion thus created by the movements of the elephants, and advanced again to oppose the Macedonian horse; but another charge by Alexander's stronger and better disciplined men broke their formation, huddled them up under the heels of the elephants, and increased the confusion tenfold. What the one hundred and fifty chariots on the left were doing all this while does not appear. There is no mention of them in the authorities beyond their place in line. There may be an error in this, or perhaps the confused mixture of elephants, cavalry and foot had prevented their making any charge whatever, as they needed space to do efficient work. Perhaps

Alexander's charge on the right dispersed them. They appear to have been of no use whatever in the battle, and the fact that no further mention is made of them looks as if there had been some change in their position prior to Alexander's attack.

Alexander's cavalry had by this time become so much disorganized by its repeated assaults and by the turmoil created by the elephants that he could no longer carry on his systematic charges; but as Cœnus had been able to join him, the united body of cavalry considerably outweighed the enemy's, not to speak of quality; and Alexander kept pressing home, though irregularly yet with extraordinary vehemence, upon the Indians and elephants. These creatures, now unmanageable, rushed again against the Macedonian phalanx, creating some considerable confusion and loss; but being driven back, for the phalangians bore themselves admirably under these novel conditions, and though much broken up, always rallied again at trumpet-call, they retired through the lines of the enemy, doing vastly more damage to their friends than they had inflicted on their foes.

The situation was most curious. Alexander and Cœnus continued their pressure on the enemy's right front, flank and rear, and though themselves much unstrung, they maintained their purpose, and their repeated charges became very fatal. The Macedonian horse showed that peculiar effect of discipline which results in the capacity to rally and reform, however serious the disaster, so soon as the immediate pressure is removed. The elephants were again and again urged forward on the phalanx; but they were received with wounds, and driven back, doing vast damage to the Indian line. The light troops under Tauron were peculiarly effective against them. The Macedonian infantry had plenty of elbow room, and could open ranks or retire from the elephants, and again close up or advance into hand to hand conflict; but the mass of the Indians was so huddled together that the men trod one upon another, and were at the mercy of the elephants when these brutes fled from the weapons of the phalanx. Finally the unwieldy creatures, unwilling longer to fight, as it were, between two fires, as with one accord retired out of action "like ships backing water" with trunks uplifted to the front, and trumpeting in terror. They were quite beyond control.

Alexander now saw that the victory was his. Keeping the phalanx in reserve but active, he continued with his horse to charge home upon the flank of the infantry line of the enemy, which was fast being hammered together into mere unwieldy masses, and gave it no chance to reform. Porus had been conspicuous for his bravery and his efforts to remedy a lost cause. But he had never fought in anything but parallel order, and had no conception of grand tactics. He could not have manœuvred his own right wing, even had he known how, because he was kept so busy by Alexander's tremendous blows upon his left. As a last effort the Indian king gathered forty yet unwounded elephants in a column, and essayed a charge on the victorious Macedonians, himself leading the van on his own huge war elephant. But Alexander met this charge with his archers and javelin-throwers, who skirmished about the column on every side, slaying the drivers and cutting the hamstrings of the elephants from behind. The effort utterly failed.

Alexander now ordered his phalanx to close ranks, link shields, and advance with pikes protended, and shouting their battle-cry, while the cavalry worked round to the rear, and charged in from the other side. The whole Indian army was a paralyzed, inert mass; it hung together from a mere habit of obedience; and out of it none but isolated individuals managed to escape through the intervals between Alexander's cavalry squadrons, or away towards the right flank.

The battle had lasted eight hours, and had been won by clean, crisp, tactical skill and wonderful use of the cavalry-arm. Perhaps no parallel can be found to such able, persistent and effective handling of horse. Alexander is above all others the pattern of a cavalry general. The conception of Cœnus' ride around the enemy's right and rear was bold, and in execution most brilliant. No cavalry officer, on the field of battle, ever performed a more dashing, clear-headed and splendid feat of arms. All Alexander's dispositions in this battle were masterly. He had left in his camp so large and excellent a force that his retreat was fully protected in case of disaster to the force in hand; he had abundant reserves in the brigades of Meleager, Attalus and Gorgias, though these indeed seem to have been tardy in crossing; and his appreciation of what himself and Cœnus could do on the level plain in which Porus had drawn up his army was full of the intellectual strength which wins the world's great victories. It may perhaps be said that Alexander's crossing with but fourteen thousand men to attack an army of nearly thrice the number savored of foolhardiness. It was certainly the reason why the battle lasted so long, and cost so heavily in killed and wounded. But this habit of taking risks was part of Alexander's nature, and success has always been held to justify risk in all but the exceptional cases.

Craterus now came up, having, though in face of the enemy, crossed the river successfully; and the other troops left on the farther side under Meleager, Attalus and Gorgias also put in an appearance, and not only made the victory a certain one, but undertook the pursuit instead of Alexander's tired men. Of Porus' army nearly twenty thousand infantry and three thousand cavalry were lost; or according to Diodorus, twelve thousand were killed and nine thousand captured. Their chariots were all broken to pieces, having been a hindrance instead of a help. The ground had probably been too deep for their evolutions. Two of Porus' sons, Spitakes, and nearly all of his prominent chieftains were killed, and all the elephants destroyed or captured. The Macedonians lost two hundred and thirty cavalry and seven hundred infantry in killed. This (over six and a half per cent.) is the heaviest loss in killed on record for an army of its size, and effectually disposes of the idea sometimes advanced that Alexander did not have to fight for his victories. It shows clearly that he was ready to fight until he won or was destroyed. To take the usual number of wounded would give us the extraordinary loss of seventy-three per cent. in killed and wounded. Still, this is credible. The wounded were numerous. "There returned to the camp scarcely a single person who was not wounded," says Curtius of another action, and it may have been the same in this case.

Porus himself was captured. Him Alexander had seen and admired during the entire battle. Conspicuously seated on his huge elephant, he led on his men with consummate bravery. After all was over, Porus, though wounded (Curtius says he had nine wounds), endeavored to make his escape. Alexander in person galloped after on Bucephalus. But the noble old animal fell in his tracks and died from overexertion, at the age, generally stated, of thirty years. As the legend goes, Bucephalus was wont to kneel down for Alexander to mount and dismount. This habit was not uncommon, for without stirrups, and with heavy armor and weapons, it would be a welcome aid. And now, rather than throw his rider in his fall, the gallant steed stopped, gently knelt for Alexander to dismount, and then rolled over dead. It is generally related that Bucephalus could be ridden, when naked, only by the king and his groom. But so soon as his trappings were on him, not even his groom could approach to mount, but only Alexander.

" When Porus, who exhibited great talent in the battle, performing the deeds not only of a general, but also of a valiant soldier, observed the slaughter of his cavalry, and some of his elephants lying dead, others, destitute of keepers, straying about in a forlorn condition, while most of his infantry had perished, he did not depart as Darius the Great King did, setting an example of flight to his men; but as long as any body of Indians remained compact in the battle, he kept up the struggle. But at last, having received a wound on the right shoulder, which part of his body alone was unprotected during the battle, he wheeled round. His coat of mail warded off the missiles from the rest of his body, being extraordinary both for its strength and the close fitting of its joints, as it was afterwards possible for those who saw him to observe. Then, indeed, he turned his elephant round and began to retire. Alexander, having seen that he was a great man and valiant in the battle, was very desirous of saving his life. He accordingly sent first to him Taxiles, the Indian, who rode up as near to the elephant which was carrying Porus as seemed to him safe, and bade him stop the beast, assuring him that it was no longer possible for him to flee, and bidding him listen to Alexander's message. But when he saw his old foe Taxiles, he wheeled round and was preparing to strike him with a javelin; and he would probably have killed him, if he had not quickly driven his horse forward out of the reach of Porus before he could strike him. But not even on this account was Alexander angry with Porus; but he kept on sending others in succession; and last of all, Meroës, an Indian, because he ascertained that he was an old friend of Porus. As soon as the latter heard the message brought to him by Meroës, being at the same time overcome by thirst, he stopped his elephant and dismounted from it. After he had drunk some water and felt refreshed, he ordered Meroës to lead him without delay to Alexander, and Meroës led him thither.

"When Alexander heard that Meroës was bringing Porus to him, he rode in front of the line, with a few of the Companions, to meet Porus; and stopping his horse, he admired his handsome figure and his stature, which reached somewhat above five cubits. He was also surprised that he did not seem to be cowed in spirit, but advanced to meet him as one brave man would meet another brave man, after having gallantly struggled in defense of his own kingdom against another king. Then, indeed, Alexander was the first to speak, bidding him say what treatment he would like to receive. The report goes that Porus replied: 'Treat me, O Alexander, in a kingly way!' Alexander, being pleased at the expression, said, 'For my own sake, O Porus, thou shalt be thus treated; but for thy own sake do thou demand what is pleasing to thee!' But Porus said that everything was included in that. Alexander, being still more pleased at this remark, not only granted him the rule over his own Indians, but also added another country to that which he had before, of larger extent than the former. Thus he treated the brave man in a kingly way, and from that time found him faithful in all things." (Arrian.)

Alexander.
(From a Phœnician Coin.)

XLII.

THE FIVE RIVERS. MAY TO JULY, B. C. 326.

ALEXANDER's policy towards the Indians was not to conquer but make allies of them; not to subdue peoples but to control rulers. He ceased ownership at the confines of the kingdom of the Great King. He reconciled Taxiles and Porus and to them committed all the territory he subdued in the Five Rivers country. He then moved into the foothills of the Caucasus, where he cut shipbuilding timber and floated it down to Craterus at Nicæa and Bucephala, new cities founded near the late battlefield. Crossing the Acesines and Hydraotis he found a number of republics. These free peoples joined hands to oppose him at Sangala, their principal city, which Alexander captured only after a stoutly contested battle and sharp siege. Wherever he advanced he subdued the country or received its submission. He then marched to the Hyphasis, purposing to cross and move as far as the Ganges. But his Macedonians had grown tired of wandering.

ALEXANDER founded two cities at the most important crossings of the Hydaspes; Nicæa near the place where the battle was fought, in commemoration of the victory, and Bucephala ten miles farther up, where he crossed the river, on the main road, in memory of his gallant horse.

"This Bucephalus," says Arrian, "had shared many hardships and incurred many dangers with Alexander during many years, being ridden by none but the king, because he rejected all other riders. He was both of unusual size and generous in mettle. The head of an ox had been engraved upon him as a distinguishing mark, and according to some this was the reason that he bore that name; but others say that though he was black he had a white mark upon his head which bore a great resemblance to the head of an ox. In the land of the Uxians this horse vanished from Alexander, who thereupon sent a proclamation throughout the country that he would kill all the inhabitants unless they brought the horse back to him. As a result of this proclamation it was immediately brought back. So great was Alexander's attachment to the horse and so great was the fear of Alexander entertained by the barbarians. Let so much honor be paid by me to this Bucephalus for the sake of his master." In this wish all good friends of the noblest of animals will join.

Alexander's mixture of the generous and the firm in his policy with the Indians was admirable. He had gained a distinct but not a fundamental control of this part of India which abutted on his Persian possessions. He had seen enough of the country to understand that he could not conquer this people out of hand. Nor had he any intention of so doing. He had control of all the territory from the Hellespont to the Indus, and could pretend to mould this into his long dreamed Graeco-Persian empire. But with India it was different. All he could pretend to do here was to make adherents and allies of the princes; not to conquer the peoples, but to control their rulers, and his acts to this end were well gauged.

Porus had in earlier days endeavored to extend his rule to the whole country between the Indus and the Hydaspes and had nearly succeeded, when the king of Taxila, fearful for the balance of power, had sought to put a limit to his advances, and the two had become active enemies. Alexander did not wish to depend on one prince alone. It was better that the power of the Five Rivers should lie between at least two; and he was wise enough to make these two princes equal in power and expert enough to reconcile them. He increased the territory and power of each, by merging the smaller principalities into theirs, and made each one content with what he held. In this manner Alexander maintained a marked control of this country.

At this time Alexander learned from Sisicottus, whom he
had made viceroy of a part of the cis-Indian district and whose
headquarters were at Aornus, of the revolt in his rear of the
Assacenians, who had murdered their governor and joined
hands to expel their new masters.   This revolt was probably

The Five River Country.

instigated by Abisares of Cashmir, who we remember had been
playing a double part, and after sundry embassies of friendship and submission to Alexander had been on the point of
joining Porus, and now that Porus was Alexander's vassal, was
again ready enough to surrender. This revolt made a disagree-
able breach in Alexander's communications which must be at
once repaired. He gave Philip, satrap of India, and Tyriaspes,
satrap of Parapamisus, orders to join forces and suppress the

revolt, instructing the other satraps in his rear to aid them. This course speedily checked a trouble which might have grown to be alarming.

Alexander remained a month in the vicinity of the Hydaspes to celebrate his victory and the funerals of the brave men who had fallen, by sacrifices and games. He then committed the building and fortifying of the cities he had projected to Craterus, and himself set out in a northeasterly direction against the Indians beyond the dominions of Porus in the foothills of the Caucasus, who were called Glaucians. Both Porus and Taxiles accompanied him. He led one half of the Companion cavalry, some picked phalangians, the horse and foot archers and Agrianians. This campaign was a direct threat at Abisares, for the conquest of this land opened the road to Cashmir, and the latter made haste to crave peace, sending another embassy and a present of forty elephants. From superabundance of work to do, Alexander was fain to overlook the past. Throughout the territory of the Glaucians all the towns and villages capitulated. Of these no fewer than thirty-seven had over five thousand population each, and some over ten thousand, a fact which shows a wonderfully prosperous condition of the country. This land he also gave over to Porus to rule, as he had previously added a large stretch to the territory of Taxiles.

In the mountain district through which this campaign led, Alexander found a fine supply of wood suitable for shipbuilding, cut a great deal of timber and floated it down to Craterus as material for the fleet he intended to make, and on which, after conquering India, he proposed to sail down to the Indus and the sea. Many deputations from other neighboring nations came to him here. These ambassadors must have been as much astonished to know Porus vanquished as to see him now held in high honor by Alexander. He was joined here by the Thracian cavalry which had been with Phrata-phernes, viceroy of Parthia and Hyrcania. He did not deem it wise to be without a sufficiency of cavalry from home, which might leaven the huge lump of Oriental horse now serving under his colors.

He next moved southerly towards the Acesines, a river flowing with the rapidity of a mountain torrent, and over two miles wide. Alexander selected the widest part of the river for his passage, because here the current was less strong. The bed was full of rocks, and the stream was a succession of eddies and rapids. There was much difficulty and loss in putting the troops over. Those who crossed with skins for floats or used them for the rafts did well enough, but the boats and some of the rafts were not so fortunate; many of them were dashed to pieces on the rocks, and a considerable number of men perished.

From beyond this river, Alexander sent Porus home to col-lect the most warlike of his troops, and all his elephants, and rejoin him. He left Cœnus with that part of the phalanx he now commanded — just how large a division is not stated — on the left bank of the Acesines River, to see to putting over the details which had been sent out on foraging expeditions, when they should return, and to hold, as it were, a bridge-head on the road along which the Macedonians were oper-ating.

There was another Porus, a cousin, says Strabo, of the Hydaspes king (the "cowardly Porus," the Macedonians dubbed him, because he deserted his relative in a season of distress), who was king of one of the tribes in the foothills. He had offered to surrender when he thought that subservi-ence to Alexander would rid him of his uncle's influence, but had again taken up arms and retired into the farther confines of his land when he found that the elder Porus was again in favor. Him Alexander set out to pursue with his light troops, leaving posts along his line of advance, at suitable intervals, so that Craterus and Cœnus might be protected in coming up, and in the foraging they were ordered to do for the army. But on reaching the Hydraotis, up which river he proposed to operate, and finding that the pursuit would be long and tedious, he detailed Hephæstion, with his own and Demetrius' hipparchies, one half of the archers, and two brigades of the phalanx, to finish the subjection of the land of this Porus, which was a district of Gandaritis, as is called the territory between the Hydaspes and Hydraotis rivers. Hephæstion was given orders to subdue other Indian tribes in this district, and to found a city on the left bank of the Acesines, at the main-road fords. Hephæstion was then to turn this territory over to the faithful Porus to govern in addition to his own.

Alexander himself then advanced on and crossed the Hydraotis, an operation which was more easily managed than the Acesines. Beyond this river he was in the land of the free Indians, the Cathæans being one of their tribes. Curiously for this tyrant-ridden part of the world, there has always been here, from time immemorial, a set of republics, or " kingless " peoples, as they were called. They were looked down upon by the subjects of the neighboring kings, but could no doubt afford to be so. Their largest city and capital, Sangala (modern Lahore), was strongly walled, and here the near-by allied tribes had met to arrest Alexander's advance in their direction. These free tribes were very warlike, and had never been subdued. Porus told Alexander that he had tried his hand against them more than once in vain, and that he would find them very obstinate in battle. Some of the qualities of the true republic appear to have been prominent among them. This report whetted Alexander's ambition to subdue them.

Turning back upon his course, Alexander marched against these confederates, and on the way, two days from the Hydraotis crossing, he passed through the city of the Adraisteans, Pimprama by name, which surrendered to him at his approach. Having in three days more, by recrossing the Hydraotis, reached Sangala, he found the barbarians drawn up on a hill in front of the city, with their wagons forming a triple line of defenses around them. The hill appears to have been precipitous on two sides, but approachable on the front, which commanded the entire surrounding country. The city was also on a hill standing sharply up out of the plain, and on its rear was protected by a lake or piece of low wet ground of some extent but no great depth.

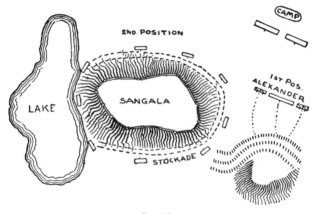

Sangala.

Alexander at once recognized that a difficult problem lay before him, and that he had not been misinformed as to the warlike qualities of these freedom-loving Indians. But he also recognized that he must not hesitate, but impose on the Indians by immediate attack, if he expected respectful submission when he had beaten them. He sent out the horse-

archers as skirmishers, to protect his advance and to allow
him to form at his leisure and without interference from the
Sangalians. He drew up his army in much the usual formation, with the cavalry and archers on the wings and the
phalanx in the centre. The royal horse-guards, led by Alexander, and Clitus' ilē (still so called) were on the right;
then came the hypaspists and Agrianians; then the phalanx
and Perdiccas' horse. Presently the rear-guard came up, and
its horse was placed on the right and left, and the infantry
troops mixed in with the phalanx in the centre.

Alexander first threw forward the cavalry of his right
wing on the Indians' left, as this seemed the least strong part
of their line, the wagons being placed less closely together.
He hoped to demoralize the enemy by a sudden onset, or perhaps get them to make a sortie, and thus secure a chance at
open field fighting. But he quickly found that cavalry was
not the arm to operate against the Indian wagon-fort. These
warriors were too shrewd to come out from their improvised
defenses. They knew the value of their position, and stood
on and among the wagons and hurled their weapons with
skill and excellent effect. So stanch was their defense
that the cavalry and light troops both recoiled from the assault. Dismounting, Alexander headed the phalanx and led
it with its fierce battle-cry and gallant rush against them.
The first row of wagons was speedily taken; but in the confined space between the first and second rows the phalangites
were unable to act to advantage; the sarissa was unadapted
to such work; a short sword or thrusting pike would have
been far more effective. They were more than once repulsed
by the Indians, who swarmed about in vast numbers; concealed themselves under both the first and second rows of
wagons; shot their arrows and cast their javelins from all
sides and with fatal aim upon the Macedonians. They showed

not the least sign of wavering, but fought with the utmost gallantry and steadiness, as if certain of and used to victory. The phalangites were not so good at this sort of fighting as at contests in the open field. Alexander rarely came so near to failure in his task. But after a long and bloody tussle, the barbarians were finally ousted from the second row of wagons. And as if despairing of success in contending against such foes, they attempted no stand at the third row, but retired into the city and closed the gates.

The walls were of such extent that Alexander could not fully surround the city, but he posted cavalry pickets on the sides he could not blockade, for he expected that the Indians would make an attempt to escape in the night. This expectation proved true, but the sortie was unsuccessful; the foremost Indians were at once cut down by the Macedonian videttes, who were alert and active, and the rest gave up the attempt and returned within walls. Alexander was now driven to something like a siege. He began by surrounding three sides of the city with a stockade which he could hold with fewer men. But the side farthest from his main camp, where lay the lake, he picketed carefully with cavalry. He prepared also to build towers and engines to override and batter down the walls. But he learned from some deserters that the enemy would try again on one of the succeeding nights to escape from the city by way of the lake, where they saw that there was no stockade, and through which, the water being shallow, they could wade. Alexander accordingly stationed Ptolemy, son of Lagus, at this point, with three chiliarchias of shield-bearing guards, the Agrianians, and one taxis of archers, giving him orders, in case the Indians made a sortie, to hold them in check at all hazards, and sound the alarm. And he instructed the rest of the forces to remain under arms and ready, upon hearing this signal, to march at an instant's notice to the spot thus indicated.

As Alexander anticipated, so the event occurred. Ptolemy had put to use many of the old wagons, and had interlocked them as an obstruction near the lake ; and at night his men blocked the roads and paths leading from the city, and threw up a mound in advance of the lake, in lieu of parts of the stockade which had been knocked down. Towards morning, in the third watch, the Indians made the expected sortie, but Ptolemy caught them as they came forth, vigorously attacked them, and, on sounding the alarm, Alexander promptly put in an appearance with the other troops. The Indians were stopped by the wagons and obstructions, and were driven back into the town, with a loss of five hundred killed.

Porus now arrived with five thousand Indian troops and a number of elephants ; sheds, towers, and rams had been built, and these military engines were being gradually advanced to the city wall, which was of brick, well constructed. A double intrenchment had now been built by the Macedonians all around the city. The walls were also gradually undermined at a number of places. Everything savored of success. But Alexander became impatient at the delays of a siege, and concluded to order a fresh assault. Preparations were carefully made, ladders were supplied in abundance to the men, and, undertaken in a moment when the Indians expected nothing less, the assault was entirely successful. The city was taken, and, under Alexander's orders to cut down all found with arms in their hands, seventeen thousand men were killed, and seventy thousand captured, with three hundred of the wagons. There is some reason to doubt these figures. The ruins of Sangala do not appear to show a city large enough to harbor so many people. Still, many may have been outside the walls. Alexander had one hundred killed and twelve hundred wounded, among them Lysimachus, the somatophylax. Sangala was razed to the ground, and the territory added to the dominion of Porus, and garrisoned by his troops.

Eumenes, Alexander's secretary, was one of the most valuable and expert officers in the army. But being a Greek, the jealousy of the Macedonians had prevented his rising to a rank for which he was eminently qualified. His name occurs rarely in Alexander's exploits. On this occasion Alexander sent him, with a guard of three hundred horse, to two cities which had joined Sangala in its opposition to Alexander, to inform them that if they at once surrendered they would receive fair treatment. But Eumenes found the cities deserted, and the tribes in abject flight. The news of the horrible butchery at Sangala belied the peaceful message which Eumenes brought; the people had a fearful dread of the Macedonians; and they could not be turned back. Alexander set out to pursue them, but they had too great a start, and the pursuit had to be given up. Those who had been left behind, however, — probably invalided, decrepit, and aged persons, — were slain by the soldiers to the number of five hundred. Such usages of war strike one as equally awful and unnecessary. But they were of every-day occurrence. The management of this land also was confided to Porus. The rest of the free Indians, now treated with a generosity by Alexander, in great contrast to the severity at Sangala, gave in their submission.

From here the army made a march to the capitals of King Sopeithes whose territory extended beyond the foothills of the Imaus and towards the sources of the Hyphasis, and of King Phegeus who reigned over neighboring peoples, at each of which places the Macedonians were received with great hospitality and rich gifts. Their dislike of the "kingless" tribes no doubt influenced their actions.

Thence Alexander descended to a suitable place on the

Hyphasis, intending to cross and subjugate the tribes beyond. For there seemed to be no limit to the king's desire to conquer, so long as any land or city or tribe remained within reach to be conquered. And the territory beyond the Hyphasis was said to be fertile and to be inhabited by a fine people, tall in stature and gallant in war, who possessed larger and fiercer elephants than were to be found anywhere else in India. Their government was a liberal aristocracy. With these people Alexander wished to become acquainted, and add them to the population owing fealty to his sceptre. He had the feeling, too, that so long as he did not reach a natural barrier, such as the sea or a desert or great mountain range, he ran danger from nations he did not subdue. He had also conceived the desire of reaching the Ganges, and of moving down this river to the Indian Ocean. Alexander himself was tireless, insatiable. But the spirit of his Macedonians had begun to flag.

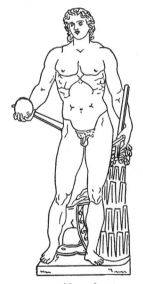

Alexander.

(From a Statue in the Smith-Barry Collection.)

XLIII.

TURNING BACK. JULY TO OCTOBER, B. C. 326.

THE Macedonian soldiers had determined to proceed no farther. They had, through their officers, certain rights of protest. These they concluded to enforce. For three months, rain had incessantly fallen, and with it the moral tone of the troops. They were ragged; their arms were worn out; of armor there was scarcely any. They were not only unwilling, they were unfit, to march farther in advance — to the Ganges and the sea, as Alexander wished them to do. Alexander's eloquence on this occasion failed. The men did nothing mutinous; they simply declined to advance. Alexander recognized the conditions. The sacrifices proved inauspicious. He agreed to return. It was well that he turned back. Much longer absence from Babylon would have seen his empire crumble into anarchy for lack of the controlling hand. Returning to the Hydaspes, he built a fleet, sacrificed, formally invested Taxiles and Porus with viceregal authority over their respective territories, and began his descent to the Indus with a pomp and ceremony and splendor never before seen. A column marched on either bank; another followed at two days' interval; the king and eight thousand men, and the baggage and camp-followers, floated down the river on a fleet of one thousand boats.

ALEXANDER had had much to contend with in the jealousies of his Macedonians. He could scarcely do a favor to an Asiatic without provoking the selfish protests of his countrymen. He had presented one thousand talents to Taxiles, whose land had furnished his army ten times as much. Said Meleager: "Must we come so far as India to find a man worthy of such a gift?" To accomplish his end, the king had grown to overlook these things, — to control his ancient temper. "Let them grumble," said he, "so long as they obey." And their obedience was marked. Near by or far away, Alexander's lieutenants acted as if they were under his eye. Of Cæsar's or Napoleon's lieutenants one could not say so much. It was with his satraps, not his generals, that Alexander had trouble. Whatever orders he issued were carried out. Marches were doubled, the most difficult mountains and rivers and deserts were crossed, toil of the most grievous undergone, the all but impossible accomplished, but Alexander's lieutenants were always on time as ordered. Perhaps no captain ever got from his subordinates such unequivocal obedience. But for all that, the army exercised its rights and wagged its tongue.

There had been growing for many months a spirit of unusual restlessness under Alexander's hungry schemes of territorial acquisition. This sort of dissatisfaction had really been at the bottom of the several conspiracies of Philotas, the pages, and Callisthenes, but now it had expanded into a different phase. There was a manifest determination among all concerned, not to disobey or mutiny or conspire, but to exert their free-born right to check the king in his ceaseless forward marches by a refusal to be led farther from home. There is nothing to prove that the Macedonian common soldier had rights anything like those which our own republican volunteers possessed as citizens; but there is a great deal which looks as if the chiefs of the Macedonians and Greek allies had much to say with regard to what they should do or where they should be led. These rights, whatever they were, now came to be exerted.

The feeling against further advance existed in the whole army, even to the warmest friends of Alexander, and the expression of it had taken the form of many meetings at which the matter had been openly discussed. The army, under the Macedonian unwritten law, may be said to have constituted, in its commanding officers, a sort of popular assembly, with undefined powers, to be sure, but none the less wielding something like a right of decision. We have repeatedly seen

Alexander appeal to it; and this was now used as a lever to enable the men and officers to so shape the movements of the army as to be able to look, at some distant period, to a return home and the enjoyment of their hardly-won riches, rather than to indefinite absence and the encountering of still greater dangers; for the rumor ran that near the head waters of the Ganges, Xandrames, an Indian prince, had blocked the way with two hundred thousand foot, twenty thousand horse, two thousand chariots, and three thousand trained elephants. No doubt all this was vastly exaggerated, but the effect remained the same. Further meetings were held, and the subject was fully ventilated. The conclusion come to by the more moderate was that they did not wish to advance farther, while the more radical declared openly that they would not advance beyond the Hyphasis. The criticisms of the soldiers often had their origin in idleness, which Alexander knew full well how to control by active work, but here it was a very different matter.

Alexander at once grasped the situation. He well understood the limitations of his own authority as well as the limitations of human endurance. He recognized that so far his Macedonians had faithfully followed him, not only from native loyalty and courage, from admiration of his military achievements, from love of war, and from the desire of sharing the wealth which had been pouring in upon them, but also from genuine affection for his person quite apart from their sense of fealty. But he also recognized that they held the constitutional right of veto, as it were, upon his decision, and that this might not be recklessly tampered with; and he further recognized that there was a point beyond which human toleration refuses to be taxed, and that his army had reached that point.

Before the danger grew into a form in which it could not

be handled, Alexander called the usual council of command-ing officers and explained to them his position. The head waters of the Ganges were not far off, said he, and on reach-ing that river, the sea would put a positive boundary to his conquests, whereas a less certain boundary must always re-main a provocation to revolt or to invasion from beyond. He invoked their ardor, patriotism and love of glory, and showed them that it was they who really ruled the land, and won its wealth, not he. But he said that he would abide by their decision and called for an expression of opinion. " Either I desire to persuade you to advance," said the king, " or to have you give me reasons for returning." After some hesitation — for Alexander was equally loved and feared and in the past more than one man had suffered for having spoken freely — Cœnus rose and expressed the feeling of all the others, or as he said, what he thought would be best for both Alexander and the army.

Of the original Macedonians, who had left Hellas, said he, few indeed were left, most having perished by disease and wounds or been left — perhaps unwillingly — in garrisons in various parts of Asia. Those "few out of many" who remained, naturally enough desired to return home to their parents, their wives and children, where they could enjoy the honors and fruits of their courage and labors. He advised Alexander, if he desired to make further conquests, to head homeward, consolidate his enormous possessions, and, waiting till times were ripe, take a fresh start with younger troops. " Self-control in the midst of success is the noblest of all virtues, O King! For thou hast nothing to fear from ene-mies, while thou art commanding and leading such an army as this; but the visitations of the deity are unexpected, and consequently men can take no precautions against them." Cœnus' speech was received with cheers by all, as it reflected the feelings of all.   Others are said by Curtius to have spoken to the same effect.

The above is the reason generally assigned by the historians for Alexander's turning back from the Hyphasis.   But Strabo and Diodorus hint at a deeper reason, namely, that the troops were exhausted, physically, mentally, and morally, by the incessant rain of the season.   Says Diodorus, probably quoting Clitarchus, an inaccurate writer but full of a species of local color : " Few Macedonians were left and these were near desperation ; the horses were footsore by the long marches ; the weapons of the soldiers dulled and broken by the number of battles ; no one had Greek clothes left : rags of barbaric and Indian booty, miserably patched together, covered the scarred bodies of these conquerors of the world ; for seventy days the most terrible rainfall had streamed from heaven, in the midst of storms and thunders."

Whoever has served through a campaign during a period of unusual storms can well picture to himself the hopeless, desperate condition of the Macedonian soldiery, and understand their refusal to proceed.   No consequences of refusal could be worse than the actual conditions.   The same low but determined pitch of mood was occasionally to be observed after the terrible slaughter of the Virginia campaign of 1864.   And that Alexander, in lieu of punishing the refusal of his Macedonians to obey his intended orders of march, — as he later punished their mutiny at Opis, — should have given way to them, well shows not only that he recognized their rights, but understood their pitiable condition, their fidelity and affection, and knew that there was abundant excuse for their want of discipline, if such indeed it was.

Alexander was much disturbed at Cœnus' voicing of the opinion of the army.   He called another meeting the next day at which he announced his intention to discharge those who desired to return home and to advance with the faithful remainder. The rest might go back to Macedon and tell their friends that they had deserted their king in the midst of his enemies. But the Macedonian army well understood its powers; the men were saddened, but remained unmoved in their determination, though their king withdrew himself from their sight and remained in his tent for three days, nursing his wrath in private. He imagined that he could once more alter their mood by this means.

But Alexander finally recognized that he must submit to a state of things which he could not control, and sought a means of gracefully doing so. The sacrificial victims proved or were ordered to be declared unpropitious to further advance, and thus having the excuse of bowing to the fiat of the gods and not to men, the king deemed it well for his own dignity to follow the indication of the sacrifices. For he was certain that his army would no longer follow him and he must decide to turn his face in the direction of home. This decision he announced to the army; and it was received with shouts and exultation. The men crowded around the king's tent and prayed blessings upon him, " because by them alone he suffered himself to be conquered."

According to Curtius and Diodorus, Alexander had endeavored to wheedle the army into a further advance. He allowed the men to indulge in a looting raid into the land of the adjoining friendly King Phegeus; while absent, made their wives and children, vast numbers of whom were always with the army, presents of all manner of valuables, amounting to fully a month's pay ; and on the return of the men, laden with booty, endeavored to persuade them, not in a conference with leaders, but in open meeting, to continue on the course he had cut out. But this has not the smack of reality. Arrian's relation is much more probable, as it comes from a better source.

It was time Alexander did turn back; for the term of his absence, and the distance he had come (from his base at Tyre to this point he had marched over nine thousand miles), not only had demoralized his soldiers, but had utterly unstrung the fidelity of many of the satraps he had left behind. When he returned to the heart of his new kingdom, he found that he must visit heavy punishments on a great number of his viceroys, and had he been gone much longer, the whole system he had so carefully established would probably have fallen to the ground for mere lack of the controlling hand. Had Alexander actually marched to the Ganges, he would have found no kingdom when he returned, if indeed that return had ever taken place. This indeed was improbable, for, when one considers the enormous stretch of desert he would have to cross to reach the Ganges, the present condition of his army and all the factors in the case, it is doubtful indeed if even his almost superhuman energy would have sufficed to put such a campaign through. Moreover, it may be suggested, in view of the entirely different manner in which he had been organizing the government of this Five River territory, whether his intention was more than a passing fancy.

Porus and Taxiles, Sopeithes and Phegeus were left all but independent; the former two in charge of enormous territories, the latter as a sort of balance of power between them. The Caucasus and the mountains on the western bank of the Indus were a far better boundary to his possessions than any which India could afford, and it is probable that Alexander had the same object in view in his political dispositions in the Five River country that he had in those made with the Bactrians and Sogdianians who were to keep in control the Scythians beyond the Jaxartes. He may perhaps have proposed a sort of raid towards the Ganges with a select small force;

but had he not in reality already determined to leave these allies to guard the real eastern boundary of his kingdom, the Indus, and turn back? The incident of the Macedonian protest was alone enough to impel his natural obstinacy to make a point of a march farther on into the bowels of India.

It was the end of August. To commemorate the event and to mark the spot where the hero arrested his conquering hand, as a thank-offering to the gods who had smiled upon his efforts and as a monument to the labors of the king and of the army, twelve altars of the shape of very high towers, but much wider, were erected and inaugurated with the greatest pomp, sacrifices, feasts and games. Alexander then gave to Porus charge also of this territory and marched back over the Hydraotis and to the Acessines, where he found the city Hephæstion was to build all but completed. This, as usual, he populated with Indians who volunteered to settle there and invalided Greek mercenaries, whom he left with abundant resources. The denizens of these new towns were no doubt given marked privileges to compensate for their change of home.

The rain had now ceased, the land began to dry, and the rice covered the lately flooded fields with a mantle of green. The soldiers rejoiced at their once more facing homeward as well as at the smiling aspect of the country.

It was here that Abisares' brother reached Alexander. He came with gifts and thirty elephants, and brought excuses from Abisares that he did not personally report to the king, for he was sick. Alexander chose to accept the excuses, and appointed Abisares satrap of the country lately his kingdom. He had no time for an expedition to chastise him ; nor was he of any great moment. Taxiles and Porus sufficed to keep him in check. Arsaces, king of the adjoining territory, likewise concluded to send in a capitulation and was placed under Abisares' authority. The proper arrangements were made for the payment of tribute by both.

Alexander then returned to the Hydaspes, where some time was spent in repairing the damage done by the floods to Bucephala and Nicæa, whose new and hastily built walls had been unable to resist the overflow and rapid current of the river. They were now made more solid and substantial. Here too he found reinforcements from Greece, consisting of six thousand cavalry and thirty thousand infantry, brought by Harpalus. There were also twenty-five thousand panoplies of complete armor, and many medicines, the latter extremely necessary. Had he sooner received these reinforcements and supplies he might, it is thought, have persuaded the army to advance across the Hyphasis.

But though Alexander, as the historians allege, had in this retreat suffered the most cruel disappointment which ever befell him, when he had accepted the inevitable, he turned his mind to utilizing the conquests he had already made, and to consolidating his empire with as much energy as he could possibly have put into the conquest of the rest of India. He now proposed to carry out his original scheme of moving down to the Indus and to reduce the people along the lower course of this river, and head back to Babylon along the coast. He had heard that some tribes near the Indus, especially the Mallians and Oxydracians, were ready to resist him; and unless the rivers, of which he held the head waters, were made absolutely his so far as the sea, his conquests at their source would be held on slight tenure. And, as always, part of his plan was to found other cities and carry with him the Hellenizing influences which he had already spread so far.

Alexander concluded to return by descending the Hydaspes, which empties into the Acesines, and thence through the

Indus to the sea. For this purpose he ordered a number of vessels to be got ready, many of them thirty-oared galleys, and others with one and a half banks of oars; flat-bottomed, deckless boats for horses, and others suitable for the men, artillery, and baggage. The Phœnicians, Cyprians, Carians and Egyptians, multitudes of whom were in the ranks, furnished plenty of shipwrights and crews.

A fact which throws into high relief the extraordinary energy and enterprise of Alexander is the unreliability of the information he was able to procure about these distant countries, in despite of which he continued to push forward. When he saw crocodiles in the Indus, and the lotus bean growing on the banks of the Acesines, he imagined and for some time believed that he had discovered the sources of the Nile, where alone he had seen or heard of these animals and plants. Among all his suite of wise men, there was none to correct this error, and it was not till some time later that he ascertained the existence of the Persian Gulf, southern Arabia, and the Red Sea.

Herodotus tells us that the vessels of Nechaus, in the seventh century B. C., left the Red Sea and made in three years a circuit of Libya; also that about 512 B. C. the vessels of Darius, son of Hystaspes, under pilotage of the Carian Scylax, floated down the Indus, sailed west, and reached the Red Sea. But this information was of the crudest. What it meant had not impressed itself on Alexander's mind.

Cœnus at this time died, and was buried with as great pomp as the circumstances allowed. It is said, however, that Alexander had not forgotten his taking up the cause of the soldiers at the Hyphasis. This scarcely accords with Alexander's character, which, though passionate, did not long harbor unkindness, and the splendid services of Cœnus, so worthily capped at the Hydaspes, must still have dwelt in his recollection.

As a last act before leaving the Five Rivers country, Alexander solemnly invested Porus with the sovereignty of all India east of the Hydaspes, so far as he had overcome it, embracing seven nations and lands containing more than two thousand cities; and clothed Taxiles with equal authority over the territory he had assigned to him. He prescribed the relations which the smaller independent princes — Sopeithes, Phegeus, Abisares — should bear to them, and the tribute all should pay.

He then got his vessels together, some eighty thirty-oared war vessels, two hundred horse transports, and seven hundred of all other kinds, river-craft, old and new, — the number is given by Arrian, on the authority of Ptolemy, as not far short of two thousand, — and gave the command of thirty-three of the war vessels, as honorable distinction, to thirty-three of his best subordinates. Of these, twenty-four were Macedonians, — the seven somatophylaxes and Peucestas, shortly to be an eighth, Craterus, the phalanx-strategos, Attalus, Nearchus of the hypaspists, a civilian Laomedon, Androsthenes, who later sailed around Arabia, and others, many of whom were probably staff officers. Among the Greeks were Eumenes, the secretary, and the king's intimate Medius. Among the foreigners, Bagoas, the Persian, and two Cyprians, sons of kings. The rest are not well-known names, or prominent. Having thus, with great ceremony and magnificence, settled the preliminaries of his departure, he himself embarked with the shield-bearing guards, the Agrianians, and the body-guard of cavalry, — some eight thousand men, all told. It is probable that the baggage and camp-followers monopolized the greater part of the small craft.

The start was made in early November. Craterus, with part of the cavalry and infantry, marched along the right bank of the river; and along the left Hephæstion led the better part, including two hundred elephants. Each of these bodies was in light marching order, and, like the modern army corps, some forty to fifty thousand strong ; while Alexander's force in the river was so placed as readily to sustain either one at need, or to enable a crossing to be made. These generals were ordered to march rapidly on the capital of Sopeithes, three days down stream, — this must have been a second potentate of the same name, — and Philip, viceroy of the region between Bactria and the Indus, was to follow as rear-guard, at an interval of three marches. The Nysæan cavalry was sent back to Nysa well rewarded. The whole fleet was placed under Nearchus as admiral. The pilot of Alexander's ship was Onesicritus. Arrian's description of the progress of this fleet is very picturesque : —

" When he had made all the necessary preparations, the army began to embark at the approach of the dawn ; while, according to custom, he offered sacrifice to the gods and to the river Hydaspes, as the prophets directed. When he had embarked he poured a libation into the river from the prow of the ship, out of a golden goblet, invoking the Acesines as well as the Hydaspes, because he had ascertained that it is the largest of all the rivers which unite with the Hydaspes, and that their confluence was not far off. He also invoked the Indus, into which the Acesines flows, after its junction with the Hydaspes. Moreover, he poured out libations to his forefather Heracles, to Ammon, and the other gods to whom he was in the habit of sacrificing, and then he ordered the signal for starting seawards to be given with the trumpet. As soon as the signal was given, they commenced the voyage in regular order ; for directions had been given at what distance apart it was necessary for the baggage vessels to be arranged, as also for the vessels conveying the horses, and for the ships of war ; so that they might not fall foul of each other by sailing down the channel at random. He did not allow even the fast-sailing ships to get out of rank by outstripping the rest. The noise of the rowing was never equaled on any other occasion, inasmuch as it proceeded from so many ships rowed at the same time ; also the shouting of the boatswains giving the time for beginning and stopping the stroke of the oars, and the clamor of the rowers, when keeping time all together, with the dashing of the oars, made a noise like a battle-cry. The banks of the river, also, being in many places higher than the ships, and collecting the sound into a narrow space, sent back to each other an echo which was very much increased by its very compression. In some parts, too, the groves of trees on each side of the river helped to swell the sound, both from the solitude and the reverberation of the noise. The horses which were visible on the decks of the transports struck the barbarians who saw them with such surprise that those of them who were present at the starting of the fleet accompanied it a long way from the place of embarkation. For horses had never before been seen on board ships in the country of India ; and the natives did not call to mind that the expedition of Dionysus into India was a naval one. The shouting of the rowers and the noise of the rowing were heard by the Indians who had already submitted to Alexander, and these came running down to the river's bank, and accompanied him, singing their native songs. For the Indians have been eminently fond of singing and dancing since the time of Dionysus and those who under his bacchic inspiration traversed the land of the Indians with him."

Three days after embarking, Alexander reached the rendezvous with Hephæstion and Craterus, and remained two days for Philip to come up. His force here is stated by Curtius at one hundred and twenty thousand men ; by Plutarch, at the same number of foot and fifteen thousand horse ; almost the only definite statement on the subject since Arbela. The following taxes are named: Cœnus, Polysperchon, Meleager, Craterus, Philotas, Alcestas, Attalus, Gorgias, Clitus, Balacrus, Philip, Peithon, Antigenes. Philip he then directed to march across to the Acesines and down that river, to assure himself of the possession of its western bank. Hephæstion and Craterus were given fresh orders as to their march, which were to sweep farther inland; and as they proceeded down the Hydaspes they reduced by force or surrender the tribes through whose land they passed. "But he himself continued his voyage down the river Hydaspes, the channel of which is nowhere less than twenty stades broad. Mooring his vessels near the banks wherever he could, he received some of the Indians dwelling near into allegiance by their voluntary surrender, while he reduced by force those who came into a trial of strength with him." (Arrian.)

Modern Statue of Alexander in the Tuileries Garden.

XLIV.

THE MALLIANS. NOVEMBER, B. C. 326, TO FEBRUARY, B. C. 325.

At the confluence of the Hydaspes with the Acesines were dangerous rapids. In these a number of ships were lost and damaged. From here Alexander undertook a campaign against the Mallians. This tribe was about to be joined by the Oxydracians, but Alexander anticipated them. He divided his army into three columns. One he himself headed, to march across a desert tract against the Mallians, for the reason that they did not expect him from that direction; on his left, Ptolemy, three marches up river, was to intercept the Mallians if they fled thither; on his right, Hephæstion, five marches down river, was to perform the like office; Nearchus and Craterus remained with the baggage and fleet. Marching across the desert with much toil, Alexander surprised the Mallians and captured Agallassa, their capital. Thence moving restlessly to and fro, he wasted the country and slew all with arms in their hands. He was too busy to subdue; he exterminated. In a number of places he found stanch opposition — and in the attack on the chief city of the Mallians (modern Multan) after a deed of personal valor worthy of Achilles, he was grievously wounded and nearly lost his life. While disabled there was great fear among the Macedonians; for who but Alexander could lead them back to their homes? The Mallian campaign was however ended. The whole country handed in its fealty.

ALEXANDER now learned that the Mallians and Oxydracians, who were the most numerous and reputed most warlike of all the Indian tribes, had put their families and treasures in the strongest cities and made vast preparations for disputing his passage over their land. Curtius gives their joint forces as ninety thousand foot, ten thousand horse and nine hundred chariots. Alexander made haste to attack this problem before these preparations were completed. In five days from his second start down river he reached a point below the confluence of the Hydaspes and Acesines where the double volume of these two rivers is suddenly driven into a narrow gorge with high banks, and flows with great rapidity. A number of his vessels were here damaged by the whirlpools and eddies in the stream, and the rapids and bad bottom came close to wrecking the entire fleet. The round ships, as the transports from their unwieldly structure were called, got through fairly well. But the long ships or war galleys suffered greatly from the oars of the lower tiers getting caught, and a number of men perished. Even Alexander's ship scarcely escaped being engulfed and the king is related to have already cast aside his mantle and upper raiment in expectation of having to swim for his life. He was forced to halt some days to repair damages. On the right bank below these rapids, in a bend of the river to the west, there was a jutting promontory which made a sort of roadstead. Here he was able to pick up much wreckage and many of the corpses.

Alexander was on the confines of the territory of the Mallians, which extends northerly of the confluence of the Acesines and Hydraotis. This tribe expected that Alexander would continue his route down river to this confluence and thence move up stream to attack them; because the stretch of land north of the confluence and between the two rivers was a desert region entirely without water and difficult to cross. But Alexander determined to do what they least expected and to march across the desert.

While repairs were being made Alexander headed an incursion some thirty miles westward into the land of some tribes known as the Sibæ, on the right bank, they being said to be about to reinforce the Mallians by crossing the river. They were some forty thousand in number, but he easily defeated them, destroyed their capital and wasted their territory as an example. He then joined the fleet and his lieutenants. Craterus he found in camp. Hephæstion and Philip were between the rivers at the confluence.

In order that the Mallians should find opposition wherever they might turn, he divided his army into several detachments. Philip's corps, the brigade of Polysperchon, the horse-bowmen and the elephants, which had been marching down the river, were now transferred to the right bank of the Acesines, as the united stream is still called, and the whole added to Craterus' force. Nearchus with the fleet was first started down the river. Craterus followed Nearchus three days later. This joint naval and military force was to form a base for future operations on the westerly side of the river. Nearchus was to land on the right bank below the point where the Acesines receives the Hydraotis, and hold the vicinity to prevent reinforcements being sent to the Mallians south of the desert, as well as to intercept any barbarian forces which attempted escape that way. The rest of the army was then divided into three parts. Alexander commanded the body which marched directly against the Mallians across the desert. It consisted of the hypaspists, archers, Agrianians, Peithon's brigade of the phalanx, the horse-archers and half of the Companion cavalry. By this march he proposed to surprise them and cut them off from Gandiritis and the Cathæan country, and drive them down towards the mouth of the Hydraotis and there have them run foul of the Macedonian forces ordered to that point. Hephæstion was sent along the left bank southerly, five marches ahead of the king, so that if the Mallians or part of them fled down stream when Alexander attacked them he could be in a position to intercept them even before they reached Craterus and Nearchus. Ptolemy followed three marches behind Alexander, so that if the Mallians or part of them fled up stream when Alexander attacked they would meet a like reception.

A rendezvous was given to all the detachments at the junction of the Hydraotis and Acesines.

These bodies thus marched in such a manner as to be able to coöperate in working against the Mallians; Nearchus and Craterus were to look after the western bank, and keep an eye on the barbarians opposite. Alexander was to march directly against the Mallians as was his wont, while Hephæstion would be within sustaining distance of his right and Ptolemy of his left flank. It should be noted that the present confluence of the Acesines (Chenab) and the Hydraotis (Ravi) is thirty miles above Multan. In Alexander's time it was just below Multan, with a branch inclosing the town and citadel. There has always been a tendency in these Indian rivers to seek channels farther west. The course of the Indus has greatly changed.

It is said that the Mallians and Oxydracians had laid aside their usual quarrels to meet the overwhelming danger and agreed to work together to resist the threatened invasion. The forces they had raised were sixty thousand foot, ten thousand horse and seven hundred chariots, and they had given mutual hostages. As the Mallian territory was the one primarily threatened, the Oxydracians would have been obliged to leave their own to join the Mallians. The joint army proposed to manœuvre under cover of the desert. But as the tribes could not agree on a common leader (being among the free Indians and, says Arrian, jealous of each other to the last degree) the confederate scheme fell through. While not vouched for on good authority this statement seems to agree with subsequent facts.

The first half day's march brought Alexander to a small water a dozen miles (one hundred stades) from the Acesines (perhaps the small river Ayek, midway between Jungh and Shorkot, eleven miles from the Chenab). Informed that this

was the last water to be had till the army reached the city to
which the largest force of the Mallians had fled, — for on the
failure of the scheme of confederation all the barbarians had
retired to their respective strongholds, — Alexander rested the

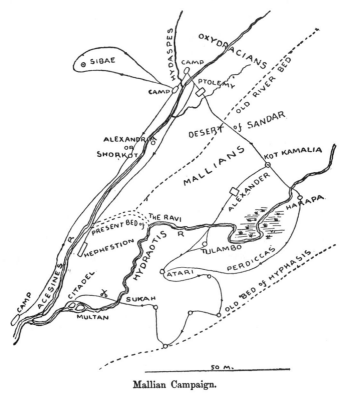

Mallian Campaign.

army and gave each man orders to fill whatever vessels he had
on hand with water to last him across the desert tract before
them. From this water on, the march occupied the balance
of this day and the succeeding night, no stop being made and
about forty-five miles (four hundred stades) being covered in
this time, a remarkable march for the twenty-four hours.
Alexander had calculated well in choosing this route so as to

surprise the Indians. They did not in the least expect him from this direction. When nearing the end of the journey, he advanced ahead of the phalanx with the cavalry and soon came in sight of the Mallian city of Agallassa (modern Kot-Kamalia) on the edge of the desert of the Sandar.

There have been numerous attempts to identify and locate the places thus made the objectives of Alexander's marches. Some have resulted happily ; many cannot be reconciled with the various statements of the ancient historians. General Alexander Cunningham, R. E., in his Ancient Geography of India, seems to be the most reliable guide ; and in all Alexander's campaigns, from the head waters of the Cophen to the delta of the Indus, much heed has been paid to his very intelligent and painstaking work. Still there are difficulties, as he himself acknowledges, in the way of many of his identifications. The route he traces, in difficult and conflicting passages, is, however, as reliable as any can be. He has largely made use of the records of the Chinese pilgrim Hwen Thsang, whose travels in India in the seventh century give the then condition of Alexander's towns, and aid materially in the process of identification.

So utterly disconcerted was the enemy at Alexander's sudden appearance that he found most of them outside the city, which was too small readily to shelter the multitude, and unarmed. Entirely unprepared for resistance, they were at the mercy of the Macedonians, who slew a vast number and drove the rest into the city, around which Alexander at once posted a cordon of cavalry, so as to hold it until the infantry could come up to begin operations against it.

On the arrival of the infantry, Alexander detached Perdiccas, with his own and Clitus' cavalry ilēs and the Agrianians, to blockade another city of the Mallians in this vicinity (Harapa, sixteen miles southeast of Kot-Kamalia, according to

Cunningham) until he himself could come to attack it. But he bade him by no means to undertake an assault, lest the rumor of its fall should too soon alarm the country. Alexander then attacked the wall of Agallassa. The enemy did not defend it to any purpose, but after a number had been killed and wounded by missiles, some retired into the citadel of the town, while the majority took to the woods. The citadel they defended gallantly for some hours against repeated partial assaults, though these were handsomely made; for this burg was situated on a height difficult of access. But Alexander ordered a final assault in force. This was so vigorously renewed, himself heading the storming party, that, under the influence of his example, who was everywhere, instinct with words of cheer and deeds of valor, the citadel was captured and its garrison of two thousand men put to the sword.

Perdiccas reached the city to which he was sent only to find it deserted by its inhabitants a short time before. Giving chase, he overtook and slew a great number of the stragglers; but most of them got away and fled to the marshes of the river Hydraotis.

Alexander, giving his men a short rest after taking Agallassa, marched with the cavalry in pursuit of the rest of the Mallians who had fled from the second city and from Agallassa. By a rapid night march he reached the Hydraotis. Here he came up with a number of stragglers of the column of fugitives, who suffered the usual fate. Crossing by the same ford to the south or left bank, he pursued in such haste that he overtook the rear-guard of the Mallians, broke it up, and slew and captured a great number. The rest made good their escape to a fortified town near by, a strong place by nature and by art (modern Tulambo). Waiting for the infantry to come up, Alexander sent Peithon, with his taxis and two ilēs of cavalry, against the latter place. Peithon captured it, and brought back all who were not slain for sale as slaves.

It is common and very natural for historians to question the propriety of waging such wars of extermination. And according to our views they are not justifiable. But it must be remembered that Alexander lived in an era when human life, as such, was not the sacred thing which the civilization of our century has made it. Even the life of a Hellene was of small consequence; these barbarians were not even considered. It is not probable that Alexander ever debated the question of cruelty; that it ever occurred to him that he was trenching on the everlasting laws of common humanity. Such a law was not at that day recognized. The extermination of a people or the devastation of a region, as a means of protecting boundaries from invasion, was then and has always been, down to this generation, within certain limits, a well recognized military scheme. And when we look at the ruthless cruelties of modern nations, practised after the Christian religion had been preached for fifteen centuries, it is less hard to palliate Alexander's acts, which proceeded by no means from a cruel nature, or lust of blood, or drunken fury, as has so often been said, but which were in pursuance of a clear and defined military policy. Nothing short of fearful examples would subdue these barbarians and semi-barbarous tribes, or deter them from rising in rebellion so soon as the conqueror turned his back. Alexander's course was now in retreat, as it were. He had not always time for careful systematic conquests. He must exterminate when he could not readily subdue. And it may perhaps be said that the influence of the trades and arts and civilization of the Greeks, which remained behind, to a greater or less extent, in every territory over which Alexander left a satrap, was of more

eventual good than the slaughter of many thousands of barbarians did harm. Perhaps Alexander had no right whatever
of conquest. That proposition is certainly capable of being
ably advocated. But he did go abroad to conquer; and once
he set forth, he was wise, in a military sense, to take the
means he did to carry through his conquests, however much
we may shudder at the awful array of figures which computes
the human souls his conquering progress swept from before
him.

While Peithon was capturing the second city, Alexander
headed an expedition against a town of the Brahmins, whither
some of the Mallians had fled (probably modern Atari,
twenty miles southwest of Tulambo, thirty-three miles northeast of Multan). No sooner had he reached the place and
marched the phalanx to the wall, in order to undermine it,
than the Indians, divining his purpose and believing that the
city wall would not long resist the Macedonians, and being,
moreover, harassed with the missiles of the light troops, retired into the citadel, thinking here to be able to make a
better defense. The Macedonians followed hard upon, and
some of them penetrated the citadel with the barbarians, but
could not hold themselves there. But they were expert sap-
pers and miners. They went to work with a will, and soon
one of the towers and a part of the wall near by were undermined and thrown down. An assault was then ordered.
When the Macedonians reached the breach, where the opposition was stoutly maintained, and were seen to hesitate in the
assault, Alexander rushed to the front, — as he could never
refrain from doing, — headed them in person, mounted the
wall first of all, carried the works, and at once captured the
citadel. The gallant defenders themselves set their habitations on fire, and, standing on the roofs, hurled their missiles
or firebrands upon the foe until they fell engulfed by the

burning walls. Here five thousand brave men perished. Sad and strange that civilization, as well as Christianity, has always needed so much blood to propagate its benignant doctrines. And yet, as Voltaire said, Alexander founded many more cities than other conquerors have destroyed.

Scarcely pausing to give his men one day's rest, though they had marched and fought almost continuously for five, Alexander moved with fresh ardor against the other tribes of the Mallians. He knew that exertion now meant quiet by and by. He found that the barbarians had all fled into the desert from their several cities, all of which he destroyed. The army was given one day more rest. He then dispatched Peithon with his infantry brigade, and Demetrius with his ilē of cavalry and some light-armed men, back to the river Hydraotis to follow it up and down, and capture all who had fled for safety into the woods and marshes which lined the banks. For many had taken refuge in these places. This work was done thoroughly; all who did not surrender were captured and killed.

While this diversion to keep his rear cleared of enemies was going on, Alexander himself led the rest of the troops against what was reputed the largest city of the Mallians, where he heard that many had taken refuge on fleeing from other towns. This was probably Multan. It was on the direct route prescribed to Hephæstion, who, however, either had no orders, or was too weak to attack it. The inhabitants had abandoned the city proper, owing to the terror inspired by the Macedonian name. For the utmost bravery appeared not to forestall defeat. They had then moved across to the north bank of the Hydraotis, had advanced up stream, and had taken up a position on the western side of the most available ford. The bank on their side was high, and they hoped to be able to arrest Alexander's crossing here, and thus protect at least a part of their territory and their capital city.

On perceiving their determination, Alexander, with his customary reckless daring, headed some squadrons of his cavalry, plunged gallantly into the current, forded the stream, and fell upon the enemy, white weapon in hand. The Indians, astonished at such a bold act by a mere handful of men, did not even wait for the foremost horsemen, of whom Alexander was always first, to reach the bank, but at once abandoned

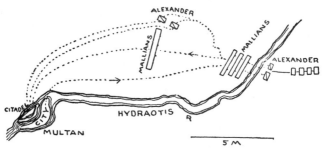

"The City of the Malli."

their position, and retired into the interior. Alexander followed upon their heels with his cavalry alone. When he had given chase some distance from the river, the Indians, recognizing the small number of their pursuers, — there were but four or five thousand Macedonian horse to fifty thousand Indians, — turned and advanced upon them in close order, presenting a very brave front. Here was a dangerous situation, but the king was used to such. The salvation of the Macedonians lay in their compact formation, their rapid manœuvring and in their being on a large plain where there was plenty of elbow-room. Instead of attempting to fight the Indians in line, Alexander quickly wheeled into column, and led his men round and round their army, coming to a front, and charging in upon their line in flank or rear wherever a chance afforded. The Macedonians could always retire in good order, reform and return to the charge. The Indians were not so active.

The light troops now arrived, and after a while the head of the phalanx was seen approaching at a rapid pace across the plain. The Indians lost courage, and fled to the citadel of their town, suffering grievous loss in the pursuit. Alexander kept close behind them, and on reaching the place, cooped them up in the citadel, first by a line of cavalry and then by the infantry as fast as it arrived. He then gave his troops a few hours' needed rest. For the infantry was exhausted by severe marching, and the cavalry equally so by marching and heavy fighting beside.

Early next day the king formed two storming columns, himself heading one and Perdiccas the other. The Indians but weakly defended the wall, and retired wholly into the citadel. This was a strong work, over a mile about, with many towers, and with the Hydraotis flowing around it. The town was separated from the citadel by a branch of the river, and all told was five miles in circumference. There is no mention in the authorities of the citadel being surrounded by the river. In this particular, Cunningham has been followed, as in all the topography of this campaign. Alexander speedily made his way into the outer circuit through a gate which he forced, but Perdiccas was unable to make much progress for want of scaling ladders. Arrived at the citadel, the Macedonians at once began to undermine the wall, and ladders were sent for hurriedly. Alexander, always impatient in his valor, seeing that the work did not advance as fast as his own desires, himself seized one of the first two scaling ladders which arrived, planted it against the wall, and ascended foremost of all, bearing his shield aloft to ward off the darts from above. He was followed on the same ladder by Peucestas, the soldier who always carried the shield brought from the temple of the Trojan Athena before him in battle, and by Leonnatus, the confidential body-guard. Up the ad-

joining ladder went Abreas, a soldier who received double
pay for his conspicuous valor. The other ladders were
delayed. Alexander, from whose fiery ardor the barbarians
retired, swung himself up on the battlements, and frayed a
place for himself with his sword. This was the affair of an
instant. The hypaspists, anxious for his safety, crowded upon
the two ladders in such number as to break them down.
Alexander was left standing with only Peucestas, Abreas and
Leonnatus upon the wall in the midst of his enemies; but so
conspicuous was his bearing and gallantry, that none came
within reach of his sword but to fall. The barbarians had
recognized him by his armor and white plumes, and the multitude of darts which fell upon him threatened his life at every
instant. The Macedonians below implored him to leap down
into their outstretched arms. Nothing daunted, however, the
descendant of the Æacidæ scorned one backward step, and
calling on every man to follow who loved him, Alexander
leaped down inside the wall, and with his three companions,
backing up against it, held his own with wonderful countenance. In a brief moment he had killed a number of
Indians, and had slain their leader who ventured against him.
But Abreas fell dead beside him with an arrow in his fore-
head, and Alexander was at the same instant pierced through
the corselet by an arrow whose point penetrated the lung.
Yet he bravely defended himself till he fell exhausted by loss
of blood, and over him, like lions at bay, but glowing with
the halo which only crowns the brave, stood Peucestas defending him with the sacred shield, and Leonnatus with his
sword, both dropping blood from countless wounds. It seemed
that the days of all three were numbered.

The Macedonians, meanwhile, some with the ladders now
arriving, some on the backs of the rest and some by means
of pegs inserted in the earth or between the bricks of the

wall, had begun to get to the top, and one by one leaped within, and surrounded the now lifeless body of Alexander. Others forced an entrance through one of the gates, and flew to the rescue. Their valor was as irresistible as their number was small. The Indians could in no wise resist their terrible onset, their war-cry doubly fierce from rage at the fate of their beloved king, to them in truth a demi-god. They were driven from the spot, and Alexander was borne back to the camp. So enraged were the Macedonians at the wounding of their king, whom they believed to be mortally struck, that they spared neither man, woman nor child in the town.

Alexander's wound was indeed grave, but his good constitution and robust health helped him, and under the care of Critodemus of Cos he recovered, much to the joy of his army. While his life was despaired of, a great deal of uncertainty and fear as to their situation must have prevailed, for Alexander was the centre-point, the motive power, the balance wheel of the entire body. Without him what could they do? How ever again reach their homes? Every man felt that no one except the king could lead them, and how much less in retreat than in advance!

At the upper camp at the confluence of the Hydaspes and Acesines, from which Alexander had started, says Arrian, it was thought for some days that Alexander was really dead, and that his captains were concealing the fact. Bad news spreads fast. The lower camp caught alarm. This threatened to give rise to lack of discipline from very fear. And here again I cannot refrain from quoting from Arrian:—

"When Alexander became acquainted with this, for fear some attempt at a revolution might be made in the army, he had himself conveyed, as soon as it could be done with safety, to the bank of the river Hydraotis, and placed in a boat to sail down the river. For the camp was at the confluence of the Hydraotis and Acesines, where Hephæstion was at the head of the army, and Nearchus of the fleet. When the ship bearing the king approached the camp, he ordered the tent covering to be removed from the stern, that he might be visible to all. But they were still incredulous, thinking, forsooth, that Alexander's corpse was being conveyed in the vessel; until at length he stretched out his hand to the multitude when the ship was nearing the bank. Then the men . raised a cheer, lifting their hands, some towards the sky, and others to the king himself. Many even shed involuntary tears at the unexpected sight. Some of the shield-bearing guards brought a litter for him when he was conveyed out of the ship; but he ordered them to fetch his horse. When he was seen again mounting his horse, the whole army reëchoed with loud clapping of hands, so that the banks of the river and the groves near them reverberated with the sound. On approaching his tent, he dismounted from his horse, so that he might be seen walking. Then the men came near, some on one side, others on the other, some touching his hands, others his knees, others only his clothes. Some only came close to get a sight of him, and went away having chanted his praise, while others threw garlands upon him, or the flowers which the country of India supplied at that season of the year."

It cannot be denied that there is a difficulty in accepting Multan as the "City of the Malli," where Alexander was wounded. The main camp was at the confluence, less than a dozen miles below Multan, and yet the troops were apparently unable to ascertain whether the king was really dead, as rumored, or only wounded. The whole paragraph just quoted looks as if the city in question were farther up the river. Moreover, Hephæstion was at the camp, in joint command with Nearchus. His route had been close to Multan from the upper camp down the left bank. Yet he had neither captured nor attacked nor masked it, nor placed his column at Alexander's disposal; nor yet ascertained the king's condition. This fact alone looks as if the city in question were far up stream. But General Cunningham has been on the ground, and has diligently compared authorities with localities. No better series of towns can be ventured on with less knowledge than his.

Alexander's officers were now emboldened to make a loyal protest against his exposing his person in battle as recklessly as had been his wont, the consequences of which had in the last battle threatened to be so fatal. With Craterus as spokesman they begged that he would leave such feats of daring to them and to the privates, though indeed none of them could vie with him in strength or skill or valor. Alexander listened to their protest, but is said secretly to have been displeased at what they said, " for," says Arrian, " he had not sufficient self-control to keep aloof from danger, through his impetuosity in battle and his passion for glory."

On this occasion a certain old Bœotian came near to him, and, quoting a line from one of the lost tragedies of Æschylus to the effect that the man who performs great deeds must also suffer, said, "O Alexander, it is the part of heroes to perform great deeds," a word which gave the king vast satisfaction, and for which he rewarded the Bœotian with his intimacy.

To this camp at the confluence of the Hydraotis and Acesines came envoys bringing the submission of the Mallians, who were thoroughly subdued by the terrible campaign just ended. Though much of their land remained unconquered, they despaired of preserving their independence. The Oxydracians, equally demoralized, though passing for the bravest of all the Indians, also came bearing the same message. Alexander demanded as hostages, to serve in his army till he

had finished the war, the one thousand best men of the Oxydracians.   These they sent with five hundred chariots, each
fitted for two warriors.   This brave and interesting people
claimed that they had been free ever since Bacchus had passed
through their land ; but that Alexander, who claimed descent
from the gods and as his deeds showed, rightly, was entitled
to their submission ; and they were glad to bring it.

Alexander appointed Philip viceroy over the Oxydracians
and the surviving Mallians, his satrapy extending to the confines of Porus and Taxiles.   Many vessels had been built
here and others were brought by the Xathrians on Alexander's order, and a much larger part of the army — seventeen
hundred cavalry Companions, ten thousand foot and the archers and Agrianians — was now transferred by water down
stream to the mouth of the Acesines where the Indus takes
up all the waters of the Five Rivers country.   Here Alexander
awaited the arrival of Perdiccas with the rest of the army.
This had marched by land and on the way had received the
submission of many tribes, the Abastanians alone needing
reduction by force.

Other nations, among them the Ossadians, likewise brought
in their submission and here too Alexander founded one more
Alexandria and began the construction of a dockyard.   The
junction of the Indus and the other great rivers seemed to
him to be a promising place for a great mart.   This city was
to be the limit of Philip's satrapy.   And he left with him all
the Thracians and such other troops as seemed to him sufficient
to hold the land and foster commerce and Hellenism.   Oxyartes, the father of Roxana, also came hither, and to him Alexander gave the viceroyalty over the Parapamisans in lieu
of the former satrap Tyriaspes, who had been exercising his
authority with cruelty and injustice.

XLV.

ALEXANDER reached the delta of the Indus after subduing the land of Oxy-canus, Sambus, and Musicanus, and chastising the Brahmins who had on several occasions instigated revolt. Here, at Patala, he established a city and dockyard ; and from here he sailed down both branches of the delta to the sea. Then he began preparations for moving back to Babylon along the coast, for he had conceived the idea that ships could sail from the mouth of the Indus to the mouth of the Euphrates, and proposed to send a fleet, and himself march that way. He dispatched Craterus, with half the army, invalids and trains, by way of Arachotia and Drangiana; and with the stronger part of the army, after subduing the border tribes, he started across the desert of Gedrosia. Near-chus, somewhat later, sailed with the fleet along the coast. No body of men had ever crossed this desert; and the provisions Alexander ordered to be sent to meet him never came to hand. The king was gravely at fault in not being sure of his supplies. On the march he dug wells at places on the coast, and left stores of provisions for Nearchus. After sixty days' march over burning sands, in which nearly all the beasts and three fourths of the men are said to have perished, Alexander reached Paura, and after a rest, returned to Pasar-gadæ and Susa. He found his kingdom all but falling to pieces for lack of the hand of the master.

CRATERUS was now put over the Acesines to the left bank of the Indus, with the elephants, and the army was collected in one body. On this bank the marching was easier, there being no mountain range, and there were more unsubdued tribes. Alexander was now entering the province of modern Sindh. Cultivation existed some distance inland, along this part of the Indus. The king headed down stream to the country of the Sogdians or Sodrians, whose capital city (modern Faxilpur) he transformed into another Alexandria, built shops and a dockyard, and made necessary repairs to the fleet. The character of the river, the people and the country here began to change. The high mountain chain on the west bent away from the river, leaving a more moderate range in places, and the Indus widened into many channels. Fruitful lowlands lined its banks. To-day, as then, this district is thickly peopled and thrifty. The main change is in the river itself, which has shifted its course to a new and western channel. In the times we are speaking of the Indus ran in the bed now called Nara.

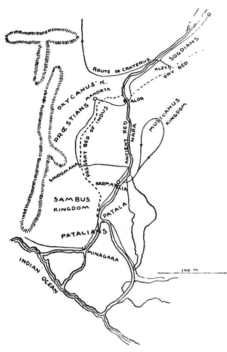

Campaign on the Lower Indus.

Alexander made Oxyartes, who had reported at headquarters, in addition to what he already controlled, the viceroy of all India from the confluence of the Acesines and Indus to the coast line, and associated with him Peithon as general, with ten thousand troops. Here, too, Craterus made preparations to march back to Persis by way of Arachotia and Drangiana, with the invalids and heavy trains. But he appears to have been delayed, perhaps by the threatened revolt of Musicanus. He apparently started later, but it was from here that led the road he followed.

Below the land of the Sogdians there had been no offer of

submission. Alexander felt that he still had much work to do, He continued down the river to the kingdom of Musicanus, who had made no tender of fealty, and who was said to be king of the most prosperous part of India, as was, to judge from the condition of to-day, a fact. To any one having the Anglo-Saxon feeling for independence, this assumption of Alexander that all kings should volunteer submission at his mere approach is grating; but the idea itself was well carried out. So rapid was his progress that he reached the borders of Musicanus before this potentate was aware that he had started from the land of the Mallians. Thus surprised, Musicanus deemed it wise to accept the inevitable, and came to meet the Macedonians with gifts and apologies. Alexander, always open to abject submission as well as flattery, forgave him his opposition, built a fortress at his capital, modern Alor, in which he placed a Macedonian garrison, and left Musicanus in possession of his ancient kingdom as satrap. This extended, in all probability, as far as modern Brahmanabad.

Thence, with the seventeen hundred horse which had been with him on the fleet, the archers and Agrianians, Alexander struck inland to the west, on a campaign against the Præstians and Oxycanus (or Portikanus), a king who had also failed to tender his submission. This territory ran as far as the foothills, and about a hundred miles north and south. The first of his two cities Alexander took at the first onset, and distributed the booty among the soldiers. The second city was the capital, Mahorta (ten miles from modern Larkhana, and forty from Alor), a place of much importance, which controlled the high road from this Indus country *via* the Gandara and Bolan passes to the plateau of Iran. Alexander was obliged to besiege this town three days, and then to storm the citadel. In the assault the barbarian king was killed. There were some elephants here, which were added to the already large herd. The other towns, numerous and mostly large and wealthy, submitted, for the Indians were cowed by Alexander's apparently superhuman successes. It is difficult to identify these cities. They are all in ruins, and there have been few to investigate the contents of the ruined mounds. In this locality, General Cunningham is still followed as the most reliable guide.

From this place Alexander was compelled to hasten against Sambus, a king who had come far up stream to tender fealty, whom he had made viceroy of the mountaineer Indians, and sent back home with favor. Sambus had long been at war with Musicanus, which fact had induced him to submit to Alexander in the hope that he would thus gain the upperhand, but when Musicanus was pardoned and received into the king's confidence, under the idea that he himself would now be the sufferer on account of the enmity of his ancient foe, he concluded to revolt from his newly-acknowledged master. On Alexander's approach, however, Sambus fled across the Indus, and his people opened the gates of his capital city, Sindomana (modern Sehwan), now on the Indus, but then sixty-five miles from the river. Sindomana was situated on a high rock, near a large lake, and in the midst of plenty; and was a city of the first importance. Alexander now returned to his fleet, left on the Indus below Alor.

He next moved against Harmatelia, a city of the Brahmins (modern Brahmanabad), near by the Indus. This was captured by the digging of a subterranean passage by which the soldiers entered the town under the walls. A number of citizens were punished with utmost severity for instigating this revolt. It was while he was conducting this campaign that Alexander learned to his surprise that Musicanus had likewise revolted and put the Macedonian garrison to the sword. When Alexander had disappeared from immediate view, Musicanus imagined he had gone for good. The Brahmins had roused the religious frenzy of this people also. Arrian calls these Brahmins the philosophers of India. They appear to have been hard to reconcile to the new régime, and excessively bitter in their antagonism. Alexander, incensed that this barbarian king should thus reward his favors, countermarched sharply against him, captured many of the cities in the southern part of his domains, razed some to the ground and sold the inhabitants into slavery, and garrisoned others; while Peithon was sent to Alor and beyond after Musicanus, who had imitated Sambus and fled into the regions east of the Indus. Having captured him, Peithon brought him to Harmatelia. Alexander ordered him to be crucified in the public roads, with a number of Brahmins who had been the prime movers in the revolt.

To offset this treachery, the ruler of the Patalians, Moëris by name, now came from the apex of the delta of the Indus and tendered submission, offering to do whatever Alexander should prescribe. This practically put an end to all opposition along the Indus. Alexander could fairly call this great river, with its mighty affluents, his own. How strong the ties which bound to him the vassals he had made might have remained, had Alexander lived to consolidate his conquests, it is hard to say; how lax they actually were was shown immediately after his death.

However uncertain or limited the information on which Alexander conceived his gigantic schemes, he none the less had a very definite general idea of what he desired to accomplish. He always looked ahead, gauged the outcome of his ventures correctly, and, after using due care, left the details to be met as they came up. From the delta of the Indus, which he next proposed to visit, Alexander's homeward

march was to be across the desert of Gedrosia. This was
an unknown route, never successfully traversed by an army,
and never attempted, except, tradition said, by Semiramis,
whose entire army perished in the passage.

To avoid having too great a force to feed in crossing this
desert, and because it was not now necessary to keep so large
a body for further military operations, which would probably
be limited in extent, Craterus, who had been kept in command of the army during Alexander's western campaign, was
now ordered to start on his overland trip with a large part of
the troops and the elephants. His route lay through Arachotia and Drangiana, and with him went a number of invalided Macedonians and Companions who were to return to

Routes of Craterus and Alexander.

Hellas, the phalanxes of Attalus, Antigenes and Meleager,
and part of the archers. This column crossed the mountain
range which runs down the west bank of the Indus from the
Cophen, separating the luxuriant tropical vegetation of India
from the barren table-lands of Persia, probably through the
pass now called Bolan.

There was an additional motive for Craterus' march, in

that many troubles and quarrels among the satraps on the Arianian uplands made the appearance of an army among them essential to restore order. Craterus had at least one third of the force which started down the Indus. On the way through Arachotia and Drangiana he was given authority to settle controversies and punish delinquents, and was especially instructed to order the satraps of the adjoining territories to send provisions to the desert of Gedrosia, through which the king was himself to march.

Alexander for the present continued down the river in his fleet, while Hephæstion, with the bulk of the army, marched down the right bank, and Peithon, having first swept the defiles in the mountains clear of hostile tribes, to protect the flanks of the army, crossed and marched, with horse-archers and Agrianians, down the left bank. The rendezvous was to be Patala, and each on his way was to provide for the future security of the country through which he passed. The delta of the Indus has so much altered the course of its waters in two thousand years that the position of Patala cannot now be identified. It may be modern Haiderabad.

Before arriving at Patala, which he reached about midsummer, Alexander learned that it was deserted. The inhabitants had fled to a man from very terror at what they heard of Alexander. But the king sent after them, captured a few prisoners, and made the latter his messengers to their fellow-citizens, and thus persuaded them to return ; whom, when they did so, he treated with the utmost generosity and helpfulness. At Patala the delta of the Indus began. Here the king transformed the city into a new Alexandria, which he left Hephæstion to fortify, built a dockyard, and sent out many days' journey into the desert to teach the inhabitants how to sink wells and thus increase their limited supply of water. These well-digging parties had many brushes with nomads, but nevertheless persevered and carried out their plan.

Alexander now determined to explore the delta of the Indus. It required as true courage and enterprise to sail down the Indus delta with Alexander's small craft, propelled alone by oars, quite ignorant of what lay beyond, and with crews which had never yet been out of the eastern Mediterranean, as it has ever required of the great discoverers to venture forth on unknown seas in search of unknown lands. There is some confusion as to which branch the king first attempted; but judging by the measures he adopted it seems probable that he began with the east branch, though Arrian calls it the right one. He detailed Leonnatus, with eight thousand foot and one thousand horse, to explore the island of Patala between the arms of the delta.

Alexander set out with his thirty-oared galleys, and some with one and one half banks of oars. After a perilous journey — for the Indus is twenty-five miles wide and subject to heavy water — he reached the open sea. Many of his vessels had been damaged, and he had been unable to procure natives for pilots a good part of the way. He was greatly astonished at the phenomenon of the tides, with which he was not familiar. Having put some distance out to sea, so as to be sure he had reached the great ocean, he returned to Patala, where he found his plans for a new city fairly completed. He then descended the west branch of the Indus. His first stop was at a point where the river broadened out into a huge lake. Here he again laid the foundations of a city and dockyard, Minagara; and proceeding to the sea, satisfied himself that this western arm was the best adapted for navigation. The details of these trips, as of the later voyage of Nearchus, are of vast interest, but scarcely belong to Alexander's military history. He then explored the coast to the west with the cavalry for a distance of a three days' journey, dug wells for the fleet he proposed to send that way, and ordering a detachment farther along for like purpose, he returned to Patala. Finding everything in progress here, he again descended to Minagara, and spent some time in collecting food for four months. The summer was drawing to a close. Alexander had been the better part of a year moving down the great river.

There is abundant internal evidence in the stories of the ancient authors that Alexander was not alone a great soldier, but that he was a statesman whose ideas were broad and whose intelligence fully grasped the extent of what could be accomplished by commerce and the arts. It is altogether probable, familiar as he must have been with the history of Tyre, with the writings of Ctesias, which, however unreliable, still were full of suggestiveness, with the statement that Scylax had sailed from the mouth of the Indus to the Red Sea, with all that the history of the Jews and Arabs could tell, and other not altogether meagre if ill-digested information of that day, that Alexander had, even before starting on the expedition, a hope that through his conquests he might concentrate the valuable trade of the East in a direction which should bring it towards the Mediterranean by an easier route than across the uplands of Iran. In endeavoring to conquer India, probably the wealth-bringing control of trade was as much the underlying motive as the greed of territory. His care in studying out the navigable character of the Indus, and subsequently that of the Persian Gulf; his later effort to send a fleet around Arabia into the Red Sea, his founding Alexandria in Egypt, all tend to show that he had great political and commercial schemes in his head which he intended should tread in the steps of his military successes. It is rather the habit of modern writers to reduce everything Alexander did, excepting military exploits, to the level of crass luck, to deny him any skill except that of the soldier, and even to base this on the fortune which often attends the gambler. And yet the great among his contemporaries all gave him credit for vast and true conceptions, and there were giants in those days. The historians who had in hand the best sources of information never doubted that his commercial sense and statecraft were as great as his power to lead men ; and it seems as if what he accomplished is better susceptible of this construction than explainable on the hypothesis of chance. For we can no more gauge his knowledge by the intelligence of to-day than measure our own petty conquests by the limitless extent of Alexander's.

Nearchus had been selected to command the fleet on account of ancient amity, as well as courage and ability. In moving from the Indus, he was to sail the fleet along the coast; the army was to march by land. Alexander had him wait for the season of favorable coasting winds which came in October, now close at hand. Nearchus, one of the friends of Alexander's youth and one of those who had been banished when he quarreled with his father, had volunteered to perform this perilous duty. The intelligence as well as the boldness of his voyage can scarcely be understood to-day, so difficult is it to place one's self in the position of those who wrought more than twenty-two centuries since. Though he had for a while imagined the Acesines to be the head waters of the Nile, the king no doubt had come to believe that the Persian Gulf could be reached from the mouth of the Indus; and it was this which Alexander desired to prove, so as to carry out his scheme of trade between India and Persia and the West, in other words, to connect the Indus and the Euphrates.

But it was a leap in the dark. The army was to march

through a desert where it was doubtful whether it could render any aid to the fleet; the bold seamen might disappear into unknown seas, and never again be heard from. Both army and fleet were forlorn hopes. It is hard to say which was the more inhospitable, the shores along which Nearchus was to sail, where alone dwelt the Ichthyophagi, or the broiling sands of the Gedrosian desert, never yet crossed by a body of men. The boldness of Nearchus' voyage is extraordinary. He had, measured by his exploit, very poor vessels at command. He had naught but sun and stars to tell him his direction. He must land each night on a shore ill-conditioned by nature and dangerous perhaps from its population. His vessels could carry but small supplies. He might sail into seas and gulfs out of which he could never find his way, or whose coasts would afford him neither food nor water. Nearchus undertook this peril at Alexander's behest. This surely looks less like greed of conquest than the true discoverer's instinct.

Alexander was the first to start. It was the close of summer. He marched with the army from Patala by way of his depot at Minagara, and in nine days reached the Arabius, about one hundred miles from the Indus. Himself with Leonnatus and Ptolemy commanded the three columns of march. The troops were one half the targeteers and archers, the phalanx, except what marched with Craterus, the agema of Companion cavalry, a squadron from each cavalry regiment and the horse-bowmen. These three columns kept near the coast and, on the way, dug wells in all the large coves from which the fleet might get water, when it should sail by. These wells were marked in such a manner as to be easily found. Hephæstion followed with the main army on a line farther inland. This division of forces was made in order to cover as wide a space as possible, and pick up as many of the barbarians as should scatter towards the desert. The Arabitians dwelt on the hither side of the river Arabius (Purali), and the Oritians on the farther side. Neither had sent ambassadors to sue for friendship, which neglect, in Alexander's code, at once placed these tribes in the rank of his enemies. The Arabitians, on learning of the approach of the Macedonians, fled towards the desert as had been anticipated. The Oritians Alexander reached in one night's march across a desert stretch beyond the Arabius. He divided his cavalry into detachments by

Oritian Campaign.

squadrons, and sent these out at given distances from each other like a huge skirmish line, in order to cover a large part of the plain, the cavalry advance being sustained by the infantry in closer order. He thus speedily covered the entire territory of the Oritians. This was an odd manœuvre, but well adapted to the conditions, which, after all said, is always the test. This was not the age of the new military art, nor was the division of an army subject to the grave danger against the barbarians, which it would be to-day against civilized nations. A small force of the well-armed and perfectly disciplined Macedonians was equal to a horde of these nomads.

The inhabitants were sold as slaves and the land was wasted wherever he met resistance, and finding the capital of the Oritians, named Rhambasia, situated in a large and fertile oasis, he left Hephæstion to found a final Alexandria there. Then, taking half the hypaspists, the Agrianians, the agema of cavalry and the horse-bowmen, he marched against some tribes of Oritians and Gedrosians who had assembled in the mountains between these two territories, to hold the passes against his advance. The barbarians, however, scarcely awaited his approach. Those who did not flee, surrendered. Over this territory Alexander left Apollophanes as viceroy, and gave him special instructions to accumulate and send forward provision for the army on its dangerous transit. For this there was ample time. Leonnatus, in command of all the Agrianians, some archers, and the Greek mercenaries, foot and horse, remained behind in Ora to await the arrival of Nearchus, not only to aid the latter, but to get the government of the land into running order. Having arranged these matters to his satisfaction, and Hephæstion having rejoined, Alexander set out to cross the desert of Gedrosia. Not long after his departure, the Oritians rose in rebellion, and, it is said, killed Apollophanes. But Leonnatus was equal to the occasion. He met and defeated the rebels in a great battle near the coast, between the Arabius and Tomerus rivers, and slew all their leaders. This pacified the new province.

The king's force was not large. It may be estimated thus : —

Alexander had in India . . . . 120,000 men
Garrisons left by the way, say 30,000
Nearchus, say 100 vessels @ 150 men each . . . 15,000
Craterus took with him some 40,000   85,000

Leaving to march with Alexander across the desert . . .   35,000 men

This march would not have involved such grievous peril and loss if the provisions which Alexander had ordered collected by Sibyrtius, satrap of part of Carmania, and by Apollophanes, satrap of Gedrosia, had been promptly got together. The latter had been especially ordered to station beeves and corn along the route. Alexander expected to be met on the way by caravans of victuals. There were none; and he must be blamed for starting on his dangerous route without a certainty of provision. He was so entirely in the habit of being

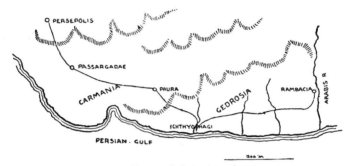

Desert of Gedrosia.

obeyed that he was wont to consider as already accomplished whatever he ordered to be done. But this does not excuse in any degree the carelessness of the present occasion. This is the only instance in all Alexander's campaigns when he failed to have a care to his rations. The satrap of Carmania appears not to have been held to blame, for Alexander afterwards added to his dignities. Perhaps he had received his orders too late.

It was a matter of tradition that Semiramis returned from her conquest of India through this desert, and that of the hundreds of thousands of which her army consisted, but twenty individuals came back with her to Babylon. Cyrus too, though incorrectly, was reputed to have crossed this desert with like sad results. Even the fanatic Islam considered Gedrosia as a boundary placed there by God, and refused to cross it. It was indeed a terrible land. Along the coast lived only the Ichthyophagi, whose huts were built of bones of the whale, shells and seaweed, and whose entire diet consisted of fish. Inland to the mountain ranges some twenty miles from the coast were sand stretches inhabited solely by jackals and wolves and insects. Beyond the mountains lay the still more terrible desert of Gedrosia. It has been said that Alexander chose this passage simply because of its difficulties — because he was minded to do greater things than Semiramis and Cyrus. This seems a partial way of looking at the matter. Is it not easier to believe that Alexander was really seeking to discover and establish the best outlet for commerce between his Indian satrapies and his Persian, and that he was willing to run a risk for this so desirable end? Unless he were to go this route, how could he prove that his great plan of commerce between India and Persia was feasible by way of the Indus, the sea and the Euphrates? How could he forsake his friend Nearchus, who was sacrificing himself to carry out the king's great schemes? How indeed would he know the extent, boundaries and resources of this coast land unless he passed this way? Was he not, in fact, compelled to choose this route, in order not to have an unconquered strip full of wandering robber tribes between his Indian satrapies and Persia? It was essential for him to march by a route along which he could sustain his fleet by digging wells, and leaving supplies at convenient places on the coast. The ancient fleets were able to sail only during the day and in fair weather; at night and in storms they were compelled to put in shore, to find water and provision. The crews of rowers and warriors were so numerous for the tonnage and the oars took up so much space, that they could carry but a limited supply of food. If he expected him to succeed, Alexander could not send Nearchus along an unknown coast without some aid. And while he might have dispatched a lieutenant on this perilous mission through the desert, this was not Alexander's way. He always undertook the most difficult task himself, and saw with his own eyes what needed to be seen.

Should the voyage of Nearchus prove that the mouth of the Indus could actually be reached by sea from the mouth of the Euphrates, the coast must be explored, wells be dug, and stations built for the purpose of opening the route to travel and commerce. How could the king intelligently direct this to be done unless personally, by a march across Gedrosia, he ascertained the actual conditions? He may no doubt be accused of undertaking a great risk without adequate provision, and this is a grave accusation. But such is the sum of his lapse, and into the danger he only led the stronger and better part of his army, leaving the rest to march under Craterus through a well-known district. What had been serious dangers to others he had easily overcome. It was natural that he should underrate the perils of Gedrosia.

The expedition, twenty years later, of Seleucus Nicator to India, for the purpose of stimulating trade between that country and Syria, seems to prove Alexander's views to have been far-sighted. Seleucus went as far as the Ganges — his road had already been opened by Alexander — and his treaties with the Indian potentates, which lasted many years, resulted in an enormous trade between the two countries. Alexander's entire scheme seems much easier to explain on the hypothesis of an idea long pondered and as well digested as the existing knowledge warranted, than on that of an adventurer or knight-errant seeking vast difficulties merely for the sake of overcoming them.

In this land of Gedrosia there was an abundance of myrrh and other spices, but naught else but suffering and death. As the army marched onward, the desert grew sandier and more sterile; brooks dried up in the sand; the heat became intolerable; vegetation ceased. Not a path of any kind existed; and the marches had to be made at night. The men were scantily provided with rations, and these were finally exhausted. Supplies, so far as they could be got, or as long as they lasted, were in part taken to the coast for the fleet; wells were dug for it, and signals erected to catch Nearchus' attention when he should sail by. One of these convoys of food to the coast, even under Alexander's own seal, was broken open by the famished soldiery in disobedience of orders, little regarding what manner of death they died. With the utmost difficulty were any fresh supplies procured, and these were carefully husbanded and left along the coast under safe charge of the most trustworthy men. The army, after a few days' march, left the coast, and struck inland. Water was often sixty and eighty miles apart. The sand was like the waves of the sea for tracklessness. Discipline broke up. The men killed the cattle used as beasts of burden and even mules and horses, and ate their flesh, saying that they had died of thirst and heat. The very animals which drew the wagons on which lay the wounded men were killed for food, and the wounded left behind. All this Alexander was fain to overlook. Worse than the thirst was the terror of reaching water, followed by the agonizing death of those who too freely drank of it.

The advance of the army was headed towards Paura, the capital of Gedrosia, which was reached in sixty days from Ora. All accounts agree that the hardships of the campaigns they had undergone were as nothing compared to the sufferings of the march across this desert. The exact amount of loss is not known; it must have been very great. It is said that but a quarter of those who started from Ora reached Paura; and these in rags and without weapons. The beasts of burden almost all perished, mostly from lack of water, but many dropped from weakness and were engulfed in the sand. The marches had to be made from water to water, and are said by Strabo to have been of two hundred, four hundred and six hundred stades, — twenty-two, forty-four and sixty-six miles, — and yet the progress was no more than ten or twelve miles a day. When they could reach the next water by a night march, they did well enough; but when the march had to be by day, the suffering was indescribable. The wagons soon got broken up, and much baggage was thrown away. The sick and weak had to be abandoned. Stragglers were rarely able to regain the column. On more than one occasion, when they camped at the brooks they reached, the sudden overflows from storms in the mountains, which are usual in this country, drowned men and swept away baggage and beasts. Alexander was wont to pitch camp a couple of miles away from water, so as to prevent both this trouble and overdrinking by the men.

It was here that Alexander, in a time of great scarcity of water, when some soldiers had gathered a little supply, and brought it to him in a helmet, refused to drink, but poured it out on the ground, saying that he would not quench his thirst when his men could not. Other authorities place the incident — or a similar one — in the pursuit of Darius. It is also said that when the army had lost the way, and the guides could not find it, Alexander himself started out with but five companions, and by moving in the direction he knew the sea must be, did actually find it and water near by. Thither he brought the army, and for a week thereafter they kept along the seashore, and then again, when the guides had oriented themselves, moved inland.

Arrived at Paura, Alexander gave the relics of his army a rest. Here he found that a number of the viceroys had, of their own motion, accumulated provisions for him on learning that he was to march through the desert. But these came too late to be of any use. It was little satisfaction to punish the careless satraps who had not forwarded the required supplies. After this the march was resumed towards Carmania, where Craterus, who had easily marched through the upper country, joined him. Winter had now set in.

Here Alexander rectified a number of abuses which had grown up since he left Persepolis, by the change of officers and the punishment of those who had proved corrupt or cruel. He celebrated his victory over the Indians and his march through the desert by feasts and games, and made Peucestas one of the somatophylaxes and afterwards viceroy of Persis. It indeed needed the arrival of supplies and the presence of old companions-in-arms to restore to the sad relics of the proud army which had but three months since left the Indus the self-respect and discipline it had lost in the march across the desert. Its terrible experiences naturally led Alexander to fear that the brave and faithful Nearchus with the fleet had fallen a prey to the dangers of the voyage. But soon came the cheering intelligence that the gallant admiral had arrived on the coast at Salmus, near the river Anamis. It was some time before he made his way up to the camp. He then came and reported his voyage to Alexander, who received him with great favor and affection, and sent him to pursue his way as far as Susiana, where he was to report again at the mouth of the Tigris. Hephæstion was ordered, with the bulk of the army, elephants, and heavy baggage, to march by a southerly route into Persis, this being warmer during the winter season, while Alexander himself, on the way to Susa, marched to Passargadæ by the direct mountain road, with his light infantry, archers, in part, and Companion cavalry.

In Persis, also, Alexander found many punishments to inflict and abuses to correct. Phrasaortes, satrap of Persis, had died, and Orxines had assumed his office, but having been guilty of pillaging and cruelty, was put to death, and Peucestas made viceroy in his stead. Atropates, viceroy of Media, came, bringing Baryaxes, who had attempted to make himself king ; and him, with his adherents, Alexander treated in like manner. Stasanor, viceroy of the Arians and Zarangians, and Phrataphernes, viceroy of the Parthians and Hyrcanians, came, bringing beasts of burden and camels at a time most opportune. These were distributed to the troops as required. Stasanor was sent back to Aria.

At Passargadæ Alexander found the tomb of Cyrus broken into, rifled of its treasures, and the corpse desecrated. But nothing could be elicited about the occurrence, even by the torture of the guard. The body was replaced in its resting place in greater state and security than before.

It was time, indeed, that Alexander should return. Everything was beginning to assume the aspect it wore so soon after his death. Sad prophecy of what would happen when there was no more Alexander ! Nothing short of the most scrupulous and exact severity in meting out justice could restore the obedient kingdom he had left. It was on the point of falling to pieces through the greed, ambition, dishonesty, cruelty and rapacity of the satraps he had created. But the people soon learned that Alexander was no respecter of persons. They made haste to lay complaints before the king, whenever these were of a nature to attract attention. In no instance was just cause of complaint thrust aside.

In Carmania the satrap Aspastes, who, five years before, had submitted to Alexander and been continued in control of his territory, was not only removed, but executed, for malfeasance, and was replaced by Tlepolemus. The Arachotian noble Ordanes was brought in chains to Persis by Craterus, and was likewise executed for plotting revolt in that satrapy, and Arachotia was added to the satrapy of Ora and Gedrosia, under Sibyrtius, Apollophanes having been deposed for neglect of the king's orders to furnish provision in Gedrosia. From Media, Heracon with the mercenary horse, Cleander with the mercenary veterans, and Sitalces with the Thracian foot, who had been in Media with Parmenio, now reported with their respective commands; but they were also accused by the Medians of misuse of their office. The two latter were found guilty of peculation, pillage, and cruelty, and were executed with six hundred of their equally guilty soldiers, who had been their agents in oppression. Heracon was at that time acquitted, but was later executed for a repeated offense of plundering. Baryaxes of Media, and Oxyathres of Parætacenæ, suffered a like fate. Philip had been killed in a mutiny in India; but the mutiny was readily suppressed, and his satrapy was given to the king of Taxila and Eudemus. Encouraged by Alexander's evident intention to be just, the people came forward more and more freely with their troubles, and none had cause to feel that he failed to receive ample justice. Evenhandedness such as this, especially when exerted against his old and now sadly-needed Macedonians, showed the Persians that Alexander meant to be their protector as well as king, and was a well-timed lesson to all satraps. It was found, also, that Harpalus, the treasurer, had been playing fast and loose with Alexander's hoarded gold. But the thief was clever enough to make good his escape from the king's wrath, conveying with him, according to Diodorus, fifty thousand talents.

It is asserted by some that Alexander often acted on insufficient or on perjured evidence. That he made mistakes in this wholesale administration of justice is altogether probable; but that his motive in punishing the delinquents was the good of the peoples under his sceptre is shown by his uniform recognition of their rights throughout his entire reign. Whatever his own course towards conquered nations, he held his satraps to strict accountability in their dealings with them.

The king now took up his march through the Persian Gates, towards the heart of his empire. In Susa, which he reached in February, after an absence of five years, he also found many things to rectify. Foremost of all, Arbulites and his son Oxathres were put to death for bad government and for despoiling the Susians. To Susa soon came Hephæstion with the heavy column of the army, and Nearchus, from his last exploring expedition. Elated at his admiral's success, Alexander is said to have contemplated a voyage not only around Arabia, but around the entire coast of Libya, as Africa was then called, as far as the Pillars of Hercules, and others to the Euxine, Scythia and the Sea of Azov. But these projects were destined to interruption.

Alexander, from an unknown Coin.

XLVI.

MUTINY. JULY, B. C. 324.

THE Macedonians had reached their goal. They could enjoy their hard-earned wealth. Alexander paid their debts — some twenty thousand talents — and made them valuable presents. He coupled this bounty with intermarriages between his chief officers and Persian noblewomen, himself wedding daughters of Darius and Ochus, thus uniting both Persian royal families. To the soldiers who had Eastern wives he was especially generous. All this was in the line of his idea of a merger of races so as to make his kingdom homogeneous. Alexander had long had many Orientals in the army. He had thirty thousand of the best youths of the East in a special phalanx. He promoted many notable Orientals to high office — as was natural and necessary. These favors to conquered peoples galled his Macedonians. Distrust between king and soldier had been growing since the Hyphasis. Now, when, at a camp council in Opis, Alexander proposed to send home all disabled Macedonians with wealth and honor, his generosity was misunderstood and met by sullen protests, as if he were trying to get rid of the men who had helped him conquer the world. This feeling broke out into mutiny. Alexander summarily put down the outbreak with the strong hand, and dismissing his Macedonians from his service in an address of wonderful power, he placed himself in the hands of his Eastern army. This act absolutely broke up the mutinous sentiment; brought grief and repentance; and the ancient love came back in double measure. Confidence was restored. Alexander had won. He was quits with the army for its refusal to cross the Hyphasis.

AFTER many years of toil and hardship, the Macedonians now saw an end to their venturesome campaigns; and the king perceived that the time had come to distribute the anticipated rewards to his faithful soldiers. Alexander was more of a dreamer on the subject of removing national distinctions than on any other. From the time he conquered Egypt his mind was constantly bent on maturing a scheme to coalesce his vast empire into one mass of equal rights and privileges.

This end he mainly sought to accomplish by what proved to be the impracticable means of introducing Macedonian customs among peoples unused to them and wedded to their old ways, and in climates to which they were unsuited; and by the still less effectual practice of fostering intermarriages of Greeks and Orientals. This last idea Alexander now próposed to inaugurate on a gigantic scale, and couple it with an equally gigantic bounty to his men. His own present marriage with Statira, Darius' eldest daughter and widow of Mentor, and with Parysatis, youngest daughter of Ochus, by which he might graft his descendants upon the two royal families of Persia, was part of this universal scheme. To Hephæstion he gave in marriage Drypetis, another daughter of Darius; to Craterus, a niece; and to eighty of his other generals, the most prominent noblewomen of the land. The names of all soldiers, some ten thousand in number, who had wedded Asiatic women were registered, and Alexander made liberal presents to them all. The marriage feasts were celebrated in the Persian manner, and all the great and distinguished from every satrapy of the empire — the world and his wife of that day — came to the banquet. There is no space to devote to a description of this almost unparalleled feast, which lasted many days. That must be sought elsewhere. On this occasion Alexander capped his generosity to his soldiers by paying all their debts, — a gift, according to Arrian and Justin, of twenty thousand talents, or not far from twenty-five million dollars of our money; or, according to Plutarch, Diodorus, and Curtius, of ten thousand talents. Those who had done exceptional service received additional rewards. A few whom Alexander chose to distinguish for bravery and merit were crowned with golden chaplets. These were the somatophylaxes and the king's chief aides and generals. First of all, Peucestas, who had saved his life among the Mallians; then

Leonnatus, who had won a victory over the Oritians at the river Tomerus ; Nearchus, who had become the most famous of admirals; Hephæstion, his bosom friend; Lysimachus, Aristonus, Perdiccas, Ptolemy and Peithon. Onesecritus, the pilot of the king's galley, was also thus honored. But there were some whom all this failed to satisfy.

Ever since Alexander started in pursuit of Darius, he had incorporated in the army a great number of Asiatic soldiers. And it seems altogether probable that they were drilled and instructed in the Macedonian manner. Some historians doubt the fact, but in no other way can we explain the marvelous results obtained in the five years' campaigning which had since been conducted. Only on this hypothesis can the essential unity of tactical action be explained. No doubt many national peculiarities were retained among the foreigners so serving ; and there must have been kept up some decided distinguishing mark between these Asiatics and the Macedonians. But we find no particular mention of Oriental detachments. The authorities mention the phalanx, the light troops, the Companion or other cavalry, and only the Daän horse-bowmen are frequently spoken of as a special corps. What Asiatics there were seem to have been distributed among the brigades of the phalanx, or to have been among the light troops, horse and foot. Nor does the proportion of light troops appear to have been increased. However this may be, whatever distinction there was it was now part of Alexander's plan to obliterate. The way was already paved. He had long ago caused to be chosen in all parts of the empire, from the choicest of the youth of Persia just reaching the age of manhood, a force numbering thirty thousand men. This body for five years had been assembling and drilling. They were known as Epigoni, the "successors," were now under command of Seleucus, and in their entire organization, drill, and equipment they conformed to the Macedonian fashion. A considerable extension of this system had been determined on by Alexander from the time of the refusal of the Macedonians to cross the Hyphasis, and he had sent orders to increase the number of these youths, to what extent is not determined. Some of them had already served with the army. He proposed to have fresh and submissive troops, and these had become, under so consummate an organizer, a powerful body, which added to pride in their calling and gratitude for the distinguished favors of the king the natural blind obedience of the Orient. The full importance of this body, so far as concerned their own relations to the fortunes of the great empire of Alexander, had perhaps not fully dawned upon the Macedonians until some time after they reached Susa, where they were brought face to face with the new corps. But now this became a fresh and unfortunate cause for suspicion and irritation on the part of the old Macedonian soldiers, who had for some time been fretting under the assumption by Alexander of the Median dress and manners and the promotion of Orientals.

There were probably left not more than twenty-five thousand Macedonians, if so many, of the two hundred thousand men who had come with the army of invasion or as reinforcements. Half of these had been in continuous service since 334 B. C. — ten long years. Most of them were utterly tired of war. They were, moreover, getting to be less easy to handle; no wonder they felt their own importance. But Alexander wanted no more Hyphasis troubles. It is not improbable that since the Hyphasis there had been a sort of moral wall building up between Alexander and his Macedonians, where before there had been perfect trustfulness. The king had hoped by his generosity, his feasts, and the abundant marriage gifts, to quell this bad feeling, but he had so far failed of success. In fact, when he offered to pay the debts of his soldiers, — and it was a frank piece of good will and entirely above-board, — it was at first suspected that he was trying to ascertain who had been extravagant, in order to punish such habits. Their ancient confidence in their king had weakened, as perhaps Alexander himself had changed. In this instance the suspicion had bred no evil; for the king at once convinced his old soldiers that he meant them naught but kindness, and had money-tables erected, where, without registering their names, each one could have the means of discharging his debts by a simple statement of their amount. In view of the enormous sum of these debts, this was a certain proof of sincerity.

But other things combined to complicate the situation. The mixing of Asiatic squadrons with the Companion cavalry, which was the easiest method of keeping up the old *cadres*, as well as of beginning the merger of races which Alexander contemplated, and the placing of distinguished Persians in the ranks of the Companion cavalry and foot-guard, added fuel to the flame of discontent. There were squadrons of Bactrian, Sogdianian, Arachotian, Zarangian, Arian and Parthian cavalry, as well as the Persian Evacæ, a choice cavalry corps, bodily incorporated with the Companion cavalry, and a fifth division of horse of mixed nationalities was now added to the body. The fact that the new-comers were especially fine men by no means drew the sting. Into the agema of foot were admitted: Artiboles and Hydarnes, sons of Mazæus; Cophen, son of Artabazus; Sisines and Phrasdamenes, sons of Phrataphernes; Histanes, Roxana's brother; Autobares and Mithrobæus; and last and most grievous, to Hystaspes of Bactria was given the command of the agema. A further grievance lay in the honors heaped upon Peucestas, who, on being made viceroy of Persis, adopted all the Oriental magnificence, and continued in the king's favor as of yore. That these new appointees were all men of standing, ability and worth, many of whom had earned their reward, was no palliation. It seemed to his old Macedonians that Alexander was losing his national character and growing to despise the men who had helped him conquer the world. All these were real grievances, to be sure; but beyond this, the Macedonians had lapsed into a chronic feeling that injustice was done them, and anything would serve its purpose.

When spring had fairly opened, Alexander sent Hephæstion with the army along the road up the Tigris to Opis, and himself ordering the fleet up to Susa, sailed with the hypaspists and agema and a few cavalry Companions down the Passitigris or Eulæus to the coast, and there founding another Alexandria on the seashore near by, sailed up the Tigris to Opis. He wished to become familiar with his new dominions. The Persians had erected dams or weirs in the Tigris to prevent a foreign fleet from invading the country. These Alexander removed, having no such fear of invasion, in order to facilitate free navigation up to Opis. This was part of his general scheme.

It was at Opis in July that dissatisfaction broke out into the great mutiny of the Macedonian soldiers. Alexander had announced a new march into Media, and, in the honest belief that he was doing an act of gratification to his veterans, he had called them together and told them that he would now discharge and send home all those who were incapacitated from further military service by age or wounds, and that he would give each man so much as to make him the object of envy to all at home. Instead of being received, as he expected, with approbation, Alexander's announcement was taken as another sign that he wished to discard his old brothers-in-arms and have Asiatics about him rather than Macedonians.

Alexander's notice had been given at a camp council called outside the town, and no doubt held in the usual or Macedonian style. He was addressing the assembled soldiers from a platform upon which he could be seen by all. That there had long been open discontent Alexander well knew ; but he hoped to allay it by just this course, and he felt that his action was generous and would be received as such. Instead of his words producing the desired effect, however, the ringleaders of the Macedonian party began a murmur of dissent which soon grew to a loud outcry of protest. Their feelings had finally broken bounds. Once their tongues were untied, their pent-up anger got the better of them, and after some other slurring remarks, the ringleaders impudently urged the king to make a clean sweep of all the Macedonians and to prosecute his wars alone. These seditious cries speedily drowned Alexander's voice and the wordy tumult of a few soon burst out into every sign of general mutiny. Astonished beyond measure at this unexpected and ungracious outbreak, and letting his naturally quick temper get the upper-hand, Alexander, unarmed as he was, leaped down from the rostrum on which he had been standing, and immediately followed by a few of his Companions who had stood beside him, he seized with his own hands upon some and ordered all the others who were apparent ringleaders to be arrested, himself singling them out, as he had been witness of the whole affair, and probably knew each man by name. Thirteen of these he ordered away to instant execution, and then again ascending the platform, he addressed the rest, who were cowed by terror at this new rôle which their king had, at their incentive, assumed : " You may every man of you go home," said he, " for aught I care. I am and always have been independent of such as you. But before you go, you shall hear what I think of you. Who were you when my father Philip found you ? Hide-clad vagabonds, feeding a few stray sheep which you had pains to guard from the border barbarians. What are you now? The kings of the earth. Who gave you cloaks instead of hides to wear? Philip. Who taught you to wield your arms so as to become the dread of your neigbors? Philip. Who gave you laws and good customs, spread abundance over your country, opened your mines, and raised you from slaves to citizens? Philip. Who made you rulers over the Thessalians and Phocians? Who humbled the Athenians and Thebans at your feet and led you triumphantly through the Peloponnesus? Philip. Who raised you to the first rank among the Hellenes? Philip. And what he did for you is little compared to what Alexander has done. Starting from home so poor that he had to borrow eight hundred talents to feed and clothe and arm you, what has Alexander given you? The dominion and wealth of Asia, Ionia, Lydia, Babylon, Susa. Even the confines of the Scythians and the Indians are yours. Who has made you viceroys, generals, captains? Alexander. Who has watched and worked so that you might sleep in security on your conquests? Alexander. And what has Alexander to show for all this, but this paltry purple robe and this worthless diadem? Does Alexander fare more sumptuously than many of you? Who among you has worked so hard as Alexander? Who can show more wounds? Let the bravest among you stand forth, and bare his breast, and your king will show you wound for wound, and yet wounds more than he. No weapon that the enemy has borne or hurled but has left its mark upon Alexander. Spear, sword, arrow, dart, stone and bolt have left, each one, its witness on Alexander's person. I have celebrated your weddings with my own. I have paid your debts. The best among you have also golden crowns. The brave dead have been magnificently buried. Their statues in eternal brass adorn the temples of the gods at home. Their parents are held in honor, and are relieved from taxes. And now I have proposed to send each one of you home loaded with spoil which will make him the envy of his native town. Ingrates! I will no more of you. Go home and tell your neighbors that you have deserted your king, Alexander, who has overcome the earth to make you powerful, to give you repute and wealth. Tell them that him, Alexander, whom no nation has yet been able to resist, ye deserted to the services of conquered foreigners. This shall be your glory and your piety to the gods. Ye are no longer my soldiers! Get you gone!"

Upon this, Alexander left the rostrum, allowing none to follow him, retired to his palace in the city, and secluded himself for three days. His orders he gave only to his Asiatic soldiers, his personal companions and the body-guard, entirely overlooking the Macedonians. The old soldiers thus discharged were utterly humbled and cast down. They were without head or counsel. Though perhaps there was some just cause of complaint, yet the magnificence of the king's anger overwhelmed them, and buried them under their own wrong.

There was for all that an element of grave danger in the situation, unless the Macedonians should decide to throw themselves on the king's mercy. For in such a body of old heroes a leader would be sure to be found, and who can say what might occur? Indeed, the body without a leader contained perhaps elements of yet greater danger. The men still had their arms, and were twenty thousand strong. But Alexander determined, as he always did, to play out the game to the end. He was ready to rely on his Orientals, and made preparations accordingly. On the third day he again called in all his Persian and Asiatic officers, and to them gave his orders, entirely ignoring the Macedonians, and making appointments as for a quite new army, organizing it in the Macedonian fashion, in phalanx and hipparchies, horse and foot agema and palace guards. He is then said to have sent word to the Macedonians to leave the camp, or if they pleased, to take up arms against him. He would show them, then, that he could do without them, but that they without him were powerless. When the Macedonians ascertained that to an entire new army which had been created of Medes and Persians all the orders were being given, that they themselves were totally ignored, as if indeed, they did not exist, they lost heart, and, running in a body to the palace, they cast their weapons down at the gates, and pleaded bitterly for pardon, exclaiming that they would not withdraw day nor night from the palace gate till Alexander had restored them to his favor.

Alexander was at length mollified. He came out to meet his veterans, forgave them, and admitted them all to their ancient honors. Then one of the Macedonians, an old and worthy "hipparch of the Companions," Kallines by name, advanced and spoke for the rest: "O king! we are grieved that thou hast admitted as kinsmen many Medes and Persians, and hast not admitted us." To which Alexander replied: "Ye are all my kinsmen," and as many as desired saluted him with a kiss, the privilege of kinsmen only, according to the Persian custom which Alexander had at this time adopted. The Macedonians then retired to their camp, shouting and exulting for very joy. This reconciliation was followed by sacrifices, and by a great feast at which the Macedonians sat next the king and the Persians below them. Of this feast nine thousand men are said to have partaken at the tables of the king. This victory over his army was probably a full compensation to Alexander for the refusal of the Macedonians to cross the Hyphasis. He had conquered the Macedonian spirit of obstinacy. He now made Orientals and Macedonians equal in the army, and no longer dreaded the mutinous spirit which at times for several years had come to the surface. But however much he honored the Persians, his old Macedonians always retained the deepest hold in his affections.

The invalided were then picked out to return to Macedonia, some ten thousand in number. Each man was paid up to such time as he would reach home, and was given a talent beside. Just how much a talent represented, it is now hard to say, but it no doubt enabled a veteran to buy himself a house or farm, and to live in ease, or comparative luxury, for the remainder of his days without toil or worry. The children of the Macedonians by Asiatic wives were left in Asia in the cause of family concord, and the king promised that all such should be brought up as Macedonians and soldiers. To the children of the dead the portions of their fathers were assured. In charge of the column moving homewards, he sent Craterus, his most trusted officer, whom he appointed to rule over Macedonia, Thrace and Thessaly. For Craterus was growing old, and was weakened by the hardest service. Polysperchon was sent second in command, and Clitus, Gorgias, Polydamas and Amadas accompanied them.

Craterus is said by Diodorus to have carried with him written instructions to build a fleet in Phœnicia and the adjacent countries, with which Alexander could later move against Carthage and other nations on the Mediterranean; and to begin a system of deportation of people from Europe into Asia and vice versa in pursuance of Alexander's general scheme. But the plan was too vast for any one but Alexander; and his successors made no attempt to carry it out.

Antipater was ordered to bring to Asia in person an equal number of young men of military age to replace the veterans who returned home. He was so instructed to come because the queen-mother, Olympias, and he were always at odds, the quarrels had of late waxed hotter, and Alexander had fears lest some harm should come of it. The king had always held his mother in great love and reverence, despite his recognition of her short-comings. In regard to Antipater's letters complaining of Olympias' mixing in public affairs, Alexander once observed: "Antipater does not know that one mother's tear wipes out a thousand letters such as this."

Alexander, from a Statue in Dresden.

XLVII.

ALEXANDER planned to visit and regulate each part of his enormous empire in turn. He had been down the Euphrates to the Gulf, and up the
Tigris to Opis. He now marched to Ecbatana. Here Hephæstion died, and
Alexander, whose grief was extreme for this friend of his soul, made his funeralia more magnificent than any before. Ptolemy and he then undertook a mid-
winter campaign against the Cossæans, mountain robbers who made insecure
the road from Ecbatana to Susa, and in a forty days' campaign subdued them.
Thence he went to Babylon, where he built a vast dockyard, began the construction of a fleet, and made large calculations for future public improvements. The new Macedo-Oriental army was organized and its discipline begun.
Eastern nobles were put in command beside his old and trusted Macedonians,
and often over them. But his work was cut summarily short. In the course
of his labors on the fleet, Alexander caught a fever, of which, after the lapse
of a few days, he died, leaving his kingdom "to the strongest," and giving his
signet-ring to Perdiccas.

IT was part of Alexander's plan to visit all parts of his
kingdom in turn. From Opis he went, about the end of August, to Ecbatana, along the straight Median road. No doubt
there was much to do in this treasury city, especially since
the flight of Harpalus. At Ecbatana Hephæstion died.
Alexander mourned greatly for this, his one friend of friends;
for as Patroclus to Achilles, so was Hephæstion to Alexander. He prepared a funeral pyre in his honor at Babylon
which is said to have cost ten thousand talents (twelve millions of dollars). His funeralia were celebrated by the most
magnificent gymnastic and musical contests he had ever
given, at a further expense of two thousand talents. Alexander is said to have crucified Glaucus, Hephæstion's doctor,

for allowing him to eat a roast fowl and wash it down with a goblet of new wine.

There had been a quarrel between Eumenes, the king's secretary, and Hephæstion; but Alexander had managed to reconcile the two. Eumenes had for seven years been Philip's secretary. For the thirteen years of Alexander's reign he filled the same position to the king. History is apt to show us its heroes surrounded by their military family and lieutenants. The civil officers one more rarely hears about. And

Alexander's Last Marches.

yet, in moving such an army as Alexander's, what efficient men they must have been! Cornelius Nepos abundantly testifies to Eumenes' ability, and he showed it after Alexander's death.

After the mourning for Hephæstion had been prolonged for many days, and the year was drawing to a close, Alexander brought himself to undertake an expedition against the Cossæans. This was rather a campaign necessary to secure the road from Susa to Ecbatana than a mere " man hunt " to rouse himself from his sorrow for Hephæstion's death. The Cossæans were á tribe of marauders northeast from Susa, who, like the Uxians, had not been subdued by Persia, but kept quiet by gifts. They never came to an open fight, but would disperse in small parties to their strongholds and hiding-places whenever attacked, and then again emerge and resume their marauding expeditions. Against these Alexander and Ptolemy, son of Lagus, marched in two columns in midwinter, for at this time these people could not take refuge in the mountain heights, but must stay in the valleys ; and, despite the ruggedness of the ground and the difficulties of snows, by sending small detachments up each valley to attack the forces there, they subdued the barbarians in a forty days' campaign, destroyed their fastnesses, and dispersed them utterly. No details of the campaign have survived.

From here Alexander returned towards Babylon, which he had selected as his future capital on account of its central position between India, Egypt, and the Mediterranean. On his way he received embassies from Lydia and Carthage, and from the Bruttians, Lucanians, and Tyrrhenians (Etruscans) of Italy, to salute him as king of Asia. The Ethiopians, Scythians of Europe, the Gauls, and the Iberians, nations whose names were heard for the first time by Macedonians, also came to pay tribute to the great conqueror, and some invoked his wisdom in settling disputes. Aristus and Asclepiades have stated that Rome also sent an embassy to congratulate Alexander ; no others mention it, and it seems scarcely probable that the freedom-loving Romans should pay court to a man they would have considered in the light of a despot. Livy doubts that contemporary Romans knew of Alexander even by report. Their horizon did not extend beyond Italy. In fact, Rome had not conquered Italy until two generations later than this.

Alexander had always been anxious to discover the topography of the Caspian Sea, and now sent a number of shipwrights, under Heraclides, into Hyrcania, to build vessels and launch them on the Caspian, ready for this use when he should be prepared to make an expedition thither.

After crossing the Tigris, Alexander was met by some Chaldæan philosophers who entreated him not to enter Babylon, as they foresaw evil to come to him if he did so; or, if he must, at least not to enter the city by the western gate. Alexander imagined some ulterior purpose in the request of the Chaldæans. He was proposing to rebuild the temple of Belus, whose revenues the Chaldæans were now appropriating, and he thought these soothsayers desired to prevent his doing what would be a manifest loss to themselves, though he could not fathom their immediate motive. He however so far heeded their counsel as to endeavor to enter the city from the east, but the shoals and marshes on this side of the city prevented his so doing. In addition to this one, there had been sundry other prophecies concerning the death of Alexander which do not particularly concern us.

In Babylon Alexander found the fleet under Nearchus which had sailed up the Euphrates to meet him, and another fleet from Phœnicia, consisting of two quinquiremes, three quadriremes, twelves triremes, and thirty triacontors, which had been taken by wagons, in parts, overland to Thapsacus, had there been joined, and thence floated down the Euphrates. The cypresses of Babylon were devoted to the building of more ships; and a harbor was excavated in Babylon large enough to contain one thousand vessels of war, and a dockyard built beside it. Recruits were got from Phœnicia and

Syria for this fleet. Alexander proposed to colonize the shores of the Persian Sea, and also to attack Arabia, because this country had sent no embassies to him, and because he coveted their territory and spices. Alexander, in fact, sent out three expeditions, designed to sail around Arabia ; but neither of the three went as far as he had commanded them to go. The trip was yet an unknown one, except from hearsay.

Not having suffered any harm from returning to Babylon, Alexander made an expedition down the Euphrates to the Pallacopas, a canal near that river running towards the sea through marshes and lowland which afford an outlet to the annual floods. Here he founded a city and established in it a number of the invalided Greek mercenaries. Thence he again returned to Babylon.

Hither Peucestas came with a force of twenty thousand Persians, Cossæans and Tarpurians, the most valiant men he could collect. Philoxenus brought an army from Caria ; Menander one from Lydia ; Menidas returned with the cavalry. The foreign soldiers were divided up into files, each headed by a Macedonian decurion, next to whom came a double-pay man, and next a ten-stater man, then twelve foreigners, and then another ten-stater man, making the sixteen deep file. The Macedonians were armed as usual. The foreigners had bows or javelins so as to fire over the heads of their front-rank men. The king did not live to fully carry this Macedonian-Asiatic organization into effect. At first blush such a disposition of troops appears to lack solidity. Alexander also held many reviews and sham fights with his fleet, in the nature of games, intended to exercise the men and ships in the duties and tactics of war.

Here, too, Alexander received favorable answer to his message to the oracle at Ammon, asking whether Hephæstion might not be worshiped as a hero. This worship was in consequence introduced, and so punctiliously carried out that Alexander even went to the length of forgiving Cleomenes many deeds of tyranny and rapacity in Egypt on the score of his acts of reverence to the newly canonized hero.

From the exposure to which Alexander had been subjected in overseeing the construction of his fleet, harbor and dockyard, he unhappily caught a low fever; but relying as he always did on his great bodily strength, he paid small heed to it, but continued to attend certain feasts which were then being held. The revelries developed a more marked feverish condition, but Alexander continued them for another day and night. He was then unable to leave the house of Medius, where he had last supped. Each morning he performed his usual sacrifice, being carried out to do this, and afterwards lying still all day. He continued his orders for the approaching expedition around Arabia into the Red Sea, — a gigantic and perilous one for those days, — and insisted on attending to all matters of business. This he persisted in doing each day, though the fever kept on the increase, and finally took a fatal form. Before his death, in June, 323 B. C., most of his old soldiers passed his couch to take a last farewell. Alexander could not speak, but he knew them, and beckoned to each one with his hand. His last words were said to be an answer to the question to whom he left his kingdom: "To the strongest!" or, as Curtius puts it, 'to the most worthy,' — his last act to give his signet-ring to Perdiccas. The rumor that he was poisoned probably had no foundation.

Alexander's embalmed body was carried by Ptolemy to Egypt, and placed in Memphis. A few years later it was removed to Alexandria.

XLVIII.

THE MAN AND SOLDIER.

ALEXANDER possessed uncommon qualities of body, head and heart. His bearing was that of a king, but he was kindly and considerate. He read much, and enjoyed the society of men of brains. He was abstinent of pleasures except drinking — the national vice. Intemperance with Alexander was occasional, not habitual. His bodily strength and activity were matched only by his extraordinary courage. He courted danger, but its excitement never clouded his intellect. He was naturally excitable and superstitious. The latter quality he kept well under control; the former sometimes ran into violence, and overcame his better nature. His two vices may be characterized as hasty temper and vanity. To these, joined with overdrinking, may be ascribed all Alexander's ill deeds. But as man and monarch, there are few with so much to their credit and less to their charge. He was not a Greek, but had a strong Hellenistic flavor. His life's idea was to conquer and then Hellenize Asia. He did the one; the other he could not do. As a soldier, Alexander was the first who conducted war in what Napoleon calls a methodical manner; as a captain and conqueror, he will always stand at the head of his peers. To him is due the credit of giving the world, on a large scale, the first lessons in the art of war. His campaigns form a text-book almost complete in its scope.

ALEXANDER was possessed of uncommon beauty. Plutarch says that Lysippus made the best portrait of him, " the inclination of the head a little on one side towards the left shoulder, and his melting eye, having been expressed by this artist with great exactness." His likeness was less fortunately caught by Apelles, who made him too dark. He was fair in complexion and ruddy, of sweet odor and agreeable in person. Above the average height, though not tall, his presence was commanding, his bearing kingly. Fond of study, he read much history, poetry and general literature. His favorite book was the Iliad, a copy of which, annotated by Aristotle, with a dagger, always lay under his pillow. In his youth he was given to music, and played well, but in later life neglected the accomplishment. He enjoyed martial music, but disliked sentimental airs. He had devoted some time to medicine, and did not lack skill as a physician. He was at all times surrounded by men of brains, and enjoyed their conversation. He understood and grasped all the science of the day. An admirer of the drama, he considered comedy lacking in the inculcation of the hardier virtues. He strictly observed his duties to the gods.

While he had no code of morals beyond the usages of that day, though indeed Plutarch credits him with more than natural chastity, Alexander was moderate, respected the rights of others, was unselfish in his dealings with women, and often showed a self-denial and continence which, in one so young and naturally of a very passionate nature, calls for the highest praise. He was abstinent of pleasures except drinking. Aristobulus says Alexander did not drink much in quantity, but enjoyed being merry. Still the Macedonian *much* was more than wisdom dictates. He was fain to talk over his wine and to sit long at table chatting with his friends, rather than overdrink. His principal meal was after dark. He ate little himself, but paid much heed to his guests. When Ada, queen of Caria, sent him, daily, curious dishes and desired to send him some skillful cooks and pastrymen, he told her that his preceptor, Leonidas, had given him the best: a night march. (*quære*, early morning walk) to prepare for breakfast, and a moderate breakfast to prepare for supper. His table was always open to, in fact was intended for his military family and friends. It is said, in Asia, to have cost 10,000 drachmas ($2,000) a day — no very great outlay for the owner of the world. Many of his officers were more extravagant and more given to luxurious living than he. But Alexander was undeniably fond of flattery at his meals, as at all other times. Indeed, he may be said to have fed on flattery rather than on rich meats.

Alexander was active, and able to endure heat and cold, hunger and thirst, trial and fatigue beyond even the stoutest. His strength and courage were altogether exceptional. Quintus Curtius says that he saved his father's life in a mutiny among the Triballi, when a mere lad, by his sole personal gallantry. "He was invincible to those things which terrify others." "His bravery did not only excel that of other kings, but even that of those who have no other virtue." He was never known to change countenance at wounds. The Mallian arrow which had penetrated his lung, was cut out without a motion on Alexander's part.

He was exceeding swift of foot, but when young would not enter the Olympic games, because he had not kings' sons to compete with. An athlete himself, he disliked professional athletes, saying that they ought to place their strength at the service of the country. He was always glad to incur hardship and danger in hunting, and is related to have slain a huge lion single-handed when in Bactria. He kept his body in good training. On the march he was habituated to shoot from his horse or chariot for practice, and to mount and dismount when at full speed. He was given to playing ball with the royal pages. He frequently marched on foot with his troops rather than make use of horse or chariot. Naturally disposed to sleep but little, he increased his watchfulness by habit. In an iron body dwelt both an intellect clear beyond compare, and a heart full of generous impulses. He was ambitious, but from high motives. His desire to conquer the world was coupled with the purpose of furthering Greek civilization. His courage was, both physically and morally, high-pitched. He actually enjoyed the delirium of battle, and its turmoils raised his intellect to its loftiest grade of clearness and activity.   His instincts were keen; his perception remarkable; his judgment all but infallible.   As an organizer of an army he was unapproached; as a leader, unapproachable in rousing the ambition and courage of his men, and in quelling their fears by his own fearlessness.   "That the soul of this king was fashioned on a superhuman pattern," says Polybius, "all men agree."

Alexander kept his agreements faithfully, and had wonderful generosity coupled with grace in giving.   He was a remarkable judge of men.   He had the rare gift of natural, convincing oratory, and of making men hang upon his lips as he spoke, and do deeds of heroism after.   He lavished money rather on his friends than on himself.

Alexander's chief attachment was for Hephæstion, with whom he had been brought up, and to whom he clung with never-changing devotion.   To Hephæstion he confided his every secret.   His affection for his mother, Olympias, never waned.   Hephæstion alone knew what Olympias wrote to Alexander.   One day when the king and his intimate had together read one of the queen-mother's letters, Alexander drew his seal ring from his finger and pressed it on Hephæstion's lips.   Next to Hephæstion came Craterus.   The former was Alexander's friend, the latter the king's.   Alexander had more love for Hephæstion, more admiration for Craterus; Hephæstion wore the same Persian dress which was adopted by Alexander, and was often his mouth-piece to the Orientals; Craterus retained his Greek dress, and was the spokesman to the king for his Macedonians.

While every inch a king, Alexander was friendly with his men; shared their toils and dangers; never asked an effort he himself did not make; never ordered a hardship of which he himself did not bear part.   His eagerness to brave danger was so marked that he could never stand idle by and see another doing deeds of valor. He invariably chose the hardest task himself. No doubt he was as conscious of his own ability to do it better than any one else, as he was of his power to endure. During the herculean pursuit of Darius, — after a march of four hundred miles in eleven days, at the close of which but sixty of his men had been able to keep beside him, — it was he who always led the van, cheered on his men, inspired all with the ambition to keep on to the very end, and who stood the heat and thirst, the fatigue and danger best of all. It was he who headed the weary handful in a charge on the Persian thousands. Such things endear a leader to his men beyond the telling.

But Alexander's temper, by inheritance quick, grew ungovernable. A naturally excitable character, coupled with a certain superstitious tendency, was the very one to suffer from a life which carried him to such a giddy height, and from successes which reached beyond the human limit. We condemn, but, looking at him as a captain, may pass over those dark hours in his life which narrate the murder of Clitus, the execution of Philotas and Parmenio, and the cruelties to Bessus and to Batis. Alexander was distinctly subject to human frailties. His vices were partly inherited, partly the outgrowth of his youth and wonderful career. But he repented quickly and sincerely of his evil deeds. When all is summed up, there are few monarchs in the world's history at whose door is cast less reproach; few of whom more that is great and good is written. Until the last few years of his life, his habits were very simple. He was not by nature fond of dress. "A prince ought to surpass his subjects rather in the culture of virtues than in the finery of his clothes," said he. But like Hannibal he was a great lover of fine arms and weapons, and of good horses. His adoption of Persian dress and manners was so largely a political requirement, that it can be hardly ascribed to personal motives, even if we fully acknowledge his overweening vanity. His public claim to superhuman lineage was not remarkable; for the descent of the Macedonian kings from Hercules was allowed by the judges at the Olympian games when Macedon was but a small kingdom.

We can get far closer to the kernel of Alexander's character by the study of those who lived nearer to his age, than by relying on the cold, statistical criticism of to-day. Altogether too much time has been devoted to belittling Alexander. The king of Macedon had innumerable enemies in Greece; Alexander had more; many outspoken ones, many backbiters. That every scintilla of ill which could be said of him was set down in malice by some one, and by hosts believed, is as natural as that his admirers should overpraise him. Arrian draws principally from the relations of Ptolemy, son of Lagus, the very best of witnesses, and of Aristobulus, also one of Alexander's officers; from the story of Nearchus and others who saw and were part of what they narrated, and from the diary of Eumenes, the secretary, and Alexander's own letters. In some respects what Alexander's laudators have said may be overdrawn, but Arrian has from them given us the only history which yields to the military man a crisp idea of how this great captain wrought; and those things which are susceptible of exaggeration are not of the essence. Losses may be diminished to place the courage of the Macedonians in higher relief; the numbers of the enemy slain may be increased. But as to what Alexander did, all agree; how he did it, Arrian best explains, and its bare recital suffices to make him in intellect, moral force, excellence of heart, and splendor of physique incomparably the first of men.

The life work of Philip had been transcendent. That of

Alexander surpasses anything in history. Words fail to describe the attributes of this monarch as a soldier. The perfection of all he did was by no means understood by his historians. But to compare his deeds with those of other captains excites our wonder. Starting with a handful of men from Macedonia, in four years one grand achievement after another and without a failure had placed at his feet the empire of the Great King. Leaving home with an enormous debt, in fifty moons he had possessed himself of all the treasures of the earth. Thence, with marvelous courage, endurance, intelligence and skill he completed the conquest of the entire then known world, marching twenty-two thousand miles in his eleven years' campaigns. And all this before he was thirty-two. There is no other instance in the world's history, it has been observed, of a small nation overrunning the earth, and impressing itself for all ages on the countries overrun. Persia had conquered the world, had threatened Greece, had in a measure asserted her authority over the islands of the Ægean, and fully over the Greek cities of the coast, and yet she went down before Alexander's sword. His health and strength were still as great as ever; his voracity for conquest greater, as well as his ability to conquer.

It is an interesting question, had he not died, what would have become of Rome. The Roman infantry was as good as his; not so their cavalry. An annually elected consul could be no match for Alexander. But the king never met in his campaigns such an opponent as the Roman Republic, nor his phalanx such a rival as the Roman legion would have been. That was reserved for Hannibal. It is altogether probable, had Alexander lived to carry his career of conquest westward, that Rome in her then condition would have succumbed to his arms, and the history of the world have been modified. For Alexander was master of the art of war; the Romans knew nothing of it until Hannibal, by dire defeat, had taught them that hard blows alone cannot stand against hard blows well delivered.

Greek civilization, to a certain degree, followed Alexander's footsteps, but it was not solely due to him. " You are a man like all of us, Alexander," said the naked Indian, " except that you abandon your home, like a meddlesome destroyer, to invade the most distant regions, enduring hardship yourself, and inflicting it on others." Alexander could never have erected a permanent kingdom on his theory of coalescing races by intermarriages and forced migrations. His Græco-Persian empire was a mere dream. Alexander was never a Greek. He had but the Greek genius and intelligence grafted on the ruder Macedonian nature; and he became, to a marked extent, Asiaticized by his conquests. His life work, as cut out by himself, was to conquer, and then to Hellenize Asia. He did the one, he could not accomplish the other aim. He did not plant a true and permanent Hellenism in a single country of Asia. Still, what he and his successors did left a decided Hellenistic flavor throughout Persia. Few of Alexander's cities have lived. They were rather fortified posts than self-sustaining marts. As a statesman, intellectual, far-seeing and broad, he yet conceived and worked on an impossible theory, and the immediate result of all his genius did not last a generation. What he might have accomplished had he lived a longer life remains a mere subject of speculation.

What has Alexander done for the art of war? When Demosthenes was asked what were the three most important qualities in an orator, he replied, " Action, action, action! " In another sense this might well be applied to the captain. No one can become a great captain without a mental and physical activity which are almost abnormal; and so soon as this exceptional power of activity wanes, the captain has come to a term of his greatness. Genius has been described as an extraordinary capacity for hard work. But this capacity is but the human element. Genius implies the divine spark. It is the personality of the great captain which makes him what he is. The maxims of war are but a meaningless page to him who cannot apply them. They are helpful just so far as the man's brain and heart, as his individuality, can carry them. It is because a great captain must first of all be a great man, and because to the lot of but few great men belongs the peculiar ability, or falls the opportunity of being great captains, that preëminent success in war is so rarely seen.

All great soldiers are cousins-german in equipment of heart and head. No man ever was, no man can by any possibility blunder into being, a great soldier without the most generous virtues of the soul, and the most distinguished powers of the intellect. The former are independence, self-reliance, ambition within proper bounds; that sort of physical bravery which not only does not know fear, but which is not even conscious that there is such a thing as courage; that greater moral quality which can hold the lives of tens of thousands of men and the destinies of a great country or cause patiently, intelligently and unflinchingly in his grasp; powers of endurance which cannot be overtaxed; the unconscious habit of ruling men and of commanding their love and admiration, coupled with the ability to stir their enthusiasm to the yielding of their last ounce of effort. The latter comprise business capacity of the very highest order, essential to the care of his troops; keen perceptions, which even in extraordinary circumstances or sudden emergencies are not to be led astray; the ability to think as quickly and accurately in the turmoil of battle as in the quiet of the bureau; the power to foresee to its ultimate conclusion the result of a strategic or tactical manœuvre; the capacity to gauge the efforts of men and of masses of men; the many-sidedness which can respond to the demands of every detail of the battlefield, while never losing sight of the one object aimed at; the mental strength which weakens not under the tax of hours and days of unequaled strain. For in truth there is no position in which man can be placed which asks so much of his intellect in so short a space as that of the general, the failure or success, the decimation or security of whose army hangs on his instant thought and unequivocal instruction under the furious and kaleidoscopic ordeal of the field. To these qualities of heart and head add one factor more — opportunity — and you have the great soldier.

Now, Alexander was the first man, the details of whose history have been handed down to us, who possessed these qualities in the very highest measure; whose opportunities were coextensive with his powers; and who out of all these wrought a methodical system of warfare from which we may learn lessons to-day. Look at what he accomplished with such meagre means! He alone has the record of uniform success with no failure. And this was not because he had weak opponents; for while the Persians were redoubtable chiefly from their numbers, the Tyrians, the tribes beyond the Caucasus, and the Indians made a bold front and good fight.

Alexander's movements were always made on a well-conceived, maturely-digested plan; and this he kept in view to the end, putting aside all minor considerations for the main object, but never losing sight of these. His grasp was as large as his problem. His base for his advance into the then known world was the entire coast-line of the then known sea. He had not Napoleon's advantage of a complete knowledge of the theatre of operations and its resources. He was compelled to study his every step forward. But he never advanced, despite his speed, without securing flanks and rear, and properly garrisoning the country on which he based. Having done this, he marched on his objective — which was wont to be the enemy's army — with a directness which was unerring. His fertility in ruse and stratagem was unbounded. He kept well concentrated; his division of forces was always warranted by the conditions, and always with a view of again concentrating. His rapidity was unparalleled. It was this which gave him such an ascendant over all his enemies. Neither winter cold nor summer heat, mountain nor desert, the widest rivers nor the most elaborate defenses, ever arrested his course; and yet his troops were always well fed. He was a master of logistics. He lived on the country he campaigned in, as entirely as Napoleon, but was careful to accumulate granaries in the most available places. He was remarkable in being able to keep the gaps in his army filled by recruits from home or enlistments of natives, and in transforming the latter into excellent soldiers. Starting from home with thirty-five thousand men, he had in the Indian campaigns no less than one hundred and thirty-five thousand, and their deeds proved the stuff that was in them.

It is true that we do not see every trivial detail of the school text-books illustrated in the campaigns of Alexander. And yet, had history vouchsafed us a fuller insight into the minutiæ of his work, it is scarcely to be doubted that we should have found as much skill in the minor as is shown in the larger operations. The results clearly prove it. But such details are not what make the captain. Few martinets have won any rank as soldiers. Details are essential; no extended operations can be successful without scrupulous attention to the last detail. What, however, places a great captain far above the rank and file of generals is something greater than this. It is the broad conception of how to do the work in hand, and its execution with intelligence and boldness. In this there is scarcely a principle illustrated by Napoleon, in which Alexander is not his prototype.

We are apt to think that the art of war is constantly improving. This is at least open to doubt. There has been an extraordinary advance in the last generation in the appliances of destruction, in the devices for making war horrible. But can it be claimed that the art of war, in its leading principles, has advanced *pari passu* with the mechanics of war? To such a state of uncertainty have modern inventions reduced even the wisest of soldiers that no one can predict on what lines the next great war will be conducted. To be said to improve, an art must become more positive, more certain. To-day we are in doubt as to many almost elementary factors in our problem. We do not know whether the best formation for infantry will be an open or a close order; whether the new powder may not call for still other tactical formations; whether cavalry has succumbed to arms of precision, or will be of more service in the future than in the past; whether higher explosives than gunpowder will be availed of; whether the spade is to play a greater or lesser rôle than it has of late; and a host of other important questions are being forced on the military man by the rapid sequence of inventions. At sea matters are still more doubtful. Expensive ironclads prove unseaworthy; big guns are damaged by a few trial shots; torpedo warfare is on trial. What will the next naval war develop? There was more certainty in arms in Alexander's era than there is to-day. For the demands to be made upon it, Alexander's methods were as perfect as Napoleon's, though no doubt inadequate to our present wants. It might be said that the art of war is in a less exact and satisfactory condition to-day than ever before. Even some of the plainest requirements of strategy as taught by Bonaparte have been qualified by modern conditions and by the size of modern armies.

Alexander's battles are tactically brilliant examples of conception and execution. The wedge at Arbela was more splendid than Macdonald's column at Wagram. It was a scintillation of genius. No parallel exists to the battle of the Hydaspes. Wonderful as Alexander's intellect was, his power of execution exceeded his power of conception. It was his ability to seize openings with a rapidity perhaps never equaled which won him his battles, rather than his mere battle plan. However excellent this, he bettered it in the execution. His will sometimes overrode his sagacity, but always in such a way as to breed success. His stubbornness bore down the opposition which his limited numbers could not overcome.

In the use of cavalry Alexander stands without a peer. No one ever hurled his cavalry on the enemy with such precision, momentum or effect. Its charge was always well-timed ; it always won. No one ever headed horse with such godlike boldness, or fought it to the bottom as he did. Had Alexander not been one of the world's great captains, he would have been the typical *beau sabreur* of the world's history.

Alexander always saw where his enemy's strength and weakness lay, and took prompt advantage of them. He utilized his victories to the full extent, and pursued with a vigor which no other has ever reached. He was equally great in sieges as in battles. The only thing he was never called on to show was the capacity to face disaster. He possessed every remarkable military attribute ; we can discover in him no military weakness. Napoleon once, in a fit of exaggeration, is said to have characterized Alexander, *the man*, as beginning with the soul of a Trajan to end with the heart of a Nero and the habits of Heliogabalus. The characterization is not only warped, but Napoleon could not cast the first stone at Alexander's personal bearing. Of *the conqueror*, the great Corsican says : " The campaigns of the son of Philip are not like those of Jenghis Khan or Tamerlane, a simple irruption, a sort of deluge ; all was calculated with depth, executed with audacity, conducted with wisdom."

As a captain, Alexander accomplished more than any man ever did. He had no equal predecessor who left him a model for action. He showed the world, first of all men, and best, how to make war. He formulated the first principles of the art, to be elaborated by Hannibal, Cæsar, Gustavus Adolphus, Turenne, Prince Eugene, Marlborough, Frederick and Napoleon. It is certain that Hannibal drew his inspiration from the deeds of the great Macedonian ; equally certain that Napoleon, robbed of his knowledge of Alexander and Hannibal and Cæsar, would never have been Napoleon. Alexander's conditions did not demand that he should approach to the requirements of modern war. But he was easily master of his trade, as, perhaps, scarce any other soldier ever was. For, as Napoleon himself aptly says, " to guess at the intentions of the enemy ; to divine his opinion of yourself ; to hide from him both your own intentions and opinion ; to mislead him by feigned manœuvres ; to invoke ruse, as well as digested schemes, so as to fight under the best conditions, — this is, and always was, the art of war."

XLIX.

THE SUCCESSORS OF ALEXANDER. EUMENES AND ANTIGONUS. PHILOPŒMEN.

ALEXANDER's lieutenants divided up his kingdom, ostensibly for his heirs. But ambition and mutual jealousies soon broke up the empire, and brought on wars. Discipline declined. Corps and armies sold themselves for gold, or betrayed their generals. Courage ebbed with discipline, and Oriental devices were adopted to eke out valor. Still, the old officers trained by Alexander showed that they were good soldiers, and their campaigns and battles bear the stamp of their great master. Fortification especially grew apace, and received its highest exemplification at the siege of Rhodes. The stratagems employed by Eumenes in manœuvring against Antigonus, and the third battle of Mantinæa, won by Philopœmen over the Spartans, are good samples of the work of the successors of Alexander. But Greece had degenerated, and with her Macedon; and finally the proud nation of Philip and Alexander, forgetful of the virtues which had made her great, sank under the sway of sturdy Rome.

ALEXANDER's lieutenants divided up his kingdom, ostensibly in trust for his heirs. But ambition and jealousies led to wars, and the great empire fell to pieces. Macedon, Egypt and Syria remained the prominent divisions, and a relic of Hellenism in the East still testified to the king's broad method. Discipline in the armies declined fast; mercenary troops multiplied, and missile-throwers, chariots and elephants crept into the line of battle. The armies became Asiaticized. Despite this, however, the wars of Alexander's immediate successors show a clear following of the great master's methods. In some minor respects, these were even improved. After the battle of Ipsus the military art declined fast. Only brilliant exceptions, of which the manœuvres of Antigonus and Eumenes and the third battle of Mantinæa are fine samples, remained to testify to its having ever existed.

Greece and Macedon were no longer what they had been. Their preëminence had departed with their patriotism.

The campaigns of Alexander in Asia had not tended to keep up the admirable spirit of discipline which Philip had created in the Macedonian army. Its contact with the riches, luxury and low moral tone of the East had sapped its hardy virtues to the core. It had needed Alexander's own wonderful power as a soldier and a king to keep this evil from destroying the army, root and branch, even during his life. Only he was capable of getting from it the work it did. That Alexander's army was no longer what it had been in earlier and simpler days was manifested by the several conspiracies which occurred in Drangiana and Bactria, the refusal of the soldiers to cross the Hyphasis, and the mutiny at Opis. On Alexander's death, there was no one capable of checking the further and rapid spread of this demoralizing evil. His generals, — the Diadochi, or successors, — Perdiccas, Antipater, Craterus, Ptolemy, Antigonus, Eumenes, Cassander, Leonnatus, Lysimachus, Seleucus, divided up the empire, ostensibly as regents and lieutenants for Alexander's half-brother Philip Arrhadæus, whom the army had chosen king, and as some say also for Alexander, his posthumous son by Roxana. But ambition for absolute control and jealousies among the Diadochi soon led to wars which were continuous and bloody, which extinguished by murder the entire family of Alexander, and which were not ended until the close of the century, at the battle of Ipsus.

But out of all this turmoil there arose several monarchies, the Eastern ones of which represented the influence of Alexander's life in their marked Hellenistic character. These monarchies were: Egypt, under Ptolemy, son of Lagus, and his descendants; Syria, under Seleucus and his descendants; Pergamon under the Attalidæ; Macedonia, under the descendants of Demetrius Poliorcetes, son of Antigonus; Bithynia, Pontus, Gallacia, Bactria, Rhodes, and the Greek cantons. In these countries Greek remained as the language of the polite world and of the government. Monuments were inscribed, and records kept in Greek; coins bore Greek legends, and the educated classes made use of the language and the manners of Hellas. In some of them Grecian art, literature and learning reached a high development; but coupled with intellectual good were mixed the elements of moral decay, and from their formation to their fall these countries bore the impress of the unreal and transitory.

The successors of Alexander soon began to indulge in extensive wars among themselves. These required enormous forces, and they were unscrupulous as to their means of gathering them. Money was poured out like water to raise armies; bribery was resorted to as a means of seducing the troops of the enemy from their allegiance; and as a result the soldiers discovered that they had a money value, and acted accordingly. Discipline became a thing of the past, and into its place stepped every vice which loosening organization is apt to engender. It was this falling-off in discipline which eventually made Greece and Macedon a prey to the Roman arms.

What had been the chief strength of Alexander's army, the Companions and the select bodies of troops chosen from the best men of the nation, gradually became a danger instead of a protection to the state. Whoever could gain over these prototypes of the Prætorian guards — and as a rule, money was the open sesame — could control the government. The demand for soldiers made the profession of arms the only one worth pursuing for a livelihood; and all Greece became a vast recruiting ground. Gold could not only buy armies of any size, but could seduce men from their allegiance. Less heed was paid to the constitution of armies; these were composed of the most heterogeneous elements, contained men of all nationalities; and missile-throwers, chariots and elephants found their uses in bolstering up declining discipline, tactical resources which Alexander had heartily despised and never used in action.

The extension of the system of mercenary troops in Greece, of which the early chapters of this work have treated, was followed by its necessary consequence. The strength of the Greeks, of which patriotism was the essence, had disappeared, and the land had sunk to a despicable level of political or military ability. A few exceptions, such as those of Pyrrhus, king of Epirus, the Achæan and Ætolian Leagues, and Sparta under Cleomenes, a hundred years after Alexander, only serve to throw into relief the deplorable condition of the land.

Alexander's magnificent plans in the East had been shipwrecked. A salvage of Hellenism remained to testify to the great conqueror's splendid projects. But soon the old national tendencies, too strong to be suppressed by an outer coating of foreign manners, began to struggle to the surface in every country he had subdued beyond the Euphrates. The descendants of Alexander's generals were with few exceptions unworthy of their sires or their sires' training; they gradually sank to the level of Oriental despots. The populations remained the same. The armies grew weak as the monarchs weakened; and the dependence on foreign accessories sapped the vigor and self-reliance of the infantry. The average soldier degenerated into a swash-buckler, a bully in peace, a coward in war.

So far as the territorial limits of Alexander's empire are concerned, these were within three generations narrowed to a small part of their original extent. The Parthians under the

Arsacidæ conquered all the lands between the Indus and Euphrates, thus making a barrier to the further encroachments of civilization. India and the southern satrapies fell away from their allegiance not long after Alexander's death. There only remained the provinces immediately adjoining the eastern Mediterranean.

But despite the gradual and certain weakening of the inner strength of the armies, the art of war itself as taught by Alexander did not at once disappear. It lasted as long as his immediate successors lived. These lieutenants of his had received too good an education in practical war to forget their trade off-hand. During the rest of the century, or until these men themselves had disappeared from the scene, we can trace a strict following out of the principles laid down by their great master. The phalanxes grew larger. The diphalangiarchias of eight thousand hoplites and tetraphalangiarchias of sixteen thousand hoplites, or with cavalry and light troops some fifteen thousand and thirty thousand strong, were not uncommon. The marshaling of the line of battle, the marches, tactical formations and evolutions remained substantially the same; and Alexander's favorite attack in oblique order, as best shown at the Hydaspes, was not infrequently employed. Generals understood how to accommodate the phalanx to the various accidents of the ground, and to make use of its strength and supplement its weakness according to the existing conditions. The various battles down to Ipsus by no means show lack of ability. In outpost and scouting duty, and the use of light cavalry and light foot, an advance may even be said to have been made. The strongest symptom of decadence — as above said — was the beginning of reliance on missile-throwing machines, not for their proper uses at rivers and defiles, as Alexander had taught, but in battle; and the employment of such useless devices as elephants and chariots.

In strategic manœuvres, these generals followed the precepts they had learned. They protected their flanks and rear; they marched directly upon their objective; they sought in battle a solution of their campaigns. Down to Ipsus, the Greeks and Macedonians generally fought bravely, if headed by a general who commanded their confidence. But the marches of the armies were accompanied by devastation and cruelties worthy only of the Orient. On the whole, these lieutenants and successors of Alexander proved themselves as apt scholars of the great master as they were faithless to the kingdom he had created for his posterity.

Of all the branches of the art, fortification and sieges grew most. In mechanics, the construction of siege devices, and ship-building, there were marked advances. Demetrius Poliorcetes, aided by the Greek Epimachus, made the siege of Rhodes one of the distinct events of that age. The constructions and machines at this siege were in size beyond anything so far known. Most celebrated is the remarkable tower built for Demetrius by Epimachus, which he named Helepolis. Each side was of fifty cubits (seventy-five feet); the height was one hundred cubits. The three sides towards the enemy were iron-plated. It rested on huge wheels, and had nine stories, connected by ladders. The windows were protected by movable blinds, through which the engines could fire. The roof story was plated, and here archers and missile-throwers were stationed. It took thirty-four hundred men to move the huge structure, which was done from within and the rear. The wonder of Demetrius' work in attack is only equaled by the skill of the defense. This was so fertile in expedients, so able and bold and persistent, that Demetrius finally deemed 'it wise to make terms.

After the battle of Ipsus (301 B. C.) tactics became Asiaticised, and the lessons of Alexander were gradually forgotten.

From now on, with a few brilliant exceptions, the decadence of the art of war in Greece was quick and certain. Not until Hannibal, whose Greek education gave him access to the record of Alexander's deeds, and whose splendid intellect enabled him to digest them, could rescue the art from oblivion and teach the Romans how to make war, was anything like the method or skill of Alexander to be seen. From the end of the fourth century B. C., the art of war disappears in Greece, to reappear in Italy under the great Carthaginian.

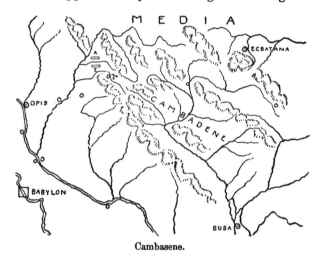

Cambasene.

An example of the campaigning of Alexander's successors is afforded by some of the manœuvres of Antigonus and Eumenes in Asia. Towards the close of 318 B. C., when the season was at hand for both to seek winter-quarters, their armies lay encamped not far apart, and separated only by a mountain torrent and some ravines. The exact locality is not known. The entire region had been so devastated that the troops were suffering for both food and forage. Eumenes had ascertained by spies whom he kept actively at work that Antigonus was proposing to break up the succeeding night for the province of Cambasene (or Corbiane), lying midway between Susa and Ecbatana, which the war had not yet drained of its riches, and whose well-watered upland character fitted it peculiarly for scattering troops in winter-quarters; for its watercourses, mountain ridges and defiles made the defense of a large section easy. Eumenes had intended later to move to Cambasene himself, and in order to head Antigonus off from his purpose, he made use of the following stratagem.

He sent several soldiers, under guise of desertion, into Antigonus' camp, to inform that general that Eumenes had made all his preparations to attack him while he was breaking camp. Eumenes meanwhile sent his baggage and pack-train forward at nightfall by a hidden circuit, and himself followed shortly after, having taken care to ration his men for a long march. He left a line of videttes opposite Antigonus, so cleverly disposed as completely to deceive this officer, who remained in line anticipating attack, until his light troops brought him word that the enemy had decamped.

Eumenes had gained a six hours' march on Antigonus. The latter followed him sharply with his entire body of cavalry, and at daybreak struck his rear-guard as it was debouching from the mountain defile through which it had made its way that night. Antigonus was unable to attack seriously, but deployed his cavalry force along the foothills, and handled it with such effectiveness and skill that Eumenes was convinced that he had the enemy's whole army to contend with, and was constrained to stop and form line. So well did Antigonus mask his weakness that his infantry gained time to come up, and both armies faced each other in full force. Each wished to fight for the possession of the road to Cambasene. An all day's battle was engaged with alternating success. The left wing of each was beaten. Night put an end to the fray; Antigonus held the battlefield, but had lost more heavily than Eumenes. This latter fact so disheartened his soldiery that he did not dare renew the struggle. He withdrew into Media for the winter. Eumenes had gained Cambasene, and there took up his winter-quarters.

He had given orders to his troops not to spread over too large a territory. But the men, heedless of orders, and far from being well under control, dispersed into hamlets so far apart as to rob the army of all power of speedy concentration in case of attack. Of this fact Antigonus became aware through the reports of his spies. He determined to fall unexpectedly on the enemy, and beat him in detail. From his own winter-quarters there led two roads to Cambasene, one long, through a thickly-settled district and well fitted to sustain an army on the march; the other by a shorter cut, through a sparsely-peopled and poor mountain country, devoid of water, and difficult to traverse. Antigonus chose the latter route because he would be less apt to be discovered, and because it debouched from the mountains directly upon the centre of Eumenes' scattered cantonments. He distributed ten days' rations to his men and forage to the cavalry, collected many water-skins to carry a water supply, and spread a report that he was about to march to Armenia. This was a very probable thing indeed, for Antigonus' army had been weakened, while that of Eumenes had grown in strength, and he had every reason to avoid his enemy, while Armenia offered him a good chance to recruit.

To further sustain the rumor spread, Antigonus set out on the road to Armenia; but he soon filed to the left and into the road leading through the mountains towards Eumenes' winter-quarters. The weather was cold. Antigonus marched at night, and allowed camp-fires to be lighted only during the day. Thus he made five marches towards Eumenes. But the

severity of the weather was such that he could no longer prevent the men from kindling fires at some part of the long
winter night. Eumenes was not careless. He had been on
the watch. Fully aware of the danger he ran from the dispersion of his troops, he sent out a large number of patrols
and spies, who soon brought him in word that numerous
camp-fires had been seen in the mountain region to the north.
This gave him ample warning of Antigonus' approach.

Eumenes' lieutenants advised him to speedily withdraw to
another part of Cambasene. But Eumenes assured them
that he could stop Antigonus' advance long enough to allow
the troops to concentrate — three or four days in any event.
He hurriedly gathered the nearest bodies of troops, and stationed them along the mountain across the path on which
Antigonus was approaching, and ordered other bodies up on
the right and left to occupy the most salient parts of the
foothills at considerable intervals, as if they had come from
different directions. To all these bodies he gave orders to
light numerous fires close together, as would be usual in a
camp, and keep these fires very bright in the first watch
(6–9 P. M.) — this being the time when the soldiers were
wont to rub their bodies with oil before the fires, as well as
cook their meals — then less so in the second watch (9–12
P. M.), and to let them gradually go out after midnight. He
thus counterfeited the presence of large bodies of troops.

Antigonus was duly informed of the existence of these
camp-fires, and was persuaded that Eumenes had concentrated.
Unwilling to encounter Eumenes' better army, unless by a
surprise, he gave up his attempt, and headed in the direction
by which he could reach a territory which would afford him
rest and shelter and food before seeking battle with the enemy. Eumenes gained abundant time to concentrate, and
went into an intrenched camp in a favorable location. Twice,

by clever stratagems, he had thus deceived Antigonus, and gained his end.

One of the last acts in the drama of Greece was among its most brilliant, — the victory by Philopœmen at Mantinæa, third battle of the name, B. C. 206. This great man, "the last of the Greeks," was strategos of the Achæan League. He was a fine type of the intelligent, diligent soldier. Livy says of him : " Philopœmen was possessed of an admirable degree of skill and experience in conducting a march and choosing his station; having made these points his principal study, not only in times of war, but likewise during peace. Whenever he was making a journey to any place, and came to a defile where the passage was difficult, it was his practice, first, to examine the nature of the ground on every side. When journeying alone, he meditated within himself; if he had company, he asked them, ' If an enemy should appear in that place, what course ought he to adopt, if they should attack him in front; what, if on this flank, or on that; what, if on the rear ; for he might happen to meet them while his men were formed with a regular front, or when they were in the loose order of march, fit only for the road.' He would proceed to examine, either in his own mind or by asking questions, ' What ground he himself would choose; what number of soldiers, or what kind of arms (which was a very material point) he ought to employ ; where he should deposit the baggage, where the soldiers' necessaries, where the unarmed multitude ; with what number and what kind of troops he should guard them ; and whether it would be better to prosecute his march as intended, or to return back by the way he came ; what spot, also, he should choose for his camp ; how large a space he should inclose within the lines; where he could be conveniently supplied with water ; where a sufficiency of forage and wood could be had ; which would be his

safest road on decamping next day; and in what form the
army should march?' In such studies and inquiries he had,
from his early years, so frequently exercised his thoughts,
that, on anything of the kind occurring, no expedient that
could be devised was new to him."

Philopœmen had spent seven years in improving the condition of the army, and had raised it far above the low ebb of
the Greek discipline of the day.   When Machanidas, tyrant

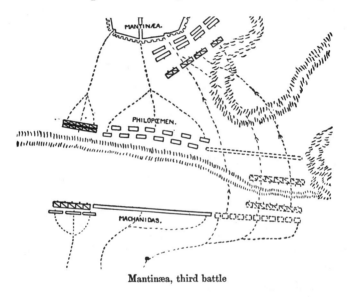

Mantinæa, third battle

of Sparta, had declared war against the League, Philopœmen
moved to Mantinæa, and there took up a position.   Machanidas concentrated at Tegea, south of Mantinæa, from which
place Epaminondas had broken up in 362 B. C. to march to
the second and most celebrated battle of this name.

When ready, Machanidas headed in three columns towards
Mantinæa.   He had a large number of missile-throwing
engines following the army.   Philopœmen moved out to meet
him, proposing to fight on his own chosen ground, which he

had carefully reconnoitred. The plain south of Mantinæa is inclosed by hills on east and west. Philopœmen drew up in rear of a ravine which crossed the plain from hill to hill, and which, wet in winter, dry in summer, and flush with the surface, was not visible from a distance. This ravine he proposed to use as a sort of field-work. It was much like the railroad-cutting at Manassas. His light infantry was on the left, and leaned on the hills, in its front the cavalry, mounted peltasts, allies and mercenaries. His phalanx was in the centre, placed checkerwise by mores, a new formation originated by Philopœmen. The cataphracti were on the right, and intended to be held as a reserve. Philopœmen made a stirring address to his men. " This day will decide," said he, " whether you will be freemen or slaves! "

Soon appeared Machanidas' three columns, the centre one apparently obliquing towards Philopœmen's right. The latter guessed that Machanidas was proposing to attack in oblique order, left reinforced, kept a close outlook, but altered nothing in his formation; but Machanidas obliqued to the right, and took up, at a distance, a parallel order of battle. Philopœmen then looked for a front attack by the Spartan phalanx; but instead of this the intervals of the phalanx opened, and the ballistas and catapults passed through, and ranged themselves before the line. Here is an instance of what had grown to be usual — the opening of a battle by the fire of artillery. Philopœmen met this threat by throwing out a skirmish line of light horse and foot in front of his phalanx in order to pick off with their arrows and sling-stones the men who served the engines. By active work the machines were silenced.

Machanidas, seeing that the light horse was all on Philopœmen's left, while the heavy horse was held in reserve upon the right, ordered his light troops from the rear of his cavalry on the right to march by the rear of the line over to the left where they might sustain his own horse. Perceiving this manœuvre, by which the enemy's right was weakened, Philopœmen ordered his mounted peltasts, backed by the allies and mercenaries, to move across the ravine at a place where he had prepared the slopes, and attack Machanidas' mercenary cavalry there stationed. The rest of both lines remained *in situ*. But the attack was not lucky. Machanidas' horse beat the lighter cavalry of Philopœmen, which retired in disorder, carrying the allies with it. Machanidas, personally in command of his horse on this wing, followed hard upon. Philopœmen's force fled towards Mantinæa, Machanidas upon its heels.

Philopœmen's line was at first disheartened by this defeat; but he himself saw that Machanidas had made a huge mistake in personally leaving the field. His own confidence re-inspired his troops. He ordered his first phalangial line to move by the flank to the left, and occupy the ground from which the mounted peltasts, allies and mercenaries had been driven, and advanced his second line into their place. This manœuvre was executed with precision. Philopœmen had cut off Machanidas from return as well as outflanked the Spartan right. Such of the mounted peltasts, allies and mercenaries as had not been scattered, and could be got together, he formed in one body, and placed in reserve in rear of his left, upon the hill slope.

Philopœmen was now about to advance on the enemy, when he saw the Spartan phalanx moving forward to cross the ravine. He decided to await their onset. Just as they reached the bottom of the ravine, and were scrambling up the rugged slope, he countercharged upon them, thrust them back, and from the height of the bank threw them into such confusion as utterly to demoralize them. He then followed

them across the ravine with part of his force, leaving a
strong body at the prepared crossing to meet Machanidas on
his return. The latter, seeking to rejoin his own army, and
surprised that his success had not won better effects, had
ployed his cavalry into a dense column, and prepared to cut
his way through; but at the last moment, perceiving their isolation, his mercenaries forsook him, and dispersed in all directions, each man seeking his own safety. Machanidas, left
alone, endeavored to escape down the ravine, but was killed
by Philopœmen. This general had won a complete victory by
cool-headed tactics, and manœuvres conceived and executed
in the heat of action.

This battle is both a fair sample of the methods of that
era and a fine exemplification of how an able commander
may make use of the accidents of the ground to gain success,
as well as by clear-headed method and personal bearing arrest
the demoralization apt to follow upon an initial failure.

But, despite that she still produced able men, Greece was
no longer herself. She had degenerated from the proud
height she occupied at the time of the Persian wars. Her
preëminence had departed with her spirit of patriotism, her
eye single to the public good, and her simple virtues, never
to return. The same hardy love of country which had given
her greatness birth, was now to be sought in the city on the
Tiber, whose legions were destined to march over the length
and breadth of the earth, as had the phalanx of Alexander.

With Greece fell Macedon. It was but a hundred and forty
years from the time Philip, backed by an army of forty thousand men, had made himself Hegemōn of Hellas, that another
Philip, defeated at Cynocephalæ, was degraded to the payment of a thousand talents of tribute, to an army and navy
of five thousand men and five ships, and forbidden to make war
outside the narrow original boundaries prescribed as his king-

dom. To this condition had the proud nation sunk, whose
soldiers, trained by the greater Philip, and led by Alexander
in campaigns such as the world has not since seen and never
can see again, had increased the skirts of Macedon to cover a
territory beyond what Greece had deemed the limits of the
earth.   A generation later Macedon was broken up.

Alexander.
(From Statue in the Chiaram Collection.)

APPENDIX A.

SOME ANCIENT MARCHES.

By whom Made.	Where Made.	Date, B. C.	Kind of Troops.	Distance, Miles.	Number of Days' March.	Distance per day, Miles.	Remarks.
Spartans.	Sparta to Marathon.	490	Infantry.	150	3 days.	50	
Ten Thousand Greeks.	Myriandrus to Thapsacus.	401	"	230	12 days.	19	
"	Retreat.	400	"	4,000	215 days.	18½	
Macedonians.	Drill Marches.	c. 350	All arms.	—	—	30	
"	Pelium to Thebes.	335	"	300	14 days.	21½	Mountain road.
"	Pella to Sestos.	334	"	350	20 days.	17½	
"	Phœnicia to Thapsacus.	331	"	200+	11 days.	19+	
"	Pursuit at Arbela.		Cavalry.	70	1 night and day.	70	
"	Uxians to Persian Gates.		All arms.	113	5 days.	22½	Bad mountain road.
"	Persian Gates to Araxes.		Cavalry.	40	1 night.	40	
"	Ecbatana to Rhage.	330	All arms.	220+	11 days.	20	
"	Pursuit of Darius.		Cavalry.	400	11 days.	36½	Hot sandy road, part desert.
"	"			175	4 days.	44	"
"	Hecatompylos to Aria.		All arms.	47	1 night.	47	Desert.
"	To Artacoana.		"	500+	20 days.	25	
"	Capture of Bessus.	329	"	75	2 days.	37½	Ptolemy's march.
"	Jaxartes to Maracanda.	"	"	150	4 days.	37½	
"	Desert of Sandar.	325	"	170	3½ days.	48½	
"			"	57	1 day.	57	Desert.

APPENDIX B.

LOSSES IN SOME ANCIENT BATTLES.

WHERE known, the losses of all noted battles are given. The wounded are mostly estimated at the usual ancient rate of ten wounded to one killed, which is low. Twelve to one would be nearer.

Battle.	Date. B. C	Number Engaged.	Nation.	Killed.	Per Cent.	Usual Per Cent.[1]	Killed and Wounded.	Per Cent.	Usual Per Cent.[2]
Marathon.	490	11,000	Greeks.	192	1¾	5	2,100	19¼	13
Platæa.	479	110,000	"	1,360	1¼	4	15,000	13½	13
Chæronæa.	338	50,000	"	2,000	4	4	18,000	36	13
Thebes.	335	33,000	Maced's.	500	1¾	4	5,500	17	13
Granicus.	334	3,000	Mac. Cav.	85	3	2	935	31	16
Issus.	333	30,000	Maced's.	450	1½	4½	5,000	16¼	13
Arbela.	331	47,000	"	500	1	4	5,500	12	13
Jaxartes.	329	6,000	"	160	2¾	7	1,160	19¼	20
Hydaspes.	326	14,000	"	930	6¾	5	10,200	73	13

[1] In a very stubbornly contested battle.   [2] As in our own Civil War.

APPENDIX C.

MARCHES OF ALEXANDER.

SOME of the distances are taken from Colonel Chesney ; some are from Kiepert's maps. Exact accuracy has not been aimed at, as the old roads and the location of many places are not known.

Routes in Greece.   Miles.

Pella to Corinth	240
Corinth to Pella	240
Pella to Danube	350
Peuce to Pelium	300
Pelium to Thebes	300
Thebes to Pella	180
Pella to Hellespont	300 1,910

Routes in Asia Minor.

Hellespont to Granicus	50
Granicus to Sardis	180

	Miles.	
Sardis to Smyrna and back	100	
Sardis to Ephesus	50	
Ephesus to Miletus	60	
Miletus to Halicarnassus	60	
Halicarnassus to Telmessus	160	
Telmessus to Phaselis	160	
Phaselis to Side	85	
Side to Termessus	85	
Termessus to Sagalassus	70	
Sagalassus to Celænæ	60	
Celænæ to Gordium	170	
Gordium to Ancyra	80	
Ancyra to Tarsus	320	
Tarsus to Rugged Cilicia and back . .	160	
Tarsus to Myriandrus	100	
Myriandrus to Issus	25	1,955

Routes in Phœnicia.

Issus to Tyre	300	
To Sidon and Libanus Campaign . .	100	
Tyre to Jerusalem	120	
Jerusalem to Gaza	60	
Gaza to Pelusium	140	720

Routes in Egypt.

Pelusium to Memphis	120	
Memphis to Alexandria	150	
Around Lake Maræotis	120	
Alexandria to Parætonium	140	
Parætonium to Temple of Jupiter Ammon .	170	
Temple of Jupiter Ammon to Memphis .	340	1,040

Route: Egypt to Persepolis.

Memphis to Gaza	260
Gaza to Tyre	135
Tyre to Thapsacus	380
Thapsacus to Bezabde	290
Bezabde to Arbela	125

	Miles.	
Arbela to Opis	180	
Opis to Babylon	90	
Babylon to Susa	230	
Susa to Uxian City	130	
Uxian City to Kal-eh-Sefid	190	
Kal-eh-Sefid to Persepolis	85	2,095

Routes in Media and the Caspian Region.

Persepolis to Ecbatana	480	
Ecbatana to Caspian Gates	285	
Caspian Gates to Hecatompylos	215	
Hecatompylos to Zadracarta	115	
Mardian Campaign	600	1,695

Routes from Caspian to Caucasus.

Zadracarta to Susia	550	
Susia to Artacoana	130	
Artacoana to Prophthasia	200	
Prophthasia to Alexandria Arachotia	450	
Alexandria Arachotia to Nicea	200	
Nicea to Alexandria ad Caucasum	35	1,565

Routes in Bactria and Sogdiana.

Alexandria ad Caucasum to Drapsaca	110	
Drapsaca to Zariaspa	220	
Zariaspa to Nautaca	205	
Nautaca to Maracanda	120	
Maracanda to Jaxartes	170	
Scythian and Seven Cities Campaigns	100	
Jaxartes to Maracanda	170	
Polytimetus Campaign	150	
Maracanda to Zariaspa	325	
Five Column Campaign	450	
Final Campaign in Sogdiana	200	
Xenippa Campaign	150	
Rock of Sisimithres and return	250	
To Sogdian Rock and Rock of Chorienes	700	
To Zariaspa	200	
To Alexandria ad Caucasum	330	3,900

Routes in Cophen Country. Miles.

	Miles	
Alexandria to Nicea	35	
Nicea to Ora	400	
Ora to Astes' Fort	100	
Astes' Fort to Aornus	75	
Aornus to Dyrta	180	
Dyrta to Indus	40	
Indus to bridge	175	1,005

Routes in Five Rivers Country.

Indus to Taxila	50	
Taxila to Hydaspes	100	
Hydaspes manœuvre	30	
Hydaspes to Glaucians	170	
Glaucians to Acesines Crossing	70	
Acesines to Hydraotis and beyond	60	
To Pimprama and Sangala	100	
To Sopeithes' and Phegeus' Kingdoms	250	
To Hyphasis	60	
To Nicæa	180	1,070

Routes on Indus.

Nicæa to confluence of Indus and Acesines	250	
Mallian Campaign	210	
Campaign and discoveries on Lower Indus	800	1,260

Route back to Susa.

Indus to Arabis	85	
Arabis to Paura	450	
Paura to Pasargadæ	400	
Pasargadæ to Susa	420	1,355

Final Routes.

Susa to sea	220	
Sea to Opis	450	
Opis to Ecbatana	330	
Cossæan Campaign, forty days, and to Susa	400	
Susa to Babylon	230	
Babylon to sea	350	
Back to Babylon	350	2,330
Total distance marched		21,900 miles.

APPENDIX D.

GENEALOGY OF ALEXANDER. (From Reineccius.)

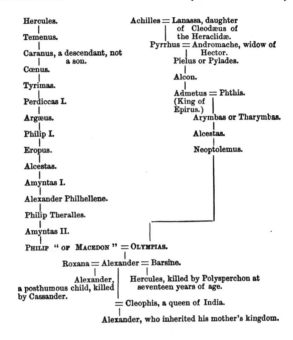

Hercules.
Temenus.
Caranus, a descendant, not a son.
Cœnus.
Tyrimas.
Perdiccas I.
Argæus.
Philip I.
Eropus.
Alcestas.
Amyntas I.
Alexander Philhellene.
Philip Theralles.
Amyntas II.

Achilles = Lanassa, daughter of Cleodæus of the Heraclidæ.
Pyrrhus = Andromache, widow of Hector.
Pielus or Pylades.
Alcon.
Admetus = Phthis.
(King of Epirus.)
Arymbas or Tharymbas.
Alcestas.
Neoptolemus.

Philip " of Macedon " = Olympias.

Roxana = Alexander = Barsine.

Alexander, a posthumous child, killed by Cassander.

Hercules, killed by Polysperchon at seventeen years of age.

= Cleophis, a queen of India.

Alexander, who inherited his mother's kingdom.

INDEX.

LIST OF DATES.

CONQUESTS OF ALEXANDER.

ENGLISH MILES.

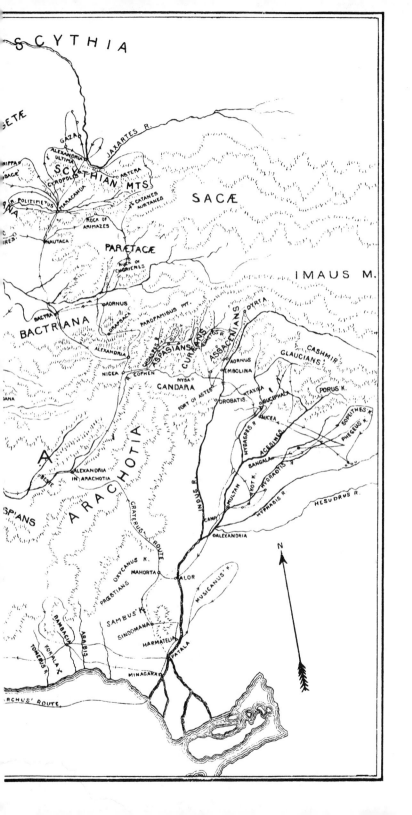